Source Code

NEWSPAPER	DATES COVERED
AD--*American Watchman and Delaware Advertiser*	1816-18, 22
AR--*American Watchman and Delaware Republican*	1812
AW--*American Watchman*	1812, 15
CI--*The Circular*	1824, 26, 35
DE--*Delaware and Eastern Shore Advertiser*, scattered, not bound. 1796-98 in Wilm Pub Library	1795-99
DF--*Delaware Free Press*	1830-31
DG--*Delaware Gazette* (or *Faithful Centinel (sic) Delaware Gazette and General Advertiser*) (1833, ? *and American Watchman*)	1809-10, 17-29, 31, 33-53
DJ--*Delaware Journal*	1829, 32
DS--*Delaware Statesman*	1811-13
FA--*The Federal Ark*	1802-04
IN--*The Intelligencer*--Dover	1821
MG--*Museum of Delaware and General Advertiser*	1804, 07-09
MN--*The Monitor*, scattered, not bound	1800, 01
MR--*Mirror of the Times*	1805, 06
MU--*Museum of Delaware*	1807
MWR--*Monitor and Wilmington Repository*	1800-01
PG--*Pennsylvania Gazette*	1729-53
WN--*Wilmingtonian*	1824-26

Delaware Genealogical Abstracts from Newspapers

Volume 3

DELAWARE
MARRIAGES
and
DEATHS
from
Newspapers

1729-1853

Delaware Genealogical Society Special Publication #10

Edited by
Mary Fallon Richards
and
John C. Richards

HERITAGE BOOKS
2006

HERITAGE BOOKS
AN IMPRINT OF HERITAGE BOOKS, INC.

Books, CDs, and more—Worldwide

For our listing of thousands of titles see our website
at
www.HeritageBooks.com

Published 2006 by
HERITAGE BOOKS, INC.
Publishing Division
65 East Main Street
Westminster, Maryland 21157-5026

Copyright © 1997 Delaware Genealogical Society
505 North Market Street
Wilmington, Delaware 19801-3091

Other books by Mary Fallon Richards and John C. Richards:

Delaware Genealogical Abstracts from Newspapers
Volume 4: Delaware Marriages and Deaths from The Delaware Gazette, 1865-1874

Delaware Genealogical Abstracts from Newspapers
Volume 5: Delaware Marriages and Deaths from The Delaware Gazette, 1875-1879

Delaware 1782 Tax Assessment and Census Lists
CD: *Delaware 1782 Tax Assessment and Census Lists*

All rights reserved. No part of this book may be reproduced or transmitted in any form or by any means, electronic or mechanical, including photocopying, recording or by any information storage and retrieval system without written permission from the author, except for the inclusion of brief quotations in a review.

International Standard Book Number: 978-0-940907-30-5

ACKNOWLEDGEMENTS

To the unknown group who did the original research which formed the basis for the bulk of this manuscript, our thanks for the hours of eye-straining and back-breaking labor which gave us so much information.

To Barbara E. Benson, Director, for permission to publish material prepared for the Historical Society of Delaware.

To Connie (Constance J. Cooper), Ellen (L. Ellen Rendle) and Ed (Edward W. Chichirichi), members of the Library staff, for cheerfully hauling heavy bound volumes of newspapers from basement stacks, for the fill-in search, and for checking some items which were puzzling or dubious. There will still be errors, but we tried to catch them, and we apologize for those we missed.

To the Board of Directors of the Delaware Genealogical Society for enthusiastic support of our efforts to make genealogical information available to the many eager seekers for their roots in Delaware.

And finally, to those very Delawareans, past and present, near and far, (with a special thanks to our numerous and growing membership), whose grateful response makes it worth the effort.

Wilmington, 19 February 1997   Mary and Jack Richards

DELAWARE MARRIAGES AND DEATHS FROM NEWSPAPERS, 1729-1853

This compilation began with the discovery of a typewritten copy of data in the collections of the Historical Society of Delaware, researched so long ago that the authors are not known and cannot be acknowledged. The Society granted permission to the Delaware Genealogical Society to publish the material. Obvious gaps were filled in by the editors' research in bound volumes at that location. The original work was copied as found, with minor attempts at corroboration. The result is not a complete listing of vital statistics, but only of those described herein. Nevertheless, it adds substantially to the meager body of published data for the period.

Bolding of surnames indicates principals in a marriage or death notice. na = no age given, ndd = no date of death, nmd = no date of marriage, NC Co = New Castle County. Editorial comments are in [ ]. 1849 - some items had been cut out of the only issue available to us.

ABBOTT, _____, at the dwelling of his son, Cyrus ABBOTT in Wilm, 12 Oct 1846, aged 70 yrs (DG 20 Oct 1846)

ABBOTT, Cyrus, to **PIERCE**, Sarah G., Miss, both of Wilm, 20 Dec 1821, by the Rev. Richard D. Hall (DG 28 Dec 1821)

ABBOTT, Cyrus, to **DENNEY**, Amy, Miss, both of Wilm, 5 May 1834, by Rev. C. S. Hedges (DG 6 May 1834)

ABBOTT, CYRUS, see **ABBOTT**, _____

ABBOTT, Elizabeth H., see **GRUBB**, George

ABBOTT, James, to **ARGOE**, M. E., in Milford, 30 Jun 1853 (DG 22 Jul 1853)

ABBOTT, Nehemiah, to **LOFLY**, Margaret, Miss, 20 Jan 1850 (DG 12 Feb 1850)

ABBOTT, Patience, see **LINCH**, David

ADAIR, Marietta, Miss, see **BURKE**, Thomas

ADAMS, Daniel J., Esq., dec'd, notice given by William LESS, of New Castle, and Robert HAMILTON, of Wilm, exec'rs (DG 4 Feb 1797)

ADAMS, James, see **ADAMS**, Martha, Mrs.

ADAMS, James F., to **RICE**, Sarah Ann F., Miss, 4 Mar 1841, by Rev. E. W. Gilbert, all of Wilm (DG 9 Mar 1841)

ADAMS, Janet K., see **MOORE**, Thomas L.

ADAMS, John, of Red Lion Hd. Edward L. STEVENSON, adm'r (DG 30 Oct 1849) see **ADAMS** Samuel H.

ADAMS, John W., of Christiana, to **DAVIS**, Mary A., Miss, of Wilm, 10 Mar 1824, by the Rev. S. W. Woolford (DG 16 Mar 1824)

ADAMS, Margaret, see **HYNDMAN**, John

ADAMS, Martha, Mrs., wife of James ADAMS, printer of Wilm, ndd (DG 12 Nov 1789)

ADAMS, Mary, see **ALLEN**, John W.

ADAMS, Roger, Sr., near Bridgeville, 5 Jul 1853, aged at least 105 yrs (DG 22 Jul 1853)

ADAMS, Samuel, to **WITSELL**, Ann, Miss, of Wilm, 27 Dec 1821, by the Rev. L, Lawrenson (DG 1 Jan 1822)

ADAMS, Samuel H., of the senior class of Delaware College, son of John ADAMS, Esq., of Northampton Co VA, after an illness of 4 days, 5 May 1845, aged 18 yrs. Body apparently sent to VA (DG 13 May 1845)

ADAMS, T. Jenifer, see **MOORE**, Thomas L.

ADAMS, William, to **FOUNTAIN**, Sally Ann, Mrs., both of NC Co, 4 Feb 1851, by Rev. T. Newman (DG 14 Feb 1851)

ADAMS, William B., of Phila, to **FIELDS**, Catharine, Miss, of Wilm, 25 Apr 1850, by Rev. Benjamin F. Templeton (DG 3 May 1850)

ADDIS, Elizabeth, Mrs., widow of John ADDIS, at her late res. in Northampton Twp., Bucks Co PA, 11 Feb 1825, in her 95th yr (Cl 11 Mar 1825)

ADDIS, John, see **ADDIS**, Elizabeth, Mrs.

ADDISON, Ann, see **ADDISON**, William

ADDISON. John, see **ADDISON**, Mary

ADDISON, Mary, Mrs., wife of John

ADDISON of Delaware City, near Port Penn, at the res. of the Hon. Samuel JEFFERSON, her son-in-law, 29 Aug 1851, in her 76th yr (DG 23 Sep 1851)

ADDISON, William, dec'd, late of Christiana Hd, notice given by Francis SAWDON, atty-in-fact for Ann ADDISON, adm'x (DG 15 Nov 1833)

ADKINS, Catharine,
see MARVEL, Theodore W.

ADYK, Catherine A.,
see DENNY, James, Esq.

AEFORD, Caroline,
see HALL, Augustus R.

AEUSPRATTS, James,
see SHIPLEY, Thomas, Esq.

AGNEW, Lydia, see TAYLOR, Mary S.

AGNEW, Mary, see TAYLOR, J. Bayard

AGNEW, Mary S., see TAYLOR, Mary S.

AHRENS, Adolph, of Balt, to WETHERALD, Anna, dau of the late Jos. WETHERALD of Wilm, 26 May 1852, by Rev. Samuel H. Worster (DG 1 Jun 1852)

AIKEN, Barbara, Miss, in Wilm, 8 Oct 1822, aged 69 yrs (DG 15 Oct 1822)

AIKEN, John, see GAMBLE, James

AIKIN, David G., formerly of Wilm, in Princeton NJ, of bilious dysentery, 9 Oct 1849, aged c 26 yrs (DG 12 Oct 1849)

AIKIN, E. T., of Wilm, to McKINGHT, Sophia, of Phila, 22 Sep 1852, by the Rev. J. Chambers (DG 28 Sep 1852)

AIKIN, Martha, in Wilm, 19 Oct 1845, aged 26 yrs (DG 31 Oct 1845)

AIKIN, Samuel M., to STEPHENS, Rebecca J., in Wilm, 27 Oct 1852, by the Rt. Rev. Alfred Lee (DG 2 Nov 1852)

AKIN, Mary, see KING, John

ALBERTSON, Eliza,
see CARUTHERS, Josiah

ALBRIGHT, Ann Maria, see BEST, John

ALCOCK, Rachel Ann J.,
see PANCOAST, Robert T.

ALDRED, Sarah Ann,
see LYBRAND, George D.

ALDRED, Thomas J.,
see LYBRAND, George D.

ALEE, Pressley, Esq., at Dover, 6 Aug 1823 (DG 12 Aug 1823)

ALEXANDER, A., Dr.,
see LITTLE, Jonathan P.

ALEXANDER, Adam, of New London Cross Roads, to EVES, Susan M., Miss, of Wilm, 10 Feb 1830, by Rev. Robert Graham (DG 12 Feb 1830)

ALEXANDER, Andrew,
see ALEXANDER, Franklin Ross

ALEXANDER, Arabella J.,
see LITTLE, Jonathan P.

ALEXANDER, Archibald, Dr., at his country seat near Wilm, 12 Aug 1822, aged 67 yrs. Served in the Rev. War, 10th VA Regt; educated Newark Academy, DE, and studied Physic with Dr. Watson in New Castle (DG 24 Sep 1822)

ALEXANDER, Charles, to TURNER, Mary, Miss, all of Wilm, 17 Dec 1846, by Rev. A. Atwood (DG 22 Dec 1846)

ALEXANDER, Franklin Ross, son of Andrew and Harriet ALEXANDER, in Elkton, 2 Aug 1853, aged 9 mos (DG 9 Aug 1853)

ALEXANDER, Harriet,
see ALEXANDER, Franklin Ross

ALEXANDER, J.,
see LAWRENCE, Alexander

ALEXANDER, James, to LOFLAND, Eliza, Miss, of Sussex, 28 Nov 1850, by Rev. James Hargis (DG 10 Dec 1850)

ALEXANDER, Loretta,
see SHUDEL, Andrew J.

ALEXANDER, Sarah, see HITCH, Spencer

ALFORD, Sarah Ann,
see TUCKER, Nathaniel

ALGEL, Ann, see ALGEL, Robert G.

ALGEL, James, see ALGEL, Robert G.

ALGEL, Robert G., son of James and Ann ALGEL, in Phila, 13 Feb 1849, aged 26 yrs (DG 16 Feb 1840)

ALLDERDICE, Abraham,
see ALLDERDICE, Barbara Shuff
see SLOAN, David R.

ALLDERDICE, Barbara Shuff, Mrs., mother of Eliza, wife of Abraham

ALLDERDICE (DG 6 Apr 1849)

ALLDERDICE, Eliza,
see ALLDERDICE, Barbara Shuff

ALLDERDICE, Jane A.,
see SLOAN, David R.

ALLDERDICE, William Hillary, of Wilm, to WINSLOW, Elizabeth, third dau of George WINSLOW, Esq., of Phila, 22 Apr 1851, by Rev. J. C. Clay DD (DG 25 Apr 1851)

ALLEE, Abraham, see ALLEE, Sarah

ALLEE, Sarah, wife of Abraham ALLEE, at Smyrna, 13 Oct 1824, aged 43 yrs 8 mos (DG 2 Nov 1824)

ALLEN, Charles,
see ARMSTRONG, William

ALLEN, Edward, colored, drowned in Holdings Mill Pond, Duck Creek, 8 Oct 1850 (DG 18 Oct 1850)

ALLEN, Jesse, to RUSHAM, Caroline, Miss, both of Pencader Hd , 24 Dec 1835, by the Rev. A. K. Russel (DG 1 Jan 1836)

ALLEN, John W., of Sussex Co, to ADAMS, Mary, 24 Dec 1852, by Rev. Isaac R. Merrill (DG 14 Jan 1853)

ALLEN, Joseah, of Darby, Del Co, PA, to DUNCAN, Mary, of New Castle, in New Castle, by Rev. Mr. Spotswood (DG 1 May 1849)

ALLEN, Martha, see HARRIS, Mason

ALLEN, Robert, his body found behind Samuel NEWLIN's blacksmith shop in Wilm, 4 Nov 1843 (DG 13 Nov 1843)

ALLEN, Samuel, to DUNLAP, Abbey, Miss, both of Wilm, on the 4th inst, by the Rev. Mr. Jones (DG 27 Mar 1849)

ALLEN, Samuel, 1 May 1849, aged 35 yrs (DG 8 May 1849)

ALLEN, Sarah L., see HILLES, William S.

ALLEN, Thomas, to SPEAKMAN, Ann, 10 Mar 1842, by Rev. J. Leach (DG 25 Mar 1842)

ALLEN, Thomas M., to WOODALL, Mary D., both of Wilm, in Trinity Ch., 21 Jul 1849, by the Rev. Mr Van Dusen (DG 24 Jul 1849)

ALLERDICE, John A., Esq., to BROWN, S. Isabella, all of Wilm, in Phila at the Washington House, 21 Mar 1850, by Rev. Dr. Gilbert (DG 26 Mar 1850)

ALLISON, Andrew, to McQUILLIN, Elizabeth Agnes, Miss, all of Wilm, in Wilm, 17 Nov 1853, by the Rev. Mr. Wynkoop (DG 22 Nov 1853)

ALLISON, Jane, see ALLISON, John

ALLISON, John, dec'd, late of Brandywine Hd, notice given by Jane ALLISON, adm'x (DS 5 Feb 1812)

ALLISTON, Margaret, Mrs., 5 May 1820 (DG 17 May 1820)

ALLMON, John, to SQUIBB, Ellen, Miss, dau of the late Robert SQUIBB, all of Stanton, DE, at New Garden, PA, 29 Jan 1829, by John W. Thomas, Esq. (DG 6 Feb 1829)

ALLMOND, Charles M., of Wilm, to SHANNON, Mary Ann, of Yellow Springs PA, 7 Sep 1848, in Vincent Church PA, by Rev. Allen J. Hires (DG 10 Oct 1848)

ALLMOND, George, to ROBINSON, Elizabeth H. Miss, both of Wilm, in Phila, 18 May 1848, by Rev. Daniel Dodge (DG 26 May 1848)

ALLMOND, Jane, see ALLMOND, R.

ALLMOND, Mary Ellen, dau of Dr. R. J. ALLMOND, 5 Oct 1848, aged 4 yrs (DG 17 Oct 1848)

ALLMOND, Mary Jane, at her father's res. in Brandywine Village, of a hemorrhage of the lungs, 26 Jan 1848, aged 21 yrs 8 mos 15 days. Born 10 May 1826. (DG 28 Jan 1848)

ALLMOND, R. J., Dr.,
see ALLMOND, Mary Ellen

ALLMOND, R., Miss, dau of Mrs. Jane ALLMOND, in Brandywine Hd, 9 Jun 1849, aged c 29 yrs (DG 19 Jun 1849)

ALLSTON, John, dec'd, late of Appoq. Hd. land adjoining that of LOWBER, John, whose land is to to be sold by sheriff, Peter B. Delany (DG 5 Mar 1827)

ALLSTON, Lydia Louisa,
see ASHCRAFT, William

ALRICH, Adeline C.,
see BEESON, Charles A.

ALRICH, Harriet S.,
see CLARK, George T.

ALRICH, Martha, consort of Peter S. ALRICH, in NC Co, 15 Apr 1853, aged c 62 yrs (DG 19 Apr 1853)

ALRICH, Peter S., see ALRICH, Martha

ALRICH, Susanna Canby,
see BUSH, William

ALRICH, Thomas C., see BUSH, William
see BEESON, Charles A.

ALRICH, Thomas C., of Wilm, to
MITCHELL, Mary C, Mrs., of Phila, at Phila,
in the 7th Presbyt Ch, by the Rev. Mr.
Ruffner (DG 2 Jul 1852)

ALRICHS, Elizabeth J., Miss,
see ELLIOTT, Benjamin

ALRICHS, Henry S., of Wilm, to MAXWELL,
Sarah B.,Miss , dau of Hugh MAXWELL,
of Lancaster, PA, at Lancaster, 1 Oct 1835,
by Rev. W. M. Davis (DG 6 Oct 1835)

ALRICHS, J. Bayard, see DEIHL, Sarah

ALRICHS, John, Dr., to WORRELL,
Elizabeth Nicosho, Miss, dau of Dr. Edward
WORRELL, 20 Jul 1852, at Delaware City,
by the Rev. E. J. May (DG 27 Jul 1852)

ALRICHS, Jonas, to CANBY, Susannah,
Miss, in Wilm, 23 Dec 1790
(DG 25 Dec 1790)

ALRICHS, Jonas, formerly of Wilm, in
Phila, 25 Jun 1847, in his 45th yr
(DG 7 Jul 1847)

ALRICHS, Mary Ann, consort of Thomas
C. ALRICHS, in Wilm, 14 Feb 1850,
aged c 50 yrs (DG 15 Feb 1850)

ALRICHS, Sarah E.,
see LOCKWOOD, Edward

ALRICHS, Thomas C.,
see ALRICHS, Mary Ann

ALRICHS, Wessell, Esq., in Pencader Hd,
16 May 1850, in his 50th yr
(DG 24 May 1850)

ALRICHS, Wm. T., of Glasgow DE, to
FRY, Sallie, L., of Phila, 4 May 1852, at
New Castle, by the Rev. J. B. Spotswood
(DG 11 May 1852)

ALRICKS, Sarah. see FARIES, George G.

ALRICKS, Susan, Mrs.,
see HAADEN (sic), John

ALSTON, Joab S., to WOODS, Mary Ann,
Miss, all of NC Co, in Phila, 10 Jun 1847,
by Rev. George Foot (DG 18 Jun 1847)

ALSTON, Stephen, atty,
see McSPARREN, Archibald

ALTER, Jacob,
see MAGEAR, Mary Catharine
see MEGEAR, Thomas J.

ALTER, Mary Catharine,
see MEGEAR, Thomas J.
see MAGEAR, Mary Catharine

AMES, Stillman, to GAMBLE, Catharine,
Miss, near Newark, 20 Nov 1829, by the
Rev. William Rider (DG 11 Dec 1829)

ANDERSON, Alexander M., at his late res.
in Brandywine Village, 4 Dec 1850
(DG 6 Dec 1850)

ANDERSON, Ann Amanda, dau of John D.
ANDERSON, Esq., aged 15 yrs 2 mos 1 day
(DG 15 Mar 1853)

ANDERSON, Charles, to DERRICKSON,
Sarah, Mrs., 4 Sep 1817, by Rev.
William Pryce (DG 6 Sep 1817)

ANDERSON, Eleanor M., Mrs., wife of
James L. ANDERSON, 5 Sep 1852,
aged 28 yrs (DG 14 Sep 1852)

ANDERSON, Elizabeth Jane, Mrs., in Wilm,
15 Jun 1853, in her 47th yr. Funeral from the
res. of her sister, Mrs. Ann MOORE,
64 King St. (DG 17 Jun 1853)

ANDERSON, George P., at the res. of his
father near Georgetown, 18 Dec 1842,
aged 25 yrs (DG 23 Dec 1842)

ANDERSON, Isaac,
see ANDERSON, William

ANDERSON, James,
see ANDERSON, Walter Scott
see WILLIAMS, Joseph
see ANDERSON, Margaret W.

ANDERSON, James, negro, who murdered
Joseph WILLIAMS, Feb last, was executed
by hanging, 31 Jul 1851 (DG 1 Aug 1851)

ANDERSON, James, of Wilm, to COLE,
Helen, Miss, of Albany NY, 28 Mar 1851,
at Albany in the 4th Presb. Ch by Rev. Dr.
Mandeville (DG 4 Apr 1851)

ANDERSON, James L.,
see ANDERSON, Eleanor M.

ANDERSON, James R., Rev., of Dover
Circuit, to TRUITT, Esther F., Miss, both
of Dover, 14 Mar 1848, by Rev. Mr. Sutton
(DG 4 Apr 1848)

ANDERSON, John, to VANGASKY, Susan,
Miss, both of Cowgill's Ville, Little Creek,
29 Jan 1824, by Rev. John Derborough
(DG 3 Feb 1824)

ANDERSON, John, at his res. in Brandywine Village, 18 Jul 1848, aged c 50 yrs (DG 28 Jul 1848)

ANDERSON, John, Capt, ship captain, native of Milford, from exposure after shipwreck on shoals at Great Egg Harbor, 4 Jan 1853, aged c 35 yrs.. Sailed from Smyrna DE. Leaves a wife and 2 children (DG 11 Jan 1853)

ANDERSON, John D., see ANDERSON, Ann Amanda

ANDERSON, John T., Capt., to POSTLES, Elen P., both of Kent Co, in Phila, 24 Oct 1847, by Rev. John S. Taylor (DG 29 Oct 1847) late of Wilm Hd. William THOMPSON, adm'r (DG 4 Feb 1853)

ANDERSON, Margaret W., dau of James ANDERSON of Sussex Co, 7 Apr 1847, in her 22nd yr (DG 7 Apr 1847)

ANDERSON, Martha K., see TOWNSEND, John T.

ANDERSON, Mary, Mrs, at the res. of her son-in-law, John WHANN, 13 Feb 1846, aged 92 yrs (DG 20 Feb 1846)

ANDERSON, Mary, see ROBINSON, Ebenezer

ANDERSON, Mary Ann, see BRENNAN, Hugh

ANDERSON, Sarah, see PRETTYMAN, Henry R.

ANDERSON, Walter Scott, at the res. of his father, James ANDERSON, near Georgetown, 17 Aug 1851, in his 19th yr (DG 9 Sep 1851)

ANDERSON, William, dec'd, late of Brandywine Hd, notice given by Isaac ANDERSON, exec'r (MR 23 May 1806)

ANDERSON, William, in Phila, 31 Dec 1852, in his 79th yr (DG 4 Jan 1853)

ANDREWS, James, Sr., Esq., editor of the *Elkton Press*, at his res. in Newark, 17 Aug 1824, aged 43 yrs (DG 27 Aug 1824)

ANDREWS, James. see SHIPLEY, Rebecca

ANDREWS, Keziah, Mrs., see HANING, George

ANDREWS, Sarah, see McCOMBS, Laurence, Rev.,

ANKINS, Susanna, see PRICE, James W.

APPLEBY, George, in Wilm, 23 Aug 1849, aged 33 yrs (DG 28 Aug 1849)

APPLEBY, John, to BARBOR, Martha Ann, Miss, both of Wilm, 16 Sep 1834, by Richard H. Bayard, Esq. (DG 19 Sep 1834)

APPLEGATE, Lydia K., Mrs., formerly of DE, in Phila, 28 Aug 1849, in her 58th yr (DG 31 Aug 1849)

APPLEGATE, William, to BATHGATE, Jane, Miss, by Rev. S. M. Gailey, 30 Aug 1849 (DG 28 Sep 1849)

APPLETON, Annie E., see HOFFECKER, John H.

APPLETON, Henry H., of Cantwell's Bridge to CRIST, Hannah M., Miss, of Bethlehem PA, at Bethlehem, 4 Dec 1851, by the Rt. Rev. Bishop Van Vleck (DG 9 Dec 1851)

APPLETON, John, see HOFFECKER, John H.

APPLETON, Joseph, formerly of Wilm, to HORNE, Susanna P., dau of Stephen HORNE, Esq., of Darbey PA, in W. Phila, 12 May 1852, by the Rev. Edgar M. Levy (DG 11 May 1852)

ARBUCKEL, Mary, see CARPENTER, James T.

ARGO, David, in Cedar Creek Hd, Sussex Co, 6 Aug 1849, na (DG 14 Aug 1849)

ARGO, John, of Milford, to HAND, Mary Virginia, Miss, of Southwark, Phila, 13 May 1850, by Rev. John C. Clay (DG 17 May 1850)

ARGOE, M. E., see ABBOTT, James

ARMOR, James Jr., to HENDRICKSON, Ann, Miss, both of NC Co, 11 Mar 1841, by Rev. J. W. McCullough (DG 16 Mar 1841)

ARMSTRONG, Ann, see MARSHALL, Edward

ARMSTRONG, Caroline S., see BATEMAN, J. H.

ARMSTRONG, Catherine, Mrs., wife of Dr. R. W. ARMSTRONG, of Wilm, 29 Apr 1816, in her 20th yr (AW 11 May 1816)

ARMSTRONG, Christopher, to MILLER, Lydia, Miss, both of NC Co, 15 Oct 1789 (DG 21 Oct 1789)

ARMSTRONG, David, keeper of a public

house in Christiana, at Christiana Bridge, 30 Aug 1826, aged 58 yrs (DG 12 Sep 1826)

ARMSTRONG, George, to ELLIOTT, Eliza, Miss, 5 Apr 1849, by the Rev. Mr. Van Dusen (DG 10 Apr 1849)

ARMSTRONG, John, to DELAPLAINE, Jane, Miss, both of Christiana Hd, 26 Sep 1816, by Rev. Dr. Read (AW 26 Sep 1816)
see GAMBLE, Elizabeth

ARMSTRONG, John B., to SWIFT, Sarah M., of NC Co, 4 Mar 1852, by Rev. J. R. Anderson (DG 16 Mar 1852)

ARMSTRONG, Lavinia,
see JUSTIS, John B.

ARMSTRONG, R. W., Dr.,
see ARMSTRONG, Catherine

ARMSTRONG, Rachel,
see SPRINGER, Joseph W.

ARMSTRONG, Rebecca,
see MORTON, Jacob G.

ARMSTRONG, Rebecca J.,
see WILTBANK, Cornelius

ARMSTRONG, Richardson H.,
see ARMSTRONG, Samuel Eugene

ARMSTRONG, Robert,
see STILLEY, John
see MORIS, Wm. H.

ARMSTRONG, Samuel Eugene, son of Richardson H. and Sarah ARMSTRONG, near Middletown DE, 23 Sep 1853, aged 2 yrs 6 mos (DG 1 Nov 1853)

ARMSTRONG, Samuel F., to VANNEMAN, Dorcas, Miss, both of Wilm, 4 Apr 1849, by the Rev. James Smithers (DG 27 Apr 1849)

ARMSTRONG, Sarah,
see ARMSTRONG, Samuel Eugene

ARMSTRONG, Sarah Jane,
see SPRINGER, John

ARMSTRONG, William, to PEARSON, Rebecca, Miss, dau of Joseph PEARSON, of the Cross Keyes, Kennett Road, 24 Nov 1821, by the Rev. Richard D. Hall (DG 30 Nov 1821)

ARMSTRONG, William, house and land in Newark for sale by Charles ALLEN, adm'r (DG 2 Mar 1827)

ARMSTRONG, William, of Delaware, to

JOHNSON, Sophie E., of Nassau, N. P., 18 Aug 1841, in Phila by Rev. Mr. Coleman (DG 27 Aug 1841)

ARNOLD, Benedict, Brig. General, "notorious throughout the world," in England (MN 8 Aug 1801)

ARTHUR, Samuel D., of NY, to MITCHELL, Mary E., Miss, of NC Co, 19 Oct 1853, near Newark, by the Rev. W. S. F. Graham (DG 28 Oct 1853)

ASH, John,
see CALDWELL, Wm. Pemberton

ASH, Sallie Amanda,
see CALDWELL, Wm. Pemberton

ASHCRAFT, William, Dr, of Cantwell's Bridge, to ALLSTON, Lydia Louisa, near St. Georges, 19 Oct 1852, by the Rev. Jas. Asperil (DG 26 Oct 1852)

ASHMEAD, C. F., see WINDLE, C. F.

ASHMEAD, Mary,
see McLANE, George R.

ASHMEAD, William,
see McLANE, George R.

ASHMEAD, William A., Rev.,
see WINDLE, C. F.

ASHMORE, J. I., to HUSTON, M. Lizzie, dau of Samuel HUSTON, all of Phila, 10 Nov 1853, by the Rev. R. Adair (DG 18 Nov 1853)

ASHTON, Lewis, in Village of Christiana, 20 Jan 1852, aged between 60 and 70 yrs (DG 23 Jan 1852)

ASHTON, Tirzah, Mrs., see COLAY, Wm.

ASKEW, F., Dr.,
see ROBINSON, Elizabeth

ASKEW, Hannah, Mrs., at the res. of Joseph MENDINHALL, in Brandywine Hd, 21 Sep 1851, aged 91 yrs 8 mos (DG 9 Sep 1851)

ASKEW, Henry Ford, M. D., to ROBINSON, Mary Hanson, Miss, both of Wilm, in Phila by George M. Dallas, Esq., Mayor (DG 23 Dec 1828)

ASKEW, Joseph, of Delaware Co PA, to HEYSER, Jane B., of NC Co, 2 Sep 1841, at Marcus Hook, by J. D. Bitting, Esq. (DG 1 Oct 1841)

ASPRIL, D. T., of Balt, to JEFFERSON, Mary Ann, Miss, eldest dau of the late Purnal JEFFERSON, of NC Co, 23 Aug 1853, in NC Co, by the Rev. James C. Howe

(DG 26 Aug 1853)

ASPRIL, Hannah, see PIPPEN, William

ASPRIL, John, see BAKER, William A.

ASPRIL, Leonard V., to McMURPHY, Mary, Miss, both of Cantwell's Bridge, 12 Oct 1843, by Rev. Thomas B. Tibbles (DG 3 Nov 1843)

ASPRIL, Mary, see BAKER, William A.

ASPY, Mary, Mrs., wife of William ASPY, Jr., native of NC Co, in Bucks Co, PA, 21 May 1833, aged 33 yrs (DG 28 May 1833)

ASPY, William, Jr., see ASPY, Mary, Mrs.

ATCHISON, G., see ATCHISON, Rhoda

ATCHISON, Rhoda, Mrs, consort of G. ATCHISON, after a short but painful illness, in Sussex Co, 8 Jul 1848, aged 44 yrs 4 mos and 13 days (DG 25 Jul 1848)

ATKINS, John, to MORRIS, Susanna, H., Miss, both of Sussex Co DE, in Phila, 31 Oct 1849, by the Rev. Jas. Allen (DG 13 Nov 1849)

ATKINS, Joseph R., to COLLINS, Eliza, Miss, both of Phila, 11 Jul 1848, by Rev. Levi Storks (DG 13 Mar 1849)

ATKINSON, Isaac, Esq., of MD, to BOOTH, Susan, Miss, dau of Chief Justice BOOTH of New Castle, 6 May 1851, by the Rev. Mr. Billopp (DG 9 May 1851)

ATKINSON, Lurania, Mrs., in Sussex Co DE, 20 Apr 1849, aged 82 yrs (DG 1 May 1849)

ATKINSON, Margaret, see HADON, William H.

ATTIX, Ann Isabel, see DISHER, William

ATTIX, Margaret, see MEEKS, Aquilla

ATWOOD, A., Rev., see FLINN, Anthony B.

ATWOOD, Hannah L., see FLINN, Anthony B.

AULD, Mary E., consort of Philip AULD and dau of Robert and Elizabeth TINDLE, 21 Nov 1847, in her 24th yr (DG 25 Nov 1847)

AULD, Philip, see AULD, Mary E.

AUSTIN, David, to CAVENDER, Elizabeth, Miss, both of Christiana Hd, 29 Dec 1843, by Rev. S. M. Gayley (DG 2 Jan 1844)

AYERS, Edward, Capt., of New Bedford, to READ, Emily, Miss, dau of the late Capt. Henry READ of Wilm, 18 May 1841, in Wilm, by Rev. John Miller (DG 18 May 1841)

AYERS, Rebecca S., see McCONAUGHY, Alexander

AYRES, J. B., Rev., see McCONAUGHY, Alexander

BABB, Thomas, at his res. in Brandywine Hd, 14 Oct 1844, aged 77 yrs (DG 25 Oct 1844)

BABB, Thomas S., of Phila, to TWEELY, Sabilda, Miss, formerly of Wilm, in Phila, 19 Dec 1847 by Rev. John Street (DG 4 Apr 1848)

BACHE, Maria C., see McLANE, Maria C.

BACHE, Richard, see McLANE, Maria C.

BACON, James W., of Phila, to YOUNG, Zeriah P., Miss, of Wilm, 8 Nov 1853, by Rev. S. R. Wynkoop (DG 11 Nov 1853)

BACON, Joseph K., to McLANE, Sallie A. H., of Newark, at Newark, 24 Aug 1852, by the Rev. J. W. Elliott (DG 31 Aug 1852)

BAGGS, Emeline, consort of George BAGGS, in Wilm, 30 Oct 1851, aged c 25 yrs (DG 4 Nov 1851)

BAGGS, George, see BAGGS, Emeline

BAGGS, James, to KURTZ, Elizabeth, both of Wilm, in Chester, 20 Oct 1853, by the Rev. J. B. Maddox (DG 28 Oct 1853)

BAIL, James S., to POOL, Charlotte, Miss, both of Del Co PA, 14 Oct 1852, by the Rev. Dr. Barrell (DG 22 Oct 1852)

BAILESS, Susan F., see HUMPHREY, Israel

BAILEY, Ann, see SHIPWAY, Charles

BAILEY, Elizabeth, Mrs., wife of John BAILEY, near Dover, 5 May 1851, na (DG 13 May 1851)

BAILEY, Hannah P., see SQUIBB, Samuel F.

BAILEY, John, of Pencader Hd, to SMITH, Tabitha N, Miss, of White Clay Creek Hd, at Christiana Bridge, 11 Jan 1825, by the Rev. E. W. Gilbert (DG14 Jan 1825)

BAILEY, John, to SHEPPERDSON, Elizabeth, Miss, both of NC Co, 9 Apr 1845,

in West Chester PA, by Rev. John B.
Clemson (DG 25 Apr 1845)
see **BAILEY**, Elizabeth

BAILEY, Lavinia, see **GRAY**, Joshua

BAILEY, Leonard F., to **THOMPSON**,
Amelia Freeman, Miss, both of Spring
Garden, 7 Sep 1851, by the Rev. A. D.
Gillette (DG 12 Sep 1851)

BAILEY, Nathan, see **BAILEY**, Sarah

BAILEY, Perry, negro convicted of rape on
Mary Ann SYTHENS, a white woman, was
hung, 8 Feb 1849, at the intersection of the
Hare's Corner and Wilm Rds
(DG 9 Feb 1849)

BAILEY, Sarah, Miss, dau of Nathan
BAILEY, of Duck Creek Hd, at the house
of L. W. STIDHAM in Wilm, 4 Jan 1853,
in her 23rd yr (DG 11 Jan 1853)

BAILEY, Thomas, to **RIGGS**, Eliza, Miss,
both of NC Co, in Wilm, 6 Nov 1848,
by Rev. M. J. Rhees (DG 10 Nov 1848)

BAILIE, James, in Phila, 31 Dec 1849,
in his 38th yr (DG 4 Jan 1850)

BAILY, _____, Mrs., consort of Mr. Edward
T. BAILY of Wilm, 29 Jan 1829, na
(DG 3 Feb 1829)

BAILY, A. Elizabeth,
see **GRIMSHAW**, Arthur H.

BAILY, Edith B., see **VALUE**, J. S.

BAILY, Edward T., of Wilm, to
WOODLAND, Mary Emma, Miss, of
Cecil Co, MD, in Elkton, MD, 21 Mar 1825,
by the Rev. Mr. Duke (DG 22 Mar 1825)

BAILY, Edward T., suddenly in Wilm,
18 May 1843 (DG 26 May 1843)
see **BAILY**, _____, Mrs.

BAILY, Hannah, see **MAHAN**, Joseph

BAILY, Isaac, of DE, to **PERKINS**, Ellen,
Miss, of Phila, in Phila, 29 Jun 1848, by
Rev. William Douglas (DG 7 Jul 1848)

BAILY, James, of Brandywine Hd, to
WETHERELL, Jane, Miss of Wilm, in
West Chester, 21 Dec 1828, by William
Everhart, Esq. (DG 26 Dec 1828)

BAILY, Jos. T., see **VALUE**, J. S.

BAILY, Joseph, Esq., ex-pres. of Bank of
Delaware, 31 Jan 1843, in Wilm
(DG 3 Feb 1843)
see **PERRY**, Charles

BAILY, Joseph P.,
see **GRIMSHAW**, Arthur H.

BAILY, Mary Elizabeth,
see **McILVAINE**, William S.

BAILY, Sarah Ann P.,
see **TAYLOR**, Isaac, Dr.,

BAIRD, William, of Wilm, to **WATSON**,
Mary Jane, Miss, formerly of Elkton MD,
in Chester, 30 Mar 1852, by the
Rev. J. W. Gibbs (DG 6 Apr 1852)

BAKER, Alexander, of Phila, to
CAMPBELL, Esther, Miss, late of Wilm, in
Phila, 28 Dec 1826, by the Rev. Dr. Wilson
(DG 2 Jan 1827)

BAKER, Alfred Lee, son of Joshua G.
and Sarah Emeline BAKER, 16 Feb 1848,
at Cedar Creek, aged 27 mos
(DG 24 Mar 1848)

BAKER, Curtis, to **CLARK**, Catharine, Miss,
both of Murderkill Hd, Kent Co, in Wilm,
23 Jan 1834 (DG 28 Jan 1834)

BAKER, Hannah, Mrs., relict of Capt.
Thomas BAKER dec'd, in Elkton MD,
3 Sep 1852, in her 70th yr
(DG 28 Sep 1852)

BAKER, Joshua G., Esq., to **ENNIS**, Sarah
Emeline, both of Cedar Creek Hd, 29 Dec
1842, in St. Matthew's Church, Cedar Creek,
by Rev. John Reynolds (DG 6 Jan 1843)
see **BAKER**, Alfred Lee

BAKER, Mary Elizabeth, infant dau of Dr.
William BAKER, 6 Sep 1826
(DG 12 Sep 1826)

BAKER, Sarah Emeline,
see **BAKER**, Alfred Lee

BAKER, Thomas, Capt.,
see **BAKER**, Hannah

BAKER, William, Dr., of Wilm, to
SCHNEIDER, Catherine, Miss, of Frankford,
PA, in Phila, 10 Jun 1823, by the Rev. Mr.
Mayers (DG 24 Jun 1823)
see **BAKER**, Mary Elizabeth

BAKER, William, in Cedar Creek Hd,
5 Mar 1850, in his 74th yr (DG 12 Mar 1850)

BAKER, William A., of Baltimore, to
ASPRIL, Mary, eldest dau of John ASPRIL,
of NC Co, 21 Nov 1850, by Rev. E. Heiner
(DG 26 Nov 1850)

BALANEY, C. D., see **BIRD**, J. H.

BALANEY, Fanny E., see **BIRD**, J. H.

BALDWIN, Charles H., to PERKINS, Elizabeth, Miss, both of Brandywine Hd, in Chester, 28 Oct 1830, by Rev. R. U. Morgan (DF 13 Nov 1830)

BALDWIN, Eli, to READ, Mary, Miss, both of NC Co, 11 Mar 1847, at Marcus Hook by Rev. Mr. Walker (DG 27 Apr 1847)

BALDWIN, Joseph, dec'd, notice given by Alexander DUNCAN, adm'r (DE 9 Apr 1798)

BALDWIN, Lewis H., to STANLEY, Phoebe Ann, both of NC Co, 23 Mar 1844, by Rev. J. M. Rhees (DG 26 Mar 1844)

BALDWIN, Lydia, dec'd, late of Wilm, notice given by William BALDWIN, exec'r (AW 30 Jul 1817)
see BALDWIN, Thomas

BALDWIN, Robert, of New Castle, to PIERCE, Sarah M, of Chester Co PA, at the Pars. in Chester PA, nmd, by the Rev. J. B. Maddux (DG 26 Oct 1852)

BALDWIN, Thomas, late of Mill Creek Hd, Lydia BALDWIN and George KLAIR, exec'rs (DG 21 Dec 1852)

BALDWIN, William, see BALDWIN, Lydia

BALDWIN, William, to MATTHEWS, Jane Y., Miss, all of Wilm, 25 Oct 1827, by John P. Peckworth (DG 30 Oct 1827)

BALDWIN, William, Capt., of Mill Creek Hd, to KIMBLE, Ann, Miss, of Chester Co, PA, 28 May 1829, by the Rev. A. K. Russel (DG 2 Jun 1829)

BALDWIN, William, to HARRIS, Caroline, Miss, all of NC Co, 1 Jul 1847, by Rev. M. J. Rhees (DG 9 Jul 1847)

BALDWIN, William Bennett, of New Garden, Chester Co PA, to HUEY, Mary Ann, Miss, of NC Co, 26 Jan 1842, at West Chester PA by Henry Fleming, Esq. (DG 4 Feb 1842)

BALL, George, to MONTGOMERY, Sarah, Miss, 10 Feb 1848, by Rev. Thomas Love (DG 15 Feb 1848)

BALL, James, to ROSS, Hannah H., both of Wilm, 20 Jan 1848, by Rev. J. R. Wynkoop (DG 26 Jan 1848)

BALL, James W., see McKNIGHT, John

BALL, Jesse, to DRAPER, Mary, Mrs., both of NC Co, in Phila, 20 Apr 1847, by the Rev. Mr. Grant (DG 30 Apr 1847)

BALL, John, see BALL, Mary

BALL, Martha, see McCREA, Samuel

BALL, Martin D., to MATTHEWS, Sarah, Miss, both of Port Penn DE, 14 Mar 1842, by the Rev. Mr. Brainard (DG 1 Apr 1842)

BALL, Mary, dau of John BALL, in Mill Creek, 10 Mar 1852, na (DG 16 Mar 1852) see RUBINCAME, John R.

BALL, Susan, at the res. of her mother in Mill Creek Hd, 14 Jul 1828, na (DG 18 Jul 1828)

BALL, William McK. Esq., formerly of NC Co, at his res. in Leona Mills TX, 13 Jun 1847, in his 48th yr (DG 10 Sep 1847)

BALLINGER, Edwin A., of Phila, to McMULLIN, Harriet A., Miss, of New Castle, 15 Jun 1853, by the Rev. J. H. Jones (DG 28 Jun 1853)

BANDERBRAAK, Lawrence, to STEVENSON, Mary, Miss, both of Wilm, in Marcus Hook PA, 2 Jan 1848, by Rev. Mr. Walker (DG 4 Jan 1847)

BANE, Mary, see WOODWARD, Samuel

BANKS, William, to McFARLIN, Mary Jane, Miss, both of NC Co, 11 Mar 1847, in Phila (DG 16 Mar 1847)

BANNAN, Edward, to FISHLER, Lydia, Miss, all of Wilm, 2 Jul 1846, by Rev. P. Reilley (DG 7 Jul 1846)

BANNARD, Jane, Mrs, after a short illness, 1 Jan 1842, aged 71 yrs (DG 7 Jan 1842)

BANNER, George, see BANNER, Thomas

BANNER, Lewis, in Mill Creek Hd, of typhoid congestive fever, 30 Mar 1843, aged 17 yrs (DG 7 Apr 1843)

BANNER, Thomas, son of George BANNER, of Wilm, of inflammation of the brain, 17 Jul 1848, aged 6 yrs (DG 28 Jul 1848)

BANNER, William W., to JACKSON, Susanna, Miss, all of Wilm, 28 Feb 1850, by Rev. William Cooper (DG 8 Mar 1850)

BANNING, Elizabeth, see ELLIOTT, Isaac S.

BANNING, George W., to PHILLIPS, Martha J., Miss, both of Sussex Co, in Milford, 2 July 1850, by Rev. Daniel Goodwin (DG 9 Jul 1850)

BANNING, Henry G., merchant of Wilm, to ESCHENBURG, Emily, Miss, dau of John

ESCHENBURG, Esq., of IL, and grand-dau of the late Hon Caesar A. Rodney, 7 Apr 1847, in Hanover St. Church by Rev. E. W. Gilbert (DG 13 Apr 1847)

BANNING, John A., see **ELLIOTT**, Isaac S.

BANNING, Nancy, see **COLLINS**, John W.

BANNING, Sallie R., see **ELLIOTT**, Isaac S.

BARBER, Peter, to **WAY**, Rachel Hanna (sic), Miss, both of Mill Creek Hd, 13 Feb 1834, by the Rev. A. K. Russel (DG 25 Feb 1834)

BARBER, Revilla, see **BODDY**, John

BARBOR, Martha Ann, see **APPLEBY**, John

BARBOUR, Abigail B., see **SUTTON**, James N. Dr.

BARBOUR, Esther A., see **CONLYN**, Thomas

BARCLAY, Andrew C., see **BARCLAY**, James

BARCLAY, James, son of Andrew C. BARCLAY, near Stanton, at the res. of John T. LONG, 27 Jun 1853, in his 34th yr (DG 8 Jul 1853)

BARDSLEY, Elizabeth, see **MANSLEY**, John G.

BARDSLEY, Sarah Ann, see **SHINN**, John

BARITT, Charles H., formerly a resident of Wilm, in Phila of consumption, 24 Apr 1848, in his 27th yr (DG 25 Apr 1848)

BARKER, Emeline S., see **BARRY**, John L.

BARKER, James P., Major, see **BARRY**, John L.

BARKER, Joseph, at the res. of George CUMMINS, Esq., in Kent Co, DE, 13 Jun 1825, aged 72 yrs (DG 21 Jun 1825) dec'd, late of NC Co, notice given by C. E. SIPPLE, adm'r C.P.A. (DG 30 Sep 1825)

BARLOW, Charles, see **BARLOW**, John

BARLOW, Emma, see **BARLOW**, John

BARLOW, George B., see **BARLOW**, John

BARLOW, Gideon E., see **BARLOW**, John

BARLOW, John, in NC Co, intestate. Mentions son, the late Nicholas BARLOW, and Lydia BARLOW, widow of Nicholas, and their children, Susan BARLOW WRIGHT, dec'd, Mary Ann BARLOW, Maria BARLOW, Lydia BARLOW, George B. BARLOW, Charles BARLOW, Louisa BARLOW, John BARLOW, Nicholas BARLOW, and Emma BARLOW. Also mentions Gideon E. BARLOW, assignee of Edward RICKARDS, who was assignee of John BARLOW. Also Gideon E. BARLOW, assignee of Thomas DEAKYNES, adm'r, who was assignee of William WRIGHT and wife (DG 4 Jan 1853)

BARLOW, Louisa, see **BARLOW**, John

BARLOW, Lydia, see **BARLOW**, John

BARLOW, Maria, see **BARLOW**, John

BARLOW, Mary Ann, see **BARLOW**, John

BARLOW, Nicholas, see **BARLOW**. John

BARLOW, Susan, see **BARLOW**, John

BARNABY, Margaret, see **JAMISON**, Alexander

BARNARD, D____, of Phila, to **WAPLES**, Ann Custis, Miss, eldest dau of Col. William D. WAPLES of Millsboro, in Millsboro, 19 Feb 1825, by the Rev. S. N. Woolford (DG 22 Feb 1825)

BARNARD, Jos. S., see **BARNARD**, Sarah

BARNARD, Sarah, Mrs., consort of Jos. S. BARNARD, Esq., at Dagsboro, 27 Nov 1853, na (DG 6 Dec 1853)

BARNARE, Moses, to **WRIGHT**, Mary Ann, Miss, both of St. Georges DE, in Phila, 21 Dec 1848, by Rev. A. Atwood (DG 5 Jan 1849)

BARNET, Henry, to **HAGUE**, Mary, Miss, both of Christiana Hd, by Benjamin F. Johnson, Esq., at his office in Marcus Hook PA (DG 30 Jul 1844)

BARNETT, James H., to **CARLISLE**, Rachel M., Miss, dau of the late William CARLISLE, of Wilm, 1 Feb 1862, by the Rev. J. Kennedy (DG 4 Feb 1842)

BARNEY, Alexander, to **GAULT**, Emma, Mrs., of Wilm, 17 Dec 1850, by Rev. Newton Heston (DG 24 Dec 1850)

BARNEY, Eliza, Mrs., late consort of St. J. Nicholas BARNEY, at Booth Hurst, near New Castle, the seat of her father, James ROGERS. Mr. Barney , U. S. Navy. is now on a cruise on the Brazilian coast. She was in her 25th yr, and died of dysentery after a 2 wk illness (DG 29 Aug 1848)

BARNEY, J. Nicholson, U. S. N., to
ROGERS, Eliza J., dau of James ROGERS,
Esq., at the res. of her father at Booth Hurst
DE, 9 Jun 1846 (DG 19 Jun 1846)

BARNEY, John, of Port Penn, to LEVIS,
Margaret, Miss, of Del. Co, PA, in Phila,
23 Sep 1818, by John Moulden, Esq.
(DG 26 Sep 1818)

BARNEY, Samuel Chase, U. S. Navy, to
DeKRAFT, Mary Eleanor, only dau of the
late Edward DeKRAFT, Esq., 14 Jun 1847,
by Rev. T. J. Thompson (DG 18 Jun 1847)

BARNEY, Solomon L. A., to COVINGTON,
Elizabeth, all of Wilm, 22 Jul 1847, by Rev.
T. J. Thompson (DG 13 Aug 1847)

BARNEY, St. J. Nicholas,
see BARNEY, Eliza

BARNEY, William Chase, to FRANCISCUS,
Ada Blanche, all of Wilm, 18 Nov 1848, by
Rev. Mr. McJilton [?] (DG 21 Nov 1848)

BARR, _____, Mrs. wife of John BARR,
at Rockland, Brandywine Hd, of dysentery,
20 Jul 1853, na (DG 26 Jul 1853)

BARR, Alexander Forrester,
see DRYDEN, John D. S.

BARR, Ann, wife of Joseph BARR, in Wilm,
9 Jun 1853, aged 36 yrs 3 mos 18 days
(DG 17 Jun 1853)

BARR, Anna Mary, dau of Joseph BARR,
in Wilm, 25 May 1845, aged 13 mos
(DG 27 May 1845)

BARR, Archimedis Jefferson, son of John H.
BARR, 17 Jul 1850, after an illness of
4 days, in his 16th yr (DG 6 Aug 1850)

BARR, Carrie D.,
see WALMSLEY, Robert Jr.

BARR, Catharine, Ann,
see BARR, Joseph

BARR, Catharine Forester,
see GIBBONS, Edward

BARR, Charles, inf. son of Joseph and
Catharine Ann BARR, Nov 16 1843, aged
19 mos and 2 days (DG 17 Nov 1843)

BARR, Elizabeth, eldest dau of Dr. M.
BARR, at the res of her father in Middle-
town, 10 Aug 1848, aged 26 yrs
(DG 18 Aug 1848)

BARR, Eugene W., youngest son of Dr.
M. BARR, in Middletown, 15 May 1844,
aged 7 yrs (DG 24 May 1844)

BARR, Forester,
see BARR, Samuel Candwell

BARR, Hannah Mary, dau of Jacob and
Rebecca BARR, in Wilm, 31 Mar 1848,
aged 4 yrs and 4 mos (DG 4 Apr 1848)

BARR, Henrietta,
see PENNINGTON, Thomas McDonough

BARR, Isaac S., grandson of Mr. William
BROWN in Wilm, 15 Jan 1851,
aged 6 yrs 8 mos (DG 17 Jan 1851)

BARR, J. A., Dr., see BARR, Mary Louisa

BARR, Jacob, see BARR, Hannah Mary

BARR, John, see BARR, _____, Mrs.

BARR, John, to McKEE, Isabella, Miss, all of
Wilm, 19 Jul 1827, by the Rev. J. B.
Peckworth (DG 24 Jul 1827)

BARR, John, to HENDERSON, Margaret
Young, Miss, both of Brandywine Hd,
17 Jan 1822, by the Rev. E. W. Gilbert
(DG 18 Jan 1822)

BARR, John H.,
see BARR, Archimedis Jefferson

BARR, Joseph, Rev.,
see DRYDEN, John D. S.

BARR, Joseph, see BARR, Ann
see GIBBONS, Edward
see BARR, Charles
see BARR, Anna Mary

BARR, Joseph M., editor of the *Delaware
Journal*, of Wilm, to JUSTIS, Hannah Mary,
Miss, of Mill Creek Hd, 10 Oct 1850, by Rev.
Mr. Batchelor (DG 15 Oct 1850)

BARR, M., Dr., see BARR, Eugene W.
see BARR, Elizabeth

BARR, Mary Louisa, dau of Dr. J. A. and
Ruth Anna BARR, at Delaware City, 9 Jun
1844, aged 3 yrs 1 mo (DG 21 Jun 1844)

BARR, Polly, see BELVILLE, Jacob

BARR, Rebecca,
see BARR, Hannah Mary

BARR, Rebecca, Mrs., in Wilm, 15 May
1849, in her 77th yr (DG 25 May 1849)

BARR, Robert, dec'd, notice given by Sarah
BARR, exec'x (DE 19 Mar 1798)

BARR, Robert M., Esq., reporter of the
Supreme Court of PA, formerly of DE,
suddenly at Reading PA, 26 Dec 1849,

aged 48 yrs (DG 1 Jan 1850)

BARR, Ruth Anna,
see BARR, Mary Louisa

BARR, Samuel, near New Castle, 27 Dec 1828, aged 92 yrs; member of the Presb. Ch for 60 yrs--elder for more than 40; survived by 89 descendants (DG 2 Jan 1829)

BARR, Samuel Candwell, son of A. Forester BARR, near Dover, 30 Aug 1852, in his 2nd yr (DG 17 Sep 1852)

BARR, Sarah, see BARR, Robert

BARR, Sarah F., see DRYDEN, John D. S.

BARRATT, Alfred, of New York, to CUMMINS, Martha, youngest dau of the late John CUMMINS, Esq., of Kent Co DE, in Phila, 20 Jun 1848, by Rev. William Suddards (DG 27 Jun 1848)

BARRATT, Andrew, see BOONE, Meriam

BARRATT, Merriam, see BOONE, Meriam,.

BARRETT, ___, Judge,
see LOCKWOOD, Sally

BARRETT, Caleb, see BARRETT, Nancy

BARRETT, Eliza,
see PRETTYMAN, Wm, the Rev.

BARRETT, Nancy, Miss, dau of Caleb BARRETT, Esq., dec'd, near Frederica, 17 Apr 1826, aged 21 yrs (DG 25 Apr 1826)

BARRETT, Sally,
see LOCKWOOD, Sally, Mrs.

BARRITT, Amanda G., dau of Wm. A. and Anna BARRITT, 22 May 1851, na (DG 23 May 1851)

BARRITT, Anna,
see BARRITT, Amanda G.

BARRITT, Elizabeth, Mrs, in Wilm, 31 Jan 1849, in her 73rd yr (DG 9 Feb 1849)

BARRITT, George C., at his res. in 4th St, Wilm, 28 Oct 1849, aged 33 yrs (DG 30 Oct 1849)

BARRITT, Wm. A.,
see BARRITT, Amanda G.

BARRON, Catharine A.,
see RAYBOLD, Clayton B.

BARRON, George,
see RAYBOLD, Clayton B.

BARROW, Denwood H.,
see HINDS, William S.

BARROW, Emelie F.,
see HINDS, William S.

BARRY, Henry, see RICE, Jane

BARRY, John L., to BARKER, Emeline S., Miss, dau of Major James P. BARKER, of Georgetown DE, in Phila, 6 Nov 1751, by the Rev. Joseph H. Smith (DG 14 Nov 1851)

BARSTOW, Simon, citizen and teacher of Wilm, 24 Oct 1828, na (DG 28 Oct 1828)

BARTHOLOMEW, Mary,
see PRICE, Thos. T.

BARTLETT, Furclose, late of Mill Creek Hd. Thos. BARTLETT, adm'r (DG 27 Jan 1852)

BARTLETT, Thos,
see BARTLETT, Furclose

BARTLEY, ___, Mr.,
see HILYARD, Simon. S.

BARTLEY, Edward P., son of James and Henrietta BARTLEY, 15 Nov 1850, aged 3 yrs 1 mo (DG 19 Nov 1850)

BARTLEY, Henrietta,
see BARTLEY, Edward P.
see BARTLEY, James Erby

BARTLEY, James,
see BARTLEY, James Erby
see BARTLEY, Edward P.

BARTLEY, James, to PIERCE, Henrietta, Miss, both of Wilm, 24 Jan 1847, by Rev. A. Atwood (DG 26 Jan 1847)

BARTLEY, James Erby, son of James and Henrietta BARTLEY, 13 Dec 1850, aged 6 mos 13 days (DG 17 Dec 1850)

BARTLEY, Margaret Jane,
see HILYARD, Simon S.

BARTON, Mary Jane,
see WILSON, George P.

BASSET, Nathan, 9 Aug 1847, in his 84th yr (DG 10 Aug 1847)

BASSETT, Elizabeth, in New Castle Hd, at the res. of Samuel BURNHAM, 13 Mar 1852, aged 100 yrs (DG 23 Mar 1852)

BASSETT, Mary, Miss, youngest dau of Hon. Richard BASSETT, 27 Aug 1807 (MU 12 Sep 1807)

BASSETT, Nathan,
see BASSETT, Sarah

BASSETT, Richard, Hon., see **BASSETT**, Mary

BASSETT, Sarah, Mrs., wife of Mr. Nathan BASSETT, in Wilm, 15 Sep 1826, aged 56 yrs (DG 19 Sep 1826)

BATEMAN, Hannah M., see **EMMORY**, Charles C.

BATEMAN, J. H., of Kent Co, to **ARMSTRONG**, Caroline S., both of NC Co, 26 Feb 1852, by the Rev. E. M. Van Deusen (DG 2 Mar 1852)

BATES, Daniel M., see **BATES**, Martin W.

BATES, Margaret H., see **BATES**, Martin W.

BATES, Martin W., youngest son of Daniel M. and Margaret H. BATES, in Wilm, 5 Oct 1849, aged 18 mos 26 days (DG 9 Oct 1849)

BATHGATE, Jane, see **APPLEGATE**, William

BATSON, George, see **MOORE**, Hester

BATTELL, French, a native of Dover and a res. of that city for more than 40 yrs, in Phila, 11 Jul 1853, na (DG 15 Jul 1853)

BATTELL, Merriam, Mrs., see **BRADY**, Benjamin, Esq.

BATTERSBY, James, dec'd, late of Wilm, notice given by Benjamin WEBB, adm'r (DG 15 Sep 1829)

BATTIN, Ann, see **McCLUEN**, John

BAUDUY, Peter, at Havana, 24 Aug 1833, aged 56 yrs (DG 1 Oct 1833)

BAUDUY, Peter 2nd, born near Wilm, at Cuba, 4 Dec 1841, aged 26 yrs (DG 31 Dec 1841)

BAXTER, Barbara Anna, see **HOLLAND**, John

BAXTER, Patrick, to **BRITTON**, Sarah, Miss, of Wilm, 24 Mar 1853, by the Rev. Mr. Breck (DG 8 Apr 1853)

BAYARD, Caroline, see **POWELL**, Barring

BAYARD, Charles, midshipman, son of Hon Richard H. BAYARD, formerly a U. S. Senator from DE, struck on the shoulder by a rock while visiting Mt. Vesuvius; arm amputated. (DG 29 Mar 1850) Long article; wound proved fatal. (DG 30 Apr 1850)

BAYARD, Isabella, Mrs., wife of Jacob BAYARD, at Frog Pond, near Smyrna, 14 Apr 1850. Burned to death while intoxicated (DG 26 Apr 1850)

BAYARD, Jacob, see **BAYARD**, Isabella

BAYARD, James A., see **SCHERMERHORN**, Cortland

BAYARD, James A. Jr. of typhoid, 17 Jul 1848, aged 23 yrs 6 mos (DG 21 Jul 1848)

BAYARD, James Ashton, of Wilm, to **FRANCIS**, Anne, Miss, dau of the late Thomas Willing FRANCIS, in Phila, 8 Jul 1823, by the Rt. Rev. Bishop White (DG 11 Jul 1823)

BAYARD, Mary Ellen, see **SCHERMERHORN**, Cortland

BAYARD, Mary Louisa, see **BECK**, William Henry

BAYARD, Richard, see **BECK**, William Henry

BAYARD, Richard H., see **POWELL**, Barring see **BAYARD**, Charles

BAYARD, Susannah, see **UNDERWOOD**, George W.

BAYARD, Thomas, see **POSTLES**, Stephen

BAYNE, Nathaniel, late of White Clay Creek Hd, Robert BAYNE, adm'r (DG 19 Jun 1849)

BAYNE, Robert, see **BAYNE**, Nathaniel

BAYS, Mary S., Mrs., 7 Jan 1853, in her 32nd yr (DG 21 Jan 1853)

BEACH, James, negro, of yellow fever (DE 18 Sep 1798)

BEACH, John Sheldon, Esq., of New Haven Conn, to **GIBBONS**, Rebecca, Miss, dau of the late William GIBBONS D. M., of Wilm, at Vernon Place in Wilm, 15 Sep 1847, by Rev. S. R. Wynkoop (DG 17 Sep 1847)

BEACK, Joseph L., to **LAKE**, Lydia Ann, Miss, both of Lewistown, in Phila, 17 Dec 1848, by Rev. C. Karsner (DG 22 Dec 1848)

BEALE, Edward F., Lieut. US Navy, to **ENGLE**, Mary, dau of the Hon. Samuel EDWARDS, in Chester, Del Co, PA, 28 Jun 1849, by the Rev. Mortimer R. Talbot of the US Navy (DG 29 Jun 1849)

BEARD, Duncan, dec'd, late of Appoq Hd, notice given by the Trustees of the 1st

Presbyterian Ch, St. Georges Hd, that they intend to petition the General Assembly to vest said Ch with certain property devised to the Ch by the last will and testament of said DUNCAN, but which for want of due execution of said will the Ch cannot now take--John HYATT, chairman of the Board (DE 24 Dec 1798)

BEARD, Mary, 17 Oct 1823, na (DG 21 Oct 1823)

BEASTON, Charles, to COCHRAN, Olivia R. M., Miss, both of Cantwell's Bridge, 19 Apr 1841, by Rev. George Foot of Port Penn (DG 23 Apr 1841)

BEASTON, Wiliam, to DAILEY, Sarah Elizabeth, Miss, all of NC Co, in Wilm, 18 Apr 1850, by Rev. M. J. Rhees (DG 23 Apr 1850)

BEATTY, Elizabeth, see BURNSIDE, John

BEAUCHAMP, Jeremiah, to DUNHAM, Mary, Mrs., both of Kent, 2 Apr 1789 (DG 11 Apr 1789)

BEAUCHAMP, Sarah A., see PALMATORY, Robert

BECK, Edward, merchant of Smyrna, to FOSTER, Mary E., of Queen Anne's Co MD, in Milford, 16 Mar 1851, by Rev. J. Bell (DG 25 Mar 1851)

BECK, John, to ROGERS, Sarah Alfonso, dau of John ROGERS, formerly of Wilm, 16 Jan 1842, at Fairmont, Phila by the Rev. F. Rafferty (28 Jan 1842)

BECK, William Henry, to BAYARD, Mary Louisa, Miss, dau of the Hon Richard BAYARD at Phila, 8 Nov 1849, by the Rev. Dr. Ducachet (DG 13 Nov 1849)

BECKLEY, Caroline, see MARTIN, Daniel

BECKLEY, Chester, of Wilm, 16 Nov 1821 (DG 30 Nov 1821)

BECKLEY, Robinson, to HODSON, Juliet, 4 Nov 1841, by Rev. S. Leach, all of Wilm (DG 12 Nov 1841)

BECKLEY, Sally Ann, see SHIPMAN, Joseph J.

BECKWORTH, Ann W., see MASON, Charles

BEDFORD, God., dec'd, late of NC Co, notice given by John STOCKTON, adm'r (DE 26 Feb 1798)

BEDFORD, Gunning, Esq., Gov. of DE, at New Castle, 30 Sep 1797 (DE 5 Oct 1797) see HACKETT, John W.

BEDFORD, Sally, see HACKETT, John W.

BEDWELL, William to HAYS, Rebekah, Miss, 5 Oct 1841, by Elder John Miller, all of Wilm (DG 8 Oct 1841)

BEE, Mary J., see RECORDS, Edward J.

BEE, Thomas, see RECORDS, Edward J.

BEEBE, John Wesley, of Phila to RIDDLE, Elizabeth Canby, Miss, of Wilm, 7 Jun 1849 in Phila by Rev. John Street (DG 19 Jun 1849)

BEEKMAN, Mary, see BIGGS, Benjamin T.

BEESON, Charles A., of Phila, to ALRICH, Adeline C., dau of Thomas C. ALRICH, of Wilm, 7 Aug 1850, by Rev. William W. Taylor (DG 16 Aug 1850)

BEESON, Edward, late of Brandywine Hd, Mary BEESON, adm'x (DG 16 Apr 1852)

BEESON, Elizabeth, widow of Jonathan BEESON, 10 Feb 1823, aged 48 yrs, leaving 1 dau and 1 son (DG 18 Feb 1823)

BEESON, Ellen, see HARKER, Thomas B.

BEESON, Jonathan, see BEESON, Elizabeth

BEESON, Joseph, see McKEE, Mary

BEESON, Mary, see BEESON, Edward

BEESON, Mary J., see GUEST, Byard

BEESON, Thomas, Esq., at his res. in Brandywine Hd, 7 May 1825, "old" (DG 13 May 1825)

BEETLE, Rebecca, see WATTS, James

BEGGS, Joseph R., son of William and Mary F. BEGGS, 2 Nov 1848, aged 5 yrs (DG 10 Nov 1848)

BEGGS, Mary F., see BEGGS, Joseph R.

BEGGS, William, see BEGGS, Joseph R.

BELL, Hannah F., see HOUSTON, David H.

BELL, Hugh, to TOPHAM, Harriet, Miss, 23 Feb 1830, by Rev. Laurence McCombe, all of NC Co (DG 26 Feb 1830)

BELL, Jacob H., to BIRCH, Margaret Jane,

DELAWARE MARRIAGES AND DEATHS FROM NEWSPAPERS, 1729-1853

Miss, both of Cantwell's Bridge, 27 Jul 1843, by Rev. William Ryder (DG 4 Aug 1843)

BELL, Margaret, see VAUGHAN, Richard

BELL, Mary Caroline, see KEENAN, John A.

BELL, Reese J., to CROCKETT, Araminta, Miss, both of Smyrna, in Phla, 6 Jun 1850, by Rev. David Shields (DG 11 Jun 1850)

BELL, Richard H., of Baltimore, to HUDSON, Sarah E., of DE, in Baltimore, 21 Oct 1847, by Rev. Mr. Lipscomb (DG 29 Oct 1847)

BELL, Wm. M., to HOFFECKER, Emlie, Miss, dau of Joseph HOFFECKER, Jr., dec'd, of Duck Creek Hd, 8 Jun 1852, by Rev. J. A. Roche (DG 15 Jun 1852)

BELLERBY, Ann, see SPACKMAN, Samuel

BELTS, Charlotte, see HARDCASTLE, Thos. H.

BELVILLE, Jacob, to BARR, Polly, Miss, both of New Castle Hd, 29 Oct 1789 (DG 4 Nov 1789)

BELVILLE, John, at New Castle, 29 Nov 1827. He was a ruling Elder of the New Castle Presbyterian Ch (DG 11 Dec 1827) Mary BELVILLE, adm'x (DG 4 Jan 1828) notice given by Henry VINING, atty-in-fact for Mary BELVILLE, adm'x (DG 4 Mar 1828)

BELVILLE, Mary, see BELVILLE, John

BENDER, Mary Ellen, see GARDNER, James S.

BENNESON, William H., Esq., attorney of Quincy Ill, to BRADLEY, Eliza, Miss, dau of Andrew BRADLEY, Esq., of Newark, 11 Jun 1846, at Newark (DG 19 Jun 1846)

BENNET, Adeline, see KING, Pennel

BENNET, Elizabeth, Miss, dau of Mr. Ezekiel BENNET, late of Brandywine, 14 May 1829, aged 17 yrs (DG 19 May 1829)

BENNET, Ezekiel, see BENNET, Elizabeth

BENNET, Gilpin, in Pennsbury Twp, Chester Co PA, 14 Oct 1849, aged c 50 yrs (DG 19 Oct 1849)

BENNET, Harriet, see KING, Pennel

BENNET, James R., to McCOY, Catharine, all of Wilm, 7 Dec 1852, by the Rev. Andrew Manship (DG 31 Dec 1852)

BENNET, Joseph, 4 Mar 1808, aged 90 yrs (MU 5 Mar 1808)

BENNET, Mary E., see DEXTER, George W.

BENNET, Mary Jane, in Stanton, 20 Jun 1853, aged 2 yrs 10 mos (DG 24 Jun 1853)

BENNET, Thomas J., to MAYFIELD, Anna Elizabeth, Mrs. both of Wilm, 24 Jan 1850, by Rev. Newton Heston (DG 1 Feb 1850)

BENNET, Titus, see KING, Pennel

BENNETT, _____, Gov., see LISLE, Henry

BENNETT, Abraham, at his res. at Chesapeake City, 24 Feb 1836 (DG 1 Mar 1836)

BENNETT, Angelo, of Barkers Landing, to ROLLAND, Elizabeth O., Miss, of Milford Hd, 4 Feb 1834, by Rev. William Barns, all of Kent Co (DG 11 Feb 1834)

BENNETT, Boadiciea (sic), see PARDEE, Isaac, the Rev.

BENNETT, C. P., see BENNETT, Joseph

BENNETT, Caleb, see PARDEE, Isaac, the Rev.

BENNETT, Caleb F., Major, see BENNETT, Caroline

BENNETT, Caleb P., see VANDEVER, Jacob B

BENNETT, Caroline, Miss, dau of Major Caleb F. BENNETT of Wilm, at New Orleans of yellow fever, ndd (DG 12 Nov 1822)

BENNETT, Charles H., to FISHLER, Mary Ann, Miss, all of Wilm, 28 Nov 1843, by Rev. J. Kennaday (DG 1 Dec 1834)

BENNETT, Charles W., Lt., USRS, to ROWAN, Mary, dau of William ROWAN, 14 Dec 1841, by Rev. E. W. Gilbert, D. D., all of Wilm (DG 17 Dec 1841)

BENNETT, Eliza, see VANDEVER, Jacob B.

BENNETT, Eliza J., see SIMPLER, Samuel

BENNETT, George, to DRAPER, Abigail, Miss, all of Sussex Co, 20 Sep 1847, by Rev. John Street (DG 24 Sep 1847)

BENNETT, George H., of NC Co near

Stanton, to **DUKE**, Emeline, of Laurel, Sussex Co, 27 Nov 1841, by Rev. Corry Chambers (DG 3 Dec 1841)

BENNETT, Jeru, Sr. at his res. in Balt Hd, Sussex Co, 24 Nov 1853, aged 86 yrs (DG 6 Dec 1853)

BENNETT, John W., of Chester Co PA, to **BOYER**, Hannah T., of NC Co, in Phila, 16 Sep 1847, by Rev. C. Karsner (DG 28 Sep 1847)

BENNETT, Joseph, notice given by C. P. **BENNETT**, exec'r (MU 18 Feb 1809)

BENNETT, Joshua L., late of Appoq. Hd, Mary H. **BENNETT**, exec'x (DG 16 Dec 1851)

BENNETT, Mary H., see **BENNETT**, Joshua L.

BENNETT, Rachel, see **MIFFLIN**, J. Biddle

BENNETT, Stephen, to **SIMPLER**, Hester A., Miss, all of Sussex Co DE, in Phila, 9 Oct 1849, by the Rev. Levi Storks (DG 16 Oct 1849)

BENNISON, Maria M., see **BENNISON**, Thomas

BENNISON, Martha A., see **BENNISON**, Thomas

BENNISON, Thomas, late of White Clay Creek Hd. Maria M. and Martha A. BENNISON, executrices (DG 20 Nov 1849)

BENSON, Catharine, see **COULTER**, John W.

BENSON, James H., of Cecil Co, MD, to **RUMFORD**, Louisa, Miss, dau of Mr. John RUMFORD of Wilm, 18 Jun 1826, by the Rev. Laurence McCoombs (DG 16 Jun 1826)

BENSON, Joseph B., to **CROCKETT**, Mary E., MIss, all of Smyrna, in Smyrna, 12 Feb 1852, by Rev. E. H. Gilroy (DG 24 Feb 1852)

BENSON, Mary, see **COULTER**, John M.

BENT, Hiram, late of Kent and formerly of Q. Annes Co MD, in St Georges DE, about a week since (DG 21 Sep 1849)

BENTON, Jacob (colored), see **BENTON**, Jane

BENTON, Jane, wife of Jacob Benton (colored), in Wilm, 21 Sep 1848, aged 70 yrs. She was born on the day of the Battle of Brandywine (DG 6 Oct 1848)

BENZEL, Adolph, see **TRANBERG**, Andrew

BERRY, Mary, see **PIERSON**, Wilson

BERRY, Thomas C., to **COLDWELL**, Marietta B., all of NC Co, 6 Aug 1845, by Rev. E. Gerry (DG 12 Aug 1845)

BESON, Lydia A., see **McGOWAN**, Patrick, Esq.

BESSE, John, Lieut., of the U. S. Revenue, to **GOLDEN**, Sarah, Miss, of Baltimore, at New Castle, 11 Feb 1830, by the Rev. William Prestman (DG 16 Feb 1830)

BEST, John, of Wilm, to **ALBRIGHT**, Ann Maria, of Lancaster PA, 1 May 1844, in Lancaster, by Elder C. H. Thomas (DG 14 May 1844)

BEST, Thompson, of Balt., formerly of Lancaster PA, to **BRACKIN**, Salina, Miss, of Wilm, in Phila, on the 48th (sic) ult. by Rev. A. Atwood (DG 2 Feb 1849)

BESWICK, Ann D., see **HYNSON**, Matthew M.

BESWICK, Mary, formerly of Milford, in Wilm, 23 Mar 1853, aged 45 yrs (DG 25 Mar 1853)

BETEHLER, Andrew J., to **SNYDER**, Harriet, Miss, all of Wilm, 5 Jun 1848, by Rev. M. J. Rhees (DG 13 Jun 1848)

BETS, Charles, to **McLACHLAN**, Eliza J., Miss, all of Wilm, 19 May 1850, by Rev. William Cooper (DG 28 May 1850)

BETSON, John, at New Castle, 13 Aug 1803, aged 53 (FA 17 Aug 1803)

BETTS, Benjamin, suddenly, 17 Apr 1824, na (DG 20 Apr 1824) late of Wilm, notice given by Mary BETTS, adm'x and Mahlon BETTS, adm'r (DG 4 May 1824)

BETTS, Charles, in Wilm, 25 Jan 1851, aged c 22 yrs (DG 31 Jan 1851)

BETTS, Edward, of Wilm, to **TATNALL**, Mary A. R., dau of Edward TATNALL of Brandywine, in Wilm, 25 Sep 1851, in Friends meeting (DG 30 Sep 1851)

BETTS, Emily, see **SMYTH**, Wiliam C.

BETTS, Hannah, wife of Jesse BETTS, in Wilm, 24 Mar 1852, aged 86 yrs (DG 30 Mar 1852)

BETTS, Jesse, see **BETTS**, Hannah

BETTS, Mahlon, see **BETTS**, Benjamin

see **SMYTH**, William C.

BETTS, Mary, see **BETTS**, Benjamin

BETTS, Sarah A., see **FOWLER**, Elias B.

BETTS, William, 1n Wilm, 27 Aug 1848, in his 22nd yr (DG 29 Aug 1848)

BEWLEY, James L., see **BLACKISTON**, Richard

BEZENOS, Zeba, drowned, 6 Jul 1845, in Cedar Creek. A Frenchman in this country for 1 month (DG 11 Jul 1845)

BIAYS, Elizabth, see **BIAYS**, Samuel

BIAYS, Samuel, dec'd, late of Wilm, notice given by Elizabeth BIAYS, adm'x (DE 19 Sep 1799)

BICKING, Richard, to **TAYLOR**, Mary Rebecca Miss, both of Wilm, in Wilm, 15 Nov 1849, by the Rev. S. R. Wynkoop (DG 23 Nov 1849)

BIDDLE, ____, Mrs., see **BIDDLE**, ____.

BIDDLE, ____, litle son of Mrs. BIDDLE, accidental drowning in Wilm, 25 Aug 1853, aged c 4 yrs (DG 30 Aug 1853)

BIDDLE, Alexander M., see **FRAZIER**, Richard A.

BIDDLE, Andrew, see **BIDDLE**, Sarah

BIDDLE, Ann Elizabeth, see **MAYFIELD**, Solomon

BIDDLE, Augustine F., dec'd, late of St. Georges Hd, sale of property by John SUTTON, adm'r (DG 19 Oct 1827)

BIDDLE, Bobias (sic) R., to **WILLIAMS**, Elizabeth B., Miss, 7 Oct 1841, by Rev. William Rider (DG 15 Oct 1841)

BIDDLE, Charles Henry, inf son of Samuel and Eliza J, BIDDLE, at New Castle, 16 Nov 1852, aged 9 mos 21 days (DG 23 Nov 1852)

BIDDLE, Eliza, see **WHILBY**, John

BIDDLE, Eliza J., see **BIDDLE**, Charles Henry

BIDDLE, Elizabeth S., see **ROBINSON**, George W.

BIDDLE, George, in Brandywine Village, 17 Jun 1849, na (DG 19 Jun 1849)

BIDDLE, Jacob, see **BIDDLE**, Rebecca see **BIDDLE**, John P.

BIDDLE, John P., student of medicine and son of Mr. Jacob BIDDLE, merchant of Milford, at his father's res. in Milford, 29 Mar 1818 (AW 11 Apr 1818)

BIDDLE, Mary Alexina Josephine, see **FRAZIER**, Richard A.

BIDDLE, Matilda, see **RIDGEWAY**, Josiah

BIDDLE, Olivia Ann, see **CAVENDER**, Lewis

BIDDLE, Rebecca, relict of the late Jacob BIDDLE, Esq., at the res. of Charles W. RIDGELY, Esq., at Georgetown, 9 Nov 1842, aged 69 yrs (DG 18 Nov 1842)

BIDDLE, Richard F., of Cecil Co MD, to **CLELAND**, Margaret Jane, Miss, of NC Co, 12 Jan 1843, by Rev. T. R. Wynkoop (DG 13 Jan 1843)

BIDDLE, Samuel, see **BIDDLE**, Charles Henry

BIDDLE, Sarah, Mrs., consort of Mr. Andrew BIDDLE, 30 Apr 1851, near Port Penn DE, na. (DG 6 May 1851)

BIDDLE, Stephen, late of Red Lion Hd, James LECOMPT, adm'r (DG 20 May 1853)

BIDDLE, Thomas, of NC Co, to **STEWART**, Sarah, Miss, dau of Mr. William STEWART near Port Penn, DE, 22 Feb 1825, by the Rev. Samuel Bell (DG 11 Mar 1825)

BIDERMAN, James Anthony, to **DuPONT**, Eveline Gabriel, Miss, both of Wilm, 14 Sep 1816, by Rev. William Weekes (AW 16 Sep 1816)

BIDWELL, Elizabeth, see **DIXON**, V. Cooper

BIGGS, Benjamin T., Major, of NC Co, to **BEEKMAN**, Mary, Miss, of Somerset Co NJ, 18 May 1853, by the Rev. W. H. Brisbane (DG 20 May 1853)

BIGNERL, Margaret, see **KNIGHT**, George H.

BIGSBY, Daniel, to **JONES**, Jane, 21 Feb 1828, by Rev. J. N. Danforth (DG 29 Feb 1828)

BILLANEY, John, to **JACKSON**, Ann, Miss, 4 Jun 1829, by the Rev. David Daily (DG 9 Jun 1829)

BILLANY, John, in Wilm, 5 Apr 1843, aged 53 yrs (DG 7 Apr 1843)

BILLENSTEIN, Jacob T., to **BROOM**, Mary

S., dau of the late Jacob BROOM, Esq., of DE, 8 Nov 1847, by Rev. N. S. Harris (DG 16 Nov 1847)

BILLING, Augusta M, see COX, Samuel K.

BILLINGHAM, Hannah B., see STANHOPE, Jacob

BINGHAM, Archibald, 6 Jul 1825, na (DG 8 Jul 1825)

BINGHAM, Margaret, see LAFOREST, John A. A.

BINGHAM, Robert, formerly of Phila, in Wilm, 15 Mar 1848, aged 38 yrs (DG 28 Mar 1848)

BIRCH, Margaret Jane, see BELL, Jacob H.

BIRD, Alfred D., formerly of DE, to LAWSON, Ellen, of the same place, 11 Dec 1850, by Rev. Kennard (DG 3 Jan 1851)

BIRD, Elizabeth, see GAILEY, Thomas

BIRD, J. H., M D, of Chicago, to BALANEY, Fanny E., dau of the late C. D. BELANEY, of New Castle, at Chicago, 2 Sep 1851, by the Rev. J. R. Hibbard (DG 9 Sep 1851)

BIRD, James T., to CLARK, Susan M., Miss, in Wilm, 9 Feb 1841, by Rev. James C. How (DG 12 Feb 1841)

BIRD, Joseph, see BIRD, Rebecca

BIRD, Lewis, to WEBSTER, Elizabeth, Miss, both of NC Co, in Phila, 1 Dec 1847, by Rev. J. Humphries (DG 14 Dec 1847)

BIRD, Lulia, dau of John C. CLARK, Esq., at the res. of her husband, Thomas BIRD, 24 Mar 1848, in her 19th yr (DG 4 Apr 1848)

BIRD, Rachel H., see CARTMELL, George T.

BIRD, Rebecca, late wife of Joseph BIRD, Mar 1843, in Brandywine Hd, aged 42 yrs (DG 7 Apr 1843)

BIRD, Rebecca Caldwell, see SMITH, William

BIRD, Robert, of Brandywine Hd, 19 Nov 1848 (DG 5 Dec 1848)

BIRD, Sarah, see SHELLEY, Joseph

BIRD, Thomas M., of Red Lion Hd, to SMITH, Fanny, of Balt, in Balt, 25 Nov 1852, by the Rt. Rev. Bishop Waugh (DG 30 Nov 1852)

BIRD, Thomas, see BIRD, Lulia

BIRD, Thomas, to CLARK, Julia A., Miss, only dau of John C. CLARK, all of Red Lion Hd, 29 Apr 1847, at Prospect Fair, by Rev. Jas. C. How (DG 30 Apr 1847)

BIRD, William, to HUSBANDS, Naomi, Mrs., both of NC Co, 24 Dec 1829, by Elder John P. Peckworth (DG 29 Dec 1829)

BIRD, William, to GRAY, Julia Ann, Miss, both of Brandywine Hd, 28 Oct 1830, by Rev. R. U. Morgan (DF 13 Nov 1830)

BISHOP, Cathern R., see DENNEY, Thomas H.

BISHOP, Cynthia, (colored), heart disease, 30 Dec 1845 (DG 2 Jan 1846)

BISHOP, James H., of Worcester MD, to LYNCH, Jane, Miss, of Sussex, 14 Sep 1842, by Rev. J. Bissey (DG 18 Nov 1842)

BISHOP, John Wesley, of Wilm Hd, George BUZINE, adm'r (DG 13 Dec 1853)

BISHOP, Uriah C., to Mrs. Hannah OCHELTREE of NC Co, at Marcus Hook, PA, 5 Feb 1834, by Rev. J. Walker (DG 11 Feb 1834)

BLACK, Charles H., Dr., in New Castle, 7 Feb 1852, aged 42 yrs (DG 10 Feb 1852)

BLACK, Eliza Jane, see JAQUETT, Isaac Grantham

BLACK, Elizabeth, at White Cottage, the res. of Schee MERRITT, Esq., near Middletown, 27 Jul 1847, aged 63 yrs (DG 3 Aug 1847)

BLACK, Elizabeth, relict of William BLACK, formerly a printer at Trenton NJ and Wilm, 1 Jan 1848, at Salem NJ, in her 81st yr (DG 21 Jan 1848)

BLACK, George, see BLACK, James

BLACK, James, dec'd, late of Mill Creek Hd, notice given by Mary BLACK, George BLACK and Thomas MONTGOMERY (DG 15 Aug 1795)

BLACK, James, Dr., see HANSON, Alexander B., Capt.

BLACK James, to WATSON, Naomi, Miss, both of Sussex Co, 30 Sep 1849, by the Rev. S. C. Palmiter (DG 25 Sep 1849)

BLACK, Jane,

see **YOUNG**, Stephen Decatur

BLACK, John Churchill,
see **JACKSON**, Mary Ann

BLACK, John G., of Frederick, MD, to **CUMMINS**, Alphonsa, Miss, second dau of John CUMMINS, Esq., of Smyrna, in Smyrna, 4 Jun 1833, by the Rev. Mr. Higby (DG 14 Jun 1833)

BLACK, John G.,
see **HANSON**, Alexander B., Capt.

BLACK, Mary, Mrs., formerly of Wilm, in Unionville PA, 13 Aug 1851, in her 82nd yr (DG 26 Aug 1851)

BLACK, Mary, see **MORRISON**, Moses
see **BLACK**, James

BLACK, Mary Ann,
see **JACKSON**, Mary Ann

BLACK, Samuel H., Dr., member of the State Legislature and Brig Gen'l of the DE militia, suddenly at New Ark, 19 Apr 1827, na (DG 24 Apr 1827)

BLACK, Samuel H., to **LINSEY**, Mary J., Miss, all of Newark, 29 Jan 1846, near Newark, by Rev. Mr. Oram (DG 10 Feb 1846)

BLACK, Susan W.,
see **HANSON**, Alexander B., Capt.

BLACK, William, dec'd, notice given by Rev. William PRYCE, Hez. NILES and Joseph JONES, adm'rs (MU 10 Nov 1804)

BLACK, William, see **BLACK**, Elizabeth

BLACKBURN, ____, Mr., ship carpenter, killed in shipyard accident in Kensington, 17 Nov 1853, na. He had lived and worked in the Wilm area (DG 18 Nov 1853)

BLACKFORD, Garret, an old and respectable citizen of Wilm, 16 Jan 1816 (AW 24 Jan 1816)

BLACKISTON, ____, colored child living with its parents, burned at a fireplace, na (DG 26 Dec 1853)

BLACKISTON, Ebenezer, at Smyrna, 11 Dec 1829, aged 63 yrs (DG 12 Jan 1830)

BLACKISTON, Richard H., late of Duck Creek Hd, James L. BEWLEY, adm'r (DG 7 Jun 1853)

BLACKLAR, Charles R., to **MILLER**, Mary Alice, Miss, of Middletown, 12 Jan 1853,

by Rev. Charles M. C. Alfresh (DG 18 Jan 1853)

BLACKWAY, Eliza, see **HAAS**, John

BLACKWELL, George,
see **BLACKWELL**, Sarah

BLACKWELL, George, to **DRAPER**, Sarah Ann, Miss, both of Wilm, 7 Apr 1851, by the Rev. A. Atwood, at the res. of Mr. R. E. Morrell (DG 11 Apr 1851)

BLACKWELL, Henry, to **BODDY**, Sarah, both of Wilm, 29 Dec 1846, by Rev. H. R. Callaway (DG 5 Jan 1847)

BLACKWELL, Sarah, late wife of George BLACKWELL, in Wilm, 7 Feb 1844 (DG 13 Feb 1844)

BLACKWELL, Stephen G., to **GRUBB**, Rebecca, Miss, both of Brandywine Hd, 26 Sep 1850, by Rev. J. B. Maddox (DG 1 Oct 1850)

BLACKWELL, William P., to **MILLER**, Jane, Miss, both of Wilm, in Phila, 14 Mar 1848, by Rev. A. Atwood (DG 21 Mar 1848)

BLACKWOOD, Ann,
see **COLEMAN**, William

BLACKWOOD, Mary W.,
see **MOORE**, Charles T.

BLACKWOOD, Rebecca,
see **GRIST**, Moses M. B.

BLAKSHAIRE, Margaret, Miss,
see **WOLLASTON**, Joshua

BLANDY, Elizabeth Martha,
see **SHAPLEIGH**, M. S.

BLANDY, Thomas,
see **SHAPLEIGH**, M. S.

BLANDY, Thomas, Esq., in Newark, 17 Aug 1849, aged c 66 yrs (DG 21 Aug 1849)

BLANEY, C. C. see **EATON**, J. H.

BLANEY, Cornelius D., late Recorder and Clerk of Orphan's Court, 6 Nov 1847. For 8 or 9 yrs Prothonotary (see Nov 9 issue) (DG 12 Nov 1847)

BLANEY, Susan C., see **EATON**, J. H.

BLAUVELT, Margaret,
see **GRIFFITH**, Edmund

BLEASDALE, John, to **MUNDOON**, Mary Elizabeth, all of Wilm, 2 Oct 1851, by Rev. Andrew Manship (DG 7 Oct 1851)

BLEST, Adeline, inf dau of James and Mary BLEST, in Wilm, 20 Feb 1850, aged c 7 yrs (DG 22 Feb 1850)

BLEST, Brian W., to SMITH, Hannah, Miss, both of Wilm, in Wilm, 18 Dec 1823, by the Rev. E. W. Gilbert (DG 23 Dec 1823)

BLEST, James, see BLEST, Adeline

BLEST, Mary, see BLEST, Adeline

BLEYER, William, to McALLISTER, Lavenia, both of Wilm, 28 Dec 1843, by Rev. P. Riley (DG 12 Jan 1844)

BLISS, Mary, see WHITELOCK, James

BLIZZARD, Geo., to BUTLER, Rebecca, Miss, all of Wilm, 5 Aug 1852, by Rev. A. Atwood (DG 10 Aug 1852)

BLIZZARD, Gideon W., to SPARKS, Mary Jane, Miss, all of Wilm, 11 Mar 1847, by Rev. A. Atwood (DG 16 Mar 1847)

BLOUNT, James, to ROBINSON, Lydia Ann, Miss, both of NC Co, in Wilm, 5 Mar 1846, by Rt. Rev. Alfred Lee (DG 13 Mar 1846)

BLUNDELLEMERSON,
see MARIM, Susan B.,

BOALER, James, son of James BOALER of Smyrna, 12 Mar 1850, in his 3rd yr (DG 19 Mar 1850)

BOCKIUS, Mary Ann,
see WEAVER, John L.

BODDY,_____, Mr., to WINGATE, Frances Ann, Miss, both of Stanton DE, 10 Sep 1849, by the Rev. Christopher Crouch (DG 25 Sep 1849)

BODDY, Ann E. dau of Benjamin BODDY, in Wilm (DG 18 Jul 1848)

BODDY, Benjamin, see BODDY, Ann E.

BODDY, Benjamin M., to LEWIS, Easther Lima, Miss, both of Wilm, 10 Mar 1846, by Rev. H. Bibighaus (DG 31 Mar 1846)

BODDY, John, to BARBER, Revilla, Miss, all of Wilm, in Phila, 4 Dec 1850, by the Rev. T. J. Thompson (DG 1 Jul 1851)

BODDY, Maggie,
see HOUSTON, Shepherd

BODDY, Margaretta, consort of Stephen BODDY, Esq., in Wilm, 25 Dec 1851, aged c 60 yrs (DG 30 Dec 1851)

BODDY, Sarah, see BLACKWELL, Henry

BODDY, Sarah Ann,
see McLEOD, Alexander

BODDY, Stephen,
see HOUSTON, Shepherd
see BRANGAN, John
see BODDY, Margaretta

BODDY, Stephen, to BROWN, Ann, Miss 4 Oct 1811, by Rev. Mr. Saunders, all of Wilm (DS 11 Oct 1811)

BODELL, John, of Wilm, to FILE, Elizabeth, Miss, of Brandywine Hd, 25 Dec 1822, by the Rev. E. W. Gilbert (DG 27 Dec 1822)

BODEN, Edward, native of Salem MA, at Smyrna, 10 Sep 1834, aged 24 yrs (DG 10 Oct 1834)

BODINE, Samuel T., to NIXON, Isabella S., Miss, dau of Jeremiah S. NIXON, Esq., all of Barker's Landing, Kent Co, 19 Dec 1833, by William Barns (DG 24 Dec 1833)

BOGAN, Fanny, in Christiana Hd, 4 Feb 1852, aged c 100 yrs (DG 13 Feb 1852)

BOGGS, John, of Welsh Tract Ch, to GRIFFITH, Mary, Mrs., nmd (DG 4 Jul 1789)

BOIES, Jeremiah S. H., Esq., formerly of Cecil Co MD, at his res. in Wilm, 28 Dec 1852, aged 56 yrs (DG 31 Dec 1852) late of Wilm city. Mary Francis (sic) Caroline BOIES, exec'x (DG 7 Jan 1853)

BOIES, Mary Francis Caroline,
see BOIES, Jeremiah S. H.

BOLTON, Elizabeth,
see HAVELLOW, John R.

BOLTON, Henry Clay, formerly of New Castle, at New Orleans, 5 Jul 1852, in his 91st yr (DG 13 Jul 1852)

BOND, William E., of Phila, to HILL, Mary Elizabeth, Miss, of Frederica DE, in Phila, 24 Jan 1848, by Alderman Brazer (DG 1 Feb 1848)

BONNEY, Maria D.,
see GILLINGHAM, Robert

BONSALL, George H., son of Israel R. BONSALL of NC Co, 20 Feb 1845, aged 5 yrs (DG 28 Feb 1845)

BONSALL, Isaac, in Wilm, 29 Jun 1829, na (DG 3 Jul 1829)

BONSALL, Israel R.,
see BONSALL, George H.

BONSALL, Jesse T., of Kennett Square, to ENGLAND, Mary A., dau of Thomas ENGLAND of Wilm, 9 May 1844, in Friends Meeting (DG 14 May 1844)

BONSALL, Stephen, of Wilm, to ZANE, Mary E., dau of Jesse S. ZANE of Phila, 5 May 1825, at Friends Meeting, Mulberry St, Phila (DG 10 May 1825)

BOON, Catharine Somers, dau of James BOON, Esq. of Georgetown, Kent Co MD, fell down the stairs, aged 8 yrs 1 mo (DG 8 Oct 1844)

BOON, James, Esq.,
see BOON, Catharine Somers

BOON, James, Esq., of Kent Co, MD, to SMITH, Charlotte, Miss, dau of the late Richard E. SMITH of NC Co, in Phila, 20 Feb 1830, by Rev. James Montgomery (DG 23 Feb 1830)

BOONE, Foster, to RILEY, Priscilla, Miss, both of Middletown DE, 27 Feb 1851, by Rev. J. R. Anderson (DG 14 Mar 1851)

BOONE, Jacob,
see BOONE, Meriam, Mrs.

BOONE, Jacob, Jr., see BROWN, Joseph

BOONE, Meriam, Mrs., wife of Jacob BOONE, Esq., and youngest dau of Andrew BARRATT, Esq., at Frederica, in Kent Co, DE, 27 Jan 1822, na (DG 5 Feb 1822)

BOONE, Sally Ann, see BROWN, Joseph

BOOTH, ____, Chief Justice,
see ATKINSON, Isaac

BOOTH, ____, Hon., see BOOTH, Ann

BOOTH, Ann, Mrs, mother of Hon. Judge BOOTH, 10 May 1846, in New Castle (DG 15 May 1846)

BOOTH, Anna,
see LOCKWOOD, Henry H.

BOOTH, Catharine A.,
see CLING, Robert A.

BOOTH, James, Hon., Chief Justice of the Court of Common Pleas, at his res. in New Castle, 3 Feb 1828, na (DG 5 Feb 1828)

BOOTH, James,
see LOCKWOOD, Henry H.
see PORTER, Alexander, Esq.
see PETERSON, Henry
see THOMAS, Samuel

BOOTH, John, to MOORE, Sarah Ann,

Miss, both of NC Co, 30 Nov 1840, by Rev. James H. McFarland (DG 8 Dec 1840)

BOOTH, Maria,
see ROGERS, James, Esq.

BOOTH, Sarah Ann,
see CLAYTON, Nelson

BOOTH, Sarah Jane, see MARTIN, John

BOOTH, Susan, see ATKINSON, Isaac

BOOTH, William, 17 Oct 1798, on list of yellow fever victims (DG 27 Oct 1798)

BOOTH, William, to ROGERS, Mary, Miss, both of New Castle, DE, dau of the late Daniel ROGERS, Esq., of Sussex Co, at Christ Church, Phila, 25 May 1825, by the Rt. Rev. Bishop White (DG 31 May 1825)

BOOTHE, Eliza, see TAYLOR, William

BOOZER, Leah, see WILSON, David J.

BORDEN, Edward P.,
see BORDEN, Mary Jane
see BORDEN, Letitia Erwin

BORDEN, Letitia Erwin, eldest dau of Edward P. and the late Mary Jane BORDEN, in Phila, 20 Sep 1849, aged 5 yrs (DG 25 Sep 1849)

BORDEN, Mary Jane, Mrs., wife of Edward P. BORDEN of Wilm, 19 Jun 1849 (DG 22 Jun 1849)
see BORDEN, Letitia Erwin

BORDLEY, Catharine, wife of John BORDLEY and dau of the late Capt. Hugh GEMMILL, at her late res., Worton, Kent Co MD, 17 Sep 1841 (DG 1 Oct 1841)

BORDLEY, John,
see BORDLEY, Catharine

BOSTICK, John, of Phila, to DICKSON, Ann, Miss, of Kent Co, 21 Apr 1853, by Dr. W. M. D. Ryan (DG 26 Apr 1853)

BOSTON, Rebecca Ann,
see JONES, Thomas W.

BOTHERMEL, Daniel, of Phila, to MORRISON, Charlotte, Miss, of Wilm, at Marcus Hook, 24 Aug 1851, by the Rev. J. Carlisle (DG 5 Sep 1851)

BOUIS, C., see JONES, Leah

BOULDEN, Ann E.,
see MILLAWAY, James

BOULDEN, David P., to CHESNUT, Ann,

Miss, 18 Nov 1828, by the Rev. John P. Peckworth, all of Wilm (DG 21 Nov 1828)

BOULDEN, David P., see BOULDEN, Eliza Jane

BOULDEN, Eliza Jane, youngest dau of David P. and Jane C. BOULDEN, in Baltimore, 7 Mar 1850 (DG 12 Mar 1850)

BOULDEN, Jane C., see BOULDEN, Eliza Jane

BOULDEN, Jane, relict of the late Levi BOULDEN, Esq., in Wilm, 8 Apr 1846, aged 75 yrs. Presbyterian (DG 21 Apr 1846)

BOULDEN, Jas. E. P., of DE, to FRANCE, Mary Virginia, dau of Capt. Richard FRANCE, of Balt, 6 Apr 1852, by the Rev. Dr. Fuller (DG 9 Apr 1852)

BOULDEN, John, woodchopper, found in the woods burned to death. "A jug of whiskey was the assassin, and the incendiary." 28 Feb 1853, na (DG 1 Mar 1853)

BOULDEN, Levi, late inspector of customs at Delaware City, at Delaware City, 22 Dec 1841, aged 73yrs (DG 7 Jan 1842) see BOULDEN, Jane

BOULDEN, Mary Ellen, Miss, 10 Nov 1845 (DG 18 Nov 1845)

BOULDEN, Matilda, see McINTIRE, Samuel

BOULDEN, N. T., of NC Co, to McCULLOUGH, Sallie, of Phila, in Phila, 4 Jan 1853, by Rev. C. D. Cooper (DG 7 Jan 1853)

BOULDEN, Nathan, see FIELD, Elenor H. see BOULDEN, William D. see FIELDS, Elenor H.

BOULDEN, Nathan, Esq., to FORD, Mary, Mrs., near Newark, 24 Nov 1835, by the Rev. A. K. Russel (DG 27 Nov 1835)

BOULDEN, Nathan, Esq., at his res. near Glasgow in NC Co, ndd, in his 67th yr, ill a few hrs. (DG 18 Apr 1848) of Pencader Hd, 14 May 1848. Shock from the death of his dau, Mrs. Elenor FIELD the previous day (DG 26 May 1848) [conflicting reports]

BOULDEN, Samuel R., see BOULDEN, Sarah A.

BOULDEN, Sarah A., Mrs., wife of Samuel R. BOULDEN, in Wilm, 19 Mar 1850, aged 28 yrs 10 mos (DG 29 Mar 1850)

BOULDEN, Suranna, Mrs., 17 Oct 1849,

at an advanced age. Bur. in the churchyard near Iron Hill (DG 23 Oct 1849)

BOULDEN, Susan, see PHILLIPS, John

BOULDEN, William D., eldest son of the late Nathan BOULDEN of NC Co, at Acala, E. Florida, 15 Sep 1849, aged 35 yrs (DG 23 Oct 1849)

BOULDIN, Benjamin, at his res. on Shipley St., 4 Dec 1833, aged 52 yrs (DG 6 Dec 1833)

BOULDIN, N. L. Dr., born in DE, in Rodney, MI, 1 Feb 1835, aged 43 yrs (DG 24 Feb 1835)

BOULDIN, Susan W., see CLARK, L. George

BOVEE, James, of Phila, to MILNER, Harriet, Miss, dau of John MILNER, Esq., of Wilm, 24 Sep 1798 (DE 1 Oct 1798)

BOWEN, Mary Ellen, see SINGLES, Edward

BOWEN, Rebecca, see KIRKEN, Jno.

BOWEN, Sarah, see GRIFFITH, Richard

BOWER, George, eldest child of George and Sarah BOWER, after a short illness, 2 Jul 1850, aged 3 yrs 8 mos 18 days (DG 9 Jul 1850)

BOWER, Sarah, see BOWER, George

BOWERS, Catharine Ann, see YATES, Charles

BOWERS, Jane L., see DEENLER, Daniel

BOWERS, John, to McCONNELL, Rachel A., Miss, both of Wilm, 10 Nov 1853, by Rev. J. Humphries (DG 18 Nov 1853)

BOWMAN, Ann, see BOWMAN, William Jr.

BOWMAN, Henry, dec'd, late of NC Co, notice given by James McCULLOUGH, F. (?), att'y in fact for Sarah BOWMAN, exec'x (DG 19 Sep 1828)

BOWMAN, Hester, see COLESBERRY, Henry, Dr.

BOWMAN, Jacob, of cholera, in Wilm, 30 Jul 1849 (DG 3 Aug 1849)

BOWMAN, Margaret, youngest dau of the late Lieut. Wm. BOWMAN, dec'd, formerly of NC Co, at the res. of John McCRACKEN in Pencader Hd, ndd, in her 39th yr (DG 3 Dec 1852)

BOWMAN, Sarah, see BOWMAN, Henry

BOWMAN, William,
see BOWMAN, William Jr.

BOWMAN, William Jr., son of William and Ann BOWMAN, at his father's res. in McDonough in NCC0, of lung disease, 18 Jun 1851, aged 20 yrs (DG 8 Jul 1851)

BOWMAN, Wm., Lieut.,
see BOWMAN, Margaret

BOYD, Elizabeth, 23 Feb 1849, aged 26 yrs (DG 13 Mar 1849).

BOYD, Harriet M., dau of Mrs. Mary Ann BOYD and the late Dr. Thomas J. BOYD, U. S. Navy, 23 Nov 1850, in her 23rd yr (DG 26 Nov 1850)

BOYD, John, Jr., of St. Georges Hd, to SMITH, Elizabeth, Miss, of Wilm, 26 Jan 1830, by Rev. Joseph Wilson (DG 5 Feb 1830)

BOYD, Margaret G., Mrs., relict of the late William BOYD, dec'd, and mother-in-law of Mr. John POWER, formerly of Wilm, at her res. in Wilm, 17 Jun 1851, aged 73 yrs (DG 20 Jun 1851)

BOYD, Mary Ann, see BOYD, Harriet M.

BOYD, Mary Stanley, Mrs., at her res. near McDonough, 29 Mar 1853, na, mother of the late surgeon Thomas J. BOYD, USN (DG 5 Apr 1853)

BOYD, Matilda J., see FETTER, Daniel

BOYD, Sarah P.,
see COMEGYS, Benjamin B.

BOYD, Thomas J., surgeon, U.S. Navy, to MONRO, Mary Ann, 2nd dau of the late George MONRO, M. D., of Wilm, 14 Oct 1824, by the Rev. E. W. Gilbert (DG 19 Oct 1824)

BOYD, Thomas J., see BOYD, Harriet M.
see BOYD, Mary Stanley

BOYD, William, at his late res. in NC Co, 14 Jun 1844 (DG 21 Jun 1844)

BOYD, William, see FETTER, Daniel
see BOYD, Margaret G.

BOYER, Emma Adelaide, inf dau of Simon W. and Sarah A. BOYER, near Head of Sassafras, 16 Sep 1849, aged 11 mos (DG 12 Oct 1849)

BOYER, Hannah T.,
see BENNETT, John W.

BOYER, Reece, to LOWNES, Alice Ann, Miss, both of NC Co, in Phila, 16 Jun 1853, by the Rev. Chas. Brown (DG 21 Jun 1853)

BOYER, Sarah A.,
see BOYER, Emma Adelaide

BOYER, Simon W.,
see BOYER, Emma Adelaide

BOYER, William, merchant, to WHITELY, Mary Kirkwood, Mrs., both of Newark, at Newark, 26 Apr 1825, by the Rev. A. K. Russel (DG 3 May 1825)

BOYER, William, merchant, at Newark, 10 Feb 1826, aged 30 yrs, buried at Head of Christiana (DG 17 Feb 1826) dec'd, late of New Ark, land for sale by sheriff, Peter B. Delaney (DG 1 May 1827)

BOYER, William R., to CAVERLY, Anna M., Miss, dau of P. CAVERLY, Esq., at Phila, 2 Jan 1816, by the Rt. Rev. Bishop White (AW 17 Jan 1816)

BOYLE, ___, Mrs,
see GORDON, William H.

BOYS, Susanna, see WILLIAMS, Henry C.

BRACKEN, Benjamin F. to CHANDLER, Hannah S., Miss, 27 Jul 1848, by Rev. M. J. Rhees (DG 1 Aug 1848)

BRACKEN, Elizabeth,
see PLANKINTON, John

BRACKEN, Hannah,
see GREEN, Edward B.

BRACKEN, Henry, to YARNALL, Susan, Miss, 8 Feb 1821 (DG 13 Feb 1821)

BRACKEN, William,
see GREEN, Edward B.

BRACKEN, William, printer, a native of Delaware and for many years lived in Phila, in Prince George's Co MD, of consumption, 20 Feb 1843, aged c 32 yrs (DG 10 Mar 1843)

BRACKEN, William, to WOODWARD, Mary Elizabeth, all of NC Co, in Phila, 28 Feb 1849, by Rev. A. D. Gillette (DG 13 Mar 1849)

BRACKETT, James,
see ROBINSON, Thomas, Esq.

BRACKETT, Maria,
see ROBINSON, Thomas, Esq.

BRACKIN, Ann Elizabeth,
see COOLING, Samuel

BRACKIN, Benjamin, to PLURIGHT, Rachel, Miss, 5 Sep 1816, by Rev. William Pryce, all of Wilm (AW 7 Sep 1816)

BRACKIN, L., to FOOTE, Jane, Miss, both of NC Co, 7 Mar 1844, by Rev. Thomas Love (DG 15 Mar 1844)

BRACKIN, Mary, late of Mill Creek Hd, Samuel C. FINLEY, adm'r (DG 14 Jun 1853)

BRACKIN, Salina, see BEST, Thompson

BRACKIN, Sarah Jane, see LEGG, James

BRACKIN, Willliam, late of Mill Creek Hd, Joseph LINDSAY and Sam'l C, FINLEY, exec'rs (DG 11 Apr 1851)

BRADEN, Leonard, to HENDERSON, Elizabeth, Miss, by Rev. William Rider at Christiana Bridge (DG 15 Oct 1841)

BRADFORD, Anna S., see BRADFORD, William Crawford

BRADFORD, E. G. see BRADFORD, Mary

BRADFORD, Edward, of Brandywine Hd, young man, drowned in the Delaware River, 24 Mar 1853, na (DG 29 Mar 1853)

BRADFORD, Edward G., Esq., to CANBY, Elizabeth, Miss, eldest dau of the late Edward CANBY, 5 Feb 1852, by Rt. Rev. Alfred Lee DD, bishop of DE (DG 10 Feb 1852)

BRADFORD, Elizabeth W., late wife of S. G. BRADFORD, Esq., of Cecil Co MD, and dau of the late Col Henry WHITELY, of Wilm, 26 Jun 1845, aged 24 yrs (DG 1 Jul 1845)

BRADFORD, Henriette Singer, Mrs., wife of the Rev. T. B. BRADFORD, at her res. in Dover, 23 Jan 1851, na (DG 28 Jan 1851)

BRADFORD, James, of Brandywine Hd, to KEENAN, Catharine A., Miss, of Wilm, 29 May 1845, by Rev. Patrick Riley (DG 3 Jun 1845)

BRADFORD, Mary, consort of E. G. BRADFORD, Esq., in Wilm, 3 Apr 1848, aged 28 yrs (DG 7 Apr 1848)

BRADFORD, Moses, Esq., to CLARK, Sarah M., in Wilm, 4 Jan 1848, by Rev. J. E. Rockwell (DG 7 Jan 1848)

BRADFORD, S. A., see MACKEY, Alexander H.

BRADFORD, S. G., see BRADFORD, Elizabeth W.

BRADFORD, Sidney G., see BRADFORD, William Crawford

BRADFORD, Sidney George, to WHITELY, Elizabeth, dau of the late Col. WHITELY, 11 Oct 1842, by Rev. William Work (DG 14 Oct 1842)

BRADFORD, Sidney George, at his res. in Middle Neck, Cecil Co MD, 1 Sep 1849, in his 32nd yr (DG 7 Sep 1849)

BRADFORD, T. B., see BRADFORD, Henrietta Singer

BRADFORD, Thomas, Mrs, see NIXON, Elizabeth

BRADFORD, William, dec'd, late of St. George's Hd., notice given by William BRADFORD, adm'r (DG 16 Oct 1796)

BRADFORD, William, to PRICE, Mary Jane, both of Elkton MD, in Baltimore, on Thursday last, by Rev. Mr. McIntyre (DG 24 Nov 1846)

BRADFORD, William, Jr., of Brandywine Hd, to MOGEE, Elenora, Miss, of Middletown DE, at Marcus Hook PA, 24 Jun 1852, by the Rev. Dr. Anderson (DG 29 Jun 1852)

BRADFORD, William Crawford, only son of Sidney G. and Anna S. BRADFORD, of Cecil Co Md., in Middletown, 26 Jun 1848, aged 10 mos 16 days (DG 11 Jul 1848)

BRADFORD, Wm. in Brandywine Hd, 20 Jul 1852, aged 65 yrs (DG 30 Jul 1852)

BRADLEY, A, see SMITH, F. Burin

BRADLEY, Adeline, dau of Andrew BRADLEY of Newark, of water in the brain, 11 Jun 1833, aged 10 yrs 5 mos 17 days (DG 16 Jun 1833)

BRADLEY, Andrew, Esq., 8 Dec 1847, at Newark (DG 14 Dec 1847)
see BENNESON, William H.
see BRADLEY, Adeline
see QUINN, John
see DOUGHERTY, James

BRADLEY, Bernard, to CANN, Emeline, Miss, 24 Dec 1844, by Rev. Mr. Hogarth (DG 10 Jan 1845)

BRADLEY, Bernard, in Wilm, 28 Jan 1848, aged 28 yrs (DG 8 Feb 1848)
see BRADLEY, Mary Anna

BRADLEY, Elenora, see WARD, J. Parrish

BRADLEY, Eliza, see BENNESON, William H.

see **KINDER**, Warren

BRADLEY, Emeline,
see **BRADLEY**, Mary Anna

BRADLEY, Isaac,
see **HUDSON**, Benjamin

BRADLEY, John F., to **MOORE**, Elizabeth, Miss, all of NC Co, 23 May 1850, by Rev. Mr. Barr (DG 31 May 1850)

BRADLEY, Mary A.,
see **DOUGHERTY**, James

BRADLEY, Mary Anna, inf dau of Bernard and Emeline BRADLEY, 7 Mar 1847 (DG 9 Mar 1847)

BRADLEY, Rebecca W.,
see **SMITH**, F. Burin

BRADLEY, Sarah, see **ROBINSON**, Jacob

BRADLEY, Sarah J.,
see **PURCELL**, William J. J.

BRADLEY, Sarah Jane,
see **JONES**, Phillip

BRADLEY, Susanna,
see **HUDSON**, Benjamin

BRADLEY, Thomas,
see **WARD**, J. Parrish

BRADUN, Elizabeth, see **CROW**, John

BRADY, Ann, Miss, of Smyrna, in Smyrna, of consumption, 4 Jan 1825, na (DG 21 Jan 1825)

BRADY, Benjamin, Esq., to **BATTELL**, Merriam, Mrs., 4 Feb 1823, by the Rev. Mr. Torbert, all of Camden, Kent Co (DG 21 Feb 1823)

BRAMAN, Sarah J.,
see **HARRISON**, Albert

BRAMBLE, George M., to **MOODY**, Eliza R., Miss, both of NC Co, 22 Jan 1846, by Rev. Dr. McCullough (DG 27 Jan 1846)

BRAMBOO, John J., to **JAQUET**, Sarah Ann, Miss, both of Newark, at Blockley, 4 Jul 1847, by Rev. John J. Baker (DG 16 Jul 1847)

BRANGAN, John, to **McCLEES**, Elizabeth, Miss, both of Brandywine Hd, 27 Apr 1844, at the house of Stephen BODDY, Esq. in Wilm, by Rev. Edward Kennard (DG 30 Apr 1844)

BRANNON, Margaret,
see **ROBINETT**, Joseph

BRASURE, Benton, to **EVANS**, Elizabeth H., both of Baltimore, Sussex Co, DE, 9 Nov 1842, by Rev. J. Bissey (DG 18 Nov 1842)

BRATTAN, Caleb, to **PHELPS**, S., Miss, both of NC Co, 17 Feb 1842, by Rev. J. Walker (DG 11 Mar 1842)

BRATTEN, Abraham, of NC Co, to **CARPENTER**, Anna, Mrs., of Wilm, by Rev. William Cooper (DG 4 Jul 1850)

BRATTON, Julia,
see **KENWORTHY**, Jonathan

BRATTON, William, to **LAYMAN**, Ann, Miss, both of NC Co, at Chester PA, 30 Oct 1847, by Rev. Levi Stokes (DG 25 Nov 1847)

BREAER, Abel, to **NEWLIN**, Elizabeth P., of Wilm, 15 Jan 1846, in West Chester PA, in the presence of Henry Fleming, Esq., by Friend's ceremony (DG 23 Jan 1846)

BRECK, Amelia Elizabeth, dau of William and Gabriella J. BRECK, at Rokeby on the Brandywine, 27 Feb 1846, aged 15 mos (DG 20 Mar 1846)

BRECK, Charles, Rev.,
see **BRECK**, Mary

BRECK, Garbiella J.,
see **BRECK**, Amelia Elizabeth

BRECK, Mary, dau of Rev. Charles BRECK of Wilm, at the res. of Dr. PENNOCK, near Rockdale, Del Co PA, 5 Aug 1853, aged c 14 yrs (DG 9 Aug 1853)

BRECK, William,
see **BRECK**, Amelia Elizabeth

BREEN, _____, Mrs., in Wilm, 29 Jul 1848, of consumption (DG 1 Aug 1848)

BREEN, James, to **McCAULEY**, Christiana, Miss, both of Wilm, 6 Nov 1821, by the Rev. Richard C. Hall (DG 13 Nov 1821)

BREEN, Philip, an aged citizen of Newport, 15 Mar 1853, aged 84 yrs (DG 18 Mar 1853) late of Christiana Hd, Connor McGUIRE, adm'r (DG 25 Mar 1853)

BRENHOLTZ, Phebe A.,
see **CAMPBELL**, Samuel

BRENN, Anna, see **BRENN**, Caroline

BRENN, Caroline, dau of Jacob and Anna BRENN, in Christiana Hd, 5 Feb 1849, aged 16 mos (DG 13 Feb 1849)

BRENN, Jacob, see **BRENN**, Caroline

BRENNAN, Hugh, to ANDERSON, Mary Ann, both of Christiana Hd, 4 Dec 1824, by the Rev. E. W. Gilbert (DG 7 Dec 1824)

BRIAN, David, see BRIAN, Hannah

BRIAN, Hannah, wife of David BRIAN, 8 Jul 1820 (DG 11 Jul 1820)

BRIAN, James, in Wilm, 11 Feb 1836, at an advanced age (DG 16 Feb 1836)

BRIAN, James, see MORRIS, Samuel, Jr.

BRIAN, Sarah H., see MORRIS, Samuel, Jr.

BRIAN, Thomas P., to MAREE, Rebecca A., Miss, both of Smyrna, in Dover by Rev. Thomas G. Murphey (DG 5 Dec 1845)

BRIGGS, Jane E., see BRISBANE, W., Rev

BRIGGS, John, see BRIGGS, Joshua H. see BRISBANE, W., Rev.

BRIGGS, Joshua H., saddler, of Wilm, 4 Sep 1826, na (DG 5 Sep 1826) notice given by John BRIGGS, adm'r (DG 2 Oct 1826)

BRIGHT, Hannah, see EVES, James, Capt.

BRIGHT, William Capt., in Phila, 21 Oct 1853, na (DG 25 Oct 1853)

BRILBANE, Catharine S., see NEWLIN, Ellis J.

BRINCKLE, John, Dr., late of Wilm, suddenly, in Phila, 9 Jan 1835, aged 71 yrs (DG 13 Jan 1835)

BRINCKLE, John R., see FERMON, Thomas see BRINCKLE, Joshua Gordon, Esq.

BRINCKLE, Joshua Gordon, Esq.,Grand Master of the Grand Lodge of Delaware, 19 Jan 1825, na (DG 21 Jan 1825) notice given by John R. BRINCKLE and Wm. D. BRINCKLE, adm'rs (DG 1 Feb 1825)

BRINCKLE, Thomas R., Dr., in Phila, 19 Jul 1853, aged 43 yrs (DG 22 Jul 1853)

BRINCKLE, William D., Dr., of Smyrna, to PHYSICK, Sarah T., Miss, youngest dau of Henry W. PHYSICK, of Wilm, 26 Apr 1821, by the Rev. George Boyd (DG 1 May 1821)

BRINCKLE, Wm. D., see BRINCKLE, Joshua Gordon, Esq.

BRINCKLOE, John, Dr., Speaker of Senate of DE, at his res. in Milford, 18 Mar 1828, aged 35 yrs; leaves a wife and children (DG 25 Mar, 1 Apr 1828)

BRINGHURST, Deborah, at her res. in Wilm, 20 Aug 1844, aged 72 yrs (DG 30 Aug 1844)

BRINGHURST, Edward, see BRINGHURST, Samuel,

BRINGHURST, James, Dr., formerly of Wilm, to RYAN, Mary, of Jerseyville, IN., 20 Mar 1850, by George Warren, Esq. (DG 12 Apr 1850)

BRINGHURST, James, see BRINGHURST, Rebecca

BRINGHURST, Joseph, druggist, in Wilm, 26 Jul 1834, aged 67 yrs (DG 29 Jul 1834)

BRINGHURST, Joseph, to RICHARDSON, Anna, 6 Oct 1842, at the house of John RICHARDSON, by Friends ceremony (DG 14 Oct 1842)

BRINGHURST, Rebecca, wife of James BRINGHURST, in Wilm, 4 Mar 1845, aged 51 yrs (DG 11 Mar 1845)

BRINGHURST, Samuel, son of Edward and Sarah BRINGHURST, 26 Oct 1834, aged 17 mos (DG 31 Oct 1834)

BRINGHURST, Sarah, see BRINGHURST, Samuel,

BRINKLE, J., Dr., see CRANS, Samuel

BRINKLE, J. G., see RODNEY, Caesar A.

BRINKLE, John, Dr., of Milford, to GORDON, Betsy, Miss, of near Dover, 6 Jan 1790, by Rev. Sydenham Thorne (DG 16 Jan 1790)

BRINKLE, Margaret Rumsey, youngest dau of Rev. S. C. BRINKLE, 16 Oct 1848, aged 16 yrs (DG 20 Oct 1848)

BRINKLE, S. C., Rev., see BRINKLE, Margaret Rumsey

BRINKLE, Wilhelmina Ridgely, see CRANS, Samuel

BRINKLOE, John P., attorney-at-law, 11 Jan 1843, at his res. in Georgetown, aged 31 yrs (DG 20 Jan 1843)

BRINTON, Caleb, at his res. in West Chester, PA, 6 Apr 1826, aged 98 yrs 6 mos 14 das; interred at Friends' Burying Ground at Birmingham, PA (DG 14 Apr 1826) see **McCAULLEY**, Wm.

BRINTON, David, dec'd, late of Wilm, notice given by David BRINTON and William BRINTON, exec'rs (MU 18 Mar 1807)

BRINTON, David, Wilm, for many years keeper of the Indian King Inn, 14 Dec 1821, in his 42nd yr, leaving a wife and 3 small children (DG 21 Dec 1821)

BRINTON, Hannah B.,
see **McCAULLEY**, Wm.

BRINTON, Jacob, Capt., to **BROOM**, Saray (sic), Miss, dau of Jacob BROOM, Esq., 26 Oct 1797, by the Rev. Mr. Clarkson, all of Wilm (DE 2 Nov 1797)

BRINTON, Mary,
see **DARLINGTON**, Chandler

BRINTON, Phebe D.,
see **HOPKINS**, George

BRINTON, Susanna F.,
see **BULLOCK**, Chalkley T.

BRINTON, William,
see **BRINTON**, David

BRISBANE, Wm, Rev., of the Phila Conf., to **BRIGGS**, Jane E., Miss, dau of John BRIGGS, Esq., of NC Co, 25 Feb 1851, by the Rev. Mr. Ruth (DG 4 Mar 1851)

BRITSON, Mary, see **BRYER**, James

BRITTENHAM, Lydia,
see **SHOCKLEY**, Elias

BRITTINGHAM, Eber, of Del Co PA, to **MEKEEVER**, Sarah Ann, Miss, of NC Co, 6 Mar 1851, by the Rev. J. C. Houston (DG 14 Mar 1851)

BRITTINGHAM, Hamilton B., son of Nathaniel BRITTINGHAM, dec'd, late of DE, in Phila, 29 Aug 1825, aged 15 yrs (DG 2 Sep 1825)

BRITTINGHAM, Mary E.,
see **SHORT**, William

BRITTINGHAM, Nathaniel,
see **BRITTINGHAM**, Hamilton B.

BRITTON, Sarah, see **BAXTER**, Patrick

BRITTS, Eliza, Mrs., wife of Isaac BRITTS, and dau of the late Caspar STICHMAN, Esq., 17 Jun 1851, aged 45 yrs (DG 20 Jun 1851)

BRITTS, Isaac, see **BRITTS**, Eliza

BROADBELT, John, see **KITNON**, John

BROADHEAD, Daniel, Gen., at his late seat in Wayne Co, PA, 15 Dec 1809, aged 73 yrs. A Colonel in the Rev. War, and for several years surveyor general of PA (DG 8 Dec 1809)

BROBSON, James, Esq., 7 Aug 1834, aged 75 yrs; b 25 Dec 1759 (DG 8 Aug 1834)

BROBSON, William P., Esq., to **STARR**, Elizabeth T., Miss, both of Wilm, at Harmony, 16 May 1825, by Rev. R. Williston (DG 20 May 1825)

BROBSON, William P. Esq., in Wilm, 19 Feb 1850. Funeral at Trinity Chapel (DG 22 Feb 1850)

BRODAWAY, Ambrose, son of Ambrose and Ann BRODAWAY, in Willow Grove, 12 Sep 1851, aged c 2 yrs (DG 23 Sep 1851)
see **BRODAWAY,** Ann

BRODAWAY, Ann, Mrs., wife of Ambrose BRODAWAY, "a few hours after her son, Ambrose." She leaves a husband and eight children (DG 23 Sep 1851)
see **BRODAWAY**, Ambrose

BROOKES, Martha,
see **CHANDLER**, James

BROOKS, Charles W., Esq., to **PIERCE**, Eliza J., both of Wilm, in Trinity Church, by Rev. W. H. Trapnell (DG 29 Oct 1850)

BROOKS, Eliza,
see **HAYES**, Henry Moore

BROOKS, Elizabeth,
see **WILSON**, James P.

BROOKS, Jesse, killed by a train near Newport. Drunk and fell across tracks (DG 30 Jul 1850)

BROOKS, John, to **MAXWELL**, Kitty, Miss, at Duck Creek Crossroads, 4 May 1789 (DG 16 May 1789)

BROOKS, John, at Duck Creek Cross Roads (DG 20 Feb 1790)

BROOKS, John R., to **WILCOX**, Ann, Miss, both of NC Co, in Chester PA, 21 Apr 1851, by the Rev. S. G. Hare (DG 29 Apr 1851)

BROOKS, Josiah,
see **SKIDMORE**, Rachel W.
see **WAY**, David B.

BROOKS, Mary, see **WAY**, David B.

BROOKS, Susan T., see CORBIT, William

BROOM, Jacob,
see BILLENSTEIN, Jacob T.
see BRINTON, Jacob, Capt.

BROOM, James, atty-at-law in Wilm, to DRIVER, Ann, Miss, dau of the late Col. DRIVER of Caroline Co, MD, "last week" in that county (FA 10 Sep 1803)
see BROOM, Thomas

BROOM, James M., Hon., 15 Jan 1850, in his 74th yr (DG 22 Jan 1850)

BROOM, James Madison, Esq.,
see BROOM Marie Ann

BROOM, Marie Ann, wife of James Madison BROOM, Esq., at New Castle, 14 Sep 1802, in her 28th yr (FA 24 Sep 1802)

BROOM, Mary S.,
see BILLENSTEIN, Jacob T.

BROOM, Saray,
see BRINTON, Jacob, Capt.

BROOM, Thomas, late of Wilm, Sale of tavern that Peter GATHONY now lives in, by exec'rs James BROOM and Peter GATHONY (PG 13 Feb 1750)

BROOMALL, Mary R.,
see MORRIS, Mary R.
see MORRIS, Daniel A.

BROOMALL, Robert,
see MORRIS, Mary R.

BROOMALL, Sarah,
see MORRIS, Mary R.

BROSIUS, Edwin, of Kennett Sq., to MARSHALL, Mary H, dau of Jno. MARSHALL of NC Co at Kennett Sq. PA, 1 May 1853, by Friends ceremony (DG 10 May 1853)

BROTHERS, Rachel,
see MORTON, Morton, Dr.

BROUGHMAN, Elizabeth,
see CURNS, John L.

BROWN, _____, Mr., of NC Co to FERGUSON, _____, Miss, of Phila, 11 May 1853, by the Rev. W. H. Brisbane (DG 17 May 1853)

BROWN, Abraham, dec'd, late of Christiana Hd, notice given by William ROBINSON, adm'r (DG 4 Feb 1797)

BROWN, Albert, in Wilm, 15 Jul 1853, after a short illness in his 18th yr (DG 19 Jul 1853)

BROWN, Ann M., see BROWN, Joseph
see BODDY, Stephen

BROWN, Anna Mary, only dau of Daniel J and Lydia BROWN, near Brick Meeting House, Cecil Co MD, 7 Mar 1851, aged 4 yrs 2 mos 11 days (DG 18 Mar 1851)

BROWN, Benjamin, dec'd, late of Wilm, notice given by John BROWN and Samuel BROWN, adm'rs (AD 18 Oct 1822)

BROWN, Benjamin, to TALLEY, Susan, Miss, both of NC Co, at Chester, PA, 13 Jun 1833, by the Rev. Joseph Walker (DG 25 Jun 1833)

BROWN, Charles, colored, 12 May 1844, aged 18 yrs. Coroner's verdict - got beyond his depth and drowned (DG 14 May 1844)

BROWN, Charlie, colored, ostler and porter of the Delaware House, 28 Mar 1848, of inflammation of the lungs (DG 31 Mar 1848)

BROWN, Daniel J.,
see BROWN, Anna Mary

BROWN, Edmund Jr, of Elkton, to KENNARD, Martha, dau of Rev. E. KENNARD, of Wilm, 30 Apr 1850, by Rev. Levi Storks (DG 7 May 1850)

BROWN, Elgar, of Salem, to REYNOLDS, Mary Jane, Miss, of St. Georges, 20 Jan 1848, by Rev. J. J. Helm (DG 4 Feb 1848)

BROWN, Elizabeth, Mrs.,
see LEWIS, James B.

BROWN, Elizabeth, see CHARLES, Daniel
see GILPIN, William

BROWN, Emeline, see KLAIR, Edmund S.

BROWN, Eugene, to HARPER, Mary, Miss, 9 Nov 1825, by the Rev. R. Williston (DG 11 Nov 1825)

BROWN, Francis, Esq., formerly Prothonotary at the Court of Common Pleas for Sussex Co, at his res. near Bridgeville, 31 Jul 1829, aged 65 yrs (DG 18 Aug 1829)

BROWN, Hannah,
see WOODWARD, William

BROWN, Huet C., at his res. near Middleford, aged c 45 yrs (DG 15 Feb 1850)

BROWN, Isaac, see BROWN, Sarah

BROWN, Isaac S., son of William BROWN of Wilm, at Cainesville IA, 17 Sep 1852, in his 40th yr, leaves a widow and 4 children (DG 14 Sep 1852)

BROWN, Jacob, 21 Mar 1846, aged 15 yrs
(DG 24 Mar 1846)

BROWN, Jacob in New Castle Hd, 10 Feb
1853, in his 61st yr (DG 15 Feb 1853)

BROWN, James Montgomery, to COWDEN,
Mary Jane, Miss, both of Delaware City,
at the Madison House, Phila, 20 Jul 1848,
by Rev. Andrew Manship (DG 25 Jul 1848)

BROWN, Jane, see WOODS, James

BROWN, John, of yellow fever
(DE 16 Sep 1798)

BROWN, John, dec'd, late of Brandywine
Hd, notice given by Benjamin ELLIOTT or
William CLOUD, exec'rs (DS 8 Jan 1812)

BROWN, John, colored. Coroner's inquest,
20 Apr 1846 - accidental drowning
(DG 24 Apr 1846)

BROWN, John, see BROWN, Benjamin

BROWN, John R., to COLLINS, Rachel,
both of Kent Co, 5 Jan 1853
(DG 1 Feb 1853)

BROWN, John T., see BROWN, Milton J.
see BROWN, Lucy

BROWN, Jonathan, colored, by over-
exertion at work, 1 Apr 1844, na
(DG 5 Apr 1844)

BROWN, Joseph, see LOFLAND, James R.

BROWN, Joseph, of Denton, MD, to
BOONE, Sally Ann, Miss, of Frederica, at
the res. of Jacob BOONE, Jr., in Frederica,
26 Jun 1826 (DG 7 Jul 1826)

BROWN, Joseph, late of Christiana Hd. Ann
M. BROWN, adm'x (DG 9 Feb 1849)

BROWN, Joseph, to FERGUSON, Mary
Jane, all of NC Co, 20 Feb 1849, by Rev.
Thos. Love (DG 27 Feb 1849)

BROWN, Lucy, inf dau of John T. and Sarah
Jane BROWN, in Christiana Hd, 29 Jul
1847, aged 11 mos 4 days (DG 3 Aug 1847)

BROWN, Lydia, see BROWN, Anna Mary

BROWN, Lydia Ann,
see RUMFORD, John G.

BROWN, Lydia Maria,
see BROWN, Milton J.

BROWN, Mary A., see WILSON, Thomas

BROWN, Mary Jane,
see PAYNTER, Alfred

BROWN, Melvina, see TWAX, Benjamin

BROWN, Milton J., inf son of John T. and
Lydia Maria BROWN, 19 Jan 1851, aged
2 mos 1 day (DG 24 Jan 1851)

BROWN, Nathaniel, to LITTLE, Sarah, Miss,
both of NC Co, 12 Nov 1846, by Rev. Dr.
McCullough (DG 17 Nov 1846)

BROWN, Rachael, see JESTER, John

BROWN, Rachel, dau of Thomas and
Rachel BROWN, 22 Oct 1851, aged 13 yrs
(DG 28 Oct 1851)

BROWN, Robert, of New Castle, to
SCHOLEY, Elizabeth, Miss, recently from
Mancher, England, 25 Dec 1851, by the
Rev. Wm. Metcalf (DG 30 Dec 1851)

BROWN, Ruth Ann, see HARTLEY, David

BROWN, S. Isabella,
see ALLERDICE, John A.

BROWN, Sallie B.,
see LOFLAND, James R.

BROWN, Samuel, see BROWN, Benjamin

BROWN, Samuel, merchant, to DAVIS,
Clarissa W., Miss, 12 May 1823,
by the Rev. E. W. Gilbert, all of Wilm
(DG 13 May 1823)

BROWN, Sarah, wife of Isaac BROWN, in
Wilm, after a short but severe indisposition,
27 Jul 1818, in her 34th yr (DG 5 Aug 1818)
see TALLEY, Caleb

BROWN, Sarah Jane, see BROWN, Lucy
see PIERCE, Thomas

BROWN, Solomon, son of Tilghman
BROWN, in Kent Co, 6 Sep 1852, aged
20 yrs (DG 28 Sep 1852)

BROWN, Thomas, in New Garden PA, near
the DE line, 21 Jun 1853, aged c 70 yrs
(DG 4 Jul 1853)
see BROWN, Rachel

BROWN, Tilghman,
see BROWN, Solomon

BROWN, William, to REYNOLDS, Ellender,
Miss, 22 May 1806, by Rev. Mr. Dodge
(MR 23 May 1806)
see BARR, Isaac S.
see BROWN, Isaac S.

BROWN, William, of Frederica, to
RIDGEWAY, Elizabeth Ann, only dau of

Joseph RIDGEWAY, 19 Jan 1843, near Canterbury, by Rev. William Conolly (DG 3 Feb 1843)

BROWNING, George, to GREEN, Elizabeth, Miss, all of Appoq. Hd, 26 Nov 1850 (DG 10 Dec 1850)

BRUCE, J. M., of Phila, to BUSH, Mary I., dau of David BUSH, Esq., of Wilm, 5 Dec 1840, by Rev. E. W. Gilbert (DG 8 Jan 1841)

BRUNON, Elizabeth Ann, see SETTLER, John

BRYAN, Catherine, Mrs., dau of the late Mr. Isaac STIDHAM, dec'd, of NC Co, 29 May 1824, aged 29 yrs (DG 8 Jun1824)

BRYAN, Elizabeth T., see LORD, Harriet M.

BRYAN, Harriet M., see LORD, Harriet M. see LORD, William H.

BRYAN, Isaac, see SMITH, Ebenezer A., Dr.

BRYAN, John C., see LORD, Harriet M. see LORD, William H.

BRYANT, William, to RUTHVIN, Sarah E., Miss, both of Wilm, 6 Sep 1849, by the Rev. Charles W. Quick (DG 11 Sep 1849)

BRYER, James, to BRITSON, Mary, Miss, all of NC Co, 5 Aug 1847, by Rev. M. J. Rhees (DG 10 Aug 1847)

BRYNBERG, Peter, see SPRINGER, John

BRYNBERG, Peter, Esq., dec'd, notice given by Robert PORTER (AW 31 Aug 1816)

BUCHANAN, Hannah, widow of James BUCHANAN, at the res. of her father, John CAMPBELL, Esq., in Slaughter Neck, 2 Aug 1850 (DG 16 Aug 1850)

BUCHANAN, James, see BUCHANAN, Hannah

BUCHANAN, Mary S., formerly of Wilm, in Phila, 23 Oct 1835, aged 46 yrs (DG 27 Oct 1835)

BUCK, Amey, see BUCK, Anthony

BUCK, Anthony. Real estate sale. Amey BUCK, surviving mortgager, John, James, and Violette BUCK, heirs at law of Anthony BUCK (DG 7 Jan 1853)

BUCK, James, see BUCK, Anthony

BUCK, John, see BUCK, Anthony

BUCK, Violette, see BUCK, Anthony

BUCKEY, Philip J. of Wilm, formerly of Washington DC, to MILLER, Mary, dau of John MILLER, Esq., at Millersville, Anne Arundel Co MD, by the Rev. C. K. Nelson (DG 29 Jun 1852)

BUCKINGHAM, Sarah J., see ROTHWELL, Abraham

BUCKINGHAM, Sarah, see HANA, Joseph

BUCKLEY, Adam, of Brandywine Hd, a dwelling house and 2 negroes to be sold by John BUCKLEY and John WILLIAMSON, exec'rs. (PG 13 Nov 1760)

BUCKLEY, Bennet, in Easton MD, 3 Feb 1843 (DG 10 Feb 1843)

BUCKLEY, Daniel, see BUCKLEY, Sarah

BUCKLEY, John, see BUCKLEY, Adam

BUCKLEY, Sarah, Mrs., consort of Daniel BUCKLEY, Esq., of Lancaster Co, PA, after a painful and lingering illness, in Wilm, na, 15 Sep 1821 (DG 21 Sep 1821)

BUCKLEY, Wm., see STATTEN, Milton

BUCKMAN, Edmund W., in Wilm, 17 Dec 1843, aged 21 yrs (DG 22 Dec 1843)

BUCKMASTER, Ellen Barrett, youngest child of Jas. S. BUCKMASTER, Esq., at Frederica, 30 Mar 1849, aged 3 yrs 4 mos (DG 6 Apr 1849)

BUCKMASTER, Jas. S., see BUCKMASTER, Ellen Barrett

BUCKMASTER, Joseph, at his res. in Dover (DG 7 Sep 1847)

BUCKMASTER, Sarah, see GOODWIN, Alexander

BUDD, Mary L., Mrs., wife of Mr. William BUDD, at Smyrna, 2 Aug 1833, na (DG 7 Aug 1833) (date is wrong on paper)

BUDD, William, see BUDD, Mary L.

BULL, Manaen, Col., see MITCHELL, Elizabeth J.

BULLEN, Henrietta R., see HAMILTON, Thos.

BULLEN, Mary, near Newark DE, 13 May 1849, in her 39th yr (DG 1 May 1849)

BULLOCK, Chalkley T., of Birmingham, to

BRINTON, Susanna F., of Wilm, at Lower Chester, Del Co PA, 12 Aug 1847, by Benjamin F. Johnson, Esq. (DG 24 Aug 1847)

BULLOCK, E. A., see REESE, William T.

BULLOCK, George, to WRIGHT, Josephine, Miss, all of Phila, 7 Oct 1851, by the Rev. Mr. G. B. Ide (DG 10 Oct 1851)

BULLOCK, Margary, see SIMMONS, George H. P.

BULLOCK, Samuel M., of Wilm, to JORDAN, Mary C., Miss, of Brandywine, 23 Oct 1845, in Penn's Grove NJ, by Carlton Passmore, Esq. (DG 28 Oct 1845)

BULLOCK, William S., Dr., of Phila, to EMLEN, Elizabeth A., of Wilm, 17 Oct 1850, at Friends meeting in Wilm (DG 22 Oct 1850)

BUNKER, Elizabeth T., Mrs. ,widow of the late Nathan BUNKER of Phila, in Wilm, 26 Jan 1851, aged c 94 yrs (DG 31 Jan 1851)

BUNKER, Nathan, see BUNKER, Elizabeth T.

BUNNELL, Henry, of Sussex Co, NJ, to FLOYD, Hannah Jane, Miss, of Middletown, DE, in Phila, 6 Jun 1849, by the Rev. Solomon Higgins (DG 12 Jun 1849)

BUNNELL, James Edwin, at the res. of father, Benjamin BURNELL (sic), Esq., 34 Logan Square, Phila, 14 Jun 1849, in his 25th yr (DG 19 Jun 1849)

BUNNER, Andrew, see McSPARREN, Archibald

BUNTING, Hannah G., see THOMAS, Evan C.

BUNTING, Rachel, Mrs., formerly of Allentown, Monmouth Co NJ, in Wilm, at the res. of her son-in-law, James P. HUGHES, 26 Apr 1853, in her 75th yr (DG 6 May 1853)

BURCHALL, Robert, of West Chester, PA, to SLACK, Jane, Miss, of Wilm, 6 Mar 1823, by the Rev. Samuel R. Greene (DG 11 Mar 1823)

BURGESS, Levi, to OZIER, Martha, both of Wilm, 3 Nov 1847, by Rev. S. R. Wynkoop (DG 5 Nov 1847)

BURGIE, Catharine, see HUSTON, John

BURGIN, Margaret, see FARIR, Samuel

BURHANS, Hezekiah, councillor-at-law, at the res. of William RICHARDS in Delaware City, 25 Apr 1847, aged 73 yrs (DG 30 Apr 1847)

BURKE, Thomas, to ADAIR, Marietta, Miss, 22 Jul 1851, by the Rev. Andrew Manship (DG 25 Jul 1851)

BURNELL, (sic), Benjamin, see BUNNELL, James Edwin

BURNHAM, Samuel, see BASSETT, Elizabeth

BURNS, Alexander, to TALLEY, Sidney, both of NC Co, 17 Jul 1842 (DG 22 Jul 1842)

BURNS, Catharine, see MORRISON, Robert

BURNS, George, of Wilm, to DARLING, Elizabeth, Miss, of New Castle, in Phila, by Rev. Ives (DG 14 May 1852)

BURNS, Joseph W., see BURNS, Mary

BURNS, Mary, dau of Joseph W. Burns, in Milford, 23 Feb 1852, aged 13 mos 27 days (DG 2 Mar 1852)

BURNS, Mary, see SWEETLAND, Daniel

BURNS, Samuel, to WHITE, Rachel, Miss, both of Cecil Co MD, 16 Aug 1852, by Rev. J. A. Roche (DG 10 Sep 1852)

BURNSIDE, John, to BEATTY, Elizabeth, Miss, both of Wilm, on the 7th inst. by Rev. Geo. Chandler (DG 13 Mar 1849)

BURRELL, William, see NOBLE, Margaret

BURRINGTON, Sarah Jane, see CANNON, Wm. W.

BURRIS, Lewis, to SIMPSON, Eliza, Miss, both of Kent Co, 5 Aug 1853, by the Rev. P. Mansfield (DG 16 Aug 1853)

BURROUGHS, George R., of Cecil Co MD, to RUMFORD, Caroline, Miss, of Brandywine Hd, 25 Mar 1845, by Rev. Joseph Walker (DG 28 Mar 1845)

BURROWS. William, of Wilm, to HUKILL, Julia, Miss, of Phila, 28 Apr 1848, by Rev. Thomas H. Quinan (DG 16 May 1848)

BURTON, _____, Dr. see McCLUNG, John

BURTON, Albert, see BURTON, Sarah

BURTON, Anna, see RODGERS, Thomas

BURTON, Benjamin,
see BURTON, Elizabeth Green

BURTON, Benjamin, Esq., merchant,
at his mansion in Sussex Co, 8 Jun 1824,
aged 49 yrs (DG 18 Jun1824)

BURTON, Benjamin, of Milton, to
TORBERT, Mary, Miss, dau of the
Rev. William TORBERT, at Laurel, DE,
24 Sep 1829, by the Rev. James A. Massey
(DG 13 Oct 1829)

BURTON, Benjamin, Esq., son of Dr. John
BURTON of Wilm, to CONWELL, Jeanette
Tatem, Miss, dau of Elias CONWELL, of
Napoleon, IN, 15 Mar 1848, at Napoleon
(DG 28 Mar 1848)

BURTON, Catharine R.,
see BURTON, Elizabeth Green

BURTON, Clementine W., consort of
S. V. BURTON, and native of Lewistown,
at Algiers opposite New Orleans,
16 Sep 1847, aged 19 yrs (DG 1 Oct 1847)

BURTON, Cornelius T., to CLIFTON,
Hannah, Miss, all of Lewes, at Lewes,
20 Aug 1851, by the Rev. D. McIlvane
(DG 12 Sep 1851)

BURTON, Deborah, Mrs., wife of Capt. John
BURTON, 26 Apr 1850, at Lewistown
(DG 3 May 1850)

BURTON, Elizabeth Green, dau of Benjamin
and Catharine R., BURTON, near Millsborough, 21 Aug 1849, aged 3 yrs
(DG 31 Aug 1849)

BURTON, Erasmus D., to SAULSBURY,
Mary Louisa, Miss, both of Kent Co DE,
14 Jun 1849 at the Union ME Ch, by the
Rev. T. J. Thompson (DG 19 Jun 1849)

BURTON, George H., son of Richard and
Ruth BURTON, in Brandywine Village, of
croup, ndd, aged 1 yr 14 days
(DG 3 May 1853)

BURTON, Henry, to MANLOVE, Mary Ann,
Miss, only dau of the Rev. John MANLOVE,
30 Mar 1843, by Rev. J. T. Cooper, all of
Dover (DG 7 Apr 1843)

BURTON, James, of Sussex Co, to COLE,
Sarah Jane, of Salem NJ, 15 Oct 1850, by
Rev. John A. Mc Kean (DG 25 Oct 1850)

BURTON, John, see KETCHUM, George A.

BURTON, John, Capt.,
see BURTON, Deborah

BURTON, John, Dr.,
see BURTON, Benjamin

BURTON, John, son of the Rev. John
BURTON, at his res. near Middletown,
15 Sep 1828, aged 32 yrs (DG 26 Sep 1828)

BURTON, Margaretta,
see McCLUNG, John

BURTON, Mary, see RODNEY, Henry F.

BURTON, Mary Jane,
see WORRALL, Stephen

BURTON, Miles, see WAPLES, Gideon

BURTON, Richard,
see BURTON, George H.

BURTON, Robert, see RODNEY, Henry F.

BURTON, Ruth,
see BURTON, George H.

BURTON, S. V.,
see BURTON, Clementine W.

BURTON, Sarah, Mrs., wife of Albert
BURTON, formerly of Lewistown DE,
in Phila, 29 Nov 1851, in her 68th yr
(DG 9 Dec 1851)
see McCONNELL, Mary
see WAPLES, Gideon

BURTON, Susan J.,
see KETCHUM, George A.

BUSH, Anna E., wife of George BUSH,
in Wilm, 9 Nov 1851, aged c 35 yrs
(DG 11 Nov 1851)

BUSH, Charles, to COX, Helen, Miss, dau
of Esau COX, both of Wilm, 12 Mar 1829,
by the Rev. Isaac Pardee (DG 17 Mar 1829)

BUSH, David, Dr., of Wilm, to PRICE, Betsy,
Miss, 5 Mar 1789 (DG 14 Mar 1789)

BUSH, David, see McLAUGHLIN, Henry
see TAYLOR, Edward
see BRUCE, J. M.

BUSH, Elizabeth, see McLEAR, John

BUSH, Elizabeth K.,
see McCOMBS, Henry S.

BUSH Eugene Elmer, son of Dr. L. P. and
Maria BUSH, of scarlet fever, 4 Dec 1851,
aged 2 yrs 4 mos (DG 12 Dec 1851)

BUSH, George, of Wilm, to JACKSON,
Mary Jane, Miss, of Baltimore, 28 Feb 1823,
by the Rev. E. W. Gilbert (DG 1 Apr 1823)

BUSH, George, see BUSH, Anna E.
see BUSH, Julia A.
see ELLIOTT, Isabella
see BUSH, Mary Jane, Mrs.

BUSH, George, to McKEAN, Sarah B., Miss, 3 Feb 1830, by Rev. Robert Adair, all of Wilm (DG 5 Feb 1830)

BUSH, George W., of Wilm, to DANFORTH, Emma K., dau of the Rev. J. N DANFORTH, of Alexandria, at Alexandria, 11 Sep 1850, by Rev. J. N. DANFORTH (DG 17 Sep 1850)

BUSH, Julia A., youngest dau of George BUSH, 26 Feb 1849, in her 3rd yr (DG 2 Mar 1849)

BUSH, L. P., Dr.,
see BUSH, Eugene Elmer
see BUSH, Lewis Potter

BUSH, Lewis Potter, son of Dr. L. P. and Maria BUSH, 7 Dec 1851, aged 7 yrs 6 mos (DG 12 Dec 1851)

BUSH, Maria, see BUSH, Eugene Elmer
see BUSH, Lewis Potter

BUSH, Martha T., see TAYLOR, Edward

BUSH, Mary, Mrs., consort of William BUSH, in Wilm, 12 May 1847, na (DG 14 May 1847)

BUSH, Mary I., see BRUCE, J. M.

BUSH, Mary Jane, Mrs., wife of Mr. George BUSH, in Wilm, 23 Jun 1823 (DG 24 Jun 1823)

BUSH, Samuel, see McLEAR, John

BUSH, William, see BUSH, Mary

BUSH, William, to ALRICH, Susanna Canby, Miss, dau of Thomas C, ALRICH, Esq., of Wilm, at the Greenhill Presby Ch, 18 Jun 1849, by the Rev. W. W. Taylor (DG 22 Jun 1849)

BUTCHER, Martha, in Phila, 26 Aug 1849, in her 77th yr (DG 28 Aug 1849)

BUTLER, Benj., 12 Jan 1821, aged 106 yrs (DG 23 Jan 1821)

BUTLER, Elizabeth,
see JEFFERSON, Asa W.
see BUTLER, William A.
see WAITE, Joseph T.

BUTLER, George W., of Carlisle, Cumberland Co PA, to GREENWOOD, Anna Elizabeth, of Wilm, 8 Feb 1852, by the Rev. Mr. Templeton (DG 13 Feb 1852)

BUTLER, James,
see BUTLER, Willam A.

BUTLER, James, in Georgetown, 19 Jan 1851, in his 55th yr (DG 21 Jan 1851)

BUTLER, James, postmaster, at his res. in Georgetown, 25 Jan 1851, na (DG 28 Jan 1851)

BUTLER, Rebecca, see BLIZZARD, Geo.

BUTLER, Sarah Elizabeth,
see MALONA, Andrew J.

BUTLER, William, to MOORE, Margaret, Miss, 11 Jan 1821 (DG 12 Jan 1821)

BUTLER, William A., son of James and Elizabeth BUTLER, in Georgetown, of bilious fever, 9 Feb 1849, in his 9th yr (DG 13 Feb 1849)

BUZBY, Charles Rossiter, son of David T. and Mary BUZBY, in Balt, of measles, 9 Apr 1852, aged 1 yr (DG 24 May 1852)

BUZBY, David T., of Wilm, to SCOTT, Mary M., of Balt, in Balt, 12 Jun 1849, by Friends ceremony (DG 15 Jun 1849)
see BUZBY, Charles Rossiter
see BUZBY, Edith Florence

BUZBY, Edith Florence, dau of David T. and Mary BUZBY, in Balt, 15 May 1852, aged 2 yrs (DG 24 May 1852)

BUZBY, Mary,
see BUZBY, Charles Rossiter
see BUZBY, Edith Florence

BUZBY, Samuel,
see TATUM, Hephzibah

BUZINE, Amanda,
see ELTONHEAD, Isaac

BUZINE, George, of Wilm, to ENOS, Rebecca M., Miss, of Southwark PA, 12 May 1841, in Phila by Rev. Thomas G. Allen (DG 14 May 1841)
see BUZINE, Susannah L.
see BISHOP, John Wesley

BUZINE, Martha, see OSBORN, William S.

BUZINE, Rebecca,
see BUZINE, Susannah L.

BUZINE, Susannah L., eldest dau of George and Rebecca BUZINE, res. 37th St, 2 Jan 1851, in her 9th yr (DG 3 Dec 1851)

BYERS, James A., of Dorchester Co MD, to ECCLESTON, Louisa, Miss, dau of John ECCLESTON, of Dover, 5 Mar 1844, by Rev. John Manlove (DG 12 Mar 1844)

BYLES, Thomas J., to NICKLE, Martha J., Miss, both of Delaware City, in Phila,

24 Nov 1853, by the Rev. D. W. Bartine (DG 20 Dec 1853)

BYRNES, Jonathan, see COX, James M.

BYRNES, Jonathan, Jr,
see BYRNES, Margaret W.
see COXE, James M.
see ROWAN, William

BYRNES, Margaret W., late consort of Jonathan BYRNES Jr, 25 Jun 1843, aged 34 yrs (DG 14 Jul 1843)

BYRNES, Sarah, see BYRNES, Thomas

BYRNES, Thomas, 6 Aug 1798, in Wilm (DE 9 Aug 1798)

BYRNES, Thomas, dec'd, late of Wilm, notice given by Sarah BYRNES, adm'x and Samuel PANCOAST and Wiliam ROBINSON, adm'rs (DG 27 Oct 1798)

COX, Ellen, Miss, see PLANK, Thomas

CADE, Hester Jane,
see HEATHER, Horatio N.

CADWALADER, Thomas,
see HOPKINSON, Thomas

CAHAL, Thomas, Jr., to VICKREY, Sarah Ann, Miss, both of Frederica, 4 Sep 1849, by the Rev. T. Newman (DG 11 Sep 1849)

CAIN, Ann, dec'd, late of Wilm, notice given by Jona. LAMBORN, exec'r (AW 1 May 1816)

CALDWELL, Ann,
see SCHRAIDER, Abraham

CALDWELL, Elizabeth,
see LATIMER, John Richardson

CALDWELL, James, near Dover, 2 Feb 1790, in his 21st yr (DG 20 Mar 1790)

CALDWELL, Rebecca Ann,
see FLEMING, George, Capt.

CALDWELL, Sarah A.,
see WELDIN, Jacob B.

CALDWELL, Wm. Pemberton, to ASH, Sallie Amanda, dau of the late John ASH, Esq., of Delaware City, at Delaware City, 25 Aug 1853, by the Rev. Hiram R. Harrold, late Rector of Christ (Ep) Ch, Delaware City (DG 30 Aug 1853)

CALHOON, Sarah Ann,
see CANNON, James R.

CALHOUN, Eliza,
see THOMPSON, Joseph J.

CALHOUN, Martha,
see GOODEN, John B.

CALLAHAN, John, to LAFFERTY, Sarah, Miss, dau of Ambrose LAFFERTY of New Castle, at St. Peter's Church, 11 Dec 1847, by Rev. John Cullen (DG 14 Dec 1847)

CALLEY, Frances A.,
see McDANIEL, Joseph

CALLOWAY, George H., to TIBBITT, Sarah Ann, 1 May 1845, by Rev. M. J. Rhees (DG 13 May 1845)

CALMONT, James M., at his res. in New Castle, 7 Oct 1824, in his 70th yr (DG 15 Oct 1824)

CALVERT, Albert L. Esq., to THOMAS, Hannah M., Miss, both of Wilm, at Morris House in Phila, 18 Jul 1848, by the Rev. Geo. Lacey (DG 8 Aug 1848)

CALVERT, H. L.,
see CALVERT, Harry Thomas

CALVERT, H. M., [fem]
see CALVERT, Harry Thomas

CALVERT, Harry Thomas, eldest son of H. L. and H. M. CALVERT, 11 Nov 1850, aged 21 mos (DG 15 Nov 1850)

CAMBWELL, John, to STUBBS, Sarah, 17 Sep 1852, in Smyrna, by Rev. P. Mansfield (DG 12 Oct 1852)

CAMERON, Margaret M.,
see ROWLAND, J. A. Dr.

CAMERON, William, to PHILLIPS, Jane, Miss, both of Wilm, on 8 Mar 1849, by Rev. J. T. Thompson (DG 13 Mar 1849)

CAMERON, William A., formerly of Millsboro, Sussex Co, 20 Jun 1852, at St. Louis MO (DG 13 Jul 1852)

CAMP, Enoch E., former editor of the Delaware Gazette, about a week or ten days ago, career data given (DG 19 Apr 1853)

CAMPBELL, Agnes,
see NORRIS, George Pepper

CAMPBELL, Catharine, in Wilm, in her 79th yr (DG 26 Jan 1848)

CAMPBELL, Charles S.,
see CAMPBELL, Sarah L.

CAMPBELL, David, to TALLEY, Elizabeth, Miss, both of Brandywine, in Brandywine by Rev. E. W. Gilbert (AW 11 Jul 1818)

CAMPBELL, David, to DENNISON, Rebecca, Miss, all of NC Co, 11 Jun 1844, by Rev. M. J. Rhees (DG 14 Jun 1844)

CAMPBELL, Eleanor,
see STILLEY, Thomas

CAMPBELL, Esther,
see BAKER, Alexander

CAMPBELL, James,
see CAMPBELL, Sarah

CAMPBELL, John,
see BUCHANAN, Hannah

CAMPBELL, Joseph, to STANTON, Sarah Ann, Miss, of Wilm, 2 Jun 1833, by the Rev. Joseph Walker (DG 11 Jun 1833)

CAMPBELL, Mary S., wife of William Campbell, Esq., at the res. of her husband, 28 Mar 1850 (DG 2 Apr 1850)

CAMPBELL, Samuel, to BRENHOLTZ, Phebe A., Miss, 10 Mar 1853, by the Rev. Dr. Dowling (DG 1 Apr 1853)

CAMPBELL, Sarah, Mrs. mother of James CAMPBELL, Esq., at Campbellville, Christiana Hd, 1 Apr 1851, aged 76 yrs (DG 8 Apr 1851)

CAMPBELL, Sarah L., dau of Charles S. CAMPBELL, 26 May 1848, aged 16 mos (DG 6 Jun 1848)

CAMPBELL, William,
see CAMPBELL, Mary S.

CAMPBELL, William, to NEALS, Rachel, Miss, both of Christiana Hd, 26 Jun 1824, by Rev. James Taylor (WN 1 Jul 1824)

CAMPBELL, William, Rev., of the Phila Annual Conf., to WHITAKER, Rachel E., dau of Francis A. WHITAKER, Esq. of Wilm, 12 Nov 1846, by Rev. J. Kennaday D. D. (DG 17 Nov 1846)

CAMPBELL, Wm., Rev., of the ME Ch and preacher in charge of Saulsbury circuit, at Saulsbury MD, 13 Aug 1849, na (DG 21 Aug 1849)

CAMPESON, Ruth Ann,
see HOOPES, Barton

CANBY, Ann, see PAXSON, Ann

CANBY, Caleb H., at the res. of his son-in-law, Cecil Co MD, 9 Apr 1852, in his 52nd yr (DG 13 Apr 1852)
see CANBY, Chas.

CANBY, Caroline A.,

see GARRETT, Henry

CANBY, Charles, see OGDEN, Clarkson

CANBY, Chas., 18 Jun 1851, of the firm of Caleb H. CANBY and Sons, in his 29th yr (DG 20 Jun 1851)

CANBY, Edmund, to PRICE, Mary T., Miss, both of Brandywine, DE, in Phila, 20 Apr 1826, by Joseph Watson, Esq. (DG 25 Apr 1826)

CANBY, Edmund, son of Mary T. CANBY, in Wilm, 1 Apr 1848, aged 13 yrs (DG 7 Apr 1848)

CANBY, Edmund, in Wilm, 3 Jul 1848, in his 45th yr (DG 7 Jul 1848)

CANBY, Edward,
see BRADFORD, Edward

CANBY, Elizabeth,
see BRADFORD, Edward

CANBY, Frances, dau of James CANBY, Esq., in Wilm, 17 Jun 1842, aged 27 yrs (DG 24 Jun 1842)

CANBY, Frances, see CLEMENT, Richard

CANBY, James, see CANBY, Frances

CANBY, James Jr., at his res., Bay Side, Kent Co MD, 13 Mar 1849, aged 42 yrs (DG 16 Mar 1849)

CANBY, Lydia, see OGDEN, Clarkson

CANBY, Margaret, see MORETON, John

CANBY, Martha, 18 Aug 1751, wife of William CANBY of Brandywine (PG 24 Aug 1751)

CANBY, Mary T., see CANBY, Edmund

CANBY, Samuel, see STAPLER, John
see CLEMENT, Richard
see PAXSON, Ann
see CROW, Michael

CANBY, Samuel, Jr., Esq., merchant of Phila, formerly of Wilm, in Birmingham, England, "of a consumption," 9 Jul 1821, in his 32nd yr (DG 28 Aug 1821)

CANBY, Susanna, see BUSH, William
see ALRICHS, Jonas

CANBY, Thomas, see WEST, Thomas

CANBY, William, see CANBY, Martha

CANN, Chandler, at his mother's res. near Christiana Bridge, 2 Feb 1844, aged 23 yrs

(DG Feb 3 1844)

CANN, Emeline, see BRADLEY, Bernard

CANN, Mary, see PECKARD, Henry L.

CANN, Rachel, see MORRISON, David

CANNON, Abraham, Sr., in Christiana Village, 16 Jul 1849, aged between 70 and 80 yrs (DG 24 Jul 1849)

CANNON, Amanda, see WEST, Edward W.

CANNON, Angeline, see SPENCER, William

CANNON, Elijah, Esq. at his res. in N.W. Fork Hd, near Horsey's Xroads, 12 May 1849, aged 70 yrs (DG 18 May 1849)

CANNON, Henry H., formerly editor of the Delaware Republican, aged 27 yrs, 19 May 1843, of a pulmonary disease, at the res. of his relative, William WILSON, near Brick Meeting House, Cecil Co MD (DG 26 May 1843)

CANNON, Isaac, of Sussex Co, brother of Jacob CANNON, who was murdered a few weeks ago, 5 May 1843 (DG 12 May 1843)

CANNON, Jacob, see CANNON, Isaac

CANNON, James R., to CALHOON, Sarah Ann, Miss, all of Sussex, 17 Feb 1850, by Rev. James Hargis (DG 26 Feb 1850)

CANNON, John D., to REYHOW, Jane, Miss, both of New Castle, 24 Dec 1835, by Elder John P. Peckworth (DG 26 Jan 1836)

CANNON, John Wiley, at New Castle, at the res. of his grandfather, John WILEY, Esq., only son of Mrs. Olivia CANNON, 22 Sep 1841, aged 24 yrs (DG 15 Oct 1841)

CANNON, Margaret, see CANNON. Mary Ann

CANNON, Mary Ann, eldest dau of William and Margaret CANNON, at Bridgeville, 28 Dec 1849, aged 18 yrs (DG 16 Jan 1850)

CANNON, Olivia, Mrs, see CANNON, John Wiley

CANNON, William, see CANNON, Mary Ann

CANNON, William, of Sussex Co, to JOYCE, Charlotte, Miss, of Anne Arundel Co MD, 22 Jun by Rev. John Reese (DG 30 Jun 1848)

CANNON, Wm. W., to BURRINGTON, Sarah Jane, Miss, both of Sussex Co, 19 Nov 1853, by the Rev. B. H. Nadall (DG 24 Nov 1853)

CANTWELL, Margaret, wife of Wm. CANTWELL, in Smyrna, 26 May 1853, in her 37th yr (DG 7 Jun 1853)

CANTWELL, Winfield Scott, in Smyrna, 27 Jun 1852, son of Wm. CANTWELL, in his 5th yr (DG 9 Jul 1852)

CANTWELL, Wm., see CANTWELL, Margaret see CANTWELL, Winfield Scott

CAPELLE, Marcus E., in Red Lion Hd, in his 59th yr (DG 16 Feb 1849)

CARE, Isabella, see McENTIRE, Thomas

CAREY, Ann, see FERRA, Charles

CAREY, Cornelius, see CAREY, Elizabeth

CAREY, Cornelius M., to SIMPSON, Elizabeth M., Miss, both of Wilm, 30 Dec 1845, by Rev. Anthony Atwood (DG 9 Jan 1846)

CAREY, Elizabeth, dau of Cornelius M. CAREY of Wilm, of croup, at the res. of her grandfather, 21 Nov 1845, aged 8 yrs 2 mos 14 days (DG 28 Nov 1845)

CAREY, Isabella, in Phila, 5 Jan 1852, in her 22nd yr (DG 9 Jan 1852)

CAREY, John, Dr., see SORDEN, John

CAREY, S. P. [fem], see SORDEN, John

CAREY, Sarah, see ENNIS, Jesse

CARLILE, James, in the village of Brandywine, 19 Aug 1823, aged 42 yrs (DG 22 Aug 1823)

CARLISLE, Nelson, see CARLISLE, William

CARLISLE, Rachel M, see BARNETT, James H.

CARLISLE, Tryphena, see CARLISLE, William

CARLISLE, William, inf son of Nelson and Tryphena CARLISLE, of congestion of the lungs, 2 Jun 1849 (DG 15 Jun 1849)

CARLISLE, Willism, see BARNETT, James H.

CARNAHAN, Elizabeth, see COOK, John

CARNAHAN, James B., Capt., of dropsy, in Wilm, 5 Feb 1845, aged c 26 yrs (DG 11 Feb 1845)

CARNAHAN, M. K., to MORRISON, Sally A., Miss, all of Wilm, 9 Nov 1843, by Rev. William Hogarth (DG 13 Nov 1843)

CARNAHAN, Margaret, see YOUNG, Thomas

CARNAHAN, Mary Jane, see WILSON, Thomas

CARNAHAN, Matthew K., see CARNAHAN, Samuel

CARNAHAN, Samuel, Presbyterian, of Wilm, after a long and lingering illness, 13 Jan 1816 (AW 17 Jan 1816)

CARNAHAN, Samuel, only child of Matthew K. CARNAHAN, at the res. of his father in Brooklyn, 3 Jun 1851, aged 3 yrs 2 mos, bur. in cem at Wilmington on the Brandywine (DG 13 Jun 1851)

CARNEY, Dyer, Esq., State Attorney and delegate to the former congress from the state, at Dover, 28 Oct 1790 (DG 30 Oct 1790)

CARPENTER, Adam, wool merchant, 20 Nov 1847, in Wilm, of lockjaw (DG 25 Nov 1847)

CARPENTER, Anna, see BRATTEN, Abraham

CARPENTER, Benjamin, of Lewiston, to SMITH, Mary Jane, Miss, of Phila, in Phila, 1 Nov 1847, by Rev. Dr. Moreton (DG 25 Nov 1847)

CARPENTER, Elizabeth, see HIPPLE, Jacob

CARPENTER, James T., to ARBUCKEL, Mary, Miss, both of Port Penn DE, in Phila, 19 Mar 1851, by Rev. John Coleman DD (DG 25 Mar 1851)

CARPENTER, John, in Centreville, 30 Sep 1852, aged c 30 yrs (DG 8 Oct 1852)

CARPENTER, Joseph C., to WALTERS, Jemima M., Miss, both of Wilm, in Wilm, 30 Jun 1825, by the Rev. E. W. Gilbert (DG 5 Jul 1825)

CARPENTER, Josephine, see SHIRKEY, John

CARPENTER, Lemuel, at Frederica, 24 Oct 1851, aged 45 yrs (DG 7 Nov 1851)

CARPENTER, Mary A., see MEREDITH, Levin

CARPENTER, Mary Q., see MARSHALL, Jacob A.

CARPENTER, Richard, a native of NC Co, in Wilm, "Wednesday last," na (DG 30 Oct 1821)

CARPENTER, Samuel, Jr., son of Samuel CARPENTER, in New Castle, 10 Sep 1835, aged 22 yrs (DG 15 Sep 1835)

CARPENTER, Samuel T., of Smyrna to THOMPSON, Emilie, D., of Wilm, Jun 1852, in St Andrew's Ch, by the Rt. Rev. Bishop Lee (DG 2 Jul 1852)

CARPENTER, Sarah J., see OWENS, Garrett

CARPENTER, Thomas H., to WERT, Mary Landreth, all of Sussex Co, 7 Jul 1853 (DG 22 Jul 1853)

CARPENTER, William, see LAROUX, John

CARR, David D., in Smyrna, 18 Oct 1849, aged 31 yrs DG 23 Oct 1849)

CARR, Joseph, Major, in Brandywine Hd, 28 Oct 1851, aged c 55 yrs (DG 4 Nov 1851)

CARR, Joseph L., in Brandywine Hd, 10 Sep 1847, in his 72nd yr (DG 17 Sep 1847)

CARR, Mary Jane, see HART, Charles W.

CARR, Susanna, see SAXTON, Isaac G.

CARROLL, _____, Mr., see MANSON, James

CARROLL, Chas. R. see MILLIGAN, George B.

CARROLL, Sophia G., see MILLIGAN, George B.

CARROW, Jonathan, see COOK, Wm. A.

CARROW, Mary Francis, see COOK, Wm. A.

CARSON, Elizabeth O., see CARSON, Francis

CARSON, Francis, youngest son of John and Elizabeth O. CARSON, in Delaware City, 26 Feb 1851, aged 9 mos (DG 4 Mar 1851)

CARSON, John, see CARSON, Francis

CARSON, Sallie Lamont, Mrs.,

see **MAITLAND**, William S.

CARSWELL, James, of Wilm, to **ENOS**, Susanna D., Miss, dau of the late John ENOS, of Phila, 19 May 1845, in Phila, by Rev. Thomas G. Allen (DG 23 May 1845)

CARSWELL, Wilson, to **SCOTT**, Eliza Jane, both of Wilm, in Phila, 24 Dec 1846, by Rev. I. T. Cooper (DG 29 Dec 1846)

CARTER, Amelia,
see **ROBINSON**, Joseph

CARTER, Amos, of Christiana Hd, to **ZEBLEY**, Mary, Miss, of Wilm, 3 Feb 1848, by Rev. S. R. Wynkoop (DG 8 Feb 1848)

CARTER, Ann, widow of the late Col. Joshua CARTER of Appoq. Hd, in Wilm at the res. of Jos. SEAL, Esq., in her 72nd yr (DG 8 May 1849)

CARTER, Edward J., to **REYBOLD**, Elizabeth, Miss, both of Kent Co, at Congress Hall, Phila, 20 Apr 1847, by Rev. A. Manship (DG 4 May 1847)

CARTER, Eliza Ann, Mrs., wife of Levi J. CARTER, in Willow Grove, 15 Nov 1851. She leaves a husband and three children (DG 21 Nov 1851)

CARTER, George, to **CERF**, Mary Ann, Miss, both of NC Co, 25 Mar 1845, by Rev. S. R. Wynkoop (DG 28 Mar 1845)

CARTER, Joshua, Col.,
see **CARTER**, Ann

CARTER, Levi J.,
see **CARTER**, Eliza Ann

CARTER, Mary Ann,
see **WILSON**, Jonathan

CARTER, Samuel, of Wilm, to **LUNGREN**, Hannah E., Miss, of Phila, 1 Aug 1848, in Phila by Rev. R. Gerry (DG 4 Aug 1848)

CARTER, Sarah T., see **SEAL**, Joseph

CARTER. Walter K., Dr., at Kenton DE, 4 Sep 1849 (DG 14 Sep 1849)

CARTHELL, Elizabeth,
see **MITCHELL**, Henry

CARTMEL, Susanna, Mrs.,
see **STILLE**, John

CARTMELL, Elizabeth,
see **HICKMAN**, William

CARTMELL, George, at his res. in Brandywine Hd, 20 Jan 1849, aged 83 yrs (DG 30 Jan 1849) Thomas CARTMELL , exec'r (DG 23 Feb 1849)

CARTMELL, George T., to **BIRD**, Rachel H., Miss, both of Brandywine Hd, NC Co, 19 Jan 1853, by the Rev. J. R. Anderson (DG 22 Mar 1853)

CARTMELL, Joseph, dec'd, late of Brandywine Hd, notice given by Thomas CARTMELL, Jr., adm'r (DG 5 Jan 1830)

CARTMELL, Thomas, dec'd, late of Brandywine Hd, notice given by William FOULK, exec'r (DS 17 Mar 1813)
see **CARTMELL**, George

CARTMELL, Thomas, Jr.,
see **CARTMELL**, Joseph

CARTWRIGHT, Matthew,
see **JACKSON**, Thomas

CARTWRIGHT, Sarah,
see **JACKSON**, Thomas

CARTY, Isaac, Esq., Col. of the DE Regt, at his habitation near Lewes Cross Roads, 15 Nov 1789, aged 53 yrs. Buried at Presbyterian meeting house; leaves a widow and 3 sons (DG 12 Dec 1789)

CARUTHERS, Josiah, of MD, to **ALBERTSON**, Eliza, Miss of Newark, "on Friday evening last," by the Rev. E. W. Gilbert (DG 27 Mar 1821)

CARY, Amelie Marim, wife of Cornelius M. CARY,at Smyrna, 31 Dec 1843, aged 24 yrs (DG 9 Jan 1844)

CARY, Andrew, see **CARY**, Mary Ann

CARY, Cornelius M.
see **CARY**, Amelia Marim

CARY, Mary Ann, Mrs., wife of Andrew CARY, in Wilm, 9 Jun 1824, aged 56 yrs (DG 15 Jun 1824)

CARY, Samuel, of NC Co, to **WILSON**, Elizabeth, Miss, of Phila, 25 Apr 1850, by Rev. J. Humphries (DG 3 May 1850)

CASHILL, Thomas, to **STAYTON**, Rhoda, Miss, all of Sussex Co, 15 Feb 1853, by Rev. McColley (DG 22 Feb 1853)

CASHO, Elizabeth, see **SCOTT**, James

CASSON, Margaret E.,
see **POSTLES**, Stephen

CASTLE, Edmund Yard, son of Rev. Joseph CASTLE, 10 Jun 1848, aged 16 mos, 13 days (DG 13 Jun 1848)

CASTLE, Joseph,
see CASTLE Edmund Yard

CASWELL, Mary,
see STOTSENBERG, John

CATHCART, William, to SPRINGER, Susan, both of New Castle, 10 May 1842, by Elder John Miller (DG 13 May 1842)

CATHERWOOD, Andrew,
see SMITH, Francis
see WALLACE, John
see LINN, John

CATS, Amelia A., see LEWIS, Thomas B.

CAUFFMAN, Julia A.,
see CHURCHMAN, Robert

CAULK, Ann, consort of CAULK, Benjamin, Esq., in Mill Creek Hd, 24 Mar 1849, na. Buried in the family burying ground in Appoq. Hd (DG 3 Apr 1849)

CAULK, Benjamin, to HANDY, Jane, Miss, both of Newark, at the res. of Dr. Thomas W. HANDY, 11 Jul 1850, by Rev. Joseph Stevens (DG 16 Jul 1850)

CAULK, Benjamin, see CAULK. Ann

CAULK, David,
see CAULK, Mary Frances

CAULK, Jacob, former sheriff of NC Co, at Delaware City, 29 Mar 1853, na (DG 1 Apr 1853)
see STAATS, James
see TURNER, George W.

CAULK, John, see WARNE, John E.

CAULK, Marriet, (sic)
see TURNER, George W.

CAULK, Mary Ann, see STAATS, James

CAULK, Mary Frances, dau of the late Mrs. Susan D. CAULK, of a ruptured blood vessel. It is desired that David CAULK, son of Mrs. CAULK, return immediately from California (DG 26 Apr 1850)

CAULK, Oliver, to WAUGH, Catherine O., Miss, 19 Aug 1841, at New Castle by Rev. S. Wynkoop (DG 27 Aug 1841)

CAULK, Sue E., see WARNE, John E.

CAULK, Susan D.,
see CAULK, Mary Frances

CAULK, Susan F., of typhoid in Pencader Hd, 4 Jan 1850, aged c 53 yrs (DG 26 Apr 1850)

CAUSEY, Elizabeth,
see FLEMING, Elizabeth

CAUSEY, Peter F.,
see FLEMING, Elizabeth

CAUSEY, Peter J.,
see CAUSEY, Sarah Marie

CAUSEY, Sarah Maria, only dau of Peter J. CAUSEY, Esq., of Milford, 6 May 1846, aged 18 mos (DG 15 May 1846)

CAVALRY, Peter, Esq., cashier of the Wilm branch of Farmers Bank, 12 Oct 1827, na (DG 16 Oct 1827)

CAVENDER, Elizabeth, see AUSTIN, David

CAVENDER, Lewis, of Smyrna, to BIDDLE, Olivia Ann, Miss, of Chesapeake City, 10 Apr 1850, by Rev. Mr. McIntire (DG 23 Apr 1850)

CAVERLY, Anna M.,
see BOYER, William R.

CAVERLY, P., Esq.,
see BOYER, William R.

CAZIER, Henry, see DEIHL, William

CAZIER, John, of DE, to POWELL, Elizabeth, Miss, of Baltimore, in Balt. "Tuesday evening last," by the Rev. Dr. Glendy (DG 21 Aug 1821)

CAZIER, Mary, see DEIHL, William

CAZIER. Olivia Ann,
see STUCKERST, William M.

CERF, Mary Ann, see CARTER, George

CHADWICK, Annie,
see JOHNSON, Geo. R.

CHADWICK, Caroline,
see CORMICHEL, James

CHADWICK, Henrietta,
see WALRAVEN, Jonas

CHADWICK, Isabella, see DUNTZE, John

CHADWICK, Radcliff,
see JOHNSON, Geo. R.

CHALFANT, Ellen L., wife of Jacob CHALFANT, in Christiana Hd, 23 Nov 1850, in her 24 th yr (DG 29 Nov 1850)

CHALFANT, Goodwin, at his res. in E. Marlborough, Chester Co PA, 16 Apr 1851, na, bur. Old Kennett Meeeting Ground (DG 25 Apr 1851)

CHALFANT, Hannah, Miss, of DE Co PA,

at St. Georges, of typhoid fever, ndd, in her 29th yr (DG 5 Oct 1849)

CHALFANT, Jacob,
see CHALFANT, Ellen L.

CHALFANT, Jacob M., of Christiana Hd, to HAYES, Sarah E., of Wilm, 15 Jun 1852, in Wilm, by Rev. Mr. Young (DG 18 Jun 1852)

CHALLENGER, Thomas, to PRICE, Sarah, Miss, 10 Jun 1823, by Rev. E. Clay, all of NC Co (DG 17 Jun 1823)

CHALTEN, John,
see CHALTEN, Phebe Ann
see CHALTEN, Sarah

CHALTEN, Phebe Ann, wife of John CHALTEN, at the second tollgate on the Wilm-Christiana Tpk near Stanton, ndd, aged 34 yrs (DG 23 Mar 1852)

CHALTEN, Sarah, 2nd dau of John CHALTEN, near Newport DE, 10 Mar 1853, aged 7 yrs 11 mos 18 days (DG 15 Apr 1853)

CHAMBERLAIN, Joseph, late of Newark (DG 18 Apr 1851)

CHAMBERLAIN, Sarah, Mrs., in Milford, 6 Nov 1852, in her 83rd yr (DG 16 Nov 1852)

CHAMBERLIN, Pierce, Rev., in Newark, 23 Aug 1850, in his 56th yr (DG 27 Aug 1850)

CHAMBERS, _____, Capt,
see McKEE, Robert L.

CHAMBERS, Corry, Rev,
see CHAMBERS, Sarah V.

CHAMBERS, David, in Mill Creek Hd, 2 Dec 1852, aged 60 yrs (DG 7 Dec 1852)

CHAMBERS, James, see MACKEY, John

CHAMBERS, John, see MACKEY, John

CHAMBERS, Sarah V., Mrs., 10 May 1841, wife of Rev. Corry CHAMBERS (DG 11 May 1841)

CHAMBERS, Susanna M.,
see McKEE, Robert L.

CHAMBERS, William, M.D., at New York, 22 Jul 1827, na. He was the inventor of a medicine for the cure of intemperance. (DG 31 Jul 1827)

CHAMPION, Rachel B., see MAULL, John

CHAMPION, Wm., see MAULL, John

CHANDLER, _____, Mrs., wife of William CHANDLER, in Wilm, 8 Apr 1834 (DG 8 Apr 1834)

CHANDLER, Adaline P., see HENDRICKSON, Joseph G.

CHANDLER, Alexander, to YATES, Margaret C., Miss, all of Wilm, in Phila, 14 Dec 1852, by Rev. William Cooper (DG 28 Dec 1852)

CHANDLER, Amer,
see CHANDLER, Sarah

CHANDLER, Amor,
see CHANDLER, Mary

CHANDLER, Benjamin,
see HYNDMAN, John
see McFARLAN, Isaac
see NOBLITT, John

CHANDLER, Benjamin, to HINDMAN, Rebecca, Miss, dau of John HINDMAN, 30 Apr 1816, by Rev. Dr. Read, all of Wilm (AW 4 May 1816)

CHANDLER, Caroline,
see JONES, Israel D.

CHANDLER, David, to CLELAND, Ellen M., both of Wilm, 22 Apr 1852, by Rev. S. L. Wynkoop (DG 27 Apr 1852)

CHANDLER, Edward G., druggist, at the res. of his brother-in-law James FULTON, in Brandywine Hd, 16 Aug 1851, in his 59th yr (DG 19 Aug 1851) of Wilm City, James FULTON, adm'r (DG 5 Sep 1851)

CHANDLER, Elizabeth,
see RUDMAN, Richard

CHANDLER, Elizabeth Head Vaux, inf dau of William Penn and Hannah S. Vaux CHANDLER (DG 28 Aug 1849)

CHANDLER, Ellen,
see PARKINSON, Richardson

CHANDLER, Gregg, to NOBLIT, Maria Louisa, Miss, dau of Dell NOBLIT, Esq., both of Wilm, 24 Apr 1834, by Rev. C. S. Hedges (DG 29 Apr 1834)

CHANDLER, Hannah, see HARPER, Mark

CHANDLER, Hannah S.,
see BRACKEN, Benjamin F.

CHANDLER, Hannah S. Vaux, see CHANDLER, Elizabeth Head Vaux

CHANDLER, James, of Woodville, Londongrove, PA, to BROOKES, Martha, of Wilm,

19 Mar 1842, in Phila, before Alderman
Thompson by Friends ceremony
(DG 1 Apr 1842)

CHANDLER, Jesse, Esq., at the res. of his son, Thomas C. CHANDLER, Christiana Hd., after an illness of one week, 14 Mar 1850, aged 64 yrs 6 mos. He was the father of William Penn CHANDLER, one of the editors of the *Del. Gazette.* Obit 19 Mar (DG 15 Mar 1850)
see HOLLINGSWORTH, Jane

CHANDLER, Jonathan, 13 Jan 1847, at his res. in Harrisburg, in his 55th yr (DG 15 Jan 1847)

CHANDLER, Joseph Eugene, inf. son of Marshall S. and Rachel CHANDLER, aged 5 wks, 5 days, 9 Feb 1844, at Fair Hill, NC Co (DG 16 Feb 1844)

CHANDLER, Joseph F., dec'd, notice given by T. S. NEWLIN, adm'r (DJ 30 Mar 1832)

CHANDLER, Lydia, relict of William CHANDLER, late of Kennett Twp, in Wilm, 16 Dec 1842, aged 81yrs (DG 23 Dec 1842)

CHANDLER, Margaret Dorothea, dau of Samuel P. and Mary Ann CHANDLER, at Willowbank in NC Co, 16 Sep 1847, aged 2 yrs (DG 17 Sep 1847)

CHANDLER, Marshall S.,
see CHANDLER, Joseph Eugene

CHANDLER, Mary, at the res. of her brother, Amor CHANDLER, in Brandywine Hd, ndd, na (DG 28 Mar 1848)

CHANDLER, Mary Ann,
see CHANDLER, Margaret Dorothea

CHANDLER, Rachel,
see CHANDLER, Joseph Eugene

CHANDLER, Rebecca A.,
see HENDRICKSON, Joseph

CHANDLER, Reece E., of Chester Co PA, to ROWE, Lucinda, Miss, dau of the Rev. Reuben ROWE, of Pickaway Co OH, 31 Dec 1850, by the Rev. Mr. Baker (DG 11 Mar 1851)

CHANDLER, Samuel P., of NC Co, to WOELPPER, Mary Ann, Miss, 2nd dau of the late David WOELPPER, Esq., of Spring Garden PA, Oct 17 1843, in Phila, by Rev. Dr. Meyer (DG 20 Oct 1843)
see CHANDLER, Margaret Dorothea

CHANDLER, Sarah, wife of Amer CHANDLER, in Brandywine Hd, 20 Feb 1853, in her 52nd yr (DG 25 Feb 1853)

see DAVIS, Alvan
see SOLOMON, Isaac

CHANDLER, Sarah H., see NOBLITT, John

CHANDLER, Thomas C.,
see CHANDLER, Jesse

CHANDLER, William, see SOLOMON, Isaac
see JONES, Israel D.
see POOLE, Richard
see CHANDLER, ____, Mrs.
see RUDMAN, Richard
see CHANDLER, Lydia

CHANDLER, William Penn, to VAUX, Hannah S., dau of the late George VAUX, 14 Jun 1848, in St. Philip's Church, Phila, by Rev. S. D. Mills (DG 16 Jun 1848)
see CHANDLER, Jesse
see CHANDLER, Elizabeth Head Vaux

CHAPMAN, John, of Spring Garden, Phila, to JONES, Ann Jane, Miss, of Smyrna, 16 Dec 1852, by the Rev. P. Meredith (DG 21 Dec 1852)

CHAPMAN, Joseph B., of Ohio, to WALRAVEN, Esther Ann, Miss, of Wilm, near Wilm, 3 Mar 1825, by the Rev. E. W. Gilbert (DG 11 Mar 1825)

CHARLES, Daniel, to BROWN, Elizabeth, Miss, both of Kent Co, DE in Dover, 13 Mar 1849 by the Rev. Mr. Allen (DG 20 Mar 1849)

CHARLES, George, to JACKSON, Hannah, Miss, both of Mill Creek Hd, 28 Dec 1843, by Rev. S. M. Gayley (DG 2 Jan 1844)

CHASE, I., to COOPER, Leah Jane, Miss, 30 Jan 1850, by Rev. J. R. Torbert (DG 12 Feb 1850)

CHASE, James R., to WILSON, Sarah, Miss, 24 Jan 1850, by Rev. J. R. Torbert (DG 12 Feb 1850)

CHASE, John, dec'd, late of St. Georges Hd, property to be sold by shff, Peter B. Delany (DG 28 Aug 1827)

CHASE, Juliana, see PHILLIPS, Nathaniel

CHASE, Mary, Miss, see ROACH, Eli

CHASTEAU, Priscilla Anna,
see JONES, James A.

CHATHAM, B. F., Dr.,
see CHATHAM, Ruhana Maria

CHATHAM, Benjamin F., M. D., of New Jersey, to COMEGYS, Mary Elizabeth, dau of ex-gov. COMEGYS, 26 May 1846, in Phila (DG 29 May 1846)

CHATHAM, Ruhana Maria, dau of Dr. B. F.
CHATHAM, in Wilm, 5 Jul 1852, in her 4th yr
(DG 13 Jul 1852)

CHATTEM, B. F.,
see CHATTEM, Cornelius Comegys

CHATTEM, Cornelius Comegys, inf son of
Dr. B. F. CHATTEM, in Wilm, 26 Sep 1851,
aged 9 mos (DG 7 Oct 1851)

CHAYTER, Aramina, inf dau of G. W.
Chayter, M. D., at her father's res,
29 Sep 1850 (DG 4 Oct 1850)

CHAYTER, G. W.,
see CHAYTER, Aramina

CHAYTOR, ____. Dr.,
see CHAYTOR, Sarah

CHAYTOR, David Atchison, son of G. W.
CHAYTOR, Capt., 23 Jul 1847, aged 1 yr
(DG 3 Aug 1847)

CHAYTOR, G. W.,
see CHAYTOR, David Atchison

CHAYTOR, George W. Dr.,
see CHAYTOR, George Washington
see CHAYTOR, Sallie

CHAYTOR, George Washington, eldest son
of Dr. George W. CHAYTOR, 12 Apr 1851,
in his 8th yr (DG 15 Apr 1851)

CHAYTOR, James, Com.,
see CHAYTOR, Sarah

CHAYTOR, Sallie, 2nd dau of Dr. Geo. W.
CHAYTOR, 21 Apr 1851, in her 10th yr
(DG 29 Apr 1851)

CHAYTOR, Sarah, widow of the late Com.
James CHAYTOR, in Wilm at the res. of
her son, Dr. CHAYTOR, 3 Jul 1853,
in her 76th yr (DG 4 Jul 1853)

CHE, Ann, see MOORE, Peter

CHEESELY, Joseph, to PHILIPS, alias
SPRINGER, Anne, Miss, 1 Feb 1821
(DG 9 Feb 1821)

CHEFFINS, Margaret J., see PRICE, John L.

CHEPPINS, John L., to FOUNTAIN,
Rebecca Jane, Miss, in Phila, 5 Jul 1852,
by Dr. Ryan (DG 13 Jul 1852)

CHESNEY, William A., to McCALL, Mary
Eliza, Miss, both of DE, 24 Feb 1848, by
Rev. Dr. Kennedy (DG 3 Mar 1848)

CHESNUT, Ann, see BOULDEN, David P.

CHESNUT, Calvin, in Baltimore, 2 Jul 1845,
aged 28 yrs (DG 8 Jul 1845)

CHESNUT, John, to RUMFORD, Sarah
Ann, Miss, 20 Apr 1824, by the Rev. Daniel
D. Lewis (DG 18 May 1824)

CHESTER, John J., in Wilm of consumption,
20 May 1850, aged 22 yrs
(DG 28 May 1850)

CHESTER, Thomas Piemson (sic),
in Wilm, 26 Feb 1852, in his 21st yr
(DG 27 Feb 1852)

CHESTNUT, William, dec'd, late of Red Lion
Hd, notice given by Henry MORTON and
Adam McGILLTON, adm'rs
(DG 10 May 1825)

CHEW, Mary, see CHEW, Samuel, Dr.

CHEW, Samuel, Dr., of Kent Co. Notice
given by Mary CHEW, admx.
(PG 5 Aug 1744)

CHIPPS, Hannah, see SEARLES, Thos.

CHRISTEE, Lydia, see DAVIS, John

CHRISTIE, Anthony, to HANDSHAW, Lydia,
Miss, all of Wilm, 24 Dec 1846, by Rev. S. R.
Wynkoop (DG 5 Mar 1847)

CHRISTIE, Catharine M., 3rd dau of Capt.
Thomas CHRISTIE of Spring Bank,
Scotland, a native of Edinburgh, on a visit
here, at Wilm, 12 Jul 1826, na
(DG 18 Jul 1826)

CHRISTIE, Mary, see STRIMPLE, Joseph

CHRISTIE, Thomas,
see CHRISTIE, Catharine M.

CHRISTY, James, of Wilm, to DOUNES,
Mary Ann, Miss, of Baltimore, 24 Mar 1845
(DG 28 Mar 1845)

CHRISTY, John V., to THOMPSON, Anne
Maria, Miss, all of NC Co, 7 May 1846,
by Rev. A. Atwood (DG 12 May 1846)

CHURCH, Nathaniel, of Phila, to JONES,
Rebecca, Mrs., of Dover, DE, in Phila,
22 Nov 1833, by the Rev. Mr. Roach
(DG 3 Dec 1833)

CHURCHMAN, Henry, of Naaman's Creek,
to REED, Sarah, Miss, dau of Alexander W.
REED, Esq., of Moyamensing, 1 Dec 1842,
in Phila, by Rev. Albert Barnes
(DG 9 Dec 1842)

CHURCHMAN, Pennell, of NY, to
MENDENHALL, Anna Ellen, of Wilm,

10 Jun 1851, by Friends ceremony in the presence of the Mayor (DG 13 Jun 1851)

CHURCHMAN, Robert, of Naaman's Creek, to CAUFFMAN, Julia A., of Phila, 26 Apr 1843, by Rev. Dr. Dorr (DG 12 May 1843)

CLANDENIRY, Elizabeth, see VANDEVER, Peter

CLARK, Adaline, see JAMES, Joseph A.

CLARK, Andrew S., to KILLINS, Mary, Miss, both of Wilm, 14 Jun 1846, by Rev. F. Reilley (DG 19 Jun 1846)
see CLARK, Ann

CLARK, Ann, late wife of Andrew S. CLARK, 15 Nov 1845, aged 24 yrs (DG 18 Nov 1845)

CLARK, Ann, see CLARK, George

CLARK, Ann, wife of John CLARK, 8 Sep 1851, aged 74 yrs (DG 9 Sep 1851)

CLARK, Ann Eliza, see CLARK, Eli

CLARK, Catharine, late wife of Nehemiah CLARK, at her res. near Dover, 10 Jul 1845, aged 65 yrs (DG 18 Jul 1845)
see BAKER, Curtis

CLARK, Eli, to CLARK, Ann Eliza, Miss, in Wilm, 25 Sep 1852, by the Rev. J. G. Collom (DG 28 Sep 1852)

CLARK, Eliza Elliott, dau of Levi H. and Susan M. CLARK, 16 Sep 1843, aged 2 yrs 2 mos (DG 22 Sep 1843)

CLARK, Elizabeth., only dau of John C. CLARK, in Red Lion Hd, ndd, aged 2 yrs (DG 19 Oct 1849)

CLARK, Elizabeth R., see CLARK, George

CLARK, Esther C., wife of Wm. CLARK, dau of Samuel PECKY, of Milestown, Phila Co PA, near Brandywine Springs, 11 Aug 1851, in her 37th yr (DG 19 Aug 1851)

CLARK, Frank Miles, son of Levi G. and Susan W. CLARK, 14 Sep 1850, aged 1 yr, 6 mos, 28 days (DG 24 Sep 1850)

CLARK, George, dec'd, late of Brandywine Hd, notice given by Ann CLARK and John TALLEY, exec'rs (DS 24 Jun 1812)

CLARK, George, see CLARK, Rebecca

CLARK, George, to CLARK, Elizabeth R., Miss, dau of Mr. Thomas CLARK, all of New Castle, 8 Oct 1851, by Rev. James C. Howe (DG 17 Oct 1851)

CLARK, George T., to ALRICH, Harriet S., both of Wilm, 3 Mar 1853, by Rev. Wm. Taylor (DG 8 Mar 1853)

CLARK, Hannah, Mrs., widow of Thomas CLARK, 4 Mar 1853, in her 54th yr. Born in Setterington, Yorkshire, Eng., dau of Mr. JACKSON. One of 8 children; immigrated 1819, m 1821 to Thomas CLARK from Leeds, Eng.; Methodist (DG 11 Mar 1853)

CLARK, Jane E., see POTTOGUE, Benjamin

CLARK, John, to TOWNSEND, Elizabeth, Miss, dau of Mrs. Ann TOWNSEND, at Dover, 31 Oct 1797, by Rev. Mr. Boyer (DE 6 Nov 1797)

CLARK, John, Esq., at Dover, 23 Nov 1821, in his 51st yr (DG 30 Nov 1821)

CLARK, John, see CLARK, Ann
see CLARK, T____, Mrs.

CLARK, John C., see CLARK, Elizabeth
see BIRD, Lulia
see BIRD, Thomas

CLARK, Jonathan R., to FITZPATRICK, Mary, Miss, both of Wilm, 25 Dec 1845, in Phila, by Rev. William Cooper (DG 9 Jan 1846)

CLARK, Julia A., see BIRD, Thomas

CLARK, L. George, of Damascus, DE, [south of Delaware City], to BOULDIN, Susan W., of Wilm, 7 Oct 1841, by Rev. Mr. Ide of Phila (DG 15 Oct 1841)

CLARK, Levi G., see CLARK, Frank Miles

CLARK, Levi H., see CLARK, Susan M.
see CLARK, Eliza Elliott

CLARK, Levi Henry, of DE to SMITH, Carrie G., Miss, 12 May 1853, by the Rev. D. E. Owen (DG 17 May 1853)

CLARK, Lulia., see BIRD, Lulia

CLARK, Mary, see CORBIT, Pennell

CLARK, Mary J., see PENNINGTON, William R.

CLARK, Matthew J., to VANGESIL, Angeline, Miss, dau of John VANGESIL, of Smyrna, 23 Dec 1850, by Rev. J. A. Roche (DG 31 Dec 1850)

CLARK, Nehemiah, see CLARK, Catharine

CLARK Rebecca, Miss, eldest dau of the late George CLARK, in Delaware City, 6 May

1852, aged c 47 yrs (DG 11 May 1852)

CLARK, Robert H., M. D., of Milford, to E. P. CUBBBAGE, of Pleasanton Abbey, at the latter place, 4 Dec, 1848, by Rev. J. Allen (DG 12 Dec 1848)

CLARK, Robert S., of Kent Co, to WILLIS, Jane H., Miss, of Richmond VA, 30 Jan 1850, by Rev. Daniel Scott (DG 8 Feb 1850)

CLARK, Sarah Ann,
see McCLEES, William K.
see PIERCE, Thomas

CLARK, Sarah M., see BRADFORD, Moses

CLARK, Susan, see REEVES, Clement

CLARK, Susan M., wife of Levi H. CLARK, in Red Lion Hd, 29 Feb 1852, aged 34 yrs (DG 5 Mar 1852)
see CLARK, Eliza Elliott
see BIRD, James T.

CLARK, Susan W.,
see CLARK, Frank Miles

CLARK, T____, Mrs., wife of John CLARK, at Frederica, in Kent Co, DE, 7 Feb 1822, na (DG 12 Feb 1822)

CLARK, Thomas, recently from England, to JACKSON, Hannah, Miss, of NC Co, 19 Dec 1821, by L. Lawrenson (DG 25 Dec 1821)

CLARK, Thomas, see CLARK, George
see REEVES, Clement
see CLARK, Hannah
see PENNINGTON, William R.

CLARK, Thomas to HARVEY, Ann, Miss, 3 Jul 1828, by Elder John P. Peckworth, all of Wilm (DG 8 Jul 1828)

CLARK, Thomas W., in Wilm, 11 Nov 1852, aged c 45 yrs (DG 16 Nov 1852)

CLARK, William, late carpenter of Brandywine Hd, dec'd, notice given by William SMITH, adm'r (AW 9 Dec 1815)

CLARK, William D., to HURLOCK, Mary F., both of NC Co, 22 Feb 1844, in Phila, by Rev. Henry A. Boardman (DG 27 Feb 1844)

CLARK, William R., in Wilm, after a long and painful illness, 21 Aug 1847, na (DG 27 Aug 1847)

CLARK, Wm., see CLARK, Esther C.

CLARKE, Ann Eliza,
see CLEMENTS, Joshua R.

CLARKE, Elizabeth,
see PENNEVILLE, Roberto

CLARKE, John, see CLEMENTS, Joshua R.
see PENNEVILL, Roberto

CLARKE, Jonathan, late of Pencader Hd. Sale of property by Peter B. Delaney, Sheriff (DG 2 Mar 1827)

CLARKE, Martha, 25 Oct 1798, on list of yellow fever victims (DG 27 Oct 1798)

CLARKE, Winlock, Lieut., U.S. Navy, while stepping from the brig *Pizarro* fell between the brig and the wharf and was drowned, 6 Apr 1810, na (His portrait is stored in the DE History Museum) (DG 7 Apr 1810)

CLARNAN, James, to CROSSON, Mary, Miss, both of Mill Creek Hd, in Wilm, 27 Dec 1821, by the Rev. E. W. Gilbert (DG 28 Dec 1821)

CLAY, Ann, Mrs., of New Castle, 14 Jun 1789, aged 66 yrs (DG 20 Jun 1789)

CLAY, David M., c 13 yrs old, found dead by hanging in the barn of David M. SANBORN, his uncle, near St. Georges. May have been an accident while playing with a rope (DG 28 Feb 1845)

CLAYTON, ____, [fem]
see YOUNG, ____, Mrs.

CLAYTON, Charles, nephew of Col. John CLAYTON,, at Dover, 31 Aug 1798, aged 19 yrs (DE 18 Sep 1798)

CLAYTON, Elizabeth,
see MAXWELL, John G., Dr.

CLAYTON, Hannah R., see DAY, John W.

CLAYTON, Harriett,
see PETERSON, Harriett

CLAYTON, Henry, to SPARKS, Mary Jane, Miss, all of Wilm, 22 Jul 1851, by the Rev. Andrew Manship (DG 25 Jul 1851)

CLAYTON, James,
see PETERSON, Harriett

CLAYTON, James F., only remaining child of the Hon, John M. CLAYTON, of erysipelas, at Buena Vista, his father's country seat, 4 Mar 1851, aged c 26 yrs (DG 7 Mar 1851)

CLAYTON, John, Col.,
see CLAYTON, Charles

CLAYTON, John L .to FARRAND, Julia P., all of Phila, 10 Nov 1853, by the Rev. Mr. Wadsworth (DG 15 Nov 1853)

CLAYTON, John M., Hon.,
see CLAYTON, James F.

CLAYTON, John M., Esq., to FISHER, Sally Ann, Miss, both of Kent Co, DE, 12 Aug 1822, by the Rev. Samuel C. Brinckle (DG 13 Sep 1822)

CLAYTON, John M.,
see CLAYTON, Sally Ann, Mrs.

CLAYTON, John, the Hon., Esq., Associate Justice of the Supreme Court, at his house near Dover, 8 Dec 1802 (FA 10 Dec 1802)

CLAYTON, Joshua, Col., of Bohemia Manor, to LOCKWOOD, Martha E., dau of Richard LOCKWOOD, all of NC Co, near Middletown, 21 Feb 1850, by Rev. H. R. Harrolds (DG 26 Feb 1850)
see CLAYTON, Lydia A.

CLAYTON, Lydia A., Mrs., wife of Col. Joshua CLAYTON and dau of Richard CLAYTON, Esq., at her res. in Bohemia Manor, NC Co, 27 Jan 1849. in her 33rd yr. Left a husband and 3 children (DG 2 Feb 1849)

CLAYTON, Maianna, (sic)
see TOWNSEND, Edward

CLAYTON, Martha, dau of Nelson CLAYTON, at the res. of her father in Bethel, 21 Mar 1853, in her 23rd yr (DG 5 Apr 1853)

CLAYTON, Mary, late wife of Reuben CLAYTON, formerly of Wilm, in Hendersonville, N C, 3 Apr 1847, aged 27 yrs (DG 18 May 1847)

CLAYTON, Nelson, of Penna., to BOOTH, Sarah Ann, Miss, of Delaware, 23 Sep 1841, by Rev. Ignatius T. Cooper at Marcus Hook PA (DG 1 Oct 1841)
see CLAYTON, Martha

CLAYTON, Reuben, see CLAYTON, Mary

CLAYTON, Richard, see CLAYTON, Lydia

CLAYTON, S. C., printer, in Wilm, 8 May 1849, aged c 50 yrs (DG 11 May 1849)

CLAYTON, Sally Ann, Mrs., wife of John M. CLAYTON, Esq.,18 Feb 1825, aged 26 yrs (DG 25 Feb 1825)

CLAYTON, Thomas,
see YOUNG, _____, Mrs.
see MAXWELL, John G., Dr.
see FRAME, Jeanette

CLEADEN, Charlotta, Mrs., 7 Oct 1846 (DG 16 Oct 1846)

CLEALAND, John, 25 Aug 1852, in his 65th yr (DG 27 Aug 1852)

CLEAVELAND, Susan H.,
see WOODS, Samuel P.

CLEAVELAND, Thomas, suddenly, at Foster's Hotel, 31 Mar 1852, na (DG 2 Apr 1852)

CLEAVER, John Jr., to GROSE, Ann, Miss, both of St. Georges Hd, on the 4th inst by Rev. Mr. McNamee (DG 13 Mar 1849)

CLEAVER, John Barr, son of William and Priscilla CLEAVER, of Port Penn, 4 Sep 1852, in his 8th yr (DG 10 Sep 1852)

CLEAVER, Priscilla,
see CLEAVER, John Barr

CLEAVER, Rachel, see PARKER, Wm. C.

CLEAVER, Thomas, of Port Penn DE, to DANIELS, Sarah, of Salem NJ, 30 Nov 1841, by T. J. Thompson (DG 10 Dec 1841)

CLEAVER, William,
see CLEAVER, John Barr

CLELAND, Elizabeth, Miss, at the res. of her mother in New Castle Hd, of consumption, 7 May 1843, aged 24 yrs (DG 12 May 1743)
see CLELAND, George

CLELAND, Ellen, see CLELAND, John

CLELAND, Ellen M.,
see CHANDLER, David

CLELAND, George, late of NC Co, 14 Jan 1827 (DG 16 Jan 1827) notice given by Elizabeth CLELAND, adm'x and John CLELAND, adm'r (DG 30 Jan 1827)

CLELAND, George D., to WELLS, Sarah A, Miss, both of NC Co, 2 Mar 1841, by Rev. S. R. Wynkoop (DG 9 Mar 1841)

CLELAND, J., see MILLER, James

CLELAND, James, in Wilm, 29 Apr 1845, aged 27 yrs (DG 29 Apr 1845)

CLELAND, Jane, see MILLER, James

CLELAND, John, Esq. at his res. near Wilm, 25 Aug 1852, in his 65th yr (DG 7 Sep 1852) late of Christiana Hd, Ellen CLELAND, exec'x (DG 17 Sep 1852)
see CLELAND, John N.

CLELAND, John, see CLELAND, George
see CLELAND, Samuel

CLELAND, John N., son of Thomas R. and

Sophia E. CLELAND, and grandson of John CLELAND, Esq., in Wilm, 17 Jul 1848, aged c 2 yrs (DG 28 Jul 1848)

CLELAND, Margaret Jane, see BIDDLE, Richard F.

CLELAND, Nelson, to ROBINSON, Ann C, Miss, both of Wilm, in Baltimore, 24 Dec 1834, by Rev. Joseph Shane (DG 30 Dec 1834)

CLELAND, Samuel, son of John CLELAND, of consumption in Wilm, 25 Dec 1847, aged 20 yrs (DG 31 Dec 1847)

CLELAND, Sophia E., see CLELAND, John N.

CLELAND, Thomas R., to WELLS, Sophia E., Miss, all of Wilm, 27 Feb 1844, by Rev. S. R. Wynkoop (DG 1 Mar 1844) see CLELAND, John N.

CLEMENT, Benjamin S., see CLEMENT, Helen see CLEMENT, Josiah F.

CLEMENT, Elizabeth, ___ May 1848, ill 3 days (DG 26 May 1848)

CLEMENT, Helen, only dau of Benjamin S. CLEMENT, 7 Apr 1835, aged 2 yrs 11 mos 23 days (DG 15 Sep 1835)

CLEMENT, Isaac, of NC Co, in Phila, 7 Jun 1842, aged 50 yrs (DG 10 Jun 1842)

CLEMENT, Josiah F., formerly of Wilm, but later of Phila, in Wilm, 17 Dec 1833, aged 40 yrs (DG 31 Dec 1833)

CLEMENT, Josiah F., only son of Benjamin S. CLEMENT, 6 Sep 1835, aged 1 yr 5 mos 5 days (DG 15 Sep 1835)

CLEMENT, Richard, merchant, to CANBY, Frances, dau of Samuel CANBY, at Friends Meeting in Wilm, 18 May 1826 (DG 26 May 1826)

CLEMENTS, Alexander, to WILDON, Dirba Ann, both of NC Co, 10 Jan 1850, by Rev. Pinor Mansfield (DG 15 Jan 1850)

CLEMENTS, Joel, of Long March MD, to LAMBDIN, Margaret, Miss, dau of Daniel LAMBDIN, presiding elder of the Wilm District of the Phila Conf. in Wilm, nmd, by Rev. T. S. Thompson (DG 28 Mar 1848)

CLEMENTS, Joshua R., to CLARKE, Ann Eliza, Miss, dau of John CLARKE, all of Dover Hd, 30 Jun 1850, by Rev. G. D. Carrow (DG 11 Jun 1850)

CLEMENTS, Thomas Jr., to DAY, Rebecca, Miss, both of Kent Co, 17 Dec 1846, by Rev. J. Anderson (DG 1 Jan 1847)

CLENDANIEL, Ann Elizabeth, see DEPUTY, Thomas A.

CLENDANIEL, Anna, see WILSON, James

CLENDANIEL, George, to GRUETT, Lydia, Miss, both of Kent, 24 Dec 1849, by Rev. J. A. Roche (DG 1 Jan 1850)

CLENDANIEL, Mary A., see WILLIAMS, Jonathan

CLENDANIEL, Wm. H. to DONOVAN, Sarah, Miss, both of Sussex Co, 13 Nov 1853, by the Rev. T. P. McColley (DG 22 Nov 1853)

CLENDENIN, Samuel E., of Pencader Hd, to GOUDY, Marie, Miss, of White Clay Creek Hd, 29 Dec 1835, by the Rev. A. K. Russel (DG 1 Jan 1836)

CLENEAY, Rhoda, see CORAM, Robert

CLESS, E. W., to GIFFER, Ruth, Miss, both of Wilm, in Wilm, 25 Mar 1841, by Rev. E. W. Gilbert (DG 30 Mar 1841)

CLIFT, Edward, son of Morgan CLIFT, Esq., of Holmesburg, to HERRING, Martha, Miss, dau of Abner HERRING of DE, 28 Nov 1850, by the Rev. Mr. Humphreys (DG 31 Jan 1851)

CLIFT, Morgan, see CLIFT, Edward

CLIFTON, Catharine A., see MAGUIRE, Thomas

CLIFTON, Daniel, see MAGUIRE, Thomas

CLIFTON, Hannah, see BURTON, Cornelius T.

CLIFTON, Sarah Ann, wife of Whittington CLIFTON, formerly of Lewes, of lockjaw, 10 Dec 1845, aged 46 yrs (DG 16 Dec 1845)

CLIFTON, Whittington, see CLIFTON, Sarah Ann

CLINE, Samuel, Jr., Esq., of Burlington Co NJ, to LEWIS, Hannah C., of Del Co PA, 24 Jan 1853, at the White Hall Hotel, by the Hon. Charles Gilpin (DG 1 Mar 1853)

CLING, Robert A., to BOOTH, Catharine A., of NC Co, 23 Nov 1847, by Rev. Dr. Kennaday (DG 17 Dec 1847)

CLING, Sarah, see DAY, John

CLING, Thos. K., of Wilm, to CURRY, Mary,

Miss, of Chester Co PA, in Phila, 3 Jan 1849, by Rev. John Bayne (DG 19 Jan 1849)

CLINTON, Hannah, see FREEMAN, Amos

CLOAK, Ebenezer, to WALCOTT, C., Miss, dau of C. C. WALCOTT, all of Smyrna DE, 2 Sep 1849, by the Rev. Joseph Mann (DG 11 Sep 1849)

CLOAK, John, Esq. of Smyrna DE to PYSER, Sarah Louisa, of Chester PA, 5 May 1841, in Phila at St. Peter's Ch by Rev. W. B. Odenheimer (DG 14 May 1841)

CLOSBY, Robert, to MORRIL, Mary A, Miss, of New Castle, 9 Sep 1851, by Rev. E. R. Williams (DG 19 Sep 1851)

CLOSE, Anna,
see SANGSTON, Thomas H.

CLOTHIER, John, to LONG, Sophia, Miss, all of NC Co, at Port Penn, 17 Jan 1850, by Rev. I. W. K. Handy (DG 8 Feb 1850)

CLOUD, Abner, see PHILLIPS, Thomas

CLOUD, Andrew M., to HENDRIKSON, Margaretta, 10 Feb 1848, by Rev. Thomas S. Love (DG 15 Feb 1848)

CLOUD, Catharine, in Wilm, 25 Apr 1852, in her 77th yr (DG 27 Apr 1852)

CLOUD, Job, drowned, body found "on Monday" (DG 24 Apr 1790)

CLOUD, John, of Chester Co, to VANDEVER, Ann Jane, Miss, of NC Co, 19 May 1847, by Rev. T. S. Griffith, M. D. (sic) (DG 11 Jun 1847)

CLOUD, Joseph, dec'd. Sale of his land on Brandywine Creek, Chester Co (PG 1 May 1729)

CLOUD, Joseph, see MOORE, Thomas

CLOUD, Priscilla, see FOULK, Stephen

CLOUD, Washington, of Wilm, to MANERING, Sarah, Miss, of Cantwell's Bridge, 23 May 1850, by Rev. J. R. Andrews (DG 7 Jun 1850)

CLOUD, William, see BROWN, John

CLOWARD, Anna Dushane, inf dau of Thomas and Eliza Jane CLOWARD, in Wilm, 10 Aug 1849, aged 1 yr (DG 21 Aug 1849)

CLOWARD, Eliza Jane,
see CLOWARD, Anna Dushane

CLOWARD, Thomas,
see CLOWARD, Anna Dushane

CLOWES, John, Esq., 2nd justice, Court of Common Pleas, in Sussex, 24 Feb 1790 (DG 3 Apr 1790)

CLUTE, Angelica. see CROPPER, Ezekiel

CLYMER, Meredith, M. D., of Phila, to GARESCHE, Virginia M., dau of J. P. GARESCHE, Esq., 13 Jun 1843, at Eden Park near Wilm, by Rev. Mr. Reilly (DG 16 Jun 1843)

CLYMER, Meredith, see CLYMER, Virginia

CLYMER, Virginia, wife of Dr. Meredith CLYMER, and dau of J. P. GARESCHE, Esq., in Phila, 29 Jul 1849, in her 24th yr (DG 3 Aug 1849)

COBOURNE, Joseph, to HAGERMAN, Hannah, Miss, both of Brandywine Hd, 15 Apr 1852, at Marcus Hook, by the Rev. J. R. Anderson (DG 11 May 1852)

COCHRAN, Adaline,
see VANDEGRIFT, James

COCHRAN, Elizabeth, Mrs, wife of Thomas COCHRAN, near Middletown, 30 Jan 1848 (DG 4 Feb 1848) Elizabeth R., wife of R. T. COCHRAN, at the res. of her husband near Middletown, 30 Jan 1848, in her 34th yr (DG 3 Mar 1848)

COCHRAN, J. T., see COCHRAN, John

COCHRAN, James, in Wilm, 31 Jan 1835, na (DG 3 Feb 1835)

COCHRAN, John, dec'd, late of NC Co, notice given by J. T. COCHRAN, adm'r, Middletown (AW 20 Apr 1816)

COCHRAN, John P., see POLK, William

COCHRAN, Olivia R. M.,
see BEASTON, Charles

COCHRAN, R. E., Lt., killed at the battle of Matamoras, 9 May 1846. He was born in NC Co, reared in Delaware City, and was a graduate of West Point (DG 29 May 1846)

COCHRAN, R. T.,
see COCHRAN, Elizabeth R.

COCHRAN, R. T., to MOODY, Elizabeth R., Miss, 1 Oct 1835, by Rev. Mr. How, all of New Castle, DE (DG 6 Oct 1835)

COCHRAN, Richard E., M.D., to EVANS, Eliza, Miss, both of NC Co, 5 May 1812, by Rev. Gideon Ferril (AR 13 May 1812)

COCHRAN, Richard Washington, of Saint Georges Hd, to SHALLCROSS, Catharine, Miss, dau of Jacob SHALLCROSS, Esq., of Oxford Twp PA, 1 May 1844, by Rev. George Sheelts (DG 7 May 1844)

COCHRAN, Thomas, see COCHRAN, Elizabeth

COCHRAN, William, to PLURIGHT, Margaret, Miss, all of Wilm, 26 Apr 1827, by Rev. John P. Peckworth (DG 8 May 1827)

COCHRAN, Wm. A. of St. Georges Hd, to SHALLCROSS, Sarah Overington, Miss, 4th dau of Jacob SHALLCROSS, Esq., of Woodland, 22 Jan 1845, at Woodland PA, by Rev. George Shuts (DG 24 Jan 1845)

COCHRAN, Wm. H., of Chester Co PA, to ROSS, Ann T., of Wilm, in West Chester PA, 1 Jan 1852 (DG 9 Jan 1852)

COCHRANE, Elizabeth M., dau of R. Thomas and Sophia A., COCHRANE, at the res. of her father near Middletown, 16 Oct 1851, aged 6 mos (DG 4 Nov 1851)

COCHRANE, R. Thomas, see COCHRANE, Elizabeth M.

COCHRANE, Sophia A., see COCHRANE, Elizabeth M.

COCHRANE, Sophia A., wife of R. Thomas COCHRANE, 21 Oct 1851 (DG 4 Nov 1851)

COCKSHOT, John, formerly an English merchant in Wilm, 17 Sep 1834, aged 82 yrs (DG 19 Sep 1834)

COFFEODE, David, of Wilm, to SIMMERS, Sarah Ann, Miss, of Chester Co PA, in Phila, 6 Sep 1849, by the Rev. John L. Grant (DG 11 Sep 1849)

COFFIN, Ebenezer, see COFFIN, Robert

COFFIN, Robert, the Boston Bard, at Rowley, MA, son of the late Ebenezer COFFIN, A.M., 7 May 1827, na (DG 18 May 1827)

COFFRODE, Daniel, see COFFRODE, Eliza Ann

COFFRODE, Eliza Ann, Miss, dau of Daniel and Elizabeth COFFRODE, in Wilm, after a short illness, 14 Jun 1853, in her 20th yr (DG 21 Jun 1853)

COFFRODE, Elizabeth, see COFFRODE, Eliza Ann

COHEE, S. G., see COHEE, Thomas

COHEE, Thomas, son of S. G. COHEE, near Wilow Grove, 21 Aug 1853, in his 12th yr (DG 26 Aug 1853)

COHEE, William, to McGEE, Harriet, Miss, all of Wilm, 16 Mar 1826, by the Rev. Mr. White (DG 21 Mar 1826)

COHOON, Maria E., see HARDASTY, George W.

COHOON, W. R., see HARDASTY, George W.

COLAY, Wm., of Camden NJ, to ASHTON, Tirzah, Mrs., late of Wilm, 1 Jul 1851, by the Rev. Mr. Ruth (DG 15 Jul 1851)

COLDWELL, Marietta B., see BERRY, Thomas C.

COLE, Ann, Mrs., relict of Thomas COLE, late of Wilm, in Phila at the res. of her son-in-law, William WRIGHT, Esq., 5 Aug 1850, in her 80th yr (DG 6 Sep 1850)

COLE, Elisha, of Wilm, to PLUMMER, Mary Ann, of Kent Co DE, 11 May 1853, by the Rev. W. B. Walton (DG 27 May 1853)

COLE, Elizabeth, formerly of Wilm, in Phila, 23 Apr 1850, in her 56th yr (DG 30 Apr 1850)

COLE, Helen, see ANDERSON, James

COLE, Henry, of Wilm, to GEORGE, Mary Ellen, Miss, second dau of Mr. GEORGE, Esq., of Balt, formerly of PA, in Balt, 6 Jul 1851, by the Rev. Mr. McCarter of Broadway Station (Balt papers please copy) (DG 23 Aug 1851)

COLE, Howard E., of Del Co PA, to KIDD, Emily, Miss, of New Castle, 8 Jul 1848, by Rev. John Street (DG 15 Aug 1848)

COLE, John R., to GOLDSBOROUGH, Lydia, Miss, both of Kent Co, 7 Aug 1853, by the Rev. P. Mansfield (DG 16 Aug 1853)

COLE, Sarah Jane, see BURTON, James

COLE, Thomas, dec'd, late of Wilm, notice given by Thomas YOUNG, adm'r (DG 6 Sep 1825)

COLE, Thomas, see COLE, Ann

COLEMAN, William L., of Wilm, to WISE, Elizabeth A., Miss, of New Castle, 30 Nov 1848, by Rev. Mr. Spotswood (DG 5 Dec 1848)

COLEMAN, William, late of Phila, carpenter. (PG 30 Mar-6 Apr 1732)

COLEMAN, William, of Phila, to
BLACKWOOD, Ann, Miss, of Wilm,
7 May 1844, by Rev. J. M. Rhees
(DG 10 May 1844)

COLESBERRY, Henry, Dr., to BOWMAN,
Hester, Miss, 11 Dec 1820
(DG 19 Dec 1820)

COLESBERRY, Henry, Dr., in NC Co,
13 Nov 1849, in his 84th yr
(DG 16 Nov 1849)

COLESBERRY, John, to TURNER, Eliz.,
Miss, 12 Dec 1820 (DG 15 Dec 1820)

COLESBERRY, Margaret,
see GOODIN, John, Jr.

COLESBERRY, William, Dr., at the res. of
his nephew, William PURVIS, 10 Oct 1848,
in his 64th yr (DG 30 Oct 1848)

COLESBURY, Henry,
see McCALLMONT, Thomas

COLESBURY, Isaac G.,
see COLESBURY, Mary

COLESBURY, Mary, wife of Isaac G.
COLESBURY, and dau of the late Alexander
REYNOLDS, Esq., of New Castle,
5 Feb 1852 (DG 10 Feb 1852)

COLESCOTT, Elizabeth,
see DOBSON, Edward

COLHOUN, John,
see THOMPSON, Stewart

COLLEY, Lydia Ann, see PYLE. Reece

COLLEY, Mary E.,
see LUCAS, Christian E.

COLLINS, Ann, Mrs.,
see MORRIS, Bevan, Capt.

COLLINS, Ann, Mrs., wife of Wm. COLLINS,
19 Sep 1820 (DG 26 Sep 1820)

COLLINS, David H.,
see COLLINS, Robert C.

COLLINS, Eliza, see ATKINS, Joseph R.

COLLINS, Elizabeth,
see FERGUSON, Robert

COLLINS, George,
see, HOLDING Samuel H.

COLLINS, George D., of Swandale Beach
DE, to WILCOX, Hannah Ashbridge, Miss,
dau of William WILCOX of Phila,
21 Nov 1850, by Rev. T. Cantwell
(DG 29 Nov 1850)

COLLINS, Henderson, to POTTER, Mary A.,
Mrs.,both of Milford, in Phila, 17 Sep 1850,
by Rev. J. Humphries (DG 24 Sep 1850)

COLLINS, Isaiah, of Brandywine, to
STURGES, Rebecca, Miss, of Wilm,
7 Sep 1808, by the Rev. William Bishop
(MU 10 Sep 1808)

COLLINS, J. P. to KNOWLES, M., Miss,
both of Sussex Co DE, 13 Jun 1853, by
the Rev. J. Smith (DG 21 Jun 1853)

COLLINS, James, dec'd, late of Wim, notice
given by Edward WORRELL, adm'r
(DG 27 Mar 1819)

COLLINS, James, Capt., at his res. near
Milford, 3 Mar 1833, aged 54 yrs
(DG 19 Mar 1833)

COLLINS, James B., of Kent Co, to
EGBERT, Martha, Miss, dau of A. EGBERT,
Esq., of NC Co, in Wilm (DG 2 Apr 1847)

COLLINS, John, Rev., Methodist, at Milton,
ndd, na (DG 24 Apr 1827)

COLLINS, John, at his res. at Potter's
Landing, Caroline Co MD, 17 Apr 1849,
aged 65 yrs (DG 1 May 1849)

COLLINS, John, Esq., see ROSS, Curtis J.

COLLINS, John, see COLLINS, Sarah

COLLINS, John W., to BANNING, Nancy,
Miss, all of Kent, 3 Jan 1850, by Rev. T. P.
McColley (DG 15 Jan 1850)

COLLINS, Martha, see ROSS, Curtis J.

COLLINS, Mary A.,
see HOLDING, Samuel H.

COLLINS, Nancy D., Mrs., dau of Daniel
GODWIN, Esq., in Milford, 21 Jun 1829,
aged 23 yrs; leaves two children
(DG 21 Jul 1829)

COLLINS, Orphua, to HOPKINS, Josiah

COLLINS, Rachel, see BROWN, John R.

COLLINS, Robert C., late of Red Lion Hd.
David H. COLLINS, adm'r (DG 4 Jan 1853)

COLLINS, Sarah, Mrs., wife of the Rev. John
COLLINS, in Milford, 25 Feb 1821
(DG 2 Mar 1821)

COLLINS, William, to PALMATORY, Sarah
A., Miss, dau of Robert PALMATORY, Esq.,
near Smyrna, 17 Mar 1833, by Rev. Mr.
Derborah of the M. E. Ch, all of that
neighborhood (DG 19 Mar 1833)

COLLINS, Wm., see **COLLINS**, Ann

COLLINSON, Elizabeth Ann, see **DAWSON**, Thomas W.

COLLISON, Stansbury, to **HITCH**, Mary A., Miss, near Bridgeville, 3 Jan 1850, by Rev. James Hargis (DG 15 Jan 1850)

COLLUM, Catharine, see **JAQUETT**, James

COLLUM, Lydia B., see **SPENCE**, Benjamin D.

COLLYER, William, to **DOWDEN**, Sarah E., Miss, all of Fieldsboro, 3 Jan 1850, by Rev. Pinor Mansfield (DG 16 Jan 1850)

COLMAN, Mary, see **HUDSON**, John

COLMARY, William Patterson, killed by lightning, 20 May 1848. Buried in Wilm and Brandywine Cemetery, IOOF member (DG 23 May 1848)

COLWELL, Eliza, see **CURREY**, Samuel

COMEGYS, _____, ex-gov., see **CHATHAM**, Benjamin F. see **RIDGLEY**, Henry M.

COMEGYS, Benjamin B., to **BOYD**, Sarah P., in Phila, 20 Apr 1847, by Rev. Dr. Parker (DG 27 Apr 1847)

COMEGYS, Cornelius P., Esq., ex-governor of DE, (born in Kent Co DE), at Dover, 27 Feb 1851 (DG 4 Mar 1851) aged 71 yrs 1 mo 12 days (DG 7 Mar 1851)

COMEGYS, Cornellus, see **COMEGYS**, Ruhamah

COMEGYS, Joseph P., see **ROWLAND**, Sarah see **DARBY**, Frances Ann

COMEGYS, Mary Elizabeth, see **CHATHAM**, Benjamin F.

COMEGYS, Millimint, (sic) see **MANN**, Thomas, Esq.

COMEGYS, Ruhamah, Mrs, wife of Cornellus COMEGYS, late governor of DE, after a short illness at the res. of Richard SEMANS of Cecilton MD (DG 29 Sep 1848)

COMEGYS, Sally Ann, see **RIDGELY**, Henry M.

COMER, Rebecca, see **RIGHTER**, William

COMFORT, Caroline, see **GREGG**, Isaac D.

COMLY, Benjamin, aged 75, to **WHITTINGTON**, Mary Ann, Miss, aged 35, both of Little Creek Landing, 29 Jan 1824, by the Rev. Patrick Conley (DG 3 Feb 1824)

COMLY, John, see **COMLY**, Martha

COMLY, Martha, relict of the late John COMLY, near Phila, "4th day morning", in her 92nd yr (DG 22 Mar 1853)

CONARD, Benjamin, to **ROBERTS**, Eliza, eldest dau of George ROBERTS, all of Chester Co, PA, at Friends Meeting, New Garden, 11 Feb 1836 (DG 16 Feb 1836)

CONAWAY, Ann F., see **SHARP**, William B.

CONAWAY, Samuel, to **FITTEN**, Ann, Miss, both of Wilm, at Marcus Hook, 31 May 1829, by the Rev. Mr. Walker (DG 9 Jun 1829)

CONCKLIN, Edith B., see **VALUE**, J. S.

CONGER, Ann, see **McCONNELL**, Mary

CONLYN, Thomas, formerly of Wilm, to **BARBOUR**, Esther A., Miss, of Carlisle PA, 23 Feb 1843, by Rev. Daniel McKinley (DG 24 Feb 1843)

CONNELLY, Henry, at his res. near Newark, 3 Nov 1826, aged 56 yrs (DG 7 Nov 1826)

CONNER, Barrat P., see **CONNER**, Mary

CONNER, George H., see **CONNER**, Kate C.

CONNER, John, to **WHEELER**, Sally Louisa, Miss, both of DE, 4 Jan 1848, by Rev. Dr. Kenneday (DG 3 Mar 1848)

CONNER, Kate C., dau of George H. and Mary A. CONNER, at Lewes, of scarlet fever, 16 Mar 1852, aged 2 yrs 5 mos (DG 30 Mar 1852)

CONNER, Margaret Anne, see **O'NEILL**, J.

CONNER, Mary, consort of Barrat P. CONNER. Bur. 29 Dec 1851, aged 51 yrs 7 mos 17 days (DG 16 Jan 1852)

CONNER, Mary A., see **CONNER**, Kate C.

CONNER, Soloman, in Dover, 25 Jan 1823, aged c 24 yrs, leaving a widow but no children (DG 31 Jan 1823)

CONNER, William, to **JACKSON**, Rebecca, Miss, both of Christiana DE, 2 Sep 1849 at the Marcus Hook Pars. by the Rev. T. A. Fernly (DG 2 Oct 1849)

CONRAD, Cecelia E.,
see JONES, Gideon F.

CONSTABLE, Mary Jane,
see GIBSON, William H.

CONSTANT, J. A.,
see DOUGLASS, James C.

CONWAY, John, father of the late senior editor of the *Delaware Gazette*, native of Ireland, at his res. in Westmoreland Co, PA, 1 Aug 1833, aged 78 yrs, leaves an aged widow with whom he lived 53 yrs
(DG 9 Aug 1833)

CONWELL, ____, Mr.,
see DAVIS, Mary Morris

CONWELL, Asa F., to MARTIN, Mary Adaline, dau of Samuel MARTIN, all of Milton DE, 23 Dec 1852, by the Rev. R. E.Kemp
(DG 14 Jan 1853)

CONWELL, Elias, see BURTON, Benjamin

CONWELL, Jeanette Tatem,
see BURTON, Benjamin

CONWELL, Mary Morris,
see DAVIS, Mary Morris

CONYNGHAN, Redmond,
see STUART, Edward

COOCH, Margaret, Mrs., consort of Gen. William COOCH, of NC Co, 4 Sep 1833, aged 65 yrs (DG 10 Sep 1833)

COOCH, William, Gen.,
see COOCH, Margaret, Mrs.

COOK, Arabella, dau of William and Mary COOK, at Harkersburg, Jasper Co, IA, 5 Aug 1852, aged 16 mos
(DG 10 Sep 1852)

COOK, Catharine, see WEBSTER, Albert

COOK, Daniel P., lately a representative in Congress from IL, at the res. of his father in Scott Co KY (DG 1 Nov 1827)

COOK, George W., to COOK, Josephine, Miss, both of Smyrna. at Beverly NJ, 19 Oct 1851 (DG 31 Oct 1851)

COOK, Henry, see PENTON, James

COOK, James, of Frederica DE, to MOORE, Catharine, Mrs., of Kent DE, 25 Jan 1849, by the Rev. John Roche (DG 6 Feb 1849)

COOK, John, to CARNAHAN, Elizabeth , Miss, 5 Apr 1810, by Rev. Dr. Read
(DG 7 Apr 1810)

COOK, Joseph, to RHODES, Martha, Miss, both of NC Co, in New Castle on the 2nd ult, by the Rev. Andrew Manship
(DG 25 Sep 1849)

COOK, Josephine, see COOK, George W.

COOK, Mary, see COOK, Arabella

COOK, Mary Ann, see PENTON, James

COOK, William, 2 Jan 1821, aged 91 yrs
(DG 23 Jan 1821)

COOK, William, see COOK, Arabella

COOK, Wm. A., to CARROW, Mary Francis, Miss, dau of Jonathan CARROW, Esq., both of Kent Co, 21 Jul 1853, by the Rev. J. J. Lewis (DG 16 Aug 1853)

COOKE, James, of Baltimore, at the Indian Queen Hotel, 14 Mar 1846, aged 30 yrs
(DG 24 Mar 1846)

COOLING, Samuel, to BRACKIN, Ann Elizabeth, Miss, all of Wilm, 26 Feb 1852, by Rev. Andrew Manship (DG 2 Mar 1852)

COOLINN, Alice A., see WIER, John W.

COOMBE, Benjamin,
see PENNINGTON, Augustus Hyland

COOMBE, Benjamin, Jr., merchant of Smyrna, to ROBINSON, Sarah, Miss, dau of Thomas ROBINSON, Esq., in Chester, PA, 12 Jun 1823, by the Rev. Richard Umstead Morgan (DG 24 Jun 1823)

COOMBE, Hannah Ann,
see TEMPLE, Thomas

COOMBE, Mary Ann,
see PENNINGTON, Augustus Hyland

COOMBE, Pennell, Rev., to PARPER, Charlotte A., dau of James PARPER, Esq., 24 May 1842, by Rev. R. Gerry
(DG 3 Jun 1842)

COOMBE, Pennel, Rev., to McCAULLEY, Elizabeth W., both of Wilm, 1 Oct 1850, by Rev. Robert Gerry (DG 4 Oct 1850)

COOMBS, ____, Rev.,
see COOMBS, Charlotte

COOMBS, Charlotte, wife of Rev. Mr. COOMBS, of typhoid fever, in Wilm, 28 Jul 1849, na (DG 31 Jul 1849)

COOPER, B. B., to SHERWOOD, Hannah, Miss, both of Kent Co, in Dover, 6 Aug 1850, by Rev. Theodore G. Murphy
(DG 16 Aug 1850)

COOPER, Elizabeth M. D.,
see VERNON, David A.

COOPER, Ezekial, see COOPER, Mary

COOPER, Hugh, see POUGE, Joseph

COOPER, Isaac, Esq., in Sussex Co,
"on the 2nd ult," in his 79th yr
(DG 15 May 1821)

COOPER, James M.,
see COOPER, Nancy

COOPER, James, see PIERCE, George

COOPER, Jane, see POUGE, Joseph

COOPER, John A., in Smyrna, of the firm of
Dunning and Cooper (DG 12 Oct 1847)

COOPER, Leah Jane, see CHASE, I.

COOPER, M. S., to PRICE, Mary Jane,
Miss, all of NC Co, 19 Feb 1846, by Rev. M.
J. Rhees (DG 24 Feb 1846)

COOPER, Mary, Mrs., relict of Ezekiel
COOPER, at her res. in Willow Grove,
14 Feb 1852, na (DG 20 Feb 1852)

COOPER, Nancy, Mrs., wife of James M.
COOPER, U. S. Navy, at Ellis Island, NY,
1 Jun 1849. a native of DE
(DG 12 Jun 1849)

COOPER, Peter L., at his res. near Willow
Grove, Kent Co, aged c 52 yrs
(DG 9 Jul 1841)

COOPER, Richard, Esq., late one of the
judges of the Supreme Court of DE, at
Passey, near Dover, DE, 29 Aug 1818
(DG 12 Sep 1818)

COOPER, Samuel, to HARISS, Sarah, Miss,
at Cantwell's Bridge, 7 Dec 1828,
by Rev. Wm. Ryder (DG 23 Dec 1828)

COOPER, Samuel B. Jr., to JACKSON,
Sarah E., Miss, dau of Fletcher JACKSON,
Esq., all of Kent, 12 Dec 1850, by Rev. G. D.
Carrow (DG 24 Dec 1850)

COOPER, Sarah,
see HORSEY, Sarah, Mrs.

COOPER, Thomas, Esq., member of the Bar
of Sussex Co and formerly of Congress from
DE, at Georgetown, 7 Nov 1829, na
(DG 13 Nov 1829)

COOPER, Thomas, formerly a distinguished
member of the theatrical profession, in Bristol
PA, at the res. of his son-in-law, Robert
TYLER, Esq., 21 Apr 1849, na

(DG 11 May 1849)

COOPER, William, 15 Aug 1847, in Dover
(DG 31 Aug 1847)

COOPER, William B.,
see HORSEY, Sarah, Mrs.

COOPER, William C., of Phila, to
SCHRADER, Gertrude, Miss, of Wilm, 8 Oct
1850, by Rev. I. C. Clay (DG 19 Feb 1850)

CORAM, Robert, to CLENEAY, Rhoda,
Miss, 10 Sep 1789 (DG 12 Sep 1789)

CORBET, James, M. D, at Cantwell's Bridge,
27 Jun 1846, aged 31 yrs (DG 7 Jul 1846)

CORBIT, Daniel, of Cantwell's Bridge, to
WILSON, Mary C., of Wilm, 15 Apr 1847,
at Friends Meeting, Wilm (DG 20 Apr 1847)
see THOMAS, Samuel

CORBIT, John, Sr., at the res. of John
COWGILL, Jr., in Little Creek Hd, Kent Co,
22 Sep 1822, in his 34th yr (DG 4 Oct 1822)

CORBIT, John, to WELLS, Rebecca, Miss,
both of Wilm, in Phila, 8 Nov 1834,
by Rev. H. White (DG 14 Nov 1834)

CORBIT, John C., Esq., of Cantwell's
Bridge, to TRIMBLE, Harriett B., Miss, dau
of Joseph TRIMBLE, Esq., of Concord, PA,
9 Dec 1824, by David Marshall, Jr., Esq.
(DG 14 Dec 1824)

CORBIT, Mary, Jr., dau of the late William
CORBIT of NC Co, at the res. of Joseph
TRIMBLE, Del Co, PA, 10 Oct 1826,
aged 26 yrs; burial in Friends Burial Ground
in Cantwell's Bridge, her native village
(DG 20 Oct 1826)

CORBIT, Mary P.,
see NAUDAIN, Andrew S.

CORBIT, Pennell, to CLARK, Mary, Miss,
near Smyrna, 22 Oct 1807, by Rev. Mr.
Pryce (MU 31 Oct 1807)

CORBIT, Thomas, after an illnes of four
days, 8 Jun 1821, in his 19th yr
(DG 14 Aug 1821)

CORBIT, William, of Wilm, to BROOKS,
Susan T., Miss, of Phila, at Hamilton Village,
PA, 28 Jan 1830, by the Rev. Mr. Kennard
(DG 2 Feb 1830)
see CORBIT, Mary, Jr.

COREY, Albert L., see COREY, Maro V.

COREY, Maro V., late of Red Lion Hd,
Albert L. COREY, adm'r (DG 18 May 1852)

DELAWARE MARRIAGES AND DEATHS FROM NEWSPAPERS, 1729-1853   53

CORKIN, Sally Ann,
see SMITHERS, John N.

CORMICHAEL, James to CHADWICK, Caroline, Miss, both of Wilm, in Wilm, 12 Nov 1851, by the Rev. E. W. Van Duesen (DG 14 Nov 1851)

CORNELIUS, Jeremiah, to JESTER, Rhoda J., Miss, all of Wilm, 21 Feb 1850, by Rev. William Cooper (DG 1 Mar 1850)

CORRIE, William, to HAVILAND, Mary, eldest dau of the late John HAVILAND, Esq., all of Wilm, 12 Mar 1849, at Grace Ch. by the Rev. Geo. Durborow (DG 16 Mar 1849)

CORSHALL, Margaret,
see JOHNSTON, John W.

COSDEN, John, to MILLAWAY, Mary Jane, both of Wilm, 18 Apr 1850, by Rev. John Roche (DG 30 Apr 1850)

COSGROVE, Hugh, late of Christiana Hd. Joseph COSGROVE and James DELAPLAINE, exec'rs (DG 21 Aug 1849)

COSGROVE, Joseph,
see COSGROVE, Hugh

COSTON, B. Franklin, inventor of Coston Gas Lights, 24 Nov 1848, in his 27th yr (DG 28 Nov 1848)

COTTER, Mary Ann, formerly of Wilm, at the res. of Thomas EASTMAN in Platteville, Wis, 7 Oct 1845, aged 36 yrs. Member of M. E. Church (DG 31 Oct 1845)

COTTINGHAM, Sarah,
see WAPLES, Gideon

COULTER, Cornelius, of Milton, to SHOCKLEY, Sarah Ann, of Milford, in Milford, 1 Oct 1849, by the Rev. Mr. Flannery (DG 9 Oct 1849)

COULTER, John M., to BENSON, Mary, Miss, of Milton, DE, 29 May 1826, by the Rev. Daniel Rigby (DG 6 Jun 1826)

COULTER, John W., Capt., to BENSON, Catharine, Miss, both of Milford, DE, 6 Apr 1821, by the Rev. Wm. Hickman (DG 13 Apr 1821)

COUNTIS, Peter, to McFARLIN, Anna Maria, Miss, both of NC Co, 22 Oct 1828, by the Rev. Thomas Barton of Chester Co, PA (DG 28 Oct 1828)

COUNTISS, James H., to PERKINS, Hannah A., both of Wilm, in Phila, 31 May 1849, by the Rev. A. Atwood (DG 5 Jun 1849)

COUNTISS, John,
see COUNTISS, Sarah Seal

COUNTISS, John, to LISTON, Sarah Ann, Miss, both of Wilm, at Marcus Hook, 28 Apr 1825, by the Rev. Mr. Walker (DG 3 May 1825)

COUNTISS, Sarah Ann,
see COUNTISS, Sarah Seal

COUNTISS, Sarah Seal, youngest dau of John and Sarah Ann COUNTISS, in Wilm, 6 May 1852, in her 4th yr (DG 14 May 1852)

COUPER, James,
see PEIRCE, George, Esq.

COUPER, James, Jr., see DICK, James

COUPER, S. M.,
see MARSHALL, Thomas

COURSE, Rebecca E.,
see WOODS, John, Esq.

COVERDALE, Esther, at the res. of her son in Pencader Hd, 22 Sep 1848, aged between 70 and 80 yrs (DG 29 Sep 1848)

COVERDALE, Harriet A.,
see GRIEVES, William V.

COVERDILL, Amelia, see STIDHAM, Daniel

COVEY, Joshua, late of CA, to MOORE, Elizabeth, Mrs., of Wilm, at Wheatland DE, 26 May 1853, by Rev. George Foote (DG 31 May 1853)

COVINGTON, Elizabeth,
see BARNEY, Solomon L. A.

COWAN, Eliza, see CRAWFORD, Thomas

COWAN, Joseph, drowned in the Brandywine, 7 Jan 1846 (DG 13 Jan 1846)

COWAN, William,
see CRAWFORD, Thomas

COWDEN, Mary Jane,
see BROWN, James Montgomery

COWDON, Mary Jane,
see BROWN, James Montgomery

COWGILL, Clayton, dec'd, notice given by John COWGILL, Jr., adm'r (IN 26 Apr 1821)

COWGILL, Daniel,
see SIPPLE, Thomas, Esq.

COWGILL, Daniel, well known in the Society of Friends, at his res. in Little Creek, Kent Co, "a few days since," in his 65th yr

(DG 5 Dec 1818)

COWGILL, Daniel, of Dover, to NAUDAIN, Mary, Miss, dau of the late Arnold NAUDAIN, of Little Creek Hd, Kent Co, near Middletown, 5 Aug 1824, by the Rev. Joseph Wilson (DG 6 Aug 1824)

COWGILL, John, , at his res. Little Creek, Kent Co DE, 10 Sep 1849, in his 78th yr (DG 14 Sep 1849)

COWGILL, John, Jr., see CORBIT, John, Sr., see COWGILL, Clayton

COWGILL, Sarah, Mrs., in Little Creek DE, 30 Dec 1852, in her 86th yr (DG 11 Jan 1853)

COWGILL, Warner, in Dover, 7 Jan 1852, aged 53 yrs (DG 9 Jan 1852)

COWGILL, William, to PLEASONTON, Hannah M., Miss, both of Kent Co, in Phila, 30 Apr 1833, by John Swift, Esq., Mayor (DG 14 May 1833)

COWGILL, Worrell, at his late res. in Kent Co, 5 Jan 1826, aged 49 yrs (DG 13 Jan 1826)

Cox, Garrett, see COX, Caroline

COX, Caroline, dau of Garrett and Elizabeth COX, in Middletown, 16 Feb 1844, aged 16 yrs (DG 27 Feb 1844)

COX, Clara Jane, inf dau of Thomas COX, of convulsions, 18 Jul 1848, aged 9 mos (DG 28 Jul 1848)

COX, Edward, see PLANK, Thomas

COX, Elizabeth, see COX, Caroline

COX, Emily, see LURN, Thomas E.

COX, Esau, brickmaker, at his res. in Wilm, 28 May 1850 (DG 4 Jun 1850)

COX, Esau, see BUSH, Charles

COX, Helen, see BUSH, Charles

COX, James Henry, to DEVOU, Anna Maria, at St Andrews Ch in Wilm, 10 Apr 1851, by the Rt. Rev. Alfred Lee (DG 11 Apr 1851)

COX, James L., see COX, Samuel B.

COX, James M., dec'd, notice given by Jonathan BYRNES, Wilm, atty-in-fact for the adm'x. (DG 13 Oct 1843)

COX, Jane A., see COX, Samuel B.

COX, John, of Phila, to HELLINGS, Sarah, Miss, of Wilm, 11 Jun 1807, by the Rev. Mr. Dodge (MU 13 Jun 1807)

COX, Mary Jane, Mrs., wife of Thomas COX, 15 Dec 1847, in Wilm (DG 14 Dec 1847)

COX, Samuel B., son of James L. and Jane A. COX, 24 Aug 1853, aged 18 yrs 11 mos 24 days (DG 9 Sep 1853)

COX, Samuel K., formerly pastor of the P. E. Church at Wilm, to BILLING, Augusta M., Miss, of Washington D. C., at Washington, 23 Dec 1847, by Rev. Levi R. Reese (DG 31 Dec 1847)

COX, Stephen T., of Montgomery Co PA, to McDANIEL, Leah Jane, of Wilm, in Wilm, by Friends ceremony in the presence of the Mayor, nmd (DG 25 Dec 1851)

COX, Thomas, see COX, Mary Jane
see COX, Clara Jane

COX, Thomas, to ROADS, Mary Jane, Miss, all of Wilm, 24 Dec 1846, by Rev. M. J. Rhees (DG 29 Sep 1846)

COXE, James M., dec'd. Notice given by Jonathan BYRNES, Jr. (DG 27 Aug 1841)

COYLE, Cornelius, of Wilm, to DUNN, Alice N., Miss, of Phila, 27 Apr 1851, by the Rev. C. Powers of St Paul's (DG 20 May 1851)

COYLE, James, to McCLELLAND, Martha A., Miss, both of NC Co, 6 Mar 1850, by Rev. Mr. James Coyle (DG 15 Mar 1850)

COYLE, Jane, see READ, Hugh

COYLE, John, of Wilm, to SCOTT, Catharine, Miss, 11 Jun 1843, in Phila, by Rev. John Coleman (DG 16 Jun 1843)

COYLE, William, to RUSSEL, Martha A., both of Wilm, 3 Jul 1848, by Rev. J. B. Clemson (DG 18 Jul 1848)

CRADDOCK, Joseph T., see CRADDOCK, Mary Jemima

CRADDOCK, Mary Jemima, wife of Joseph T. CRADDOCK, in Phila, 22 Dec 1852, in her 35th yr (DG 24 Dec 1852)

CRAIG, Anna, Mrs., wife of Walter CRAIG, 3 Apr 1849, in her 28th yr (DG 10 Apr 1849)

CRAIG, Frederick, in Wilm, 4 Jul 1841, aged 85 yrs 5 mo, 20 days. Editorial in this issue (DG 9 Jul 1841)

CRAIG, John, to RUST, Lydia, Miss, 3 Feb 1850, by Rev. J. R. Torbert

(DG 12 Feb 1850)

CRAIG, John A., Col., of Kennett Twp., PA, to CUSTILOW, Elizabeth, Miss, of Mill Creek Hd, 12 Apr 1821, by the Rev. E. W. Gilbert (DG 13 Apr 1821)

CRAIG, Rebecca, see DEVOU, Peter

CRAIG, Walter, see CRAIG, Anna

CRAIGE, William S., to WOOTSTON, Anna W., both of Wilm, in Phila, 15 Jun 1852, in the presence of Hon Charles Gilpin, Mayor (DG 18 Jun 1852)

CRAMER, Mary, see HAZLET, Bennet

CRANOR, Joshua, Esq., near Milford, 22 Apr 1852, aged 65 yrs (DG 4 May 1852)

CRANS, Samuel, to BRINKLE, Wilhelmina Ridgely, Miss, only dau of the late Dr. J. BRINKLE, 21 Mar 1847, by Rev. John Coleman (DG 17 Sep 1847)

CRANSTON, Joseph, see REID, Hannah

HARKER, John Newton, late of Wilm Hd. Joshua S. VALENTINE, adm'r (DG 9 Jan 1852)

CRAUCH, Wilhelmina, 10 Dec 1850, aged c 14 yrs. (DG 13 Dec 1850)

CRAWFORD, ____, Rev. Dr., see CRAWFORD, J. A.

CRAWFORD, A. B., see GORHAM, Eleazer S.

CRAWFORD, Alexander B., to SHAKESPEAR, Rebecca, both of NC Co, DE, 22 Mar 1849, by Rev. B. Ayres (DG 27 Mar 1849)

CRAWFORD, Barney A., of Wilm, to CRAWFORD, Maria, Miss, second dau of Mr. James CRAWFORD of Milford Cross Roads, at that place, 17 Mar 1835, by the Rev. A. K. Russel (DG 20 Mar 1835)

CRAWFORD, Ebenezer K., to HOOK, Mahala H., both of Wilm, in Marcus Hook PA, 4 Jul 1844, by Rev. J. B. Ayers (DG 9 Jul 1844)

CRAWFORD, J. A., Rev., to GILBERT, Susie Munro, dau of the late Rev. Dr. GILBERT, all of Wilm, 18 Aug 1853, by the Rev. Dr. CRAWFORD (DG 26 Aug 1853)

CRAWFORD, James, see CRAWFORD, Barney A.

CRAWFORD, Margaret Ann,

see JONES, Samuel M.

CRAWFORD, Maria, see CRAWFORD, Barney A.

CRAWFORD, Samuel C., of Chester Co PA, to GROOME, Evalina, Miss, of Wilm, in W. Chester PA, 1 May 1849, by Rev. Alfred S. Patten (DG 8 May 1849)

CRAWFORD, T. F., of New Orleans, LA, to JANVIER, Louisa, youngest dau of the late John JANVIER of New Castle, 28 Oct 1851, by Rev. Henry A. Boardman DD (DG 4 Nov 1851)

CRAWFORD, Thomas, of NC Co, to COWAN, Eliza, Miss, youngest dau of William COWAN of Cowantown, Cecil Co, MD, at that place, 5 Jun 1834, by the Rev. A. K. Russel (DG 10 Jun 1834)

CRAWFORD, Willamina H., see MACKEY, Haslett

CRAWFORD, William R., of Baltimore, merchant, to MERRITT, Sarah Vance, Miss, dau of Dr. Benjamin MERRITT, late of NC Co, at Phila, 9 Mar 1818, by Rev. Dr. Parker (AW 14 Mar 1818)

CRAWFORD, Wm. H., of NY, to JONES, Anna Maria, Miss, youngest dau of David T. JONES, Esq., formerly of Wilm, 7 Oct 1849, by the Rev. J. T. Seely (DG 19 Oct 1849) see MACKEY, Alexander H. see MACKEY, Haslett C.

CRAWFORD, Wm. W., of Wilm, to FOREST, Anne, Miss, of same, 2 Sep 1853, by the Rev. Dr. Hand of Chester PA (DG 6 Sep 1853)

CREED, John B., to VAULES, Mary E., Miss, both of Milford DE, 27 Feb 1851, by the Rev. S. C. Palmiter (DG 4 Mar 1851)

CREEMER, Jacob, dec'd, late of Wilm, notice given by Archibald HAMILTON, Esq., atty-in-fact for Jacob DUNTON, adm'r (DG 28 Jul 1829)

CREERY, Margaret, Mrs, in Wilm, 22 Mar 1848, aged 65 yrs (DG 4 Apr 1848)

CREERY, William, to PRICE, Mary, Miss, dau of Capt. PRICE of Brandywine, 26 Aug 1835, by Elder John P. Peckworth (DG 4 Sep 1835)

CREGG, Jesse, see SIMMONS, Lydia

CRIPPEN, Edward I., of Newark DE, to MADDOCK, Mary L., dau of William L. MADDOCK of Phila, 2 Dec 1851, by the Rev. Samuel N. Hollowell of Beverly NJ

(DG 5 Dec 1851)

CRIPPEN, James, to LAMBSON, Sarah Ann, Miss, both of NC Co, 2 Dec 1845, by Rev. Dr. John Kennaday (DG 5 Dec 1845)

CRIPPEN, Silas, at his late res. in New Castle Hd after a lingering illness, 30 Nov 1841, aged 48 yrs (DG 10 Dec 1841)

CRIPPEN, Silas, to HAMILTON, Eliza, Miss, of NC Co, at Marcus Hook PA, 14 May 1840, by Rev. Samuel Walker (DG 22 Feb 1841)

CRIPS, Cornelius, 24 Oct 1798, on list of yellow fever victims (DG 27 Oct 1798)

CRISDEN, Stephen, colored, from Vangesel's Corner, Duck Creek Hd, drunk, fell from tongue of ox cart and was run over by wheel (DG 18 Oct 1850)

CRIST, Hannah M., see APPLETON, Henry H.

CROASDALE, Howard, to STARR, Melinda, both of Wilm, 30 Dec 1852, by Rev. J. R. Anderson (DG 14 Jan 1853)

CROCKETT, Araminta, see BELL, Reese J.

CROCKETT, Mary E., see BENSON, Joseph B.

CROCKETT, Robert D., to REGISTER, Eunity, dau of Mr. Francis REGISTER, all of Kent Co DE, 11 Nov 1851, by Rev. Enos R. Williams (DG 14 Nov 1851)

CROMPTON, John, of Phila, to NEAL, Ann, Mrs., of NC Co, near Wilm, 16 Aug 1852, by the Rev. Wm. Mullin (DG 24 Aug 1852)

CRONSBERRY, Mary, see FREEMAN, John

CROOKSHANKS, John, see CROOKSHANKS, Mary Ann

CROOKSHANKS, Mary Ann, wife of John CROOKSHANKS, Esq., and dau of Hyland B. PENINGTON, of bilious cholic, in Baltimore, 26 Dec 1845 (DG 9 Jan 1846)

CROPPER, Ezekiel, of Phila, to CLUTE, Angelica, Miss, of DE, 25 Jun 1850, by Rev. Dr. Castle (DG 2 Jul 1850)

CROSBY, Reuben H., to MARSHALL, Emily J., Miss, dau of Capt. Aaron MARSHALL, of Milton, 14 Aug 1850, by Rev. G. W. Kennedy (DG 20 Aug 1850)

CROSLEY, Granville, to GOLD, Elizabeth, of Christiana Hd, DE, in Chester, PA, 8 May 1834, by Samuel Smith, Esq. (DG 13 May 1834)

CROSLEY, Joseph, in Wilm, 25 May 1849, aged c 100 yrs (DG 5 Jun 1849)

CROSLEY, Joseph, see CROSLEY, Mary

CROSLEY, Mary, relict of Joseph CROSLEY, in Wilm, 6 Apr 1852, aged 80 yrs (DG 11 May 1852)

CROSSGROVE, Charles, in Christiana Hd, 5 Sep 1852, aged c 45 yrs (DG 10 Sep 1852)

CROSSMORE, John, to WILLIS, Mary, Miss, both of NC Co, 8 Dec 1842, by Rev. Corry Chambers (DG 16 Dec 1842)

CROSSON, Mary, see CLARNAN, James

CROW, Andrew J., to WOLFE, Mary E., Miss, all of Wilm, 5 Feb 1850, by Rev. J. E. Rockwell (DG 8 Feb 1850)

CROW, John, Esq., of New Castle, to BRADUN (sic), Elizabeth, Miss, near Wilm, 18 Nov 1807, by Rev. Mr. Pryce (MU 21 Nov 1807)

CROW, John, Esq., for many years a member of the Legislature of DE, at New Castle, 23 Aug 1826, na (DG 25 Aug 1826) notice given by John MOODY, adm'r (DG 12 Sep 1826)

CROW, Michael, an Irishman in the employ of John HOLLINGSWORTH on the farm of Samuel CANBY in Christiana Hd, from the effects of heat, 22 Jun 1853, na. Had been in this country only ten days (DG 24 Jun 1853)

CROW, Owen C., to EWING, Mary. Miss, both of NC Co, in Wilm, 4 Nov 1834, by Rev. Mr. Staats (DG 10 Nov 1834)

CROW, Rebecca, Mrs., at Bohemia Manor, 29 Aug 1849, in her 73rd yr (DG 4 Sep 1849)

CROW, Sarah, see SAUNDERS, Charles

CROW, Thomas, eldest son of Thos. CROW of Wilm, 25 Jan 1790, aged 16 yrs. Buried Presbyterian ground (DG 30 Jan 1790)

CROW, Thomas, to NEWLIN, Eliza, Miss, both of Wilm, 20 Mar 1823, by the Rev. E. W. Gilbert (DG 25 Mar 1823)

CROWS, Fanny C., wife of James CROWS, of Paris, Oneida Co, NY, at the hotel of Mr Jones in New Garden, Chester Co PA, of heart disease, 18 Jan 1851

(DG 21 Jan 1851)

CROWS, James, see CROWS, Fanny C.

CROZIER, Eli, of Wilm, to MORELAND, Margaretta A., Miss, of New York, in New York, 1 Apr 1850, by Rt. Rev. Bishop Weston (DG 9 Apr 1850)

CROZIER, Elizabeth, see MARSHALL, Samuel

CROZIER, Jane, see RILEY, Thomas S.

CROZIER, Sarah Ann, see SMITH, Samuel P.

CRUMP, Sarah F., see STRAIN, Isaac

CRUSUN, Wm., to DAVIS, Sarah E., all of Kent Co, 2 Mar 1852, by the Rev. P. Mansfield (DG 16 Mar 1852)

CRUTHERS, Rebecca, see McGUIRE, Hugh

CUBBAGE, E. P., see CLARK, Robert H.

CULIN, Adam, see CULIN, Elizabeth

CULIN, Elizabeth, dau of Adam and Rebecca CULIN, at Delaware City, 13 Jun 1848, in her 6th yr (DG 23 Jun 1848)

CULIN, Rebecca, see CULIN, Elizabeth

CULLEN, Ann, see LANE, Nathaniel

CULLEN, Charles M., Esq., at his res. in Lewistown, 5 Apr 1828, na (DG 15 Apr 1828)

CULLEN, Chas. M., of Georgetown DE, to WAUGH, Virginia C., only dau of the Rt. Rev. Bishop WAUGH of Phila, 4 May 1853, by the father of the bride (DG 10 May 1853)

CULLEY, Elizabeth, see FORD, Samuel

CULLEY, Wm., to FRAME, Ruth Ann, both of Brandywine Springs, 5 Mar 1851, by the Rev. Mr. Love (DG 18 Mar 1851)

CULLISON, Elizabeth, see POLK, William

CULLISON, Micajah, see POLK, William

CUMMINGS, Lydia A., see PLEASANTON, John

CUMMINGS, William C., of Wilm, a carpenter, laboring under temporary mental derangment, drowned near Arch St. Wharf in Phila. Body found 18 Feb 1847. Leaves a widow, several children (DG 19 Feb 1847)

CUMMINS, Alexander, to ELLSBURY, Rebecca, Miss, both of Wilm. 17 Oct 1844, by Rev. S. R. Wynkoop (DG 25 Oct 1844)

CUMMINS, Alphonsa, see BLACK, John G.

CUMMINS, Anna W., see KIRKPATRICK, Robert B.

CUMMINS, David J, of Smyrna, to POLK, Juliet M., youngest dau of William POLK, Esq., of Cantwell's Bridge, at Cantwell's Bridge, 29 Jun 1852, by the Rev. Mr. Handy (DG 2 Jul 1852)

CUMMINS, Eveline M., see CUMMINS, Florence

CUMMINS, Florence, youngest dau of George W. CUMMINS and Eveline M, his wife, in Smyrna, of dysentery, 22 Jun 1851, aged 2 yrs 4 mos 26 days (DG 8 Jul 1851)

CUMMINS, George, Esq., at his farm near Smyrna, 22 Sep 1827, in his 63rd yr (DG 28 Sep 1827) Farmer, of Duck Creek Hd, former member of the General Assembly, in his 69th yr (DG 1 Oct 1827) see BARKER, Joseph

CUMMINS, George W., see CUMMINS, Florence

CUMMINS, John, Esq., of Smyrna, from bilious fever, 28 Jul 1833, na (DG 30 Jul 1833)

CUMMINS, John, see BARRATT, Alfred see BLACK, John G. see KIRKPATRICK, Robert B.

CUMMINS, Lydia, see RHODES, William

CUMMINS, Martha, see BARRATT, Alfred

CUMMINS, Susan, see FISHER, Samuel M., Dr.,

CUMMINS, William C., to LENDERMAN, Margaret, Miss, both of Brandywine, 10 Oct 1833, by Elder John P. Peckworth (DG 15 Oct 1833)

CUMMMINS, William to JOHNSON, Sarah Ann, both of Wilm, 15 Mar 1849, by the Rev. S. R. Wynkoop (DG 20 Mar 1849)

CUNNINGHAM, ____, Mrs., in Cecil Co MD, near Newark, 18 Aug 1853, aged c 80 yrs (DG 23 Aug 1853)

CUNNINGHAM, John W., see MENOUGH, Isaac

CUNNINGHAM, Martha, see CURRY, Alexander

CUNNINGHAM, Mary, see ROSS, David

CURLETT, _____ Mrs., mother of Lewis
CURLETT, in Wilm, 1 Mar 1843
(DG 7 Apr 1843)

CURLETT, Lewis,
see STEPHENS, Samuel

CURLETT, Lewis,
see CURLETT, _____ Mrs.

CURLEY, Henry R., of Baltimore, to
WINTERHALTER, Sarah, Miss, eldest dau
of George WINTERHALTER, of Wilm,
30 Sep 1847, by Rev. P Reilly
(DG 5 Oct 1847)

CURNS, John L., to BOUGHMAN,
Elizabeth, Miss, all of Wilm, 15 Apr 1851,
by Rev. A. Atwood (DG 18 Apr 1851)

CURNS, John L., Capt.,
see CURNS, Sarah Elizabeth

CURNS, Sarah Elizabeth, Mrs. consort of
Capt. John L. CURNS, in Wilm,
12 Apr 1852, aged 22 yrs (DG 23 Apr 1852)

CURRAN, John, to QUINN, Eliza J. Miss,
both of Wilm, in Phila, 8 Sep 1853, by the
Rev. D. W. Bartine (DG 13 Sep 1853)

CURRENDER, John, to OGLE, Elizabeth,
Miss, both of White Clay Creek Hd,
22 Feb 1830, by the Rev. A. K. Russel
(DG 23 Feb 1830)

CURREY, Samuel, to COLWELL, Eliza,
Miss, both of Brandywine, 10 Dec 1846, by
Rev. S. R. Wynkoop (DG 15 Dec 1846)

CURRY, Alexander, to CUNNINGHAM,
Martha, Miss, both of Cecil Co, MD,
14 May 1829, by the Rev. A. K. Russel
(DG 19 May 1829)

CURRY, John, to FOULK, Candace, Miss,
both of NC Co, 22 Feb 1853, by the Rev.
John Thompson (DG 25 Feb 1853)

CURRY, Mary, see CLING, Thos. K.

CURRY, Robert, to TAYLOR, Elizabeth,
Miss, 27 Aug 1820 (DG 29 Aug 1820)

CURTIS, _____, Mrs,
see HOOKER, Sarah H.

CURTIS, Geo. B.,
see CURTIS, Lucretia M.

CURTIS, Harriet M., in Newark, 31 Dec
1851, aged c 30 yrs (DG 6 Jan 1852)

CURTIS, James, 19 May 1850, in Wilm
(DG 28 May 1850)

CURTIS, Lucretia M., Mrs., wife of Geo. B.
CURTIS, recently from Columbus GA,
12 Sep 1853, at her mother's res., South
Natic MA, na (DG 20 Sep 1853)

CUSHMAN, William H. W., Rep. from
LaSalle Co., to RODNEY, Hannah C., Miss,
dau of the late Hon. C.A. RODNEY, 9 Feb
1843, in Springfield, IL (DG 10 Mar 1843)

CUSHMAN, William H.,
see RATTLE, Francis

CUSTILOW, Elizabeth,
see CRAIG, John A., Col.

CUSTIS, George W. N., of Marion IN,
to WELLS, Sarah E., Miss, of Wilm,
18 Jan 1853, by Rev. J. A. Roche
(DG 25 Jan 1853)

DAILEY, Sarah Elizabeth,
see BEASTON, William

DAISY, Mary, see ROZELL, Isaac

DALBEY, Sarah, see PENROSE, H.

DALE, Margaret, see DALE, Richard C.

DALE, Richard, to PRESS, Ellen, Miss, both
of NC Co, 5 Oct 1843, by Rev. W. R. Work
(DG 27 Oct 1843)

DALE, Richard C., of Wilm, after a short
and severe indisposition, 10 May 1818
(AW 13 May 1818) long obit
(AW 16 May 1818) notice given by Margaret
DALE, adm'x (AW 24 Jun 1818)

DALRYMPLE, Charles W., to DUVAL,
Sarah Ann, Miss, all of Wilm, 6 Aug 1848,
by Rev. A. A. Reese (DG 11 Aug 1848)

DALZELL, James,
see DALZELL, Mary Ann
see DALZELL, William Henry

DALZELL, Mary Ann, Mrs, late wife of
James DALZELL of Phila, and dau of the late
Stephen F. TOWNSEND of NC Co, 26 Jun
1841, aged 27 yrs, at the res. of John
PEACH near Newark (DG 2 Jul 1841)

DALZELL, William Henry, son of James
DALZELL, 14 Nov 1843, of scarlet fever,
aged 4 yrs and 17 days (DG 17 Nov 1843)

DANBY, Sarah Ann,
see WOODROW, James

DANFORTH, Emma K.,
see BUSH, George W.

DANFORTH, J. N.,
see BUSH, George W.

DANFORTH, Joshua N., the Rev., Pastor of the Fourth Presbyterian Ch, Washington DC, to **WHILDIN**, Jane J., Mrs., dau of Thomas JANVIER, Esq., of New Castle, at New Castle, 6 Aug 1829, by the Rev. William Bell (DG 11 Aug 1829)

DANIELS, Sarah, see **CLEAVER**, Thomas

DARBY, Frances Ann, Miss, dau of the late John M. DARBY of Milford, in Dover, at the res. of Joseph P. COMEGYS, 15 Oct 1848, in her 24th yr (DG 24 Oct 1848)

DARBY, John M.,
see **DARBY**, Frances Ann

DARBY, John M., at his res. in Milford, 26 Apr 1847, in his 46th yr (DG 4 May 1847)

DARBY, John, of Camden, DE, to **LEWIS**, Sarah, Miss, near the same place, 24 Feb 1825, by the Rev. Vincent Offley (DG 4 Mar 1825)

DARLEY, John, Esq., at his res.,Wren's Nest, DE, 5 Jan 1853, in his 78th yr (DG 14 Jan 1853)

DARLING, Elizabeth, see **BURNS**, George

DARLING, James, at New Castle, 21 Apr 1850, aged c 40 yrs (DG 26 Apr 1850) aged 46 yrs (DG 14 Jun 1850)

DARLINGTON, Abel, to **NEILS**, Mary, Miss, both of Chester Co, PA, in Wilm, 23 Feb 1828, by the Rev. John Hagany (DG 7 Mar 1828)

DARLINGTON, Chandler, of Wilm, to **BRINTON**, Mary, Miss, of Del Co PA, 1 Sep 1853 at Isaac Powell's White House Hotel, by the Hon. Charles Gilpin, Mayor (DG 6 Sep 1853)

DARLINGTON, Edward, to **LANGDON**, Susan M., all of Wilm, 25 Feb 1852, by Rev. J. A. Roche (DG 2 Mar 1852)

DARLINGTON, Edward C., of Lancaster, to **HAWLEY**, Mary L., dau of the late Capt. L. HAWLEY, formerly of Wilm, 11 Dec 1851, in St Lukes Ch, Phila, by the Rev. Jos. M. Lybrand (DG 16 Dec 1851)

DARLINGTON, Edward G.,
see **DARLINGTON**, Emily

DARLINGTON, Emily, wife of Edward G. DARLINGTON, Editor of the Lancaster *Examiner*, and dau of the late Judge FRANKLIN and sister of the Rev. Walter FRANKLIN, 24 Jan 1850 (DG 1 Feb 1850)

DARLINTTON [?], Job, of South Bradford, Chester Co PA, to **HUEY**, Linda, of Christiana Hd, 15 Jan 1849, by Friends ceremony, at the res. of the late John HUEY (DG 2 Mar 1849)

DARRACH, William, Dr., of Phila, to **MONROE**, Margaretta, Miss, dau of the late Dr. George MONROE of Wilm, in Wilm, 26 Apr 1826, by Rev. E. W. Gilbert (WN 27 Apr 1826) to **MONRO**, Margaretta, Miss, dau of the late Dr. George MONRO of Wilm, 26 Apr 1826, by the Rev. E. W. Gilbert (DG 28 Apr 1826)

DARRAGH, Alexander P.,
see **NEWTON**, Thomas

DARRAGH, Margaret P.,
see **NEWTON**, Thomas

DAUPHIN, J. B.,
see **MacPHERSON**, Alexander McIntosh

DAUPHIN, John, son of the late Joseph DAUPHIN of Wilm, at the Agricultural School near Germantown, PA, 22 Oct 1849 (DG 26 Oct 1849)

DAUPHIN, Joseph, see **DAUPHIN**, John

DAUPHIN, Joseph, son of Joseph DAUPHIN, aged 4 yrs 2 mos 14 days, 14 Sep 1841, in Wilm, (DG 17 Sep 1841)

DAUPHIN, Joseph, suddenly, in Wilm, 5 Feb 1843, (DG 10 Feb 1843)

DAUPHIN, Susan,
see **MacPHERSON**, Alexander McIntosh

DAVID, John, see **LATIMER**, Thos.

DAVID, Martha in Pencader Hd, 8 Feb 1849, in her 77th yr, (DG 16 Feb 1849)

DAVID, Mary, see **THOMAS**, William

DAVID, Mary J., see **HASEL**, Isaac

DAVID, Susanna, see **LATIMER**, Thos.

DAVIDS, James J., dentist of Elkton MD, to **TURNER**, Elizabeth G., dau of J. M. TURNER of Wilm, 6 Sep 1847, by Rev. Mr. Castle (DG 7 Sep 1847)

DAVIDSON, Amos E.,
see **DAVIDSON**, George A.

DAVIDSON, George A., constable, stabbed by a negro, lived in Delaware City, aged c 23 yrs, leaves a wife and two children (DG 11 May 1852) late of Red Lion Hd, Amos E. DAVIDSON, adm'r (DG 22 Jun 1852)

DAVIDSON, John,

see **GREEN**, George W.

DAVIDSON, John, of Marcus Hook, PA, to **HENDRICKSON**, Mary Ann, Miss, of NC Co, in Phila, 12 Nov 1835, by Rev. Thomas G. Allen (DG 17 Nov 1835)

DAVIDSON, Letitia A., see **JOHNSON**, Stephen

DAVIDSON, Louisa A., see **HADDOCK**, Samuel

DAVIDSON, Lydia, see **GREEN**, George W.

DAVIDSON, Mary J., see **JACKSON**, George B.

DAVIDSON, Richard C., to **WILSON**, Sarah, Mrs., both of Sussex Co, 7 Oct 1821, by the Rev. Samuel Jester (DG 16 Oct 1821)

DAVIS, ____, Mrs, wife of Lt. Alonzo B. DAVIS of the U. S. Navy, in Wilm, of the prevailing fever, 14 Jul 1848 (DG 18 Jul 1848)

DAVIS, Alexander, see **DAVIS**, Mary Morris

DAVIS, Alonzo B., see **DAVIS**, ____

DAVIS, Alvan, of Newark, DE, to **CHANDLER**, Sarah, Miss, of Wilm, formerly of New Garden PA, in Phila, 14 Feb 1851, by the Rev. J. N. C. Grier (DG 21 Feb 1851)

DAVIS, Amer, at Auburn, DE [near Yorklyn, NC Co], in his 69th yr (DG 20 Jul 1847)

DAVIS, Catharine, see **ROBINETT**, David
see **DICKERSON**, Nehemiah

DAVIS, Clarissa, see **BROWN**, Samuel

DAVIS, Colburn P., to **JEFFRIES**, Martha J, Miss, 25 Apr 1850, by Rev. M. J. Rhees (DG 30 Apr 1850)

DAVIS, Eli, of Chester Co, PA, to **STEEL**, Margaret, Mrs., of NC Co, near Newark, 16 Feb 1830, by the Rev. A. K. Russel (DG 23 Feb 1830)

DAVIS, Eliza, see **WRIGHT**, W. W.

DAVIS, Elizabeth,
see **SMITH**, Samuel, Capt.
see **WATKINS**, Josiah
see **WAY**, Thomas

DAVIS, Emily, **HOFFAY**, B.

DAVIS, Emma F., see **LOFLAND**, M. G.

DAVIS, Geo., see **LOFLAND**, M. G.

DAVIS, George, to **LOFLAND**, Mary M., Miss, dau of Dr. J. P. LOFLAND, all of Milford, 20 Dec 1848, by Rev. Mr. Flarney (DG 26 Dec 1848)

DAVIS, Henry,
see **HENDRICKSON**, Peregrine

DAVIS, Henry, in Milford Neck, 19 Nov 1848, aged 58 yrs (DG 5 Dec 1848)

DAVIS, Hetty Ann, see **PHILLIPS**, John M.

DAVIS, Isaac, to **McCAIN**, Eliza Jane, Miss, both of Phila, 1 Apr 1852, by Alderman J. Thompson (DG 6 Apr 1852)

DAVIS, James, Esq., of Kent, DE, to **NUTTER**, Sophia Louisa, Miss, of Somerset, MD, 2 Oct 1821, by the Rev. Dr. Read (DG 5 Oct 1821)

DAVIS, James, to **YOUNG**, Rebecca, Miss, all of NC Co, at Chester, PA, 27 Apr 1834, by Abraham Kerlin, Esq. (DG 29 Apr 1834) Same people, but 26 Apr 1834, by Samuel Smith, Esq. (DG 6 May 1834)

DAVIS, Jane, see **DAVIS**, Laetitia Patton

DAVIS, Jane, see **MORRISON**, Joseph

DAVIS, John, to **CHRISTEE**, Lydia, Miss, both of NC Co, 9 May 1835, by Elder John P. Peckworth (DG 12 May 1835)

DAVIS, John W., son of Mrs. Kittura DAVIS, 7 Jul 1852, in his 21st yr (DG 20 Jul 1852)

DAVIS, John Wesley, to **SHUSTER**, Mary, Miss, both of NC Co, 15 Sep 1849, by Rev. Andrew Manship (DG 25 Sep 1849)

DAVIS, Joseph S., to **HUDSON**, Mary, Miss, dau of Dr. Benjamin HUDSON, all of Sussex, in Baltimore, 25 Jan 1848, by Rev. A. Webster (DG 1 Feb 1848)

DAVIS, Joseph, see **SHARP**, Elizabeth J.
see **DAVIS**, Laetitia Patton

DAVIS, Kessiah, see **STEVENSON**, Jacob

DAVIS, Kittura, see **DAVIS**, John W.

DAVIS, Laetitia Patton, dau of Joseph and Jane Davis, 15 Aug 1851, in her 4th yr (DG 15 Aug 1851)

DAVIS, Manlove, see **DAVIS**, Martha

DAVIS, Margaret L.,
see **POSTLES**, James H.

DAVIS, Martha, dau of Manlove and Mary DAVIS, near Middletown, 22 Oct 1853, aged 10 mos (DG 1 Nov 1853)

DAVIS, Mary, see DAVIS, Martha

DAVIS, Mary A., see ADAMS, John W.

DAVIS, Mary Morris, late wife of Alexander DAVIS, and dau of the late Mr. CONWELL, near Milton, of inflammation of the lungs, 22 Mar 1845. Leaves 7 children, the youngest aged 3 mo. (DG 18 Mar 1845)

DAVIS, Nehemiah, of Milford, to McCURDY, Martha M., of Phila, 3 Sep 1850, by Rev. Thomas J. Thompson (DG 10 Sep 1850)

DAVIS, Outen, see THOMAS, William C.

DAVIS, Outten, Esq., at his res. near Middletown, 23 Sep 1847, aged 75 yrs (DG 28 Sep 1847)

DAVIS, Robert to FRAME, Anna, Miss, both of Sussex, 9 Jan 1850, by Rev. T. P. McColley (DG 15 Jan 1850)

DAVIS, Ruth Hannah, see WOOLSON, William R.

DAVIS, Samuel, of Wilm, to THOMPSON, Elizabeth, Miss, of Del Co PA, in Phila, 4 Dec 1851 (DG 9 Dec 1851)

DAVIS, Sarah, see DRAPER, Lemuel

DAVIS, Sarah Ann, see THOMAS, William C.

DAVIS, Sarah E., see CRUSON, Wm.

DAVIS, Sarah K., see TRAINOR, Joseph W.

DAVIS, Theodore L., to HAYS, Emeline N., Miss, both of NC Co, 15 Aug 1853, by the Rev. M. D. Kurtz (DG 19 Aug 1853)

DAWES, Edward, see MINCHALL, Moses

DAWSON, John, see SLEVER, Philip

DAWSON, Michael, see DAWSON, Sarah, Mrs.

DAWSON, Nancy, Miss, dau of William DAWSON, 13 Oct 1850, in Kent Co. (DG 22 Oct 1850)

DAWSON, Sarah, Mrs, widow of Michael DAWSON, member of the Methodist Ch, 1 Feb 1823 (DG 4 Feb 1823)

DAWSON, Thomas W., to COLLINSON, Elizabeth Ann, both of Seaford, 30 Jun 1850, by Rev. James Hargis (DG 16 Jul 1850)

DAWSON, Willard H., to HERRING, Sarah A., Miss, 24 Dec 1846, near Canterbury, by Rev. Jesse Thompson (DG 1 Jan 1847)

DAWSON, William, dec'd, late of White Clay Creek Hd, notice given by Michael NAGEL (MN 20 Sep 1800)

DAWSON, William, see DAWSON, Nancy

DAY, C. H. B., to WARREN, Mary, Miss, of Kent Co, 3 Dec 1850, by Rev. G. D. Carrow (DG 24 Dec 1850)

DAY, Eliza, see WARRINGTON, David

DAY, Emeline, see LOFLAND, Elias

DAY, Francis, 25 Oct 1818, from a wound in the right side and arm from a fowling piece fired by John RUTTER. Verdict, wilful murder; prisoner put in New Castle jail. (DG 28 Oct 1818)

DAY, George, to LOWE, Jessie, Miss, all of Wilm, 2 Nov 1852, by J. A. Roche (DG 5 Nov 1852)

DAY, Joan, near Stanton, 23 Dec 1848, aged 35 yrs (DG 5 Jan 1849)

DAY, John, see LOFLAND. Elias

DAY, John, to CLING, Sarah, Miss, both of Christiana Hd, 21 Dec 1809, by Rev. Mr. Pryce (DG 23 Dec 1809)

DAY, John R., to RUSSEL, Sallie A., Miss, nmd, by the Rev. Daniel Godwin (DG 14 Jan 1853)

DAY, John W., to CLAYTON, Hannah R., Miss, both of Brandywine Hd, in Phila, on Thursday evening, by Rev. John M. Grant (DG 20 Oct 1848)

DAY, Joseph W., to RICE, Matilda, Miss, youngest dau of William RICE, Esq., all of Wilm, 8 Apr 1850, by Rev. J. E. Rockwell (DG 12 Apr 1850)

DAY, Margaret R., see MAGINNIS, William

DAY, Mary, see MOUSLEY, William

DAY, Rebecca, see CLEMENTS, Thomas Jr.

DAZAY, Jesse, of Delaware, a hero of the Revolution, 30 Jan 1849, aged 94 yrs (DG 9 Feb 1849)

DEAKYNE, Catharine, see FLEMING, E. J.

DEAKYNE, Emily, see WALKER, Wilson W.

DEAKYNE, Jacob, to FLEMING, Catharine,

Miss, dau of Joseph FLEMING, Esq., all of NC Co, at her father's res., 16 Nov 1848, by Rev. Thomas Sumption (DG 5 Dec 1848)

DEAKYNE, Nancy, 9 Oct 1847, at her res. in Appoq. Hd (DG 18 Oct 1847)

DEAKYNE, Peter S., of New Castle, DE, to GALLAGHER, Mary Ann, Miss, of Phila, in Phila, 22 Mar 1849, by Rev. Thomas Brainerd (DG 6 Apr 1840)

DEAKYNE, Wm. S., to STAATS, Sarah E., both of NC Co, in Phila, 5 Apr 1953, by the Rev. S. Higgins (DG 8 Apr 1853)

DEAKYNES, Thomas, see BARLOW, John

DEAL, Sarah, see HENRY, John J.

DEAN, Mary Emily, inf dau of Saulsbury DEAN, in Dover, 4 Mar 1853, na (DG 8 Mar 1853)

DEAN, Rachel, see WALLS, Campbell, Esq.

DEAN, Saulsbury, see DEAN, Mary Emily

DEAN, William, Rev., of Dorchester Co MD, aged 82 yrs, to SELLERS, ____, the widow, of Seaford, 8 Jul 1846, by Rev.William Morgan (DG 14 Jul 1846)

DEDFORD, Elizabeth, dau of William SCOTT of Gloucester Co, East NJ, at the res. of her son Willliam [WINDELL or DEDFORD?], ndd, aged 95. Married (1) Jonathan WINDELL, Rev. War soldier, who died 1786, leaving 9 children and Rev. War Certificates. She m (2) Samuel DEDFORD, "alias fortune hunter, who married her for those Certificates...spent all and left her..." (DG 19 Aug 1823)

DEDFORD, Samuel, see DEDFORD, Elizabeth

DEDIER, Elizabeth, see UNRUH, Abraham

DEENLER, Daniel, to BOWERS, Jane L., Miss, both of Wilm, 22 Feb 1846, in Phila, by Rev. H. G. King (DG 5 Mar 1846)

DEHAVEN, Jacob, see HURLEY, H.

DEHAVEN, Louisa L., see HURLEY, H.

DEIHL, Sarah, late of St Georges Hd, J. Bayard ALRICHS, adm'r (DG 4 Oct 1853)

DEIHL, William, to CAZIER, Mary, Miss, both of NC Co, at Mt. Vernon, the res. of Henry CAZIER, by Rev. James McIntire of Elkton. nmd (DG 23 May 1848)

DeKRAFT, Edward, see BARNEY, Samuel Chase

DeKRAFT, Mary Eleanor, see BARNEY, Samuel Chase

DeLANEY, Peter B., see DeLANEY, Peter

DeLANEY, Peter B., Sr., 22 Nov 1845, aged 66 yrs (DG 28 Nov 1845)

DELANEY, Levin W., to WOOTEN, Martha E., both of Sussex, 4 Nov 1846, at Laurel, by Rev. Jacob B. Smith (DG 15 Jan 1847)

DeLANY, Peter, Dr., of the navy, in Laguna, Mexico, of yellow fever, 10 Sep 1847. Practiced in New Castle and later near Brandywine Springs A writer, also, and son of Peter B. DeLANEY, Esq., formerly sheriff of NC Co.(DG 10 Sep 1847)

DeLANY, Sarah E., see MERRITT, John, M. D.

DELANY, P. B., see MERRITT, John, M. D.

DELAPLAIN, James, see JEFFERIES, Henry see GAMBLE, Elizabeth

DELAPLAINE, James, see COSGROVE, Joseph

DELAPLAINE, Jane, see ARMSTRONG, John

DELAPLAINE, Mary, see GREGG, John

DELAPLAINE, Nehemiah, see GREGG, John

DELAPLAINE, Sarah, see TURNER, Joseph

DELE VAN, Rosanna, see PANADER, Henry

DELL, Mary Jane, see MARVEL, Ruben G.

DELLIN, James, to KING, Mary E, both of New Castle, at the pars. in Chester, 17 Feb 1853, by the Rev. J. B. Maddux (DG 1 Mar 1853)

DEMPSEY, Margaret, see NELSON, Robert

DEMPSTER, Lydia Ann, see JUMP, Wm. L.

DENN, George, of Wilm, to SIMKINS, Abigail, Miss, of Upper Penn's Neck, 12 Dec 1833, by Lewis Green,., Esq. (DG 31 Dec 1833)

DENN, George, of Wilm, to HOWELL,

DELAWARE MARRIAGES AND DEATHS FROM NEWSPAPERS, 1729-1853

Sidney E., dau of Joseph HOWELL, of Phila, at Friends Meeting on Orange St in Phila, 2 Jul 1834 (DG 8 Jul 1834)

DENNEY, Amy, see ABBOTT, Cyrus

DENNEY, Mary Ann, Mrs., at her late res. on Orange St. between 2nd and 3rd, 18 Feb 1844, aged 52 yrs 1 mo 1 day (DG 23 Feb 1844)

DENNEY, Sarah, see WALKER, Robert Jr.

DENNEY, Thomas H., to BISHOP, Cathern (sic) R., Miss, all of Kent Co, 3 Mar 1846, by Rev. Joseph Mason (DG 13 Mar 1846)

DENNIS, Augustus H., to RITCHIE, Elizabeth Jane, Miss, all of Wilm, 29 Feb 1844, by Rev. J. Kennaday (DG 5 Mar 1844)

DENNISON, _____. inf son of James DENNISON, in Wilm, 6 Jun 1848, aged 3 mos (DG 13 Jun 1848)

DENNISON, James,
see DENNISON, _____
see DENNISON, Zachary T.

DENNISON, Jesse, Mason, in Wilm, 1 Jul 1848, aged 52 yrs (DG 28 Jul 1848)

DENNISON, Mary, see DENNISON, Robert

DENNISON, Rebecca,
see CAMPBELL, David
see JOHNSON, Moses

DENNISON, Robert, to DENNISON, Mary, Miss, both of Wilm, 1 Jan 1852, by Rev. S. R. Wynkoop (DG 9 Jan 1852)

DENNISON, Thomas, Rev, in Newark, 21 Oct 1849, aged c 75 yrs (DG 26 Oct 1849)

DENNISON, Zachary T., son of James DENNISON, 19 May 1848, aged 13 mos 9 days (DG 2 Jun 1848)

DENNY, Ann G, wife and mother, at the res. of her husband, Collins DENNY, of Wilm, 15 Mar 1845, aged 47 yrs (DG 18 Mar 1845)

DENNY, Ann Jane, wife of Timothy P. DENNY, near Milford, 27 Aug 1849, na (DG 11 Sep 1849)

DENNY, Charles Griffin, to JAQUES, Sarah Maria, Miss, dau of Dr. Gideon JAQUES, all of Wilm, in Phila, 9 Apr 1828, by Joseph Watson, Esq., Mayor (DG 15 Apr 1828)

DENNY, Collins, see DENNY, Ann G.
see DENNY, Elizabeth
see REGISTER, Samuel B.
see STRATTAN, William R.

DENNY, Elizabeth, second dau of Collins DENNY, 21 Feb 1848, in Wilm (DG 25 Feb 1848)

DENNY, Evalina,
see STRATTAN, William R.

DENNY, Georgianna, see DENNY, Jacob

DENNY, Jacob, to DENNY, Georgianna, Miss, both of NC Co, 11 Dec 1849, by Rev. S. R. Wynkoop (DG 14 Dec 1849)

DENNY, Jacob, butcher, in Wilm, 16 Oct 1852, aged c 35 yrs (DG 19 Oct 1852)

DENNY, James, Esq., of Thoroughfare Neck, Kent Co, to ADYK, Catherine A., Miss, of Smyrna, at Smyrna, 26 Mar 1833, by Rev. Ephraim Jefferson (DG 2 Apr 1833)

DENNY, Mary S.,
see REGISTER, Samuel B.

DENNY, Rebecca A., see SMITH, James L.

DENNY, Robert, 21 Feb 1841, at his res. between Smyrna and Dover, aged 31yrs (DG 2 Mar 1841)

DENNY, Timothy P.,
see DENNY, Ann Jane

DENNY, W. Collins, 25 Aug 1848, of typhoid (DG 29 Aug 1848)

DENORMANDIE, A. E., formerly of Wilm, to TAYLOR, Mary Jane, both of Phoenixville, 26 May 1849, by Rev. H. R. Gallaway (DG 12 Jun 1849)

DENORMANDIE, Julian H, to JUAN, Susan, all of Wilm, 9 May 1851, before Hon C. P. Evans, Mayor (DG 13 May 1851)

DENT, Elizabeth, see HARLAN, Joshua

DEPUTY, _____, Mrs,
see DEPUTY, Nathaniel

DEPUTY, _____, Mrs. from near Middletown, on the campground at the Red Lion Camp, 12 Aug 1851, na (DG 19 Aug 1851)

DEPUTY, _____, Mrs, wife of Nathaniel DEPUTY, in Milton DE, 17 Aug 1853, na (DG 30 Aug 1853)

DEPUTY, Abraham, to DEPUTY, Elizabeth, Miss, all of Cedar Creek Hd, Sussex Co, DE, 26 Dec 1848, by the Rev. T. P. McColley (DG 6 Feb 1849)

DEPUTY, Charles M., to GRAY, Isabella T., Miss, both of NC Co, 1 Nov 1849, by the Rev. P. Coombe (DG 9 Nov 1849)

DEPUTY, Elias, to SAWDEN, Jane, Miss, both of NC Co, 6 Nov 1751, by the Rev. Dr. Hodgson (DG 14 Nov 1851)

DEPUTY, Elizabeth, see DEPUTY, Abraham

DEPUTY, James P., to LINDAL, Eliza, 20 Apr 1853, by the Rev. D. Godwin (DG 3 May 1853)

DEPUTY, John, to WATSON, Emeline Truitt, Miss, both of Sussex Co, near Milford, 23 Feb 1836, by Rev. Corry Chambers (DG 1 Mar 1836)

DEPUTY, Joshua, see ELLISON, James M.

DEPUTY, Nathaniel, see DEPUTY, _____, Mrs.

DEPUTY, Nathaniel, husband of the late Mrs. DEPUTY, 18 Aug 1853, na (DG 30 Aug 1853)

DEPUTY, Sarah J., see ELLISON, James M.

DEPUTY, Thomas A., to CLENDANIEL, Ann Elizabeth, all of Cedar Creek Hd, 14 Jan 1849, by the Rev. T. P. McColley (DG 6 Feb 1849)

DePUY, _____, Dr., see O'DANIEL, William F.

DePUY, Elizabeth Eves, see O'DANIEL, William F.

DERICK, Samuel, see SCHULEE, John M.

DERICKSON, Jacob, see DERICKSON, Sarah

DERICKSON, Jehu. F., to WILLIAMS, Margaret E., Miss, both of Balt Hd, Sussex Co, 5 Oct 1863, by the Rev. Lemuel Hall (DG 21 Oct 1853)

DERICKSON, Martha, see HARVEY, Amor

DERICKSON, Mary, see REYNOLDS, Roger

DERICKSON, Sarah, Mrs., consort of the late Jacob DERICKSON, at her res. in Wilm, 12 Mar 1847, in her 76th yr (DG 19 Mar 1847)

DERICKSON, Sarah Ann, youngest dau of David and Ann PENNEY of Brandywine Hd, 22 Feb 1829, aged 24 yrs (DG 27 Feb 1829)

DERICKSON, William Z., to LYNAM, Sarah K., Miss, both of NC Co, 22 Feb 1844, by Rev. J. W. McCullough (DG 27 Feb 1844)

DERRAHAM, Pearce, to HUGHES, Nancy, Miss, both of Middletown, 17 Jun 1824, by the Rev. D. Crouch (DG 22 Jun1824)

DERRICK, Ann, see RUMER, John

DERRICK, Eliza, see WEBSTER, Richard A.

DERRICK, John A. J., to WELDE, Lydia A., Miss, both of Wilm, 31 May 1852, by the Rev. Levi G. Beck (DG 4 Jun 1852)

DERRICKSON, Elizabeth, see HUXLEY, Elisha see LYNAM, James K.

DERRICKSON, Emily Jane, Miss, at her father's res., from severe burns, 18 Jul 1833, na, Methodist (DG 2 Aug 1833)

DERRICKSON, Israel P., 8 Apr 1850, in Wilm, aged 44 yrs (DG 12 Apr 1850)

DERRICKSON, Jacob, in Mill Creek Hd, 7 Nov 1851, aged c 71 yrs (DG 11 Nov 1851)

DERRICKSON, Jacob, see DERRICKSON, Mary see HUXLEY, Elisha

DERRICKSON, James, to WEIR, Mercer, Miss, of Wilm, 18 Dec 1821, by the Rev. L. Lawrenson (DG 28 Dec 1821)

DERRICKSON, James, Dr., late of Sussex Co, ndd, but "funeral to be held by Seaford Lodge at his late res. in Laurel, 11 Nov 1824, according to the Institution of Masonry. Funeral sermon by Samuel Rawleigh at the Presb. Ch." Notice given by Elisha Wright, secretary (DG 2 Nov 1824)

DERRICKSON, Joseph, see GALLASPIE (sic), _____, Major

DERRICKSON, Joseph S., to PENNEY, Sarah Ann, Miss, 10 Nov 1825, by the Rev. R. Williston (DG 11 Nov 1825)

DERRICKSON, Mary, relict of Jacob DERRICKSON, in Mill Creek Hd, 20 May 1853, aged c 70 yrs (DG 24 May 1853)

DERRICKSON, Mary Ann, see KOLLOCK, James P. W.

DERRICKSON, Mary B., see HANSON, Joseph H.

DERRICKSON, Sarah, Mrs., see ANDERSON, Charles

DERRICKSON, William B., 15 Nov 1850, in his 48th yr (DG 17 Dec 1850)

DERRICKSON, William R. Capt., of

Southwark, at Phila, after a lingering illness, 3 Jul 1853, in his 40th yr (DG 4 Jul 1853)

DERRY, Ann McKim, 2nd dau of James and Jane DERRY, 18 Jun 1841, aged 6 yrs (DG 2 Jul 1841)

DERRY, James, see DERRY, Jane McNeal see DERRY, Ann McKim

DERRY, Jane, see DERRY, Ann McKim

DERRY, Jane McNeal, youngest dau of the late Valentine McNEAL, and wife of James DERRY, in Wilm, 21 Apr 1852, na (DG 23 Apr 1852)

DeSANDRAN, Alexander Gardon, to POGY, Mary E., Miss, of Brandywine, at Red Clay Creek, 25 Oct 1817, by Rev. Mr. Kenney (AW 1 Nov 1817)

DESAQUE, L., see KEEMLE(?), Samuel Ralph

DESAUQUE, Francis, Capt., of Phila, to LOCKERMAN, Ann P., Miss, of Wilm, 31 May 1827, by the Rev. P. Connelly (DG 8 Jun 1827)

DESAUQUE, Mary Louisa, see KEEMLE(?), Samuel Ralph

DESHONG, M. W., see WILLS, Henry

DETERLINE, Peter, to LUFF, Sarah, Miss, all of Wilm, 31 May 1827, by the Rev. J. P. Peckworth (DG 8 Jun 1827)

DEVELAN, Ann, 19 Oct 1798, on list of yellow fever victims (DG 27 Oct 1798)

DEVINE, _____, Mr., another of the men injured in the recent explosion at DuPont's, ndd, na (DG 19 Mar 1852)

DEVOU, Anna Maria, see COX, James Henry

DEVOU, James L., see SEAL, Joshua

DEVOU, Mary W., see SEAL, Joshua

DEVOU, Peter, to CRAIG, Rebecca, Miss, both of Wilm, in Wilm, 31 Dec 1823, by the Rev. E. W. Gilbert (DG 2 Jan 1824)

DEWDELE, Francis (sic) Ann, see THARP, Reuben - credibility in question

DEWEES, Cornelius, at his res. near Camden DE, 16 Nov 1851, aged c 30 yrs. Leaves a wife and several children (DG 25 Nov 1851)

DEWEES, William C., of Kent Co, to MASSEY, Mary Ann, Miss, of Wilm, 29 Nov 1846, in Phila, by Rev. James A. MASSEY (DG 4 Dec 1846)

DEWEESE, Daniel, 25 Oct 1848, at the res. of J. F. ZEBLEY (DG 27 Oct 1848)

DEXTER, George W., to BENNET, Mary E., both of NC Co, 21 Nov 1850, by Rev. T. Newman (DG 6 Dec 1850)

DICK, James, dec'd, late of White Clay Creek Hd, notice given by James COUPER, Jr., adm'r (FA 17 Mar 1804)

DICKENSON, Mary, see PAS WATERS, John

DICKENSON, Morris, Esq., to PHILLIPS, Eliza, both of NC Co, DE, at the Mansion House, W. Chester PA, 1 May 1851, before Henry Fleming, Esq. (DG 9 May 1851)

DICKENSON, Stockley, to JOHNSON, Elizabeth, Miss, 21 Oct 1841, by Rev. S. M. Gayley (DG 5 Nov 1841)

DICKERSON, Alfred A., to ROBINSON, Amelia, Miss, dau of the late John ROBINSON, Esq., all of Balt, 1 Nov 1849, in Balt by the Rev. S. P. Hill (DG 9 Nov 1849)

DICKERSON, George, to PRETTYMAN, Zippy, Miss, in Georgetown, 12 Mar 1835, by the Rev. J. R. Torbert (DG 20 Mar 1835)

DICKERSON, George Henry, in Phila. 7 Dec 1849, aged 2 yrs 11 mos 22 das (DG 11 Dec 1849)

DICKERSON, Nancy, see DUTTON, Levin

DICKERSON, Nehemiah, of Phila, to DAVIS, Catherine, Miss, of Newark DE, 9 Jan 1853, by Rev. John Rush (DG 14 Jan 1853)

DICKINSON, Afir, see HUMBERT, Fredrick

DICKINSON, Francis, of Phila, to IRVIN, Eliza, Miss, of Wilm, 14 Nov 1822, by the Rev. E. W. Gilbert (DG 19 Nov 1822)

DICKINSON, John, Esq., 14 Feb 1808. Buried in Friends Burying Ground, Wilm (MU 20 Feb 1808) notice given by Sally Norris DICKINSON, exec'x (MU 23 Jul 1808)

DICKINSON, Sally Norris, see DICKINSON, John, Esq.,

DICKINSON, William, formerly of DE, in Quaker Neck MD, 20 Sep 1847, in his 63rd yr (DG 5 Oct 1847)

DICKSON, Ann, see BOSTICK, John

DICKSON, Benjamin W., in Smyrna, 14 Jan 1849, in his 56th yr (DG 23 Feb 1849)

DICKSON, David, to SIMPSON, Margaret Jane, 10 Sep 1844, by Rev. M. J. Rhees (DG 13 Sep 1844)

DICKSON, Deborah, see DICKSON, William

DICKSON, Elizabeth Baynard, only dau of George B. and Mary J. DICKSON, at Dover of measles, 16 Jun 1848, aged 11 wks, 1 day (DG 23 Jun 1848)

DICKSON, George B., see DICKSON, Elizabeth Baynard

DICKSON, John, of a pulmonary complaint, at his late res. near Newark, 12 Nov 1823, na (DG 18 Nov 1823)

DICKSON, John H., dec'd, late of White Clay Creek Hd, notice given by Isaac PRICE, exec'r (DG 17 Feb 1824)

DICKSON, Mary J., see DICKSON, Eliabeth Baynard

DICKSON, William, dec'd, late of Christiana Bride (sic) notice given by Deborah DICKSON and James McCALLMONT, adm'rs (DE 15 Jul 1795)

DIEHL, Elizabeth, see HATCH, William H.

DIEHL, George S., at Delaware City, to SMITH, Mary, of Kent Co MD, 26 Oct 1852, by the Rev. Dr. Murray (DG 16 Nov 1852)

DIEHL, Joseph, late of St. Georges Hd, Sarah DIEHL, adm'x (DG 13 Apr 1852)

DIEHL, Sarah, see DIEHL, Joseph

DILL, Lemuel, to WOOTEN, Sarah E., Miss, all of Kent Co, 3 Jan 1850, by Rev. T. J. Quigley (DG 15 Jan 1850)

DILWORTH, Adaline L., see NICHOLS, John

DINGEE, Eliza, see GILMORE, James

DINGEE, Mary Ann, see McLENEGAN, Isaiah

DINGEY, David, to MILES, Mary, Miss, 31 Dec 1828, by Mr. John P. Peckworth, all of Wilm (DG 2 Jan 1829)

DINGEY, Joanna B., see NOBLE, William

DINGLE, William C., Dr., of Millsborough, Sussex Co DE, in Milford of congestive fever, 3 Dec 1846, aged 43 yrs (DG 15 Dec 1846)

DINGY, Elizabeth, see HOEKSMAN, George

DISHER, William, of Phila, to ATTIX, Ann Isabel, of Kent Co, in Phila, 23 Apr 1848, by J. B. Nichols (DG 12 May 1848)

DITTUS, Andrew Jackson, son of the late Robert and Mary DITTUS, 12 Jan 1852, aged 6 yrs 4 days (DG 23 Jan 1852)

DITTUS, Mary, see DITTUS, Andrew Jackson see DITTUS,Mary Emma

DITTUS, Mary Emma, dau of the late Robert and Mary DITTUS, 17 Jan 1852, aged 8 yrs 1 mo 17 days (DG 23 Jan 1852)

DITTUS, Robert, see DITTUS, Andrew Jackson see DITTUS, Mary Emma

DIVIN, Charles, of Christiana Bridge, to JUSTIS, ____, Mrs., of Swanwick, NC Co, 6 Apr 1789 (DG 11 Apr 1789)

DIVINE, Mary Ann, see KEARNS, John F.

DIXON, Rebecca, see DIXON, John

DIXON, Aaron, to HARBESON, Anna, Miss, both of Chester Co PA, 8 Jan 1848, by Hon. Alexander Porter (DG 8 Feb 1848)

DIXON, Alexander H., of NC Co, to MILES, Ruth Ann, Miss, of Chester Co, PA, 10 Feb 1836, by Jno. T. Deury, Esq. (DG 23 Feb 1836)

DIXON, Ann, see SENEX, Nehemiah

DIXON, Anna Elizabeth, dau of James M. and Rebecca DIXON, in Wilm, 19 Nov 1849, aged 1 yr 8 mos (DG 23 Nov 1849)

DIXON, Hannah C., see STATTEN, Milton

DIXON, Isaac, Sr., at his house in Wilm, 20 Dec 1816 (AW 21 Dec 1816)

DIXON, James M., see DIXON, Anna Elizabeth

DIXON, James M., see DIXON, John

DIXON, Jasher (sic) E., see DIXON, Rose W.

DIXON, John, see DIXON, Mary

DIXON, John, son of James M. and Rebecca DIXON, in Wilm, 10 May 1849, aged c 14 mos (DG 11 May 1849)

DIXON, John, tyler [doorkeeper] of St. John's

Lodge # 2, A.F. & A.M., at New Castle, 16 Apr 1824, aged 78 yrs. Buried in Masonic Form (DG 16 Apr 1824)

DIXON, Joseph S.,
see GREENWALT, Henry

DIXON, Mary Ann,
see PASCHALL, Henry M.

DIXON, Mary Ellen,
see GREENWALT, Henry

DIXON, Mary, see STROP, Lewis D.

DIXON, Mary, widow of John DIXON, at her res. in Wilm, 10 Oct 1844, aged 65 yrs (DG 18 Oct 1844)

DIXON, Rebecca,
see DIXON, Anna Elizabeth

DIXON, Rose W., dec'd, late of Mill Creek Hd, NC Co, notice given by Jasher (sic) E. DIXON, adm'r (DG 21 Mar 1834)

DIXON, Samuel, see STATTEN, Milton

DIXON, Sarah C., see LLOYD, James

DIXON, Thomas, to SIMMONS, Lydia Ann, all of Wilm, 29 Mar 1844, by Rev. S. R. Wynkoop (DG 2 Apr 1844)

DIXON, Thos., to RAYHOW, Eliza, Miss, in Wilm, 11 Aug 1851, by the Rt. Rev. Alfred Lee (DG 12 Sep 1851)

DIXON, V. Cooper, to BIDWELL, Elizabeth, Miss, all of Appoq Hd, 22 Mar 1849, by the Rev. Thomas Sumption (DG 3 Apr 1849)

DIXSON, William,
see UNDERWOOD, William

DOBSON, Edward, of MD, to COLESCOTT, Elizabeth, Kent Co DE, 25 Nov 1847, by Rev. Jesse Thompson (DG 14 Dec 1847)

DODD, D., editor of the *Sussex News*, to JONES, P. D., Miss, of Georgetown, at the res. of George KOLLOCK, Esq., 6 Sep 1853, by Rev. Jonathan R. Torbert (DG 13 Sep 1853)

DODSWORTH, Mary,
see LANGLEY, Joseph B.

DOLBOW, Emeline, Miss, dau of King and Margaret DOLBOW, in Wilm, 20 Feb 1843 (DG 24 Feb 1843)

DOLBOW, King, see DOLBOW, Emeline

DOLBOW, Margaret,
see DOLBOW, Emeline

DOLBY, Lydia, 21 May 1850, in her 17th yr (DG 18 Jun 1850)

DONALDSON, Sarah, Mrs., 6 Jul 1825, "an aged...citizen" (DG 8 Jul 1825)

DONALDSON, Sarah, late of Wilm, John HEDGES, adm'r (DG 6 Nov 1849)

DONAVAN, James I., to POTTER, Rachel A., Miss, both of Kent Co, DE, 22 Mar 1849, by the Rev. T. P. McColley (DG 10 Apr 1849)

DONNALDSON, Margaret, in Wilm, 14 Sep 1849, aged c 75 yrs (DG 18 Sep 1849)

DONNELL, Elizabeth,
see OCHELTREE, John

DONOVAN, Sarah,
see CLENDANIEL, Wm. H.

DORSEY, Mary Agnes,
see WOLLASTON, William

dosSANTOS, A. F., of Phila, to REILEY, Mary Ann, Miss, of Wilm, 31 Jan 1850, by Rev. F. Reiley (DG 22 Feb 1850)

DOUGHERTY, Charles, Jr., to HOLLAND, Ellen J., Miss, both of Christiana Hd, at St. Joseph's Chapel, Brandywine, on the 2nd ult, by Rev. J. S. Walsh (DG 28 Aug 1849)

DOUGHERTY, James, of Wilm, to BRADLEY, Mary A., third dau of the late Andrew BRADLEY of Newark DE, at Newark, 25 Sep 1849, by James P Wilson DD (DG 28 Sep 1849)

DOUGHERTY, James, drowned in the Brandywine below DuPonts Powder Mill, ndd, aged c 22 yrs (DG 13 Sep 1853)

DOUGHERTY, Patrick, working near factories of Mrs. DuPont on Brandywine, injured in a sandbank cave-in, 22 Aug 1848 (DG 25 Aug 1848)

DOUGHERTY, Sarah Ann,
see WELDON, Christopher

DOUGHTEN, Stephen,
see DOUGHTEN, William

DOUGHTEN, William, late of White Clay Creek Hd, dec'd, notice given by Stephen DOUGHTEN and William DOUGHTEN, adm'rs (DG 14 Jun 1825)

DOUGHTON, James, to DOWNES, Elizabeth A., Miss, both of NC Co, at Cantwell's Bridge, 18 Apr 1848, by Rev. James Cuningham (DG 16 May 1848)

DOUGLAS, Robert, of yellow fever

(DE 16 Sep 1798)

DOUGLASS, James C., US Navy, to SINCLAIR, Ellen, dau of William SINCLAIR, Esq., US Navy, at Locust Wood, at the res. of J. A. CONSTANT, Esq., on the Hudson (DG 13 Nov 1849)

DOUNES, Mary Ann, see CHRISTY, James

D'OUVILLE, Auguste [fem], see D'OUVILLE, Marie Alexandrine Olympe

D'OUVILLE, Jumonville, see D'OUVILLE, Marie Alesandrine Olympe

D'OUVILLE, Marie Alexandrine Olympe, second dau of Jumonville and Auguste D'OUVILLE, professor of music, 15 Apr 1849, na (DG 24 Apr 1849)

DOWDEN, Sarah E., see COLLYER, William

DOWLIN, Christopher, drowned in the Brandywine, while bathing with some other boys near Bancroft's Bank, 15 Jun 1852, na (DG 25 Jun 1852)

DOWN, Mary G., see WHITEMAN, Thomas

DOWNES, _____, Mrs., see DOWNES, Thomas F.

DOWNES, Elizabeth A., see DOUGHTON, James

DOWNES, Mary Emeline, see FOSTER, William

DOWNES, Thomas F., eldest son of Mrs. DOWNES of Red Lion, DE, of yellow fever, on board the Brig *Morgiana* on her passage from Auxcayes to Wilm (DG 12 Nov 1822)

DOWNING, Elizabeth, see TURNER, Solomon

DOWNING, Geo. S., see PRICE, Samuel Jr.

DOWNING, George S., see PRICE, Mary A.

DOWNING, John H., formerly of Wilm, at the res. of his mother in Coatesville PA, 31 Jul 1842 (DG 5 Aug 1842)

DOWNING, Joseph, formerly of Pottsville, to JOHNSON, Margaret J., formerly of Wilm, 15 Apr 1851, by Rev. J. D. Clay (DG 22 Apr 1851)

DOWNING, Mary A., see PRICE, Mary A. see PRICE, Samuel Jr.

DOWNING, Samuel S., to STAPLER, Mary, dau of Stephen M. STAPLER, 27 May 1852,

by Friends ceremony (DG 1 Jun 1852)

DOWNY, Sarah Ann, see GREEN, John H.

DRAPER, Abigail, see BENNETT, George

DRAPER, Henry, merchant of Smyrna, 1 Jul 1820, aged 48 yrs (DG 11 Jul 1820)

DRAPER, James, fell from the steam packet *E. I. Dupont* when within 2 or 3 miles of the Christiana, 17 Aug 1846. Leaves a wife and several small children who reside in Christiana Village (DG 21 Aug 1846)

DRAPER, John R., Col., at his res. in South Milford, 12 Aug 1848, in his 43rd yr (DG 1 Sep 1848)

DRAPER, Joseph, to INSKIP, Martha, Miss, dau of Mr. Edward INSKIP, all of Wilm, 10 Nov 1829, by Elder John P. Peckworth (DG 13 Nov 1829)

DRAPER, Lemuel, to DAVIS, Sarah, Miss, both of Milton, DE, 25 Nov 1824, by the Rev. William Hickman (DG 30 Nov 1824)

DRAPER, Mary, see BALL, Jesse

DRAPER, Mary Malvina, see SAPP, George W.

DRAPER, Sarah Ann, see BLACKWELL, George see LAYTON, Joshua

DRENNEN, John, of Newark, to LINDSEY, Mary, Miss, dau of the late Mr. William LINDSEY, near Newark, 2 July 1835, by the Rev. A. K. Russel (DG 7 Jul 1835)

DRIVER, _____, Col., see BROOM, James

DRIVER, Ann, see BROOM, James

DRIVER, John M., son of Joshua E. DRIVER, Esq., in Wilm, 11 Sep 1848, in his 14th yr (DG 22 Sep 1848)

DRIVER, Joshua E., see DRIVER, John M.

DRUMMOND, Do., see DRUMMOND, Duncan

DRUMMOND, Duncan, late of NC Co. Pay debts to Thomas McKEAN of New Castle (PG 4 Feb 1762). Victoria McPHERSON, housekeeper, has embezzled the estate. Do. DRUMMOND, adm'r (PG 4 Feb 1762)

DRYDEN, John D. S., Esq., of Palmyra MO, to BARR, Sarah F., dau of Rev. Joseph BARR of Newark, 15 Apr 1847, at the res. of her brother, Alexander Forrester BARR, of Marion Co MO, by H. H. Hayes

(DG 7 May 1847)

DuBOIS, Amy, see **DUBOIS**, Susan Sparks

DuBOIS, Edward,
see **DuBOIS**, Susan Sparks

DuBOIS, Edward, of Phila, to **SPARKS**, Amy, of Wilm, 19 Aug 1841, in Wilm, by the Rev. Mr. Gerry (DG 10 Sep 1841)

DuBOIS, Susan Sparks, inf dau of Edward and Amy DuBOIS, 15 Dec 1852, aged 7 mos 15 days. Funeral from the res. of her grandfather, George SPARKS, 25 Poplar St (DG 17 Dec 1852)

DUBOIS, Hannah Ann, see **SMITH**, Joseph

DUBOIS, Mary, dau of Robert DUBOIS, 11 Oct 1848, aged 14 yrs (DG 17 Oct 1848)

DUBOIS, Robert, see **DUBOIS**, Mary

DUFF, Thomas, see **MIDDLETON**, Robert

DUFFIELD, Samuel, Dr., of Lancaster Co, to **MORRIS**, Maria, Miss, of NC Co, in Lancaster at the First Presbyt Ch, by the Rev. Dr. Wilson (DG 30 Dec 1825)

DUFFIELD, Thomas, a child, 22 Oct 1798, on list of yellow fever victims (DG 27 Oct 1798)

DUGAN, Mary I., see **MANSFIELD**, Edward

DUGAN, Thomas E.,
see **MANSFIELD**, Edward

DUKE, Emeline, see **BENNETT**, George H.

DULANEY, William W., of Laurel, to **TUNNELL**, Ann, Miss, dau of Mr. TUNNELL, of Dagsborough DE, 6 Apr 1845, near Laurel, by Rev. John Long (DG 11 Apr 1845)

DUNBAR, _____, drowned, while sailing on the Delaware River, 17 Aug 1851, na, res. of Porter's Alley, Wilm (DG 19 Aug 1851)

DUNCAN, Alexander,
see **BALDWIN**, Joseph

DUNCAN, Benjamin,
see **DUNCAN**, John Henry

DUNCAN, Eliza,
see **STEVENSON**, Thomas Collins

DUNCAN, Elizabeth, Mrs., in Wilm, 14 Nov 1851, in her 78th yr (DG 21 Nov 1851)

DUNCAN, J. W., to **WOOLSTON**, E. S., Mrs., both of Phila, at West Chester, 7 Nov 1833, by Rev. Mr. Stevens

(DG 12 Nov 1833)

DUNCAN, James, see **DUNCAN**, Margaret

DUNCAN, John, of Wilm, 30 Sep 1852, in his 76th yr (DG 8 Oct 1852)

DUNCAN, John Henry, son of Benjamin W. DUNCAN, near the Brandywine Springs, 21 Feb 1849, in his 13th yr (DG 27 Feb 1849)

DUNCAN, Margaret, wife of James DUNCAN, in New Castle, 5 Oct 1852, in her 67th yr (DG 8 Oct 1852)

DUNCAN, Mary, see **ALLEN**, Joseah

DUNCAN, Sally S.,
see **PLUMLY**, Thomas C.

DUNHAM, Mary, Mrs.,
see **BEAUCHAMP**, Jeremiah

DUNLAP, Abbey, see **ALLEN**, Samuel

DUNLAP, Adelia P., see **JUSTICE**, Lewis C.

DUNLAP, Bernard, 24 Aug 1851, in his 35th yr (DG 29 Aug 1851)

DUNLAP, Bernard, late of Brandywine Hd, Ellen DUNLAP, adm'x (DG 16 Sep 1851)

DUNLAP, Ellen, see **DUNLAP**, Bernard

DUNLAP, Francis P.,
see **JUSTICE**, Lewis C.

DUNLAP, Peggy, see **LONGHEAD**, William

DUNLAP, Samuel, dec'd, notice given by Benjamin HERSEY, adm'r (MU 21 Nov 1807)

DUNLAY, Francis, see **DUNLAY**, Jane

DUNLAY, Jane, wife of Francis DUNLAY, in Delaware City, 11 Jul 1850, aged c 50 yrs (DG 23 Jul 1850)

DUNN, Alice N., see **COYLE**, Cornelius

DUNN, Henry, while working on new RR depot, ndd, na. Leaves a wife and two or three children (DG 13 Apr 1852)

DUNN, Thomas,
see **MONTGOMERY**, John

DUNNING, Charles H., of Talbot Co Md, to **KARSNER**, Ella J., of Chesapeake City, at same, 30 Nov 1853, by the Rev. Mr. KARSNER (DG 6 Dec 1853)

DUNNING, Emma E.,
see **SPEARMAN**, Simon

DUNNING, Isaac T.,
see KOLLOCK, James P. W.

DUNNING, James A., to STEVENSON,
Margaret Ann, Miss, dau of Thomas
STEVENSON, all of Dover, 1 Sep 1847,
by Rev. H. Sutton (DG 3 Sep 1847)

DUNNING, James, see SPEARMAN, Simon

DUNNING, John W., to SHORT, Mary, Miss,
both of Kent Co, 27 Mar 1851, by the Rev.
E. R. Williams (DG 8 Apr 1851)

DUNNING, Julia A., ,
see ROBINSON, Julia A.
see ROBINSON, John

DUNNING, Mary E., see WOLFE, William P.

DUNNING, William,
see ROBINSON, Julia A.
see ROBINSON, John

DUNOTT, Eliza Ann,
see PENNINGTON, Hyland B., Jr.

DUNOTT, Miller, 13 May 1845, aged 53 yrs.
Buried Public Cem. (DG 13 May 1845)

DUNTON, Jacob, see CREEMER, Jacob

DUNTZE, John, to CHADWICK, Isabella,
Miss, 9 Mar 1847, by Rt. Rev. Alfred Lee
(DG 12 Mar 1847)

DuPONT, Alexis Irenee,
see DuPONT, Thomas Mackie

DuPONT, Alfred V., of DE, to LAMMOT,
Margaretta Elizabeth, Miss, dau of Daniel
LAMMOT of Phila, in Phila, 31 Oct 1824,
by the Rev. M. M. Carll (DG 2 Nov 1824)

DuPONT, Charles Irenee, Esq., to VAN
DYKE, Dorcas Montgomery, Miss, dau of t
he Hon. Nicholas VAN DYKE, all of NC Co,
at New Castle, 5 Oct 1824, by the Rev. Mr.
Prestman. Generals Lafayette and Suite
were present (DG 8 Oct 1824)
see DuPONT, Victor

DuPONT, Eleuthere Irenee, of Brandywine,
in Phila, 31 Oct 1834, aged 63 yrs
(DG 4 Nov 1834)

DuPONT, Eveline Gabriel,
see BIDERMAN, James Anthony

DuPONT, Joanna,
see DuPONT, Thomas Mackie

DuPONT, Julia Sophia,
see SHUBRICK, Irvine, Esq.

DuPONT, Thomas Mackie, youngest son of
Alexis Irenee and Joanna DuPONT, at
Harley, near Wilm, 3 Oct 1853, aged 13 mos
(DG 7 Oct 1853)

DuPONT, Victor, Esq., of Brandywine Hd,
Dir. of the Bank of the U. S., several times
member of the State Legislature, in Phila,
30 Jan 1827 (DG 2 Feb 1827)
Charles I. DuPONT, adm'r, Louviers,
Brandywine Hd (DG 3 Apr 1827)

DuPONT, Victor, to HOUNSFIELD, Alice,
Miss, 16 Oct 1851, by the Rev. Wm. Benade
(DG 21 Oct 1851)
see SHUBRICK, Irvine, Esq.

DURBIN, Augusta,
see WHITAKER, William M.

DURBIN, J. P., Rev.,
see HARPER, Fletcher, Jr.
see WHITAKER, William M.,

DURBIN, Margaret C.,
see HARPER, Fletcher, Jr.

DURBOROW, John, Rev.,
see DURBOROW, Margaret, Mrs.

DURBOROW, Margaret, Mrs., wife of Rev.
John DURBOROW, near Smyrna,
19 Aug 1833, na (DG 3 Sep 1833)

DURNIN, _____, Mrs., wife of Mr. John
DURNIN, keeper of the Golden Swan Inn, in
Wilm, 28 Aug 1825, na (DG 30 Aug 1825)

DURNIN, John, see DURNIN, _____, Mrs.

DuSOLLE, _____, of Phila, to FORD, Sarah
Ann, Miss, dau of the late Robert FORD,
Esq., of Wilm, 24 Dec 1833, by Rev. William
C. Mead, D. D. (DG 31 Dec 1833)

DUTTON, Eliza Jane,
see WALTER, John H.

DUTTON, Jacob,
see DUTTON, James Bishop

DUTTON, James Bishop, son of Jacob
and Orinda DUTTON, in Brandywine,
2 Apr 1847, aged 2 yrs and 8 mos
(DG 27 Apr 1847)

DUTTON, James, see SMITH, Joseph
see DUTTON, Joseph

DUTTON, Joseph, dec'd, late of Brandywine
Hd, notice given by James DUTTON, adm'r
(DG 8 Oct 1822)

DUTTON, Levin, to DICKERSON, Nancy,
Miss, 20 Jan 1850, by Rev. J. A. Torbert
(DG 12 Feb 1850)

DUTTON, Orinda,
see DUTTON, James Bishop

DUVAL, Sarah Ann,
see DALRYMPLE, Charles W.

EAKIN, Robert, to UXLEY, Elizabeth, Miss, 12 Sep 1820 (DG 15 Sep 1820)

EAKIN, William, in Wilm, 8 Jan 1829, aged 22 yrs (DG 16 Jan 1829)

EARL, Lydia, see SMITH, Joseph, Esq.

EARLE, James Tilghman, of MD, to JOHNS, Ann, dau of the Hon Kensey JOHNS Jr., Chancellor of this state, 16 Dec 1841, by Rev. Dr. JOHNS (DG 24 Dec 1841)

EARLY, James, to SHEARER, Catharine, both of New Castle, 29 Dec 1850, by Rev. Mr. Kelly (DG 3 Jan 1851)

EASTBURN, Amos, late of Mill Creek hd, Mary Jane EASTBURN and David EASTBURN, exec'rs (DG 24 Jun 1853)

EASTBURN, Charles, of Phila, to SMITH, Lydia, Mrs, of Wilm, 22 Oct 1845, in Phila by Alderman Palmer (DG 21 Oct 1845)

EASTBURN, David,
see EASTBURN, Amos

EASTBURN, Mary Jane,
see EASTBURN, Amos

EASTER, John, see FIELD, John A. Jr.

EASTER, Susan R. M.,
see FIELD, John A., Jr.

EASTMAN, Thomas,
see COTTER, Mary Ann

EATON, J. H., 1st Lt, 3rd Reg, U. S. Inf., to BLANEY, Susan C., dau of C. C. BLANEY, Esq., at New Castle, 6 Jun 1845, by Rev. J. H. Spottswood (DG 6 Jun 1845)

EBERBACH, John C., of Wilm, to FUTCHER, Margaret L., of Lewistown, 2 Sep 1847, by Rev. John Kennaday (DG 14 Sep 1847)

ECCLES, Edwin O., to LORE, Amanda F., dau of Eldad LORE, Esq., all of Cantwell's Bridge, in Phila, by Rev. Jas. Cunningham (DG 16 May 1848)

ECCLES, Samuel, of Christiana Bridge, DE, to HALL, Margaret C., Miss, of Darby, PA, 27 Mar 1834, by Rev. Joseph Lybrand (DG 1 Apr 1834)

ECCLESTON, J. H.,
see STEVENS, Edwin J.

ECCLESTON, John, see BYERS, James A.

ECCLESTON, Louisa,
see BYERS, James A.

ECCLESTON, Sarah E.,
see STAPLEFORD, William

ECCLESTON, Sarah Hooper,
see STEVENS, Edwin J.

ECKLE, Elizabeth, Mrs. in Phila, suddenly, 7 Sep 1853, in her 76th yr (DG 16 Sep 1853)

ECKLIN, Joseph M., to MARCHBANK, Mary Ann, Miss, both of Chester Co PA, 4 May 1847, by Rev. S. R. Wynkoop (DG 7 May 1847)

EDDOWES, Eleanor, dau of the late Ralph EDDOWES, at the res. of her brother, Mr. John EDDOWES, near Middletown, 2 Sep 1833, na (DG 13 Sep 1833)

EDDOWES, John,
see EDDOWES, Eleanor

EDDOWES, Ralph,
see EDDOWES, Eleanor

EDEN, Nancy, "from the tent," of yellow fever (DE 18 Sep 1798)

EDINBOROUGH, Sarah Dunbar,
see ELLIOTT, Thomas

EDMONDSON, Caroline R.,
see SMITH, Joseph E.

EDMONDSON, Lydia, in Wilm, at the res. of her sister, Ann REYNOLDS, 22 May 1849, in her 80th yr (DG 25 May 1849)

EDMUNDSON, Clarissa A.,
see MURGATROYD, Benjamin

EDWARDS, Charles C.,
see EDWARDS, Charles Franklin

EDWARDS, Charles Franklin, son of Charles C. and Mary Ann EDWARDS, in NC Co, 20 Jan 1849, in his 4th yr (DG 6 Feb 1849)

EDWARDS, George, late of Dover Hd, J. W. F. JACKSON, adm'r (DG 22 Feb 1853)

EDWARDS, J. Dr., to GARRETT, Anna M., dau of Thomas GARRETT, of Wilm, at Auburn CA, 20 Nov 1852, by Friends ceremony, in the presence of the Mayor (DG 31 Dec 1852)

EDWARDS, James W., of Phila, to

FLETCHER, Hannah, Miss, of Wilm,
28 Sep 1833, by Rev. Joseph Lyburn
(DG 1 Oct 1833)

EDWARDS, John, to HAWKE, Ann, Miss,
both of NC Co, 10 Feb 1848, at Pennsbury
Township PA, by Hugh Passmore, JP
(DG 26 Feb 1850)

EDWARDS, Joseph, to MORRISON,
Isabella, both of Wilm, 24 Feb 1848, by
Rev. T. J. Thompson (DG 7 Mar 1848)
see WEER, Mary

EDWARDS, Mary, see WEER, Mary
see BEALE, Edward F.

EDWARDS, Mary A., see KIRBY, John W.

EDWARDS, Mary Ann,
see EDWARDS, Charles Franklin

EDWARDS, Moses S., member of IOOF, at
Mrs. Sharpe's Hotel in Wilm, 28 Nov 1845.
Buried East Fallowfield PA (DG 5 Dec 1845)

EDWARDS, Samuel,
see BEALE, Edward F.

EDWARDS, Sarah, Miss, in Wilm,
24 Jan 1847, aged 64 yrs (DG 2 Feb 1847)

EDWARDS, Thomas, to LEVY, Margaret,
both of Brandywine Hd, 15 May 1833,
by Samuel Smith, Esq., of Chester
(DG 21 May 1833)

EGBERT, A., see COLLINS, James B.

EGBERT, Abraham, Esq.,
see McMECHEN, Mary, Mrs.

EGBERT, Abraham, see TYSON, Jacob
see TYSON, Isaac

EGBERT, Helena, see LEE, Israel S.

EGBERT, Martha, see COLLINS, James B.

EGBERT, Phebe, see HALL, Joseph L.

EGBERT, Rachel, see MOUNT, Wiliam G.

EGLEE, Charles, formerly of Wilm, merchant
of Glen Cove, Oyster Bay, Long Island, at
that place, 28 May 1835, na
(DG 30 Jun 1835)

EGNER, Charles,
see JARETTE, Joseph
see HART, Theophilus

EGNER, Matilda, see HART, Theophilus

EIJASON (sic), James J., to HANSON,
Lydia Ann, Miss, both of NC Co, in Phila,
21 May 1849, by Rev. Dr. Kennaday
(DG 12 Jun 1849)

EISONBRY, Charles S., to WALLS, Sarah
Ann, Miss, both of Smyrna, 8 Nov 1853, by
the Rev. T. C. Murphey (DG 15 Nov 1853)

ELBERSON, John, pilot, in Wilm,
25 Mar 1807 (MU 28 Mar 1807)

ELDRIDGE, Mary M.,
see PIERCE, William H.

ELDRIDGE, Tustin [Trustin?], of Phila, to
PIERCE, Ruth Ann, Miss, of Wilm,
19 Oct 1847, by Rev. M. J. Rhees
(DG 22 Oct 1847)

ELIASON, Andrew,
see ELIASON, James J.

ELIASON, James J., Andrew ELIASON,
adm'r (DG 18 Nov 1851) late of Pencader
Hd (DG 9 Jan 1852)

ELINGSWORTH, Nancy, Mrs., 11 Jul 1852,
aged 65 yrs (DG 20 Jul 1852)

ELLEGOOD, J. H.,
see ROWENS, Francis R.

ELLEGOOD, Joshua A., Esq., at his res.
near Concord DE, of a disease of the heart,
24 May 1845, aged 60 yrs
(DG 30 May 1845)

ELLEGOOD, Margaret, Mrs., at her res.
in Broad Creek Hd, 12 Jan 1851,
in her 82nd yr (DG 21 Jan 1851)

ELLEGOOD, Mary E.,
see ROWENS, Francis R.

ELLINGSWORTH, Sarah,
see POSTLES, Wm. R.

ELLIOT, Hugh, see ELLIOT, Mary S.

ELLIOT, J. Cloud, to PLATT, Lavinia dau of
John PLATT, Esq., both of NC Co, in West
Chester, 29 Oct 1851, by Rev. Alfred
Cookman (DG 4 Nov 1851)

ELLIOT, James, see ELLIOT, John

ELLIOT, John, late of Wilm. James ELLIOT,
adm'r (DG 27 Jul 1849)

ELLIOT, Joseph P., of Phila, to MIFFLIN,
Jane R., Miss, dau of Hon James L. MIFFLIN
of IN, in Newark, 15 Jul 1851, at the Village
Ch by the Rev. George Foot
(DG 22 Jul 1851)

ELLIOT, Mary S., wife of Hugh ELLIOT,
in Phila, 22 Jan 1852 (DG 27 Jan 1852)

ELLIOTT, A., son of Francis and Hannah

ELLIOTT, of bilious fever, 2 July 1848, aged 13 yrs 5 mos 17 days (DG 28 Jul 1848)

ELLIOTT, Anna Mary, see TALLEY, William T.

ELLIOTT, Benjamin, to ALRICHS, Elizabeth J., both of NC Co, in Phila, 25 Feb 1841, by Rev. Robert Adair (DG 2 Mar 1841)
see ELLIOTT, Cloud
see BROWN, John

ELLIOTT, Cloud, dec'd, late of Brandywine Hd, notice given by Benjamin ELLIOTT, adm'r (DG 4 May1824)

ELLIOTT, Edward, 5 Jan 1846, in Brandywine Vilage (DG 9 Jan 1846)

ELLIOTT, Eliza, see ARMSTRONG, George

ELLIOTT, Elizabeth, see SHARPLEY, Elizabeth

ELLIOTT, Francis, see ELLIOTT, A.

ELLIOTT, George W., at Canterbury, Kent Co, 7 Nov 1842, an aged and respected man (DG 18 Nov 1842)

ELLIOTT, Hannah, see ELLIOTT, A.

ELLIOTT, Isaac S., to BANNING, Elizabeth, Miss, both of NC Co, 6 Mar 1843, dau of John A. BANNING, Esq., by Rev. Mr. Love (DG 10 Mar 1843)

ELLIOTT, Isaac S., to BANNING, Sallie R., dau of John A. BANNING, Esq., of NC Co, 30 Nov 1852, by the Rev. Samuel C. Brinckle (DG 3 Dec 1852)

ELLIOTT, Isabella, dec'd, late of Brandywine Hd, notice given by George BUSH, exec'r (DG 16 Oct 1829)

ELLIOTT, Jane, Miss, at her late res. in Brandywine Hd, 31 Jan 1825, aged 68 yrs (DG 8 Feb 1825)
see ELLIOTT, Mark

ELLIOTT, John, to SHIELDS, Susanna, of Wilm, in Phila, 4 Oct 1847, by Rev. A. Atwood (DG 18 Oct 1847)

ELLIOTT, John in Wilm, 15 Jun 1849, aged c 83 yrs (DG 19 Jun 1849)
see LANDERS, John

ELLIOTT, Mark, dec'd, late of Brandywine Hd, notice given by Jane ELLIOTT, exec'x 14 Aug 1790 (DG 21 Aug 1790)

ELLIOTT, Martha Georgiana, see PALMER, Daniel C.

ELLIOTT, Peggy, see WELSH, John

ELLIOTT, Thomas, to EDINBOROUGH, Sarah Dunbar, Miss, both of NC Co, 19 Mar 1821, by the Rev. Richard D. Hall (DG 20 Mar 1821)

ELLIOTT, Washington, formerly of Brandywine Hd, but for the last 18 yrs a res. of Mississippi, near Vicksburg, 24 Mar 1850 (DG 13 Sep 1850)

ELLIOTT, Wm., Col, see SHARPLEY, Elizabeth

ELLIOTT, Wm., to McNEY, Isabella, in NC Hd, 2 Aug 1853, by the Rev. Mr. Billopp (DG 9 Aug 1853)

ELLIS, Matilda, see RICHARDS, F. De B.

ELLISON, James M., of NC Co, to DEPUTY, Sarah J., dau of Joshua DEPUTY, Esq., of Kent Co DE, 6 Jun 1850, by Rev. M. E. Ellison of the NJ Conf. (DG 11 Jun 1850)

ELLSBURY, Rebecca, see CUMMINS, Alexander

ELMER, Nancy P., see WHITELY, William

ELMER, William, see WHITELEY, Elizabeth Caroline see WHITELY, William

ELTONHEAD, Isaac, of Frankford PA, to BUZINE, Amanda, Miss, formerly of Wilm, in Frankford, 20 Sep 1851, by the Rev. Wm. Cooper (DG 26 Sep 1851)

EMERSON, Jane, see EMERSON, John Carlile

EMERSON, John Carlile, son of Jonathan and Jane EMERSON, at his father's res. in Smyrna, of dysentery, 25 Jun 1851, aged c 4 mos (DG 8 Jul 1851)

EMERSON, Jonathan, see EMERSON, John Carlile

EMERSON, Manlove, Esq., at his res. in Little Creek,15 Oct 1802 (FA 19 Oct 1802)

EMERSON, Vincent, M. D., to MARVEL, Elizabeth, Miss, eldest dau of Thomas J. MARVEL, Esq., all of Willow Grove, Kent Co DE, 21 Mar 1850, by Rev. Peter Meredith (DG 5 Apr 1850)

EMLEN, Elizabeth A., see BULLOCK, William S.

EMMORY, Charles C., to BATEMAN, Hannah M., Miss, in Phila, 14 Sep 1833, by Rev. J. Rusling, all of Kent Co, DE

(DG 17 Sep 1833)

EMORY, Charles C., to HARRIS, Caroline, Miss, dau of Abel HARRIS, Esq., all of Kent Co, DE, in Phila, 10 May 1829, by Rev. Solomon Higgins (DG 19 May 1829)

EMPSON, Bayard, negro, who murdered Joseph WILLIAMS, Feb last, was executed by hanging ,31 Jul 1851 (DG 1 Aug 1851) see WILLIAMS, Joseph

EMPSON, Mary, see EMPSON, William

EMPSON, William, late of Brandywine Hd. Household furnishings to be sold by Joshua NORTH and Mary EMPSON, exec'rs. Notice given for debtors to meet at house of Joshua LITTLER in Wilm (PG 1 Nov 1759)

ENGLAND, Ann Eliza, dau of Joseph ENGLAND, Esq., at White Clay Creek, 20 May 1827, in her 23rd yr (DG 1 Jun 1827)

ENGLAND, Bethia E., in Wilm, 19 Jul 1852, na (DG 23 Jul 1852)

ENGLAND, Eliza, see ENGLAND, Joseph

ENGLAND, Elizabeth A., see GUTHRIE, Alexander

ENGLAND, James, to YOUNG, Sarah, Miss, 30 Apr 1835, by Elder John P. Peckworth, all of Wilm (DG 5 May 1835)

ENGLAND, Joseph, see ENGLAND, Ann Eliza

ENGLAND, Joseph, Esq., "old," a State Senator at the time of his death, at his res. in Mill Creek Hd, recently (DG 2 May 1828) dec'd, late of Mill Creek Hd, notice given by Eliza ENGLAND, adm'x (DG 6 Jan 1829)

ENGLAND, Mary A., see BONSALL, Jesse T.

ENGLAND, Thomas, see BONSALL, Jesse T.

ENGLAND, Thomas H., of Wilm, to KIMMEY, Elizabeth S., of Camden DE, 4 Dec 1844, in Phila by Mayor McCall (DG 27 Dec 1844)

ENGLE, Mary. see BEALE, Edward F.

ENGLES, _____, Mr., 1st Mate of the ship Farwell, killed by Thomas FORRES, Scotsman, in a mutiny near Marcus Hook, 30 Dec 1844. Buried in Presb. graveyard, New Castle (DG 31 Dec 1844)

ENGLES, Abigail, see ENGLES, Elizabeth

ENGLES, Elizabeth, only dau of John and Abigail ENGLES, of consumption, 1 Apr 1850, in her 23rd yr (DG 12 Apr 1850)

ENGLES, John, see ENGLES, Elizabeth

ENGLISH, Henry, of Newport, to PHILE, Eliza Jane, Miss, of New York, 1 Aug 1850, by Rev. William Pauline (DG 6 Aug 1850)

ENNIS, _____, Mrs. consort of Wm. B. ENNIS, in Indian River Hd, 16 Nov 1853, na (DG 29 Nov 1853)

ENNIS, Jesse, to CAREY, Sarah, Miss, near Milton, 29 Jan 1835, by Rev. Daniel Jesper (DG 24 Feb 1835)

ENNIS, Rebecca F., see SPENCER, John W.

ENNIS, Sarah Emeline, see BAKER, Joshua G.

ENNIS, Wm. B., see ENNIS, _____, Mrs.

ENOS, Charity B., see PIERCE, Walter

ENOS, John, see CARSWELL, James

ENOS, Mary Jane, see GALE, Isaac Jr.

ENOS, Rebecca M., see ENOS, Susanna K.

ENOS, Robert, see QUIN, William

ENOS, Susanna D., see CARSWELL, James

ENOS, Susanna K., inf dau of Wm. J. and Rebecca M. ENOS, in Wilm, 20 Apr 1853, aged 9 mos (DG 26 Apr 1853)

ENOS, Syraphina, at Glasgow, 6 Jan 1853, aged c 40 yrs (DG 14 Jan 1853)

ENOS, William, in Brandywine Hd, 6 May 1843, aged 25 yrs (DG 12 May 1843)

ENOS, William J., to KIRKMAM, Rebecca M., Miss, both of Wilm, in West Chester, 3 Sep 1851, by the Rev. John B. Clemson (DG 9 Sep 1851)

ENOS, Wm. J., see ENOS, Susanna K.

ERSKINE, William, dec'd, late of Wilm, blacksmith, notice given by John FLEMING, acting exec'r (DG 16 Sep 1818)

ERWIN, James, see ERWIN, John

ERWIN, John, a former cabinet maker, an old and respectable inhabitant of Wilm,

31 May 1797, aged 70 yrs
(DG 31 May 1797) of a lingering illness,
(DE 1 Jun 1797) notice given by James
ERWIN for Lettice ERWIN, exec'r
(DE 27 Nov 1797)

ERWIN, Lettice, see ERWIN, John

ESCHENBERG, John, Esq., of Germany, merchant, to RODNEY, Eliza, Miss, second dau of the late Caesar A. RODNEY, at Buenos Aires, 2 Jun 1824
(DG 10 Aug 1824)

ESCHENBURG, Emily,
see BANNING, Henry G.

ESCHENBURG, John,
see BANNING, Henry G.

ESCHINBURG, Eliza,
see ESCHINBURG, Harman

ESCHINBURG, Harman, youngest son of John and Eliza ESCHINBURG, at Nevada City, CA, of congestion of the brain, 16 Dec 1850, aged 18 yrs 6 mos (DG 25 Feb 1851)

ESCHINBURG, John,
see ESCHINBURG, Harman

ESHER, Sarah Anna,
see PEIRCE, Joseph W.

ESTELL, Naomi,
see WARRINGTON, Thomas J.

EVANS, ____, Mrs., relict of the late Wm. EVANS, in Newark, 20 Apr 1853, aged c 75 yrs (DG 26 Apr 1853)

EVANS, Edward R., to PRICE, Sally, Miss, eldest dau of Isaac PRICE, Esq., at Harmony Mills, 12 Mar 1829, by the Rev. S. W. Presstman (DG 20 Mar 1829)

EVANS, Edward, late of Christiana Hd. Sale of property by Peter B. Delaney, sheriff (DG 2 Mar 1827)

EVANS, Eliza,
see COCHRAN, Richard E., M. D.
see LEECH, Isaac Jr.

EVANS, Elizabeth H.,
see BRASURE, Benton

EVANS, John, of New Albany IN, to LOWE, Rachel H., Miss, of Wilm, 20 Mar 1846, by Rev. Dr. Kennaday (DG 31 Mar 1846)

EVANS, John W.,
see UNDERWOOD, Annabella

EVANS, Martha, see GREEN, Jacob

EVANS, Mary Jane,
see STEPHENS, Alexander

EVANS, Purnell, of Port Penn, to PETTIT, Hannah, Miss, of Cumberland Co NJ, 8 Dec 1847, by Rev. Dr. Kennaday (DG 17 Dec 1847)

EVANS, Robert, to McMULLEN, Ann, Miss, 20 Jul 1826, by Rev. Mr. Williston (DG 25 Jul 1826)

EVANS, Ruth, see SIMMONS, George

EVANS, Sarah, see SPRINGER, Joseph

EVANS, William D., of Newark, to PREVOST, Mary J. M., dau of Lewis M. PREVOST, Esq., of Hunterton Co NJ, 20 May 1845, in Phila, by Rev. Mr. Sherwood (DG 27 May 1845)

EVANS, Wm., see EVANS, ____, Mrs.

EVERITT, Benj., Esq.,
see SMITH, Purnell Fletcher, the Rev.

EVERITT, Mary Wright,
see SMITH, Purnell Fletcher, the Rev.

EVERSOLE, A. S., Rev., MD, of the MD annual Conf, to WALLACE, Elizabeth, Miss, of Seaford DE, 7 Jul 1853, by the Rev. Theophilus Burton (DG 22 Jul 1853)

EVERSON, Eliza,
see EVERSON, Joseph Henry

EVERSON, Hanna,
see WHETSTONE, Samuel

EVERSON, John,
see EVERSON, Joseph Henry

EVERSON, Joseph Henry, a promising son of John and Eliza EVERSON, in NC Hd, 10 Feb 1846, aged c 5 yrs (DG 20 Feb 1846)

EVES, A., see WILLET, Allen W.

EVES, Abraham, Esq., member of First Baptist Church, in Wilm, 14 Nov 1846, aged 75 yrs (DG 20 Nov 1846)

EVES, Abraham, of Wilm, nephew of Major Spencer D. EVES, in San Francisco, of dysentery, 24 Nov 1851, na
(DG 10 Jan 1851)

EVES, Abraham, see RAY, John T. Dr.
see STIDHAM, Jonas
see EVES, Anna Mary

EVES, Anna Mary, Miss, dau of Mr. Abraham EVES, in New Castle Hd, 18 Jul 1824, na (DG 20 Jul 1824)

EVES, Bethia F., see MORROW, James

EVES, Eliza J., see RAY, John T, Dr.

EVES, Elizabeth,
see STIDHAM, Jonas Spencer

EVES, Henrietta, see WILLET, Allen W.

EVES, James, Capt., of Wilm, to BRIGHT, Hannah, Miss, of Boston, in Boston, 4 Nov 1822, by the Rev. Dr. Baldwin (DG 12 Nov 1822)

EVES, John D., to HIGGINS, Harriott, Miss, 30 Nov 1820 (DG 8 Dec 1820)

EVES, Mary C., see GILLESPIE, Thomas

EVES, Rebecca, see ROSS, Richard

EVES, Rebecca N,
see McCRONE, William B.

EVES, Samuel B., formerly of Wilm, in Houston, Texas, 8 Jul 1842, na (DG 5 Aug 1842)

EVES, Sarah,
see STIDHAM, Jonas Spencer
see STIDHAM, Jonas

EVES, Spencer D., to PORTER, Elizabeth, Miss,16 Sep 1835, by Rev. Arthur Granger, all of Wilm (DG 22 Sep 1835)

EVES, Spencer D., see EVES, Abraham

EVES, Susan B., see MARTIN, Nathan S.

EVES, Susan M., see ALEXANDER, Adam

EVES, William D., of Chester Co, PA, to GILLESPIE, Mary, Miss, dau of George GILLESPIE, Esq., of Newark, near Newark, nmd, by the Rev. A. K. Russel (DG 23 Jun 1829)
see MORROW, James

EWELL, D. F., see EWELL, Mary H.

EWELL, Mary H., Mrs, consort of the Rev. D. F. EWELL, in Vienna, of consumption, 14 Jan 1853, aged 22 yrs 2 mos 9 days (DG 1 Mar 1853)

EWING, Brinckley, see EWING, Mary, Mrs.

EWING, Mary, Mrs., relict of the late Brinckley EWING, dec'd, at the res. of her son in Georgetown, 28 Sep 1833, aged c 86 yrs (DG 15 Oct 1833)
see CROW, Owen C.

FAHAR, Mary Ann, see LOFFMAN, George

FAIRLAMB, N. Walter, of Del. Co PA, to MARSHALL, Sallie, formerly of Marcus Hook PA, 28 Dec 1852, by Rev. John McDowell (DG 4 Jan 1853)

FAIRLAMB, Susan P.,
see HARLAN, Samuel, Jr.

FARIES, Alexander, in Smyrna, 10 Apr 1850, aged 75 yrs 3 mos 16 days (DG 23 Apr 1850)

FARIES, George G., to ALRICKS, Sarah, Miss, both of Wilm, 17 Sep 1816, by Rev. William Wickes (AW 21 Sep 1816)

FARIR, Samuel, to BURGIN, Margaret, Miss, both of Red Lion Hd, 22 Apr 1848, by Rev. S. R. Wynkoop (DG 25 Apr 1848)

FARIS, Jacob, see WILLIAMS, Peter, Esq.

FARQUHAR, Alexander. Sale of land in Dover. Orchards, grist mill, 400 acres, by exec'rs James GORRELL and Mary GORRELL (PG 16 Jul 1741)

FARR, Sarah H., see YOUNG, William H.

FARRA, Daniel, Jr., of Wilm, to McCULLOUGH, Sarah A., Miss, of New Castle, in New Castle, 31 Jan 1850, by Rev. Thomas Billop (DG 5 Mar 1850)

FARRA, David W., to SIMPSON, Mary, Miss, 28 May 1846, by Rev. Dr. Kennaday (DG 5 Jun 1846)

FARRA, Harriet F., see VINCENT, Francis

FARRA, John, see VINCENT, Francis

FARRADAY, Mary Ann, see IVINS, Francis

FARRAND, Julia P.,
see CLAYTON, John L.

FARREN, Charles,
see FARREN, Mary Therisha

FARREN, Margaret,
see FARREN, Mary Therisha

FARREN, Mary Therisha, infant dau of Charles and Margaret FARREN, at the res. of her parents, 27 Mar 1851, na (DG 1 Apr 1851)

FARRIS, Jacob, see JAMES, Margaret

FARRIS, Margaret, see JAMES, Margaret

FARSON, John, to WILDS, Mary, Miss, both of Kent, 28 Sep 1820 (DG 10 Oct 1820)

FARWELL, A., Dr., at the res. of his brother-in-law near Wilm, 24 May 1851, na (DG 27 May 1851)

FAUCET, John,
see FAUCET, William Jacobs

FAUCET, William Jacobs, son of John FAUCET, in Milton, 3 Apr 1850, aged 7 yrs 8 mos (DG 23 Apr 1850)

FAUCETT, Henry, to SMITH, Prudence J., dau of Isaac SMITH, 19 Dec 1850, at Smith's Mills, Brandywine Hd, by the Rt. Rev. A. Lee (DG 7 Jan 1851)

FAUCETT, Nathan Y., to SMITH, Isabella, Miss, 9 Jan 1845, in Wilm, by Rev. Bishop Lee (DG 10 Jan 1845)

FAUST, Henry Atwood, son of Henry and Margaret FAUST, of scarlet fever, 10 Dec 1851, aged 3 yrs 1 mo (DG 16 Dec 1851)

FAUST, Henry, see FAUST, Henry Atwood

FAUST, Margaret,
see FAUST, Henry Atwood

FAY, P., of Wilm, to McCABE, Bridget, of Phila, 5 Aug 1852, by the Rev. Mr. Strohan (DG 10 Aug 1852)

FEBIGER, Christian, of Cincinnati, Ohio, to TATNALL, Sarah, second dau of Edward TATNALL, Esq. of Brandywine Hd, 23 Apr 1844, at the house of William WARNER, in Wilm, by the Mayor (DG 26 Apr 1844)

FELL, Courtland J., in Phila, aged 45 yrs (DG 24 Oct 1848)

FELL, Watson, of DE, to REYNOLDS, Lydia Ann, Miss, of MD, 26 Mar 1850 (DG 9 Apr 1850)

FENIMORE, Allen,
see FENIMORE, Margaret

FENIMORE, Margaret, dau of Allen FENIMORE, of Burlington Co NJ, in Wilm, 4 Apr 1848, in her 16th yr (DG 28 Apr 1848)

FENNELL, James, teacher of elocution, in Phila, "lived to see his friends of his prosperity abandon him when poverty came to his door" (AW 22 Jun 1816)

FENWICK, Eliza A., see SHORT, John

FENWICK, Virginia, Miss,
see McMINN, George Monroe

FERCUM, Mary Louisa,
see McCORMACK, Alexander

FERGUSON, _____, see BROWN, _____

FERGUSON, _____, wife of Robert FERGUSON, in Christiana Hd, 10 Feb 1853, na (DG 15 Feb 1853)

FERGUSON, Basset, Esq., State Senator from NC Co, at his late res. in Appoq Hd, 20 Nov 1853, in his 51st yr (DG 2 Dec 1853) Richard FERGUSON, adm'r (DG 16 Dec 1853)
see LYNAM, John

FERGUSON, Eliza, see LUTON, Ebenezer

FERGUSON, Mary Jane,
see BROWN, Joseph

FERGUSON, Richard,
see FERGUSON, Basset

FERGUSON, Robert, to COLLINS, Elizabeth, Miss, 1 Nov 1825, by the Rev. R. Williston (DG 11 Nov 1825)
see FERGUSON, _____.

FERMON, Thomas, dec'd, employed by John R. BRINCKLE, notice given by same (DG 18 Jul 1826)

FERRA, Charles, to CAREY, Ann, Miss, at Naaman's Creek, 15 Mar 1821, by the Rev. J. Rusling (DG 20 Mar 1821)

FERRELL, Gideon, the Rev., of Pencader, 22 Aug 1820 (DG 22 Aug 1820)

FERRIN, Ann, Miss, in Wilm, 5 Oct 1841 (DG 8 Oct 1841)

FERRIS, David, see WAY, Joshua

FERRIS, John, of Wilm, in Wilm, 24 Oct 1828, an old citizen (DG 28 Oct 1828)

FERRIS, Mary, see SELLARS, William

FERRIS, Zeba, see SELLARS, William

FERRIS, Ziba, to MEGEAR, Eliza, dau of Michael MEGEAR, all of Wilm, 14 Nov 1816, at the Friends Meeting (AW 16 Nov 1816)
see JOHNSON, John

FERRISS, Benj., see FERRISS, John

FERRISS, Edith, see FERRISS, Ziba

FERRISS, John, dec'd, late of Wilm, notice given by Eli HILLIS and Benj. FERRISS, exec'rs (DG 16 Jan 1829)

FERRISS, John, Sr., see FERRISS, Ziba

FERRISS, Ziba, dec'd, notice given by John FERRISS, Sr., and Edith FERRISS, exec'rs (DG 4 Feb 1797)

FERRY, William, drowned in the Brandywine below DuPonts Powder Mill, ndd, aged c 22 yrs (DG 13 Sep 1853)

FETTER, Daniel, merchant of New Orleans, to BOYD, Matilda J., Miss, 9 Dec 1843, at the res. of William BOYD (DG 15 Dec 1843)

FIELD, Elenor H., Mrs., dau of Nathan BOULDEN of Pencader Hd, in New York, 13 May 1848, of consumption (DG 26 May 1848) see FIELDS, Elenor H.

FIELD, Elenor, see BOULDEN, Nathan

FIELD, John A., Jr., to EASTER, Susan R. M., (late a pupil of the Wesleyan Female Seminary in Wilm), dau of the late John EASTER, all of Baltimore, 13 Jan 1846, at St. Andrew's, by Rev. Dr. Dorsey (DG 20 Jan 1846)

FIELDS, A. C., Rev., see HERMANCE, John P.

FIELDS, Abraham, dec'd, late of Appoq. Hd, notice by Sarah FIELDS, adm'x (FA 4 Jan 1804)

FIELDS, Benjamin, at his res. on Block Marsh Farm, near Middletown DE, 23 Jun 1842, aged 46 yrs (DG 1 Jul 1842) see HAZELL, William B.

FIELDS, Catharine, see ADAMS, William B.

FIELDS, Daniel, of Newark DE, to WRIGHT, Harriet P., of Dorchester Co MD, in Dorchester Co, 8 Sep 1852, by the Rev. T. P. Barber (DG 1 Oct 1852)

FIELDS, Elenor H., Miss, dau of Nathan BOULDEN, Esq., in New York City, 13 Apr 1848, in her 29th yr (DG 18 Apr 1848) see FIELD, Elenor H.

FIELDS, Sarah, see FIELDS, Abraham see HERMANCE, John P.

FIELDS, Sarah J., see HAZELL, William B.

FILAR, Sarah A., see WALTON Thomas

FILBERT, Anna M., see McDOWELL, Elijah

FILE, Elizabeth, see BODELL, John

FILE, Jonathan, formerly of Wilm, 28 Oct 1848, at New Orleans, aged 27 yrs (DG 10 Nov 1848)

FILE, Mary, see O'DANIEL, George

FILER, John, in Wilm from consumption, 26 May 1850 (DG 28 May 1850)

FINCHER, _____, Mrs, wife of George FINCHER, near the village of Brandywine, ndd, na (DG 21 Jan 1848)

FINCHER, George, see FINCHER, _____, Mrs.

FINCHER, George, to HOLMES, Catharine, Miss, all of NC Co, in Wilm 25 Mar 1849, by the Rev. M. Rhees (DG 3 Apr 1849)

FINCHER, Sarah, see REDGRAVE, Samuel

FINLEY, John, the Rev., see WEST, Wrexham, Esq.

FINLEY, Joseph, to REECE, Delia, Miss, 21 Dec 1820 (DG 22 Dec 1820)

FINLEY, Martha G., see WEST, Wrexham, Esq.

FINLEY, Samuel C., see BRACKIN, Mary

FINLEY, Sam'l C., see BRACKIN, Willliam

FINN, John, see RODGERS, Thomas

FINNEY, _____, son of William FINNEY of Wilm, drowned near Upper Wharf, on the Christiana, 27 Jul 1844, aged between 8 and 9 yrs (DG 30 Jul 1844)

FINNEY, David T., see FINNEY, Washington L.

FINNEY, John, see FRENCH, David

FINNEY, Washington L., Esq., notice given by David T. FINNEY and Lewis NEAL, exec'rs (FA 10 Mar 1804)

FINNEY, William, see FINNEY, _____

FIPPS, Charlotte, wife of Cornelius FIPPS, 15 Oct 1848, in her 35th yr (DG 20 Oct 1848)

FIPPS, Cornelius, see FIPPS, Charlotte

FIPPS, Cornelius, to PERRY, Charlotte, Miss, all of Wilm, 16 May 1847, in St. Paul's M. E. Church, by Rev. Joseph Castle (DG 18 May 1847)

FIRESTONE, Sarah, see PEDRICK, William H.

FISHER, _____, Judge, see MAXFIELD, Joseph Jr.

FISHER, Edward, Esq., merchant of Carthage MO, formerly of Kent Co, to SANDERS, Arabella, dau of William SANDERS, Esq., of Carthage, at Carthage, 18 Jun 1848, by Rev. M. Robinson (DG 22 Aug 1848)

DELAWARE MARRIAGES AND DEATHS FROM NEWSPAPERS, 1729-1853

FISHER, Elizabeth R.,
see TALLEY, John Henderson

FISHER, Hannah C., see PIERCE, Alfred

FISHER, Henry, to ROBINSON, Margaret Jane, 24 Apr 1845, in Wilm, by Rev. M. J. Rhees (DG 13 May 1845)

FISHER, John, Hon., Judge of the District Court of the U. S. for the DE Dist., at his res. near Smyrna, 22 Apr 1823
(DG 25 Apr 1823)
see SHERER, William

FISHER, John C., of pulmonary consumption, at Milford, 31 May 1848, in his 22nd yr (DG 2 Jun 1848) at Hotel Hudson Burr in Milford, 30 May 1848, aged 21 yrs 7 mos 24 days (DG 13 Jun 1848)

FISHER, Lavinia Rodney,
see SHERER, William

FISHER, Robert, clerk in Treasury Dept. of the office of the Fifth auditor in Washington, a native of Delaware, in Washington, after a short illness, 11 Nov 1823, na
(DG 18 Nov 1823)

FISHER, Sally Ann,
see CLAYTON, John M., Esq.,

FISHER, Samuel M., Dr., to CUMMINS, Susan W., Miss, 5 May 1835, by Elder John P. Peckworth, all of Smyrna
(DG 12 May 1835)

FISHER, William H., to PITT, Emma, Miss, all of Wilm, 9 Dec 1852, by Rev. J. Roche
(DG 14 Dec 1852)

FISHER, Williamina,
see MAXFIELD, Joseph Jr.

FISHLER, Lydia, see BANNAN, Edward

FISHLER, Mary Ann,
see BENNETT, Charles H.

FITTEN, Ann, see CONAWAY, Samuel

FITZHUGH, Philip Aylett, Dr., of Middlesex, to TANKARD, Georgiana, of Northhampton Co, VA, 17 Apr 1849, by the Rev. John Ufford (DG 1 May 1849)

FITZPATRICK, Mary,
see CLARK, Jonathan R.

FITZPATRICK, Thomas, late of Christiana Hd, John S. WALSH, exec'r
(DG 19 Oct 1852)

FITZRANDOLPH, Elizabeth,
see THOMAS, Randolph

FITZSIMMONS, Joseph, to JOHNSON, Rebecca, Miss, both of Christiana Hd, 13 May 1845, by Rev. Mr. Cox
(DG 23 May 1845)

FLAGLER, Albert, to HARDY, Mary Ann, Miss, both of Wilm, 1 Oct 1849, by the Rev. Caleb J. Good (DG 6 Nov 1849)

FLAMER, Solomon, to MOORE, Ann, Miss, both of Wilm, 12 Sep 1850, by Rev. J. E. Rockwell (DG 17 Sep 1850)

FLEESON, Thomas, eldest son of Rev. Thomas FLEESON, of Wilm, 14 Oct 1789, aged 15 yrs. Buried in the Baptist Burying Ground (DG 28 Oct 1789)

FLEESON, Thomas, Rev.,
see FLEESON, Thomas

FLEMING, Adam, to FLEMING, Eve, 25 Jul 1835, by Rev. Owen Lloyd
(in some doubt) (DG 24 Jul 1835)

FLEMING, Alexa Rebecca Ann,
see REYNOLDS, Aaron

FLEMING, Anna J., see MURPHY, Samuel

FLEMING, Catharine,
see DEAKYNE, Jacob

FLEMING, Charles T.,
see FLEMING, Elizabeth

FLEMING, E. J., to DEAKYNE, Catharine, Miss both of Appoq. Hd., 2 Mar 1848, by Rev. T. Sumption (DG 31 Mar 1848)

FLEMING, Edward, 18 yrs, son of Mr. John FLEMING, merchant (MN 8 Aug 1801)

FLEMING, Elias, of NC Co, to JANE, Sarah, of Gloucester Co NJ, 19 Feb 1852, by Alderman C. Brazier at his res., 61 N. 5th St
(DG 2 Mar 1852)

FLEMING, Elizabeth, Mrs., late wife of Charles T. FLEMING, and sister of Peter F. CAUSEY, Esq., in Milford, 16 May 1847
(DG 25 May 1847)

FLEMING, Eve,
see FLEMING, Adam (in some doubt)

FLEMING, George, Capt., of Smyrna, to CALDWELL, Rebecca Ann, Miss, of Wilm, 29 Feb 1844, by Rev. John D. Onins
(DG 5 Mar 1844)

FLEMING, George, Capt., at the res. of his father, Joseph FLEMING, Esq., near Smyrna, 26 Mar 1847, aged 28 yrs
(DG 2 Apr 1847)

FLEMING, Gilbert R., see LISLE, Mary Ann

FLEMING, John, Wilm merchant, 5 Jan 1827. Notice given by Allen THOMSON and James GARDNER, exec'rs (DG 9 Jan 1827)
see ERSKINE, William
see FLEMING, Edward

FLEMING, John, Sr., near DuPont Mills, Brandywine, of typhus fever, 15 Sep 1834, aged c 60 yrs (DG 16 Sep 1834)
see FLEMING, Samuel

FLEMING, Joseph, see FLEMING, George
see DEAKYNE, Jacob

FLEMING, Marcellus, to HOLLINGSWORTH, Martha, Miss, all of Wilm, 14 Oct 1847, by Rev. T. J. Thompson (DG 18 Oct 1847)

FLEMING, Mary,
see WILLIAMS, John, of Phila
see FLEMING, Wilhelmina Donnan

FLEMING, Samuel, son of the late John FLEMING, Sr., near DuPont Mills, Brandywine, 5 Sep 1834, aged 19 yrs (DG 16 Sep 1834)

FLEMING, Sarah Francis, in Phila of heart disease, 3 May 1848, aged 6 yrs 2 mos 14 days (DG 9 May 1848)

FLEMING, Wilhelmina Donnan, inf. dau of William S. and Mary Clementina FLEMING, in Christiana Hd, 30 Aug 1843 (DG 15 Sep 1843)

FLEMING, William H., of Columbia Co NY, to LISLE, Caroline B., of Wilm, 20 Nov 1848, by Rev. E. Van Dusen, in Chester PA (DG 23 Nov 1848)

FLEMING, William S.,
see FLEMING, Wilhelmina Donnan

FLETCHER, Charles, suddenly, 30 Mar 1845 (DG 1 Apr 1845)

FLETCHER, Hannah,
see EDWARDS, James W.

FLEU, Catherine, see FLEU, George W.

FLEU, George W., son of Simon and Catherine FLEU, in Wilm 10 May 1848, aged 5 yrs (DG 16 May 1848)

FLEU, Simon, see FLEU, George W.

FLINN, Abigail A., see HAYS, James P.

FLINN, Anthony B., to ATWOOD, Hannah L., all of Wilm, 1 Dec 1853, by Rev. A. ATWOOD (DG 6 Dec 1853)

FLINN, Daniel B., to PENNEPACKER, Margaret A., all of Wilm, at the Baptist Publication Rooms, Phila, 15 May 1850, by Rev. B. R. Loxley (DG 21 May 1850)

FLINN, Elizabeth, see KLEIN, George M.

FLINN, Elizabeth C.,
see HOLLINGSWORTH, Abner

FLINN, Isaac W., to LITTLE, Mary E., Miss, all of NC Co, 2 Dec 1851, by Rev. A. Atwood (DG 5 Dec 1851)

FLINN, John, see KLEIN, George M.

FLINN, Martha J., see GAUSE, John T.

FLINN, Robert B., to LYNAM, Joanna S., Miss, both of NC Co, 28 Feb 1851, by Rev. Wm. Cooper (DG 4 Mar 1851)

FLINTHAM, George, of Cecil Co MD, to STEWART, Sarah Ann, Miss, of NC Co, on board steamboat Kent on her passage to Phila, 25 Mar 1846, by Rev. J. Mason (DG 31 Mar 1846)

FLOYD, ____, Mrs, late wife of Samuel FLOYD, now of Wilm, formerly of Middletown DE, 29 Dec 1842 (DG 6 Jan 1843)

FLOYD, Hannah Jane,
see BUNNELL, Henry

FLOYD, Samuel, see FLOYD, ____, Mrs.

FLOYD, Wm. H. of Boston MA, to FOREMAN, Mary A. Miss, of Wilm DE, 16 Nov 1853, by the Rev. Roche (DG 22 Nov 1853)

FOARD, Chris, see SMITH, Thomas W.

FOARD, Edward, see NOBLE, Margaret

FOARD, Mary, see SMITH, Thomas W.

FOLS, Ezekiel, to HUMPHRIES, Martha S., Miss, 3 Oct 1816, by Rev. William Wickes (AW 5 Oct 1816)

FOOT, David L., at the res. of his brother near Stanton, 14 Feb 1836, na (DG 19 Feb 1836)

FOOT, Esther and FOOT, William, dec'd, late of Mill Creek Hd, notice given by James FOOT (DE 2 Aug 1798)

FOOT, George, see MOORE, William E.

FOOT, Hannah, of yellow fever (DE 20 Sep 1798)

FOOT, Harriet, see MOORE, William E.

FOOT, James, see FOOT, William
see FOOT, Esther

FOOT, Margaret, 21 Oct 1798, on list of
yellow fever victims (DG 27 Oct 1798)

FOOT, Thomas, of Christiana Hd, to
GREGG, Lydia, Miss, of Wilm, in Phila,
17 Dec 1846, by Mr. Garey
(DG 22 Dec 1846)

FOOT, William and FOOT, Esther, dec'd,
late of Mill Creek Hd, notice given by James
FOOT (DE 2 Aug 1798)

FOOTE, Benjamin, to RUMER, Martha, all of
Mill Creek Hd, at St James Ch, 25 Mar 1852,
by Rev. Mr. Bachelor (DG 27 Apr 1852)

FOOTE, Eliza, see WINGATE, Thompson

FOOTE, Elizabeth Robinson, wife of James
FOOTE of Mill Creek Hd, 1 Apr 1851, na
(DG 4 Apr 1851)

FOOTE, James, of DE, to ROBINSON,
Elizabeth, Miss, of Phila, 24 Jan 1850, by
Rev. John Chambers (DG 1 Feb 1850)
see FOOTE, Elizabeth Robinson

FOOTE, Jane, see BRACKIN, L.

FOPPLES, Elizabeth,
see GARRETSON, James B.

FORBES, Thomas, mutineer on the ship
Farwell, near New Castle, shot by the
captain, 30 Dec 1844 (DG 31 Dec 1844)
see ENGLES, _____

FORD, Eliza S., see FORD, Wm. Henry

FORD, Emily, see JOHNSON, Absalom

FORD, Franklin, to PHLEGER, Anna A.,
Miss, all of Wilm, 26 Oct 1847, by Rev. M. J.
Rhees (DG 29 Oct 1847)

FORD, Frederick, formerly of NC Co, DE, in
Cincinnati, 27 Aug 1849, in his 18th yr
(DG 26 Oct 1849)

FORD, Jeremiah, to FRIST, Susan, Miss,
both of NC Co, 11 Feb 1834,
by Elder John P. Peckworth
(DG 14 Feb 1834)

FORD, Jesse, Rev., see GRUBB, Lewis H.

FORD, John H., see FORD, Wm. Henry

FORD, Martha, see GUYER, John L.

FORD, Mary, see FRAME, Thomas
see GRUBB, Lewis H.

FORD, Mary, Mrs.,
see BOULDEN, Nathan, Esq.

FORD, Robert, see DuSOLLE, _____

FORD, Samuel, to Miss Elizabeth CULLEY,
all of Wilm, "on Thursday evening,"
22 or 29 Nov 1821, by the Rev. L.
Lawrenson (DG 30 Nov 1821)

FORD, Sarah Ann, see DuSOLLE, _____

FORD, Susannah,
see JEFFERSON, Enos H.

FORD, William, to SMITH, Jane, Miss, both
of Wilm, 9 Dec 1823, by the Rev. J. Potts
(DG 16 Dec 1823)

FORD, William, formerly of Christiana Hd, at
the Insane Hospital, Phila Co, 18 Feb 1847,
aged c 60 yrs (DG 23 Feb 1847)

FORD, Wm., to REED, Martha, Miss, both
of Kent Co, in Dover, 23 Aug 1853, by the
Rev. Mr. E. R. Hera (DG 6 Sep 1853)

FORD, Wm. Henry, son of John H. and
Eliza S. FORD, in Phila, 30 Sep 1853,
aged 3 yrs (DG 7 Oct 1853)

FOREMAN, Albert, to NICHOLSON, Jane,
Miss, in Wilm, 6 Apr 1848, by Rev. M. J.
Rhees (DG 25 Apr 1848)

FOREMAN, Cassar, dau of John
FOREMAN, 10 Oct 1848, aged 3 yrs
(DG 17 Oct 1848)

FOREMAN, Ellen D.,
see STIDHAM, Jonas B.

FOREMAN, John, see FOREMAN, Cassar

FOREMAN, Mary A.,
see FLOYD, Wm. H.

FOREMAN, Samuel R., in Wilm,
12 Jan 1853, aged 7 yrs 7 mos 1 day
(DG 28 Jan 1853)

FOREST, Anne, see CRAWFORD, Wm. W.

FORMAN, Elizabeth, see WAY, Joseph C.

FORMAN, John, in Christiana Hd,
14 Apr 1850, aged 60 yrs (DG 23 Apr 1850)

FORMAN, John, the Rev., of Georgetown,
DE, to RICHARDS, Elizabeth, Mrs , of
Worcester Co, MD, 24 May 1821, by the
Rev. Wm. M. Stone (DG 1 Jun 1821)

FORMAN, Mary,
see PORTER, Alexander, Esq.

FORMAN, Thomas Marsh,
see PORTER, Alexander, Esq.

FORREST, Martha, see WHITE, William

FORREST, Mary, see RUSSELL, George

FORREST, William, to PARVIS, Margaret,
Miss, 29 Oct 1835, by Rev. H. Adams,
rector of Trinity Ch (DG 3 Nov 1835)

FORRESTER, Alexander, Dr., dec'd, notice
given by Catharine FORRESTER and Clara
FORRESTER, adm'xes (DG 24 May 1817)

FORRESTER, Catharine,
see FORRESTER, Alexander

FORRESTER, Clara,
see FORRESTER, Alexander

FORWARD, Margaret, see PHILLIPS, Lewis

FORWOOD, Amer G., to MILLER, Mary E.,
Miss, of Brandywine Hd, at the res. of Mr.
Joseph MILLER, 18 Mar 1852, by Rev.
Andrew Manship (DG 23 Mar 1852)

FORWOOD, Jehu, see GUEST, Henry

FORWOOD, Valentine, to WELDIN,
Hannah, Miss, both of Brandywine Hd,
in Wilm, 14 Jun 1829, by the Rev. Isaac
Pardee (DG 19 Jun 1829)

FOSTER, Cathrine Mary, inf dau of John
and Mary FOSTER (DG 10 Nov 1848)

FOSTER, Ebben H., son of Hiram FOSTER,
20 Jul 1848, aged 15 mos (DG 8 Aug 1848)

FOSTER, Hiram, see FOSTER, Ebben H.

FOSTER, Hiram E., to KIRKPATRICK,
Mary, 16 Jul 1846, in Wilm (DG 24 Jul 1846)

FOSTER, John,
see FOSTER, Cathrine Mary
see FOSTER, Mary

FOSTER, Mary,
see FOSTER, Cathrine Mary

FOSTER, Mary E., see BECK, Edward

FOSTER, Mary, wife of John FOSTER,
proprietor of the Indian Queen Hotel, in Wilm,
16 Dec 1851, in her 53rd yr
(DG 19 Dec 1851)

FOSTER, Ruth Ann, see ROSE, David

FOSTER, William, of Queen Anne's Co, MD,
to DOWNES, Mary Emeline, Miss, of NC Co,
DE, at the res. of Mrs. Mary SIMMONS, near
Christiana, 9 Nov 1824, by the Rev. Mr.
Holdick of New Castle (DG 12 Nov 1824)

FOUGERAY, Henry J., of Phila to MILBY,
Sarah, Miss, dau of Arthur MILBY, Esq.,
of Milton DE, 25 Oct 1827, by the
Rev. William Torbert (DG 30 Oct 1827)

FOULK, Ann E., see KING, John A.

FOULK, Candace, see CURRY, John

FOULK, Elizabeth, see SINEX, Thomas

FOULK, Jacob, see FOULK, William

FOULK, John, to STOREY, Elizabeth, Miss,
all of NC Co, 15 Mar 1821, by the Rev.
Richard D. Hall (DG 23 Mar 1821)
see FOULK, William

FOULK, Mary Emma, 10 Mar 1847,
in her 11th yr (DG 16 Mar 1847)

FOULK, Mary P., see JONES, Abraham S.

FOULK, Stephen, to CLOUD, Priscilla, Miss,
of Delaware Co, PA, 15 Mar 1821, by the
Rev. Richard D. Hall (DG 20 Mar 1821)

FOULK, William,
see CARTMELL, Thomas

FOULK, William, dec'd, late of NC Co,
notice given by John FOULK and Jacob
FOULK, adm'rs (DG 27 Mar 1819)

FOULKE, John, to JACKSON, Candice,
Miss, in Wilm, 22 Jan 1807, by the Rev.
Mr. Pryce (MU 24 Jan 1807)

FOUNTAIN, Rebecca Jane,
see CHEPPINS, John L.

FOUNTAIN, Sally Ann, see ADAMS, William

FOWLER, Ann, see LOFLAND, Edward C.

FOWLER, Elias B., of Kent Co, to BETTS,
Sarah A., of Sussex Co, in Milford,
2 Jan 1851, by the Rev. T. P. McColley
(DG 14 Jan 1851)

FOWLER, James, of Wilm, to WILLIAMS,
Mary, Miss, of Phila, in Phila, 11 Nov 1828,
by John Shaw, Esq. (DG 21 Nov 1828)

FOWLER, Susan, 18 Aug 1850, in her 62nd
yr (DG 27 Aug 1850)

FOWLER, Thos., to LYNCH, Margaret,
Miss, both of Kent Co, nmd, by the Rev.
T. P. McColley (DG 8 Mar 1853)

FOWLER, William M., of Chestertown, MD,
to STROUP, Eliza, Miss, of Christiana, DE, at
Wilm, 29 May 1834, by Rev. Joseph Rusling

(DG 3 Jun 1834)

FOX, Aaron, of Del. Co PA, to SMITH, Sarah E., of DE, 27 Oct 1847, by J. P. Haines, Esq. (DG 16 Nov 1847)

FOX, Anne Maria,
see STEPHENS, George W.

FOX, Cecilia M., see McINALL, Edward

FOX, Eliza, see GARRETSON, Henry G.

FOX, Emily A., see GEAR, William H.

FOX, James, Jr., of Wilm, to HEUSEMAN, Letitia, S., Miss, youngest dau of Daniel HEUSEMAN, Esq., of Phila, in Phila 10 Jul 1849, by the Rev. J. C. Clay, DD (DG 24 Jul 1849)

FOX, James, see STEPHENS, George W.

FOX, Lewis, see SULLIVAN, John

FOX, Sophia E., see SULLIVAN, John

FOX, Thomas, to LOWBER, Catherine R., Miss, both of Wilm, 27 Nov 1851, by the Rev. Mr. Cosgrove (DG 2 Dec 1851)

FRAME, Anna, see DAVIS, Robert

FRAME, Elizabeth,
see WILLIAMS, Nathaniel

FRAME, George, Esq., one of the best practical land surveyors in the US, at his res. near Millsboro, 13 Sept 1845, aged 48 yrs (DG 7 Oct 1845)
see WILSON, Manlove D.

FRAME, Jeanette, Mrs, relict of the late Robert FRAME, and dau of Hon Thomas CLAYTON, late a U. S. Senator from DE, at her res. on King St., , of consumption, 12 Jul 1848 (DG 14 Jul 1848)

FRAME, Mary Y., see WILSON, Manlove D.

FRAME, Robert, Esq., from Dover, one of our most distinguished lawyers, 19 Mar 1847, aged c 47 yrs (DG 23 Mar 1847)
FRAME, Robert, see FRAME, Jeanette

FRAME, Ruth Ann, see CULLEY, Wm.

FRAME, Samuel, of Kennett, Chester Co, to STOKES, Ann Elizabeth, Miss, of NC Co, 5 May 1853, in W. Chester, by the Rev. C. Karsner (DG 13 May 1853)

FRAME, Thomas, to FORD, Mary, Miss, both of Chester Co PA, 27 Jan 1847, by Rev. A. Atwood (DG 29 Jan 1847)

FRANCE, G. W., Dr., of Balt, to GLASS, Mary J, Miss, of Wilm, at Wheeling VA, 16 Nov 1853, by Rev. Wm. Armstrong (DG 24 Nov 1853)

FRANCE, Mary Virginia,
see BOULDEN, Jas. E. P.

FRANCE, Richard, Capt,
see BOULDEN, E. P.

FRANCES, Sarah, dau of William S. FRANCES, 3 May 1848, in Phila (DG 16 May 1848)

FRANCES, William S.,
see FRANCES, Sarah

FRANCIS, Alfred, Esq., of NC Co, after a protracted illness, at the res. of his mother-in-law in Phila, 24 Jan 1842, aged 27 yrs (DG 28 Jan 1842)

FRANCIS, Anne,
see BAYARD, James Ashton

FRANCIS, Henry, to LAIN, Mary, Miss, dau of Mr. James LAIN, both of Wilm, in Phila, 30 May 1852, by Rev. John Ruth (DG 4 Jun 1852)

FRANCIS, Mary, see RATCLIFF, Samuel

FRANCIS, Thomas Willing,
see BAYARD, James Ashton

FRANCIS, William, to HANKINS, Abigail, both of Appoq. Hd, at Cantwells Bridge, 11 Nov 1851, by the Rev. H. R. Harrold (DG 21 Nov 1851)

FRANCISCUS, Ada Blanche,
see BARNEY, William Chase

FRANK, Auston F., to HARMAN, Rosanna, Miss, all of Wilm, in Baltimore, 20 Apr 1846, by Rev. S. A. Roszel (DG 28 Apr 1846)

FRANKLIN, Emily,
see DARLINGTON, Emily

FRANKLIN, _____, Judge,
see DARLINGTON, Emily

FRANKLIN, Walter, Rev.
see DARLINGTON, Emily

FRARY, Emily Eliza,
see WOODWALL, Allen

FRAZER, Albert, son of James FRAZER, at New Castle, 9 Feb 1835, aged 4 yrs 4 mos 14 days (DG 20 Feb 1835)

FRAZER, Ann, Miss, in Wilm, 5 Apr 1843 (DG 7 Apr 1843)

FRAZER, Elizabeth V.,
see FRAZER, Hannah
see WOODS, John

FRAZER, Hannah, late of St. Georges Hd, dec'd, notice given by Elizabeth V. FRAZER, adm'x (DG 6 May 1825)

FRAZER, James,
see FRAZER, Albert
see FRAZER, William,

FRAZER, John, to STIDHAM, Ingebur, Miss, both of Wilm, in Wilm, 26 Mar 1833, by the Rev. E. W. Gilbert (DG 29 Mar 1833)
see FRAZER, Rebecca

FRAZER, Rebecca, 2nd dau of John FRAZER, Esq., at Elm Cottage, res. of her father near Dover, 7 Jun 1847, aged 19 yrs (DG 29 Jun 1847)

FRAZER, William, Esq., dec'd, late of New Castle, notice to present claims to Evan Thomas, Register, New Castle, or Pennel Corbitt, of Cantwell's Bridge, given by William C. FRAZER, adm'r (AW 14 Mar 1818)

FRAZER, William, son of Mr. James FRAZER, in New Castle, 25 or 26 Feb 1835, aged 23 yrs (DG 3 Mar 1835)

FRAZER, William C.,
see FRAZER, William, Esq.

FRAZIER, _____, Dr.,
see FRAZIER, Richard A.

FRAZIER, Hannah, dec'd, late of St. Georges Hd, shff's sale (DG 11 May 1827)

FRAZIER, John, near Dover, 29 Nov 1850, aged c 55 yrs (DG 6 Dec 1850) Esq., long obit, no dates or places (DG 10 Jan 1851)
see SPRUANCE, Enoch Jr.

FRAZIER, Mary Elizabeth,
see SPRUANCE, Enoch Jr.

FRAZIER, Richard A., son of Dr. FRAZIER, Kent Co MD, to BIDDLE, Mary Alexina Josephine, Miss, only dau of Alexander M. BIDDLE, at her father's res. near St. Georges, 11 Dec 1850, by Rev. N. Patterson (DG 13 Dec 1850)

FRED, Benjamin, of Wilm, to PATTERSON, Mary, Miss, of Upper Penn's Neck, NJ, 7 Nov 1821, by the Rev. William Biddle (DG 16 Nov 1821)

FREDD, Lydia, see JOHNSON, Elias

FREEMAN, Amos, to CLINTON, Hannah, Miss, at Christiana Bridge, 23 Nov 1809, by Rev. Mr. Pryce of Wilm (DG 25 Nov 1809)

FREEMAN, John, of Phila, to CRONSBERRY, Mary, Miss of NC Co, 21 Mar 1842, in Trinity Church by Rev. J. W. McCullough (DG 8 Apr 1842)

FREEMAN, John, to ROBINSON, Mary Jane, Miss, 9 Oct 1841, by Rev. S. M. Gayley, all of Wilm (DG 29 Oct 1841)

FREEZE, Edward M, to MORROW, Sarah A., Miss, both of Wilm, in Phila, 29 Apr 1852, by the Rev. E. Miller (DG 4 May 1852)

FREEZE, Jefferson, of Pottsville PA, to JONES, Sarah J., dau of John JONES of NC Co, 18 May 1847, by Rev. Thomas H. Stockton (DG 25 May 1847)

FREEZE, Lydia, see HAZLITT, James A.

FREEZE, Sarah, see ROSSELL, William

FRENCH, A. J., of New Orleans LA, merchant, to PORTER, Permelia C., Miss, youngest dau of Alexander PORTER, Esq., 24 Jul 1845, in Wilm, by Rev. Mr. Hogarth (DG 25 Jul 1845)

FRENCH, David, Esq., late of New Castle. Notice given by John FINNEY and John LEGATE, exec'rs (PG 20 Jan 1742-3)

FRENCH, Elizabeth L., Mrs.,
see LITHERBURY, William H.

FRENCH, Mary, Mrs., in Wilm, 20 Mar 1848, in her 56th yr (DG 28 Mar 1848)

FRENCH, Mary Jane,
see WILLIAMSON, William P.

FRICK, Charles F., of Phila, to MILLS, Charlotte Ann, dau of Mr. Allen MILLS of Wilm, in Phila, 3 Sep 1833, by the Rev. James Montgomery, D. D. (DG 6 Sep 1833)

FRIEL, Daniel, see RICE, Robert

FRIES, H. C., Rev., of Frankford PA, to GREEN, Matilda, Miss, dau of Dr. Stephen GREEN of Laurel DE, 16 Sep 1841, by Rev. C. H. Mustard   (DG 24 Sep 1841)

FRIEZE, Christian, a wood corder, a Swede, lived in Wilm for about 50 yrs, aged 90 yrs, buried at Old Swedes (DG 3 Dec 1850)

FRIST, Catharine, see FRIST, Elizabeth

FRIST, Elizabeth, dau of Mrs. Catherine and Henry FRIST, in Wilm, 24 Jan 1853, in her 2nd yr (DG 28 Jan 1853)

FRIST, Esther Ann, see SPRINGER, Levi H.

FRIST, Henry, see FRIST, Elizabeth

FRIST, Mary, see ROBINSON, J.

FRIST, Susan, see FORD, Jeremiah

FRIST, Thos., of Balt, to HOLMS, Sarah E., of Wilm, 8 Sep 1851, by the Rev. E. R. Williams (DG 19 Sep 1851)

FROMBERG, Susan Maria, see RODNEY, Thomas M., Esq.

FRY, Elizabeth J., Miss, late of Phila, at New Castle, 14 Mar 1853, na (DG 22 Mar 1853)

FRY, Sallie L., see ALRICHS, Wm. T.

FULLERTON, James, of Baltimore, to MURPHY, Mary, Miss, of New Castle, 13 Jan 1846, in Phila, at St. John's Cath'l, by Rev. F. T. Gartland (DG 20 Jan 1846)

FULLMEAL, Andrew, to HINTON, Eliza Ann, all of Wilm, 25 Apr 1850, by Rev. Wiliam Cooper (DG 3 May 1850)

FULLMER, Anna, see SCHOTT, Nicholas

FULLMER, John, see SCHOTT, Nicholas

FULTON, James, see CHANDLER, Edward G.

FULTON, Maria, see PHILIPS, Isaac J.

FURBEE, Jacob, Esq., husband, father, at his late res. in Dover, 11 Aug 1826, aged 68 yrs (DG 29 Aug 1826)

FUREY, John S., Esq., schoolmaster, late of Phila, in Kent Co, DE, recently (DG 28 Feb 1834)

FUTCHER, Margaret L., see EBERBACH, John C.

GAFFORD, Samuel, dec'd, late of Wilm, notice given by George SIMMONS, adm'r (DG 14 Oct 1828)

GAILEY, Thomas, to BIRD, Elizabeth, Miss, both of DE, May 31 1849, by the Rev. John Street (DG 12 Jun 1849)

GAILEY, William in Wilm, 13 Jun 1848, in his 70th yr (DG 16 Jun 1848)

GAISFORD, George, to WILLIS, Mary, 26 May 1841, by Elder John Miller, all of Wilm (DG 28 May 1841)

GALAGHER, Francina Schrader, at the res. of her grandfather, Abraham SCHRADER, 3 Apr 1846, aged 4 yrs 5 mos 20 days (DG 7 Apr 1846)

GALBREATH, Jacob, late of Christiana Hd, in Brandywine Hd, 23 July 1848, in his 79th yr (DG 1 Aug 1848)

GALBREATH, James F., see NORMAN, Emily A.;

GALBREATH, Robert, to JACKSON, Rebecca, Miss, both of Brandywine Hd, 22 May 1828, by Elder John P. Peckworth (DG 27 May 1828)

GALBREATH, Samuel, to McCLINTOCK, Eliza, Miss, both of Brandywine Hd, in Wilm, 20 Apr 1825, by the Rev. E. W. Gilbert (DG 22 Apr 1825)

GALBREATH, Samuel, of Muskingum Co OH, but formerly of DE, in Bedford Co PA, while on the way to DE to see his friends, 26 May 1852, in his 55th yr (DG 11 Jun 1852)

GALE, Isaac, Jr., to ENOS, Mary Jane, Miss, of Millington and formerly of Smyrna, in Millington, 27 Sep 1849, by the Rev. Mr. Townsend (DG 12 Oct 1849)

GALIGNA, Mary, see WILLS, Henry

GALLAGHER, Alice Ann, see ROBERTS, Hugh

GALLAGHER, Charles H., to WILSON, Rebecca, H., Miss, all of Wilm, 9 Apr 1846, by Rt. Rev. Alfred Lee in St. Andrew's Ch. (DG 14 Apr 1846)

GALLAGHER, David, Dr., a native of DE, at New Washington, Galveston Bay, TX, 24 Jan 1851 (DG 28 Mar 1851)

GALLAGHER, Mary Ann, see DEAKYNE, Peter S.

GALLAGHER, Thomas, to MATHEWSON, Margaret J., Miss, both of Brandywine, in Wilm, 4 May 1848, by Rev. S. M. Gayley (DG 9 May 1848)

GALLASPIE (sic), _____, Major, dec'd, late of Mill Creek Hd, notice given by Joseph DERRICKSON, adm'r (DG 6 May 1834)

GALLAWAY, John W., to WILLIAMSON, Mary S., Miss, both of Wilm, 27 Jun 1847, by Rev. S. R. Wynkoop (DG 13 Jul 1847)

GALLAWAY, Martha Jane, see SIMPSON, James A.

GALLUP, Charles, Esq., of NC Co, at the res. of his son on Spesutia Island, Harford Co, MD, 9 Nov 1826, aged 70 yrs; descendant of early settlers of New England (DG 1 Dec 1826)

GAMBLE, Catharine, see AMES, Stillman

GAMBLE, Elizabeth, widow, in NC Co, near Centreville, 27 Dec 1850, in her 71st yr. Born in Ireland, Res'd in NC Co c 40 yrs, Presb. (DG 10 Jan 1851) late of Christiana Hd, James DELAPLAIN and John ARMSTRONG, exec'rs (DG 4 Feb 1851)

GAMBLE, James, dec'd, late of Port Penn, notice given by John AIKEN, adm'r (DE 10 May, 13 Jun 1796)

GAMBLE, John, see McCONNELL, Mary

GAMBLE, Rebecca, see SMITH, Louis

GAMBLE, Robert M., see SMITH, Louis

GANBY, William, boy, of yellow fever (DE 20 Sep 1798)

GANT, John, see WARNER, Mary

GARDEN, Anna M., see GARDEN, William R.

GARDEN, Francis R., of Pine Grove, Brandywine Hd, to WALDIE, Annie E., Miss, eldest dau of the late Adam WALDIE, Esq., of Phila, at the First Unitarian Church, Phila, 13 Apr 1848, by Rev. William H. Furness (DG 25 Apr 1848)

GARDEN, W. A., Dr., of Wilm, to MOULDER, Hannah W., dau of the late John N. MOULDER, of Washington DC, in Wilm, 1 Oct 1850, by Rev. W. Blackwood (DG 8 Oct 1850)

GARDEN, William, see GARDEN, William R.

GARDEN, William R., inf son of Dr. William and Anna M GARDEN, at the res. of his parents, Pinegrove, Brandywine Hd, 26 Jul 1852, aged 5 mos 10 days (DG 30 Jul 1852)

GARDINER, Rachel M., see HAMBBLETON, Alexander

GARDNER, _____, Mrs., wife of James GARDNER, merchant of Wilm, 25 Aug 1823 (DG 26 Aug 1823)

GARDNER, George, former auctioneer in Wilm, died in Covington KY, a few weeks ago of cholera (DG 2 Aug 1850)

GARDNER, George W., Esq., see GARDNER, Thomas T.

GARDNER, James, at his res. near Wilm, 26 Sep 1844, aged 68 yrs (DG 1 Oct 1844) see FLEMING, John see GARDNER, _____

GARDNER, James S., of Wilm, to BENDER, Mary Ellen, Miss, of Camden NJ, 22 Sep 1945, by Rev. Edward H. Thomas (DG 3 Oct 1845)

GARDNER, John M., see GARDNER, Rebecca A.

GARDNER, Mary Ann, Mrs., wife of Robert W. GARDNER and dau of Thomas RUMFORD, all of Wilm DE, in Logan Co IL, 24 Feb 1852, aged 44 yrs (DG 9 Mar 1852)

GARDNER, Rebecca A., inf dau of John M. and Rebecca GARDNER, 22 Jul 1848 (DG 28 Jul 1848)

GARDNER, Robert W., see GARDNER, Mary Ann

GARDNER, Thomas T., inf son of George W. GARDNER, Esq., 19 Oct 1841, in Wilm (DG 22 Oct 1841)

GARESCHE, J. P., see CLYMER, Meredith see CLYMER, Virginia

GARESCHE, Virginia, see CLYMER, Virginia

GARESCHE, Virginia M., see CLYMER, Meredith

GARESCHE, Vital M, late of St. Louis and formerly a res. of Wilm, in Havana, 4 Apr 1844 (DG 26 Apr 1844)

GARLAND, Mary, see McFARLIN, Wm. W. see TURNER, John N.

GARLAND, Rebecca, see TRUMAN, Thomas

GARRET, David, of Cecil Co MD, to WILSON, Catharine, of NC Co, 8 Aug 1850, by Rev. Charles H. Plummer (DG 22 Oct 1850)

GARRET, Sarah Ann, see WILKINSON, Nathan

GARRET, Thomas, to MENDINHALL, Rachel, both of Wilm, at Friends Meeting Hall, West St, 7 Jan 1830 (DG 12 Jan 1830)

GARRET, William, see WILKINSON, Nathan

GARRETSON, Charles, formerly of York, PA, to NEALIS, Anne E., Miss, of Wilm, at Marcus Hook PA, 10 Feb 1850, by Rev. Theophilus Jones (DG 19 Feb 1850)

GARRETSON, Cornelius L., of Wilm, to RUPP, Catharine E., dau of Daniel RUPP, 3 Oct 1844, in York PA by Rev. H. Douglass (DG 18 Oct 1844)

GARRETSON, Cornelius L, in Wilm,
10 Mar 1848, of typhoid fever
(DG 14 Mar 1848)

GARRETSON, Elizabeth,
see GARRETSON, Rebecca Martin

GARRETSON, Elizabeth M., wife of William
GARRETSON and dau of the late Thomas
MOORE, 9 Dec 1852, na (DG 14 Dec 1852)

GARRETSON, Henry, dec'd, late of
Newport, DE, notice given by John L.
MORRIS, adm'r (DG 12 Jul 1833)

GARRETSON, Henry G., of Wilm, to FOX,
Eliza, of Schuylkill Co PA, 23 May 1853, by
the Rev. J. B. Maddux (DG 31 May 1853)

GARRETSON, Jacob M., of Wilm to TILL,
Catharine, Miss, of Phila, 21 May 1851, by
the Rev. Joseph Castle (DG 6 Jun 1851)
see GARRETSON, Mary Ann

GARRETSON, James B., to FOPPLES,
Elizabeth, Miss, formerly of Wilm, in Phila,
7 May 1834, by the Rev. Mr. Wiltbanks
(DG 13 May 1834)

GARRETSON, Leonard, in Wilm, 26 May
1846 (DG 29 May 1846)

GARRETSON, Mary Ann, Mrs, wife of Jacob
M. GARRETSON, in Wilm, of consumption,
19 Jul 1850, aged 45 yrs 7 mos
(DG 26 Jul 1850)

GARRETSON, Rebecca Martin, dau of
William and Elizabeth GARRETSON, at
Wilm, 30 Jul 1852, aged 11 mos 5 days
(DG 27 Aug 1852)

GARRETSON, Susanna,
see ZIMMERMAN, Charles W.

GARRETSON, William, to MOORE,
Elizabeth, Miss, dau of Thomas MOORE,
25 Apr 1850, by Rev. A. Lee
(DG 30 Apr 1850)
see GARRETSON, Elizabeth M.
see GARRETSON, Rebecca Martin

GARRETT, Anna, see SMITH, John D.

GARRETT, Anna M.,
see EDWARDS, J., Dr.

GARRETT, Gideon M., to MOORE,
Margaret, Miss, 15 Mar 1807, in Wilm,
by the Rev. Mr. Pryce (MU 21 Mar 1807)

GARRETT, Henry, to CANBY, Caroline A.,
all of Wilm, 7 May 1846, according to the
order of the Society of Friends
(DG 12 May 1846)

GARRETT, Horatio, see GARRETT, John

GARRETT, John, dec'd, late of Christiana
Hd, notice given by Levi GARRETT and
Horatio GARRETT, exec'rs
(MU 14 Jan 1809)

GARRETT, Levi, see GARRETT, John

GARRETT, Margaret M.,
see McCOLLIN, James G.

GARRETT, Sarah S.,
see HEWES, Edward C.

GARRETT, Thomas,
see EDWARDS, J., Dr
see HEWES, Sarah G.
see McCOLLIN, James G.
see WEBB, Benjamin

GARRETT, Wm. A., formerly of Balt, to
GUYER, Mary Elizabeth, Miss, of Wilm, in
Wilm, 31 Mar 1853, by the Rev. Mr. Pollock
(DG 26 Apr 1853)

GARRISH, Mary A., see VARE, Japhet

GARRISON, Charles, to JOHNSON,
Sarah Ann, Miss, of Phila, in Baltimore,
19 Nov 1846, by Rev. James G. Hamner
(DG 24 Nov 1846)

GARY, Philip, at his res. in Smyrna,
30 Jan 1853, aged 50 yrs (DG 8 Feb 1853)

GATCHELL, David, Jr., at his res. in Oxford,
Chester Co PA, 10 Nov 1852, aged 30 yrs
(DG 19 Nov 1852)

GATHONY, Peter, see BROOM, Thomas

GAULT, Emma, see BARNEY, Alexander

GAUNT, John, in Wilm, of typhoid,
17 Aug 1848, aged 69 (DG 18 Aug 1848)

GAUNT, John, at his late res. in French St,
between 4th and 5th, 20 Aug 1849, na
(DG 28 Aug 1849)

GAUNT, Mersa A., see LODGE, John W.

GAUNT, Samuel J., see LODGE, John W.

GAUSE, Harlan, at his res. near Kennett Sq.,
10 Apr 1852, aged 59 yrs
(DG 16 Apr 1852)

GAUSE, Jesse, see HESTON, Newton

GAUSE, John T., to FLINN, Martha J., both
of Wilm, 27 Jan 1848, by Rev. J. Castle
(DG 4 Feb 1848)

GAUSE, Martha Johnson,
see HESTON, Newton

GAUSE, Washington, of Brandywine Hd, to SMITH, Rebecca R., of Wilm, 7 Jan 1847, by Rev. A. Atwood (DG 15 Jan 1847)

GAUZE, O. B., of Wilm, to POWELL, H. M., Miss, of Salem Co NJ, 27 Apr 1848 (DG 16 May 1848)

GAW, Chambers, at the res. of Dr. SUTTON in St. Georges, 14 Oct 1844, aged 84 yrs. Served during the Revolution (DG 18 Oct 1844)

GEAR, William H., to FOX, Emily A., Miss, both of Wilm, at Jones Red Lion Hotel, Phila, 1 Nov 1848, by Rev. Mr. Cuyler (DG 10 Nov 1848)

GEBHART, Benjamin F., to MONTGOMERY, Margaret Ann, Miss, both of Mill Creek Hd, in Phila, 21 Jul 1847, by Rev. H. Bibighause (DG 30 Jul 1847)

GEDDES, George H., Capt., 4 May 1846, in Wilm (DG 8 May 1846)

GEDDES, Henry, Capt., Inspector of Revenue for Port Penn, in Port Penn, 30 Nov 1833, at an advanced age (DG 3 Dec 1833) (Obit, 13 Dec)

GEDDES, Jane, see SHOEMAKER, Charles

GEDDES, Rachel, see KING, James

GEDDES, Susan, see THOMAS, Tristram

GEDDES, William, see THOMAS, Tristram

GEMMELL, Eliza, wife of Hugh GEMMELL, at the res. of her husband in New Castle Hd, 7 Feb 1826, na (DG 14 Feb 1826)

GEMMELL, Hugh, see GEMMELL, Eliza

GEMMIL, David W., see GEMMIL, Elizabeth Hamilton

GEMMIL, Elizabeth A., see GEMMIL, Elizabeth Hamilton

GEMMIL, Elizabeth Hamilton, dau of Elizabeth A. and David W. GEMMIL, at the res. of her parents in N C Hd, of scarlet fever, 30 Jan 1849, in her 3rd yr (DG 6 Feb 1849)

GEMMILL, Ann E., see PLATT, George, Esq.,

GEMMILL, Catharine, see BORDLEY, Catharine

GEMMILL, Hugh, Capt., 6 Dec 1822 (DG 10 Dec 1822)
see BORDLEY, Catharine
see GEMMILL, Jane, Mrs.

see PLATT, George, Esq.,

GEMMILL, Hugh, of NC Co, to HODGSON, Eliza, Miss, dau of James B. HODGSON, Esq., Chester Co, PA, 15 Feb 1825, by the Rev. Mr. Robert Graham (DG 22 Feb 1825)

GEMMILL, Jane, Mrs., relict of the late Capt. Hugh GEMMILL, at Newark, DE, 17 Aug 1826, aged 54 yrs (DG 25 Aug 1826)

GEMMILL, Margaret Ann, late wife of Dr. William M. GEMMILL, and dau of John SUTTON, Esq., of St. Georges DE, 8 Jan 1847, at her res. in Kennard's Point, Eastern Shore of MD, in her 41st year (DG 12 Jan 1847)

GEMMILL, William M., see GEMMILL, Margaret Ann

GEORGE, _____. Mr., see COLE, Henry

GEORGE, Jonathan E., to McMULLEN, Sarah, all of NC Co, 7 Jan 1851, by Rev. J. G. Callom (DG 7 Jan 1851)

GEORGE, Mary Ellen, see COLE, Henry

GEORGE, Rachel T., see GRIFFIN, Jno. R.

GEST, Abraham, see GEST, Samuel D.

GEST, Elizabeth, in Christiana Hd, near Wilm, 4 Jul 1850 (DG 9 Jul 1850)

GEST, Samuel D., dec'd, late of Wilm, notice given by Abraham GEST, adm'r (MU 30 May 1807)

GEST, William, to GRUBB, Rebecca, Miss, all of Brandywine Hd, 5 Sep 1847, by Rev. John B. Clemson (DG 17 Sep 1847)

GETTY, Eliza, see RICKETTS, P. C.

GETTY, John A., see RICKETTS, P. C.

GIBBINS, Elizabeth, see TOWNSEND, Washington

GIBBINS, William, see TOWNSEND, Washington

GIBBONS, Caroline, see TATTNALL, Henry L.
see STUART, James

GIBBONS, Edward, of Contra Costa, formerly of Wilm, to BARR, Catharine Forester, eldest dau of Joseph BARR of Newark, 20 Oct 1852, on board the steamer *Golden Gate* at San Francisco CA (DG 3 Dec 1852)

GIBBONS, Francis Turpin, late of Seaford,

son of the late Dr. John GIBBONS, at Monterey, Alta, CA, 21 Nov 1849, aged 34 yrs (DG 26 Feb 1850)

GIBBONS, John,
see **GIBBONS**, Francis Turpin
see **GIBBONS**, Washington M.

GIBBONS, Mary T.,
see **TAYLOR**, Edward W.

GIBBONS, Rebecca,
see **BEACH**, John Sheldon

GIBBONS, Sarah Ellan, Miss,
see **THOMPSON**, James

GIBBONS, Washington M., son of the late John GIBBONS, M. D., at Seaford DE, 14 Aug 1844, aged 25 yrs (DG 10 Sep 1844)

GIBBONS, William,
see **THOMPSON**, James
see **BEACH**, John Sheldon

GIBBS, Eliza Jane, see **SILTER**, William Jr.

GIBERSON, Mary,
see **PENNINGTON**, James

GIBSON, Ann Jane. see **TAYLOR**, Robert

GIBSON, James, baker, of Wilm, 10 Sep 1827, na (DG 11 Sep 1827) notice given by John GORDON, adm'r (DG 9 Oct 1827)

GIBSON, James, M. D., of Chester Co PA, to **MACKEY**, Sarah Ann, Miss, of Wilm, 9 Jun 1846, by Rev. S. R. Wynkoop (DG 16 Jun 1846)

GIBSON, William H., to **CONSTABLE**, Mary Jane, Miss, of Baltimore, 13 Aug 1850, by Rev. P. Coker (DG 20 Aug 1850)

GIFFEN, James, see **GIFFIN**, James

GIFFEN, Mary, see **GIFFIN**, James

GIFFER, Ruth, Miss, see **CLESS**, E. W.

GIFFIN, Hannah S., see **JONES**, David T.

GIFFIN, James, near Mt. Pleasant, in Mill Creek Hd, 11 Mar 1852, aged c 60 yrs (DG 16 Mar 1852) late of Mill Creek Hd, Mary and James GIFFEN exec'rs (DG 23 Mar 1852)

GIFFIN, Mary Ann, see **KIRKMAN**, John

GIFFIN, Rachel, see **KENNARD**, William

GIFFING, Harriet, dau of Thomas and Sarah GIFFING, in Wilm, 19 Feb 1850, aged c 11 yrs (DG 22 Feb 1850)

GIFFING, Sarah, see **GIFFING**, Harriet

GIFFING, Susanna, Mrs, formerly of Wilm, at the res. of her son-in-law, John HARRIS in Manayunk PA, 6 Jun 1850, aged 80 yrs (DG 14 Jun 1850)

GIFFING, Thomas, see **GIFFING**, Harriet

GILBERT, ___, Rev. Dr.,
see **WRIGHT**, Mary G.
see **CRAWFORD**, J. A.

GILBERT, E. W., D. D., Rev., pres. of Del College, to **SINGER**, Mary Ann, Miss, dau of the late John SINGER, Esq., of Phila, 16 Dec 1844, by Rev. Thomas F. Bradford (DG 24 Dec 1844)

GILBERT, Joseph S., late of Mill Creek Hd, Eli MOTE, exec'r (DG 10 Aug 1852)

GILBERT, Mary
see **WRIGHT**, Mary G.

GILBERT, Mary Ann, in Mill Creek Hd, aged 30 yrs (DG 17 Jan 1851)

GILBERT, Susie Munro,
see **CRAWFORD**, J. A.

GILDERSLEEVE, George, merchant, at his res. in Canterbury, of consumption, 11 Oct 1828, aged 27 yrs; leaves a wife, son, brother...(DG 21 Oct 1828)

GILFREY, Sarah Elizabeth Fisher,
see **GILL**, John R.

GILL, George, see **GILL**, James

GILL, James, son of George GILL, 4 Aug 1847, aged 4 yrs (DG 10 Aug 1847)

GILL, John R., to **GILFREY**, Sarah Elizabeth Fisher, all of NC Co, in St. Ann's Ch, Middletown, 23 Mar 1852, by Rev. H. R. Harrold (DG 26 Mar 1852)

GILL, Joseph, to **SPRINGER**, Rebecca, Miss, both of NC Co, 13 Dec 1821, at Mr. John Plumley's Hotel, by the Rev. Richard D. Hall (DG 18 Dec 1821)

GILL, Joseph B., Esq., of Gloster (sic) Co NJ, to **KNIGHT**, Hannah W., of Wilm, in Balt, 16 Apr 1861, by Rev. Wm. Hirst (DG 22 Apr 1851)

GILL, Rachel, see **POGUE**, David

GILL, Thomas, Sr., formerly of DE, at St. Mary's, New Brunswick, 17 Jul 1833, aged 77 yrs (DG 7 Aug 1833)

GILLAM, Simon, see **MARRIOTT**, Sarah

GILLES, Elizabeth T., see **GILLES**, Mary

GILLES, John P., see **GILLES**, Mary

GILLES, Mary, dau of John P. and Elizabeth T. GILLES, 20 Jul 1851, aged 3 yrs (DG 22 Jul 1851)

GILLESPIE, Elexene Adkins, wife of Thos. GILLESPIE, 20 Oct 1852, aged 29 yrs (DG 26 Oct 1852)

GILLESPIE, Elizabeth, see **HODGSON**, James

GILLESPIE, George, see **EVES**, William D.

GILLESPIE, Mary, see **EVES**, William D.

GILLESPIE, Thomas, of Newark, to **EVES**, Mary C., Miss, of Wilm, in Wilm, 6 Aug 1833, by the Rev. E. W. Gilbert (DG 9 Aug 1833)

GILLESPIE, Thos., see **GILLESPIE**, Elexene

GILLESPY, George, Maj., to **HANNAH**, Sarah, Mrs., both of the vicinity of Newark, DE, 15 Mar 1829, by the Rev. J. J. Hagany (DG 27 Mar 1829)

GILLETT, Hannah, Mrs, wife of Ignatius GILLETT, of Wilm, 16 Dec 1846, aged 32 yrs (DG 15 Dec 1846)

GILLETT, Ignatius, see **GILLETT**, Hannah

GILLINGHAM, Ann, see **GILPIN**, John F.

GILLINGHAM, Joseph, see **GILPIN**, John F.

GILLINGHAM, Robert, of Phila, to **BONNEY**, Maria D., Miss, of Wilm, in Wilm, 25 Oct 1848, by Rev. M. J. Rhees (DG 27 Oct 1848)

GILLIS, John P., Lt. US Navy, to **TATNALL**, Elizabeth, dau of Edward TATNALL, Brandywine, 7 Dec 1841, in Wilm, by N. G. Williamson, Mayor (DG 10 Dec 1841)

GILMORE, Anne, see **MEEKINGS**, Jesse

GILMORE, James, to **DINGEE**, Eliza , Miss, "Thursday evening last" [1 Nov 1821], by the Rev. L. Lawrence (DG 6 Nov 1821)

GILPIN, ____, Atty-general, see **WOLLASTON**, Joshua H.

GILPIN, Abigail, see **WOOLWORTH**, Richard C.

GILPIN, Charles L., formerly of Wilm, to **WADDINGTON**, Mary Elizabeth, dau of Wm. WADDINGTON, Esq., all of St Louis MO, in Christ Ch. St Louis, 28 Jan 1852, by the Rt. Rev. Bishop Hawks (DG 13 Feb 1852)

GILPIN, Edward, see **WOOLWORTH**, Richard C. see **STAPLER**, John see **MASSEY**, Elizabeth

GILPIN, Edward W., Esq., of Wilm, to **LAMMOT**, Elenora Adelaide, dau of Daniel LAMMOT, Esq., 15 Mar 1842, at Lenni, Delaware Co PA (DG 25 Mar 1842)

GILPIN, Elizabeth, see **MAURY**, Matthew, Esq.

GILPIN, Elizabeth P., wife of Henry L. GILPIN, after a short illness, 14 Jun 1850, in her 42nd yr (DG 21 Jun 1850)

GILPIN, Hannah, in Wilm, 27 Nov 1841, aged 77 yrs (DG 3 Dec 1841)

GILPIN, Henry D. of Phila, to **JOHNSON**, Eliza, of Louisiana, at Kentmere near Wilm, 3 Sep 1835, by the Rev. Mr. Adams (DG 4 Sep 1835)

GILPIN, Henry L., see **GILPIN**, Elizabeth P.

GILPIN, J. F., see **GILPIN**, Mary, Mrs.

GILPIN, John F., to **LOVERING**, Mary, Miss, in Phila, 23 Nov 1820 (DG 28 Nov 1820)

GILPIN, John F., of Wilm, to **GILLINGHAM**, Ann , dau of Joseph GILLINGHAM, of Bellevieu, near Holmesburg, at that place, 12 Jun 1833, by the Rev. George Sheets (DG 16 Jun 1833)

GILPIN, Joseph, 1 Jan 1793, aged 88 yrs 9 mos. Buried in Friends Burying Ground, leaves 9 children, 76 grandchildren and 37 greatgrandchildren (DG 3 Jan 1793)

GILPIN, Joseph C., see **NICHOLLS**, Hannah

GILPIN, Joshua, see **MAURY**, Matthew

GILPIN, Josiah H., merchant of Wilm, to **MOFFIT**, Martha T., Miss, dau of William MOFFIT, Esq., late of Kent Co, MD, dec'd, 3 Apr 1825, by the Rev. Purnell F. Smith (DG 18 Apr 1825)

GILPIN, Josiah H., formerly of Wilm, at his res. in Kent Co. MD, 13 Apr 1845, aged 48 yrs (DG 25 Apr 1845) see **GILPIN**, Sarah

GILPIN, Lydia Z., see **VAUGHAN**, John D.

GILPIN, Mary, Mrs., wife of Mr. J. F. GILPIN, grocer, in Wilm, 12 May 1824

(Cl 14 May 1824)(DG 18 May1824)

GILPIN, R. B., see **WOOD**, W. Dewees

GILPIN, Richard B., to **PORTER**, Ann R., Miss, 13 Aug 1824, by the Rev. E. W. Gilbert, all of Wlm (DG 27 Aug 1824)

GILPIN, Rosalind H., see **WOOD**, W. Dewees

GILPIN, Samuel S., formerly of Wlm, to **MORTON**, Elizabeth, Miss, dau of Thomas MORTON of Newburgh, at Newburgh, 26 Jul 1833 (DG 13 Aug 1833)

GILPIN, Sarah, wife of Josiah H. GILPIN, at her res. in Kent Co MD, 12 Apr 1845, na (DG 25 Apr 1845)

GILPIN, Thomas, 3 Mar 1853, in Phila, in his 72nd yr (DG 8 Mar 1853) see **GREATRAKE**, Lawrence

GILPIN, Vincent, see **WILLIAMS**, Peter

GILPIN, Vincent, to **ROBINSON**, Naomi, dau of Mr. Joseph ROBINSON, all of Wlm, in Phila, 14 Nov 1822, by Robert Wharton, Esq. (DG 19 Nov 1822)

GILPIN, William, to **BROWN**, Elizabeth, Miss, 8 May 1831, by Rev. J. P. Peckworth, all of Wilm (DF 14 May 1831)

GINN, _____, dau of Jacob GINN, at Harmony Mills in White Clay Creek Hd, caught in the mill's cog wheels, 2 Aug 1851, aged c 8 yrs (DG 5 Aug 1851)

GINN, Elizabeth of Pencader Hd, killed by lightning, 9 Jun 1851 (DG 13 Jun 1851)

GINN, Isaac, to **POTTER**, Elizabeth, Miss, both of Rockland, Brandywine Hd, 16 Mar 1843, at Marcus Hook PA by Rev. Mr. Daly (DG 7 Apr 1843)

GIRTLER, Lydia, see **THOMAS**, Edward

GIRVIN, Charles, young, unmarried RR engineer, native of Elkton MD, engine derailed, ran into the Brandywine, 8 Jul 1853 (DG 12 Jul 1853)

GIVEN, James, dec'd, late of Christiana Hd, notice given by Isaac STEVENSON, adm'r (FA 3 Mar 1804)

GIVEN, William, dec'd, late of NC Co, notice given by Isaac STEVENSON, adm'r (FA 3 Mar 1804)

GIVENS, Archibald, see **GIVENS**, Isabella

GIVENS, Isabella, dau of Archibald GIVENS,
in Wilm, 29 Oct 1851, of croup, in her third yr (DG 4 Nov 1851)

GLASFORD, Abel, see **ROTHERAM**, Joseph

GLASGOW, James, dec'd, late of NC Co, notice given by Isabella IRWIN, adm'x, David IRWIN, adm'r (DE 12 Mar 1798)

GLASS, Mary J., see **FRANCE**, G. W.

GLEN, Edward J., M. D., of Newark, at the res. of his brother-in-law, David LEWIS, 27 Jan 1850, in his 40th yr (DG 1 Feb 1850)

GLENN, John, to **KNIGHT**, Phebe, Miss, both of Glasgow, DE, 20 Dec 1825, by the Rev. John Sharpley (DG 30 Dec 1825)

GLOVER, Henry, of Brandywine Hd, to **HALL**, Eliza, of Chester PA, 21 Nov 1841 at Lower Chichester PA by Benjamin F. Johnson, Esq. (DG 3 Dec 1841)

GODFREY, Mary E., Mrs., wife of Nathaniel D. GODFREY and dau of Edward SHORT, near Dagsborough, 30 Dec 1850, in her 22nd yr (DG 17 Jan 1851)

GODFREY, Nathaniel D., see **GODFREY**, Mary E.

GODWIN, Daniel, see **COLLINS**, Nancy D., Mrs.

GODWIN, Nancy, see **COLLINS**, Nancy D., Mrs.

GOFORTH, John, the Rev., see **LAWRENSON**, Lawrence, the Rev.

GOLD, Elizabeth, see **CROSLEY**, Granville

GOLDEN, Sarah, see **BESSE**, John, Lieut.

GOLDSBOROUGH, Caroline, wife of Charles GOLDSBOROUGH of Wilm, died of consumption 5 May 1848, aged 67 yrs 7 mos (DG 16 May 1848)

GOLDSBOROUGH, Charles, see **GOLDSBOROUGH**, Caroline

GOLDSBOROUGH, G. W., Dr, of Seaford to **REYNOLDS**, Ann, eldest dau of the Rev. Prof. J. REYNOLDS, rector of Christ Church, Milford, 12 Aug 1841, in Phila, by Rev. John C. Clay, D. D. (DG 27 Aug 1841)

GOLDSBOROUGH, Lydia, see **COLE**, John R.

GOLT, James, at Forest Landing, 25 Jul 1853 (DG 2 Aug 1853)

GOODALL, Sarah, formerly of Wilm, at the

res. of John F. ZEBLEY, in NY, 26 Jun 1853, in her 20th yr (DG 1 Jul 1853)

GOODEN, John B., near Elkton, to
CALHOUN, Martha, Miss, of NC Co,
29 Apr 1852, by the Rev. Mr. Townsend
(DG 4 May 1852)

GOODES, Thomas A., in Phila, 22 Aug 1840, in his 24th yr (DG 28 Aug 1849)

GOODIN, John, Jr., of Phila, to
COLESBERRY, Margaret, of New Castle, 6 Nov 1827, in New Castle, by the Rev. Mr. Pressman (DG 13 Nov 1827)

GOODING, Abraham, see NOXON, Thomas

GOODLY, Jonas, of NC Co, to
HAGERROTON, Catharine N., Mrs,
(DG 2 Jan 1849)

GOODMAN, Esther S., wife of George GOODMAN and dau of the late Jesse Z. ZANE, of Wilm, 22 Aug 1853, at Niles MI, na (DG 26 Aug 1853)

GOODMAN, George,
see GOODMAN, Esther S.

GOODWIN, Alexander, to BUCKMASTER, Sarah, Miss, both of Dover, 2 Feb 1848, by Rev. T. J. Thompson (DG 8 Feb 1848)

GORDON, Betsy, see BRINKLE, John, Dr.

GORDON, Catharine,
see PRICE, James E.

GORDON, James, see GIBSON, James

GORDON, John,
see MONGES, John Armand
see O'DONALD, Martha
see PRICE, James E.,
see GIBSON, James

GORDON, Polly, Miss, 25 Sep 1793 (DG 28 Sep 1793)

GORDON, Rebecca, descendant of one of the ancient families of Delaware, widow of Robert M. GORDON, at Port Penn, 31 Jan 1844, aged 58 yrs. Leaves a mother aged 93 yrs (DG 23 Feb 1844)

GORDON, Robert M.,
see GORDON, Rebecca

GORDON, Sidnay Ann Cecilia,
see MONGES, John Armand

GORDON, William H., to MOODY, Rachel Rebecca, Miss, of PA, at the res of Mrs. BOYLE, in Phila, 10 May 1846, by Rev. Mr. Street (DG 22 May 1846)

GORGAS, Ann, wife of John GORGAS, 8 Aug 1848 (DG 8 Aug 1848)

GORGAS, John, see GORGAS, Ann

GORHAM, Eleazer S., at the res. of A. B. CRAWFORD, Esq., at Newark, 4 Aug 1850, aged 20 yrs (DG 16 Aug 1850)

GORRELL, James,
see FARQUHAR, Alexander

GORRELL, Mary,
see FARQUHAR, Alexander

GOSLIN, Lucillia, in Sourth Milford, 5 Nov 1848, aged 82 yrs (DG 10 Nov 1848)

GOSSLER, Susan, see SUTTON, James N.

GOTT, Mary Ann, see RILEY, Joseph

GOUDY, Marie,
see CLENDENIN, Samuel E.

GOULD, _____, little dau of Joseph GOULD, from burns caused by the upsetting of a fluid lamp, 6 Jan 1851, na (DG 10 Jan 1851)

GOULD, Joseph, see GOULD, _____.

GOULD, Rachel, see GOULD, Strainge

GOULD, Strainge, dec'd, late of Christiana Hd, notice given by Rachel GOULD, adm'x (DE 5 Feb1798) (DE 26 Feb 1798)

GOVER, Robert, of Baltimore, to MORRIS, Lydia L., Miss, dau of the late Capt. James P. MORRIS, formerly of Delaware, in St. Louis, 2 Aug 1846, by Rt. Rev. Bishop Harks (DG 21 Aug 1846)

GOWAN, Mary A.,
see PRETTYMAN, Thomas J.

GRAFF, Abraham, see GRAFF, Catharine

GRAFF, Catharine, formerly a res. of Lancaster Co PA, widow of the late Abraham GRAFF, near Wilm, 26 Jan 1846, aged 90 yrs. (DG 6 Feb 1846)

GRAGG, Hugh, in Wilm after a long and painful illness, 30 Mar 1850, in his 24th yr (DG 9 Apr 1850)

GRAHAM, Ann, 24 Oct 1798, on list of yellow fever victims (DG 27 Oct 1798)

GRAHAM, Ellen D., Mrs., widow of the late William S. GRAHAM, of Newark DE, in Phila, 29 Sep 1849, aged 39 yrs. Bur. in Newark (DG 5 Oct 1849)

GRAHAM, Emory, Rev., of Vernon, to
SAPP, Elizabeth, Miss, near Berrytown,
Kent Co DE, 14 May 1848, by Rev.
Richard H. Meriken (DG 16 Jun 1848)

GRAHAM, Henry, to McNATT, Mary, all of
Kent Co, 17 Feb 1853, by the Rev. Emory
GRAHAM (DG 8 Mar 1853)

GRAHAM, Mary, see HART, Geo. H.

GRAHAM, R. Montgomery, MD,
see HART, Geo. H.

GRAHAM, Sarah Ann,
see MURDOCK, James Jr.

GRAHAM, Walter S., Rev., Pres. of Del
College, to LECHE, Elizabeth E., Miss, eldest
dau of David LECHE, Esq., of Balt, 10 Jun
1852, by the Rev. Dr. Thomas Brainard
(DG 15 Jun 1852)

GRAHAM, William Henry, a native of
Vernon, DE, at St. Marks, West Florida,
6 Dec 1834, aged 18 yrs 9 mos 15 days
(DG 13 Feb 1835)

GRAHAM, William S., A. M., formerly
Principal of Newark Academy, 10 Oct 1847,
at Harrisburg (DG 12 Oct 1847)
see GRAHAM, Ellen D.

GRASSEL, Susanna, known as nurse
Grassel, 22 Dec 1848, in her 91st yr
(DG 29 Dec 1848)

GRAVES, David,
see ROBINSON, James H.

GRAVES, Eli, farmer, at his res. in Christiana
Hd, 13 Aug 1849 (DG 17 Aug 1849)
late of Wilm, Lewis GRAVES, adm'r
(DG 14 Sep 1849)

GRAVES, Lewis, see GRAVES, Eli

GRAVES, Margaret, Mrs., widow of the
late Thomas GRAVES, near Loveville DE,
31 Dec 1850, in her 68th yr
(DG 10 Jan 1851)

GRAVES, Maria P., consort of Robert
GRAVES, at the almshouse, 20 Jul 1849,
aged 38 yrs (DG 24 Jul 1849)

GRAVES, Rebecca,
see SPRINGER, George

GRAVES, Robert, see GRAVES, Maria P.

GRAVES, Thomas, of Mill Creek Hd,
29 Apr 1844, aged 63 yrs (DG 29 Apr 1844)
see GRAVES, Margaret

GRAY, _____, Mrs., mother of Rev. W. L.
GRAY of Smyrna, in Smyrna, 12 Aug 1849,
in her 74th yr (DG 21 Aug 1849)

GRAY, _____, Mrs., wife of William GRAY,
in S. Milford, on the 39th ult (sic)
(DG 12 Sep 1851)

GRAY, Andrew, of Murderkill, to
McCLYMONT, Nancy, Miss, dau of James
McCLYMONT, Esq., of Cambden (sic),
15 Feb 1798, by Rev. Mr. McKee
(DE 26 Feb 1798)
see WILSON, _____, Mrs.
see WILSON, Elijah

GRAY, Andrew C., Esq., of New Castle, to
SCOFIELD, Elizabeth M., Miss, dau of
Frederick SCOFIELD, Esq., of Phila, 8 Oct
1833, by Rev. Mr. Judson (DG 11 Oct 1833)

GRAY, Ann, see WILSON, Elijah

GRAY, Elizabeth, wife of Joshua GRAY, in
Cedar Creek Hd, Sussex Co, 25 Sep 1852,
aged c 33 yrs (DG 28 Sep 1852)
see HOLLAND, David
see GRAY, John B.

GRAY, Elizabeth C., see WOTTEN, Isaac

GRAY, George W., of Phila, to
THOMPSON, Mary Ann, dau of the late
Daniel WOLFE of Lewestown DE, 6 Dec
1841, in Phila by Rev. Robert Adair
(DG 10 Dec 1841)

GRAY, Hannah S., see GREEN, Emor R

GRAY, Isabella, see DEPUTY, Charles M.

GRAY, John B., to GRAY, Elizabeth, Miss,
both of NC Co, 15 Mar 1846, by Rt. Rev.
Alfred Lee (DG 31 Mar 1846)

GRAY, Joshua, to BAILEY, Lavinia, Miss,
30 Jan 1850, by Rev. J. R. Torbert
(DG 12 Feb 1850)
see GRAY, Elizabeth

GRAY, Julia Ann, see BIRD, William

GRAY, Sarah B., see PALMER, John

GRAY, W. L., see GRAY, _____, Mrs.

GRAY, Welcome, Esq., 24 May 1846,
aged c 60 yrs. Buried Friends Burial Ground
(DG 29 May 1846)

GRAY, William, see PALMER, John
see GRAY, _____, Mrs.

GRAY, William C., formerly of Wilm, to
McMILLEN, Sarah Jane, of Louisville, KY,
at Louisville, 22 Feb 1849, by the Rev. Mr.
Williams (DG 20 Mar 1849)

GRAY, Wm., to MOORE, Rebecca S., both of NC Co, in Phila, 22 Jan 1852, by Rev. G. R. Crooks (DG 27 Jan 1852)

GREATRAKE, George,
see GREATRAKE, Lawrence

GREATRAKE, Lawrence, of the Brandywine paper mill, lately dec'd, notice, requesting payment to George GREATRAKE, given by Thomas GILPIN, exec'r (AW 19 Jul 1817)

GREATRAKE, Mary, see ROBERTS, John

GREEN, ____, Dr., see GREEN, Caroline

GREEN, ____, Mrs. Jesse,
see GUNBY, Mary, Mrs.
see KENNEY, Jeremiah F.

GREEN, ____.Mrs. N., see MORRIS, Ann

GREEN, Ann T., see GREEN, Sarah M.

GREEN, Caroline, dau of Dr. ____ GREEN, in Laurel, recently, aged 14 yrs (DG 24 Sep 1833)

GREEN, Charles, to WILSON, Susan, Miss, both of Brandywine, 21 May 1846, by Rev. S. R. Wynkoop (DG 29 May 1846)

GREEN, Cuthbert, S., Dr., of Middletown (DG 24 Nov 1843)

GREEN, David, to MITCHELL, Hannah, Miss, 15 Feb 1821 (DG 20 Feb 1821)

GREEN, Edward, see GREEN, Elmira

GREEN, Edward B., of Delaware Co PA, to BRACKEN, Hannah, Miss, dau of William BRACKEN, Esq., of Brackenville [near Hockessin], NC Co, 1 Jan 1844 (DG 9 Jan 1844)

GREEN, Elizabeth,
see BROWNING, George
see KENNEY, Jeremiah F.

GREEN, Elmira, Mrs, wife of Mr. Edward GREEN, 16 Sep 1847, in Dover (DG 28 Sep 1847)

GREEN, Emeline, see LONG, Henry

GREEN, Emor R., of Chester Co PA, to GRAY, Hannah S., Miss, of NC Co, at Chester PA, 31 Jan 1849, by Rev. Charles W. Quick (DG 6 Feb 1849)

GREEN, George W., to DAVIDSON, Lydia, Miss, eldest dau of John DAVIDSON, Esq., near Georgetown, 11 Sep 1834, by the Rev. Jonathan R. Torbert (DG 19 Sep 1834)
see GREEN, Sophia Jane

GREEN, Jacob, to EVANS, Martha, Miss, both of Wilm, in Phila, 26 Sep 1850, by Rev. S. Higgins (DG 1 Sep 1850)
see REDDEN, Abraham

GREEN, James, to RUSSELL, Ruth 7 Dec 1826, by the Rev. Mr. Macombe, all of Wilm (DG 12 Dec 1826)

GREEN, James, to WHITE, Margaret, both of Rockland, 14 Mar 1845, by Rev. S. M. Gayley (DG 18 Mar 1845)

GREEN, James, laborer, killed by a bank falling on him at Madison St. near Delaware Ave, 1 Feb 1848 (DG 4 Feb 1848)

GREEN, Jesse, Maj. Gen., to MARTIN, Sophia, Miss, dau of Capt H. MARTIN, of Seaford, 9 Jun 1846, by Rev. J McKimm (DG 16 Jun 1846)

GREEN, Jesse, Major-General, at his res. in Concord, DE, 21 Aug 1834, aged 68 yrs. ...served 30 yrs in the Legislature (DG 2 Sep 1834)
see GUNBY, Mary, Mrs.
see KENNEY, Jeremiah F.
see LONG, Henry

GREEN, John, at Cantwell's Bridge, 11 Apr 1828, na (DG 15 Apr 1828)

GREEN, John, Esq., in Milford, 25 Sep 1852, aged 49 yrs (DG 28 Sep 1852)

GREEN, John H., to DOWNY, Sarah Ann, all of Cantwell's Bridge, at Cantwell's Bridge, 10 Mar 1852, by the Rev. H. R. Harrold, Rector of St. Ann's Ch, Middletown (DG 26 Mar 1852)

GREEN, Mark, Dr., see GREEN, Sarah M.

GREEN, Mary, Miss, eldest dau of Mrs. Mary Ann GREEN of NC Co, 13 Feb 1826, na (DG 21 Feb 1826)
see MORRISON, Henry
see GUNBY, Mary

GREEN, Mary Ann, wife of the late William W. GREEN, of DE, 17 Dec 1850 (DG 31 Dec 1850)
see GREEN, Mary

GREEN, Matilda, see FRIES, H. C., Rev.

GREEN, Rachel, see HANDY, Kendal

GREEN, Rachel Ann, see McCALL, Josiah

GREEN, Sarah M., Miss, dau of the late Dr. Mark and Ann T. GREEN, at Milford, Methodist, of pulmonary disease, 4 Sep 1844, aged 23 yrs (DG 1 Oct 1844)

GREEN, Sophia Jane, Mrs., wife of Col George W. GREEN, at Seaford, at the res. of her father, Capt Hugh MARTIN, of Concord, Sussex Co, 9 Jan 1851, in her 22nd yr (DG 21 Jan 1851)

GREEN, Stephen, Dr., see FRIES, H. C.

GREEN, William W., see GREEN, Mary Ann

GREENE, Charles G., Esq., junior editor of the *National Palladium,* Phila, to HILL, Charlotte Elizabeth, dau of the late Capt. Samuel HILL at Boston, 24 Oct 1827, by the Rev. Mr. Pierpont (DG 30 Oct 1827)

GREENE, Jemimah, Mrs., widow of the late Rev. Samuel R. GREENE, formerly of Wilm, in Phila, 19 Apr 1827, na (DG 24 Apr 1827)

GREENE, Samuel R., see GREENE, Jemimiah, Mrs.

GREENE, Samuel R., the Rev., in Phila, 17 Sep 1826, aged 36 yrs (DG 22 Sep 1826)

GREENFIELD, Amos, to GRUBB, Elizabeth Ann, of NC Co, 2 Oct 1841, at Marcus Hook PA, by Rev. J. Walker (DG 22 Oct 1841)

GREENHALGH. Ann, see SPEAR. Springer

GREENWALT, Elizabeth, see HAWTHORN, William

GREENWALT, Henry, merchant of Dauphin PA, to DIXON, Mary Ellen, dau of Joseph S. DIXON, Esq., formerly of Wilm, in Wilm, 17 Apr 1850, in the Presb. Ch by Rev. J. E. Rockwell (DG 19 Apr 1850)

GREENWALT, Joseph, to McMICHAEL, Mary, Miss, both of NC Co, 7 Jul 1835, by the Rev. A. K. Russel (DG 10 Jul 1835)

GREENWALT, Margaret, Mrs., Newark DE, 6 Mar 1853, aged 40 yrs 8 mos (DG 5 Apr 1853)

GREENWOOD, Anna Elizabeth, see BUTLER, George W.

GREENWOOD, William, of Wilm, to ROBERTSON, Charlotte, of Chester PA, 25 Dec 1852, by Rev. J. Duncan (DG 4 Jan 1853)

GREGG Abraham, late of Pencader Hd. Jane R. GREGG, exec'x (DG 29 Jun 1849)

GREGG, Edmund C., to STIDHAM, Ingeber Ann, Miss, of Wilm, 27 Jan 1846, by Rev. J. Kennedy (DG 30 Jan 1846)

GREGG, George, in Wilm, 6 May 1852, aged c 43 yrs (DG 11 May 1852)

GREGG, Hiram, son of Salomon GREGG of Chester Co, in Wilm at Sharpe's Hotel, 4 Jun 1847, aged 25 yrs (DG 22 Jun 1847)

GREGG, Margaret, in Wilm, 22 Jan 1852, aged c 55 yrs (DG 27 Jan 1852)

GREGG, Isaac D., to COMFORT, Caroline, Miss, all of Wilm, in Phila, 5 May 1847, by Rev. S. A. Clark (DG 11 May 1847)

GREGG, Jane R., see GREGG, Abraham

GREGG, Jesse, see UNDERWOOD, Elizabeth

GREGG, John, of Kennett, Chester Co PA, to HARKER, Sarah Ann, Miss, dau of Mr. Jeremiah HARKER of Brandywine Hd, in Chester, 31 Dec 1823, by Samuel Smith, Esq. (DG 2 Jan 1824)

GREGG, John, to DELAPLAINE, Mary, Miss, dau of Nehemiah DELAPLAINE, both of Brandywine Hd, 3 Feb 1842, by the Rev. Corry Chambers (DG 11 Feb 1842) see GREGG, Mary

GREGG, John D., formerly of Chester Co, PA, at his res. in the village of Brandywine, 30 Aug 1834, aged 32 yrs (DG 12 Sep 1834) dec'd, notice given by Sarah Ann GREGG, adm'x (DG 30 Sep 1834)

GREGG, Lydia, see FOOT, Thomas

GREGG, Mary, wife of John GREGG, in Christiana Hd, of consumption, 17 Aug 1851, na (DG 2 Sep 1851) see LECARPENTIER, Charles

GREGG, Salomon, see GREGG, Hiram

GREGG, Samuel, res. of Christiana Hd, 13 Jan 1830, "old" (DG 19 Jan 1830)

GREGG, Samuel, Esq., in Christiana Hd, 15 Aug 1849, age 78 yrs (DG 21 Aug 1849)

GREGG, Samuel, see WAY, Caleb see McCULLOUGH, James

GREGG, Sarah Ann, see GREGG, John D.

GREGORY, William, of Phila, to NELSON, Mary, Miss, 21 Feb 1846, in Wilm, by Rev. S. R. Wynkoop (DG 24 Feb 1846)

GREY, _____, Mrs., see RODGERS, Elizabeth

GRIER, Ann, see LINDLE, Ann

GRIER, James, Capt., see LINDLE, Ann

GRIEVES, William V., to COVERDALE, Harriet A., Miss, both of Smyrna, 8 Nov 1853, by the Rev. T. C. Murphey (DG 15 Nov 1853)

GRIFFIN, Eliza, see LAWS, Joshua

GRIFFIN, Jno. R., to GEORGE, Rachel T., both of Kent Co DE, 8 Jul 1851, by T. Newman (DG 18 Jul 1851)

GRIFFIN, John A., Esq., of Wilm, to HINTZE, Henrietta Hellen (sic), Miss, dau of F. B. HINTZE of Baltimore, 16 Jul 1846, in Baltimore (DG 24 Jul 1846)

GRIFFIN, Thomas, Rev., at New York, 17 Aug 1826, na (DG 22 Aug 1826)

GRIFFITH, Alethea, Mrs., see MASTEN, Hezekiah

GRIFFITH, David B., of Newark DE, to SUTTON, Julia Ann, Miss, dau of John SUTTON, Jr. of St Georges, at St Georges, 27 Apr 1852, by the Rev. James C. Howe (DG 4 May 1852)

GRIFFITH, Edmund, to BLAUVELT, Margaret, Miss, both of New York, in Wilm, 28 Mar 1846, by Rev. S. R. Wynkoop (DG 31 Mar 1846)

GRIFFITH, Joseph, see LOCKWOOD, William Jr.

GRIFFITH, Lizzie, W., see LOCKWOOD, William Jr.

GRIFFITH, Mary, see BOGGS, John

GRIFFITH, Richard, to BOWEN, Sarah, Miss, of Wilm, by John Larkin Jr., Esq. (DG 11 Jun 1850)

GRIMES, Elizabeth Ann, see STOKES, John B.

GRIMES, Sarah Ann, see HITCHENS, Myers B.

GRIMSHAW, Arthur H., M. D., to BAILY, A. Elizabeth, dau of Joseph P. BAILY, Esq., 10 Apr 1850, at St. Andrew's, by the Rt. Rev. Alfred Lee DD (DG 12 Apr 1850)

GRIMSHAW, Arthur H., see GRIMSHAW, James

GRIMSHAW, James, Dr., late of New Cumberland PA, at the res. of his brother in Wilm, of consumption, 6 Jun 1853, in his 37th yr. Funeral from the house of Dr. Arthur H. GRIMSHAW, on Market St bet 8th and 9th (DG 7 Jun 1853)

GRINER, John, to SHIPLEY, Susanna,

Miss, in Wilm, 9 Jun 1853, by the Rt. Rev. A. Lee (DG 14 Jun 1853)

GRIST, Moses M. B., to BLACKWOOD, Rebecca, Miss, all of Wilm, 23 Sep 1851, by the Rev. J. A. Roche (DG 26 Sep 1851)

GROHE, ____, Mr., professor and teacher of music, in Wilm, ndd. aged 40 yrs. (DG 13 Jul 1847)

GROOME, Evalina, see CRAWFORD, Samuel C.

GROOME, Samuel, merchant, in Wilm, 14 Mar 1828, aged 51 yrs; bur. at Episcpal Ch. in Wilm (DG 28 Mar 1828)

GROSE, Ann, see CLEAVER, John Jr.

GROSE, Jacob, late of St. Georges Hd. Philip J. GROSE, adm'r (DG 3 Feb 1852)

GROSE, Philip J., see GROSE, Jacob

GROVES, John, Capt., late of Wilm, in his 42nd yr, in Phila, 20 Aug 1849 (DG 21 Aug 1849) Thomas YOUNG, exec'r (DG 12 Oct 1849)

GROVES, Jonathan, see WILLIAMS, John

GRUBB, Adam, to MEGAW, Rachel, Miss, both of Brandywine Hd, in Chester PA, 19 Aug 1847, by Rev. A. B. Hard (DG 7 Sep 1847)

GRUBB, Amer, see GRUBB, James

GRUBB, Amor, in Brandywine Hd, 31 Mar 1850, aged 50 yrs (DG 9 Apr 1850)

GRUBB, Bayard, see GRUBB, James

GRUBB, Beulah C., wife of Wellington GRUBB, in Wilm, 10 Sep 1852, aged c 39 yrs (DG 14 Sep 1852)

GRUBB, Edward, in Wilm, 20 Feb 1845 (DG 25 Feb 1845)

GRUBB, Elizabeth Ann, see GREENFIELD, Amos

GRUBB, George, to ABBOTT, Elizabeth H., Miss, of Wilm, 22 Nov 1846, by Rev. Dr. Kennaday (DG 1 Dec 1846) see GRUBB, George Allmond

GRUBB, George Allmond, only son of George and Susannah GRUBB, of measles, 18 Jul 1848, aged 3 mos (DG 28 Jul 1848)

GRUBB, H. W., of Brandywine Hd, to SHILLING, Sidney, Miss, of Rural Dale, Muskingum Co, OH, in Rural Dale,

18 Aug 1853 (DG 16 Sep 1853)

GRUBB, Hannah, dau of the late Joseph GRUBB of Wilm, 17 Nov 1848, in Phila (DG 28 Nov 1848)

GRUBB, James, of B'wine Hd, Amer GRUBB, Bayard GRUBB and James GRUBB, exec'rs (DG 20 Apr 1827) see WOOD, William

GRUBB, James, to PERKINS, Ann , Miss, 8 Apr 1828, by Elder John P. Peckworth, all of Wilm (DG 11 Apr 1828)

GRUBB, Joseph, see GRUBB, Hannah

GRUBB, Letitia Glover, Miss, of Brandywine Hd, 3 Mar 1834, aged 25 yrs (DG 18 Mar 1834)

GRUBB, Lewis H., to FORD, Mary, Miss, dau of Rev. Jesse FORD, all of Brandywine Hd, 6 May 1843, by Rev. Ignatius Cooper (DG 12 May 1843)

GRUBB, Lewis T., to HARPER, Keziah E., both of NC Co, in Phila, 23 Sep 1847, by Rev. John A. Roach (DG 1 Oct 1847)

GRUBB, Rebecca, see BLACKWELL, Stephen G. see GEST, William

GRUBB, Samuel S., see STORY, Betty

GRUBB, Susannah, see GRUBB, George Allmond

GRUBB, Wellington, in Wilm, of erysipelas, 11 Feb 1853, in his 43rd yr (DG 15 Feb 1853) see GRUBB, Beulah

GRUBBS, William F., in Brandywine Hd, 31 Jul 1849, aged 77 yrs (DG 14 Aug 1849)

GRUETT, Lydia, see CLENDANIEL, George

GUEST, Byard, to BEESON, Mary J., both of NC Co, at Marcus Hook PA, 21 Apr 1853, by the Rev. W. H. Brisbane (DG 17 May 1853)

GUEST, Henry, dec'd, late of Brandywine Hd, notice given by Jehu FORWOOD, adm'r (AW 27 Apr 1816)

GULEY, Lewis H., of Phila, to WASHINGTON, Mary Ann, Miss, of Christiana Hd, 23 Dec 1824, by Rev. R. Williston (DG 28 Dec 1824)

GUMMERS, Elizabeth, dau of the late John GUMMERS, in Wilm, 16 Apr 1848, in her 25th yr (DG 21 Apr 1848)

GUMMERS, John, see GUMMERS, Elizabeth

GUNBY, James, Capt., "a revolutionary character"... worthy member of the Baptist Ch for nearly 50 years, at his res. in Sussex Co, 14 Jan 1824, aged 77 yrs (DG 27 Jan 1824) see GUNBY, Mary, Mrs.

GUNBY, Mary, Mrs., late consort of James GUNBY, Esq., and mother of Mrs. GREEN, relict of Gen Jesse GREEN, at her res. in Broad Creek Hd, Sussex Co, 18 Sep 1834, aged 76, Baptist for 40 yrs (DG 30 Sep 1834)

GUTHRIE, _____, Mrs., wife of Mr. James GUTHRIE of Wilm, 7 Jan 1834, na (DG 10 Jan 1834)

GUTHRIE, Alexander, to ENGLAND, Elizabeth A., Miss, all of NC Co, 30 Nov 1848, by Rev. John Bayne (DG 5 Dec 1848) see GUTHRIE, Elizabeth, Mrs.

GUTHRIE, Annie F., see VERNON, George W.

GUTHRIE, Elizabeth, Mrs., wife of Alexander GUTHRIE, in Mill Creek Hd, 27 Jan 1835, na (DG 3 Mar 1835)

GUTHRIE, Hannah Marie L., dau of William and Maria GUTHRIE, at New Castle, of scarlet Fever, 10 Feb 1835, aged 5 yrs (DG 13 Mar 1835)

GUTHRIE, James, see GUTHRIE, _____, Mrs.

GUTHRIE, Maria, see GUTHRIE, Hannah Marie L. see GUTHRIE, Thomas Magens

GUTHRIE, Thomas Magens, son of William and Maria GUTHRIE, 27 Feb 1835, aged 3 yrs (DG 13 Mar 1835)

GUTHRIE, William, see GUTHRIE, Hannah Marie L. see GUTHRIE, Thomas Magens

GUTHRIE, William A., to TAYLOR, Mary A., Miss, both of New Castle, 12 Mar 1846, by Rev. William Ryder (DG 24 Mar 1846)

GUY, Julia Ann, see KIRK, Marshall

GUYER, John L., to FORD, Martha, Miss, all of Wilm, 22 Apr 1846, by Rev. A. Atwood (DG 28 Apr 1846)

GUYER, Mary Elizabeth, see GARRETT, Wm. A.

GWINCHEWSKI, Felix Gustavus, a Polish patriot and exile, in Phila, 3 Oct 1849. Bur in Wilm and Brandywine Cem. He taught and lived in Wilm (DG 9 Oct 1849)

HAADEN (sic), John, to ALRICKS, Susan, Mrs., 19 Mar 1807, by Rev. Mr. Pryce (MU 21 Mar 1807)

HAAS, John to BLACKWAY, Eliza, Miss, in Wilm, 28 Jun 1853, by Rev. Mr Gerry (DG 1 Jul 1853)

HABERSTROPH, Xavier, 10 Oct 1848, aged 43 yrs (DG 17 Oct 1848)

HACKET, Isaac, disease of heart and exposure, ndd (DG 4 Jul 1848)

HACKETT, John W., merchant of Centreville, MD, to BEDFORD, Sally, Miss, 14 Feb 1804, at Lombardy, the seat of Gunning BEDFORD, Esq., by Rev. Mr. Read (FA 18 Feb 1804)

HACKETT, Maria, drowned while sailing with a party of young people on the Christiana, 30 May 1852, na (DG 1 Jun 1852)

HADDEN, Charles, see HADDEN, John

HADDEN, Elizabeth C., see MENOUGH, John

HADDEN, John, dec'd, late of Wilm, notice given by Susana HADDEN, exec'x, and William SMITH, exec'r (AR 13 May 1812)

HADDEN, John, son of Charles and Mary HADDEN, in Smyrna, 17 May 1853, aged c 2 yrs (DG 27 May 1853)

HADDEN, Mary, see HADDEN, John

HADDEN, Susana, see HADDEN, John

HADDEN, Susanna Canby, 29 Feb 1848, in Wilm (DG 7 Mar 1848)

HADDOCK, Henry, to RITCHIE, Sarah, Miss, in Wilm, 4 Jul 1853, by the Rt. Rev. A. Lee (DG 4 Jul 1853)

HADDOCK, John G., to MORAN, Elizabeth G., Miss, both of Wilm, in Wilm, 14 Jan 1852 (DG 16 Jan 1852)

HADDOCK, Samuel, to DAVIDSON, Louisa A., all of NC Co, 29 Jul 1847, by Rev. M. J. Rhees (DG 3 Aug 1847)

HADON, William R., to ATKINSON, Margaret, both of Wilm, 17 May 1852, by Wm. Hemphill Jones, Mayor (DG 28 May 1852)

HAGANY, Joseph, in Phila, 19 Mar 1846, aged 45 yrs (DG 24 Mar 1846)

HAGERMAN, Hannah, see COBOURNE, Joseph

HAGERROTON, Catharine N., see GOODLY, Jonas

HAGUE, Eliza, see WILLIAMSON, John

HAGUE, Eliza M, see HAGUE, W. F.

HAGUE, Mary, see BARNET, Henry

HAGUE, W. F., son of Eliza M. HAGUE, in Wilm, 7 Jun 1847, aged 2 yrs (DG 8 Jun 1847)

HAINES, Elizabeth, see PYLE, Joseph

HAINES, Mary, see SEITZ, George

HALFINANN, Angeline, see HALFINANN, Angeline Redman

HALFINANN, Angeline Redman, dau of Herbert and Angeline HALFINANN, in Phila, of croup, 15 Oct 1849, aged 3 yrs 4 mos (DG 19 Oct 1849)

HALFINANN, Herbert, see HALFINANN, Angeline Redman

HALL, _____, Mrs., wife of John HALL of Christiana Bridge (DG 1 Aug 1789)

HALL, Ann, Mrs., wife of David HALL, near Smyrna, 6 Apr 1833, aged 29 yrs (DG 23 Apr 1833)

HALL, Augustus R., to AEFORD, Caroline, Miss, all of Phila, 14 Sep 1847, by Rev. J. Chambers (DG 1 Oct 1847)

HALL, David, see HALL, Ann, Mrs.

HALL. Eliza, see GLOVER, Henry

HALL, Eliza M., dau of the late Purnel HALL, Esq., in Milford, 24 Dec 1852, in her 11th yr (DG 14 Jan 1853)

HALL, George, Rev., to HICKMAN, Mary Caroline, Miss, eldest dau of George HICKMAN, all of Sussex, at Lewes, 18 Apr 1850, by Rev. Chas. W. Quick (DG 30 Apr 1850)

HALL. George P., see SPENCER, James

HALL, Henrietta, dau of the late John HALL, in Wilm, 23 Apr 1852, aged 18 yrs (DG 27 Apr 1852)

HALL, Henry, Dr., Surgeon of the U. S. Army to RODNEY, Hester, Miss, dau of

Caleb RODNEY, Esq.,at Lewis, 29 May 1823, by the Rev. John RODNEY (DG 10 Jun 1823)

HALL, Jacob, dec'd, late of Christiana Hd, notice given by John WHITEMAN, exec'r (DG 17 Feb 1826)

HALL, Joel, to MORTON, Emeline, Miss, 7 Dec 1826, by the Rev. Mr. Hagany, all of Wilm (DG 12 Dec 1826)

HALL, John, of Christiana Bridge, to REECE, Lucretia, Miss, of the same, 25 Nov 1789 (DG 28 Nov 1789)
see HALL, _____, Mrs.
see ISRAEL, Joseph

HALL, John, of Christiana, to OGDEN, Orpha, Miss, of Derby, PA, at Marcus Hook, PA, 27 Dec 1821, by J. Walker, Esq. (DG 8 Jan 1822)

HALL, John, proprietor of the Indian Queen Hotel, in Wilm, 19 Jun 1850, aged c 55 yrs (DG 21 Jun 1855)
see HALL, Henrietta

HALL, John, Jr.,
see QUANDRILLE, John

HALL, John W., merchant of Frederica DE, to WARREN, Caroline, only dau of Samuel WARREN Jr., near that place, 15 Nov 1842, by Rev. William Conely (DG 18 Nov 1842)

HALL, Joseph L., to EGBERT, Phebe, Miss, both of Christiana Hd, at the Washington Hotel in West Chester PA, 19 Feb 1846, by the Rev. David E. Gardiner (DG 3 Mar 1846)

HALL, Margaret C., see ECCLES, Samuel

HALL, Margaret F.,
see MARSHALL, John P.

HALL, Perry Pilmore, only child of Rev. Richard D. Hall, of Wilm, 27 Dec 1812, in his 6th yr (DG 28 Dec 1821)

HALL, Peter, Esq., at his res. in Milton, 27 Jan 1835, aged 72 yrs (DG 10 Feb 1835)

HALL, Purnel, see HALL, Eliza M.

HALL, Willard, Esq., to HILLYARD, Harriet, Miss, at Dover, 11 Apr 1826, by Rev. Jacob Moore (AW 14 Apr 1826)

HALSTEAD, Benjamim, Rev., of New Harmony, Ind, to HANDY, Ann, Miss, dau of Thomas W. HANDY, M. D. of Newark, 8 Nov 1842, at Newark, by Rev. Prof. Allen (DG 18 Nov 1842)

HAMAN, Catherine,
see SHAKESPEARE, William M.

HAMAN, John, to McMULLEN, Harriet, both of NC Co, 12 Feb 1852, by Rev. J. G. Collom (DG 27 Feb 1852)

HAMBBLETON,(sic), Alexander, to GARDINER, Rachel M., Miss, all of Wilm, 25 Dec 1851, by the Rev. Andrew Manship (DG 30 Dec 1851)

HAMBLY, Richard, dec'd, late of St. Georges Hd, notice given by Richard HAMBLY, adm'r (DG 4 Feb 1797)

HAMBY, Ann R., see TORBETT, Peter

HAMILTON, A., see HAMILTON, Susan

HAMILTON, A. Boyd, to NAUDAIN, Catharine, dau of Dr. A. NAUDAIN, 18 Dec 1845, in Phila (DG 23 Dec 1845)
see HAMILTON, Susan

HAMILTON, Ann, Mrs., wife of Robert HAMILTON, Esq.,at Ellerslie, Brandywine Hd, 1 Sep 1825, aged 66 yrs (DG 13 Sep 1825)

HAMILTON, Ann E.,
see HUTCHINSON, Mahlon Jr.

HAMILTON, Ann Jane,
see MERCER, John C.

HAMILTON, Archibald, Esq., of Wilm, 4 Oct 1841 (DG 8 Oct 1841)
see CREEMER, Jacob

HAMILTON, Charles, mate, of the brig Gazette of Baltimore, native of Wilm, at Havana, 6 Jul 1825, na (DG 22 Jul 1825)
see HUTCHINSON, Mahlon Jr.

HAMILTON, Eleanor,
see HOOPES, Joseph

HAMILTON, Eliza, see CRIPPEN, Silas

HAMILTON, James, stage driver for Mr. Anderson for the past six yrs, in Wilm, 19 Jan 1816, in his 36th yr (AW 24 Jan 1816)

HAMILTON, James, in Wilm, 12 Mar 1824, aged 68 yrs (DG 23 Mar 1824)

HAMILTON, James, Capt., of Phila, son of the late Robert HAMILTON, Esq., of Wilm, at sea on board the ship Globe in Lat. 44 N, Long. 30.10, out 14 days from Liverpool, 10 Jul 1826, na (DG 15 Aug 1826)

HAMILTON, James C. Sale of land (formerly the old Blue Ball Tavern property) on the Wilm - Kennett Turnpike (DG 3 Jan 1851)

HAMILTON, Jane, aged 80 yrs. Inquest at Log Meeting House in Christiana Hd. Body interred about three weeks ago. (DG 28 Mar 1851)

HAMILTON, John, late master of the ship *Delaware*, of Phila, formerly of Wilm, at Liverpool, 23 Jan 1828, aged 48 yrs (DG 18 Mar 1828)

HAMILTON, John, see MERCER, John C.

HAMILTON, John, in Phila, 17 Nov 1848, aged 48 yrs (DG 28 Nov 1848)

HAMILTON, Philip, of New York, to McLANE, Rebecca, dau of Hon. Louis McLANE, 29 Dec 1842, at Bohemia, Cecil Co MD, (DG 6 Jan 1843)

HAMILTON, Robert,
see HAMILTON, James, Capt.
see HAMILTON, Ann, Mrs.
see ADAMS, Daniel J., Esq.,

HAMILTON, Robert, Esq., of Wilm, 22 Jul 1826, in his 71st yr (WN 10 Aug 1826) aged 71 yrs (DG 25 Jul 1826) obit (DG 8 Aug 1826)

HAMILTON, Susan, Miss, sister of the late A. HAMILTON, Esq., in Wilm, 19 Dec 1850, in her 65th yr (DG 24 Dec 1850)

HAMILTON, Thomas, the Rev., of New York, to YOUNG, Margaretta M., Miss, dau of William YOUNG, Esq., at Rockland near Wilm, 26 May 1807, by the Rev. Joseph Shaw (MU 30 May 1807)

HAMILTON, Thos., to BULLEN, Henrietta R., Miss, 14 Jul 1849, by the Rev. M. J. Rhees (DG 20 Jul 1849)

HAMM, Susan B., see PURNELL, James S.

HAMMITT, Anna Margaret, youngest dau of Thomas and Rebecca HAMMITT, 10 Nov 1842, aged 4 yrs 4 mos (DG 18 Nov 1842)

HAMMITT, Rebecca,
see HAMMITT, Anna Margaret

HAMMITT, Thomas,
see HAMMITT, Anna Margaret

HAMMOND, Alexina, see RATLIFF, William

HAMMOND, Nicholas.
see PETERSON, Henry

HAMMOND, William, to KOLLOCK, Martha, Miss dau of George KOLLOCK, Esq., all of Georgetown, DE, 17 May 1834, by Rev. Jonathan R. Torbert (DG 27 May 1834)

HAMON, Jacob, to MORRISON, Mary Ann, Miss, both of Wilm, 7 Apr 1835, by Elder John P. Peckworth (DG 10 Apr 1835)

HAMON, James H., to RICHARDSON, Susan, Miss, both of Wilm, 3 Mar 1853, by the Rev. S. R. Wynkoop (DG 8 Mar 1853)

HAMPTON, Anna, in Brandywine Hd, 23 Jun 1848, in her 24th yr (DG 27 Jun 1848)

HAMPTON, Edward H., of Bucks Co PA to SLEEPER, Anna W.of NC Co, 28 Nov 1845, by the Mayor (DG 2 Dec 1845)

HAMPTON, Susanna D.,
see HIGHAM, Edward

HANA, Joseph, to BUCKINGHAM, Sarah, Miss, both of Mill Creek Hd, 6 Nov 1823, by _____ Thomas, Esq. (DG 11 Nov 1823)

HANBEY, Benjamin F., to KENDALL, Martha C., Miss, both of Brandywine Hd, at Marcus Hook parsonage, 7 Feb 1850, by Rev. T. A. Fernley (DG 19 Feb 1850)

HANBY, Clark, see HANBY, Susana

HANBY, Richard, dec'd, late of Brandywine Hd, notice given by Charles ROBINSON, adm'r (DG 13 Nov 1829)

HANBY, Susana, Mrs, late wife of Clark HANBY, dau of Ewemon TAYLOR, 16 Nov 1843 (DG 1 Dec 1843)

HANBY, William, Esq., at his res. in Brandywine Hd, 7 Feb 1847, aged 78 yrs (DG 16 Feb 1847)

HANCE, John R., to HOWARD, Elizabeth N., Miss, both of Kent Co MD, in Wilm, 10 Jun 1847, by Rev. T. J. Thompson (DG 22 Jun 1847)

HANCE, Samuel, at the res. of his father in Bethel, Brandywine Hd, 20 Aug 1847, aged 17 yrs (DG 7 Sep 1847)

HANCOCK, Henry,
see HANCOCK, William Henry

HANCOCK, William Henry, son of Henry HANCOCK, in Centreville, 15 Nov 1848, aged 5 yrs (DG 28 Nov 1848)

HAND, Mary Viginia, see ARGO, John

HAND, Rachel, see SCOTT, Henry

HANDSHAW, Lydia,
see CHRISTIE, Anthony

HANDY, _____, Dr. Sale of real estate (DG 14 Jan 1853)

HANDY, Ann,
see HALSTEAD, Benjamin, Rev.

HANDY, Benjamin R., of Newark, to PRICE,
Martha R., Miss, of Cecil Co MD, 22 May
1850, by the Mayor of Phila
(DG 31 May 1850)

HANDY, Isaac Henry, M. D., of NC Co, to
NASSAU, Mary Ann, dau of William
NASSAU, Esq., of Phila, in Phila, 2 Jul 1833,
by the Rev. Charles W. NASSAU of
Montgomery Square, PA (DG 2 Jul 1833)

HANDY, Isaac, W. K., Rev., of Port Penn
DE, to MARTIN, Sallie S., dau of the late
Dr. John S. MARTIN, at Snow Hill MD,
11 Jun 1850, by Rev. Mr. Olinstead
(DG 28 Jun 1850)

HANDY, Jane, see CAULK, Benjamin

HANDY, Kendal, to GREEN, Rachel, Miss,
24 Aug 1849, by Rev. S. M. Gailey
(DG 28 Sep 1849)

HANDY, Margaret, see MOORE, George K.

HANDY, Sarah A.,
see HANDY, Thomas W.

HANDY, Thomas W., Dr., at his res. in
Newark, 27 Jun 1851, in his 75th yr (Balt
papers please copy) (DG 1 Jul 1851)
late of White Clay Creek Hd, Sarah A.
HANDY adm'x (DG 18 Jul 1851)
see CAULK, Benjamin

HANING, George, to ANDREWS, Keziah,
Mrs., both of Wilm, 12 Oct 1809,
by Rev. Dr. Read (DG 18 Oct 1809)

HANKINS, Abigail, see FRANCIS, William

HANN, John W., dec'd, "A Santa Fe
prisoner" (DG 23 Jan 1852)

HANNA, Davis, see HANNA, John

HANNA, Eleanor, Mrs., in Wilm, 21 May
1848, in her 89th yr (DG 27 Jun 1848)

HANNA, John, late of Mill Creek Hd, Davis
HANNA and Samuel HANNA, adm'rs
(DG 3 Jun 1853)

HANNA, Leah,
see HANNA, Thomas

HANNA, Robert, see SPRINGER, Margaret

HANNA, Samuel, see HANNA, John

HANNA, Sarah, Mrs., in Wilm, 10 Feb 1835,
aged c 55 (DG 17 Feb 1835)

HANNA, Thomas, late of Mill Creek Hd,
Leah HANNA, adm'x (DG 1 Jul 1853)

HANNAH, Sarah, Mrs.,
see GILLESPY, George, Maj.

HANNAH, Thomas, to McDANIEL, Leah,
Miss, both of NC Co, 20 Dec 1827, by
John P. Peckworth (DG 28 Dec 1827)

HANNAN, John, late gunner in U. S.
Revenue Marine Service, in Wilm, 24 May
1848, in his 46th yr (DG 26 May 1848)

HANNUM, James, see HANNUM, Robert

HANNUM, Robert, late of Wilm. House and
inn to be sold by James HANNUM and
Thomas HANNUM (PG 15 Mar 1759)

HANNUM, Thomas, see HANNUM, Robert

HANSON, Alexander B., Capt., to BLACK,
Susan W, Miss, only dau of the late Dr.
James BLACK, at the res. of Mr. John G.
BLACK, 22 Dec 1829, by the Rev. Mr.
Piggot, all of Kent Co, MD (DG 29 Dec 1829)

HANSON, Alpheus T., in New Castle,
25 May 1850, aged c 25 yrs
(DG 31 May 1850)

HANSON, Benj. R., of DE, to NORWOOD,
Lucretia L. D., 3rd dau of the late Thomas D.
NORWOOD, of Anne Arundel Co MD, 1 Jan
1850, in the Methodist Prot. Ch, W. Balt,
by Rev. J. J. Murray (DG 8 Jan 1850)

HANSON, Benjamin, see HANSON, Mary

HANSON, E. G., Mrs.,
see HANSON, R. Ellie

HANSON, John, of Middletown, to NEWLIN,
Ann, Miss, of Wilm, in Phila, 26 Nov 1848,
by Rev. J. F. Berg, D. D. (DG 28 Nov 1848)

HANSON, Joseph H., to DERRICKSON,
Mary B., Miss, 30 Apr 1844, at Cantwell's
Bridge, by the Rev. Mr. Tyng
(DG 3 May 1844)

HANSON, Levi, (of) near Middletown to
TURNER, Eliza, Miss, of White Hall near
Red Lion, DE, 21 Dec 1822, by the Rev.
John B. Latta (DG 24 Dec 1822)

HANSON, Lydia Ann,
see EIJASON (sic), James J.

HANSON, Mary, Mrs., wife of Benjamin
HANSON, of Middletown, 9 Mar 1848,
in Middletown (DG 28 Mar 1848)

HANSON, R. Ellie, Miss, only child of Mrs.
E. G. HANSON, 9 Apr 1853, at New Castle,

in her 26th yr (DG 26 Apr 1853)

HANSON, Thomas P., of DE, to HUTAIRE, Eary (sic), of Balt., 23 Jan 1849, by Rev. L. R. Deloul (DG 6 Feb 1849)

HANSON, Timothy, 20 Oct 1798, on list of yellow fever victims (DG 27 Oct 1798)

HARBESON, Anna, see DIXON, Aaron

HARDASTY, George W., of Kent Co, to COHOON, Maria E., Miss, dau of W. R. COHOON, Esq., of Smyrna, 29 Oct 1852, by Rev. H., E. Gilroy (DG 19 Nov 1852)

HARDCASTLE, Amanda M., see MANLOVE, John P.

HARDCASTLE, Edward B., merchant of Denton, Caroline Co, MD, to LOCKWOOD, Mary Ann, Miss, dau of Caleb LOCKWOOD, Esq., of Whiteleysburg, Kent Co, DE, 12 Nov 1822, by the Rev. John Durborough (DG 19 Nov 1822)

HARDCASTLE, Mary, 22 Apr 1850, in Wilm (DG 26 Apr 1850)

HARDCASTLE, Philip, to SIPPLE, Elizabeth, Miss, dau of Mr. Garret SIPPLE, at Dover, 2 Nov 1797, by Rev. Mr. Johnstone (DE 6 Nov 1797)

HARDCASTLE, Thomas J., a native of Camden, DE, at Natchez of yellow fever, 10 Dec 1825, aged 24 yrs (DG 23 Dec 1825)

HARDCASTLE, Thos. H., to BELTS, Charlotte, Miss, both of NC Co, 14 Aug 1851, at the res. of the administrator, Hodgsons Farms, Chester Co PA, by the Rev. C. H. Plummer (DG 12 Aug 1851)

HARDY, Mary Ann, see FLAGLER, Albert

HARDY, Prudence J. L., see McDOWELL, Samuel C.

HARE, John N., son of William N. HARE, after a very brief illness, 11 Nov 1847, aged c 3 yrs (DG 25 Nov 1847)

HARE, William N., see HARE, John N.

HARGADINE, Julia Ann, see WRIGHT, Robert

HARISS, Sarah, see COOPER, Samuel

HARKER, Ann, see RUMSEY, Ann

HARKER, Ezekiel, in Wilm, after a brief illness, 4 Oct 1847, aged 51 yrs (DG 8 Oct 1847)

HARKER, Henrietta, Miss, dau of Dr. Jeremiah HARKER, in Brandywine Hd, 20 Feb 1830, aged 16 yrs (DG 26 Feb 1830)

HARKER, Jemima, Mrs., mother of the editor of the Delaware Gazette, in Phila, 31 Mar 1825, aged 57 yrs; member of the Baptist Ch (DG 5 Apr 1825)

HARKER, Jeremiah, see GREGG, John

HARKER, Jeremiah, Dr., see HARKER, Henrietta, Miss

HARKER, John Newton, 27 Oct 1851, in his 43rd yr, at his res. in Wilm, b 25 Dec 1808; 25 yrs with the Delaware Gazette, editor (DG 31 Oct 1851) late of Wilm Hd, Joshua S. VALENTINE, adm'r (DG 18 Nov 1851)

HARKER, Joseph, infant son of the editor of the Delaware Gazette, 29 Jun 1828, aged 16 mos (DG 4 Jul 1828)

HARKER, Margaretta, see PRETZNER, Henry

HARKER, Samuel, see WRIGHT, Ezekiel
see RUMSEY, Ann
see HARKER, Jemima, Mrs.
see HARKER, Joseph
see HARKER, Samuel, Jr.

HARKER, Samuel, Jr., infant son of the Editor of the Delaware Gazette, 11 Apr 1829 (DG 14 Apr 1829)

HARKER, Sarah Ann, see GREGG, John

HARKER, Thomas B., to BEESON, Ellen, Miss, both of Brandywine Hd, 7 Jan 1830, by Rev. R. U. Morgan (DG 19 Jan 1830)

HARLAN, C., Dr., to MONTGOMERY, Eliza, both of Mill Creek Hd, 7 Nov 1842, by Rev. Thomas Love (DG 18 Nov 1842)

HARLAN, John, in Mill Creek Hd, 24 Dec 1851, aged 78 yrs (DG 30 Dec 1851)

HARLAN, Joshua, of Wilm, to DENT, Elizabeth W, Miss, of Baltimore, in Baltimore, 20 Apr 1829, by the Rev. Mr. Finley (DG 24 Apr 1829)

HARLAN, Mary, see MARSHALL, John
see HUSTON, William

HARLAN, Samuel, Jr., to FAIRLAMB, Susan P., Miss, both of Wilm, 5 Jan 1830, by the Rev. R. U. Morgan (DG 12 Jan 1830)

HARLAN, Thomas W., of Doe Run, Chester Co, PA, to PERKINS, Catharine, Miss, of Wilm, in Phila, 12 Apr 1849, by Rev. A.

Atwood (DG 20 Apr 1849)

HARMAN, Jacob, to NEWLIN, Jane, Miss, both of Wilm, in Wilm, 10 Apr 1823, by the Rev. E. W. Gilbert (DG 22 Apr 1823)

HARMAN, Rosanna, see FRANK, Auston F.

HARPER, Elizabeth, Mrs., wife of Mr. James HARPER, after a short illness, 7 Oct 1802, in her 19th yr; married only 3 mos (FA 12 Oct 1802)

HARPER, Fletcher, Jr., of NY, to DURBIN, Margaret C., youngest dau of the Rev. Dr. DURBIN, 3 Apr 1851, at Trinity ME Ch, by the Rev. J. P. DURBIN DD (DG 11 Apr 1851)

HARPER, Francis B., see SPICER, Geo. W.

HARPER, James, see HARPER Elizabeth, Mrs.

HARPER, John, in South Milford, after a protracted illness, 20 Feb 1850 (DG 26 Feb 1850)

HARPER, Joseph, Esq., to RUTHERAM, Catharine, Miss, 24 May 1817, by Rev. William Pryce, all of Wilm (DG 28 May 1817)

HARPER, Joseph, Esq., Rev. War veteran of 9 engagements, in Dover where he had resided for c 40 yrs, 9 Jun 1824, aged 68 yrs (DG 15 Jun 1824)

HARPER, Joseph, at his res. near Dover, 15 Sep 1825, aged 25 yrs (DG 23 Sep 1825)

HARPER, Keziah E., see GRUBB, Lewis T.

HARPER, Mark, of Phila Co, to CHANDLER, Hannah, Miss, of NC Co, 7 Jul 1835, by the Rev. A. K. Russel (DG 10 Jul 1835)

HARPER, Mary, see BROWN, Eugene

HARPER, Matilda J., see SPICER, Geo. W.

HARRIGAN, Wesley, to READ, Ellen, Miss, both of Brandywine, in Phila, 15 May 1848, by Rev. Mr. Kerr (DG 6 Jun 1848)

HARRINGTON, Elizabeth, late wife of William HARRINGTON, at her res. near Canterbury, Kent Co DE, 25 Jul 1843, aged 47 yrs (DG 25 Aug 1843)

HARRINGTON, Jonathan, to THOMAS, Sarah J., both of Kent Co, 11 Jan 1853 (DG 1 Feb 1853)

HARRINGTON, S. M., see SIPPLE, Caleb E.

HARRINGTON, Sarah, see SIPPLE, James D.

HARRINGTON, William, see HARRINGTON, Elizabeth

HARRIS, Abel, see EMORY, Charles C.

HARRIS, Ann L., see HOPKINS, James

HARRIS, Barney, Jr., of Brandywine Village, to SHAKESPEARE, Mary Ann, Miss, of Wilm, 6 Nov 1823, by the Rev. J. Potts (DG 11 Nov 1823)

HARRIS, Benton, Major, see HARRIS, Louisa Maria

HARRIS, Caroline, see EMORY, Charles C. see BALDWIN, William

HARRIS, Catharine A., see HARRIS, Lester Anderson

HARRIS, Catharine Marion, see SHARPE, Solomon, M. D.

HARRIS, Ella A., see SWIGGET, William

HARRIS, George S., to THOMPSON, Ann M. Miss, both of Phila, 10 Oct 1849, by the Rev. Mr. Bradford (DG 12 Oct 1849)

HARRIS, Hetty Ann, see PHILLIPS, John M.

HARRIS, James A., Esq., at his res., Hackle Barney, near Drawbridge, Sussex Co, 26 Jun 1846, aged 44 yrs (DG 7 Jul 1846)

HARRIS, Jesse, of Brandywine to WARNER, Lydia Ann, Miss, of Wilm, at Chester, 19 Dec 1822, by Samuel Smith, Esq. (DG 27 Dec 1822)

HARRIS, John, see HARRIS, Margaret see GIFFING, Susanna

HARRIS, John A., see HARRIS, Lester Anderson

HARRIS, John E., of Wilm, to HASTINGS, Mary D., Miss, formerly of New Castle, in Phila, 29 Jul 1852, by the Rev. W. Ramsey (DG 10 Aug 1852)

HARRIS, Lester Anderson, son of John A. and Catharine A. HARRIS, 1 Jul 1848, in Wilm (DG 4 Jul 1848)

HARRIS, Louisa Maria, youngest dau of Major Benton HARRIS, at her father's res. in Georgetown, after a short illness, 23 Feb 1828, na (DG 29 Feb 1828)

HARRIS, Margaret, dau of John HARRIS, Esq., in Wilm, 17 Apr 1849, na

(DG 20 Apr 1849)

HARRIS, Mason, to ALLEN, Martha, Miss, both of Q. Anne's MD, 29 Dec 1852, by Rev. H. E. Gilroy (DG 11 Jan 1853)

HARRISON, Albert, of Phila, to BRAMAN, Sarah J., Miss, of Wilm, in Phila, on the 48th (sic) ult., by Rev. A. Atwood (DG 30 Jan 1849)

HARRISON, Hester, see WARE, John

HARRITY, _____, son of Mr. HARRITY, slipped and fell while playing, ndd, aged c 3 yrs (DG 13 Jun 1851)

HARRY, Nathan H., see KEECH, John

HART, Anna Maria, see TOWNSEND, Samuel

HART, Charles W., to CARR, Mary Jane, Miss, both of Christiana Hd, 29 Nov 1849, at the Marcus Hook Pars. by Rev. T. A. Fernley (DG 11 Dec 1849)

HART, Geo. H., to GRAHAM, Mary, dau of the late R. Montgomery GRAHAM, MD, all of Wilm, at Marcus Hook PA, 1 Jul 1851, by the Rev. J. Walker (DG 11 Jul 1851)

HART, Jacob, at the res. of his brother, William HART, in Brandywine Hd, of typhus fever, 1 Nov 1843, aged 23 yrs (DG 17 Nov 1843)

HART, Theophilus P., to EGNER, Matilda, Miss, dau of Charles EGNER, Esq., of Ellerslie Place, NC Co, 2 May 1843, by Rev. Mr. Newton, rector of St. Paul's Ch, Phila (DG 12 May 1843)

HART, William, see HART, Jacob

HARTES, Richard, to RAMBO, Margaret, Miss, of NC Co, 21 Mar 1848, by Rev. M. J. Rhees (DG 31 Mar 1848)

HARTING, Cyrus, of Strasburg PA, to WOODALL, Lizzy, Miss, of Wilm, in Phila, 2 Apr 1852, by Rev. Henry Ducachet DD, rector of St Stephens Ch (DG 27 Apr 1852)

HARTLEY, Ann, in Wilm, 18 Nov 1848, aged 54 yrs (DG 5 Dec 1848)

HARTLEY, Cornelia P., see PALMER, Levick

HARTLEY, David, to BROWN, Ruth Ann, Miss, all of Wilm, 22 Feb 1844, by the Mayor (DG 27 Feb 1844)

HARTLEY, Henry C., 14 Nov 1848, in his 17th yr (DG 21 Nov 1848)

HARTLEY, Joseph C., merchant, to WILSON, Rebecca, Miss, all of Wilm, 26 Jan 1809, by Rev. Dr. Read (MU 28 Jan 1809)

HARTLEY, Milton, in Wilm, 23 Nov 1848, in his 26th yr (DG 28 Nov 1848)

HARTLY, Rebecca, see SEBO, John

HARTMAN, Isabella C., Mrs., wife of Newton HARTMAN, and eldest dau of the late Rev. Joseph LYBRAND, in Phila, 21 Jan 1852, in her 31st yr (DG 27 Jan 1852)

HARTMAN, Newton, see HARTMAN, Isabella C.

HARTT, Dennis, dec'd, notice given by George WEBSTER, adm'r (DE 18 Sep 1797)

HARTZELL, Susan, in Wilm, 2 Jul 1846, aged 28 yrs (DG 26 Jun 1846)

HARVEY, Amor, to DERICKSON, Martha, 1 Apr 1834, by the Rev. Isaac Pardee, all of Wilm (DG 4 Apr 1834)

HARVEY, Ann, see CLARK, Thomas

HARVEY, Charles, see HARVEY, Job

HARVEY, Edmund A., to HUXLEY, Sarah, Miss, dau of Elisha HUXLEY, Esq., of Phila, 2 Nov 1843 in Phila by Rev. Mr. Coleman (DG 13 Nov 1843)

HARVEY, Isaac, Jr., see HARVEY, Job

HARVEY, Job, dec'd, late of Wilm, notice given by Isaac HARVEY, Jr., Samuel D. HARVEY and Charles HARVEY, exec'rs (AW 13 Nov 1816)

HARVEY, Lea R.(or Lear) of Chester Co PA, to SHARPLESS, Hannah M., Miss, of DE, in Phila, 13 Sep 1851, by Alderman Henry Simpson (DG 16 Sep 1851)

HARVEY, Mary, see STANLEY, Charles

HARVEY, Samuel D., see HARVEY, Job

HARVEY, Sarah Ann, see JOHNSON, Asbury Mitchell

HARVEY, Thomas, keeper of the light, at the lighthouse, 11 Dec 1848, aged 35 yrs (DG 26 Dec 1848) see REED, Elizabeth

HARVEY, Thomas E., to WALKER, Susan, Miss, in Phila, 6 Mar 1834, by the Rev. Mr. Barnes, all of Dover Hd (DG 21 Mar 1834)

DELAWARE MARRIAGES AND DEATHS FROM NEWSPAPERS, 1729-1853   105

HARVEY, William, to HOLLAND, Mary Ann, Miss, both of Wilm, 6 Mar 1846, by Rev. Isaac R. Merrill of Chester PA (DG 13 Mar 1846)

HASEL, Isaac, to DAVID, Mary J., both of Kent Co, 3 Aug 1853, by the Rev. P. Mansfield (DG 16 Aug 1853)

HASLETT, _____, Gov., see HENDERSON, George

HASLETT, Jemima, see HENDERSON, George

HASSAN, Peter, of Mill Creek Hd, John PEACH, exec'r (DG 17 Jun 1851)

HASTINGS, Ann, see SIDDY, James

HASTINGS, Elizabeth B., see MILLS, Joseph

HASTINGS, Fidelia A., see HOGARTH, William, Rev.

HASTINGS, Jesse, see HASTINGS, Nancy

HASTINGS, Mary D., see HARRIS, John E.

HASTINGS, Nancy, wife of Jesse HASTINGS, in New Castle, 2 Oct 1849, in her 61st yr (DG 12 Oct 1849)

HASTINGS, Sarah, see TAYLOR, Robert

HATCH, William H., to DIEHL, Elizabeth, Miss, both of NC Co, 7 Dec 1846, by Rev. Mr. Foote (DG 15 Dec 1846)

HATFIELD, Joseph, to TRUITT, Eliza, Miss, both of Sussex, 30 Nov 1848, by Rev. Mr. Spottswood (DG 5 Dec 1848)

HATSEL, John V., to WRIGHT, Margaret A, Miss, both of Smyrna, in Salem NJ, 17 Oct 1850, by Rev. Mr. Hitchens (DG 22 Oct 1850)

HATTON, Enos, of Chester Co PA, to WALKER, Elizabeth, of Wilm, at Powell's White Hall Hotel, Phila, 17 Oct 1850, by Friends ceremony on the presence of Alderman J. Mitchell (DG 22 Oct 1850)

HATTON, Mary Jane, at New Castle, 9 Sep 1849, aged c 5 yrs (DG 14 Sep 1849)

HAUGHEY, Charles H., at his res. in St. Georges Hd, 7 Oct 1842, na. Presbyterian (DG 21 Oct 1842)

HAUGHEY, James of DE, to MOULDER, Sarah Jane, Miss, youngest dau of William MOULDER, Esq., of the Northern Liberties, Phila, 4 Mar 1824, by the Rev. Mr. Hoff (DG 5 Mar 1824)

HAUGHEY, Sarah, of Wilm, from congestion of the lungs, 19 May 1850 (DG 24 May 1850)

HAUGHEY, William, Esq., to RIDDLE, Mary, Miss, 1 Mar 1804 by Rev. John Latta, notice given by N. JOHNS (FA 3 Mar 1804) DENIED (FA 7 Mar 1804)

HAULEY, Harriet, see PETITDEMANGE, John

HAVELLOW, John R., to BOLTON, Elizabeth, Miss, both of Glasgow DE, 18 Mar 1852, by Rev. S. R. Wynkoop (DG 23 Mar 1852)

HAVILAND, Emma, see WRIGHT, W. Roderick

HAVILAND, John, see CORRIE, William

HAVILAND, Joseph, see WRIGHT, W. Roderick

HAVILAND, Mary, see CORRIE, William

HAWKE, Ann, see EDWARDS, John

HAWKE, John, to PAINTER, Rachel, Miss, both of NC Co, 10 Feb 1850, at Pennsbury Township PA, by Hugh Passmore, JP (DG 26 Feb 1850)

HAWKINS, Benjamin, Col., the venerable, agent for Indian Affairs, 6 Jun 1816 (AW 22 Jun 1816)

HAWKINS, Hannah, youngest dau of Mary HAWKINS, 10 Jul 1841, aged 7 yrs 10 mos 10 days (DG 16 Jul 1841)

HAWKINS, Lucy, see MILNOR, George A.

HAWKINS, Mary, see HAWKINS, Hannah

HAWKINS, Rebecca, wife of Thomas HAWKINS, in Wilm, 15 Dec 1824, in her 42nd yr. Leaves husband and 8 children; member of the Methodist Ch (DG 24 Dec 1824)

HAWKINS, Sarah, see MORROW, John

HAWKINS, Thomas, see HAWKINS, Rebecca

HAWKINS, Thomas, Sr., to McCANNON, Mary, Miss, 20 Oct 1825, by the Rev. Mr. White, all of NC Co (DG 26 Oct 1825)

HAWLEY, L., Capt., see DARLINGTON, Edward C.

HAWLEY, Mary L.,

see **DARLINGTON**, Edward C.

HAWTHORN, Emeline, see **PEACH**, John

HAWTHORN, William, to **GREENWALT**, Elizabeth, Miss, both of NC Co, 22 Nov 1833, by the Rev. A. K. Russel (DG DG 26 Nov 1833)

HAY, Forbes S., of Newark DE, to **LAUNY**, Catharine A., Miss, of Phila, on 57 Sep (sic) 1849, by the Rev. Henry D, Moore (DG 19 Oct 1849)

HAYES, Ann, see **HAYES**, Manlove

HAYES, Caroline A., at Cantwell's Bridge, 6 Oct 1848, aged 19 yrs (DG 14 Oct 1848)

HAYES, Eliza Jane, see **HOOLAHAN**, James

HAYES, Geo. Washington to **ZEBLEY**, Margaret, Miss, both of Wilm, 7 Apr 1853, by the Rev. S. R. Wynkoop (DG 15 Apr 1853)

HAYES, Henry Moore, Proprietor of the Elk Forge, to **BROOKS**, Eliza, Miss, both of Cecil Co, MD, in Wilm, 20 Apr 1821, by the Rev. Richard D. Hall (DG 24 Apr 1821)

HAYES, Jane, Mrs., widow of John **HAYES**, in the Village of Brandywine, 28 Jan 1849, in her 76th yr (DG 9 Feb 1849)

HAYES, John, see **HAYES**, Jane see **HAYES**, Rachel

HAYES, John, Sr., in Brandywine Village, 23 Sep 1842, aged 75 yrs (DG 30 Sep 1842) late of the Village of Brandywine, notice given by John HAYS and Louis W. HAYS, adm'rs (DG 21 Oct 1842) see **HOOLAHAN**, James

HAYES, Manlove, dec'd, late of Cantwell's Bridge, notice given by Ann HAYES, adm'x, Purnel TATMAN, adm'r (DG 12 Aug 1831)

HAYES, Manlove, Esq., at his res. near Dover, 9 Jul 1849, in his 81st yr (DG 13 Jul 1849)

HAYES, Mary C., see **LYNCH**, Amos W.

HAYES, Myers, to **MOODY**, Sarah E., Miss, both of Christiana Hd, at Chester, 11 Nov 1830 (DF 20 Nov 1830)

HAYES, Phebe E., see **MATLACK**, Charles P.

HAYES, Rachel, Mrs., relict of the late John HAYES, Esq., cashier of the Bank of Delaware, after a short illness, 2 Apr 1813 (DS 6 Apr 1813)

HAYES, Rhoda, see **MENDENHALL**, Edward S.

HAYES, Samuel, Esq., of Cecil Co, MD, to **WARRINGTON**, Ann B., Miss, of Wilm, 9 Dec 1824, by the Rev. E. W. Gilbert (DG 14 Dec 1824) (Cl 17 Dec 1824)

HAYES, Sarah E., see **CHALFANT**, Jacob M.

HAYES, Stephen, see **PEDRECK**, Joshua

HAYHURST, Edward, son of Thomas and Martha HAYHURST, in Phila, 7 Jan 1849, in his 25th yr (DG 16 Jan 1849)

HAYHURST, Martha, see **HAYHURST**, Edward

HAYHURST, Thomas, see **HAYHURST**, Edward

HAYHURST, Warren Mifflin, printer, in Kennett Square PA, 21 Sep 1845, aged 21 yrs (DG 10 Sep 1845)

HAYMAN, Giles, see **HAYMAN**, Nicholas

HAYMAN, Jacob, see **HAYMAN**, William Henry

HAYMAN, John, see **HAYMAN**, Nicholas

HAYMAN, Mary, see **HAYMAN**, William Henry

HAYMAN, Nicholas, late of Christiana Bridge, left the country and is reported dead. Sons: John, Giles, Nicholas and Peter (PG 30 Jul 1752)

HAYMAN, Nicholas [2], see **HAYMAN**, Nicholas

HAYMAN, Peter, see **HAYMAN**, Nicholas

HAYMAN, William Henry, second son of Jacob and Mary HAYMAN, at the res. of his father in Wilm, 1 Nov 1842, aged 4 yrs 3 mos 1 day (DG 8 Nov 1842)

HAYS, Addis, see **STEWART**, Samuel

HAYS, Emeline N. see **DAVIS**, Theodore L.

HAYS, James P., to **FLINN**, Abigail A., Miss, both of Wilm, 21 Dec 1848, by Rev. S. R. Wynkoop (DG 26 Dec 1848)

HAYS, John, of Wilm, to **RATCLIFF**, Elizabeth, Miss, of Sussex Co, 16 Jan 1851, by Rev. T. P. McColley (DG 28 Jan 1851)

HAYS, John, see HAYES, John Sr.

HAYS, John, son of Reuben HAYS, 3 Aug 1848, aged 3 yrs (DG 15 Aug 1848)

HAYS, Louis W., see HAYES, John Sr.

HAYS, Manlove, see TATMAN, Collins, Esq.

HAYS, Martha J., see TAYLOR, Franklin

HAYS, Mary Ann, see STEWART, Samuel

HAYS, Rebekah, see BEDWELL, William

HAYS, Reuben, see HAYS, John

HAYS, Sarah, dau of the late MACBETH, John, of Newark, at Grand Gulf, Miss., of congestive fever, 13 Aug 1851, aged c 50 yrs (DG 5 Sep 1851)

HAYS, Susan, see WOODS, James

HAYS, William, of Phila, to LOTT, Agnes, Miss., of NC Co, 29 May 1833, by the Rev. Joseph Walker (DG 11 Jun 1833)

HAYWARD, James F., Dr., of Charleston SC, to PRESSTMAN, Maria T., Miss, of Balt, in Balt, 4 Nov 1851, at the house of I. R. TRIMBLE, Esq., by the Rt. Rev. Alfred Lee, Bishop of DE (DG 7 Nov 1851)

HAZARD, Phebe, see THOMAS, Evan Henry, Esq.

HAZEL, Elizabeth, Mrs., wife of James HAZEL, Esq., near Blackiston's Xroads, 28 Nov 1851, na (DG 5 Dec 1851)

HAZEL, James, see HAZEL, Elizabeth

HAZELL, William B, merchant, to FIELDS, Sarah J., dau of Benjamin FIELDS, Esq., 27 Jul 1843, near Middletown, by Rev. F. B. Tibbles (DG 18 Aug 1843)

HAZLET, Bennet, of Wilm, to CRAMER, Mary, Miss, of Kensington, 18 May 1853, by the Rev. Robert J. Black (DG 24 May 1853)

HAZLET, George M., see HAZLET, Sarah L.

HAZLET, Sarah L., Mrs., wife of George N. HAZLET, in Brandywine Village, 6 Jan 1851, in her 56th yr (DG 24 Jan 1851)

HAZLET, Thomas S., to SMITH, Jerusha, Miss, of Wilm, 23 Mar 1853 by the Rev. George Chandler (DG 29 Mar 1853)

HAZLITT, James A., to FREEZE, Lydia, Miss, 22 May 1828, by Elder John P. Peckworth, all of Wilm (DG 27 May 1828)

HAZWELL, George R., to KIRBY, Sarah H., Miss, 22 Feb 1847, by Rev. Mr. Dorr (DG 26 Feb 1847)

HAZZARD, David, see WOLFE, Erasmus D.

HAZZARD, John, Esq.,Major, long an active merchant and a member of the M. E. Ch upward of 30 yrs, at his res. in Milton, DE, 26 Dec 1825, aged 73 yrs (DG 3 Jan 1826)

HAZZARD, John F., formerly of Sussex Co, to TYNER, Louisiana, of Brookville IN, 24 Feb 1853, by the Rev. T. M. Eddy (DG 8 Mar 1853)

HAZZARD, Maria, see WOLFE, Erasmus D.

HEADOCK John, of Marcus Hook, to McCLINTOCK, Isabella, of Wilm, 12 Jan 1851, at Marcus Hook, by the Rev. Henry H. Bean (DG 21 Jan 1851)

HEAGLES, Joseph, a German, found dead in a lot in Newark. Carpet weaver by trade. Took laudanum (DG 11 Jul 1845)

HEALD, Henry, overseer of the Poorhouse of NC Co, of bilious fever, 5 Dec 1829, aged 51 yrs (DG 11 Dec 1829)

HEALD, Jacob, see PRICE, Isaiah

HEALD, Joshua T., to PUSEY, Hannah, all of Wilm, 18 Apr 1844, at the house of Jonas PUSEY, in accordance with the order of the Society of Friends (DG 23 Apr 1844)

HEALD, Lydia, see PRICE, Isaiah

HEALD, Mary, Mrs., in Phila, 24 Oct 1848, aged 54 yrs. Obit Nov 3 (DG 30 Oct 1848)

HEARN, Joseph J., to WALLER, Amanda W., both of Sussex, 1 Dec 1846, in St. John's Church, Little Hell [near Little Heaven] by Rev. Jacob B. Smith (DG 15 Jan 1847)

HEATHCOTE, Andrew, of Chester, PA, to ROBINSON, Elizabeth J., Miss, of NC Co, 28 Jun 1853, by the Rev. Wm. E. Moore (DG 4 Jul 1853)

HEATHER, Horatio N., of Kent Co, to CADE, Hester Jane, Miss, of Sussex Co, in Phila, 8 Nov 1834, by Rev. C. Pitman (DG 18 Nov 1834)

HEAZLITT, John, of Phila, to ROBINSON, Ann, Miss, of Wilm, 4 Jan 1827, by the Rev. John P. Peckworth (DG 5 Jan 1827)

HEDGES, Adeline, dau of John and Elizabeth HEDGES, in Wilm, 30 Jul 1853, na (DG 30 Dec 1853) late of Wilm Hd, Urban D. HEDGES, adm'r (DG 23 Sep 1853)

HEDGES, Elizabeth,
see HEDGES, Adeline

HEDGES, Elizabeth, wife of John HEDGES, in Wilm, 28 Dec 1853, in her 76th yr (DG 30 Dec 1853)

HEDGES, Hannah, Mrs., relict of the late Joseph HEDGES, at the res. of her son-in-law, William TOWNSEND, 16 Apr 1829, aged 87 yrs (DG 17 Apr 1829)

HEDGES, Hannah F.,
see STROUD, James

HEDGES, John, see HEDGES, Adeline
see DONALDSON, Sarah
see HEDGES, Elizabeth

HEDGES, Joseph, see HEDGES, Hannah

HEDGES, Urban D.,
see HEDGES, Adeline

HEDRICK, John, 18 Sep 1824, na (DG 21 Sep 1824)

HEDRICK, Lewis B., 25 Nov 1842, aged 30 yrs (DG 2 Dec 1842)

HELFORD, Washington C., a native of DE, at Fort Gibson, by the accidental discharge of a pistol, ndd, na (DG 23 Jan 1835)

HELLINGS, Sarah, see COX, John

HELMHOLD, Edward R.,
see HELMHOLD, Eliza Jane

HELMHOLD, Eliza Jane, dau of Edward R. and Louisa HELMHOLD, 18 Nov 1848 (DG 5 Dec 1848)

HELMHOLD, Louisa,
see HELMHOLD, Eliza Jane

HELMS, Hugh, 2 Dec 1848, in his 56th yr (DG 8 Dec 1848)

HEMPHILL, Elizabeth, Mrs., widow of the late William HEMPHILL, Esq., merchant of Wilm, 11 Dec 1825, aged 80 yrs (DG 6 Dec 1825)notice given by James HEMPHILL, adm'r (DG 28 Apr 1826)

HEMPHILL, James,
see HEMPHILL, Elizabeth

HEMPHILL, James, Esq., in Phila, 4 Apr 1833, aged 59 yrs (DG 9 Apr 1833)

HEMPHILL, James, infant son of John HEMPHILL, in Phila, 8 Apr 1826, aged 16 mos; brought to Wilm for burial (DG 11 Apr 1826)

HEMPHILL, John, see HEMPHILL, James

HEMPHILL, Margaret,
see SANDERS, John F.

HEMPHILL, William,
see HEMPHILL, Elizabeth, Mrs.

HEMPHILL, William, Esq., merchant, res. 102 Market St, 10 Feb 1823, in his 81st yr (DG 11 Feb 1823) obit (DG 14 Feb 1823)

HENDERSON, Elizabeth,
see BRADEN Leonard

HENDERSON, George, to HASLETT, Jemima, Miss, dau of the late Gov. HASLETT of DE, both of Phila, at Georgetown, 10 Sep 1835, by the Rev. John R. Torbert (DG 29 Sep 1835)

HENDERSON, Hannah,
see HENDERSON, James

HENDERSON, James, dec'd, late of Wilm, notice given by Hannah HENDERSON, adm'x (DG 2 Apr 1833)

HENDERSON, Levi, of Delaware, to PARRIS, Jane, Miss, of Port Penn, 28 Sep 1841, by Rev. A. D. Gillette (DG 15 Oct 1841)

HENDERSON, Margaret Young,
see BARR, John

HENDERSON, Mary,
see MYERS, Alexander

HENDERSON, William, of Wilm, to HOLSTON, Amy D., of Brandywine, 14 May 1841, by Rev. R. Gerry (DG 9 Jul 1841)

HENDRICKS, Christopher, n, 13 Feb 1789, aged over 100 yrs (DG 14 Feb 1789)

HENDRICKSON, Ann, Miss,
see ARMOR, James Jr.

HENDRICKSON, Anna Walter, 25 Nov 1845, aged 12 yrs (DG 2 Dec 1845)

HENDRICKSON, David, to JONES, Margaret, Miss, both of NC Co, 20 Dec 1827, by John P. Peckworth (DG 28 Dec 1827)

HENDRICKSON, Eliza Ann, at Newport, 18 Feb 1849, in her 12th yr (DG 2 Mar 1849)

HENDRICKSON, Isaac,
see HENDRICKSON, Joseph

HENDRICKSON, John S., to PERRY, Jane, Miss, both of Wilm, 6 Mar 1833, by the Rev. E. W. Gilbert (DG 12 Mar 1833)

HENDRICKSON, Joseph, to CHANDLER,

Rebecca A., Miss, both of NC Co,
2 Feb 1830, by Dr. J. J. Janneway of Phila
(DG 5 Feb 1830)

HENDRICKSON, Joseph, at Oak Hill,
Christiana Hd, 31 Dec 1852, aged 78 yrs
(DG 7 Jan 1853) Isaac HENDRICKSON,
exec'r (DG 18 Jan 1853)

HENDRICKSON, Joseph G., Esq., to
CHANDLER, Adaline P., both of NC Co,
12 Sep 1850, by Rev. S. R. Wynkoop
(DG 20 Sep 1850)
see HENDRICKSON Rebecca

HENDRICKSON, Joseph, Jr., to MERVINE,
Caroline, Miss, in Phila, 27 Jul 1851, by the
Rev. J. D. Duplee (DG 1 Aug 1851)

HENDRICKSON, Margaret A.,
see McCLARY, Thomas

HENDRICKSON, Margaretta,
see CLOUD, Andrew M.

HENDRICKSON, Mary Ann,
see DAVIDSON, John

HENDRICKSON, Peregrine, Esq., at his
res. near Middletown, 18 May 1851,
aged c 63 yrs; late of Appoq Hd,
Henry DAVIS, adm'r (DG 27 May 1851)

HENDRICKSON, Peter, at his res. in
Christiana Hd, after a short illness,
9 Jun 1843, aged 67 yrs (DG 9 Jun 1843)

HENDRICKSON, Peter, to McCULLOUGH,
Deborah, Miss, both of Christiana Hd, in
Wilm, 4 Mar 1824, by the Rev. E. W. Gilbert
(DG 9 Mar 1824)

HENDRICKSON, Rebecca, wife of Joseph
G. HENDRICKSON, in Christiana Hd,
20 Aug 1849, aged 37 yrs
(DG 28 Aug 1849)

HENDRICKSON, Sarah, of yellow fever
(DE 17 Sep 1798)

HENDRICKSON, Sarah Ann,
see SUTTON, Isaac F.

HENDRICKSON, William H., to VERNON,
Ann Maria, Miss, both of Wilm, at New
London PA, 20 Sep 1849, by the Rev.
Mr. DuBoise (DG 25 Sep 1849)

HENDRIX, Eliza Ann, see PERKINS, J. D.

HENNONS, Nancy, Mrs, wife of Rhodes S.
HENNONS, in Milford, 15 Feb 1853,
in her 49th yr (DG 22 Feb 1853)

HENNONS, Rhodes S.,
see HENNONS, Nancy

HENRY, Catharine, see PORTER, Robert

HENRY, Eliza, see PORTER, Scott

HENRY, Ida, only child of Sarah and John J.
HENRY, in Red Lion Hd, of croup, 20 Nov
1853, aged 2 yrs 4 mos (DG 29 Nov 1853)

HENRY, John J., to DEAL, Sarah, Miss,
both of NC Co, at the res. of W. F.
O'DANIEL, in Wilm by Rev. S. R. Wynkoop
(DG 9 Jan 1846)
see HENRY, Ida

HENRY, Margaret, see McDANIEL, Joseph

HENRY, Martha, see PORTER, Robert

HENRY, Sarah, see HENRY, Ida

HENSHAW, Elizabeth,
see McCALL, John S.

HERDMAN, Eliza Ann,
see WALKER, John W.

HERDMAN, John, to MOORE, Eliza Jane
Magee, Miss, dau of John MOORE, all of NC
Co, 27 Dec 1843, by Rev. W. R. Work
(DG 5 Jan 1844)

HERDMAN, John, in Newark, of
consumption, 24 Jul 1850, in his 47th yr
(DG 30 Jul 1850)

HERDMAN, William, Esq., at his res. in
Christiana Hd, aged 69 yrs (DG 2 Sep 1842)
see PHILLIPS, Robert

HERMANCE, John P., of NY, to FIELDS,
Sarah, Miss, of Newark, 30 Apr 1851, by
the Rev. A. C. FIELDS (DG 6 May 1851)

HERN, Jonathan, to LERMAN, Sarah
Elizabeth, both of Laurel DE, 20 Oct 1851,
on board the schooner *Watchman* by Rev.
Fielder Israel (DG 24 Oct 1851)

HERON, Alexander,
see JOHNSON, Benjamin
see WILLIER, Henry R.

HERON, Alexina,
see JOHNSON, Benjamin

HERON, Mary Elizabeth,
see WILLIER, Henry R.

HERONS, William, carpenter by trade,
native of Wilm, 12 Feb 1741, lost overboard
from steamer *Augusta* near New Orleans
(DG 26 Feb 1841)

HERRETT, Abilony, see KELLER, George

HERRING, Abner, see THORP, Henry

see **CLIFT**, Edward

HERRING, Anna Maria, for many years a resident of NC Co, wife of Langford HERRING, at her res. in Vine St. Phila, 8 Feb 1844, aged 71 yrs (DG 23 Feb 1844)

HERRING, Elizabeth J., see **THORP**, Henry

HERRING, Langford, see **HERRING**, Anna Maria

HERRING, Margaret Ann, see **OSKINS**, William H.

HERRING, Martha, Miss, see **CLIFT**, Edward

HERRING, Sarah A., see **DAWSON**, Willard H.

HERSEY, Benjamin, see **DUNLAP**, Samuel

HERSEY, Solomon, of Wilm, 29 Aug 1847 (DG 31 Aug 1847)

HESS, Hiram R., of Phila, to **POWELL**, Martha, Miss, of Wilm, at Chester, PA, 8 Jun 1835, by Samuel Smith, Esq. (DG 23 Jun 1835) see **HESS**, Martha P.

HESS, Martha P., Mrs., wife of Hiram R. Hess, 8 Mar 1852, in her 35th yr, Catholic (DG 23 Mar 1852)

HESSEMER, Philip, to **ISRAEL**, Maria, Miss, all of Wilm, in Phila, 17 May 1847, by Rev. T. G. Allen (DG 21 May 1847)

HESTON, Elizabeth, see **HESTON**, Susan Emma

HESTON, Mahlon K., see **HESTON**, Susan Emma

HESTON, Newton, Rev., of the Phila Conf., to **GAUSE**, Martha Johnson, Miss, dau of Jesse GAUSE, of Wilm, 16 Oct 1851, in St. Paul's ME Ch, Wilm, by Rev. F. A. Hodgson DD (DG 21 Oct 1851)

HESTON, Susan Emma, dau of Mahlon K. and Elizabeth HESTON, in Mason Co IL, 18 Jul 1853, of lung disease, aged 6 yrs 2 mos 8 days (DG 26 Aug 1853)

HEUSEMAN, Daniel, see **FOX**, James Jr.

HEUSEMAN, Letitia S., see **FOX**, James Jr.

HEVERIN, Outten L., to **WEBB**, Elizabeth A., Miss, both of Kent Co, 3 May 1848, by Rev. James Allen (DG 12 May 1848)

HEVERN, William, late of Appoq Hd, Benjamin McKAY, Sr., adm'r (DG 19 Oct 1852)

HEWES, Edward C. to **GARRETT**, Sarah S., of Wilm, 9 Sep 1841, at Friend's Meeting House (DG 17 Sep 1841)

HEWES, Edward C., formerly of Elk Iron Works, Cecil Co MD, of cholera, in San Francisco, 30 Nov 1850 (DG 14 Jan 1851)

HEWES, Sarah G., dau of Thomas GARRETT, in Wilm, 4 Sep 1853, aged 34 yrs (DG 6 Sep 1853)

HEWS, Joseph, see **WAY**, Joshua

HEYLIN, Frances V., see **HICKMAN**, William M.

HEYLIN, I. Newton, see **HICKMAN**, William M.

HEYSER, Jane B., see **ASKEW**, Joseph

HICKMAN, Charlotte R., see **SPEAKMAN**, Lewis

HICKMAN, Eliza, see **HICKMAN**, Mary see **HICKMAN**, Hiram

HICKMAN, George, at his res. in Lewes, 7 Aug 1851, in his 74th yr (DG 12 Aug 1851) see **HALL**, George see **HICKMAN**, Sarah

HICKMAN, Hiram, son of William and Eliza HICKMAN, ill 5 days of scarlet fever, at New London Cross-Roads, 19 Feb 1850, aged 1 yr 6 mos (DG 5 Mar 1850)

HICKMAN, John H., to **SCOTT**, Sarepta, both of Kent Co, 30 Dec 1852 (DG 1 Feb 1853)

HICKMAN, Joseph, see **VAN BURKELOW**, John

HICKMAN, Margaret H., see **LILLAGORE**, Theodore W.

HICKMAN, Mary, dau of William and Eliza HICKMAN, ill 5 days of scarlet fever, 19 Feb 1850, at New London Cross-Roads, aged 4 yrs (DG 5 Mar 1850) see **HICKMAN**, Sarah

HICKMAN, Mary Caroline, see **HALL**, George

HICKMAN, Patience, see **VAN BURKELOW**, John

HICKMAN, Phoebe Ann, negro, died suddenly, of lung inflammation, aged

17 yrs; inquest 6 Aug 1853, natural causes (DG 9 Aug 1853)

HICKMAN, Sarah, Miss, eldest dau of George and Mary HICKMAN, aged 21 yrs 3 mos 10 days, 2 Feb 1842, at her father's res. near Lewes, after a lingering illness (DG 11 Feb 1842)
see McCOMMON, Thomas

HICKMAN, William, of Smyrna, to CARTMELL, Elizabeth, Miss, of Brandywine Hd, 16 Dec 1809, by the Rev. Wm. Pryce (DG 23 Dec 1809)

HICKMAN, William, to KIRK, Elizabeth, Miss, both of Wilm, in Wilm, 27 Apr 1824, by the Rev. E. W. Gilbert (DG 30 Apr 1824)
see HICKMAN, Mary
see HICKMAN, Hiram

HICKMAN, William M., of Lewes, to HEYLIN, Frances V., Miss, dau of the late I. Newton HEYLIN of IL, 21 Nov 1853, at the res. of T. Broom SMITH, Esq., Phila, by the Rev. James G. Shinn (DG 24 Nov 1853)

HICKS, F. A.(fem),
see HICKS, Robert Derwood

HICKS, Henry, Esq., in Wilm, 24 Jun 1853, in his 55th yr (DG 28 Jun 1853) Obit-Born in Dorchester Co MD, public service career data given (DG 4 Jul 1853)

HICKS, R. D., see HICKS, Robert Derwood

HICKS, Robert Denwood, son of R. D. and F. A. HICKS, in Wilm, 5 Jan 1850, aged 3 yrs 9 mos 22 days (DG 8 Jan 1850)

HICKS, Robert M., to LIVINGSTON, Margaret, Miss, both of Milford, 8 Sep 1850, by Rev. Mr. Aspril (DG 31 Dec 1850)

HIDE, J. B., to LAWRENCE, Mary, Miss, both of Wilm, in Chester, 28 Feb 1852, by Rev. J. W. Gibbs (DG 2 Mar 1852)

HIGBE, _____, Mrs., widow of James HIGBE, shortly after her husband, ndd, na (DG 16 Aug 1853)

HIGBEE, James, of Brandywine, to PETERSON, Margaret, Miss, in Wilm, nmd (DG 2 Apr 1847)

HIGBE, James, of Brandywine Village, ndd, na (DG 16 Aug 1853)
see HIGBE, _____, Mrs.

HIGBY, Daniel, see HIGBY, Mary

HIGBY, Mary, only dau of the Rev. Daniel HIGBY, ndd, na (DG 6 Apr 1827)

HIGGINBOTHAM, Edward G., Dr., of Richmond VA, to THOMSON, Julia A., dau of Dr. James W. THOMSON, of Wilm, 3 Nov 1853, by the Rt. Rev. Alfred Lee (DG 8 Nov 1853)

HIGGINS, Ann M., see JENKS, M. H.

HIGGINS, Anthony, Esq., at his late mansion in Cox's Neck, Red Lion Hd, 1 May 1824, in his 60th yr (Cl 14 May 1824)

HIGGINS, George, see McCLUNG, John R.

HIGGINS, Harriott, see EVES, John D.

HIGGINS, Jacob K., merchant of Wilm, to MURRAY, Martha J. of Phila, 15 Nov 1835, by Rev. J. Rusling (DG 17 Nov 1835)

HIGGINS, James Edward, only child of Rev. Solomon HIGGINS, 27 Jul 1827, aged 1 yr 24 days (DG 7 Aug 1827)

HIGGINS, John, of St. Georges to SAWYER, Ann, Miss, of New Castle, in Phila, 12 Nov 1822, by S. Badger, Esq. (DG 19 Nov 1822)

HIGGINS, John,
see RAYMOND, Benjamin, Esq.

HIGGINS, John, Col., at his res. in Red Lion Hd., 10 Jul 1848, after a protracted illness (DG 14 Jul 1848)

HIGGINS, Joseph, in Mill Creek Hd, 6 Jan 1853, aged 84 yrs (DG 18 Jan 1853)

HIGGINS, Patrick, an aged and worthy citizen, found dead in the Christiana, 29 Aug 1847 (DG 31 Aug 1847)

HIGGINS, Ruth Ann,
see McCLUNG, John R.

HIGGINS, S., Dr., to STEVENSON, Margaret, Miss, 26 Mar 1833, by Rev. Mr. Lybrand, all of Wilm (DG 29 Mar 1833)

HIGGINS, Samuel, of St Georges Hd, 10 Mar 1798, at Christiana Bridge (DE 12 Mar 1798)

HIGGINS, Sarah, see TITUS, Thomas

HIGGINS, Solomon, Rev.,
see HIGGINS, James Edward

HIGGINS, Thomas, to KELLEY, Elizabeth, Miss, both of Mill Creek Hd, 20 Apr 1852, by Rev. S. R. Wynkoop (DG 23 Apr 1852)

HIGHAM, Edward, to HAMPTON, Susanna D., all of Wilm, 16 Apr 1844, by Rev. M. J. Rhees (DG 19 Apr 1844)

HIGHAM, Mary, see LEE, Joseph

HILL, Absalom, to JESTER, Rachael D., Miss, all of Sussex Co, 15 Feb 1853, by Rev. McColley (DG 22 Feb 1853)

HILL, Caroline, see WIGGINS, Alexander M.

HILL, Charlotte Elizabeth, see GREENE, Charles G.

HILL, George, see WIGGINS, Alexander M.

HILL, George Lewis, son of James HILL, in Smyrna, 10 Jan 1853, in his 4th yr (DG 18 Jan 1853)

HILL, George P., to SPENCER, Elizabeth I., Miss, all of Wilm, 4 May 1851, by the Rev. Andrew Manship (DG 9 May 1851)

HILL, Jacob M., merchant of Cowgillsville, Kent Co, DE, to LAWS, Amelia, Miss, dau of the late Outen LAWS, Esq., of St. Jones' Neck, at the house of John PLEASANTON, Esq.,12 Feb 1824, by the Rev. John Durborough (DG 17 Feb 1824)

HILL, James, see HILL, George Lewis

HILL, John, colored, results of coroner's inquest, by O. D.Jester, Cor., death from too free use of spiritous liquors and exposure, 7 June 1847 (DG 11 Jun 1847)

HILL, John P., in Smyrna, 9 Apr 1821, in his 23rd yr (DG 20 Apr 1821)

HILL, Lavinia Ann, see VINCINGER, William

HILL, Mary Elizabeth, see BOND, William E.

HILL, Samuel, see GREEENE, Charles G.

HILL, Samuel V., of NC Co, to SHOEMAKER, Hester Ann, Miss, dau of Charles SHOEMAKER, Esq., of Phila, in Phila, 8 Nov 1849, by the Rev. A.D. Gillette (DG 16 Nov 1849)

HILLES, William S., of Wilm, to ALLEN, Sarah L., of Atleboro, Bucks Co Pa, 17 May 1849, at Friends meeting in Atleboro (DG 25 May 1849)

HILLIS, Eli, see FERRISS, John

HILLMAN, Benjamin, in Wilm, 25 Nov 1852, in his 74th yr (DG 30 Nov 1852)

HILLMAN, Mary Ellen, see THORNTON, Thomas [Thos.]

HILLMAN, Thomas, see THORNTON, Thos.

HILLYARD, Harriet, see HALL, Willard

HILT, William, to RITCHIE, Eliza, Miss, in Wilm, 30 Apr 1829, by the Rev. Isaac Pardee (DG 5 May 1829)

HILYARD, Simon S., to BARTLEY, Margaret Jane, all of New Castle, 8 Sep 1853, at the res. of Mr.BARTLEY of New Castle, by Rev. W. B. Walton (DG 16 Sep 1853)

HILYARD, Thomas S., Esq., 21 May 1841, at his res. near Dover, aged 49 yrs (DG 28 May 1841)

HIMSBY, Amos, see HIMSBY, Sarah Ann

HIMSBY, Sarah Ann, widow of the dec'd Amos HIMSBY, 20 Jul 1853, at Templeville MD, aged 78 yrs (DG 2 Aug 1853)

HINCHMAN, George, see HINCHMAN, Mary

HINCHMAN, Mary, only child of George HINCHMAN, 5 Oct 1846, aged c 10 yrs (DG16 Oct 1846)

HINDMAN, J., Col., of the U. S. Army, to HYATT, Susan, Miss, dau of the late John HYATT, Esq., of DE, in Phila, 12 Jul 1825, by the Rt. Rev. Bishop White (DG 19 Jul 1825)

HINDMAN, John, see CHANDLER, Benjamin

HINDMAN, Rebecca, see CHANDLER, Benjamin

HINDS, William S., to BARROW, Emelie M., both of Phila, dau of Denwood H. BARROW, in Phila, at High St. ME Ch, 6 Jan 1853, by Rev. Benjamin F. Brook (DG 14 Jan 1853)

HINES, Samuel R., to McWHORTER, Elizabeth J. Miss, dau of the late David McWHORTER, both of Delaware City, in Phila, 4 Jul 1853, by the Rev. Alexander Macklin (DG 12 Jul 1853)

HINES, Sarah, see SMITH, William

HINES, Susanna, see KIRBY, Thomas

HINKSON, Washington, see TRANOR, Mary

HINTON, Eliza Ann, see FULLMEAL, Andrew

HINTZE, F. B., see GRIFFIN, John A.

HINTZE, Henrietta Hellen (sic),

see **GRIFFIN**, John A.

HIPPLE, Jacob, late of Montgomery Co PA, to **CARPENTER**, Elizabeth, Miss, of Centerville DE, at Chester PA, 23 Jan 1851, by the Rev. Mr. Gibbs (DG 4 Mar 1851)

HIRONS, John, see **VEASEY**, George Clinton

HIRONS, John, Sr., 27 Jul 1829, na (DG 28 Jul 1829)

HIRONS, Lydia Gilpin, see **VEASEY**, George Clinton

HITCH, Mary A., see **COLLISON**, Stansbury

HITCH, Spencer, to **ALEXANDER**, arah, Mrs., of Kent Co, 29 Oct 1850, by Rev. James Aspril (DG 5 Oct 1850)

HITCHENS, Myers B., to **GRIMES**, Sarah Ann, Miss, both of NC Co, 3 Dec 1850, by Rev. Andrew Manship (DG 6 Dec 1850)

HITCHINGS, Lucinda, see **MORTON**, Isaac H.

HOBART, ___. Mrs., see **WALTER**, Richard Gilpin

HOBSON, Francis, see **SHARP**, Elizabeth J.

HOCKER, William, in Wilm, 20 Sep 1835, aged c 21 yrs. In the employ of Alexander PORTER as a coach driver, he was kicked in the abdomen by a horse, which caused his death after about 26 hours. Born in England; is said to have a father living in Wayne Co, PA (DG 22 Sep 1835)

HODGE, Isabella B., see **KINSLEY**, Robert

HODGSON, Eliza, see **GEMMILL**, Hugh

HODGSON, George, near the new bridge on the Brandywine in Christiana Hd (DG 27 Mar 1849)

HODGSON, George W., of Cantwell's Bridge to **MINNER**, Margaret A., Miss, formerly of Frederica, in Wilm, 9 Oct 1849, by the Rev. Wm. Cooper (DG 16 Oct 1849)

HODGSON, James, of Chester co, PA, to **GILLESPIE**, Elizabeth, Miss, of NC Co, near Newark, 15 Feb 1827, by the Rev. A. K. Russell (DG 16 Feb 1827)

HODGSON, James B., see **GEMMILL**, Hugh

HODGSON, Margaret B., see **SMITH**, Elwood E.

HODSON, Juliet, see **BECKLEY**, Robinson

HODSON, Mary, see **RANKIN**, Parker

HODSON, Robert W., to **JORDAN**, Amanda, Miss, both of Wilm, 21 Dec 1845, by Rev. James Meredith (DG 16 Jan 1846)

HOEKSMAN, George, of Phila, to **DINGY**, Elizabeth, Miss, of Wilm, on the 28th inst. by Rev. M. J. Reese (DG 13 Mar 1849)

HOFFAY, B., to **DAVIS**, Emily, Miss, both of Wilm, 12 Mar 1844, at the house of Jesse M. JUSTIS in Marcus Hook, by B. F. Johnson, Esq. (DG 19 Mar 1844)

HOFFAY, Mary T., see **McINTYRE**, Thomas Jr.

HOFFAY, Victoria, in Wilm, 19 Jan 1844, aged 46 yrs 4 mos 1 day. Leaves husband and family (DG 23 Jan 1844)

HOFFECKER, Arraminta, dau of James P. and Jessephia HOFFECKER, in Raymond's Neck, [south of Woodland Beach] 29 Jan 1851, aged 4 yrs 10 days (DG 14 Feb 1851)

HOFFECKER, Emlie, see **BELL**, Wm. M.

HOFFECKER, Henry D., late of St. Georges Hd. Mary H. HOFFECKER, exec'x (DG 3 Jan 1852)

HOFFECKER, James, to **WINDLE**, Elizabeth, both of Kent Co, 12 Jan 1853 (DG 1 Feb 1853)

HOFFECKER, James P., see **HOFFECKER**, Arraminta

HOFFECKER, Jessephia, see **HOFFECKER**, Arraminta

HOFFECKER, John H., of Smyrna, to **APPLETON**, Annie E., Miss, only dau of Mr. John APPLETON, of Cantwell's Bridge at Cantwell's Bridge, 19 May 1853, by the Rev. Joseph Aspril (DG 24 May 1853)

HOFFECKER, Joseph, see **HUFFINGTON**, Jesse S. see **BELL**, Wm. M.

HOFFECKER, Joseph Jr, see **SUMPTION**, Charles

HOFFECKER, Joseph V., to **SAVIN**, Susan A., Miss, dau of the late Wm. SAVIN, Esq., all of Duck Creek Hd, Kent Co, 8 Mar 1853, by the Rev. G. W. Lybrand (DG 15 Mar 1853)

HOFFECKER, Mary, see **HUFFINGTON**, Jesse S.

HOFFECKER, Mary H.,
see **HOFFECKER**, Henry D.

HOFFMAN, Caroline, see **NETHERY**, Lea J.

HOGARTH, Julia Sophia, dau of the Rev. William HOGARTH, in Geneva, NY, 11 Mar 1849, in her 4th yr (DG 23 Mar 1849)

HOGARTH, William, Rev., of Wilm, to **HASTINGS**, Fidelia A., Miss, of Geneva, N. Y., 26 Apr 1842, in Geneva by Rev. P. C. Hay (DG 6 May 1842)
see **HOGARTH**, Julia Sophia

HOGG, Catherine, see **POLK**, Robert

HOGG, James, in Wilm, after a lingering illness, 25 Aug 1844 (DG 30 Aug 1844)
see **HOGG**, Samuel

HOGG, Jane, Mrs., in Wilm, 9 Jul 1852, in her 90th yr (DG 16 Jul 1852)

HOGG, Samuel, tallow chandler, dec'd, late of Wilm, notice given by James HOGG, exec'r (DE 11 Jan 1798)

HOGG, Wm. C., in Wilm, 17 Jun 1849, na (DG 19 Jun 1849)

HOLCOMB, Chauncey P., son of Chauncey P. and Rebecca HOLCOMB, in New Castle Hd, 10 Apr 1850, aged 15 mos (DG 12 Apr 1850)
see **HOLCOMB**, Rebecca

HOLCOMB, Rebecca, wife of Chauncey P. HOLCOMB, and dau of the late Bankson TAYLOR of Phila, at the res. of her husband near New Castle, 3 Nov 1851, in her 34th yr (DG 7 Nov 1851)
see **HOLCOMB**, Chauncey P.

HOLCOMBE, George, member of the House of Congress, at his res. in Allentown NJ, of consumption, ndd, na (DG 22 Jan 1828)

HOLDING, Ebenezer B., of Smyrna DE, to **SMITH**, Martha Phedora, Miss, of Smyrna, 15 Jul 1851, by the Rev. P. Carpenter (*Phila Ledger* please copy) (DG 18 Jul 1851)
see **HOLDING**, Henrietta

HOLDING, Henrietta, wife of Ebenezer B. HOLDING, 24 Feb 1848, in her 22nd yr. Leaves inf dau, affectionate husband, several brothers and sisters, and a wide circle of friends (DG 17 Mar 1848)

HOLDING, Samuel H., to **COLLINS**, Mary A., dau of George COLLINS, Esq., of NC Co, 7 Nov 1844, in Phila by Rev. J. D. Onens (DG 12 Nov 1844)

HOLLAND, Amanda, Mrs, wife of William HOLLAND, 9 Feb 1847, of consumption (DG 16 Feb 1847)

HOLLAND, David, to **GRAY**, Elizabeth, Miss, both of Sussex, 27 Mar 1850, by Rev. T. P. McColley (DG 2 Apr 1850)

HOLLAND, Eliza Jane, Mrs., consort of Ruben HOLLAND, 27 Oct 1844, in Wilm (DG 29 Oct 1844)

HOLLAND, Ellen J.,
see **DOUGHERTY**, Charles Jr.

HOLLAND, Henry, to **STARLING**, Martha, Miss, 17 Dec 1842, by Rev. Mr. Lowe, all of NC Co (DG 23 Dec 1842)

HOLLAND. John, at his res. near New Bridge on the Brandywine, after a short illness, 13 Oct 1846 (DG 20 Oct 1846)

HOLLAND, John, of Brandywine, NC Co to **BAXTER**, Barbara Anna, Miss, at Phila, 23 Dec 1848, by Rev. M. Clighten (DG 5 Jan 1849)

HOLLAND, John, to **PETTIMAGUE** (sic) [PETTIDEMANGE?], Mary Ann, Miss, both of Christiana Hd, 22 Mar 1824, by the Rev. P. Kenny (DG 26 Mar 1824)

HOLLAND, Mary Ann,
see **HARVEY**, William

HOLLAND, Mary E., see **NULL**, William

HOLLAND, Ruben,
see **HOLLAND**, Eliza Jane

HOLLAND, Thomas, late of White Clay Creek Hd, John WHAN, exec'r (DG 28 Dec 1852)

HOLLAND, William,
see **HOLLAND**, Amanda

HOLLAND, William, 11 Jan 1848, at E. I. DuPont's Bank (DG 28 Jan 1848)

HOLLEN, James, widower with two daughters, in a barn fire in Mill Creek Hd, 27 Oct 1848 (DG 30 Oct 1848)

HOLLIDAY, Nancy,
see **REDGRAVES**, Abraham

HOLLINGSWORTH, Abner, to **FLINN**, Elizabeth C., Miss, all of NC Co, in Wilm, 1 Nov 1849 (DG 6 Nov 1849)

HOLLINGSWORTH, Anna R.,
see **HOLLINGSWORTH**, Henry F.
see **HOLLINGSWORTH**, Julia Lee

HOLLINGSWORTH, Eli, in Wilm, 24 Dec 1851, aged c 70 yrs (DG 30 Dec 1851) see **HOLLINGSWORTH**, Lydia C.

HOLLINGSWORTH, Elijah,
see **HOLLINGSWORTH**, Julia Lee
see **HOLLINGSWORTH**, Henry F.

HOLLINGSWORTH, Ferdinand, to **HYNDMAN**, Anna Maria, both of Wilm, 18 Feb 1847, in the First Presb. Church, by Rev. S. R. Wynkoop (DG 19 Feb 1847)

HOLLINGSWORTH, Ferdinand, to **SPRINGER**, Mary Ann, Mrs., both of Wilm, in Phila, 8 Oct 1849, by Rev. Robert Adair (DG 19 Oct 1849)

HOLLINGSWORTH, Ferdinand, near Dover, 20 Sep 1853, aged 40 yrs (DG 23 Sep 1853)
see **HOLLINGSWORTH**, William C.

HOLLINGSWORTH, Francis, at the res. of John L. STAM in Chestertown after a short illness, 15 Mar 1850, in his 44th yr (DG 22 Mar 1850)

HOLLINGSWORTH, Henry F., son of Elijah and Anna R. HOLLINGSWORTH, in Wilm, 10 Aug 1849, aged 2 yrs (DG 14 Aug 1849)

HOLLINGSWORTH, Jane, dec'd, late of Christiana Hd, notice given by Jesse CHANDLER, exec'r (DG 2 Apr 1833)

HOLLINGSWORTH, Joel, in Christiana Hd, 15 Apr 1848, in his 56th yr (DG 25 Apr 1848)

HOLLINGSWORTH, John,
see **CROW**, Michael

HOLLINGSWORTH, Julia Lee, inf dau of Elijah and Anna R. HOLLINGSWORTH, in Wilm, 19 Feb 1851, na (DG 21 Feb 1851)

HOLLINGSWORTH, Lydia C., Mrs. wife of Eli HOLLINGSWORTH, in Wilm, 25 Jan 1851, in her 64th yr (DG 31 Jan 1851)

HOLLINGSWORTH, Martha,
see **FLEMING**, Marcellus

HOLLINGSWORTH, Mary Ann, see **HOLLINGSWORTH**, William C.

HOLLINGSWORTH, William C., inf son of Ferdinand and Mary Ann HOLLINGSWORTH, near Camden DE, 30 Oct 1850 (DG 8 Nov 1850)

HOLLINGSWORTH, Wm. Penn, formerly of Wilm, to **WHITEMAN**, Amanda, Miss, dau of Wm. WHITEMAN of Phila, in Phila, 18 Jan 1853, by the Rev. Jos. F. Berg (DG 21 Jan 1853)

HOLME, Charles, keeper of the tollgate on the Wilm and Lancaster turnpike, 19 Feb 1849 (DG 27 Feb 1849)

HOLMES, Catharine, see **FINCHER**, George

HOLMES, Edmund A., to **WHITE**, Ann Matilda, dau of Ambrose WHITE, Esq., all of Phila, 19 Nov 1827, by the Rev. Dr. Wilson (DG 23 Nov 1827)

HOLMES, Rachel, see **KELLY**, Abraham

HOLMES, Thomas, to **RHODES**, Mary, Miss, all of NC Co, in Christiana, 3 Sept 1846, by Rev. Mr. Rider (DG 8 Sep 1846)

HOLMS, Sarah E., see **FRIST**, Thos.

HOLSTEIN, James J., to **SCOUT**, Sarah Ann, Miss, all of Smyrna, 26 Oct 1851, by the Rev. H. E. Gilroy (DG 31 Oct 1851)

HOLSTON, Amy D.,
see **HENDERSON**, William

HOLTON, Catharine, Mrs, in Wilm, 12 Oct 1846, na (DG 16 Oct 1846)

HOLTON, Charles, dec'd, late of Wilm, notice given by Thomas MENDENHALL, adm'r (DE 10 Dec 1798)

HOLTON, Elizabeth, see **HOLTON**, William

HOLTON, William, dec'd, late of Wilm, notice given by Elizabeth HOLTON, adm'x (DG 3 Jun 1834)

HOLTZBECHER, Eliza,
see **HOLTZBECHER**, F. H.

HOLTZBECHER, F. H., dec'd, late of NC Co, notice given by Eliza, Lewis and George HOLTZBECHER, exec'rs (DG 3 Jan 1834) [Check **HOLTZBECKER**]

HOLTZBECHER, George,
see **HOLTZBECHER**, F. H.

HOLTZBECHER, L:ewis,
see **HOLTZBECHER**, F. H.

HOLTZBECKER, F. W., at Hermitage, 13 Dec 1833, na (DG 17 Dec 1833)

HOLTZBECKER, Lewis, at his res. near Stanton, of inflammation of the brain, 1 May 1849, aged c 40 yrs (DG 4 May 1849)

HOLTZBECKER, Marianna Margaritta, eldest dau of F. H. HOLZBECKER near Newark, NC Co, DE, of bilious fever, 19 Aug 1822, aged 22 yrs (DG 24 Sep 1822)

HOLZBECKER, F. H.,
see **HOLTZBECKER**, Marianna Margaritta

HOOK, Mahala H.,
see CRAWFORD, Ebenezer K.

HOOK, Minerva, see WALTON, Alfred

HOOK, Thomas H. Jr., to WHARTON, Hetty Ann, Miss, all of Sussex Co DE, near Laurel, 18 Aug 1847, by Rev. H. C. Fries (DG 24 Aug 1847)

HOOKER, Sarah H., Miss, sister of the late Mrs. CURTIS of Newark, in Bridgewater, MA, 12 Jul 1852, of consumption, aged 24 yrs (DG 20 Jul 1852)

HOOLAHAN, James, of Phila, to HAYES, Eliza Jane, Miss, only dau of John HAYES, Sr., of Brandywine Hd, 3 Feb 1842, by Rev. F. Reilley (DG 11 Feb 1842)

HOOPES, Barton, of Chester Co PA, to CAMPESON, Ruth Ann, of NC Co, 23 Aug 1848, by Friends ceremony in the presence of the mayor of Wilm (DG 25 Aug 1848)

HOOPES, Daniel, see WEBB, Christian

HOOPES, Ezra, see LOWNES, George
see OTLEY, Abner

HOOPES, Jonathan, of Kennett, Chester Co PA, to MENDENHALL, Martha Matilda, of NC Co, 1 Mar 1849, by Friends ceremony, before James Daniel, Esq.(DG 16 Mar 1849)

HOOPES, Joseph, to HAMILTON, Eleanor, Miss, both of Wilm, 5 Apr 1798, by Rev. Mr. Clarkson (DE 9 Apr 1798)

HOOPES, Mary Ann, see MOORE, Edward

HOOPES, Sarah, see WEBB, Christian

HOOTEN, Isaac, to VANDEVER, Rebecca, Miss, dau of Thomas VANDEVER, both of Brandywine Hd, 18 Dec 1828, by the Rev. James Pardee (DG 23 Dec 1828)

HOOTEN, Isaac, late of Brandywine Hd, Rebecca HOOTEN, adm'x (DG 26 Oct 1852)

HOOTEN, Jacob, in Wilm, 16 Apr 1850, in his 82nd yr (DG 23 Apr 1850)

HOOTEN, Rebecca, see HOOTEN. Isaac

HOPE, Thomas, broker, late of Wilm, in Phila, 28 Aug 1826, aged 50 yrs 6 mos (DG 29 Aug 1826)

HOPKINS, Betty, Mrs.,
see WARRINGTON, James P.

HOPKINS, George, to BRINTON, Phebe D.,
Miss, 28 Dec 1820 (DG 29 Dec 1820)

HOPKINS, Hetty E., see WHITE, Benj.

HOPKINS, James, see HOPKINS, Margaret

HOPKINS, James, to HARRIS, Ann L., Mrs, all of Sussex, 31 Dec 1846, near Millsboro, by Rev. H. C. Fries (DG 8 Dec 1847)

HOPKINS, Josiah, to COLLINS, Orphua, Miss, 24 Jan 1850, by Rev. J. A. Torbert (DG 12 Feb 1850)

HOPKINS, Margaret, dau of James and Mary HOPKINS, in Kent Co, 15 Jun 1848, aged 3 yrs 11 mos (DG 30 Jun 1848)

HOPKINS, Mary, see HOPKINS, Margaret

HOPKINS, Robert, at Seaford DE, 31 Aug 1844, aged 53 yrs (DG 10 Sep 1844)

HOPKINSON, Mary,
see HOPKINSON, Thomas

HOPKINSON, Thomas, late of Phila. Sale of land of the branches of Blackbird Creek, NC Co. Apply to Mary HOPKINSON, Dr. Thomas CADWALADER, Richard PETERS, or Charles WILLING (PG 14 Dec 1752)

HOPPLE, Emanda T., see KING, Smiley

HORN, Elizabeth Gesner, dau of Peter HORN, in Wilm,13 Dec 1844, aged 22 mos 23 days (DG 17 Dec 1844)

HORN, Mary A., see MILLIGAN, Samuel

HORN, Peter, in Wilm, 24 Jul 1849, in his 55th yr (DG 27 Jul 1849)
see HORN, Elizabeth Gesner
see WEST, Jane

HORN, Sarah Jane,
see PHILLIPS, William W.

HORN, Susan Ann P.,
see MASON, Jonathan P.

HORN, William, father of Wm M. HORN, 10 Jun 1853, at Haverford, Del Co PA, na (DG 21 Jun 1853)

HORN, William M. to YEATES, Letitia, D., Miss, by Elder John Miller, all of Wilm, 10 Dec 1840 (DG 11 Dec 1840)

HORN, Wm. M., see HORN, William

HORNE, Stephen, see APPLETON, Joseph

HORNE, Susanna P.,
see APPLETON, Joseph

HORSEY, Sarah, Mrs., wife of Thomas

HORSEY, Esq., at the res. of her father, the Hon. William B. COOPER, near Laurel, Sussex Co, 14 Dec 1822, recently married and the only remaining child of her father (DG 24 Dec 1822)

HORSEY, Thomas, Esq.,
see HORSEY, Sarah, Mrs.

HORSEY, Thomas C., , at his father's res. in Sussex Co, 18 Sep 1849, aged 33 yrs (DG 19 Oct 1849)

HORTON, Ann, see LOWERY, Ann T.,

HORTON, Ann T., see LOWERY, Ann T., see LOWERY, _____

HORTON, Ebenezer, see LOWERY, Ann T.,

HOSACK, Sarah, in Wilm, at the res. of David L. MOODY, 13 Dec 1842, aged 67 yrs (DG 16 Dec 1842)

HOSEA, James W., of Laurel DE, to WATTS, Elizabeth L., Miss, dau of George WATTS, Esq., of Phila, in Phila, 16 Oct 1851, by the Rev. Chas. D. Cooper (DG 21 Oct 1851)

HOSEA, John, Esq., near Laurel, Sussex Co, 11 May 1852, in his 60th yr (DG 24 May 1852)

HOSKINS, Edward B., of Wilm, to STEEL, Sarah H., Miss, of Upper Oxford, PA, 11 May 1843, at Marshalton,PA, by Rev. A. John (DG 26 May 1843)

HOSKINS, George,
see HOSKINS, Phebe D.

HOSKINS, Harriet C.,
see TAYLOR, Thomas

HOSKINS, Phebe D., consort of George HOSKINS, Esq., 14 Jun 1847, in her 54th yr (DG 2 Jul 1847)

HOSSENGER, Catharine, Miss, dau of Peter HOSSENGER, near Newark, 1 Feb 1825, aged 20 yrs 11 mos (CI 16 Feb 1825)

HOSSENGER, Peter,
see HOSSENGER, Catharine

HOSSINGER, Jane, Mrs., relict of the late Peter HOSSINGER, of Newark DE in Phila, 10 Jul 1853, in her 81st yr (DG 15 Jul 1853)

HOSSINGER, Peter,
see HOSSINGER, Jane

HOTTON, William, of yellow fever (DE 16 Sep 1798)

HOUNSFIELD, Alice, see DuPONT, Victor

HOUSTEN, Joseph William, son of Liston HOUSTEN, Esq., at his father's res. in Kent Co, 11 Jan 1851, aged 16 yrs (DG 21 Jan 1851)

HOUSTEN, Liston,
see HOUSTEN, Joseph William

HOUSTON, David H., to BELL, Hannah F., Miss, 8 Dec 1842, at Lewes, by the Rev. C. A. Mustard (DG 9 Dec 1842)

HOUSTON, George,
see HUMPHRIES, Richard

HOUSTON, John T., son of David H. HOUSTON, 9 Aug 1847, at Lewes (DG 20 Aug 1847)

HOUSTON, Samuel, of Wilm, died at sea on board the Brig *Hero*, arrived at Boston (AW 8 Nov 1817)

HOUSTON, Shepherd, of Lewes, to BODDY, Maggie, youngest dau of Stephen BODDY, Esq., of Wilm, in Wilm, 19 May 1852, by Rev. J. A. Roche (DG 24 May 1852)

HOWARD, _____, Mrs., see LAMN, Thos.

HOWARD, Elizabeth, see MILNOR, Mahlon

HOWARD, Elizabeth N.,
see HANCE, John R.

HOWARD, Jane Russell,
see PARKER, Henry L.

HOWARD, Sarah Ann,
see OLIVER, Thomas, Jr.

HOWARD, Spencer, to MACKLAN, Ann , Miss, both of the vicinity of Newark, DE, 16 Mar 1829, by the Rev. J. J. Hagany (DG 27 Mar 1829)

HOWARD, Thomas,
see OLIVER, Thomas, Jr.
see PARKER, Henry L.

HOWELL, Courtland, to WILLIAMSON, Elvina, Miss, dau of the late Hon. Nicholas G. WILLIAMSON of Wilm, 14 Sep 1847, in Phila (DG 17 Sep 1847)

HOWELL, Enos, in St. Georges, 19 Oct 1829, "old" (DG 23 Oct 1829)

HOWELL, Joseph, see DENN, George

HOWELL, Margaret, see PEIRCE, John Lee

HOWELL, Mary, see LAWS, Thomas

HOWELL, Sidney E, see DENN, George

HOYT, Wm J., of Phila, to SCHIFFELY, Susan M., Miss, youngest dau of Prof. Fred'k SCHIFFELY, late of Wilm, 6 Jul 1851, by Rev. J. C. Clay (DG 29 Jul 1851)

HUBBARD, Elizabeth A., see SWAIN, John W.

HUDSON, ___, Mrs., in S. Milford 30 Aug 1851, "at an advanced age" (DG 12 Sep 1851)

HUDSON, A. Ella, see PRETTYMAN, John S.

HUDSON, Asay, to TUCKER, Elizabeth Ann, both of Kent Co, 28 Dec 1852 (DG 1 Feb 1853)

HUDSON, Benjamin, of Baltimore, to BRADLEY, Susanna, dau of Isaac BRADLEY of Sussex Co, 22 Feb 1847, by Rev. Mr. Owens (DG 9 Mar 1847)

HUDSON, Benjamin, Dr., see DAVIS, Joseph S.

HUDSON, Henry, Esq., at his res. of many years in Milford, of typhus fever, 4 Jan 1851, in his 60th yr (DG 14 Jan 1851)

HUDSON, John, to COLMAN, Mary, Miss, all of Kent Co, 12 Jun 1850, by Rev. John A. Roche (DG 2 Jul 1850)

HUDSON, Mary, see DAVIS, Joseph S.

HUDSON, Nathaniel, to McCABE, Elizabeth, Miss, dau of Garritson McCABE, all of Balt Hd, Sussex Co, 24 Nov 1853, by the Rev. Isaac T. Atkins (DG 6 Dec 1853)

HUDSON, Polly, near Milford, at the res. of her brother-in-law, 12 Nov 1848, in her 60th yr (DG 28 Nov 1848)

HUDSON, Sarah E., see BELL, Richard H.

HUET, Mary A., see LINDAL, William

HUEY, John, see DARLINTTON, Job

HUEY, Linda, see DARLINTTON, Job

HUEY, Mary Ann, see BALDWIN, William Bennett

HUEY, William, farmer in Brandywine Hd near Smith's Bridge, in Christiana Hd, killed by falling tree, leaves a wife and several brothers and sisters, ndd, na (DG 27 Aug 1852)

HUFFINGTON, Jesse S., of Duck Creek Hd,

to HOFFECKER, Mary, Miss, dau of Joseph HOFFECKER Sr., of Smyrna, 25 Nov 1850, by Rev. J. Riche (DG 6 Dec 1850)

HUGGINS, Mary, Mrs., 28 Dec 1821, aged almost 80 yrs (DG 1 Jan 1822)

HUGHES, Elias, an old pensioner at the Navy Asylum in Phila, 5 May 1848 (DG 12 May 1848)

HUGHES, Harriet, see KIRBY, Arnold

HUGHES, Hester Ann, see LONG, Jeremiah

HUGHES, James P., see BUNTING, Rachel

HUGHES, John, see SHAW, Joseph

HUGHES, Mary, see SHAW, Joseph

HUGHES, Nancy, see DERRAHAM, Pearce

HUGHES, William H., to REYNOLDS, Mary W., both of DE, 27 Oct 1847, by Rev. A. Atwood (DG 5 Nov 1847)

HUGHLETT, William, 2 Feb 1850, in Mill Creek Hd. (DG 12 Feb 1850)

HUGHS, Maria, see PRITCHARD, John

HUKILL, Julia, see BURROWS, William

HULL, Thomas F., in Wilm, 10 Oct 1850, aged 28 yrs (DG 25 Oct 1850)

HUMBERT, Fredrick, to DICKINSON, Afir, Miss, both of Cantwell's Bridge, NC Co, 13 Dec 1852, at the Arch St. House, Phila, by the Rev. E. J. Way (DG 17 Dec 1852)

HUMPHREY, Israel, to BAILESS, Susan F., Miss, both of New Castle, in New Castle, 18 May 1848, by Rev. Mr. Hallowell (DG 23 May 1848)

HUMPHRIES, Elizabeth, see HUMPHRIES, William C.

HUMPHRIES, Martha S., see FOLS, Ezekiel

HUMPHRIES, Richard, dec'd, late of NC Co, notice given by George HOUSTON, adm'r, St. Georges Hd (DG 13 Mar 1827) George HOUSTON of St Georges Hd, adm'r (DG 27 Mar 1827)

HUMPHRIES, William C., son of William and Elizabeth HUMPHRIES, formerly of DE, in Phila, 26 Oct 1849, aged 7 yrs (DG 30 Oct 1849)

HUNN, John, see JUMP, Isaac, M. D. see JUMP, Margaret

HUNN, Margaret, see JUMP, Margaret

HUNN, Margaret M, see JUMP, Isaac, M. D.

HUNN, Patience, see JENKINS, George

HUNTER, Elizabeth R.,
see WRIGHT, James R.

HUNTER, Emily, see ORR, William P.

HUNTER, Georgiana, late wife of Capt. Henry D. HUNTER, 5 Jun 1843, aged 27 yrs (DG 9 Jun 1843)

HUNTER, Henry D.,
see HUNTER, Georgiana

HUNTER, Joseph A., to SOLOMON, Martha, Miss, 22 May 1833, by Rev. Joseph Lybrand, all of Wilm (DG 28 May 1833)

HUNTER, Mary, see PARKE, Francis, Esq.

HUNTER, Sarah, see RUSLING, Joseph

HUNTSMAN, William, to MATTER, Hannah, both of NC Co, at Pennsburg, Chester Co PA, 7 Nov 1846, by Hugh Passmore, Esq. (DG 24 Nov 1846)

HUNTZBERGER, Enos, of Baltimore, to SIMPSON, Elizabeth M., Miss, of Wilm, 1 Jan 1850, by Rev. J. E. Rockwell (DG 8 Jan 1850)

HURLEY, George, to MURPHY, Martha, Miss, both of Milford, DE in Christiana, 15 Apr 1849, by Rev. Joseph Barr (DG 24 Apr 1849)

HURLEY, H., of Washington DC, to DEHAVEN, Louisa L., Miss, 2nd dau of Jacob DEHAVEN of Newark, 2 Dec 1852, by the Rev. S. Townsend (DG 21 Dec 1852)

HURLOCK, Abraham, to PARSONS, Sarah A., dau of Isaac PARSONS, all of Kent Co, MD, 12 Jun 1849, by Rev. Mr. Wright (DG 15 Jun 1849)

HURLOCK, Jacob, at his res. near Blackbird, 14 Jul 1853, in his 76th yr (DG 22 Jul 1853)

HURLOCK, Mary F., see CLARK, William D.

HURST, James M., to SPEAKMAN, Mary G., Miss, both of NC Co, 5 Jun 1851, by Rev. J. G. Collin (DG 10 Jun 1851)

HUSBANDS, Adolphus, at his res. in Brandywine Hd, 21 Mar 1846, aged c 70 yrs (DG 24 Mar 1846)

HUSBANDS, John, to HUSBANDS, Mary, Miss, both of Brandywine Hd, 16 Mar 1843, by Rev. Mr. Daly (DG 7 Apr 1843)

HUSBANDS, Mary, see HUSBANDS, John

HUSBANDS, Naomi, Mrs.,
see BIRD, William

HUSBANDS, Wm., to WILSON, Jane,. Miss, both of Christiana Hd, in Old Chester, 13 May 1849, "A somewhat curious match, as the husband's step-mother is the bride's sister." (DG 5 Jun 1849)

HUSLER, Catherine,
see RHINEHOLT, Jacob

HUSLER, John, dec'd, property in New Ark for sale by Benjamin WAITSON, adm'r (DG 20 Nov 1827)

HUSTON, Edward S., of DE, to REDFIELD, Mary Ann, Miss, dau of Belen REDFIELD of Deptford NJ, at Camden NJ, 15 Jan 1852, by Rev. T. R. Taylor (DG 23 Jan 1852)

HUSTON, Ellen, see STROUP, Uriah

HUSTON, John, dec'd, late of Brandywine Hd, notice given by Richard RAMBO, adm'r (DG 2 Oct 1829)

HUSTON, John, to BURGIE, Catharine, Miss, both of Wilm, 24 Jan 1850, by Rev. P. Riley (DG 5 Feb 1855)

HUSTON, M. Lizzie, see ASHMORE, J. I.

HUSTON, Margaret, see KERSEY, Gerard

HUSTON, Samuel, see ASHMORE, J. I.

HUSTON, William, to HARLAN, Mary, Miss, both of Christiana Hd, in Wilm, 31 Mar 1825, by the Rev. E. W. Gilbert (DG 1 Apr 1825)

HUTAIRE, Eary (?),
see HANSON, Thomas P.

HUTCHINS, Benedic, a native of DE, long resident in Ohio, in Putnam, OH, 14 Dec 1825, aged 51 yrs (DG 30 Dec 1825)

HUTCHINSON, James L., Jr., of Phila, to LINCOLN, Rebecca L., Miss, of DE, 28 Mar 1852, by the Rev. C. W. Shields (DG 2 Apr 1852)

HUTCHINSON, James, late a travelling merchant, dec'd, notice given by James LEA, Jr., adm'r (DG 25 Feb 1797)

HUTCHINSON, Mahlon, Jr., of Bordentown, to HAMILTON, Ann E., Miss, dau of the late Capt. Charles HAMILTON of Wilm,

27 Mar 1844, in Phila, by Rev. John Hall (DG 2 Apr 1844)

HUTCHINSON, Thomas, to MANLOVE, Ann Elizabeth, Miss, all of Dover, 16 Jun 1853, by the Rev. J. P. Walter (DG 28 Jun 1853)

HUTCHISSON, Joseph, to LYNAM, Catharine A., Miss, eldest dau of John LYNAM, Esq., of Appoq. Hd, 30 Nov 1848, by Rev. T. J. Thompson (DG 5 Dec 1848)

HUTHWAITE, Ebenezer, late of St Georges Hd, Wm. G. JOHNSTON, adm'r (DG 30 Aug 1853)

HUTTON, Mary E., see WALKER, George W.

HUTTON, Nehemiah B., to STIDHAM, Catharine, Miss, both of Wilm, in Phila, 17 Sep 1849, by the Rev. D. Shields (DG 12 Oct 1849)

HUTTON, Sarah Ann, see STARR, Jacob

HUTTON, Susanna, see WHITEMAN, Charles W.

HUXLEY, Elisha, to DERRICKSON, Elizabeth, Miss, dau of Jacob DERRICKSON, of Brandywine Village, 29 Nov 1821, by the Rev. R. D. Hall (DG 4 Dec 1821)
see HUXLEY, Elizabeth
see HARVEY, Edmund A.
see WILSON, James F.
see SMITH, John Fleming

HUXLEY, Elizabeth, Mrs., wife of Mr. Elisha HUXLEY, in Wilm, 21 Nov 1824, aged 25 yrs. Leaves a husband and two little children... (DG 23 Nov 1824)
see WILSON, James F.

HUXLEY, Martha, see SMITH, John Fleming

HUXLEY, Sarah, see HARVEY, Edmund A.

HYATT, Ann, see HYATT, Francis

HYATT, Elizabeth, wife of T. HYATT, in Wilm, 17 Dec 1847, aged 39 yrs (DG 21 Dec 1847)

HYATT, Francis, of Cantwell's Bridge, to WITSELL, Ann, Miss, of Newport, 31 Jan 1822, by the Rev. L. Lawrenson (DG 5 Feb 1822)

HYATT, Francis, dec'd, late of Cantwell's Bridge, notice given by Ann HYATT, adm'x (AW 14 Apr 1826)

HYATT, Francis A., to ROSE, Serena Jane, Miss, both of Cantwell's Bridge, NC Co, 20 May 1849, by Rev. A. Atwood (DG 15 Jun 1849)

HYATT, John, dec'd, late of Pencader Hd, notice given by Sarah HYATT, exec'x, and Lewis WATSON and Solomon UNDERWOOD, exec'rs (MR 27 Feb 1805)
see HINDMAN, J., Col.
see BEARD, Duncan

HYATT, John T., U. S. Custom House Officer, to PUNCH, Ellen, Mrs., all of Wilm, 31 Dec 1849 (DG 4 Jan 1850)

HYATT, Samuel, at his res. near Bordentown NJ, 22 Feb 1850, in his 50th yr. Remains taken to Cantwell's Bridge (DG 5 Mar 1850)

HYATT, Sarah, in Wilm, 16 Mar 1850, in her 80th yr (DG 19 Mar 1850)
see HYATT, John

HYATT, Susan, see HINDMAN, J., Col.

HYATT, T., see HYATT, Elizabeth

HYLAND, Christian, see HYLAND, Jane

HYLAND, Jane, Miss, dau of Christian HYLAND, after a lingering illness, 17 Jan 1846 (DG 20 Jan 1846)

HYLAND, Thomas B., to ROBINSON, Jane E., Miss, both of Wilm, 8 Sep 1850, in Marcus Hook PA, by Rev. Mr. Walker (DG 10 Sep 1850)

HYLETT, James, to RUSSOM, Mary Jane, all of NC Co, 5 Apr 1849, by Rev. M. J. Rhees (DG 10 Apr 1849)

HYNDMAN, Anna Maria, see HOLLINGSWORTH, Ferdinand

HYNDMAN, John, late of Wilm. Benjamin CHANDLER and Margaret ADAMS, exec'rs (DG 3 Apr 1849)

HYNOLDS, Elizabeth, see SPRINGER, Peter, Esq.

HYNSON, Martha (colored), exposure from lying out at night (DG 11 Apr 1845)

HYNSON, Matthew M., to BESWICK, Ann D., Miss, both of Milford, 2 Oct 1828, by the Rev. John Jones (DG 21 Oct 1828)

INGRAM, Leah Jane, see JEFFERSON, William

INGRAM, Nathaniel, at his res. near Millsboro, Sussex Co, 23 Mar 1852, na (DG 2 Apr 1852)

DELAWARE MARRIAGES AND DEATHS FROM NEWSPAPERS, 1729-1853

INLAN, George D., son of William INLAN, in Wilm, 4 Jun 1848, aged 4 yrs (DG 13 Jun 1848)

INLAN, William, see INLAN, George D.

INSKIP, Edward, see DRAPER, Joseph

INSKIP, Martha, see DRAPER, Joseph

IRELAN, David, see IRELAN, David Ormond

IRELAN, David Ormond, son of David and the late Elanore Matilda IRELAN, in Phila, of scarlet fever, 11 Mar 1851, aged 11 mos 16 days (DG 14 Mar 1851)

IRELAN, Elanore Matilda, see IRELAN, David

IRONS, Joshue H., see LAYTON, Joseph A.

IRONS, Mary Ann, see LAYTON, Joseph A.

IRONS, William, to RASH, Elizabeth, Miss, both of Dover, 25 Jan 1848, by Rev. Mr. Murphy (DG 4 Feb 1848)

IRVIN, Eliza, see DICKINSON, Francis

IRVIN, Ellen, see MORRISON, John

IRVINS, Thomas, to PRIMROSE, Catharine, Miss, both of Wilm, 23 Apr 1844, in Phila, by Rev. Mr. Douglas (DG 3 May 1844)

IRWIN, David, see GLASGOW, James

IRWIN, Isabella, see GLASGOW, James

ISAACS, W. G., to VANNEMAN, Mary, Miss, of Wilm, in Chester, 20 May 1849, by the Rev. Walker (DG 29 Jun 1849)

ISRAEL, George, of Phila, to PATTERSON, Amey Eliza, Miss, dau of Mrs. Abigail PATTERSON of Wilm, 6 Aug 1822, by the Rev. Dr. Read (DG 9 Aug 1822)

ISRAEL, Joseph, dec'd, late of NC Co, sale of property in the village of Christiana by Susanna ISRAEL and John HALL, exec'rs (MU 23 Jan 1808)

ISRAEL, Maria, see HESSEMER, Philip

ISRAEL, Susanna, see ISRAEL, Joseph

IVINS, Francis, to FARRADAY, Mary Ann, Miss, both of Wilm, 4 Feb 1847, by Rev. S. R. Wynkoop (DG 9 Feb 1847)

I'ANSON, Mary Elizabeth, eldest dau of Richard M. I'ANSON, at Wilm, 6 Apr 1833, aged 15 yrs (DG 16 Apr 1833)

I'ANSON, Richard M., see I'ANSON, Mary Elizabeth

JACK, Charles, see JACK, Hetty

JACK, Hetty, wife of Charles JACK, 29 Nov1841, aged 26 yrs (DG 3 Dec 1841)

JACKSON, ____, Mr., see CLARK, Hannah

JACKSON, Abijah S., of Wilm, late of the Army of Mexico, to LAMBORN, Elizabeth J., Miss, dau of the late Levis LAMBORN, Esq., of NC Co, at West Chester PA, 27 Nov 1848, by John S. Haines, Esq. (DG 5 Dec 1848)

JACKSON, Ann, see BILLANEY, John

JACKSON, Bryan, of New Castle Hd, to SOLOMON, Jane, Miss, of Wilm, 14 Jan 1830, by the Rev. Mr. Daley (DG 15 Jan 1830)

JACKSON, Candice, see FOULKE, John

JACKSON, E., Mrs., see MARTIN, Eliza

JACKSON, Elizabeth, see SAMPLE, Jesse

JACKSON, Elizabeth V., see SEEDS, Joseph R. D.

JACKSON, Erasmus, to McCULLOUGH, Betsey, Miss, both of New Castle, at New Castle, 5 Mar 1798 (DE 12 Mar 1798)

JACKSON, Fletcher, see COOPER, Samuel B. Jr.

JACKSON, George B., of Dover, to DAVIDSON, Mary J., Miss, of Camden, 8 Jun 1845, in the Presb Church, Dover, by Rev. Thomas G. Murphey (DG 13 Jun 1845)

JACKSON, Hannah, see CLARK, Hannah see CHARLES, George see CLARK, Thomas

JACKSON, Hannah C., dau of Richard JACKSON, 22 Feb 1853, in New Castle Hd, na (DG 1 Mar 1853) at Claremont, NC Co, 22 Feb 1853, in her 15th yr (DG 8 Mar 1853)

JACKSON, J. W. F., see EDWARDS, George

JACKSON, Jos., see JACKSON, Mary Ann

JACKSON, Levi, respectable and industrious mechanic of Wilm, committed suicide by taking a large dose of arsenic, 26 Oct 1844.

No reason given (DG 1 Nov 1844)

JACKSON, Martha, wife of Wayne JACKSON, in Wilm, 30 Aug 1849, aged 24 yrs (DG 4 Sep 1849)

JACKSON, Mary,
see SPENCER, Richard B.
see REED, James
see PLATT, John

JACKSON, Mary Ann, wife of Jos. JACKSON and dau of the late John Churchill BLACK, of Cedar Neck, Sussex Co DE, aged 38 yrs (DG 14 Sep 1849)

JACKSON, Mary Jane, see BUSH, George

JACKSON, Patty, colored, suicide by hanging at Gregg's Hotel in Brandywine Village, 9 Jul 1834 (DG 11 Jul 1834)

JACKSON, Rebecca,
see CONNER, William
see GALBREATH, Robert

JACKSON, Resdon, late of White Clay Creek Hd, William H. SHORTT, adm'r (DG 16 Jul 1852)

JACKSON, Richard,
see JACKSON, Hannah C.

JACKSON, Samuel P., of Phila, to YOUNG, Sarah A, Miss, of Wilm, 26 Aug 1852, by Rev. F. Hodgson (DG 31 Aug 1852)
see YOUNG, Robert

JACKSON, Sarah A., Mrs., wife of Thomas JACKSON of Duck Creek, 15 Nov 1851, na (DG 25 Nov 1851)

JACKSON, Sarah E.,
see COOPER, Samuel B. Jr.

JACKSON, Susanna,
see BANNER, William W.

JACKSON, Thomas, of Wilm, to CARTWRIGHT, Sarah, eldest dau of Matthew CARTWRIGHT, of Phila, 24 Sep 1850, by Rev. George Boyd, DD (DG 1 Oct 1850)

JACKSON, Thomas, in Wilm, 23 Apr 1852, in his 19th yr (DG 27 Apr 1852)
see JACKSON, Sarah A.

JACKSON, Wayne, see JACkSON, Martha

JACOBS, Charles W., Rev., of the Methodist Protestant Ch, in Easton, MD, 20 Jul 1833, aged 21 yrs (DG 26 Jul 1833)

JACOBS, Maria, see SHARP, Evans J.

JACOBS, Thomas, Esq., to WILLIAMS, Elizabeth, Miss, all of Northwest Fork Hd, Sussex Co, near Seaford, 20 Aug 1852, by the Rev. Dr. Wm. Morgan (DG 3 Sep 1852)

JACOBS, William, to LEECH, Sarah, both of Wilm, in Chester, 20 Mar 1853, by the Rev. J. B. Maddux (DG 28 Oct 1853)

JACQUET, _____, dec'd, vendue by Susannah JACQUET, "her father's estate" (DG 11 Sep 1790)

JACQUET, Susannah,
see JACQUET, _____

JAGGARD, Elizabeth,
see McFARLAND, Richard

JAGGARD, Thomas,
see McFARLAND, Richard

JAMES, Ann, see JEFFERSON, Elihu, Esq.

JAMES, Joseph A., to CLARK, Adaline, Miss, both of Wilm, at the White Hall Hotel, W. Chester PA, 14 Sep 1853, by Rev. Levi Parmely (DG 23 Sep 1853)

JAMES, Levis J., of Wilm, to LAWRENCE, Mary E., of Phila, 5 Jan 1850, by Rev. T. R. Taylor of Phila (DG 16 Jan 1850)

JAMES, Margaret, Mrs., in Phila, 16 Aug 1849, in her 98th yr (DG 21 Aug 1849)

JAMES, Margaret, Mrs., near Glasgow, at the res. of her brother, Jacob FARRIS, 17 Feb 1851, aged 86 yrs (DG 21 Feb 1851)

JAMES, Mary, Mrs., in Wilm, 15 Oct 1833, aged c 83 yrs; no children; generous bequests to St. Andrews P. E. Ch (DG 5 Nov 1833)

JAMES, Samuel. Dispute over proposed sale of Arbitinton Iron works and land at Christiana Bridge (PG 10 Sep 1741)

JAMISON, Alexander, to BARNABY, Margaret, Miss, of NC Co, by Rev. M. J. Rhees (DG 27 Jan 1846)

JANE, Sarah, see FLEMING, Elias

JANVIER, C. Louisa,
see WHITAKER, J. Addison

JANVIER, Edward G., late of Pencader Hd. Abraham VANDERGRIFT, adm'r, the widow having renounced (DG 7 Feb 1851)

JANVIER, Eliza, Mrs, 8 Feb 1847 (DG 12 Feb 1847)

JANVIER, Eliza Jane,

see **SUTTON**, James N., Dr.
see **SUTTON**, Eliza Jane

JANVIER, Eliza S., consort of the late
William JANVIER, in Wilm, 8 Mar 1847
(DG 12 Mar 1847)

JANVIER, Emily, see **JANVIER**, George

JANVIER, Francis, to **MERISS**, Sally, Miss,
at Christiana Bridge, 11 Jan 1798, by Rev.
Mr. Barr (DE 15 Jan 1798)

JANVIER, Francis, dec'd, late of New Castle,
notice given by John JANVIER and Philip
JANVIER, exec'rs (DE 13 Dec 1798)
and Joseph TATLOW, Esq.,
of New Castle (DE 22 Aug 1799)
see **THOMPSON**, Thomas

JANVIER, George, to **PAYNTER**, Catharine,
Miss, dau of David PAYNTER, at New
Castle, 30 Mar 1826, by the Rev. Joshua N.
Danforth (DG 4 Apr 1826)

JANVIER, George, of Phila, to **JANVIER**,
Emily, Miss, of NC Co, at McDonough,
10 Oct 1850, by Rev. H. C. Fries
(DG 22 Oct 1850)

JANVIER, Geo, see **WHITAKER**, J. Addison

JANVIER, Henry, at the res. of his father in
Pencader Hd, 18 May 1847, in his 19th yr
(DG 8 Jun 1847)

JANVIER, Jane C.,
see **DANFORTH**, Joshua N., the Rev.

JANVIER, John, in New Castle, 5 Mar 1846,
aged 75 yrs (DG 10 Mar 1846)

JANVIER, John, at Cantwell's Bridge,
23 Apr 1850, aged c 75 yrs
(DG 26 Apr 1850)

JANVIER, John,
see **SUTTON**, James N., Dr.
see **CRAWFORD**, T. F.
see **SUTTON**, Eliza Jane
see **JANVIER**, Francis

JANVIER, Joseph, formerly of New Castle
and late of Wilm, at Baltimore, 18 Apr 1846,
aged 85 yrs (DG 28 Apr 1846)

JANVIER, Louisa, see **CRAWFORD**, T. F.

JANVIER, Mary G., see **ROBESON**, John L.

JANVIER, Philip, see **JANVIER**, Francis

JANVIER, Rebecca,
see **MARLEY**, Richard McW.

JANVIER, Thomas,
see **DANFORTH**, Joshua N., the Rev.
see **ROBESON**, John L.

JANVIER, Thomas, Jr., Esq., at his res. near
Newark, 4 Dec 1843, aged 40 yrs
(DG 15 Dec 1843)

JANVIER, William, see **JANVIER**, Eliza S.

JANVIER, William B., merchant, in
New Castle, 30 Sep 1848, aged 50 yrs
(DG 10 Oct 1848) Wm. B., Esq.,
see **MARLEY**, Richard McW.

JAQUES, Gideon,
see **DENNY**, Charles Griffin

JAQUES, Sarah Maria,
see **DENNY**, Charles Griffin

JAQUET, Sarah Ann,
see **BRAMBOO**, John J.

JAQUETT, Amy, see **JOHNSON**, Thomas

JAQUETT, Catharine W., in Phila,
20 Apr 1849, aged 60 yrs (DG 27 Apr 1849)

JAQUETT, Eliza P., Mrs., at Long Neck
Farm near Wilm, of influenza, 4 May 1834,
aged 64 yrs (DG 6 May 1834)

JAQUETT, Isaac Grantham, to **BLACK**,
Eliza Jane, Miss, both of Wilm, 30 Nov 1824,
by the Rev. E. W. Gilbert (DG 7 Dec 1824)

JAQUETT, James, of Mill Pond Xroads, NC
Co to **COLLUM**, Catharine, Mrs., of Cecil Co
MD, 10 Apr 1853, by Rev. Mr. Barton
(DG 26 Apr 1853)

JAQUETT, Jane, see **WATTERS**, Michael

JAQUETT, Thomas, in Wilm, 7 Apr 1835,
aged 45 yrs (DG 10 Apr 1835)

JAQUETTE, Peter, Major, distinguished
officer, Rev. war, at his res. near Wilm,
13 Sep 1834, na (DG 16 Sep 1834)

JARETTE, Joseph, of Montgomery Co PA,
to **SPARKS**, Christiana, of DE, at Ellerslie,
seat of Charles EGNER, Esq., 11 Sep 1847,
by Rev. S. R. Wynkoop. Total age of this
couple exceeds 160 yrs (DG 14 Sep 1847)

JEANDELL, William T., one of the
proprietors of the *Delaware Republican*,
to **KIRK**, Rachel, Miss, of Schuykill Twnp,
Chester Co PA, in Phoenixville, PA,
25 Apr 1843, by Rev. T. W. Johnson
(DG 5 May 1843)

JEFFERIES, Bennett,
see **JEFFERIES**, Henry

JEFFERIES, Henry, dec'd. Notice given by Bennett JEFFERIES and James DELAPLAIN, exrs. (DG 22 May 1846)

JEFFERIES, James V., to **MENDINHALL**, Phebe, dau of Joseph MENDINHALL, all of Wilm, 29 Nov 1849, by Mayor Jones, Phila (DG 4 Dec 1849)

JEFFERIS, Emmor, to **ROBINSON**, Ann, Miss, both of Wilm, at Chester PA, 28 May 1827, by Samuel Smith, Esq. (DG 1 Jun 1827)
see **JEFFERIS**, Henry

JEFFERIS, Henry, inf son of Emmor JEFFERIS, in Wilm, 9 Jul 1848 (DG 18 Jul 1848)

JEFFERIS, James,
see **PERRY**, Malinda B.

JEFFERIS, Jervas, in Wilm, of dysentery, 6 Aug 1851, aged 36 yrs (DG 8 Aug 1851)

JEFFERIS, John C., to **TORBERT**, Catharine, both of Wilm, 1 Jan 1851, by Friends ceremony, in the presence of the Mayor (DG 3 Jan 1851)

JEFFERIS, Joseph P., to **McCAULLEY**, Mary Sinclair, Miss, eldest dau of William McCAULLEY, Esq., in Wilm, 17 Apr 1850, by Rev. Pennell Coombe (DG 19 Apr 1850)

JEFFERIS, Malinda B.,
see **PERRY**, Malinda B.

JEFFERIS, Malinda, see **PERRY**, Henry C.

JEFFERIS, Oliver, to **WILLIS**, Jane, Miss, of Wilm, 7 Mar 1852, by Rev. Nicholas Paterson (DG 12 Mar 1852)

JEFFERIS, William R., Esq. to **SHUSTER**, Harriet, Miss., both of Wilm, in Phila, 13 Mar 1851, by the Rev. Joseph Castle (DG 21 Mar 1851)

JEFFERS, John, see **USHER**, John

JEFFERSON, _____, Mr.,
see **JOSEPH**, Thomas

JEFFERSON, Asa W., to **BUTLER**, Elizabeth, Miss, both of Sussex, in Georgetown, 28 Dec 1847, by Rev. Jonathan R. Torbert (DG 4 Jan 1848)

JEFFERSON, Caroline, eldest dau of Rev. Ephraim JEFFERSON, at Smyrna, 5 Sep 1833, na (DG 10 Sep 1833)

JEFFERSON, Elihu, Esq., to **JAMES**, Ann, Miss, both of NC Co, at Elkton, 17 May 1829, by the Rev. Wm. Rider (DG 26 May 1829)

see **WHILBY**, John

JEFFERSON, Enos H., of Wilm, to **FORD**, Susannah, Miss, of Baltimore, at Marcus Hook PA, 14 Sep 1848, by Rev. Stephen Townsend (DG 29 Sep 1848)

JEFFERSON, Ephraim, Rev.,
see **JEFFERSON**, Caroline

JEFFERSON Isaac P., the only surviving son of the late Warren JEFFERSON, at his res. near Concord DE, 10 Feb 1849, in his 34th yr (DG 23 Feb 1849)

JEFFERSON, James, to **READ**, Sarah Ann, Miss, both of Port Penn, in Phila, 15 Jan 1834, by the Rev. George Chandler (DG 21 Jan 1834)

JEFFERSON, Job, at his res. near Georgetown, 20 Jul 1828, aged 81 yrs; had 10 children, 56 g'children, 18 g'g'children; left an aged widow, the companion of 57 yrs (DG 5 Aug 1828)

JEFFERSON, John C., at the res. of his father, Warren JEFFERSON, 23 Nov 1846, aged 33 yrs 7 mos 13 days (DG 15 Dec 1846)

JEFFERSON, Mary,
see **JEFFERSON**, Robert

JEFFERSON, Mary Ann,
see **ASPRIL**, D. T.

JEFFERSON, Purnal, see **ASPRIL**, D. T.

JEFFERSON, Purnell, 9 May 1851, near Port Penn, in his 60th yr (DG 20 May 1851) late of St Georges Hd, Samuel JEFFERSON, adm'r (DG 6 Jun 1851)

JEFFERSON, Robert, to **JEFFERSON**, Mary, Miss, near Georgetown, DE, 4 Mar 1835, by the Rev. J. R. Torbert (DG 13 Mar 1835)

JEFFERSON, Samuel,
see **ADDISON**, Mary
see **JEFFERSON**, Purnell
see **WOODS**, Sarah Ann

JEFFERSON, Sarah,
see **JOSEPH**, Thomas

JEFFERSON, Warren, citizen of Sussex Co, member of the state senate and 1840 candidate for governor. Temporary derangement of the mind--Shot himself through the heart, 4 May 1848 (DG 9,12, 26 May 1848)
see **JEFFERSON**, John C.
see **JEFFERSON**, Isaac P.

JEFFERSON, William, to **INGRAM**, Leah

Jane, Miss, both of Sussex Co, in Milford, 9 Jan 1851, by the Rev. T. P. McColley (DG 14 Jan 1851)

JEFFERY, John, train derailed at Grubb's Landing, died 8 Jul 1853 (DG 12 Jul 1853)

JEFFRIES, James, of the Forks of Brandywine, to VANDEVER, Perthena, Miss, eldest dau of Mr. Thomas VANDEVER of Brandywine Hd, 10 Jan 1822, by the Rev. Richard D. Hall (DG 18 Jan 1822)

JEFFRIES, Martha J., see DAVIS, Colburn P.

JEHU, Mary, see MOODY, Mary

JENKINS, George, to HUNN, Patience, Miss, both of Camden, in Phila, 19 Aug 1824, by Joseph Watson, Esq., Mayor (DG 24 Aug 1824)

JENKINS, Harriet, see TEMPLE, Henry M

JENKINS, Jonathan, see RIDGELY, Henry see JUMP, Isaac, M. D.

JENKINS, Peter, "good old," colored, member of Meth. Ch., in Milford, 12 Feb 1826, "advanced age" (DG 28 Feb 1826)

JENKINS, Ruth Anna, see JUMP, Isaac

JENKINS, Virginia E., see RIDGELY, Henry

JENKS, M. H., Hon., of Newton, Bucks Co, PA, to HIGGINS, Ann M., late of New Castle DE, in Phila, 25 Jun 1851, by Friends ceremony (DG 1 Jul 1851)

JESS, Thomas, of NJ, 16 May 1807, in Wilm (MU 23 May 1807)

JESTER, Charles, see JESTER, Rebecca

JESTER, Else A, see PERRY, William H.

JESTER, John S., to McILVANE, Mary Jane, Miss, all of Kent Co DE, at Florence, 20 Sep 1849, by the Rev. Jos. J. Lewis (DG 25 Sep 1849)

JESTER, John, to BROWN, Rachael, in Smyrna, 6 Nov 1851, by the Rev. Dr. Perkins (DG 25 Nov 1851)

JESTER, Jonathan, to SAXTON, Deborah, 14 Dec 1852 (DG 14 Jan 1853)

JESTER, Mary, see McKINZEY, John

JESTER, Peter, near Smyrna, 7 Nov 1852, na (DG 16 Nov 1852)

JESTER, Rachel D., see HILL, Absalom

JESTER, Rebecca, Mrs., wife of Mr. Charles JESTER, of Milford Neck, 20 Mar 1850 (DG 2 Apr 1850)

JESTER, Rhoda J., see CORNELIUS, Jeremiah

JEWELL, Isaac, to VEACH, Elizabeth, Miss, all of New Castle DE, 13 Jan 1849, by Rev. Levi Storks (DG 30 Jan 1849)

JEWETT, William H., of Skaneateles NY, to RIDDLE, Eliza, eldest dau of John RIDDLE, Esq., of Wilm, 26 May 1842, by Rev. R. Wynkoop (DG 3 Jun 1842)

JOHNS, _____, Chancellor, see QUIN, William

JOHNS, _____, Dr., Register of Wills of Kent Co, brother of Elizabeth JOHNS, 1 Jun 1824, na, leaving an infant son (DG 11 Jun 1824)

JOHNS, _____, Rev. Dr., see EARLE, James Tilghman

JOHNS, Ann, see EARLE, James Tilghman

JOHNS, Delia, see ROGERS, James -- DENIED

JOHNS, Elizabeth, sister of the late Dr. JOHNS, of "illness caused by fatigue at attending the infant son of her brother," at Dover, 7 Jun 1824, na (DG 11 Jun 1824)

JOHNS, K., see SHOAL, Andrew,

JOHNS, Kensey, at his res. in Everdal, near Baltimore, 4 Apr 1846 (DG 21 Apr 1846)

JOHNS, Kensey, Jr., see VAN DYKE, Nicholas see EARLE, James Tilghman see McCALLMONT, James, Dr.

JOHNS, Kensey, Hon, formerly Chancellor of the State of DE, in New Castle, in his 60th yr (DG 2 Jan 1849) see STUART, David

JOHNS, N., see ROGERS, James see HAUGHEY, William

JOHNS, Susan, see STUART, David

JOHNSON, _____, engineer of the steamboat *Rainbow*, drowned in the Christiana, 26 May 1843. Leaves a wife and family (DG 2 Jun 1843)

JOHNSON, Abigail, see SMITH, Joseph

JOHNSON, Absalom, to FORD, Emily, all of Wilm, 1 Aug 1844, by Rev. M. J. Rhees

(DG 6 Aug 1844)

JOHNSON, Alexander,
see JOHNSON, Mary Ann

JOHNSON, Ann, see MAGEE, Peter

JOHNSON, Anna, Mrs., near Milford, 21 Jun 1852, aged 93 yrs (DG 13 Jul 1852)

JOHNSON, Asbury Mitchell, to HARVEY, Sarah Ann, Miss, both of Mill Creek Hd, 22 Sep 1844, at Pennsville, Chester Co PA, by Charles Henry Plummer, Evangelist (DG 24 Sep 1844)

JOHNSON, Benjamin, of Wilm, to HERON, Alexina, youngest dau of Alexander HERON, of Baltimore, 27 Mar 1845, in Baltimore, by Rev. Mr. Duncan (DG 28 Mar 1845)

JOHNSON, C. P., editor of the *Delaware Gazette*, to YOUNG, Martha B., dau of Thomas YOUNG, Esq., in Wilm, 28 Jul 1853, by the Rev. G. D. Carrow (DG 2 Aug 1853)

JOHNSON, Catharine, relict of the late Dr. William JOHNSON, at her res. near Cantwell's Bridge, 12 Mar 1844, aged 77 yrs (DG 19 Mar 1844)

JOHNSON, Christopher, to SINGER, Margaret, Miss, 5 Apr 1810, by Rev. Dr. Read (DG 7 Apr 1810)

JOHNSON, Elias, to FREDD, Lydia, Miss, all of Wilm, 22 Feb 1821, by the Rev. J. Rusling (DG 2 Mar 1821)

JOHNSON, Elijah, to REECE, Mary Jane, Miss, both of Wilm, 12 Nov 1848 (DG 21 Nov 1848)

JOHNSON, Eliza J., Mrs., wife of George JOHNSON, in Wilm 31 Jul 1852, in her 23rd yr (DG 13 Aug 1852)

JOHNSON, Eliza, see GILPIN, Henry D.

JOHNSON, Elizabeth, 29 Sep 1847, aged 68 yrs (DG 5 Oct 1847)
see RAMBO, Jacob
see DICKENSON, Stockley

JOHNSON, Geo. R., USN, of Norfolk, to CHADWICK, Annie, dau of Radcliff CHADWICK of Wilm, in Wilm, 10 Mar 1852, by the Rt. Rev. Alfred Lee, Bishop of DE (DG 12 Mar 1852)

JOHNSON, George, at his res. in Kent Co DE, after a protracted illness, 22 Jan 1850 (DG 29 Jan 1850)
see JOHNSON, Eliza J.

JOHNSON, Hugh, to McCALL, Margaret, Miss, 8 Feb 1821 (DG 13 Feb 1821)

JOHNSON, James. All persons owing debts to, pay to William SHAW, Esq., in New Castle (PG 27 Apr-4 May 1738)

JOHNSON, James, 19 Oct 1833, na "long a ... citizen of Wilm" (DG 22 Oct 1833)

JOHNSON, John, in Wilm, after a short illness, 10 May 1812 (AR 13 May 1812)

JOHNSON, John, dec'd, notice given by Ziba FERRIS, adm'r (AW 25 Oct 1817)

JOHNSON, John, Dr., to PORTER, Eleanor B., Miss, dau of Mr. Robert PORTER, proprietor of the *Circular,* 22 Dec 1824, by the Rev. E. W. Gilbert, all of Wilm (DG 24 Dec 1824)

JOHNSON, John A., see RAMBO, Jacob

JOHNSON, Joshua, to JONES, Hannah, Miss, both of Wilm, in Phila, 5 Aug 1826, by Alderman Binns (DG 11 Aug 1826)

JOHNSON, Julia, dau of Dr. Wm. JOHNSON, 18 Apr 1849 (DG 24 Apr 1849)

JOHNSON, Lavenia Jane,
see PEPPER, Peter J.

JOHNSON, Margaret J.,
see DOWNING, Joseph

JOHNSON, Margaret L.,
see SINEY, Charles

JOHNSON, Mary Ann, Miss, near Milford, at the res. of her brother, Alexander JOHNSON, 22 Oct 1849 (DG 16 Jan 1850)

JOHNSON, Moses, to DENNISON, Rebecca, Miss, 10 Apr 1828, by Elder John P. Peckworth, all of Wilm (DG 11 Apr 1828)

JOHNSON, Nathan, to WRIGHT, Lydiamira, Miss, both of St. Georges, 24 Feb 1848, by Rev. John L. Taylor (DG 7 Mar 1848)

JOHNSON, Nathaniel H., to SIMPLER, Elizabeth Jane, Miss, both of Sussex, in Milford by Rev. Silas C. Palmitery (DG 2 Apr 1850)

JOHNSON, Peter, in Wilm, 25 Nov 1850, aged c 60 yrs. (DG 29 Nov 1850)
see MURPHY, Arthur

JOHNSON, Rachel, see PRICE, William

JOHNSON, Rebecca,
see FITZSIMMONS, Joseph

DELAWARE MARRIAGES AND DEATHS FROM NEWSPAPERS, 1729-1853

JOHNSON, Robert W., to SPARKS, Susan, Miss, all of Wilm, 13 Oct 1846, by Rev. A. Atwood (DG 16 Oct 1846)

JOHNSON, Samuel, sadler, formerly of Marietta, PA, in Wilm, at the house of Mr. James WATSON, 12 Aug 1826, aged 23 yrs (DG 18 Aug 1826)
see JOHNSON, Sophia

JOHNSON, Sarah,
see PRETTYMAN, George

JOHNSON, Sarah Ann,
see CUMMINS, William
see GARRISON, Charles

JOHNSON, Sophia, dau of Samuel JOHNSON, Esq., formerly of New Castle, at the res. of her father in Phila, 15 Feb 1850 (DG 22 Feb 1850)

JOHNSON, Sophie E.,
see ARMSTRONG, William

JOHNSON, Stephen, to DAVIDSON, Letitia A., all of NC Co, in Wilm, 27 May 1846, by Rev. M. J. Rhees (DG 29 May 1846)

JOHNSON, T. Sheward, Esq., to THOMPSON, Helen D., Miss, both of Wilm, 19 Jun 1851, in Trinity Chapel by the Rector, Rev. E. M. Van Dusen (DG 20 Jun 1851)

JOHNSON, Thomas, to JAQUETT, Amy, Miss, in Wilm, 17 Jun 1847, by Rt. Rev. A. Lee (DG 29 Jun 1847)

JOHNSON, William, Dr,
see JOHNSON, Catharine

JOHNSON, William, of Salem, NJ, to McCLANE, Mary, Miss, of Wilm, 25 Sep 1809, by Rev. Daniel Dodge (DG 27 Sep 1809)

JOHNSON, William, to WITSELL, Catharine, Miss, 11 Dec 1828, by Rev. Solomon Higgins, all of Wilm (DG 23 Dec 1828)

JOHNSON, William, to THOMPSON, Sarah, both of NC Co, at Friends' Meeting, New Garden, 14 Nov 1833 (DG 19 Nov 1833)

JOHNSON, William, to TALLEY, Julia Ann, Miss, both of Wilm, in Phila, 9 Nov 1848, by Rev. A. Atwood (DG 10 Nov 1848)

JOHNSON, Wm., see JOHNSON, Julia

JOHNSTON, Charles, in the Village of Brandywine, 18 Aug 1853, in his 21st yr (DG 23 Aug 1853)

JOHNSTON, Ellen, see NONES, Jefferson

JOHNSTON, John W., to CORSHALL, Margaret, both of Wilm, in Chester PA, 4 Jul 1848, by Rev. John Shields (DG 21 Jul 1848)

JOHNSTON, Margaret, see KERN, George

JOHNSTON, Peter,
see McMANAMY, Bernard

JOHNSTON, Samuel W., to WALLS, Lydia, Miss, near Georgtown, 11 Mar 1835, by the Rev. J. R. Torbert (DG 20 Mar 1835)

JOHNSTON, William,
see WALLACE, Thomas

JOHNSTON, Wm. G.,
see HUTHWAITE, Ebenezer

JONES, Abraham S., of Wilm, to FOULK, Mary P., of Mill Creek Hd, in Phila, 10 Jan 1850, by Rev. Levi Stokes (DG 22 Jan 1850)

JONES, Alexander, of Smyrna, to McCRONE, Hannah Mary, dau of John McCRONE Jr, 2 Apr 1846, in Bethel Baptist Church, near Hare's Corner, by Rev. Joseph Smart (DG 3 Apr 1846)

JONES, Ann, see JONES, Fanny

JONES, Ann Jane, see CHAPMAN, John

JONES, Anna Maria,
see CRAWFORD, Wm. H.

JONES, Charles, in Wilm, 27 Dec 1850, aged c 50 yrs. Leaves a wife and only dau (DG 14 Jan 1851)
see JONES, Elizabeth

JONES, Cora, only child of Lt. James Hemphill JONES, U. S. Marine Corps, in Wilm after a few hours illness, 1 Jan 1850, aged 4 yrs (DG 4 Jan 1859)

JONES. James Hemphill,
see JONES, Cora

JONES, David H., of Laurel DE, to READ, Agnes, Miss, of Balt, in Balt, 2 Jul 1852, by the Rev. J. McKenzie Riley (DG 27 Jul 1852)

JONES, David T., to GIFFIN, Hannah S., Miss, 13 Dec 1821, by the Rev. Richard D. Hall, all of Wilm (DG 18 Dec 1821)
see CRAWFORD, Wm. H.

JONES, E. I., to SUTTON, Margaret J., Miss, dau of John SUTTON Jr., both of St. Georges DE, 20 Jun 1848, by Rev. James L. Howe (DG 27 Jun 1848)

JONES, Ebenezer, Esq., formerly of DE, of consumption, 1 Nov 1847, at Joliet Ill, in his 78th yr (DG 23 Nov 1847)

JONES, Ebenezer, to THOMAS, Hester A., Miss. both of Brandywine Village, 29 Mar 1849 by Rev. E. Kennard (DG 6 Apr 1849)

JONES, Edward C., Rev., of Georgetown D. C., to O'DANIEL, Maria Louisa B., dau of Francis O'DANIEL, Esq., of Wilm, 27 Mar 1845, in St. Andrews Church, by Rt. Rev. Bishop Lee (DG 1 Apr 1845)

JONES, Elizabeth, dau of Charles JONES, at the res. of her father in Appoq. Hd, of measles and inflammation of the breast, 26 Jan 1842, aged 7 yrs (DG 1 Apr 1842)

JONES, Elizabeth Hemphill, see POPE, Elizabeth Hemphill

JONES, Evan, to RICHARDS, Frances, all of Wilm, at the Philadelphia Hotel, (Pettet's), New York, 20 Jan 1836, by Ald. Labaugh (DG 26 Jan 1836)

JONES, Fanny, only child of John and Ann JONES, in Wilm, 9 Aug 1850, in her 6th yr (DG 16 Aug 1850)

JONES, Frances Ann, see REED, John G.

JONES, G. W., to WILSON, Eliza A., Miss, all of NC Co, 12 Oct 1843, by Rev. John Taylor of Phila (DG 20 Oct 1843)

JONES, George, to MACMULLEN, Anna Maria, Mrs., all of Wilm, in Wilm, 18 Nov 1823, by the Rev. E. W. Gilbert (DG 21 Nov 1823)

JONES, George, of Elkton, MD, to NAFF, Joanna, Miss, of Wilm, 15 Oct 1829, by the Rev. Isaac Pardee (DG 16 Oct 1829)

JONES, George, at Elkton, 17 Aug 1848, aged 76 yrs (DG 1 Sep 1848)

JONES, George B., son of John B. and Sarah Jane JONES, in Wilm, 21 Jul 1848, aged c 2 yrs (DG 28 Jul 1848)

JONES, George C., Dr., of Rokeby DE, to SCHEETZ, Caroline A., Miss, youngest dau of the Rev. George SCHEETZ of Frankford PA, 22 Apr 1851, in St Marks Ch, Frankford, by the Rt. Rev. Alonzo Potter DD and LLD (DG 25 Apr 1851)

JONES, Gideon F., to CONRAD, Cecelia E, all of Phila, 3 Jun 1850, by Rev. A. D. Gillett (DG 7 Jun 1850)

JONES, H. Sophia, see WYNNE, Peter

JONES, Hannah, dau of Philip and Sarah Jane JONES, 19 Apr 1851, in her third yr (DG 9 May 1851)

JONES, Hannah, Mrs., consort of Mr. Joseph JONES of West Chester, PA, at the res. of her father, Mr. Isaac SOLOMON in Wilm, no date, aged 34 yrs (DG 16 Apr 1833)

JONES, Hannah, see MASDEN, Benjamin see JOHNSON, Joshua

JONES, Hannah Ann, see PETERSON, Henry W.

JONES, Hester Ann, aged 33 yrs (DG 12 Jun 1849)

JONES, Isaac, dec'd, notice given by Peter WEYANT, Henry MOORE (DG 12 Aug 1831)

JONES, Israel, in Wilm, 20 Dec 1834, na (DG 23 Dec 1834)   notice given by Ruben WEBB and William CHANDLER, exec'rs (DG 25 Sep 1835)

JONES, Israel D., to CHANDLER, Caroline, both of Wilm, at Chester, 25 Jul 1826, by Samuel Smith, Esq. (WN 10 Aug 1826)

JONES, Israel D., to THOMSON, Margaret, both of Wilm, at the house of John J. THURLOW, 16 May 1833 (DG 21 May 1833)

JONES, James, a native of Delaware, seaman on board the brig *Columbia,* at Baltimore from Porto Cabello. Fell from the masthead, 6 Jun 1842 and was killed, na (DG 17 Jun 1842)

JONES, James A., to CHASTEAU, Priscilla Anna, Miss, both of Baltimore, 24 May 1848, by Rev. Mr. Trapnell (DG 2 Jun 1848)

JONES, James H., to PATTERSON, Margaret R., 27 Sep 1842, by Rev. William Hogarth, all of Wilm (DG 30 Sep 1842)

JONES, Jane, see BIGSBY, Daniel

JONES, Jefferson P. son of Wm. G. JONES of Wilm, at San Juan del Sud, Central America, 7 Dec 1852, in his 26th yr (DG 25 Mar 1853)

JONES, Jessie G., formerly of Wilm, in Phila, 9 Apr 1852, aged 62 yrs (DG 16 Apr 1852)

JONES, John, formerly of Wilm, to SHOUP, Ann Maria, of Upton, Franklin Co PA, 6 Jun 1844, by Rev. Marshal Davey (DG 11 Jun 1844)

JONES, John, jeweler from Phila, train derailed at Grubb's Landing, died 6 Jul 1853

(DG 12 Jul 1853)

JONES, John, see JONES, Priscilla
see FREEZE, Jefferson
see JONES, Fanny

JONES, John B., see JONES, George B.

JONES, John C., of Duck Creek Hd,
24 Oct 1853, na (DG 1 Nov 1853)

JONES, Joseph, see JONES, Hannah, Mrs.
see BLACK, William

JONES, Kendal, inf son of Dr. Waiteman
and Mary E. JONES, 29 Jun 1852, at
"Woodland" near Vernon DE,
aged 8 mos 8 days (DG 13 Jul 1852)

JONES, Leah, in Baltimore, at the res.
of C. BOUIS, of consumption,10 Nov 1842,
aged 30 yrs (DG 18 Nov 1842)

JONES, Margaret,
see HEDRICKSON, David

JONES, Martha, see WARD, Thomas

JONES, Mary E., see JONES, Kendal
see STROUD, Samuel, Jr.

JONES, Mary Hemphill, Mrs., wife of Morgan
JONES, Esq., of erysipelas super- induced
by scarlet fever, 22 Feb 1834, aged 55 yrs
(DG 25 Feb 1834) Obit (DG 28 Feb 1834)

JONES, Mary, see SIMMONS, William

JONES, Morgan,
see POPE, Elizabeth Hemphill
see JONES, Mary Hemphill, Mrs.

JONES, P. D., see DODD, D.

JONES, Phillip, of Wilm, to BRADLEY,
Sarah Jane, Miss, of Newark, 18 Apr 1843,
at Newark, by Rev. S. R. Wynkoop
(DG 21 Apr 1843)
see JONES, Hannah
see TWEED, Curtis

JONES, Philip C.,
see OVERLEY, Thomas W.

JONES, Priscilla, Miss, dau of John JONES
of Wilm, 18 May 1810, na
(DG 19 May 1810)

JONES, Purnell, to LANE, Betsy, Mrs.,
all of Milford, 21 Mar 1852, by the Rev.
G. W. Kennedy (DG 30 Mar 1852)

JONES, Rebecca, Mrs.,
see CHURCH, Nathaniel

JONES, Robert M., to RAUGHLEY, Rachel,
both of Kent Co, 16 Mar 1853

(DG 29 Mar 1853)

JONES, Sally, see MILLIGAN, Robert, Esq.

JONES, Samuel M., to CRAWFORD,
Margaret Ann, Miss, both of New Castle,
24 Jan 1847, at Christiana Bridge, by Rev.
William Ryder (DG 2 Feb 1847)

JONES, Sarah J., see FREEZE, Jefferson

JONES, Sarah Jane, see STRATTON, Isaac
see JONES, George B.
see RICE, Jacob
see JONES, Hannah

JONES, Susan, see MALONEY, Thomas

JONES, T., Mr., see MASDEN, Benjamin

JONES, Thomas, see STORY, James

JONES, Thomas W., to BOSTON, Rebecca
Ann, both of NC Co, 12 Feb 1850, by Rev.
A. D. Gillette (DG 19 Feb 1850)

JONES, Waiteman, Dr.,
see JONES, Kendal

JONES, Wm. G.,
see JONES, Jefferson P.

JORDAN, Amanda,
see HODSON, Robert W.

JORDAN, Mary C.,
see BULLOCK, Samuel M.

JORDAN, Rachel, dec'd, see ALLSTON, on
adjoining land

JORDAN, Samuel, see PRINCE, John

JORDAN, Thomas J., of Harrisburg, to
WILSON, Jane, Miss, dau of D. C. WILSON,
of Wilm (DG 11 Oct 1850)

JORDON, Emily, see MORROW, Robert B.

JOSEPH, George W., to VENT, Ella, Miss,
both of Georgetown, 13 Jul 1853, by the
Rev. J. R. Torbert (DG 26 Jul 1853)

JOSEPH, Thomas, to JEFFERSON, Sarah,
Miss, dau of Mr. JEFFERSON of Job,
19 Jun 1834, by Rev. Jonathan R. Torbert,
all of Sussex Co (DG 1 Jul 1834)

JOSHLIN, William, to NEWLOVE, Sina, Mrs,
both of Wilm, 14 Nov 1845, by Alexander
Porter, Mayor (DG 18 Nov 1845)

JOSLIN, Thomas, to MAYER, Elizabeth,
Miss, both of Wilm, in Chester PA,
16 Apr 1851, by Rev. Newton Heston
(DG 22 Apr 1851)

JOURDAN, John A.,
see JOURDAN, Mary Jane

JOURDAN, John H., of Wilm, to
STRICKLAND, Louisa, Miss, of Strickersville,
Chester Co PA, 30 Jul 1846, by Rev. Mr.
Dubois (DG 11 Aug 1846)

JOURDAN, Mary Jane, inf dau of John A.
and Susanna JOURDAN, in Wilm,
23 Jun 1847 (DG 29 Jun 1847)

JOURDAN, Susanna,
see JOURDAN, Mary Jane

JOYCE, Charlotte, see CANNON, William

JUAN, Susan,
see DENORMANDIE, Julian H.

JUMP, Isaac, M. D., of Dover, to JENKINS,
Ruth Anna, dau of Jonathan JENKINS of
Camden DE, 1 Nov 1843, in Phila , before
his Honor the mayor (DG 13 Nov 1843)

JUMP, Isaac, M. D., of Dover, to HUNN,
Margaret M., only dau of John HUNN, Esq.,
of NY, 6 Jan 1846, in New York City by Rev.
James Johnston of Framingham, Mass
(DG 13 Jan 1846)

JUMP, Isaac, see JUMP, Ruthana
see JUMP, Margaret

JUMP, Margaret, wife of Dr. Isaac JUMP,
and only dau of John HUNN, Esq., of
NY City, at Dover DE, 17 Sep 1849,
in her 25th yr (DG 18 Sep 1849)

JUMP, Ruthanna, wife of Isaac JUMP, M.
D., at her res. in Dover after a short illness,
27 Jun 1844 (DG 4 Jul 1844)

JUMP, Wm. L. to DEMPSTER, Lydia Ann,
dau of Alexander DEMPSTER, of Milford,
26 Dec 1852 (DG 14 Jan 1853)

JUSTICE, Lewis C., of Brandywine Springs,
to DUNLAP, Adelia P., Miss, dau of Francis
D. DUNLAP, Esq., of Delaware City, at
Delaware City, 21 Feb 1850, by Rev. H. E.
Harrolds (DG 26 Feb 1850)

JUSTIS, _____, Mrs., see DIVIN, Charles

JUSTIS, Augustus, aged 23 yrs, native of
DE, and recently a student at law in the office
of Messrs. Skinner and Hoyne, 13 Aug 1847,
at the house of A. NEELY, Esq., in Chicago
(DG 31 Aug 1847)

JUSTIS, Hannah Mary,
see BARR, Joseph M.

JUSTIS, Jesse M., see HOFFAY, B.
see McINTYRE, Thomas Jr.

JUSTIS, John, see MILLS, George

JUSTIS, John B., to ARMSTRONG, Lavinia,
Miss, both of NC Co, 2 Feb 1843, by
Rev. J. W. McCullough (DG 10 Feb 1843)

JUSTIS, Justa,
see SPRINGER, John
see SPRINGER, Anna

JUSTIS, Lewis C., see SPRINGER, Isaac

JUSTIS, Mary, Mrs, in Wilm, 25 Oct 1848,
aged 71 yrs (DG 30 Oct 1848)

JUSTIS, Sarah, Mrs, in Phila, 3 Jan 1851,
in her 87th yr (DG 7 Jan 1851)

JUSTISSON, Rebecca,
see PHILLIPS, John R.

KANE, Mary, see KANE, Michael

KANE, Michael, to KANE, Mary, Miss,
23 Nov 1848, by Mayor Huffington
(DG 28 Nov 1848)

KAPELLE, Elizabeth,
see LATIMER, John Richardson

KAPELLE, Michael,
see LATIMER, John Richardson

KARR, Isabella, see SPEAKMAN, James E.

KARSNER, _____, Rev.,
see DUNNING, Charles H.

KARSNER, Ella J.,
see DUNNING, Charles H.

KATES, Eliza A., see WILSON, John E.

KATES, George,
see KATES, Henry Harper

KATES, Henry Harper, son of George and
Jane KATES, in Wilm, aged 1 mo 19 days
(DG 22 Nov 1850)

KATES, Jane, see KATES, Henry Harper

KATES, Rebecca, see LOGAN, Asher B.

KEAN, Margaret Jane,
see WILSON, Margaret Jane, Mrs.

KEAN, Mary, dau of the late Thomas KEAN,
in Wilm, 17 Nov 1852, na. Funeral from the
res. of her brother Matthew KEAN
(DG 19 Nov 1852)

KEAN, Matthew, see KEAN, Mary

KEAN, Thomas,
see WILSON, Margaret Jane, Mrs.
see KEAN, Mary

see **WILSON**, William

KEARNS, John F., of Baltimore, to **DIVINE**, Mary Ann, Miss, of New Castle, in Baltimore, 10 June 1850, (DG 18 Jun 1850)

KEDDY, John, the Rev., on a visit to Wilm from England, 2 Oct 1826, aged 57 yrs (DG 10 Oct 1826)

KEE, Joseph, to **THOMAS**, Sarah, all of Smyrna, 13 Jan 1853 (DG 1 Feb 1853)

KEECH John, late of Christiana Hd, Nathan H. HARRY, adm'r (DG 7 Aug 1849)

KEEMLE(?), Samuel Ralph, to **DESAUQUE**, Mary Louisa, dau of the late L. DESAUQUE, at St Phillips Ch, 18 Mar 1851, by the Rev. Charles D. Cooper (DG 21 Mar 1851)

KEEN, Joseph, to **STEWART**, Eliza Ann, Miss, both of NC Co, 21 May 1835, by Elder John P. Peckworth (DG 26 May 1835)

KEEN, Nancy, see **ROBB**, John

KEENAN, Catharine A., see **BRADFORD**, James

KEENAN, John A., to **BELL**, Mary Caroline, Miss, 9 May 1843, by Rev. Patrick Reilly, all of Wilm (DG 12 May 1843)

KEENAN, Mark, see **MULLIN**, Isaac

KEENAN, Mary Ann, see **MULLIN**, Isaac

KEERS, John, of Phila, to **PHILLIPS**, Ann, Miss, of Wilm, 20 Jul 1851, at Marcus Hook PA, by the Rev. Henry H. Bean (DG 29 Aug 1851)

KEES, Richard, dec'd, see ALLSTON, John, on adjoining land

KEITH, Gennett, see **SAPPINGTON**, Samuel

KELLAM, Arthur, to **WARRINGTON**, Mary Ann, Miss, both of Balt, 26 Feb 1853, by the Rev. Mr. Ownes (DG 4 Mar 1853)

KELLER, George, to **HERRETT**, Abilony, Miss, 10 May 1823, by the Rev. Samuel Greene (DG 13 May 1823)

KELLEY, Clark, to **McDOWELL**, Josephine, both of Delaware City, 29 Aug 1850, in Salem [NJ], by Rev. R. F. Young (DG 10 Sep 1850)

KELLEY, Elizabeth, see **HIGGINS**, Thomas

KELLEY, Ezekiel C., to **POINSETT**, Catharine D., Miss, dau of Asa POINSETT, all of Wilm, 27 Mar 1851, by Rev. Andrew Manship (DG 4 Apr 1851) see **KELLEY**, Susan Ann

KELLEY, Mary, see **WOOLSON**, John L.

KELLEY, Susan Ann, Mrs., wife of Ezekiel C. Kelley, in Wilm, 5 Nov 1848, aged 32 yrs 3 mos 14 days (DG 10 Nov 1848)

KELLO, Charles E., to **LINDEL**, Rachel, Miss, all of Wilm, 7 Oct 1847, by Rev. T. J. Thompson (DG 12 Oct 1847)

KELLUM, Margaret, see **LAING**, John F.

KELLY, Abraham, to **HOLMES**, Rachel, Miss, both of Brandywine, 3 Aug 1846, by George W. Bartram, Esq. (DG 11 Aug 1846)

KELLY, Alexander, see **KELLY**, Samuel Harlan

KELLY, E. C., see **MEHARGE**, Mary

KELLY, Hannah, Mrs., wife of James KELLY, 26 Oct 1852, aged 24 yrs (DG 29 Oct 1852)

KELLY, James, at Smyrna Landing, 23 Sep 1849, na (DG 2 Oct 1849) see **KELLY**, Hannah

KELLY, Luke, to **MURPHY**, Catherine Ann, Miss, dau of John MURPHY of Wilm, 24 Apr 1843, by Rev. P. Riley (DG 28 Apr 1843)

KELLY, Margaret Ann, see **KELLY**, Samuel Harlan

KELLY, Samuel Harlan, inf son of Alexander and Margaret Ann KELLY, in Wilm, 22 Feb 1852, aged 1 yr 2 days (DG 27 Feb 1852)

KELLY, Sarah, see **RITTENHOUSE**, William

KENDALL, Emily H., in Wilm, 17 Mar 1845, aged 22 yrs (DG 21 Mar 1845)

KENDALL, John, 1 Dec 1845, aged 80 yrs (DG 2 Dec 1845) see **KENDALL**, Mary

KENDALL, Martha C., see **HANBEY**, Benjamin F.

KENDALL, Mary, widow of the late John KENDALL of Wilm, in Londonderry Twp, 11 Apr 1853, in her 84th yr (DG 29 Apr 1853)

KENDRICK, William G. W. to **STODDART**, A. Louisa, all of Wilm, 27 Feb 1849, by the Rev. Dr. Castle (DG 2 Mar 1849)

KENNADY, David, dec'd, late of Kent Co, notice given by Margaret KENNADY and William KENNADY, exec'rs (FA 30 Jul 1803)

KENNADY, Margaret, see KENNADY, David

KENNADY, William, see KENNADY, David

KENNARD, Anna F., see RAYMOND, Seymore

KENNARD, E., Rev., see BROWN, Edmund Jr.

KENNARD, Edward, to SOLOMON, Ruth, Miss, 7 Dec 1824, by the Rev. S. Sharp, all of Wilm (DG 14 Dec 1824)

KENNARD, Martha, see BROWN, Edmund Jr.

KENNARD, William Groom, to SIMMONS, Hannah H., Miss, both of Wilm, in Phila, 2 Nov 1848, by Rev. A. Atwood (DG Nov 10 1848)

KENNARD, William, of Baltimore, formerly of Wilm, to GIFFIN, Rachel, Miss, of Wilm, "on Thursday evening last,"[6th?] by Rev. L. Lawrenson (DG 11 Dec 1821)

KENNEDY, Eleanor Darrach, consort of William KENNEDY, at Smyrna, "on Saturday last" (AW 23 Feb 1818)

KENNEDY, Elizabeth, see KENNEDY, Elma J.

KENNEDY, Elma J., only child of George and Elizabeth KENNEDY, in Smyrna, 16 Jun 1852, aged 18 mos (DG 10 Aug 1852)

KENNEDY, George, see KENNEDY, Elma J.

KENNEDY, Mary Ann, see KENNEDY, Mary Guire

KENNEDY, Mary Guire, dau of William and Mary Ann KENNEDY, at the res. of her father in St Georges Hd, 24 Nov 1849, aged 19 yrs (DG 29 Nov 1849)

KENNEDY, William, see KENNEDY, Eleanor Darrach see KENNEDY, Mary Guire

KENNEY, Jeremiah F., of Laurel, DE, to GREEN, Elizabeth, Miss, dau of the late Gen. Jesse GREEN of Concord, 28 Jan 1835, by Rev. Mr. Hamilton (DG 10 Feb 1835)

KENT, Margaret Louisa, see TRAYNOR, Thomas

KENWORTHY, Jonathan, to BRATTON, Julia, 21 Jun 1843, by Rev. S. M. Gayley, all of NC Co (DG 7 Jul 1843)

KEPLEY, Thomas L., to NEWLIN, Sarah E., Miss, both of NC Co, 5 Oct 1845, in West Chester PA, by Rev. T. S. Griffith (DG 10 Oct 1845)

KERN, George, of Phila, to JOHNSTON, Margaret, Miss, of Wilm, in Phila, 23 May 1833, by Rev. Gilbert Livingston (DG 28 May 1833)

KERNS, Cassanda S., see ROLLINS, Carlusine J.

KERNS, James D., of Chester Co PA, to MIDDLETON, Sarah H., Miss, of Centreville DE, at Chester, 11 Aug 1850, by Rev. N. Heston (DG 20 Aug 1850)

KERNS, James D., of Chester Co PA, to MIDDLETON, Sarah H., of Centreville DE, 11 Sep 1850 (DG 17 Sep 1850) ??

KERSEY, Gerard, to HUSTON, Margaret, all of Wilm, in Wilm, 24 Oct 1849, by the Rev. W. Lord (DG 9 Nov 1849)

KERSHAW, Betty, see TAYLOR, James

KETCHUM, George A., M. D., of Mobile AL, to BURTON, Susan J., dau of Dr. John BURTON, 23 Nov 1848, by Rev. S. R. Wynkoop (DG 28 Nov 1848)

KEYS, William, to MEREDITH, Martha, Miss, both of Smyrna DE, in Phila, 31 Oct 1849, by Rev. Bishop (DG 13 Nov 1849)

KIDD, Emily, see COLE, Howard E.

KIDD, G. W., see KIDD, Mary Jane

KIDD, Margaret Jane, see McPHERSON, Lewis

KIDD, Mary Jane, wife of G. W. KIDD of Wilm, at Port Deposit MD, 25 Sep 1849 (DG 28 Sep 1849)

KILGORE, Charles Ayars, inf son of Joseph and Margaret KILGORE, of croup, at Newport, 1 Mar 1852, aged 1 yr 3 mos 12 days (DG 5 Mar 1852)

KILGORE, Joseph, see KILGORE, Charles Ayars

KILGORE, Margaret, see KILGORE, Charles Ayars

KILLAM, Charles, to KIRKPATRICK, Anna R., Miss, all of NC Co, 30 Dec 1847, by Rev. M. J. Rhees (DG 4 Jan 1848)

DELAWARE MARRIAGES AND DEATHS FROM NEWSPAPERS, 1729-1853

KILLEN, Rebecca, Mrs., consort of the Hon. William KILLEN, chief justice, Dover, 7 Jan 1790, aged 60 yrs. Buried Presbyterian burying ground (DG 6 Feb 1790)

KILLEN, William, the Hon., see KILLEN, Rebecca, Mrs.

KILLINGSWORTH, John, see KILLINGSWORTH, Mary Jane

KILLINGSWORTH, Mary Jane, consort of John KILLINGSWORTH, 14 Jun 1850, in Wilm (DG 18 Jun 1850)

KILLINS, Mary, see CLARK, Andrew S.

KILPATRICK, Eliza Ann, see MOGEE, William

KIMBER, Mary Jane, Mrs., formerly of Wilm, in Phila, 2 Jun 1851, aged 31 yrs (DG 20 Jun 1851)

KIMBLE, Ann, see BALDWIN, William, Capt.

KIMES, Benjamin F., to SMITH, Mary I., Miss, both of Wilm, in W. Chester, 10 Jul 1849 (DG 20 Jul 1849)

KIMMEY, Abraham, Capt., to PRIDE, Sarah, Miss, both of Milton, 19 Feb 1835, by Rev. John J. Conwill (DG 24 Feb 1835)

KIMMEY, David B., of Dover, DE, at White Oak Encampment, 200 miles west of Jefferson Barracks, MO, on their march to Fort Gibson under the command of Capt. Noon from Pittsburg, PA, 27 May 1834, aged 22 yrs (DG 17 Mar 1835)

KIMMEY, Elizabeth S., see ENGLAND, Thomas H.

KIMMEY, James, near Dover, 9 May 1851 (DG 13 May 1851)

KIMMEY, Joseph, of St. Jones Neck, 20 Dec 1802 (FA 24 Dec 1802)

KINCAID, Blair, to RAY, Jane, Mrs., both of NC Co, 17 Mar 1835, by Elder John P. Peckworth (DG 24 Mar 1835)

KINCH, ____, Mrs, relict of Michael KINCH, in Newport, 7 Nov 1851, aged between 65 and 70 yrs (DG 11 Nov 1851)

KINCH, Michael, at Newport, 18 Aug 1850, at a very advanced age (DG 20 Aug 1850) see KINCH, ____, Mrs.

KINDER, John, see LAYTON, Thomas W.

KINDER, Mary W.,
see LAYTON, Thomas W.

KINDER, Rhoda Ann, see NOBLE, William

KINDER, Warren, to BRADLEY, Eliza, Mrs., all of N. W. Fork Hd, in Bridgeville, 24 Aug 1848, by Rev. Wiliam Davis (DG 1 Sep 1848)

KING, Catharine, drowned in the Delaware River near New Castle, 21 Jun 1853, while swimming with a young man named Thomas REDING, "a young lady" (DG 24 Jun 1853)

KING, Edward, to LONG, Sarah, Miss, both of Chandlerville, 11 Mar 1851, by John J. Jones (DG 21 Mar 1851)

KING, Emily, see PORTER, Alexander

KING, James, of Wilm, to GEDDES, Rachel, Miss, of Phila, 8 Dec 1840, by Rev. Mr. Sorin (DG 11 Dec 1840)

KING, John, Esq., to AKIN, Mary, Miss, all of NC Co, in Phila, 26 Apr 1850, by Rev. S. R. Wynkoop (DG 3 May 1850)

KING, John, see KING, Mary

KING, John A., to FOULK, Ann E., Miss, of Wilm, 6 May 1845, in Phila, by Rev. William Cooper (DG 16 May 1845)

KING, Lucretia, see ORELL, James K.

KING, Margaret, see WEST, Stockley

KING, Mary, wife of John KING, at Newport DE, 5 Sep 1853, in her 33rd yr (DG 9 Sep 1853)

KING, Mary Ann, see LINDSEY, George

KING, Mary E., see DELLIN, James

KING, Pennel, of New Castle, to BENNET, Adeline, dau of Titus and Harriet BENNET of West Chester PA, 4 Jul 1848, by Rev. Pennel Combs (DG 18 Jul 1848)

KING, Rufus, Hon., in NY, 29 Apr 1827, in his 73rd yr (DG 1 May 1827)

KING, Smiley, to HOPPLE, Emanda T., Miss, both of Wilm, 17 Nov 1842, by Rev. C. C. Park (DG 18 Nov 1842)

KING, Temperance R., see SHAW, William

KINGSBERRY, Nathan, at Milton, 12 Apr 1846, aged 55 yrs (DG 17 Apr 1846) New York papers please copy.

KINKEAD, Amelia, Mrs., 29 Jan 1843, in Wilm, aged 45 yrs (DG 3 Feb 1843)

KINKEAD, Amelia J., see POLK, John P.

KINKEAD, George B., formerly of Elkton MD, to WINDLE, Lydia A., of Wilm, in Wilm, 26 Mar 1846, by Rev. William Hogarth (DG 3 Apr 1846)

KINKEAD, William, see POLK, John P.

KINNEY, Edward, son of Michael KINNEY, in Wilm, 31 Jul 1852, aged 8 mos (DG 3 Aug 1852)

KINNEY, Michael, see KINNEY, Edward

KINSLEY, Robert, of Phila, to HODGE, Isabella B., Miss, of Kent Co, 26 Sep 1847, by Rev. G. S. Nickets (sic) (DG 5 Oct 1847)

KIRBY, Arnold, to HUGHES, Harriet, both of NC Co, 21 Feb 1850, by Alderman George Erety (DG 26 Feb 1850)

KIRBY, John W. to EDWARDS, Mary A, both of NC Co, 9 Dec 1851, by Rev. S. G. Hare (DG 6 Jan 1852)

KIRBY, Sarah H., see HAZWELL, George R.

KIRBY, Thomas, to HINES, Susanna, both of Kent Co MD, in Milford, 8 Sep 1851, by the Rev. P. Mansfield (DG 9 Sep 1851)

KIRK, Amy, near Centreville MD, 3 Mar 1849, aged 78 yrs (DG 13 Mar 1849)

KIRK, Caleb, see UNDERWOOD, William

KIRK, Elizabeth, see HICKMAN, William

KIRK, Hannah, Mrs., in Brandywine, 26 May 1848, aged 70 yrs (DG 6 Jun 1848)

KIRK, Jane F., see STARR, Jacob, Capt.

KIRK, John, blacksmith, 21 Sep 1793, aged c 40 yrs. Buried Friends Burying Gr. (DG 28 Sep 1793)

KIRK, Jonathan, dec'd, late of Wilm, notice given by William KIRK, adm'r (MU 18 Oct 1808)

KIRK, Marshall, to GUY, Julia Ann, Miss, both of NC Co, at Pennsbury Township, Chester Co PA,19 Dec 1849, by Hugh Passmore, JP (DG 26 Feb 1850)

KIRK, Rachel, see JEANDELL, William T.

KIRK, Samuel, formerly of Wilm, to SUTER, Sarah, Miss, second dau of Henry SUTER, Esq., of Baltimore, 6 Oct 1833, by Rev. Mr. Gibbons (DG 11 Oct 1833)

KIRK, William, dec'd, notice given by William KIRK or David C. WILSON (DS 7 Sep 1811) see KIRK, Jonathan

KIRKBRIDE, Richard, of Ship *Swanwick*, to MOFFITT, Jane, Miss, of Phila (DE 19 Sep 1799)

KIRKEN, Jno, of Delaware City, to BOWEN, Rebecca, Miss, of same, in Phila, 13 Sep 1853 (DG 23 Sep 1853)

KIRKMAN, John, to GIFFIN, Mary Ann, 14 Apr 1847, by Rev. A. Atwood (DG 20 Apr 1847)

KIRKMAN, Rebecca M., see ENOS, William J.

KIRKPATRICK, Anna R., see KILLAM, Charles

KIRKPATRICK, David M., M. D., of Pittsburg, PA, to PATTERSON,Susannah Maria, Miss, of Wilm, "Wednesday morning last," by the Rev. Dr. Read (DG 8 Jun 1821)

KIRKPATRICK, Harrison, of Wilm, to LOVE, Mary R., of Delaware Co PA, 2 Apr 1848, in Phila by Alderman Lurz (DG 12 May 1848)

KIRKPATRICK, Mary, see FOSTER, Hiram E.

KIRKPATRICK, Robert B., to CUMMINS, Anna W., dau of the late John CUMMINS, Esq., of DE, in Phila, 14 Oct 1847, by Rev. William Suddaro (DG 18 Oct 1847)

KIRKPATRICK, Sarah J., see MAHAFFY, William A.

KITNON, John, in New Castle Hd, at the res. of John BROADBELT, 19 Mar 1852, aged 75 yrs (DG 23 Mar 1852)

KLAIR, Edmund S., to BROWN, Emeline, Miss, both of NC Co, in West Chester, 6 Mar 1851, by the Rev. Wm. Moore (DG 14 Mar 1851)

KLAIR, George, see BALDWIN, Thomas

KLEIN, George M., Esq., of Lancaster PA, to FLINN, Elizabeth, Miss, dau of John FLINN of Wilm, 17 Jun 1847, by the Rev. Robert Perry (DG 22 Jun 1847)

KNIGHT, Diel, to TRAUX, Sarah, Miss, both of Wilm, 18 Feb 1847, by Rev. A. Atwood (DG 26 Feb 1847)

KNIGHT, Emmor, see KNIGHT, Mary W.

KNIGHT, George H., of Southwark, to

BIGNERL, Margaret, Miss, of Lewiston DE, in Phila, 10 Aug 1849, by the Rev. S. H. Nickels (DG 14 Aug 1849)

KNIGHT, Hannah W., see GILL, Joseph B.

KNIGHT, Joseph C., of NC Co, to MILLEGAN, Mary Ann, Miss, of Phila, in Phila, 28 Mar 1850, by Rev. William Ramsey (DG 2 Apr 1850)

KNIGHT, Mary W., widow of Emmor KNIGHT, 18 Jul 1848 (DG 25 Jul 1848)

KNIGHT, Phebe, see GLENN, John

KNOTT, Eliza Jane, dau of Thomas and Mary Jane KNOTT, in Wilm, 22 Jul 1852, aged 2 yrs 10 mos (DG 3 Aug 1852)

KNOTT, Mary Jane, see KNOTT, Eliza Jane

KNOTT, Thomas, see KNOTT, Eliza Jane

KNOWLES, Daniel, at his res. in Nanticoke Hd, 18 Nov 1853, aged c 50 yrs (DG 29 Nov 1853)

KNOWLES, Ephraim, to MURRAY, Margaret, Miss, both of Pencader Hd, 10 May 1824, by the Rev. E. W. Gilbert (DG 14 May 1824) same, except 11 May 1824 (Cl 14 May 1824)

KNOWLES, Isaac Henry, to WINGATE, Luranah, Miss, both of Sussex Co, at Laurel, 25 Sep 1846, by Rev. Henry C. Frise (DG 13 Oct 1846)

KNOWLES, M., see COLLINS, J. P.

KNOX, James, to MURRY, Mary, both of Newark, in Newark Academy, 29 Jan 1852, by W. S. F. S. Graham (DG 10 Feb 1852)

KNOX, Rebecca, Mrs., dau of the late John REEDER of Sussex Co, 14 Mar 1849, in her 70th yr (DG 30 Mar 1849)

KOLLOCK, Elizabeth, Mrs., relict of the late Major Philip KOLLOCK, at Georgetown, 8 Jan 1835, aged 87; left 5 children, 46 g'children, 76 g'g'children (DG 13 Jan 1835)

KOLLOCK, Elizabeth, late wife of James P. W. KOLLOCK, at her res. in Georgetown, 12 Mar 1845, aged 51 yrs (DG 18 Mar 1845)

KOLLOCK, George, see HAMMOND, William

KOLLOCK, George, see DODD, D.

KOLLOCK, James P. W., Esq., to DERRICKSON, Mary Ann, Miss, both of Georgetown, at the res. of Mr. Isaac T. DUNNING, 22 Sep 1853, by the Rev. J. R. Torbert (DG 4 Oct 1853)

KOLLOCK, James P. W., see KOLLOCK, Elizabeth

KOLLOCK, Martha, see HAMMOND, William

KOLLOCK, Penelope, see WALTONE, (sic), Paynter

KOLLOCK, Philip, see KOLLOCK, Elizabeth see KOLLOCK, Philip L.

KOLLOCK, Philip L., son of Mr. Philip KOLLOCK, formerly of Lewistown, in Phila, 24 Apr 1835, aged 22 yrs (DG 1 May 1835)

KOLLOCK, Philips, see WALTONE, (sic), Paynter see KOLLOCK, Elizabeth, Mrs.

KOLLOCK, Rebecca, wife of the late Simon KOLLOCK, aged 64 yrs, 11 Mar 1846, at St. Georges (DG 20 Mar 1846)

KOLLOCK, Sarah, see MESSICK, George

KOLLOCK, Simon, in the Village of St. Georges after a short illness, 4 Mar 1846, aged 67 yrs (DG 10 Mar 1846) see KOLLOCK, Rebecca

KUHNS, Benjamin, of Delaware City, to NAUMAN, Ann Mary, of Lancaster, at Lancaster, 14 Apr 1853, by the Rev. N. A, Keyes (DG 26 Apr 1853)

KULP, Eli S., at St. Georges DE, of cholera, 5 Jul 1849, in his 49th yr (DG 10 Jul 1849)

KURNS, Thomas to McGUIRE, Rebecca Ann, Miss, both of Newport, 22 Oct 1829, by the Rev. John P. Peckworth (DG 27 Oct 1829)

KURTZ, Elizabeth, see BAGGS, James

KYLE, Henry, of Co Derry, Ireland, in an explosion of a powder mill at DuPont, 20 Jun 1834, na (DG 23 Jun 1834)

KYLE, Robert, to NOWLAND, Francis. all of Delaware, 22 May 1845, by Rev. James McIntire (DG 27 May 1845)

LACKEY, Deborah, Mrs., formerly of Chester Co PA, in Wilm, 12 Sep 1849, aged c 70 yrs (DG 18 Sep 1849)

LACKEY, James C., son of Milton LACKEY, 11 Oct 1847, in Wilm (DG 15 Oct 1847)

LACKEY, Milton, see LACKEY, James C.

LACKEY, Samuel, in Wilm, 12 Dec 1843, aged 26 yrs (DG 22 Dec 1843)

LACKLIN, George, to WHITE, Armanica, Miss, both of Wilm, nmd, by Rev. Mr. Green (DG 14 Mar 1851)

LACY, Eleanor, see WOLFE, David R.

LAFFERTY, Ambrose, see CALLAHAN, John

LAFFERTY, Anne, see ROWLAND, James

LAFFERTY, Jacob, see LAFFERTY, Sarah Louisa

LAFFERTY, James, see PALMER, John

LAFFERTY, Louisa, see LAFFERTY, Sarah Louisa

LAFFERTY, Sarah, see CALLAHAN, John

LAFFERTY, Sarah Louisa, dau of Jacob and Louisa LAFFERTY, in Wilm, 3 Dec 1847, aged 3 yrs and 4 mos (DG 14 Dec 1847)

LAFOREST, John A. A., of Wilm, to BINGHAM, Margaret, Miss, of Brandywine Hd., at Chester, 10 Jan 1822, by John Caldwell, Esq. (DG 15 Jan 1822)

LAIN, James, see FRANCIS, Henry

LAIN, Mary, see VERNON, Alfred see FRANCIS, Henry

LAING, John F., to KELLUM, Margaret, Miss, both of NC Co, in Marcus Hook, PA, 14 Jan 1830, by Rev. Benjamin F. Johnson, Esq. (DG 19 Jan 1830)

LAIRD, John, a sawyer... ate dinner and died...leaves a wife and children, 14 Dec 1850 (DG 17 Dec 1850)

LAKE, Lydia Ann, see BEACK, Joseph L.

LAKE, Rachel, of yellow fever (DE 17 Sep 1798)

LAMB, Clementine, Miss, in Phila, 3 Oct 1849, in her 23rd yr (DG 9 Oct 1849)

LAMB, Luke, see McILVAIN, John S.

LAMB, Margaret R., see SMITH, Thomas J. F.

LAMB, Martha, see McILVAIN, John S.

LAMBDEN, _____, Miss,
see MESSICK, John W.

LAMBDEN, Charles W., of DE, to MEWSHAW, Alaethea, of Baltimore, 15 Apr 1847, by Rev. B. F. Brook (DG 20 Apr 1847)

LAMBDEN, Joshua J., see MESSICK, John W.

LAMBDEN, L. A., to MESSICK, Elizabeth, Miss, 22 Jul 1851, all of Sussex Co (DG 12 Aug 1851)

LAMBDIN, Daniel, see CLEMENTS, Joel

LAMBDIN, John S., see WARNER, Thomas J.

LAMBDIN, Margaret, see CLEMENTS, Joel

LAMBDIN, Thomas J., of Smyrna, to ROGERS, Wilhelmina, S., Miss, of Phila, 24 Dec 1846, by Rev. M. J. Rhees (DG 25 Dec 1846)

LAMBOIRN, Cyrus, see MORRIS, John

LAMBORN, _____, Mrs., wife of Mr. Eli LAMBORN, innkeeper of Wilm, res. Market St., very unexpectedly, 9 Dec 1822 (DG 10 Dec 1822)

LAMBORN, Carson, in Christiana Hd, 1 Oct 1848, aged 33 yrs (DG 17 Oct 1848)

LAMBORN, Eli, see LAMBORN, _____, Mrs.

LAMBORN, Eli, inn-keeper and contractor for carrying the mail between Wilm and Georgetown, Wilm and Phila and Wilm and Elkton, 20 Sep 1825, na (DG 23 Sep 1825) dec'd, land in Christiana Hd, to be sold by shff (DG 19 Jun 1827)

LAMBORN, Elizabeth J., see JACKSON, Abijah S.

LAMBORN, Jona., see CAIN, Ann

LAMBORN, Levis, see JACKSON, Abijah S.

LAMBSON, Sarah Ann, see CRIPPEN, James

LAMMOT, Allen, son of Ferdinand LAMMOT, 28 Feb 1845, aged 29 mos (DG 7 Mar 1845)

LAMMOT, D. Jr., to MURGUIONDO, Lola, dau of the late Prudencio MURGUIONDO, Esq., at Wilm, 5 May 1853, by the Rt. Rev. Alfred Lee DD (DG 10 May 1853)

LAMMOT, Daniel, see GILPIN, Edward W. see DUPONT, Alfred V.

LAMMOT, Elenora Adelaide,
see GILPIN, Edward W., Esq.

LAMMOT, Ferdinand, see LAMMOT, Allen

LAMMOT, Margaretta Elizabeth,
see DUPONT, Alfred V.

LAMN, Thos., aged 24, to HOWARD,
_____, Mrs., aged 72, both of Kent,
12 Sep 1820 (sic) (DG 22 Sep 1820)

LAMONT, J., see MAITLAND, William S.

LAMONT, Sallie, see MAITLAND, William S.

LAMPBUGH [?], Thomas, to WALKER, Sarah Ann, Miss, both of NC Co, in DE, 1 May 1851, by the Rev. T. A. Fernley (DG 6 May 1851)

LAMPLUGH, Margaret, consort of Thomas LAMPLUGH, at Newport, 23 Apr 1850 (DG 26 Apr 1850)

LAMPLUGH, Thomas,
see LAMPLUGH, Margaret

LANCASTER, Ignatius T., of Charles Co MD, to SPEARMAN, Elizabeth, Miss, dau of Simon SPEARMAN, Esq., of Smyrna, 25 Jun 1846, at Smyrna (DG 7 Jul 1846)

LAND, Charlotte Wright, dau of Thomas and Mary Ann LAND, in Wilm, 21 Aug 1848, aged 2 yrs (DG 25 Aug 1848)

LAND, John, see LAND, Samuel

LAND, Mary Ann,
see LAND, Charlotte Wright

LAND, Samuel, late of NC Co. Sale of 1/5 of his lands and tenements by his brother, John LAND (PG 2 Jun 1757)

LAND, Thomas,
see LAND, Charlotte Wright

LANDERS, John, dec'd, late of Brandywine Hd., notice given by John ELLIOTT and William SMITH, exec'rs (MU 30 Jul 1808)

LANDRETH, David, Jr., of Phila Co, PA, to RODNEY, Eliza dau of Caleb RODNEY, Esq., at Lewis, 18 May 1825, by the Rev. John RODNEY of Easton, PA (DG 27 May 1825)

LANE, Betsy, see JONES, Purnell

LANE, Gilpin, son of Jesse LANE, in Wilm, 9 Oct 1851, in his 4th yr (DG 17 Oct 1851)

LANE, Jesse, see LANE, Gilpin

LANE, Mary E., see VOSS, William H.

LANE, Mary Jane,
see WHITELOCK, John M.

LANE, Nathaniel, Esq., to CULLEN, Ann, Miss, in Frederica, 23 Aug 1849, by the Rev. Joseph I. Lewis (DG 4 Sep 1849)

LANE, Ruth Ann, see WRIGHT, Crispus S.

LANGDON, Susan M.,
see DARLINGTON, Edward

LANGLEY, Joseph B., to DODSWORTH, Mary, both of NC Co, 11 Mar 1841, by Rev. Joseph Lybrand (DG 12 Mar 1841)

LANGLEY, Thomas, 31 Jul 1847, aged 30 yrs (DG 10 Aug 1847)

LARKIN, _____, Mrs. William, merchant of Wilm, 27 July 1829, na (DG 28 Jul 1829)
see LARKIN, William

LARKIN, Rosanna, Mrs., consort of William LARKIN, merchant, of Wilm, 10 Feb 1828, na (DG 12 Feb 1828)

LARKIN, Thomas, see LARKIN, William

LARKIN, William, merchant, dec'd, late of Wilm, notice given by John RODGERS, exec'r, for payments to be made to Thomas H. LARKIN (DG 14 Aug 1829)
see LARKIN, _____, Mrs. William

LARKIN, William, see LARKIN, Rosanna

LAROUX, John, dec'd, late of NC Co, notice given by William CARPENTER, exec'r (DE 26 May 1798)

LATIMER, Henry, Esq., of Newport, to RICHARDSON, Nancy, Miss, of Wilm, 26 Feb 1789 (DG 28 Feb 1789)
see MOODY, William

LATIMER, James,
see MIDDLETON, Robert

LATIMER, James, Jr.,
see LATIMER, Sarah R.,

LATIMER, John Richardson, to CALDWELL, Elizabeth dau of the late Michael KAPELLE, at Phila, 15 Jul 1834, by Rev. Alfred Barnes (DG 25 Jul 1834) [No way to determine whether CALDWELL is her middle name or a previous married name, as she is not called "Mrs."]

LATIMER, John, see McKINLY, John, Dr.

LATIMER, Sarah R., dec'd, notice given by James LATIMER, Jr., exec'r (DG 5 May 1829)

LATIMER, Thos., merchant of Newport, to DAVID, Susanna, Miss, dau of John DAVID, silversmith of Phila, in Phila, nmd, by Rt. Rev. William White (DG 18 Dec 1790)

LATTOMUS, Angeline, see SCOTT, William

LAUDERS, Mary Ann, see WASSEN, William

LAUNY, Catharine, see HAY, Forbes S.

LAVERY, John, in Wilm, of consumption, 10 Dec 1845, aged 33 yrs (DG 16 Dec 1845)

LAWRENCE, Alexander, eldest son of the late Capt Alexander LAWRENCE, formerly of Bridgeton NJ, to LAWRENCE, Sarah Ann, Miss, of Delaware City DE, in Phila, at the res. of J. ALEXANDER, Esq., 26 Nov 1851, by Alderman C. Brazer (DG 2 Dec 1851)

LAWRENCE, Andrew, dec'd, late of Red Lion Hd, notice given by Abel NILES, adm'r (DG 5 Jan 1793)

LAWRENCE, Mary, see HIDE, J. B.

LAWRENCE, Mary E., see JAMES, Levis J..

LAWRENCE, Sarah Ann, see LAWRENCE, Alexander

LAWRENSON, Lawrence, the Rev., of the M. E. Ch, at the house of the Rev. John GOFORTH, Port Deposit, of gangrene of the throat, 4 Apr 1829 (DG 14 Apr 1829)

LAWS, _____, Mrs., wife of Mr. Ledowick LAWS of Little Creek; 20 Dec 1802, leaves numerous family of small children (FA 24 Dec 1802)

LAWS, Amelia, see HILL, Jacob M.

LAWS, Clement, see WEST, Charles C.
see MIFFLIN, Elizabeth
see ROWLAND, Samuel J.

LAWS, Elizabeth, see MIFFLIN, Elizabeth

LAWS, John, dec'd, late of Pencader Hd, notice given by Robert RHODES, adm'r (WN 14 Dec 1826)

LAWS, Joshua, to GRIFFIN, Eliza, 3 Mar 1842, by Rev. William Rider (DG 18 Mar 1842)

LAWS, Ledowick, see LAWS, _____, Mrs.

LAWS, Lydia, see WEST, Charles C.,

LAWS, Mary, see ROWLAND, Samuel J.

LAWS, Outen, Esq., see HILL, Jacob M.

LAWS, Sarah B., Mrs., wife of Wm. M. LAWS, Bohemia, 11 Sep 1820 (DG 22 Sep 1820)

LAWS, Thomas, to HOWELL, Mary, Miss, both of St. Georges, at Christiana Bridge, 19 Nov 1829, by the Rev. William Rider (DG 11 Dec 1829)

LAWS, Wm. M., see LAWS, Sarah B.

LAWSON, Ellen, see BIRD, Alfred D.

LAYMAN, Ann, see BRATTON, William

LAYMAN, Rachel, see NICHOLSON, William, Esq.

LAYTON, Caleb S., see LAYTON, Sarah Elizabeth

LAYTON, Henry A., late of Phila, to SMITH, Sarah E., of Georgetown DE, at Georgetown, 1 Dec 1852, by Rev. John L. McKim (DG 10 Dec 1852)

LAYTON, Hughitt, Esq., in Dover Hd, 15 Jan 1853, aged 74 yrs (DG 1 Feb 1853)

LAYTON, John M., to MORRIS, Sarah, Miss, 1 Feb 1821 (DG 9 Feb 1821)

LAYTON, Joseph A., M. D., to IRONS, Mary Ann, Miss, eldest dau of Capt. Joshua H. IRONS, at the res. of her ather near Millsborough, 11 Nov 1847, by Rev. Henry C. Fries (DG 19 Nov 1847)

LAYTON, Joshua, of Milford, to DRAPER, Sarah Ann, Miss, of Smyrna, 20 Dec 1821, by the Rev. Richard D. Hall (DG 25 Dec 1821)

LAYTON, Joshua S., at his res. in S. Milford, 25 Mar 1849, aged 48 yrs 2 mos 11 days (DG 3 Apr 1849)
see LAYTON, Sally Ann

LAYTON, Lowder, see SMITH, _____, the Rev. Mr.

LAYTON, Sally Ann, late wife of Joshua S. LAYTON, in Georgetown, 25 Apr 1844, aged 40 yrs (DG 30 Apr 1844)

LAYTON, Samuel H., merchant, to LONG, Elizabeth, Miss, dau of the late Capt. John LONG, all of Sussex Co, 24 Jun 1848, by Rev. John R. Torbert (DG 18 Jul 1848)

LAYTON, Sarah Elizabeth, dau of the Hon Caleb S. LAYTON of Georgetown, on a visit to Lewes, 31 Jul 1845, aged 17 yrs (DG 5 Aug 1845)

LAYTON, Sarah S.,
see MATTHEWS, Joseph S.

LAYTON, Thomas W., to KINDER, Mary
W., Miss, dau of John KINDER, all of Sussex
Co DE, 17 May 1853, by Rev. Isaac Merrill
(DG 24 May 1853)

LAYTON, William Joseph, at the res. of Dr.
John R. SUDLAR, in Bridgeville, Sussex Co,
9 Jul 1852, aged c 23 yrs (DG 16 Jul 1852)
Changed to LAYTON, Joseph W., at the
home of Dr. John R. SUDLER, aged 24 yrs
(DG 20 Jul 1852)

LAZELERE, Benjamin F., to ROCHE, Ann
Eliza, Miss, both of Wilm, 7 Oct 1841, in New
Castle by Rev. Mr. Decker (DG 15 Oct 1841)

LEA, James, formerly of Wilm, in Cincinnati,
OH, 30 Sep 1825, aged 66 yrs
(DG 18 Oct 1825)

LEA, James, Jr.,
see HUTCHINSON, James
see SHEWARD, James

LEA, Thomas, Esq., formerly one of the
millers at Brandywine, at that place
4 Sep 1823 (DG 9 Sep 1823)

LECARPENTIER, Charles, late of Rouen,
France, to GREGG, Mary, Miss, of NC Co,
13 Apr 1847, by Rev. S. R. Wynkoop
(DG 20 Apr 1847)

LECATT, Nancy, see SMART, Alexander

LECHE, David, see GRAHAM, Walter S.

LECHE, Elizaeth E.,
see GRAHAM, Walter S.

LECOMPT, James,
see BIDDLE, Stephen

LEE, Alfred, Bishop of DE,
see LEE, Layton
see LEE, Elizabeth Leighton

LEE, Ann, see McFADDEN, William L.

LEE, Elizabeth Leighton, child of Alfred
and Julia W. LEE, in Wilm, 12 Nov 1850,
aged 12 mos (DG 15 Nov 1850)

LEE, Elizabeth, Mrs., relict of James LEE,
formerly of Wilm, in Cincinnati, OH,
13 Mar 1833, aged 71 yrs
(DG 26 Mar 1833)

LEE, Israel S., formerly of Cape May Co NJ,
to EGBERT, Helena, Miss, of Wilm, 30 Oct
1851, by Rev. A. Atwood (DG 4 Nov 1851)

LEE, James, see LEE, Elizabeth, Mrs.

LEE, Joseph, to HIGHAM, Mary, Miss,
22 Mar 1829, by Elder John P. Peckworth,
all of Wilm (DG 24 Mar 1829)

LEE, Julia W., see LEE, Elizabeth Leighton

LEE, Layton, son of Rt. Rev. Alfred LEE
Bishop of DE, in Phila 13 Feb 1853,
aged c 15 yrs (DG 15 Feb 1853)

LEECH, Isaac Jr., of KIngsessing, Pa, to
EVANS, Eliza, Miss, of Moyamensing, PA,
1 May 1849, by the Rev. Samuel C. Brinkle
(DG 8 May 1849)

LEECH, Sarah, see JACOBS, William

LEES, Samuel, to VANAMAN, Harriet, Miss,
all of Wilm, 28 Nov 1843, by Rev. J.
Kennaday (DG 1 Dec 1834)

LEFORGE, _____, Mrs., relict of the late
John LEFORGE of Wilm, at Phila, of a
lingering illness, ndd, na. Buried in Wilm
(DG 1 Apr 1797)

LEFORGE, John,
see LEFORGE, _____, Mrs.

LEGATE, John, late of New Castle.
Controversy about a payment he made
before death. Archibald McSPARRAN, adm'r
(PG 1 Sep 1744)
see FRENCH, David

LEGG, _____, Capt, keeper of the
Brandywine Light in Delaware Bay,
18 Dec 1852, na (DG 24 Dec 1852)

LEGG, Emeline, see THOMAS, James

LEGG, Frances, see WILSON, David

LEGG, James, to BRACKIN, Sarah Jane,
all of Wilm, 18 Nov 1852, by Rev. Andrew
Manship (DG 23 Nov 1852)

LEKITES, _____, Mrs., in S. Milford,
4 Oct 1849, na (DG 9 Oct 1849)

LEMMON, David, to McCLURE, Sarah
Jane, Miss, both of Wilm, 8 Dec 1851,
by Rev. S. R. Wynkoop (DG 12 Dec 1851)

LEMON, John, of Chester Co PA, to
SIMMONS, Sarah, Miss, of Wilm,
30 Jul 1846, in Chester PA, by George W.
Bartram, Esq. (DG 11 Aug 1846)

LENDERMAN, Margaret,
see CUMMINS, William C.

LENOIR, Francis, see LENOIR, Julian

LENOIR, Julian, dau of Francis LENOIR,
aged 9 yrs (DG 8 Aug 1848)

LENTNER, George C.,
see WHITE, Alphonso

LENTNER, Ura, see WHITE, Alphonso

LEONARD, John, at Bridgeville,
15 Dec 1847 (DG 17 Dec 1847)

LERMAN, Sarah Elizabeth,
see HERN, Jonathan

LESLEY, Henry Voorhees, of Glenallen, to STEWART, Ellen F., dau of the late J. STEWART of Port Penn, 8 Jun 1846, by Rev. Geo. Fort (DG 16 Jun 1846)

LESLIE, Alexander, to ROSS, Rebecca, Miss, both of Chester Co PA, 4 Apr 1844, by Rev. S. R. Wynkoop (DG 16 Apr 1844)

LESS, William,
see ADAMS, Daniel J., Esq.,

LEST, Lewis, to McCOY, Elizabeth, Miss, both of Wilm, 15 Dec 1846, by Rev. S. R. Wynkoop (DG 15 Dec 1846)

LETHERBURY, Perygrine, near Smyrna, of bilious dysentery, 9 Jul 1851, in his 60th yr (DG 18 Jul 1851)

LEVICK, Mary, see WEST, Luke

LEVIS, Margaret, see BARNEY, John

LEVY, _____, Judge,
see LEVY, Mary, Mrs.

LEVY, Margaret, see EDWARDS, Thomas

LEVY, Martha Mary Anne,
see MILLIGAN, John J.

LEVY, Mary, Mrs, relict of the late Judge LEVY of Phila, in Wilm, 20 Aug 1850, in her 87th yr (DG 27 Aug 1850)

LEWES, Thomas H., near Dover, 21 Oct 1853, aged 35 yrs (DG 28 Oct 1853)

LEWIS, Albert G.,
see LEWIS, Catherine Ann

LEWIS, Amey, Mrs., relict of Joel LEWIS, in Christiana, where she had lived nearly 50 yrs, 5 Oct 1826, aged 73 yrs (DG 10 Oct 1826)

LEWIS, Catherine Ann, Mrs, consort of Albert G. LEWIS, at New Ark, 3 Jul 1847; leaves husband and children
(DG 9 Jul 1847)

LEWIS. David, see GLEN, Edward J.

LEWIS, Easther Lima,
see BODDY, Benjamin M.

LEWIS, Hannah C., see CLINE, Samuel Jr.

LEWIS, James B., of DE, to BROWN, Elizabeth, Mrs., at Baltimore, (nmd)
(DG 20 Dec 1825)

LEWIS, James W., to MORRIS, Sarah B., all of Lewis, Sussex Co, 9 Aug 1853, by the Rev. C. H. Mustard (DG 26 Aug 1853)

LEWIS, Joel, see LEWIS, Amey, Mrs.
see ROTHERAM, Joseph

LEWIS, John, to WINKS, Ann, both of Wilm, in Balt, 3 Jun 1852, by the Rev. Francis McCartney (DG 20 Jul 1852)

LEWIS, Josiah, see LEWIS, Stephen

LEWIS, Kendall M., see TATE, William

LEWIS, Luranah M., see TATE, William

LEWIS, Margaret W.,
see WALLACE, A., Rev.

LEWIS, Mary, see NEWITT, Alexander

LEWIS, Samuel G., of Wilm, to ROBERTS, Emily, in New Garden, Chester Co PA, 12 Mar 1851, by Mayor Charles Gilpin
(DG 18 Mar 1851)

LEWIS, Sarah, see DARBY, John

LEWIS, Stephen. House and tanyard in New Castle to be sold or let by Benjamin SWETT and Josiah LEWIS, adm'rs
(PG 15 Sep 1743)

LEWIS, Thomas B., to CATS, Amelia A., both of Camden, at Camden, 16 Dec 1851, by the Rev. James Flannery
(DG 23 Dec 1851)

LEWIS, Tillie, see SWARTZ, J. A., Dr.

LEWIS, William, of Balt, to McDOLE, Sophia, Miss, of Port Deposit, MD, 23 Oct 1853, by the Rev. M. D. Kurtz
(DG 28 Oct 1853)

LILLAGORE, Theodore W., to HICKMAN, Margaret H., Miss, all of Phila, 16 Feb 1853, by the Rev. A. Johns (DG 4 Mar 1853)

LINCH, David, to ABBOTT, Patience, both of Sussex Co, 16 Dec 1852
(DG 14 Jan 1853)

LINCOLN, Rebecca,
see HUTCHINSON, James L.

LINDAL, Eliza, see DEPUTY, James P.

LINDAL, William, to HUET, Mary A, Miss, in Milford, 22 Jul 1852 (DG 10 Aug 1852)

LINDEL, Rachel, see KELLO, Charles E.

LINDLE, Ann, wife of Fisher LINDLE, and eldest dau of Capt James GRIER, near Frederica, 18 Jul 1852, aged 26 yrs (DG 27 Jul 1852)

LINDLE, Fisher, see LINDLE, Ann

LINDSAY, Joseph,
see LINDSAY, Mary Ann
see BRACKIN, William

LINDSAY, Mary Ann, dau of Joseph LINDSAY, in Mill Creek Hd, 9 Feb 1853, na (DG 15 Feb 1853)

LINDSEY, Elizabeth E.,
see OCHELTREE, Maxwell B.

LINDSEY, George, to KING, Mary Ann, Miss, both of Newlin Twp, Chester Co PA, at Marshallton, 6 Jul 1853, by Albert Way, Esq. (DG 26 Jul 1853)

LINDSEY, Mary, see DRENNEN, John

LINDSEY, Susan, see THOMAS, John H.

LINDSEY, William, see DRENNEN, John

LINGEL, Samuel, to MILLS, Elizabeth C., Miss, dau of Mr. Allen MILLS of Wilm, at Marcus Hook, PA, 21 May 1834, by Rev. Joseph Walker (DG 27 May 1834)

LINGO, Cornelius B., to WALLS, Eliza A., Miss, both of Sussex Co, 13 Oct 1853, by the Rev. C. H. Mustard (DG 28 Oct 1853)

LINN, John, dec'd, late of Wilm, travelling merchant, notice given by Andrew CATHERWOOD (DE 14 May 1798)

LINSEY, Mary J., see BLACK, Samuel H.

LIRK, Anna Jane.
see LIRK, William O'Daniel

LIRK, John T., see LIRK, William O'Daniel

LIRK, William O'Daniel, son of John T. and Anna Jane LIRK, in Wilm, 18 Mar 1850, aged 13 mos 6 days (DG 26 Mar 1850)

LISLE, Caroline B.,
see FLEMING, William H.

LISLE, Henry, eldest grandson of the late Gov. BENNETT, at Natchez, Miss., 7 Feb 1849, in his 31st yr (DG 2 Mar 1849)

LISLE, Mary Ann, wife of Gilbert R. FLEMING, Esq., in Jersey City, 7 Sep 1848, in her 29th yr. Buried in NJ. (DG 15 Sep 1848)

LISTER, James S., Dr., to TOWNSEND, Susan, Miss, at Frederica, 21 Oct 1823, by the Rev. Zedekiah Davis (DG 28 Oct 1823)

LISTON, Margaret, Mrs, consort of William LISTON, formerly of Appoq. Hd, at South Bend Ind, 18 Jan 1846 (DG 24 Feb 1846)

LISTON, Sarah Ann, see COUNTISS, John

LISTON, William, formerly of NC Co, at South Bend IN, 5 Jan 1847, aged 65 yrs (DG 22 Jan 1847)
see LISTON, Margaret

LITHERBURY, William H., formerly of Smyrna DE, to FRENCH, Elizabeth L., Mrs., of Wilm, in Phila, 3 Apr 1851, by the Rev. Mr. Woodward (DG 11 Jul 1851)

LITTLE, James, dec'd, late of Mill Creek Hd, NC Co, notice given by John LITTLE, adm'r (DG 15 Aug 1826)

LITTLE, John, see LITTLE, James

LITTLE, Jonathan P., of Phila, to ALEXANDER, Arabella J., Miss, dau of Dr. A. ALEXANDER of Fairfield, 22 May 1817, at Fairfield by Rev. Dr. Reed (DG 28 May 1817)

LITTLE, Mary E., see FLINN, Isaac W.

LITTLE, Rebecca, see ROBINSON, Jacob

LITTLE, Sarah, see BROWN, Nathaniel

LITTLE, William, late of Duck Creek. Notice given by William McCREA, adm'r, Phila (PG 26 Apr 1746)

LITTLER, Joshua, see EMPSON, William
see McFERSON, Daniel

LITTLETON, Elizabeth,
see WILSON, Robert

LIVINGSTON, Francis,
see LIVINGSTON, James

LIVINGSTON, James, Esq. at his res. in Pencader Hd, NC Co, 17 Feb 1852, na (DG 20 Feb 1852) Sarah and Francis LIVINGSTON, exec'rs (DG 5 Mar 1852)

LIVINGSTON, Margaret,
see HICKS, Robert M.

LIVINGSTON, Sarah,
see LIVINGSTON, James

LLOYD, James, of Chester Co PA, to DIXON, Sarah C., Miss, of NC Co, 1 Jun 1843, by Rev. Corry Chambers (DG 9 Jun 1843)

LLOYD, Mary Ann, see RUSSELL, Levi

LOBB, Benjamin, in Wilm, from apoplexy, 27 Feb 1850, aged 72 yrs (DG 1 Mar 1850)

LOBB, Joseph, late of Mill Creek Hd, Joshua PARKER, adm'r (DG 13 Feb 1852)

LOCK, Sarah E., see McKINLEY, Daniel S.

LOCKARD, Mathew, to WALKER, Mary Ann, dau of Robert WALKER, Esq., in Mill Creek Hd, 26 Apr 1849, by Rev. Thomas Love (DG 8 May 1849)

LOCKE, Anna, Mrs., for the last 22 yrs a res. of Balt, in Wilm, 29 Oct 1849, in her 50th yr (DG 16 Nov 1849)

LOCKERMAN, ____, Mr., in Dover, 19 Mar 1850, an aged citizen of Dover (DG 22 Mar 1850)

LOCKERMAN, Ann, Mrs., relict of the late Vincent E. LOCKERMAN of Dover, at Baskingridge, NJ, 20 Apr 1826, na (DG 19 May 1826)
see DESAQUE, Francis

LOCKERMAN, Eliza, see MILLER, Joseph, Esq.

LOCKERMAN, James C., to RING, Ann C., Miss, both of Wilm., 20 May 1824, by the Rev. D. D. Lewis (DG 21 May 1824)

LOCKERMAN, James C., in Wilm, 2 Dec 1828, aged 26 yrs (DG 9 Dec 1828)

LOCKERMAN, Mary, see LOCKERMAN, Matthew R.,

LOCKERMAN, Mathew R., bookseller, 1 Dec 1816 (AW 4 Dec 1816) dec'd, late of Wilm, notice given by Mary LOCKERMAN, adm'x (DG 22 Nov 1817)

LOCKERMAN, Nicholas, Esq., in Dover, 20 Mar 1850, in his 67th yr (DG 5 Apr 1850) see NIXON, Elizabeth

LOCKERMAN, Sarah, see WILLIAMSON, Nicholas G., Esq.,

LOCKERMAN, Sarah C., see THOMAS, Joseph, M. D.

LOCKERMAN, Vincent, see NIXON, Elizabeth

LOCKERMAN, Vincent E., see LOCKERMAN, Ann, Mrs.

LOCKERT, Margaret, Mrs, of New Castle, at the res. of James THOMAS in Wilm, 18 Jan 1842, aged 85 yrs (DG 28 Jan 1842)

LOCKWOOD, Benjamin, at his res. near Dagsborough, 24 Jul 1822, aged 97 yrs 2 mos 18 das. He was born 25 Apr 1725 (old style) ... Near the Trap, Worcester Co, MD ....one of the founders of the Protestant Episcopal Church, Prince George's, built ca 1756, near Dagsborough...7 children, 1 son and 6 daus, all married...(DG 9 Aug 1822)

LOCKWOOD, Caleb, see HARDCASTLE, Edward B.

LOCKWOOD, Edward, late of Middletown, to ALRICHS, Sarah E., Miss, late of NC Co, 3 Jun 1845, by Rev. George Foot (DG 3 Jun 1845)

LOCKWOOD, Henry H., U. S. N., to BOOTH, Anna, eldest dau of Hon James BOOTH, at New Castle, 2 Oct 1845, by Rev. T. Billopp (DG 7 Oct 1845)

LOCKWOOD, Martha E., see CLAYTON, Joshua

LOCKWOOD, Mary Ann, see HARDCASTLE, Edward B.

LOCKWOOD, Richard, to WILSON, Mary, Miss, both of Middletown, in Wilm, 30 Oct 1817, by Rev. Thomas Reed (AW 1 Nov 1817)
see CLAYTON, Joshua
see TATMAN, Cyrus

LOCKWOOD, Sally, Mrs., wife of William LOCKWOOD, and last surviving dau of the late Judge BARRETT, at the seat of her husband near Camden, DE, 16 Nov 1825, aged 33 yrs; m 20 Oct 1825; bur. family burying ground (DG 25 Nov 1825)

LOCKWOOD, Sarah Frances, see TATMAN, Cyrus

LOCKWOOD, Thomas, see WARREN, Penelope

LOCKWOOD, Thomas B., see LOCKWOOD, William

LOCKWOOD, William, see LOCKWOOD, Sally, Mrs.

LOCKWOOD, William, inf son of Thomas B. LOCKWOOD, in Smyrna, 1 Aug 1852, aged 12 mos (DG 10 Aug 1852)

LOCKWOOD, William Jr., of Middletown, to GRIFFITH, Lizzie W., Miss, only dau of Joseph GRIFFITH, Esq., near Newark DE, 2 Dec 1851, by the Rev. Thomas Barton (DG 9 Dec 1851)

LOCKWOOD, William K., see TRUITT, George

LODGE, George, see **LODGE**, Samuel

LODGE, Henry H., of NC Co, to **VALE**, Caroline F., Miss, dau of George VALE, Esq., late of Phila, 1 Feb 1847, in Phila by Rev. Mr. Ridgely (DG 23 Feb 1847)

LODGE, Henry, see **LODGE**, Samuel

LODGE, John, see **LONG**, Sarah Ann

LODGE, John W., of NC Co, to **GAUNT**, Mersa A., dau of Samuel J. GAUNT, of Springfield, Burlington Co NJ, 25 Dec 1851, by Wm. Irick, Esq., in Springfield (DG 6 Jan 1852)

LODGE, Mary, see **LONG**, Sarah Ann

LODGE, Samuel, dec'd, late of Brandywine Hd, notice given by Henry LODGE and George LODGE, exec'rs (DG 15 Dec 1819)

LODGE, Samuel W., late of Wilm, to **STEVENSON**, Mary B., dau of James STEVENSON, Esq., of Augustine DE, in Phila,14 Apr 1845, by Rev. Asher Moore (DG 20 Mar 1846)

LODGE, Sarah Ann, see **LONG**, Sarah Ann

LOE, William, of Burrsville MD, to **WILLEY**, Julia Ann, Mrs., of Milford DE, 3 Mar 1852, by the Rev. Richard H. Merriken (DG 16 Mar 1852)

LOFFMAN, George, to **FAHAR**, Mary Ann, Miss, both of Wilm, in Chester, 3 Apr 1852, by the Rev. J. W. Gibbs (DG 13 Apr 1852)

LOFLAND, Asa, see **McGONIGAL**, William

LOFLAND, Edward C., to **FOWLER**, Ann, Miss, both of Milford, 7 Jul 1848, by Rev. J. B. Clemson (DG 18 Jul 1848)

LOFLAND, Elias, to **DAY**, Emeline, Miss, eldest dau of John DAY, Esq., 20 Sep 1841, by Rev. Jnoa R. Torbert (DG 8 Oct 1841)

LOFLAND, Eliza, see **ALEXANDER**, James

LOFLAND, Hester Ann, see **McGONIGAL**, William

LOFLAND, Hiram, of Milford, 30 Dec 1848. in Phila, in his 19th yr (DG 16 Jan 1849)

LOFLAND, Isaac, to **STUARD**, Ann E., in Milford, 24 Jun 1852, by the Rev. T. P. McColley (DG 20 Jul 1852)

LOFLAND, J. P., see **DAVIS**, George

LOFLAND, James P., of Milford, to **LOWBER**, Mary G., Miss, at the res. of Mrs. Sarah MAXWELL near Canterbury, 4 Mar 1823 (DG 11 Mar 1823)

LOFLAND, James P., Dr., of Milford, in Phila, 7 Aug 1851, an old and respectable citizen of Milford (DG 12 Aug 1851)

LOFLAND, James R., Esq., of Milford, to **BROWN**, Sallie B., only dau of Joseph BROWN of Phila, 27 May 1852, at the third Presbyt Ch, by the Rev. Thos. Brainard (DG 1 Jun 1852)

LOFLAND, Luke, soldier of the American Revolution, at his res. near the town of Milton, 24 May 1850 (DG 18 Jun 1850)

LOFLAND, M. G., Dr., of Milford, to **DAVIS**, Emma F., second dau of Geo DAVIS, Esq., of Smyrna, 16 Nov 1853, by the Rev. Thos. C Murphy (DG 18 Nov 1853)

LOFLAND, Mary M., see **DAVIS**, George

LOFLAND, Purnell, of Dover, to **WEST**, Elizabeth H., Miss, dau of the late Richard WEST of Lewes, at Lewes, by Rev. C. H. Mustard, nmd (DG 6 Jun 1848)

LOFLY, Margaret, see **ABBOT**, Nehemiah

LOGAN, Asher B., see **LOGAN**, Sarah Elizabeth

LOGAN, Asher B., to **KATES**, Rebecca, Miss, both of Wilm, in Wilm, 13 Jan 1848, by Rev. T. J. Thompson (DG 21 Jan 1848)

LOGAN, E. H., of East Fallowfield, Chester Co PA, to **SPRINGER**, Sarah E, Miss, of Brandywine Springs, 14 Mar 1850, by Rev. A. S. Patton (DG 22 Mar 1850)

LOGAN, Margaret, see **LOGAN**. Sarah Elizabeth

LOGAN, Sarah Elizabeth, dau of Asher B. and Margaret LOGAN, in Wilm, 29 Jan 1845, aged 1 yr 6 mos (DG 31 Jan 1845)

LOGRAM, John, to **ROBBINS**, Elizabeth, all of Sussex Co DE, 11 Jan 1853 (DG 11 Feb 1853)

LONG, Daniel, youth, at the mouth of Shellpot Creek, res. Spruce St bet 5th and 6th, 2 Aug 1853, aged c 17 yrs (DG 5 Aug 1853)

LONG, Elizabeth, see **LAYTON**, Samuel H.

LONG, Henry, of Baltimore, to GREEN, Emeline, Miss, dau of Col. Jesse GREEN, at the house of her father in Concord, Sussex Co, 5 Aug 1822 (DG 16 Aug 1822)

LONG, Jeremiah, to HUGHES, Hester Ann, Miss, all of Bridgeville, 24 Nov 1850, by Rev. James Hargis (DG 6 Dec 1850)

LONG, John, Rev., see LONG, Sarah Ann

LONG, John, see LAYTON, Samuel H.

LONG, Sarah, see KING, Edward
see LYNAM, John

LONG, Sarah Ann, wife of Rev. John LONG, and dau of John and Mary LODGE of Brandywine Hd, at Seaford, nmd, aged 28 yrs (DG 31 Jan 1845)

LONG, Sophia, see CLOTHIER, John

LONGFELLOW, Sarah C.,
see WILMER, James C.

LONGFELLOW, Wm. H., of Kent Co DE, to PRICE, Elizabeth P. O., Miss, of W Chester PA, 14 Apr 1853, by the Rev. Mr. Clarke (DG 13 May 1853)

LONGHEAD, William, merchant, to DUNLAP, Peggy, Miss, both of New Castle Hd, 16 Oct 1789 (DG 21 Oct 1789)

LORD, Harriet M., wife of Wm. H. LORD, and dau of John C. and Elizabeth T. BRYAN, of DE, of heart disease, at Holly Springs, MS, 13 Jan 1851, na (DG 31 Jan 1851)

LORD, Wm. H., see LORD, Harriet M.

LORE, Amanda F.,
see ECCLES, Edwin O.

LORE, Ann W., see VOSHELL, John C.

LORE, Anna Matilda,
see PRICE, T. Roberts

LORE, Auley, in Appoq. Hd, 18 Aug 1849, aged c 58 yrs (DG 21 Aug 1849) Born at Dividing Creek, Cumberland Co NJ, 23 May 1792, came to DE 1828, died at his res. near Blackbird, aged 57 yrs (DG 31 Aug 1849). Eldad LORE, adm'r (DG 4 Sep 1849)
see LORE, Emma

LORE, Eldad, of cholera morbus, lived at Cantwell's Bridge, 21 Jul 1850, at Marcus Hook PA (DG 26 Jul 1850)
see LORE, Auley
see ECCLES, Edwin O.

LORE, Emma, dau of Mrs. Sarah LORE, at the res. of her late grandfather, the late Aulley LORE, near Blackbird, aged c 10 yrs (DG 22 Oct 1850)

LORE, Furman, at Cantwell's Bridge, 3 Apr 1853, aged 31 yrs (DG 15 Apr 1853) late of St Georges Hd, Priscilla A. LORE, adm'x (DG 23 Aug 1853)

LORE, Priscilla A., see LORE, Furman

LORE, Sarah, see LORE, Emma

LORE, Seth, Capt, see PRICE, T. Roberts

LOTT, Agnes, see HAYS, William

LOUD, William H., of Phila, to BRYAN, Harriet M., dau of John C. BRYAN, Esq., 15 Sep 1841 (sic) at the dwelling of John C. BRYAN, Esq., of Brandywine Hd, by Rev. Mr. Talbot (DG 10 Sep 1841)

LOURY, Mary Jane,
see SUPPLEE, Andrew

LOVE, Mary E., see SPRINGER, Stephan

LOVE, Mary R.,
see KIRKPATRICK, Harrison

LOVE, Thomas, see SPRINGER, Stephen

LOVELL, Anna Mary,
see SPRINGER, Peter

LOVELL, Eliza A.,
see MORRISON, George, the Rev.

LOVELL, William, butcher, near Wilm, 24 Jul 1849, in his 36th yr (DG 27 Jul 1849) see MORRISON, George, the Rev.

LOVERING, Mary, see GILPIN, John F.

LOWBER, Ann,
see MITCHELL, Patience J.

LOWBER, Catherine R.,
see FOX, Thomas

LOWBER, John, Justice of the Peace, Dover, 24 Apr 1821, in his 58th yr (IN 26 Apr 1821)
see TEMPLE, William
see ALLSTON, John

LOWBER, Kate, see TEMPLE, William

LOWBER, Mary G.,
see LOFLAND, James P.

LOWBER, Michael,
see MITCHELL, Patience J.

LOWBER, Patience J.,
see MITCHELL, Patience J.

LOWE, _____, inf dau of the recently deceased Ann Maria LOWE, 22 Aug 1850, aged 15 mos (DG 10 Sep 1850)

LOWE, Ann Maria, Mrs., consort of William W. LOWE, and dau of Capt. John M. PHILLIPS of DE, near Greensborough, Caroline Co MD, 14 Aug 1850, in her 20th yr (DG 10 Sep 1850)

LOWE, Ann Marie, see LOWE, _____

LOWE, Elizabeth,
see LOWE, Mary Elizabeth

LOWE, Jessie, see DAY, George

LOWE, John T., in Wilm, 3 Mar 1847, in his 28th yr (DG 9 Mar 1847)
see LOWE, Mary Elizabeth

LOWE, Mary Elizabeth, dau of Elizabeth and John T. LOWE, 21 Dec 1846, in her 6th yr (DG 5 Jan 1847)

LOWE, Rachel H., see EVANS, John

LOWE Washington, in Wilm, 4 Jun 1849. Fun. from the res. of his brother, Wm. G. LOWE (DG 5 Jun 1849)

LOWE, William W., see LOWE, Ann Maria

LOWE, Wm. G., see LOWE, Washington

LOWERY, _____, child (sex not noted) of Ann T. and Thomas LOWERY, 4 Sep 1835, aged 8 mos 28 days (DG 13 Oct 1835)

LOWERY, Ann T., wife of Thomas C. LOWERY, of Milford, DE, dau of Ebenezer and Ann HORTON of Cumberland Co, NJ, 27 Aug 1835, aged 29 yrs 10 mos 28 days (DG 13 Oct 1835)
see LOWERY, _____

LOWERY, Justus,
see PROCTER, George W.

LOWERY, Mary E., see LUFF, John L.

LOWERY, Sallie,
see PROCTER, George W.

LOWERY, Thomas C.,
see LOWERY, Ann T.,
see LOWERY, _____

LOWLER, Jane B., see TAYLOR, John

LOWNES, Alice Ann, see BOYER, Reece

LOWNES, George, dec'd, late of Wilm, notice given by Ezra HOOPES, adm'r (DG 2 Feb 1827)

LOWTHER, Angelina S. wife of David D. LOWTHER and dau of Charles and Margareta PORTER, 10 Feb 1853, aged 35 yrs 2 mos 16 days (DG 8 Mar 1853)

LOWTHER, David D.,
see LOWTHER, Angelina S.

LOWTHER, Mary,
see SPEAKMAN, John N.

LOWTHER, Moses, son of Wm. L. LOWTHER, of typhoid fever, near Brandywine Hd, 24 Aug 1853, in his 21st yr (DG 2 Sep 1853)

LOWTHER, Wm. L.,
see LOWTHER, Moses

LOYD, Mary Ann, see PIERCE, Edward B.

LUCAS, Christian E., to COLLEY, Mary E., Miss, both of NC Co, 3 Jul 1853, by the Rev. J. Humphries (DG 2 Aug 1853)

LUCAS, Eliza,
see MONTGOMERY, James Jr.

LUDWICK, James G., to VIRDEN, Sarah Ann, Miss, both formerly of Frederica, 14 Apr 1848, by Rev. C. Karsner (DG 14 Apr 1848)

LUFF, John L., to LOWERY, Mary E., Miss, 28 Apr 1842, by Rev. R. Wynkoop, all of Wilm (DG 6 May 1842)

LUFF, Mary E, wife of Nathaniel LUFF, at Frederica, 9 Oct 1849, in her 26th yr (DG 19 Oct 1849)

LUFF, Mary E., see LUFF, Mary Jane

LUFF, Mary Jane, inf dau of Nathaniel and Mary E. LUFF, at Frederica, 27 Sep 1849 (DG 19 Oct 1849)

LUFF, Nathaniel,
see LUFF, William George
see LUFF, Mary Jane see LUFF, Mary E.

LUFF, Rebecca,
see LUFF, William George

LUFF, Sarah, see DETERLINE, Peter

LUFF, William George, infant son of Nathaniel and Rebecca LUFF of Frederica DE, 5 Apr 1853, na (DG 12 Apr 1853)

LUFFMAN, James B., Capt., of Wilm, in New York of fever contracted in the West Indies, 10 Aug 1847, aged 30 yrs (DG 17 Aug 1847)

LUKENS, Rebecca J.,

see **NORTH**, George L.

LULL, Nathaniel, of Frederica, DE, to **THOMPSON**, Mary E. Miss, the amiable dau of John THOMPSON, merchant, of Milford Neck DE, 31 Aug 1847, by Rev. T. P. McColley (DG 10 Sep 1847)

LUM, Benjamin Franklin, son of Isaac **LUM**, in Pencader Hd., 28 Sep 1848, in his 8th yr (DG 29 Sep 1848)

LUM, Isaac, see **LUM**, Benjamin Franklin

LUNBECK, Silas, to **McLAUGHLIN**, Rachel, all of Wilm, 9 Sep 1847, by the Mayor (DG 17 Sep 1847)

LUNGREN, Hannah E., see **CARTER**, Samuel

LURN, Thomas E., to **COX**, Emily, Miss, both of Middletown DE, 13 Feb 1849, by Rev. John Henry (DG 20 Feb 1849)

LUTON, Ebenezer, to **FERGUSON**, Eliza, Miss, both of Cecil Co MD, 4 Aug 1827, by John P. Peckworth (DG 10 Aug 1827)

LYBRAND, George D., Rev., of the Phila Conference, to **ALDRED**, Sarah Ann, eldest dau of Thomas J. ALDRED, Esq., Chester Co PA, 20 Mar 1848, by Rev. Mr. McFarlan (DG 24 Mar 1848)

LYBRAND, J., Rev., in Phila, 24 Apr 1844, aged 51 yrs (DG 30 Apr 1844) see **LYBRAND**, Mary

LYBRAND, Joseph, Rev., see **HARTMAN**, Isabella C.

LYBRAND, Mary, Miss, dau of the late Rev. J. LYBRAND, at the res. of her mother in Phila, 21 Aug 1846, aged 19 yrs, ill 36 hrs (DG 21 Aug 1846)

LYLE, Rebecca, see **VINING**, Henry

LYMAN, Thomas, to **ROBINSON**, Elenor, Miss, both of Christiana Hd, 1 Feb 1807, by Rev. Thomas Greer (MU 7 Feb 1807)

LYNAM, Catharine A., see **HUTCHISSON**, Joseph

LYNAM, Ellen. see **OGLE**. Benjamin

LYNAM, Emma S., see **PORTER**, James T.

LYNAM James K., to **DERRICKSON**, Elizabeth, Miss, all of NC Co, 1 Dec 1853, by Rev. A. Atwood (DG 6 Dec 1853)

LYNAM, Joanna S., see **FLINN**, Robert B.

LYNAM, John, to **LONG**, Sarah, Miss, 23 Nov 1820 (DG 28 Nov 1820) see **HUTCHISSON**, Joseph

LYNAM, John, late of Appoq. Hd, **FERGUSON**, Bassett, exec'r (DG 4 Jul 1851)

LYNAM, John R., to **McFARLAN**, Eliza, Miss, both of NC Co, 5 Nov 1829, by Rev. William Ryder (DG 17 Nov 1829)

LYNAM, Robert T., of Mill Creek Hd, to **MEDILL**, Margaret, Miss, of White Clay Creek Hd, 25 Apr 1850 (DG 30 Apr 1850)

LYNAM, Sarah K., see **DERICKSON**, William Z.

LYNAM, William R., see **OGLE**, Benjamin G.

LYNCH, Amos W., merchant of Middletown, to **HAYES**, Mary C., of Cantwell's Bridge, 19 Aug 1846, at Cantwell's Bridge (DG 21 Aug 1846)

LYNCH, Christoppher, to **SKEGGS**, Ann Malvina, at New Castle, 18 Feb 1828, by the Rev. J. N. Danforth (DG 29 Feb 1828)

LYNCH, Hugh, 27 Jul 1851, in Christiana Hd. aged c 70 yrs (DG 1 Aug 1851)

LYNCH, James W., to **RUST**, Harriet Jane, both of Sussex Co, 18 May 1853, by Rev. John Hough (DG 31 May 1853)

LYNCH, Jane, see **BISHOP**, James H.

LYNCH, Margaret, see **FOWLER**, Thos.

LYNCH, Thomas, to **McGARDY**, Julia, Miss, 2 Dec 1842, by Rev. Patrick Reilley, all of NC Co (DG 23 Dec 1842)

MACBETH, John, dec'd, late of NC Co, notice given by Henry WHITELEY, atty-in-fact for the adm'r (AW 27 Nov 1816) see **HAYS**, Sarah

MACBETH, Sarah, see **HAYS**, Sarah

MACKEY, Alexander H., of Talbot Co MD, to **BRADFORD**, S. A., Mrs., eldest dau of Wm H. CRAWFORD, Esq., of NC Co, at Easton MD, 6 Apr 1853, by the Rev. H. M. Mason DD (DG 19 Apr 1853)

MACKEY, Haslett, C., of Talbot Co MD, to **CRAWFORD**, Willamina H., dau of Wm. H. CRAWFORD, Esq., of NC Co, 26 Jan 1852, by Rev. H. R. Harrold, rector of St. Anne's Ch., Middletown (DG 30 Jan 1852)

MACKEY, John, Capt, late clerk of NC Co,

before his death purchased a house in which Capt. James CHAMBERS, since dec'd, brother of John CHAMBERS, lived. House was purchased in the name of John MACKEY, in trust for the use of said John CHAMBERS, merchant of Antigua (PG 15 Jun 1749)

MACKEY, Maria, see PENNINGTON, John

MACKEY, Sarah Ann, see GIBSON, James

MACKLAN, Ann, see HOWARD, Spencer

MACKLEM, Catharine, Mrs, wife of Matthew MACKLEM, 8 Jun 1841, in Newark, aged 47 yrs (DG 18 Jun 1841)

MACKLEM, Isaac M., late of Mill Creek Hd, William MACKLEM, adm'r (DG 4 Feb 1853)

MACKLEM, Matthew, see MACKLEM, Catharine

MACKLEM, William, see MACKLEM, Isaac M.

MACMULLEN, Anna Maria, see JONES, George

MacPHERSON, Alexander McIntosh, of Phila, merchant, to DAUPHIN, Susan, Miss, dau of the late J. B. DAUPHIN, of Wilm, 31 Oct 1829, by Rev. G. H. Coit (DG 3 Nov 1829)

MACY, Silnamus J., son of Wm. H. MACY, merchant, to RIDGWAY, Caroline, dau of Thomas RIDGWAY of Phila, 27 Oct 1853, at 353 Arch St, Phila, by Friends ceremony (DG 1 Nov 1853)

MACY, Wm. H., see MACY, Silnamus

MADDOCK, Mary L., see CRIPPEN, Edward I.

MADDOCK, William L., see CRIPPEN, Edward I.

MAGEAR, Mary Catharine, wife of Thomas J. MAGEAR, formerly of Wilm, and dau of Jacob ALTER, in Phila, 1 Nov 1847, in her 25th yr (DG 5 Nov 1847)

MAGEAR, Thomas J., see MAGEAR, Mary Catharine

MAGEE, George, to MURPHY, Elizabeth, Miss, 16 Jun 1825, by the Rev. Henry White, all of Wilm (DG 21 Jun 1825)

MAGEE, James, of Brandywine, to MENOUGH, Mary, Miss, of New Castle Hd, 13 Feb 1822, by the Rev. E. W. Gilbert (DG 15 Feb 1822)

MAGEE, John, of Newark, to MOORE, Eliza Jane, Miss, eldest dau of Mr. John MOORE of White Clay Creek Hd, 1 Jan 1835, by the Rev. A. K. Russel (DG 6 Jan 1835)

MAGEE, Peter, to JOHNSON, Ann, both of Sussex Co, 7 Jul 1853 (DG 22 Jul 1853)

MAGENS, William, of New Castle, to SOLOMON, Sarah Ann, Miss, of Wilm, 10 Jan 1827, by the Rev. Mr. McCombs (DG 19 Jan 1827)

MAGINNES, Ellen B., see WILLET, Gideon W.

MAGINNIS, William, to DAY, Margaret R., Miss, both of Brandywine Hd, 9 Mar 1843, by Rev. Alfred Lee (DG 17 Mar 1843)

MAGUIRE, Anna Rachel, see McCOY, Washington

MAGUIRE, Thomas, of Southwark, to CLIFTON, Catharine A., Miss, dau of Daniel CLIFTON of Lewes DE, 13 Jun 1841, in Phila by Rev. A Kennady (DG 24 Sep 1841)

MAHAFFY, William A., to KIRKPATRICK, Sarah J., both of Wilm, 16 Dec 1847, by Rev. S. R. Wynkoop (DG 21 Dec 1847)

MAHAN, Joseph, of Elkton, to BAILY, Hannah, Miss, 11 May 1820 (DG 17 May 1820)

MAHANY, James L., to STROUP, Sarah, Miss, both of Wilm, 20 Mar 1849, by the Rev. J. Castle (DG 23 Mar 1849)

MAHON, Richard, dec'd, late of Mill Creek Hd, NC Co, notice given by James MENDENHALL and David WILSON, exec'rs (DG 25 Feb 1834)

MAILLY, Augustine, see MAILLY, Mary Constance

MAILLY, Constance Marguerite, Dame, b 14 Jun 1776, at Bours St Laurant, Canton de Bage, Dept. de l'Ain, France, later of Lyons. Had been res. in DE for 12 yrs, d in Wilm, 21 Jan 1851 (DG 24 Jan 1851)

MAILLY, Mary Ann, see MAILLY, Mary Constance

MAILLY, Mary Constance, only dau of Augustine and Mary Ann MAILLY, 25 Feb 1848, in her 7th yr (DG 29 Feb 1848)

MAITLAND, William S., of the U. S. Army to CARSON, Sallie Lamont, Mrs., eldest dau of Mr. J. LAMONT of Belfast, Ireland, at

Smyrna, 22 Mar 1828, by the Rev. John P. Robinson (DG 25 Mar 1828)

MAJOR, Thomas, to SMITH, Sarah, Miss, of Wilm, 1 Feb 1834, by the Rev. Joseph Walker (DG 11 Feb 1834)

MAKIM, Alicia, dau of John MAKIM, 19 May 1848, aged 17 yrs (DG 2 Jun 1848)

MAKIM, John, see MAKIM, Alicia

MAKINS, John, see MAKINS, Virginia

MAKINS, Virginia, dau of John MAKINS, in Wilm, 8 Jun 1848, aged 9 yrs (DG 13 Jun 1848)

MALCOM, John, to SMITH, Sarah, both of Brandywine Hd, 9 Jan 1853, by Rev. J. R. Anderson (DG 14 Jan 1853)

MALONA, Andrew J., to BUTLER, Sarah Elizabeth, Miss, 8 Jul 1852, by the Rev. T. P. McColley (DG 20 Jul 1852)

MALONE, John S., to PIERSON, Sarah, Miss, both of Brandywine, 2 Feb 1822, by the Rev. L. Lawrenson (DG 12 Feb 1822)

MALONEY, Catharine, in Wilm, of apoplexy, 25 Dec 1853, aged 33 yrs (DG 30 Dec 1853)

MALONEY, John, of Brandywine Village, of convulsions, 18 Jul 1848, aged 40 yrs (DG 28 Jul 1848)

MALONEY, Mary A, see ROCHE, James L.

MALONEY, Thomas, to JONES, Susan, Miss, both of Kent Co, 15 Dec 1849, by Rev. J. A. Roche (DG 1 Jan 1850)

MANERING, Sarah, see CLOUD, Washington

MANLOVE, Elizabeth, see HUTCHINSON, Thomas

MANLOVE, James, to McDANEL, Sallie C., Miss, both of Dover, in Phila, 1 Dec 1853, by the Rev. George Duffield, Jr. (DG 6 Dec 1853)

MANLOVE, John P., of Dover, to HARDCASTLE, Amanda M., Miss, of Caroline Co MD, 26 May 1845, in Phila, by Rev. Charles Brown (DG 3 Jun 1845)

MANLOVE, John, Rev., see BURTON, Henry

MANLOVE, Mary Ann, see BURTON, Henry

MANN, James M., at the res. of William POLK, Cantwell's Bridge, NC Co, after a short and severe illness, 27 Nov 1822, in his 43rd yr (DG 10 Dec 1822) dec'd, land in St Georges and Appoq. Hds, sold by sheriff (DG 15 Jan 1828)

MANN, Joseph, see MANN, Susan

MANN, Susan, consort of Rev. Joseph MANN, 23 Jan 1850, in her 42nd yr (DG 29 Jan 1850)

MANN, Thomas, Esq., of Kent Co, MD, to COMEGYS, Millimint (sic), Miss, of McAllister's Ferry, 29 Aug 1822, by the Rev. W. Smith (DG 6 Sep 1822)

MANSFIELD, Ann, Mrs., consort of Mr. Piner MANSFIELD, merchant of Smyrna, at Smyrna, 13 Jan 1823 (DG 24 Jan 1823)

MANSFIELD, Edward, Esq., edtior of the *Kent News*, to DUGAN, Mary I., Miss, dau of the late Thomas E. DUGAN, in Chestertown MD, 28 Nov 1849, by the Rev. Mr. McFaden (DG 11 Dec 1849)

MANSFIELD, Mary Letitia, eldest dau of Gen. Richard MANSFIELD of St. Georges Hd, at her father's res, 4 Oct 1841 (DG 15 Oct 1841)

MANSFIELD, Piner, see MANSFIELD, Ann

MANSFIELD, Richard, Gen., see MANSFIELD, Mary Letitia

MANSLEY, John G., of NC Co, to BARDSLEY, Elizabeth, Mrs., of Phila, 24 Mar 1850, by Rev. I. Humphries (DG 2 Apr 1850)

MANSON, James, who rid post from Dover to Phila. Notice given to pay debts to James MANSON, the deceased['s] father, Mr. CARROLL, who now rides post, Mr. John PRIOR, or Master STEWART, tavern keeper in St. Georges (PG 26 Jun 1760)

MANY, James, to MURPHY, Susan M., both of New Castle, in Wilm, 28 Sep 1848, by Rev. P. Reilly (DG 10 Oct 1848)

MARCHBANK, Mary Ann, see ECKLIN, Joseph W.

MARCHBANK, Samuel, highly respected citizen of Delaware, 14 Jul 1846, aboard the schooner *William Polk* bound for Boston (DG 28 Jul 1846)

MAREE, John, at his res. near Stanton, 8 Feb 1852, aged 37 yrs (DG 5 Mar 1852) late of White Clay Creek Hd, Margaret

MAREE, adm'x (DG 16 Mar 1852)
see WARRINGTON, Stephen

MAREE, Margaret, see MAREE, John

MAREE, Rebecca A.,
see BRIAN, Thomas P.

MARIM, Charles, see MARIM, Susan B.

MARIM, Susan B., Mrs., wife of Charles
MARIM, Esq., at her res. near Dover,
20 Dec 1834, aged 29 yrs
(DG 30 Dec 1834) "B." is Blundellemerson
(DG 6 Jan 1835)

MARIN, Henry, eldest son of Thomas
MARIN, 24 Feb 1836, aged 16 yrs
(DG 1 Mar 1836)

MARIN, Thomas, see MARIN, Henry

MARINOR, Matilda, see RIBLER, John

MARIS, Barclay, in Wilm, 8 Jan 1853,
in his 17th yr (DG 18 Jan 1853)

MARIS, George,
see MARIS, Mary Elizabeth

MARIS, Mary Elizabeth, dau of Mr. George
MARIS, merchant of Baltimore, in Wilm,
10 Oct 1828, aged 22 yrs (DG 10 Oct 1828)

MARLEY, Benjamin, dec'd, late of New
Castle Hd, notice given by Louisa MARLEY,
adm'x (DG 23 Sep 1828)

MARLEY, Louisa,
see MARLEY, Benjamin

MARLEY, Richard McW., to JANVIER,
Rebecca, Miss, eldest dau of the late
Wm. B. JANVIER, Esq., at New Castle,
17 Apr 1849, by Rev. Mr. Spotswood
(DG 27 Apr 1849)

MAROT, Elizabeth, see MAROT, Joseph

MAROT, Joseph, dec'd, late of Wilm, notice
given by Elizabeth MAROT, adm'x, and John
WHITE, adm'r (DE 6 Dec 1798)

MARR, Elizabeth A., dau of William and
Elizabeth MARR, in Wilm, 16 Jun 1853,
aged 7 yrs 11 mos (DG 24 Jun 1853)

MARR, Elizabeth, see MARR, Elizabeth A

MARR, William, see MARR, Elizabeth A.

MARRIOTT, Sarah, dec'd, late of the
borough of Bristol, PA, formerly of Wilm,
notice given by Isaac PAXSON, Simon
GILLAM, Jonathan WILLIS, exec'rs
(AW 15 May 1816)

MARSEL, Mary B.,

MARSH, Ann May, Miss, wife of the late Dr.
Joseph MARSH, and only dau of Wiliam
SHANKLAND, at her res. near Lewestown,
12 Apr 1847, na (DG 11 May 1847)

MARSH, Caroline,
see MARSH, Erasmus D.

MARSH, Comfort,
see MARSH, William Thomas

MARSH, Deborah, wife of Dr. R. C.
MARSH, near Smith's Bridge on the
Brandywine, 17 Sep 1853, na
(DG 7 Oct 1853)

MARSH, Erasmus D., son of Peter
and Caroline MARSH, 28 Jul 1849,
aged 18 mos, (DG 3 Aug 1849)

MARSH, John
see MARSH, William Thomas

MARSH, John, to WALKER, Mary, both of
Wilm, 8 May 1845, by Rev. S. R. Wynkoop
(DG 13 May 1845)

MARSH, Joseph, Dr.,
see MARSH, Ann May

MARSH, Peter, of Lewes and Rehoboth Hd,
26 Jul 1851, of dysentery, in his 50th yr
(DG 1 Aug 1851)
see MARSH, Erasmus D.

MARSH, R. C., Dr.,
see MARSH, Deborah

MARSH, William Thomas, son of John
and Comfort MARSH, at Eden Park Farm,
aged 10 mos 6 days (DG 10 Sep 1841)

MARSHALL, Aaron,
see CROSBY, Reuben H.

MARSHALL, Ann,
see VINCENT, Thomas M.

MARSHALL, Daniel,
see MARSHALL, David

MARSHALL, David, lost about 6 wks ago
from the shallop Happy Returns of New
Castle. Give notice to George MONROE
at New Castle. Reward paid by Daniel
MARSHALL (PG 2 Dec 1748)

MARSHALL, Edward, to ARMSTRONG,
Ann, Miss, both of Christiana Hd,
28 Oct 1830 , by Rev. R. U. Morgan
(DF 13 Nov 1830)

MARSHALL, Emily J.,
see CROSBY, Reuben H.

MARSHALL, Helen, Miss, eldest dau of John MARSHALL, in Lewes, 9 Nov 1851, aged 22 yrs (DG 18 Nov 1851) eldest dau of Hon. John MARSHALL, at her father's res. in Lewes, 9 Nov 1851, aged 22 yrs 3 mos (DG 25 Nov 1851)

MARSHALL, Henry W., of Wilm, to ROOT, Mary Ann, Miss, of Phila, 2 May 1852, by Rev. R. S. Norris (DG 28 May 1852)

MARSHALL, Jacob A., to CARPENTER, Mary Q., Miss, both of Lewes, 3 Sep 1850, by Rev. Cornelius Mustard (DG 24 Sep 1850)

MARSHALL, Jno., see BROSIUS, Edwin

MARSHALL, John, to HARLAN, Mary, both of NC Co, 15 Feb 1845, by David C. Wilson, Mayor (DG 25 Feb 1845)
see MARSHALL, Helen

MARSHALL, John P., to HALL, Margaret F., both of Sussex Co, 14 Apr 1847, by Rev. Cornelius Mustard (DG 4 May 1847)

MARSHALL, Maria,
see McCULLOUGH, Thomas

MARSHALL, Mary H.,
see BROSIUS, Edwin

MARSHALL, Sallie,
see FAIRLAMB, N. Walter

MARSHALL, Samuel, of Staunton, to CROZIER, Elizabeth, Mrs., of Wilm, 24 Dec 1812, by Rev. Daniel Dodge (DS 30 Dec 1812)

MARSHALL, Samuel. Sale at Newport on the Christiana Creek, a lot, brick house for entertainment, wharf, storehouse and personal effects. Sarah MARSHALL, adm'x (PG 15 Jul 1741)

MARSHALL, Sarah,
see MARSHALL, Samuel

MARSHALL, Thomas, dec'd, notice given by S. M. COUPER, atty-in-fact for the adm'x (DG 17 Feb 1829)

MARSHALL, Wm. Dr., of Georgetown, to McCOLLEY, Lina, Miss, of Milford, in Milford, 22 Nov 1853, by her father, Rev. T. P. McCOLLEY (DG 29 Nov 1853)

MARTER, I. B., to RAYMOND, Mary E., Miss, dau of T. C. RAYMOND, Esq., formerly of Smyrna, in Phila, 17 May 1853, by the Rev. D. B. Bartine (DG 27 May 1853)

MARTIN, Arthur, to TALLEY, Mary, Miss, both of NC Co, 5 Feb 1846, in Wilm, by Rev. M. J. Rhees (DG 10 Feb 1846)

MARTIN, Daniel, to BECKLEY, Caroline, Miss, of Wilm, 13 Jan 1834, by the Rev. Joseph Walker (DG 11 Feb 1834)

MARTIN, Edmund Nevill, son of James I. MARTIN, of Deer Park Hall, DE, 15 Jan 1850, aged 7 yrs 10 mos 1 day (DG 22 Jan 1850)

MARTIN, Eleuthere J., to RANKIN, Maria J., Miss, both of NC Co, by Rev. Arthur Granger (DG 29 May 1835)

MARTIN, Eliza, Miss, at the home of her relative, Mrs. E. JACKSON of Wilm, aged 40 yrs (DG 15 Dec 1843)

MARTIN, Eliza, see WELDON, John A.

MARTIN, Elizabeth, see WEBB, Joseph

MARTIN, Emma, see SCHOFIELD, James

MARTIN, H., Capt., see GREEN, Jesse

MARTIN, Hugh, Capt.,
see GREEN, Sophia Jane

MARTIN, J. Willis, of Wilm, to REGISTER, Malvina, dau of Robert REGISTER, late of DE, in Phila, 23 Nov 1848, at Friends Mtg House on Green St (DG 5 Dec 1848)

MARTIN, James, of Cecil Co MD, to ROBINSON, Sally Ann, of NC Co, in Smyrna, 11 Jan 1853 (DG 1 Feb 1853)

MARTIN, James I.,
see MARTIN, Edmund Nevill

MARTIN, John, to BOOTH, Sarah Jane, Miss, both of New Castle, in New Castle, 7 Feb 1850, by Rev. Andrew Manship (DG 15 Feb 1850)

MARTIN, John, see MARTIN, Rebecca

MARTIN, John S.,
see HANDY, Isaac W. K.

MARTIN, Luther, the Hon., "the illustrious patriot and jurist," at NY, 10 Jul 1826, aged 82 yrs, (DG 14 Jul 1826)
see SCOTT, Mary T.

MARTIN, Mary Adaline,
see CONWELL, Asa F.

MARTIN, Nathan S., of Phila, to EVES, Susan B. of Wilm, 22 Sep 1852, by Rev. Jos. Smith (DG 28 Sep 1852)

MARTIN, O. B., Capt, to SWIGGETTE, Sarah J, Miss, both formerly of DE,

DELAWARE MARRIAGES AND DEATHS FROM NEWSPAPERS, 1729-1853   151

27 Apr 1852, at Christ Ch in Balt, by the Rev. Mr. Killen (DG 4 May 1852)

MARTIN, Orlando H., see MARTIN, Sarah S.

MARTIN, Pascal Allen, to UUMAN, Emelia, Miss, dau of the late John James UUMAN, of Wilm, in New York at St. George's Church, 3 Apr 1850, by Rev. Dr. Tyng (DG 23 Apr 1850)

MARTIN, Rebecca, member of Soc. of Friends, widow of John MARTIN, dec'd, at the res. of her son-in-law, Thomas MOORE, 15 Jun 1849, in her 94th yr (DG 19 Jun 1849)

MARTIN, Sallie S., see HANDY, W. K.

MARTIN, Samuel, see CONWELL, Asa F.

MARTIN, Sarah S., formerly of DE, but recently of Balt, consort of Capt Orlando H. MARTIN, in Balt, 20 Nov 1849, aged 28 yrs (DG 23 Nov 1849)

MARTIN, Sophia, see GREEN, Jesse

MARTIN, Sophia Jane, see GREEN, Sophia Jane

MARTIN, Thomas, in Wilm, 13 Jan 1850, aged 71 yrs (DG 22 Jan 1850)

MARTIN, William, of Christiana Hd, 21 Jan 1850, aged 80 yrs (DG 1 Feb 1850)

MARVEL, Elizabeth, see EMERSON, Vincent

MARVEL, John G., at his res. near Cecilton, Cecil Co MD, of bilious pleurisy and liver disease, 11 Feb 1847, aged 44 yrs (DG 19 Feb 1847)

MARVEL, Philip, of Wilm, to McCARTNEY, Alice, of Elkton, MD, in Phila 22 Mar 1849, by the Rev. R. Gerry (DG 27 Mar 1849)

MARVEL, Phillip, Capt., at his res. near Millsboro after a protracted illness, aged 71 yrs 6 mos 10 days (DG 23 Aug 1850)

MARVEL, Ruben G., to DELL, Mary Jane, Miss, both of Willow Grove, Kent Co DE, 25 May 1848, in Dover, by Rev. G. Asay (DG 2 Jun 1848)

MARVEL, Theodore W., to ADKINS, Catharine, Miss, 20 Nov 1846, near Millsboro, by Rev. H. C. Fries, all of Sussex Co (DG 8 Jan 1847)

MARVEL, Thomas J., see EMERSON, Vincent

MARVEL, William, near Georgetown, 15 Jan 1848, aged 82 yrs. He left the wife of his youth and age to mourn her loss (DG 1 Feb 1848)

MARVILL, Milley Ann, see MARVILL, William

MARVILL, Nathaniel H., son of Capt Philip MARVILL at the res. of his father near Millsborough, 6 Mar 1843, aged 32 yrs (DG 17 Mar 1843)

MARVILL, Philip, see MARVILL, Nathaniel H.

MARVILL, William, to MARVILL, Milley Ann, Miss, both of Kent Co, 16 Jan 1851, by the Rev. T. P. McColley (DG 28 Jan 1851)

MARVIN, Ebenezer, to OGLE, Jane, Miss, both of White Clay Creek Hd, NC Co, 6 Feb 1834, by the Rev. A. K. Russel (DG 11 Feb 1834)

MARVIN, Ebenezer, to WEST, Mary, Miss, 29 Mar 1849, by the Rev. Joseph Barr (DG 3 Apr 1849)

MASDEN, Benjamin, Esq., merchant of Phila, to JONES, Hannah, Miss, dau of Mr. T. JONES, of DE, in Phila, "Thursday last," by the Rev. Dr. Boyd (DG 29 May 1821)

MASON, Ann, Mrs., in Wilm, 15 Feb 1851, aged 67 yrs (DG 18 Feb 1851)

MASON, Isaac, at Dover, 12 May 1851, aged 87 yrs (DG 20 May 1851)

MASON, Catharine, wife of Charles MASON, Esq., 5 Jul 1834, aged 37 yrs (DG 29 Jul 1834)

MASON, Catharine Jane, dau of Park MASON, 27 Dec 1841, after a short illness (DG 7 Jan 1842)

MASON, Charles, of Milford, DE, to BECKWORTH, Ann W., Miss, of Phila, 8 Nov 1835, by Dr. Thomas Dunn (DG 13 Nov 1835) see MASON, Catharine

MASON, Charles C., Esq., of Altoonar, Blair Co, formerly of Wilm, to MATLACK, Sarah A., Miss, of W. Chester Pa, at the res. of A. MATSINGER, Esq., 12 Oct 1853, by the Hon. Charles Gilpin, Mayor (DG 18 Oct 1853)

MASON, Daniel, in Milford, 25 Apr 1852, aged c 75 yrs (DG 30 Apr 1852)

MASON, John, in Wilm of consumption, 30 Jun 1835, aged 35 yrs (DG 3 Jul 1835)

MASON, Jonathan P., to HORN, Susan Ann P., both of Wilm, 29 Mar 1852, by the Rev. John A. McKean (DG 13 Apr 1852)

MASON, Mary E.,
see THAWLEY, Samuel Jr.

MASON, Park,
see MASON, Catharine Jane

MASON, Taylor, in Wilm, of croup, 6 Nov 1851, aged 3 yrs 10 mos (DG 11 Nov 1851)

MASON, Washington, to SLACK, Rebecca, Miss, all of Wilm, 26 Oct 1843, by Rev. M. J. Rhees (DG 3 Nov 1843)

MASON, William, seaman, of Seaford, on board ship *Madison* on her passage from Havre to Hampton Roads, 17 Dec 1829 (DG 12 Jan 1830)

MASON, Wm. of Easton, to WHITE, Mary A., dau of John WHITE, Esq., of Smyrna, 17 Apr 1849, in Smyrna, by the Rev. Dr. Perkins (DG 27 Apr 1849)

MASSEY, Elizabeth D.,
see SPEAKMAN, Eber

MASSEY, Elizabeth, wife of Thomas MASSEY, at her late dwelling near Wilm, 25 Aug 1823, funeral from the home of Edward GILPIN (DG 26 Aug 1823)

MASSEY, Henry P., to PRICE, Susan A., Miss, both of NC Co, 29 Jan 1850, by Rev. Dr. Furness (DG 5 Feb 1850)

MASSEY, James A., Rev.,
see DEWEES, William C.

MASSEY, Joshua, to PHILLIPS, Sarah, Miss, 24 Oct 1816, by Rev. William Pryce (AW 30 Oct 1816)

MASSEY, Lewis Howard, son of William B. and Rebecca A. MASSEY, in Wilm, 31 Aug 1852, aged c 3 yrs (DG 3 Sep 1852)

MASSEY, Mary Ann,
see DEWEES, William C.

MASSEY, Rebecca A.,
see MASSEY, Lewis Howard

MASSEY, Thomas,
see MASSEY, Elizabeth

MASSEY, William B., to READEL, Rebecca Ann, Miss, both of Wilm, 2 Dec 1841, by Rev. S. Leach (DG 10 Dec 1841)
see MASSEY, Lewis Howard

MASTEN, Hezekiah, of St. Georges Hd, to GRIFFITH, Alethea, Mrs., of Cecil Co, MD, 16 Nov 1821, by the Rev. Sharpley (DG 20 Nov 1821)

MATHESON, Gilbert, to STUART, Mary, Miss, both of NC Co, 22 Sep 1846, by Rev. S. M. Gayley (DG 2 Oct 1846)

MATHEWS, Eliza, see SMITH, Allen

MATHEWS, John, , Esq., member of the Levy Court, NC Co, at his res. in Appoq Hd, 3 Mar 1834, aged 31 yrs (DG 11 Mar 1834)

MATHEWSON, Margaret J.,
see GALLAGHER, Thomas

MATHIAS, John. Trustee's sale in Cecil Co MD (DG 4 Jan 1853)

MATHIEU, Anne M.,
see RANDOLPH, B. Harrison

MATHIEU, J. E. Capt.,
see RANDOLPH, B. Harrison

MATLACK, Charles P., to HAYES, Phebe E., Miss, all of Wilm, 19 Jun 1849, by Rev. M. J. Rhees (DG 22 Jun 1849)

MATLACK, Sarah A.,
see MASON, Charles C.

MATLOIX, Sarah Jane, in Wilm, 20th inst., na (DG 2 Jan 1849)

MATSINGER, A., see MASON, Charles C.

MATSON, George, of Chester Co, PA, to WALTERS, Elizabeth, Miss, 8 Mar 1798, by Rev. Mr. Clarkson (DE 12 Mar 1798)

MATTER, Hannah,
see HUNTSMAN, William

MATTES, _____, Mrs., wife of Valentine MATTES, in Appoq. Hd, 18 Oct 1849, na (DG 26 Oct 1849)

MATTES, Valentine,
see MATTES, _____, Mrs.

MATTHEWS, Artemissia,
see TOWNSEND, Joseph R.

MATTHEWS, Eliza, see SIMPSON, William

MATTHEWS, Elizabeth, only dau of Capt. John MATTHEWS, 6 Nov 1821, na, the same day as her father, see his notice (DG 20 Nov 1821)

MATTHEWS, Jane Y.,
see BALDWIN, William

MATTHEWS, John, Capt., in Appoq. Hd, after a lingering illness, 6 Nov 1821. Burial

DELAWARE MARRIAGES AND DEATHS FROM NEWSPAPERS, 1729-1853   153

in Presbyterian Ch ground near Smyrna (DG 20 Nov 1821) see **MATTHEWS**, Elizabeth

MATTHEWS, Joseph S., of Delaware City, to **LAYTON**, Sarah S., Miss, of Milford, 6 Nov 1848, by Rev. Mr. McKimp [?] (DG 10 Nov 1848)

MATTHEWS, Margaret Jane, see **WIGGLESWORTH**, Joseph

MATTHEWS, Mary J., see **VANDYKE**, William S.

MATTHEWS, Sarah, see **BALL**, Martin D.

MATTHEWSON, Margaret, see **GALLAGHER**, Thomas

MAULL, _____, Gov., 3 May 1846, at Milton (DG 5 May 1846)

MAULL, James, see **STEEL**, James

MAULL, John, of Lewistown DE, to **CHAMPION**, Rachel B., Miss, dau of Wm. CHAMPION, of Phila, in Phila, 7 Jun 1849, by the Rev. J. C. Clay (DG 18 Sep 1849)

MAULL, Penelope K., see **STEEL**, James

MAURY, Matthew, Esq., of New York, to **GILPIN**, Elizabeth, dau of Joshua GILPIN, Esq., 2 Jun 1841, at Kentmere on the Brandywine, by Rev. J. W. McCullough (DG 11 Jun 1841)

MAXFIELD, Joseph, Jr., to **FISHER**, Williamina, dau of the late Judge FISHER of Delaware, 17 Jun 1847, by Rev. Samuel C. Brinkle (DG 22 Jun 1847)

MAXWELL, Hugh, see **ALRICHS**, Henry S.

MAXWELL, John G., Dr., of Canterbury, to **CLAYTON**, Elizabeth, Miss, dau of Thomas CLAYTON, Esq., Dover, 27 Feb 1825, by the Rev. Mr. Dale (DG 4 Mar 1825)

MAXWELL, Kitty, see **BROOKS**, John

MAXWELL, Margaret, see **NICHOLSON**, Isaac J.

MAXWELL, Mary, see **PETERSON**, Charles B.

MAXWELL, Sarah, Mrs., see **LOFLAND**, James P.

MAXWELL, Sarah B., see **ALRICHS**, Henry S.

MAY, Elenora, see **PARSONS**, Henry R.

MAY, Joshua, see **PARSONS**, Henry R.

MAY, Mary A., see **PEIRCE**, Caleb

MAY, Thomas P., the Rev., see **PEIRCE**, Caleb

MAYBIN, A. W., Rev., see **MAYBIN**, Joseph A.

MAYBIN, Joseph A., of Newark, to **WALDIE**, Mary A., of Wilm, 25 May 1853, by the Rev. Wm. A. W. MAYBIN (DG 31 May 1853)

MAYDIN, Eunice, at the res. of James H. RAY, near Newark, 25 Nov 1852, in her 58th yr (DG 30 Nov 1852)

MAYER, Elizabeth, see **JOSLIN**, Thomas

MAYFIELD, Anna Elizabeth, see **BENNET**, Thomas J.

MAYFIELD, Solomon, at his late res. in Wilm, 5 Sep 1849, aged 27 yrs (DG 7 Sep 1849)

MAYFIELD, Solomon, of Wilm, to **BIDDLE**, Ann Elizabeth, Miss, of Roxborough, PA, in Phila, 4 Nov 1847, by Rev. Thomas Winter (DG 12 Nov 1847)

McALLISTER, Lavenia, see **BLEYER**, William

McALLISTER, Margaret, see **RIGHTER**, John

McALLISTER, Sarah, Mrs, at the res. of her son-in-law, Lewis WILSON, 17 Feb 1848, aged 80 yrs (DG 7 Mar 1848) see **WILSON**, Lewis

McANALL, James, to **VANEMAN**, Rebecca, Miss, 4 Feb 1827, by the Rev. John P. Peckworth, all of Wilm (DG 6 Feb 1827)

McBRIDE, Hugh, killed by explosion in J. P. Garesche Powder Mills, 10 Apr 1845 (DG 11 Apr 1845)

McCABE, Bridget, see **FAY**, P.

McCABE, Elizabeth, see **HUDSON**, Nathaniel

McCABE, Garritson, see **HUDSON**, Nathaniel

McCABE, Mary, suddenly, near her res. in Mill Creek Hd, 20 Mar 1850. Leaves a large family (DG 26 Mar 1850)

McCAFFERTY, Alexander, in Wilm, 2 Apr 1847, aged 75 yrs (DG 20 Apr 1847)

McCAFFERTY, Susan,
see McCAIG, John N.

McCAIG, John N., to McCAFFERTY, Susan, Miss, both of Brandywine, in the Meth. Ch at Newark, 5 Apr 1853, by the Rev. Joseph T. Brown (DG 12 Apr 1853)

McCAIN, Eliza Jane, see DAVIS, Isaac

McCALL, _____, little son of John McCALL, tailor, in 4th St. between Market and Shipley St, 8 Jan 1851, na. Burned to death playing with fire (DG 10 Jan 1851)

McCALL, Adaline,
see MITCHELL, Passmore H.

McCALL, Andrew,
see McCALL, Louisa, Mrs.,
see McCALL, Elenor

McCALL, Charles, see McCALL, James B.

McCALL, David, see McCALL, Martha

McCALL, Elenor, Mrs., relict of Andrew McCALL, in Camden NJ, 26 Nov 1849, in her 72nd yr (DG 29 Nov 1849)

McCALL, James B., son of Charles and M. N. McCALL, 30 Jul 1847, aged 19 mos (DG 3 Aug 1847)

McCALL, John, see McCALL, _____.

McCALL, John S., to HENSHAW, Elizabeth, Miss, of NC Co, 6 Jan 1846, in Wilm (DG 27 Jan 1846)

McCALL, Josiah, to GREEN, Rachel Ann, Miss, both of Wilm, 15 Sep 1850, by Rev. Newton Heston (DG 24 Sep 1850)

McCALL, Louisa, Mrs., wife of Andrew McCALL and dau of George S. SHUGART, in Smyrna, 21 May 1833, aged 21 yrs (DG 28 May 1833)

McCALL, M. M., see McCALL, James B.

McCALL, Margaret, see JOHNSON, Hugh

McCALL, Martha, inf dau of David and Mary McCALL, at her father's res. in Wilm, 13 Mar 1848, aged c 4 mos (DG 14 Mar 1848)

McCALL, Mary, see McCALL, Martha

McCALL, Mary Eliza,
see CHESNEY, William A.

McCALL, Mary Jane,
see RICHARDSON, Jacob

McCALL, Ralph, to WALKER, Mary Ann,
both of Wilm, 6 Jun 1848, by Rev. J. Castle (DG 9 Jun 1848)

McCALL, William, 25 Aug 1844 (DG 30 Aug 1844)

McCALLION, David, drowned in the Brandywine, 7 Jan 1846 (DG 13 Jan 1846)

McCALLMONT, Anna,
see THOMSON, Allan
see McCALLMONT, James, Dr.

McCALLMONT, James,
see DICKSON, William

McCALLMONT, James, Dr,
see THOMSON, Allan

McCALLMONT, James, Dr., dec'd, notice given by Kensey JOHNS, Jr., atty-in-fact for Anna McCALLMONT and Sarah McCALLMONT, adm'ces (DG 11 Jan 1825)

McCALLMONT, Sarah,
see McCALLMONT, James, Dr.

McCALLMONT, Thomas, dec'd, late of NC Co, notice given by Henry COLESBURY, adm'r (DG 3 Jun 1825)

McCANDLES, Eleanor,
see MOORE, John D.

McCANLESS, Susan,
see MURPHY, Bernard

McCANN, Bernard, Jr., formerly of Wilm, in Phila, 9 Jan 1853, in his 32nd yr (DG 14 Jan 1853)

McCANNON, Charles, drowned in the Brandywine (DG 13 Mar 1846)

McCANNON, Mary,
see HAWKINS, Thomas, Sr.

McCARNAN, Bernard, formerly of Wilm, in Phila, 13 Dec 1850 (DG 17 Dec 1850)

McCARRON, Charles,
see MELLEN, Patrick

McCARTNEY, Alice, see MARVEL, Philip

McCARTNEY, Mary,
see WILKINSON, James

McCAULEY, Absalom, of Cecil Co MD, to TYRREL, Olivia Ann, Miss, of NC Co, 19 Feb 1846, by Rev. James Hare (DG 31 Mar 1846)

McCAULEY, Alexander, formerly of St. Georges Hd, at his res. in Tippecanoe Grove, Brandywine Hd, 2 Feb 1841, aged 71 yrs. A Methodist (DG 5 Feb 1841)

McCAULEY, Christiana,
see BREEN, James

McCAULLEY, Anna, dau of William McCAULLEY, 30 Mar 1843, aged 9 yrs (DG 7 Apr 1843)

McCAULLEY, Elizabeth Mary, Miss, dau of Samuel McCAULLEY, Esq., 19 Mar 1846, aged 16 yrs (DG 24 Mar 1846)

McCAULLEY, Elizabeth W.,
see COOMBE, Pennel

McCAULLEY, Mary Sinclair,
see JEFFERIS, Joseph P.

McCAULLEY, Samuel,
see McCAULLEY, Susanna

McCAULLEY, Samuel,
see McCAULLEY, Elizabeth Mary

McCAULLEY, Sarah L., Mrs., wife of William McCAULLEY, and dau of the late Samuel SINCLAIR, Esq., of Kennet, Chester Co PA, in Wilm, 11 Aug 1851, age 48 yrs (DG 12 Aug 1851)

McCAULLEY, Susanna K., at the res. of her father, Samuel McCAULLEY, Esq., 17 Feb 1847, aged 17 yrs (DG 23 Feb 1847)

McCAULLEY, William,
see McCAULLEY, Sarah L.
see JEFFERIS, Joseph P.
see McCAULLEY, Anna

McCAULLEY, William, merchant, Brandywine, to SINCLAIR, Sarah, Miss, dau of Samuel SINCLAIR, Esq., of Kennett Twp, Chester Co, PA, in Lancaster, PA, 12 Jan 1824, by Nathaniel Lightner, Alderman (DG 20 Jan 1824)

McCAULLEY, Wm., Esq., of Wilm, to BRINTON, Hannah B., dau of Caleb BRINTON, of East Bradford Twp, Chester Co, 19 Jul 1853, by the Rev. J. N. Grier (DG 22 Jul 1853)

McCAY, John, late of Appoq Hd, Benj. McCAY, exec'r (DG 30 Dec 1853)

McCLAIN, Andrew L. to SCOTT, Arrabella, Miss, both of Wilm, 27 May 1849, by Rev. A. B. Hard (DG 8 Jun 1849)

McCLANE, Mary, see JOHNSON, William

McCLARY, Elizabeth, 20 Oct 1798, on list of yellow fever victims (DG 27 Oct 1798)

McCLARY, Thomas, of Wilm, to HENDRICKSON, Margaret A., Miss, of Delmore, at Delmore, near Wilm,
14 Mar 1850, by Rev. S. R. Wynkoop (DG 15 Mar 1850)

McCLAY, Alexander, in Wilm, 23 Sep 1853, in his 44th yr (DG 27 Sep 1853)

McCLEES, Elizabeth, see BRANGAN, John

McCLEES, Herbert, inf son of Wm. K. McCLEES, 27 Mar 1852, aged 5 mos (DG 2 Apr 1852)

McCLEES, William K., to CLARK, Sarah Ann, Miss, both of Wilm, 10 Dec 1846, by Rev. J. Kennaday, D. D. (DG 15 Dec 1846)

McCLEES, Wm. K.,
see McCLEES, Herbert

McCLELLAND, Martha A.,
see COYLE, James

McCLELLAND, William, of Newark, DE, to STUART, Margaret, Miss, of Elkton, in Elkton, 17 Apr 1849, by Rev. Mr. Barton (DG 24 Apr 1849)

McCLEMENT, Alexander, Esq., clerk of the Bank of Smyrna for more than 20 yrs, of bilious dysentery, 28 Jun 1851, in his 67th yr (DG 8 Jul 1851)

McCLENNAN, Eliza,
see TAYLOR, James T.

McCLINTOCK, Eliza,
see GALBREATH, Samuel

McCLINTOCK, Isabella,
see HEADOCK, John

McCLOUD, William, a miller at Isaac Jones Snuff Mill, on 25 Oct 1790, walking up the bank was taken with a fit (as supposed), being shortly afterwards found in the Brandywine. Immediate assistance proved ineffectual (DG 30 Oct 1790)

McCLUEN, John, of Wilm, to BATTIN, Ann, Miss, of Williston, Chester Co PA, 15 Jan 1846, in Phila, by John Swift, Mayor (DG 13 Feb 1846)

McCLUGHAN, John, Capt., of Wilm. Notice given by John McKINLY, assisting exec'r (PG 26 Mar 1761)

McCLUNG, Elizabeth H., dau of William and Mary H. McCLUNG, in Wilm, 4 Jan 1841, aged 4 yrs (DG 8 Jan 1841)

McCLUNG, John,
see McCLUNG, Wm. Linn

McCLUNG, John, Gen., of Wilm, to BURTON, Margaretta, Miss, dau of Dr.

BURTON of Phila, in Phila, 12 Oct 1847, by Rev. S. R. Wynkoop (DG 15 Oct 1847)

McCLUNG, John R., MD, of New Garden, Chester Co PA, to HIGGINS, Ruth Ann, dau of George HIGGINS, 1 Jan 1851, by the Rev. George HIGGINS of Montgomery Co PA (DG 3 Jan 1851)

McCLUNG, Margaretta H., see McCLUNG, Wm. Linn

McCLUNG, Mary, see McCLUNG, Susan Keen

McCLUNG, Mary H., see McCLUNG, Elizabeth H.

McCLUNG, Mary H., consort of Wm. McCLUNG, 15 Aug 1853, in her 40th yr (DG 23 Aug 1853)

McCLUNG, Rebecca, see McCLUNG, William

McCLUNG, Susan Keen, youngest dau of Wm. and Mary McCLUNG, in Wilm, 4 Apr 1852, aged 14 mos 10 days (DG 9 Apr 1852)

McCLUNG, Wesley, in Wilm, 12 Jan 1830, aged 31 yrs (DG 15 Jan 1830)

McCLUNG, William, see McCLUNG, Elizabeth H.

McCLUNG, William, dec'd, late of Wilm, notice given by Rebecca McCLUNG, adm'x (DS 24 Jul 1813)

McCLUNG, Wm., see McCLUNG, Susan Keen

McCLUNG, Wm., see McCLUNG, Mary H.

McCLUNG, Wm. Linn, inf son of John and Margaretta H. McCLUNG, at the res. of John RODNEY, Esq., Lewes, 20 Aug 1852, na (DG 24 Aug 1852)

McCLURE, Sarah Jane, see LEMMON, David

McCLYMONT, _____, Mrs., consort of William McCLYMONT, Esq., 20 Dec 1802, (FA 24 Dec 1802)

McCLYMONT, James, Esq., see GRAY, Andrew

McCLYMONT, Nancy, see GRAY, Andrew

McCLYMONT, William, Esq., see McCLYMONT, _____, Mrs.

McCOLAM, master of the sloop ANN, drowned in C and D Canal 15 May 1848 (DG 19 May 1848)

McCOLLEY, Andrew J., see McCOLLEY, Francis Bertrum

McCOLLEY, Anthdelina, Mrs., widow of the late Robert W. McCOLLEY of Sussex Co, near Georgetown, 26 Oct 1825, aged 84 yrs; mother of 18 children, 9 now living, 61 g'children and 65 g'g'children (DG 6 Dec 1825)

McCOLLEY, Francis Bertrum, youngest son of Andrew J. McCOLLEY, in Milford, 6 Nov 1852, in his 2nd yr (DG 16 Nov 1852)

McCOLLEY, Lina, see MARSHALL, Wm.

McCOLLEY, Robert W., see McCOLLEY, Anthdelina, Mrs.

McCOLLEY, T. P., see MARSHALL, Wm.

McCOLLIN, James G., of Phila, to GARRETT, Margaret M., dau of Thomas GARRETT of Wilm, 17 Aug 1848, by Friends ceremony (DG 25 Aug 1848)

McCOMB, Thomas, a boy, 17 Oct 1798, on list of yellow fever victims (DG 27 Oct 1798)

McCOMBS, Henry S., to BUSH, Elizabeth K., only dau of Charles BUSH, Esq., all of Wllm, 16 Jun 1853, by the Rev. A. D. Pollock (DG 17 Jun 1853)

McCOMBS, Laurence, Rev., of the Phila Conference of the M. E. Ch, to ANDREWS, Sarah, Miss, of Phila, in Phila, by the Rev. Joseph Rusling (DG 9 Apr 1833)

McCOMMON, Thomas, to HICKMAN, Sarah, Miss, both of New Castle, 29 May 1817 in New Castle by Rev. William Pryce (DG 31 May 1817)

McCONAUGHY, Alexander, see McCONAUGHY, James Ayers

McCONAUGHY, Alexander, to AYERS, Rebecca S., dau of Rev. J. B. AYRES, all of Delaware City, 20 Jun 1850, by Rev. J. D. Long (DG 28 Jun 1850)

McCONAUGHY, James Ayers, inf son of Alexander and Rebecca McCONAUGHY, in Delaware City, 25 Jul 1851, aged 3 mos (DG 8 Aug 1851)

McCONAUGHY, Rebecca, see McCONAUGHY, James Ayers

McCONEGHAY, Mary, see PENNINGTON, Samuel

DELAWARE MARRIAGES AND DEATHS FROM NEWSPAPERS, 1729-1853   157

McCONNELL, ____, Mr.,
see McMAKIN, Catharine

McCONNELL, Eliza,
see SOMERS, Chalkley

McCONNELL, Hannah,
see McCONNELL, Mary

McCONNELL, Hannah, formerly of Wilm, after a short illness in Richmond VA, 8 Jan 1844, aged 70 yrs (DG 13 Feb 1844)

McCONNELL, Mary, late of New Castle, died intestate. Heirs to appear at Orphan's Court: John GAMBLE, Ann CONGER, Sarah BURTON, Hannah McCONNELL (DG 13 Jan 1852)

McCONNELL, Rachel A.,
see BOWERS, John

McCONNELL, Thomas, formerly of Wilm, at Richmond, VA, ndd, aged 48 yrs (DG 25 Jan 1825)

McCOOL, George, dec'd, late of Red Lion Hd, notice given by Abel NILES, adm'r (DG 5 Jan 1793)

McCOOL, John Sr., late of NC Co. Notice given by John MEARIS, exec'r (PG 14 Jan 1762)

McCORKLE, George, of Wilm, to PENNY, Mary, Miss, of Brandywine Hd, 6 Nov 1823, by the Rev. E. W. Gilbert (DG 14 Nov 1823)

McCORKLE, William, late mate of the brig Mary, of Phila, and native of Wilm, of fever after being shipwrecked at Cow Island, Mosquito Shore, Central America, 4 Apr 1827, na (DG 22 May 1827)

McCORMACK, Alexander, of Halifax NS, to FERCUM, Mary Louisa, Miss,of Smyrna DE, in Phila, 27 Aug 1849, by the Rev. Mr. Allen (DG 7 Sep 1849)

McCORMACK, Henry C., in Sussex Co, 7 Sep 1849, in his 31st yr (DG 14 Sep 1849)

McCORMACK, Henry C., son of the late James McCORMACK, in Sussex Co DE, 7 Sep 1849, in his 31st yr (DG 11 Sep 1849)

McCORMACK, James,
see McCORMACK, Henry C.

McCORMICH, Holt, accidentally drowned in the Brandywine at Henry Clay Factory, 22 Oct 1850   (DG 25 Oct 1850)

McCORMICK, Lewis, of NC Co, to PASS, Rebecca Ellen, Miss, of London, Britain Twp, Chester Co PA, in Phila, 31 May 1849, by

the Rev. C. H. Plummer (DG 9 Oct 1849)

McCOY, Abigail E., see WEIR, John H.

McCOY, Catharine,
see THOMPSON, Robert
see BENNET, James R.

McCOY, Eliza, see RICHARDS, William

McCOY, Elizabeth,
see McCOY, Nathaniel
see LEST, Lewis

McCOY, Isabella, see OGLE, Thomas

McCOY, James, see McCOY, Sarah
see McCOY, Nathaniel

McCOY, James, to MORRISON, Ellizabeth, Miss, youngest dau of Mr. Douglas MORRISON, both of White Clay Creek Hd, near Newark, DE, Tuesday evening last (DG 17 or 25 Nov 1834), by the Rev. A. K. Russel (DG 28 Nov 1834)

McCOY, Jane,
see MURDAUGH, Alexander

McCOY, Mary Ann, see ROWAN, Henry

McCOY, Nathaniel, eldest son of James and Elizabeth McCOY, in Wilm, 15 Aug 1853, aged 17 yrs 11 mos 7 days (DG 23 Aug 1853)

McCOY, Nathaniel, of Wilm, to WALKER, Mary, Miss,of Red Lion Hd, 18 Dec 1828, by Elder John P. Peckworth (DG 23 Dec 1828)

McCOY, Robert, to SAMPLE, Jane, Miss, both of White Clay Creek Hd, 26 Jun 1834, by the Rev. A. K. Russel (DG 1 Jul 1834)

McCOY, Sarah, wife of James McCOY, in Phila "on Wednesday morning" (4 Jul 1849) aged 52 yrs (DG 10 Jul 1849) day of paper, Tuesday

McCOY, Washington, to MAGUIRE, Anna Rebecca, both of Wiim, 8 Apr 1851, by Rev. A. Manship (DG 18 Apr 1851)

McCRACKEN, Amelia Jane,
see WARE, Robinson

McCRACKEN, Elizabeth,
see McCRACKEN, John, Esq.

McCRACKEN, John,
see BOWMAN, Margaret

McCRACKEN, John, Esq., Justice of the Peace, at his res. near Buck Tavern,

[= Summit Bridge, 6 mi N of Middletown] "a short time since," na (DG 28 Feb 1826) late of St. Georges Hd, dec'd, notice given by Elizabeth McCRACKEN, adm'x (DG 12 May 1826)

McCREA, Joseph, of NC Co, 7 Mar 1849, aged 43 yrs (DG 27 Mar 1849)

McCREA, Samuel, of Cecil Co MD, to BALL, Martha, Miss, of NC Co, 12 Dec 1848, by Rev. E. Kennard (DG 22 Dec 1848)

McCREA, William, see LITTLE, William

McCRONE, Hannah, Mrs., consort of John McCRONE, Jr., near New Castle, 8 Mar 1834, aged 46...member of the Baptist Ch (DG 14 Mar 1834)

McCRONE, Hannah Mary, see JONES, Alexander

McCRONE, John, to NORWOOD, Elizabeth, Mrs., both of Appoq. Hd., 21 Feb 1850, by Rev. J. Hamilton (DG 1 Mar 1850)

McCRONE, John Jr, see JONES, Alexander see McCRONE, Hannah

McCRONE, William B., of Red Lion, to EVES, Rebecca N., Miss, of Wilm, 28 Dec 1847, by Rev. S. R. Wynkoop (DG 31 Dec 1847)

McCULLOUGH, Betsey, see JACKSON, Erasmus

McCULLOUGH, Catharine, see VANDEVER, Peter B.

McCULLOUGH, Deborah, see HENDRICKSON, Peter

McCULLOUGH, James, of yellow fever (DE 20 Sep 1798)

McCULLOUGH, James, dec'd, late of Christiana Hd, notice given by Samuel GREGG, adm'r (MU 7 Feb 1807)

McCULLOUGH, James, see BOWMAN, Henry see MORTON, Andrew

McCULLOUGH, Sallie, see BOULDEN, N. T.

McCULLOUGH, Sarah A., see FARRA, Daniel Jr.

McCULLOUGH, Thomas, to MARSHALL, Maria, Miss,of Christiana Hd, 6 Nov 1823, by the Rev. E. W. Gilbert (DG 14 Nov 1823)

McCURDY, Ann, see STOOPS, Samuel

McCURDY, Martha M., see DAVIS, Nehemiah

McDANEL, Margaret, in Chritiana Hd, 18 Mar 1848, aged c 60 yrs (DG 24 Mar 1848)

McDANEL, Sallie C., see MANLOVE, James

McDANIEL, Archibald, dec'd, late of Mill Creek Hd, notice given by Samuel McDANIEL, adm'r (DG 22 Mar 1825)

McDANIEL, Catharine, see PARIS, William

McDANIEL, Joseph, to HENRY, Margaret , Miss, 19 Mar 1807, by Rev. Mr. Pryce (MU 21 Mar 1807)

McDANIEL, Joseph, of Dover, to CALLEY, Frances A., Miss, of Kent Co, 6 Dec 1843, in Phila, by His Honor the Mayor (DG 15 Dec 1843)

McDANIEL, Leah Jane, see COX, Stephen T.

McDANIEL, Lear, see HANNAH, Thomas

McDANIEL, Martha, dau of Springer McDANIEL, at Stanton, 25 Sep 1853, in her 18th yr (DG 18 Oct 1853)

McDANIEL, Samuel, see McDANIEL, Archibald

McDANIEL, Springer, see McDANIEL, Martha

McDANIEL, Susan, near Thomas' Chapel, 9 Oct 1853, in her 27th yr (DG 28 Oct 1853)

McDANIELS, Albert G., to WHITECRAFT, Isabella C., all of Wilm, 26 Sep 1846, by Rev. A. Atwood (DG 29 Sep 1846)

McDANNIEL, Emma, see WATT, William

McDOLE, Sophia, see LEWIS, William

McDONALD, James, "from the tent," of yellow fever (DE 18 Sep 1798)

McDONOUGH, Lucy Ann, Mrs., wife of Adm. Thomas McDONOUGH, in Middletown, CT, of a liver complaint, ndd, aged 35 yrs (DG 16 Aug 1825)

McDONOUGH, Lydia, see ROBERTS, Lydia

McDONOUGH, Thomas, see ROBERTS, Lydia

DELAWARE MARRIAGES AND DEATHS FROM NEWSPAPERS, 1729-1853

McDONOUGH, Thomas, Commodore, U. S. Navy, on board Brig *Edwin*, 10 Nov 1825, na (DG 29 Nov 1825) Funeral (DG 2 Dec 1825) see **PENNINGTON**, Thomas McDonough as "Adm." **McDONOUGH**, see **McDONOUGH**, Lucy Ann, Mrs.

McDOWELL, Ann, of Phila, in Wilm, 10 Jun 1848, in her 71st yr (DG 16 Jun 1848)

McDOWELL, Elijah, to **FILBERT**, Anna M., both of Balt Co MD, 22 Nov 1852, by the Rev. F. Hodgson (DG 3 Dec 1852)

McDOWELL, Esther Ann, late wife of Philip McDOWELL, near Wilm, 7 Nov 1843 (DG 13 Nov 1843)

McDOWELL, John, of Christiana Hd, to **McGOVERN**, Ann, Miss, of Wilm, 23 Oct 1850, by Rev. P. Reilly (DG 29 Oct 1850)

McDOWELL, Josephine, see **KELLEY**, Clark

McDOWELL, Martha, see **PRICE**, Isaac S.

McDOWELL, Mary Collins, see **SPOONER**, Charles A.

McDOWELL, Mary M., see **POLK**, Robert

McDOWELL, Philip, see **McDOWELL**, Esther Ann

McDOWELL, Samuel C., to **HARDY**, Prudence J. L. Miss, 22 Sep 1853, by Rev. A. Atwood, all of Wilm (DG 27 Sep 1853)

McDOWELL, Thomas, see **WELLS**, Arthur A., Capt.

McDOWELL, Thomas, Esq., see **SPOONER**, Charles A.

McELREE, Charles W., only child of J. H. and Sallie A. McELREE, 19 Feb 1852, aged 3 mos (DG 24 Feb 1852)

McELREE, J. H., see **McELREE**, Charles W.

McELREE, Sallie A., see **McELREE**, Charles W.

McELWEE, Barton, see **McELWEE**, James

McELWEE, James, late of Mill Creek Hd, Barton McELWEE, adm'r (DG 12 Apr 1853)

McENTIRE, Thomas, to **CARE**, Isabella, Miss, both of NC Co, 14 Mar 1852, by Rev. Andrew Manship (DG 23 Mar 1852)

McEVOY, Mary Ann, at New Castle, 25 Dec 1850, aged c 30 yrs (DG 3 Jan 1851)

McFADDEN, William L., of Phila, to **LEE**, Ann, Miss, of Wilm, in Wilm, 5 Jul 1847, by Rev. Joseph Castle (DG 15 Oct 1847)

McFADDON, Mary A., see **WINGATE**, John A.

McFARLAN, Edward, to **McMULLEN**, Mary Jane, Miss, in New Castle Hd, 28 Nov 1848, by Rev. M. J. Rhees (DG 1 Dec 1848)

McFARLAN, Eliza, see **LYNAM**, John R.

McFARLAN, Isaac, dec'd, late of Christiana Hd, notice given by Benjamin CHANDLER, adm'r (DG 15 Nov 1833)

McFARLAN, Robert, 19 May 1843, at Rockland on the Brandywine (DG 26 May 1843)

McFARLAND, Anna, see **McFARLIN**, William T.

McFARLAND, Richard, formerly of Elkton MD, to **JAGGARD**, Elizabeth, Miss, eldest dau of Thomas JAGGARD, Esq., of NC Co, 22 Nov 1853, by the Rev. W. S. F. Graham (DG 29 Nov 1853)

McFARLAND, Robert, see **McFARLIN**, William T.

McFARLIN, Alexander, Esq., of Appoq. Hd, 14 Jan 1823, in his 55th yr (DG 31 Jan 1823)

McFARLIN, Anna Maria, see **COUNTIS**, Peter

McFARLIN, Mary Jane, see **BANKS**, William

McFARLIN, Robert, to **STEVENSON**, Anna, Miss, both of Wilm, 2 Oct 1845, in Phila (DG 7 Oct 1845)

McFARLIN, Thomas, of NC Co to **YOUNG**, Fanny L. of Phila, in Phila, 4 Jun 1849, by Rev. A. D. Gillette (DG 15 Jun 1849)

McFARLIN, William T., inf son of Robert and Anna McFARLAND (sic), of contusion of the brain, 15 Jun 1847, aged 11 mos 11 days (DG 22 Jun 1847)

McFARLIN, Wm. W., of Wilm, to **GARLAND**, Mary, Miss, formerly of NY city, at New Trier, IL, 10 Aug 1851, by the Rev. Thomas Milmore (DG 23 Aug 1851)

McFERSON, Daniel [2], see **McFERSON**, Daniel

McFERSON, Daniel. Two lots to be sold by John and Daniel McFERSON, exec'rs, at the house of Joshua LITTLER (PG 23 Oct 1760)

McFERSON, John, see McFERSON, Daniel

McGARDY, Julia, see LYNCH, Thomas

McGEE, Harriet, see COHEE, William

McGEE, James, innkeeper, in Wilm, 16 Aug 1826, aged 59 yrs (DG 22 Aug 1826)

McGEE, Levin J., to PRIDE, Elizabeth, all of Sussex Co, 17 May 1853, by the Rev. C. H. Mustard (DG 31 May 1853)

McGEE, Mary, see WHELDON, Richard

McGILL, Mary, a child, 17 Oct 1798, on list of yellow fever victims (DG 27 Oct 1798)

McGILLTON, Adam, see CHESTNUT, William

McGINLEY, Patrick, laborer, killed by a bank falling on him at Madison St. near Delaware Ave, 1 Feb 1848 (DG 4 Feb 1848)

McGINN, Jane, at Newport, after a short illness, 4 Dec 1842, aged 85 yrs (DG 9 Dec 1842)

McGINN, Paul, innkeeper, at Newport, 4 Apr 1828, na (DG 8 Apr 1828)

McGINNIS, Rebecca, see REYNOLDS, Thomas P.

McGLAUGHLIN, Caroline, see SMITH, Charles C.

McGLAUGHLIN, James, late of Brandywine Hd, Josiah SPARKS, adm'r (DG 7 Oct 1851)

McGONIGAL, William, to LOFLAND, Hester Ann, Miss, dau of Asa LOFLAND, all of St. Jones Neck, Kent Co, 20 Jan 1848, by Rev. E. R. Williams (DG 26 Jan 1848)

McGORLEY John, of Wilm, on the RR near Northeast MD, 1 Nov 1852, na (DG 5 Nov 1852)

McGORLIE, Patrick, in Wilm, 3 Aug 1852, in his 75th yr (DG 10 Aug 1852)

McGOVERN, _____, Mrs, consort of Hugh McGOVERN, in Wilm, 26 Jul 1848 (DG 28 Jul 1848)

McGOVERN, Ann, see McDOWELL, John

McGOVERN, Hugh, see MONAGHAN, Julia A. F.

see McGOVERN, _____, Mrs.

McGOVERN, Julia A. F., see MONAGHAN, James J.

McGOWAN, Patrick, Esq., of New York, to BESON, Lydia A., Miss, of Wilm, 26 Sep 1841, by the Rev. P. Riley (DG 1 Oct 1841)

McGRA (sic), John, see THOMPSON, Thomas

McGUIGAN, Barnerd (sic), see McGUIGAN, Catharine

McGUIGAN, Catharine, Miss (sic), of Wilm, widow of Barnerd (sic) McGUIGAN, suddenly, 2 Aug 1846, aged c 35 yrs (DG 11 Aug 1846)

McGUIRE, Connor, see BREEN, Philip

McGUIRE, Hugh, to CRUTHERS, Rebecca, Miss, both of Wilm, 24 Apr 1843, in Wilm, by Rev. P. Riley (DG 28 Apr 1843)

McGUIRE, Rebecca Ann, see KURNS, Thomas

McILHENNY, Alexander, a laborer on the first section of the Wilminton and Susquehanna RR, killed by the falling of a large mass of earth, 16 Feb 1836 (DG 19 Feb 1836)

McILVAIN, John S., to LAMB, Martha, Miss, dau of Luke LAMB, all of Sussex Co, 20 Sep 1841, by Rev. Jnoa R. Torbert (DG 8 Oct 1841)

McILVAINE, Hester J., see McILVAINE, Thomas Asbury

McILVAINE, Thomas Asbury, only son of Thomas H. and Hester J. McILVAINE, of Kent Co DE, drowned in the mill pond near White House, 20 Dec 1852, in his 12th yr (DG 11 Jan 1853)

McILVAINE, Thomas H., see McILVAINE, Thomas Asbury

McILVAINE, William S., to BAILY, Mary Elizabeth, all of Kent Co, 5 Mar 1851, by Rev. J. Flannery (DG 1 Apr 1851)

McILVANE, Mary Jane, see JESTER, John S.

McINALL, Edward, to FOX, Cecilia M., Miss, both of Wilm, 26 Sep 1847, at St. Mary's Church, Phila, by Rev. M. Carter (DG 1 Oct 1847)

McINTIRE, Harding, in Delaware City, 15 Feb 1853, in his 17th yr (DG 8 Mar 1853)

DELAWARE MARRIAGES AND DEATHS FROM NEWSPAPERS, 1729-1853   161

McINTIRE, James, Rev.,
see McINTIRE, Samuel

McINTIRE, John, to READ, Isabella, Miss, both of New Castle, in Wilm, 13 Dec 1828, by the Rev. E. W. Gilbert (DG 2 Jan 1829)

McINTIRE, Mary, Mrs.,
see SHORT, Abraham C.

McINTIRE, Peter, of Wilm, in Mobile, 1 Apr 1847 (DG 20 Apr 1847)

McINTIRE, Samuel, of Cecil Co MD, to BOULDEN, Matilda, Miss, of NC Co, 7 Mar 1844, by Rev. James McINTIRE (DG 12 Mar 1844)

McINTYRE, Elizabeth, see OGDEN, Edward

McINTYRE, James A., to SEEDS, Phebe Ann, Miss, both of Wilm, 13 Oct 1846, by Rev. S. R. Wynkoop (DG 16 Oct 1846)

McINTYRE, Thomas Jr., to HOFFAY, Mary T., of Wilm, 12 Mar 1844, at the house of Jesse M. JUSTIS in Marcus Hook by B. F. Johnson, Esq. (DG 12 Mar 1844)

McKAIG, Amy A.,
see VALENTINE, W. William

McKAY, Benj., see McCAY, John

McKAY, Benjamin Sr,
see HEVERN, William

McKEAN, James B., late Burgess of Wilm, after a painful illness, 4 Aug 1826 (WN 10 Aug 1826) James, Esq., late first Burgess of Wilm, 4 Aug 1826, na (DG 8 Aug 1826) notice given by Sarah P. McKEAN, exec'x or her atty, Robert P. ROBINSON (DG 12 Sep 1826)

McKEAN, Sarah, see McKEAN, James

McKEAN, Sarah B., see BUSH, George

McKEAN, Thomas, to McPHERSON, Jane, Miss, both of Christiana Hd, 4 Mar 1847, by Rev. S. M. Gayley (DG 9 Mar 1847)
see DRUMMOND, Duncan

McKEE, _____, consort of Dr. William McKEE and mother-in-law to the Hon. H. M. RIDGELY, our Representative in Congress, on Tuesday (DS 12 Jan 1812)

McKEE, _____, Mr., 16 Aug 1751 (PG 24 Aug 1751)

McKEE, Edmund H., see McKEE, Mary A.

McKEE, Emmit V., of dysentery, in Wilm, 14 Jul 1848, aged 2 yrs (DG 28 Jul 1848)

McKEE, Isabella, see BARR, John

McKEE, James dec'd, late of Brandywine Hd, notice given by John McKEE (DS 7 Mar 1812)

McKEE, James, to REYNOLDS, Hannah, Miss, 20 Oct 1825, by the Rev. Daniel D. Lewis, all of Wilm (DG 1 Nov 1825)

McKEE, John, see McKEE, James

McKEE, Lydia, see POWELL, John

McKEE, Marian J., see MURPHEY, John B.

McKEE, Mary, dec'd, late of Brandywine HD, notice given by Joseph BEESON, adm'r D.B.N., C.T.A. (DG 16 Sep 1825)

McKEE, Mary A., wife of Edmund H. McKEE, 12 Mar 1848, in Phila (DG 21 Mar 1848)

McKEE, Robert L., of Bridgeton, NJ, formerly of Wilm, to CHAMBERS, Susannah M., Miss, dau of Capt. CHAMBERS of Phila, 16 Oct 1834, by Joel S. Robinson, Esq. (DG 28 Oct 1834)

McKEE, William, Dr., see McKEE, _____

McKEE, William, Dr., at his farm near Wilm, 13 Jan 1816 (AW 17 Jan 1816)

McKENNA, James, to TOY, Mary, Miss, both of Brandywine, 13 Apr 1850, by Rev. J. S. Walsh (DG 23 Apr 1850)

McKENNAN, Elizabeth,
see POINSETT, Asa

McKENNAN, John, dec'd, notice given by Thomas McKENNAN, Mill Creek Hd (AW 24 Sep 1817)

McKENNAN, Thomas, in Wilm, 29 Feb 1852, in his 74th yr (DG 5 Mar 1852)
see McKENNAN, John

McKENNEY, Barbara Ann, wife of Michael McKENNEY, and dau of J. A. WELDIN, in Brandywine Village, 13 Aug 1848, aged 19 yrs (DG 15 Aug 1848)

McKENNEY, Michael,
see McKENNEY, Barbara Ann

McKENNON, Thomas, of NC Co, to OCHELTREE, Isabella, Miss, of Wilm, 28 Aug 1816, by Rev. Thomas Read (AW 31 Aug 1816)

McKINLEY, Mary Jane,
see PEDRICK, T. Sargent

McKINLY, Jane, see McKINLY, John, Dr.

McKINLY, John, Dr., dec'd, notice given by John LATIMER, for Jane McKINLY, exec'x (DE 3 May, 7 Sep 1797)

McKINLY, John, see McCLUGHAN, John

McKINSEY, Sarah Ann, see MOORE, George W.

McKINZEY, John, of Elkton, MD, to JESTER, Mary, Miss, of NC Co, 21 May 1843, near Elkton, by Rev. James McIntire (DG 26 May 1843)

McKNIGHT, Elenor, Mrs., widow, late of Phila, "Sunday last," aged 88 yrs Presbyterian Church (DG 11 Dec 1790)

McKNIGHT, John, at his res. in Mill creek Hd, 8 May 1851, in his 67th yr (DG 13 May 1851)

McKNIGHT, John, late of Mill Creek Hd. James W. BALL, exec'r (DG 13 May 1851)

McKNIGHT, Sophia, see AIKIN, E. T.

McKOWAN, William Alvord, to TAYLOR, Sarah B., Miss, both of DE, 9 Jun 1850, by Rev. Ezra Stiles Ely, DD (DG 14 Jun 1850)

McLAGHLAN, Eliza J., see BETS, Charles

McLANE, Allan, see McLANE, Maria C.

McLANE, Allen, Col., collector of the port, in Wilm, 22 May 1829, aged 83 yrs; born in Phila, 8 Aug 1746; to Kent Co, DE, 1771; served during Rev. War (DG 26 May 1829) see McLANE, Allen, Dr.

McLANE, Allen, Dr., native of Kent Co, youngest son of Col Allen McLANE of the American Revolution, 11 Feb 1845. Buried Methodist Church Yard (DG 14 Feb 1845) see McLANE, Catharine Ann, Mrs. see WORRELL, Rebecca

McLANE, Catharine Ann, Mrs., consort of Dr. Allen McLANE of Wilm, and dau of George READ, Esq., 16 Jan 1826, na (DG 17 Jan 1826)

McLANE, George R., M. D., of Wilm, to ASHMEAD, Mary, dau of the late William ASHMEAD of Phila, 16 Jul 1844, at Lancaster PA, by Rev. Joseph Barr (DG 19 Jul 1844)

McLANE, John, in Wilm, 17 Dec 1852, in his 50th yr (DG 21 Dec 1852)

McLANE, Joshua, see McLANE, Rebecca

McLANE, Louis, see HAMILTON, Phillip

McLANE, Maria C., Mrs. wife of Allan McLANE, USN, and dau of the late Richard BACHE of Phila, 6 Apr 1851, on board the ship *Fremont*. Bur in Valparaiso (DG 27 Jun 1851)

McLANE, Rebecca, see WORRELL, Rebecca

McLANE, Rebecca, relict of the late Joshua McLANE, in Wilm, 4 Jun 1853, in her 92nd yr (DG 17 Jun 1853)

McLANE, Rebecca, see HAMILTON, Philip

McLANE, Sallie A. H., see BACON, Joseph K.

McLAUGHLIN, Henry, Capt., of Wilm. Notice given by David BUSH, adm'r (PG 12 Mar 1740-41)

McLAUGHLIN, Joel., late of Brandywine Hd, John MELLON, exec'r (DG 28 Oct 1851)

McLAUGHLIN, Margaret, see SAYERS, William

McLAUGHLIN, Owen, in Brandywine Hd, 26 Mar 1848, aged 70 yrs (DG 4 Apr 1848)

McLAUGHLIN, Rachel, see LUNBECK, Silas

McLEAR, Elizabeth B, wife of John McLEAR, 27 Mar 1846, in Wilm, aged 45 yrs (DG 3 Apr 1846)

McLEAR, John, merchant, to BUSH, Elizabeth, Miss, dau of Capt. Samuel BUSH, all of Wilm, 26 Nov 1829, by Rev. Robert Adair (DG 1 Dec 1829) see McLEAR, Elizabeth B.

McLEAR, Susannah P., 10 Dec 1849, aged 84 yrs (DG 14 Dec 1849)

McLENEGAN, Isaiah, to DINGEE, Mary Ann, Miss, 8 Jan 1824, by the Rev. John Potts, all of Wilm (DG 13 Jan 1824)

McLEOD, Alexander, to BODDY, Sarah Ann, Mrs., in Wilm, 2 Sep 1849, by the Rev. S. R. Wynkoop (DG 11 Sep 1849)

McMAKIN, Catharine, a little orphan girl, niece of Mr. McCONNELL, res. Front St, burnt to death there, while cooking breakfast, 15 Feb 1853 (DG 25 Feb 1853)

McMAN, John, near Newark, DE, 10 Apr 1849, in his 73rd yr (DG 1 May 1849)

McMANEMY, Bernard, dec'd, [no location],

DELAWARE MARRIAGES AND DEATHS FROM NEWSPAPERS, 1729-1853

notice given by Peter JOHNSTON, adm'r (DG 24 Sep 1827)

McMANN, John, near Newark DE, 10 Apr 1849, in his 73rd yr (DG 8 May 1849)

McMANN, Susan, see MORRISON, Samuel

McMANUS, Philip, late of Appoq Hd, Samuel PLATT, adm'r (DG 3 Oct 1851)

McMANUS, Phillip, late of Appoq. Hd. Samuel PLATT, adm'r (DG 31 Oct 1851)

McMARTIN, D.J., of Wilm, to STEWART, Catharine, Miss, of Perth, Fulton Co, NY, in Perth, 6 Nov 1849, by the Rev. J. M. Graham (DG 9 Nov 1849)

McMARTIN, Flora, see STIMSON, S. L.

McMECHEN, Mary, Mrs., dec'd, notice given by Isaac PRICE and Abraham EGBERT, Esq., of Christiana Bridge (DG 16 Aug 1822)

McMICHAEL, James, at Stanton, 4 Oct 1848, in his 50th yr (DG 20 Oct 1848)

McMICHAEL, Mary, see GREENWALT, Joseph

McMILLEN, Sarah Jane, see GRAY, William C.

McMINN, George Monroe, of Delaware City, to FENWICK, Virginia, Miss, in Phila, 3 Jul 1851, by the Rev. Ignatius T. Cooper (DG 11 Jul 1851)

McMULLEN, Ann, see EVANS, Robert

McMULLEN, Harriet, see HAMAN, John

McMULLEN, John C., 4 Jun 1849, in his 33rd yr (DG 5 Jun 1849)

McMULLEN, Mary Jane, see McFARLAN, Edward

McMULLEN, Robert, of New Castle Hd, to TOPHAM, Sarah C., of Wilm, 17 Dec 1846, by Rev. Dr. Kennaday (DG 22 Dec 1846)

McMULLEN, Samuel, to ROWAN, Mary C., dau of Henry ROWAN, Esq., all of NC Co, 8 Jul 1851, by the Rev. Joseph Barr (DG 15 Jul 1851)

McMULLEN, Sarah, see GEORGE, Jonathan E.

McMULLEN, Sarah P., see SPRINGER, Lewis

McMULLIN, Harriet A., see BALLINGER, Edwin A.

McMURPHEY, John, see McMURPHEY, Priscilla

McMURPHEY, Mary A. formerly of Delaware, of consumption, 2 Mar 1844 (DG 15 Mar 1844)

McMURPHEY, Priscilla, wife of John McMURPHEY, of Appoq. Hd, 10 Jan 1853, na (DG 18 Jan 1853)

McMURPHY, Mary, see ASPRIL, Leonard V.

McNATT, Mary, see GRAHAM, Henry

McNEAL, Elizabeth, in Phila, 20 Aug 1850. Buried in Wilm (DG 27 Aug 1850)

McNEAL, Jane, see DERRY, Jane McNeal

McNEAL, Valentine, 25 Jul 1834, na (DG 29 Jul 1834) Obit (DG 12 Aug 1834) see DERRY, Jane McNeal

McNEAL, Valentine, Jr., at his father's res., 7 Jul 1833, aged 30 yrs (DG 9 Jul 1833)

McNEIR, Emily Maury, dau of Thomas S. and Emily R. McNEIR of Wilm, 24 Nov 1853, aged 11 mos (DG 29 Nov 1853)

McNEIR, Emily R., see McNEIR, Emily Maury

McNEIR, Thomas S., see McNEIR, Emily Maury

McNEVIN, John, see McNEVIN, Mary Jane

McNEVIN, Mary Jane, dau of John McNEVIN, in Brandywine Village, 14 Oct 1835, aged 5 mos 8 days (DG 20 Oct 1835)

McNEY, Isabella, see ELLIOTT, Wm.

McNIGHT, Ann, "from the tent," of yellow fever (DE 18 Sep 1798)

McPHERRAN, Robert, at his res. in Milton DE, 11 Sep 1843, aged 46 yrs (DG 15 Sep 1843)

McPHERSON, James, see McPHERSON, Susannah

McPHERSON, Jane, see McKEAN, Thomas

McPHERSON, Lewis, of Norfolk, VA, to KIDD, Margaret Jane, Miss, of New Castle, in Wilm, 20 Jan 1822, by the Rev. Dr. Read (DG 22 Jan 1822)

McPHERSON, Susannah, late wife of James McPHERSON, near Middletown,

9 Sep 1843 (DG 15 Sep 1843)

McPHERSON, Victoria,
see DRUMMOND, Duncan

McQUILLEN, Elizabeth Agnes,
see ALLISON, Andrew

McSPARRAN, Archibald,
see LEGATE, John

McSPARREN, Archibald, dec'd, late of Kent Co, pay to Stephen ALSTON, atty, in Dover, notice given by Andrew BUNNER, adm'r (DG 31 Oct 1789)

McWHORTER, Ann Jane, see McWHORTER, Mary Elizabeth

McWHORTER, David,
see HINES, Samuel R.

McWHORTER, Elizabeth J.,
see HINES, Samuel R.

McWHORTER, Leontine,
see McWHORTER, Mary Elizabeth

McWHORTER, Mary Elizabeth, only dau of Leontine and Ann Jane McWHORTER, 6 Oct 1843, aged 3 yrs (DG 20 Oct 1843)

MEACHEM, Sarah E.,
see SPARKS, George W.

MEARIS, John, see McCOOL, John Sr.

MEDILL, Margaret, see LYNAM, Robert T.

MEEKINGS, Jesse, to GILMORE, Anne, Miss, all of NC Co, at Cantwell's Bridge, 22 Jun 1850, by Rev. J. R. Anderson (DG 4 Jul 1850)

MEEKINS, Robert, Capt., of Dorsett [?] Co MD to ROACH, Margaret, Miss, of Wilm, 20 Sep 1841, by Rev. S. R. Wynkoop (DG 24 Sep 1841)

MEEKINS, Sarah Ann,
see RUMFORD, Washington

MEEKS, Aquilla, of Kent Co, to ATTIX, Margaret, Miss, late of Delaware, 6 Oct 1846, by Rev. Mr. Sheaves (DG 20 Oct 1846)

MEETEER, William, Capt., Pres. of the Citizens Union Line Steam Boat Co, in Baltimore, 11 Apr 1833, na (DG 16 Apr 1833)

MEGATTAGAN, Phebe,
see TWINING, Isaac

MEGAW, Rachel, see GRUBB, Adam

MEGEAR, Eliza, see FERRIS, Ziba

MEGEAR, Michael, see FERRIS, Ziba

MEGEAR, Thomas J., to ALTER, Mary Catharine, dau of Jacob ALTER, Esq., 8 Aug 1842, at the res. of her father in Phila, by Rev. Mr. Mayer (DG 12 Aug 1842)

MEGGISON, Rebecca,
see SAWYER, George

MEGINNIES, Edward, of West Chester, PA, to SOLOMON, Leah, Miss, youngest dau of Mr. Isaac SOLOMON of Wilm, in Wilm, 3 Oct 1833, by Rev. Mr. Lybrand (DG 11 Oct 1833)

MEGONIGAL, Narcissa,
see PENROSE, Barton

MEHARGE, Mary, Mrs., of erysipelas, in Wilm at the res. of her son-in-law, E. C. KELLY, 6 May 1848, in her 67th yr (DG 16 May 1848)

MEKEEVER, Sarah Ann,
see BRITTINGHAM, Eber

MELLEN, Patrick, dec'd, late of Wilm, notice given by Bernard MURPHY, adm'r D.B.N. of Charles McCARRON (DG 27 Jan 1829)

MELLIER, Adolph,
see SMETHURST, Charles H.

MELLIER, Lena P.,
see SMETHURST, Charles H.

MELLON, Henry, in Wilm, 9 Feb 1850, aged 50 yrs (DG 19 Feb 1850)

MELLON, John, see McLAUGHLIN, Joel

MELRICK, Emma, dau of John and Sarah MELRICK, in Wilm, 25 Apr 1852, aged c 1 yr (DG 30 Apr 1852)

MELRICK, John, see MELRICK, Emma

MELRICK, Sarah, see MELRICK, Emma

MELVIN, Alexander, of Smyrna, in Phila, 12 Apr 1850 (DG 23 Apr 1850)

MENDENHALL, Anna Ellen,
see CHURCHMAN, Pennell

MENDENHALL, Charles, Dr., Asst. Surgeon, U. S. Army, and son of Capt. Thomas MENDENHALL of Wilm, at the Post of Fort Crawford, Prairie du Chien, after a short illness, ___ Oct 1823, aged 29 yrs (DG 16 Dec 1823)

MENDENHALL, Cyrus, Jr., to MOORE,

Minerva W., Miss, both of Newark DE, 25 Dec 1848, in Camden NJ, by the Rev. D. W. Bartine (DG 11 Sep 1849)

MENDENHALL, Edward S., to HAYES, Rhoda, Miss, both of New Castle Hd, at Phila, 10 Jan 1822, by the Rev. Dr. Ely (DG 15 Jan 1822)

MENDENHALL, Eli,
see PRITCHETT, Jesse

MENDENHALL, James,
see MAHON, Richard

MENDENHALL, Margaret,
see MENDENHALL, Milton

MENDENHALL, Martha Matilda,
see HOOPES, Jonathan

MENDENHALL, Milton, son of William and Margaret MENDENHALL (DG 23 Apr 1850)

MENDENHALL, Sarah, Mrs., wife of Wm. MENDENHALL, at the res. of her husband in Mill Creek Hd, 4 May 1851, aged 45 yrs (DG 9 May 1851)

MENDENHALL, Susan, dau of Capt. Thomas MENDENHALL, 14 Aug 1825, aged 22 yrs (DG 16 Aug 1825)

MENDENHALL, Thomas,
see OLIVER, John
see HOLTON, Charles
see MENDENHALL, Charles
see MENDENHALL, Susan

MENDENHALL, William,
see MENDENHALL, Milton

MENDENHALL, William A., of Wilm, to STIDHAM, Anna, dau of Mr. Isaac STIDHAM, dec'd, late of New Castle Hd, 12 Aug 1824, by the Rev. William Smith (DG 20 Aug 1824)

MENDENHALL, Wm.,
see MENDENHALL, Sarah

MENDINHALL, Benj.,
see MENDINHALL, Hannah

MENDINHALL, Elizabeth W.,
see REYNOLDS, John T.

MENDINHALL, Hannah, Mrs., relict of Benj. MENDINHALL, 24 Mar 1810, "advanced age." Burial in the Friends ground. Lived five years with the family of the Rev. Wm. PRYCE (DG 27 Mar 1810)

MENDINHALL, Jesse,
see STROUD, _____, Mrs.

MENDINHALL, Jesse, in Wilm, 16 Nov 1852, aged c 52 yrs (DG 19 Nov 1852)

MENDINHALL, Joseph,
see ASKEW, Hannah
see JEFFERIES, James V.

MENDINHALL, Phebe,
see JEFFERIES, James V.

MENDINHALL, Philip, to TAYLOR, Amy, Miss, 21 Nov 1820 (DG 28 Nov 1820)

MENDINHALL, Rachel,
see GARRET, Thomas

MENOUGH, Isaac, late of White Clay Creek Hd, farm to be sold by John MENOUGH and John W. CUNNINGHAM, exec'rs (DG 4 Dec 1827)

MENOUGH, John, of New London Xroads, to HADDEN, Elizabeth C., Miss of Wilm, in Wilm, 23 Oct 1834, by the Rev. E. W. Gilbert (DG 28 Oct 1834)

MENOUGH, John, see MENOUGH, Isaac

MENOUGH, Mary, see MAGEE, James

MERCER, James R., to SMITH, Mary, Miss, both of Cantwell's Bridge, at Marcus Hook PA, 19 Aug 1847, by Rev. J. Walker (DG 17 Aug 1847)

MERCER, John C., to HAMILTON, Ann Jane, dau of John HAMILTON, 9 Nov 1843, in Phila, by Rev. Dr. Cuyler (DG 17 Nov 1843)

MERCER, Margaret S., see WRIT, John W.

MEREDITH, Catharine Keppele, wife of the Hon. Wm. M. MEREDITH, in Phila, 26 Jun 1853, in her 53rd yr (DG 1 Jul 1853)

MEREDITH, James, to MORTON, Ann, Miss, both of NC Co, 7 Jun 1827, by John P. Peckworth (DG 12 Jun 1827)

MEREDITH, John, to PARSONS, Amelia, Miss, all of Kent, 3 Jan 1850, by Rev. Daniel Goodwin (DG 15 Jan 1850)

MEREDITH, Levin, to CARPENTER, Mary A., 23 Dec 1852 (DG 14 Jan 1853)

MEREDITH, Martha, see KEYS, William

MEREDITH, Samuel, dec'd, late of Christiana Hd, notice given by John QUINBY, adm'r (DG 13 Jun 1828)

MEREDITH, Wm. M.,
see MEREDITH, Catharine Keppele

MERISS, Sally, see JANVIER, Francis

MERRIHEW, Joseph, Capt., in Wilm, after an illness of 26 hrs, 8 Jun 1821, in his 52nd yr (DG 12 Jun 1821)

MERRILL, William, Rev., to WHITE, Ada, 16 Mar 1853, by Silas C. Palmiter (DG 29 Mar 1853)

MERRITT, Benjamin, Dr., see CRAWFORD, William R.

MERRITT, Caleb S., to WITTENBERG, Emma C., in New York City, 17 Oct 1847, by Rev. O. E. Skinner (DG 22 Oct 1847)

MERRITT, Elizabeth, Mrs., at Havre de Grace MD, 27 Jul 1851, in her 38th yr (DG 29 Jul 1851)

MERRITT, Elizabeth Noxon, see WILLITTS, Horatio N.

MERRITT, John, see PERKINS, Thomas, Esq.

MERRITT, John, M. D., to DeLANEY, Sarah E., dau of Maj. P. B. DeLANY, 25 Jun 1844, by Rev. Mr. Spotswood (DG 4 Jul 1844)

MERRITT, Sarah Vance, see CRAWFORD, William R.

MERRITT, Schee, see BLACK, Elizabeth

MERRITT, Thomas Schee, see WILLITTS, Horatio N.

MERROT, Ann, see WHITELOCK, Isaac

MERVINE, Caroline, Miss, see HENDRICKSON, Joseph, Jr.

MESSICK, Ann, Mrs., in Milford, 25 Feb 1851, na (DG 4 Mar 1851)

MESSICK, Elizabeth, see LAMBDEN, L. A.

MESSICK, George, to KOLLOCK, Sarah, Miss, 15 Sep 1841, by Rev. H. C. Fries, all of Sussex Co (DG 24 Sep 1841)

MESSICK, John W., of J(?), to LAMBDEN, _____, Miss, dau of Joshua J, LAMBDEN, all of Sussex Co, 1 Aug 1851 (DG 12 Aug 1851)

MESSICK, Samuel T., near Laurel DE, 20 Jul 1849, in his 25th yr (DG 27 Jul 1849)

MESSICK, Stansbury, at Seaford, DE, prob 29 Dec 1852, "Wed. last", aged 25 or 26 yrs. A sailor (DG 4 Jan 1853)

MESSIK. James B., to SHORT, Rebecca, Miss, both of NC Co, in Wilm, 19 Apr 1849, by Rev. William Cooper (DG 27 Apr 1849)

METZ, Geo. W., see ROBINSON, A. Gilbert

METZ, Harriet, see TAYLOR, Samuel

METZ, Susan Amelia, see ROBINSON, A. Gilbert

METZ, W., Gen., see ROBINSON, A. Gilbert

MEWSHAW, Alaethea, see LAMBDEN, Charles W.

MIDDLETON, Hannah, see RIGHTER, John

MIDDLETON, Robert, late of Wilm, shallopman. Notice given by James LATIMER, Thomas WALLACE, Thomas DUFF (PG 2 Sep 1762)

MIDDLETON, Sarah H., see KERNS, James D.

MIFFLIN, Elizabeth Johns, see NEWBOLD, Joshua

MIFFLIN, Elizabeth, wife of Warner MIFFLIN, of Kent Co, and dau of the late Clement LAWS of Phila, in Wilm, 31 Aug 1835, aged 28 yrs (DG 1 Sep 1835)

MIFFLIN, J. Biddle, formerly of DE, to BENNETT, Rachel, Miss, of Phila, in Phila, by Rev. J. H. Jones (DG 1 Aug 1848)

MIFFLIN, James L., see MITCHELL, James Y. see ELLIOT, Joseph P.

MIFFLIN, Jane R., see ELLIOT, Joseph P.

MIFFLIN, Sarah L., see MITCHELL, James Y.

MIFFLIN, Warner, at Camden DE, 2 Apr 1848, aged 71 yrs (DG 28 Apr 1848) see NEWBOLD, Joshua see MIFFLIN, Elizabeth

MILBY, Arthur, see FOUGERAY, Hanry J.

MILBY, Catharine, see SPARE, James

MILBY, Sarah, see FOUGERAY, Henry J.

MILES, Jane W., see THOMPSON, Wm.

MILES, John, Esq., late of the City of Phila, Edward SHEPPARD, adm'r (DG 16 Mar 1852)

MILES, John, Esq., late of Phila, Henry L. SMALLEY, adm'r (DG 13 Feb 1852)

MILES, Mary see DINGEY, David

MILES, Ruth Ann, see DIXON, Alexander H.

MILEWARD, George, late of Pencader Hd, soon after his arrival in San Frncisco in the ship *Susan B Owens* from Phila (DG 12 Feb 1850)

MILLAWAY, James, of Smyrna, to BOULDEN, Ann E., of Glasgow, 31 May 1850, by Rev. J. Humphries (DG 7 Jun 1850)

MILLAWAY, Mary Jane, see COSDEN, John

MILLEGAN, Mary Ann, see KNIGHT, Joseph C.

MILLER, _____, son of Martin MILLER, burned to death while father was burning brush, 25 Nov 1842, aged 4 yrs (DG 2 Dec 1842)

MILLER, _____, a young man, knocked overboard by a boom and drowned in DE Bay near Lewes a few days ago (DG 30 Aug 1850)

MILLER, Ann, near Wilm, 16 Aug 1847, at an advanced age (DG 20 Aug 1847)

MILLER, Ann, see MILLER, Peter S.

MILLER, Ann, Mrs, near Wilm, 11 Aug 1847 (DG 27 Aug 1847)

MILLER, Ann, Mrs., see MILLER, Robert

MILLER, Anthony, to SMITH, Lavinia, both of Wilm, 18 Nov 1851, by the Rev. E. M. Van Duesen (DG 21 Nov 1851)

MILLER, Caleb, see MILLER, James Walter see MILLER, Samuel Patterson

MILLER, Catharine, dau of John and Mary MILLER, at Newark, 12 Jul 1835, aged 17 mos (DG 17 Jul 1835)

MILLER, Charles Kinch, inf son of Joseph and Sarah MILLER, at Newport, 25 Jul 1852, aged 1 yr 1 mo 22 days (DG 10 Aug 1852)

MILLER, Daniel H., Esq., Pres., Bank of Penn. Twp., PA, late Rep. to Congress from PA, 24 Apr 1831, in his 48th yr (DF 30 Apr 1831)

MILLER, Daniel J., formerly of Wilm, in Balt, when a fly-wheel burst, ndd, na. His father resides near Bridgeton NJ (DG 10 Dec 1852)

MILLER, Eleanor, see MILLER, George

MILLER, Elizabeth, Mrs., of Phila, when clothing caught fire at the Fayette Hotel, Wilm, 24 Apr 1829, aged 67 yrs; bur. in Friends Burying Ground (Wilm?) (DG 28 Apr 1829)

MILLER, Elizabeth, see MILLER, Robert

MILLER, Ellis, see SMITH, _____, the Rev. Mr.

MILLER, George, dec'd, late of Wilm, notice given by Eleanor MILLER (DE 22 Aug 1799)

MILLER, George, in Brandywine Hd, of dysentery, 26 Aug 1851, in his 87th yr (DG 26 Aug 1851)

MILLER, Jacob, in Wilm, 13 Jul 1848, aged 60 yrs (DG 18 Jul 1848)

MILLER, James, Capt., see WALTER, Ebe. Jr.

MILLER, James, Esq., of Chester Co PA, to CLELAND, Jane, Miss, dau of J. CLELAND, Esq., of Wilm, 28 Feb 1850, by Rev. S. R. Wynkoop (DG 1 Mar 1850)

MILLER, James, to TODD, Martha, 30 Jul 1853, by the Rev. Wm C. Cooley, all of Christiana (DG 5 Aug 1853)

MILLER, James Walter, son of Caleb and Julia Ann MILLER of Stanton, of croup, 28 Oct 1851, aged 4 yrs 1 mo 11 days (DG 13 Feb 1852)

MILLER, Jane, see BLACKWELL, William P.

MILLER John, Elder, 30 May 1842, aged 40 yrs (DG 3 Jun 1842)

MILLER, John, see MILLER, Margaret see MILLER, Catharine see MILLER, Mary see BUCKEY, Philip J.

MILLER, Joseph, Esq., to LOCKERMAN, Eliza, Miss, both of Dover, 5 Mar 1798, by Rev. Samuel Keene (DE 12 Mar 1798) (see 6 Sep issue for MILLER's death)

MILLER, Joseph, of Dover, 4 Sep 1798, in Wilm (DE 6 Sep 1798) (note marriage, 5 Mar 1798) notice given by John PATTEN, adm'r (DE 6 Dec 1798)

MILLER, Joseph, see MILLER, Peter S. see MILLER, Charles Kinch see FORWOOD, Amer G.

MILLER, Julia Ann, see MILLER, James Walter see MILLER, Samuel Patterson

MILLER, Lydia, see ARMSTRONG, Christopher

MILLER, Margaret, Mrs., spouse of Rev. Mr. John MILLER of Kent, 22 Nov 1789, in her 60th yr (DG 12 Dec 1789)

MILLER, Martin, see MILLER, _____.

MILLER, Mary, consort of John MILLER, in Newark, 9 May 1851 (DG 13 May 1851)
see MILLER, Catharine
see PENNINGTON, Isaac
see BUCKEY, Philip J.

MILLER, Mary Alice,
see BLACKLAR, Charles R.

MILLER, Mary Ann, see WALTER, Ebe. Jr.

MILLER, Mary E., see FORWOOD, Amer G.

MILLER, Peter S., of Wilm, son of Joseph and Ann MILLER, 21 Oct 1841, aged 14 yrs (DG 22 Oct 1841)

MILLER, Rebecca, in Wilm , ndd, aged 85 yrs (DG 10 Feb 1846)
Rebecca, see WALL, Joseph

MILLER, Richard, to SPENCER, Anna, Miss, both lately of England, 16 Jul 1853, by Rev. S. R. Wynkoop (DG 26 Jul 1853)

MILLER, Robert, d. in Kent Co near Dover. His fulling mill to be lett. For terms, apply to Thomas NIXON, living near, or Elizabeth MILLER, on the premises (PG 10 Jul 1760)

MILLER, Robert, to MILLER, Ann, Mrs., 5 Dec 1816, by Rev. William Pryce (AW 7 Dec 1816)

MILLER, Samuel,
see ROBINSON, Elizabeth

MILLER, Samuel Patterson, son of Caleb and Julia Ann MILLER of Stanton, of croup, 31 Jan 1852, aged 1 yr 5 mos 9 days (DG 13 Feb 1852)

MILLER, Sarah,
see MILLER, Charles Kinch

MILLER, William, late of New Castle Hd, Thomas TURNER, exec'r (DG 7 May 1852)

MILLER, William, to WALKER, Elizabeth, Miss, 6 Mar 1820 (DG 8 Apr 1820)

MILLES, John, Esq., counsellor-at-law in Phila, to SMITH, Hannah Wager, Miss, dau of William T. SMITH, Esq., of Christiana, DE, in Phila, 30 Jun 1829, by the Rev. P. F. Mayer, D. D. (DG 3 Jul 1829)

MILLIGAN, Elizabeth, see STEVENS, Daniel

MILLIGAN, George B., Esq., formerly a resident of DE, 16 Mar 1841, died of hypertrophia of the heart in New Orleans, aged 50 yrs (DG 6 Apr 1841)

MILLIGAN, George B., to CARROLL, Sophia G., dau of Chas. R. CARROLL, Esq., of Balt, in Balt, 5 Feb 1852, by the Rev. Dr. Wyatt (DG 13 Feb 1852)

MILLIGAN, Jas. C., to SANFORD, Mary D., dau of the late, Whiting SANFORD of Laurel, at the Arch St Presbyt Ch, 25 Nov 1851, by the Rev. Charles Wadsworth (DG 25 Nov 1851)

MILLIGAN, John J., to LEVY, Martha Mary Anne, Miss, 1 Feb 1821 (DG 9 Feb 1821)

MILLIGAN, Robert, Esq., to JONES, Sally, Miss, "a young lady possessed with every good quality...joined with a large fortune," in New Castle, 2 Apr 1789 (DG 11 Apr 1789)

MILLIGAN, Samuel, of Newark NJ, to HORN, Mary A., Miss, formerly of Wilm, in Newark NJ, 29 Sep 1853, by the Rev. Mr. Van Horn (DG 21 Oct 1853)

MILLS, Allen, see LINGEL, Samuel
see FRICK, Charles F.

MILLS, Charlotte Ann,
see FRICK, Charles F.

MILLS, Elizabeth C., see LINGEL, Samuel

MILLS, George, 18 Oct 1798, on list of yellow fever victims (DG 27 Oct 1798) dec'd, late of Wilm, notice given by John JUSTIS, adm'r (DE 22 Aug 1799)

MILLS, Hannah C., youngest dau of John MILLS, in Wilm, of croup, 11 Feb 1853, in her 7th yr (DG 22 Feb 1853)

MILLS, John, see MILLS, Hannah C.

MILLS, Joseph, of Camden NJ, to HASTINGS, Elizabeth B., Miss, of Wilm, 31 Jul 1852, in Wllm, by the Rev. Andrew Manship (DG 10 Aug 1852)

MILLS, Martha, commonly known as Old Matty, at Stanton, 21 Jan 1842, aged 109 yrs (DG 29 Jan 1842)

MILMAN, Eliza, see SPENCER, Joseph

MILNER, Harriet, see BOVEE, James

MILNER, John, see BOVEE, James

MILNER, Thomas, to STEVENSON, Elizabeth J., Miss, both of Wilm, 9 Jun 1852, by Rev. F. Hodgson (DG 11 Jun 1852) (DG 15 Jun 1852)

MILNOR, George A, of Phila, to **HAWKINS**, Lucy, of Wilm, at Rochester NY, 7 Jul 1852, at the res. of Asa SPRAGUE, Esq., by the Rev. Henry W. Lee (DG 13 Jul 1852)

MILNOR, Mahlon, to **HOWARD**, Elizabeth, in Phila, 28 Nov 1850, by Rev. Mr. Bruen (DG 10 Dec 1850)

MILWARD, Thomas, to **ROBINETT**, Sarah E., both of Wilm, in Phila, 31 Mar 1853, by the Rev. Dr. German (DG 5 Apr 1853)

MINCHALL, Moses. Notice given by Edward DAWES. adm'r (PG 26 Mar 1761)

MINNER, Margaret A., see **HODGSON**, George W.

MINNER, Pitkin, at his res. in Seaford, 9 Aug 1851, aged 69 yrs (DG 2 Sep 1851)

MINOS, George, of Milford, 22 Mar 1850 (DG 2 Apr 1850)

MIRLER, George E., to **MOUSLEY**, Alice, Miss, both of NC Co, 17 Sep 1851, by the Rev. E. M. Van Duesen (DG 19 Sep 1851)

MITCHELL, Amor C., see **MITCHELL**, Edward Passmore

MITCHELL, Ann, see **SHACKLEY**, Joseph

MITCHELL, Charles, see **SEMANS**, Edward

MITCHELL, Charles W., see **MITCHELL**, Patience J.

MITCHELL, Edward Passmore, son of Amor C. and Martha J, MITCHELL, 5 Aug 1852, aged 1 yr 4 mos (DG 10 Aug 1852)

MITCHELL, Elizabeth J., Miss, youngest dau of the late Nathaniel MITCHELL, Esq., former Gov. of DE, at the res. of Col. Manaen BULL, in Sussex Co, 8 Feb 1828, na (DG 22 Feb 1828)

MITCHELL, Ez'l, see MITCHELL, John

MITCHELL, George E., Col, see **MITCHELL**, Mary H.

MITCHELL, Hannah, see **GREEN**, David

MITCHELL, Henry, to **CARTHELL**, Elizabeth, Miss, both of Wilm, 25 Feb 1841, in Wilm by E. W. Gilbert (DG 2 Mar 1841)

MITCHELL, James Y., of Phila, to **MIFFLIN**, Sarah L., dau of the Hon James L. MIFFLIN, of IN, in Newark DE, 15 Jul 1851, at the Village Ch, by the Rev. George Foot (DG 22 Jul 1851)

MITCHELL, John, in Dorchester Co, MD, 3 Jun 1816, aged 106 yrs and 9 mos (AW 22 Jun 1816)

MITCHELL, John, late of Dorchester Co Md, Peter ROBINSON and Ez'l MITCHELL, Adm'rs (DG 23 Mar 1827)

MITCHELL, Martha E., see **WILSON**, William M.

MITCHELL, Martha J., see **MITCHELL**, Edward Passmore

MITCHELL, Mary C., see **ALRICH**, Thomas C.

MITCHELL, Mary E., see **ARTHUR**, Samuel D.

MITCHELL, Mary H., consort of Col. George E. MITCHELL, late of the US Army, and rep. in Congress, at Fair Hill Farm, Cecil Co MD, 21 Apr 1827, in her 35th yr (DG 27 Apr 1827)

MITCHELL, Nathaniel, see MITCHELL, Elizabeth J.

MITCHELL, Passmore H., to **McCALL**, Adaline, Miss, both of Wilm, in Phila, 18 Aug 1853, by the Rev. D. W. Bartine (DG 13 Sep 1853)

MITCHELL, Patience J., wife of Charles W. MITCHELL, and dau of Michael and Ann LOWBER, in Phila, 12 Dec 1850, in her 26th yr (DG 17 Dec 1850)

MITCHELL, Sallie, see **SEMANS**, Edward

MITCHELL, Sarah, see **ROBINSON**, Peter

MITCHELL, Thomas, late of Mill Creek Hd. William L WILSON, adm'r (DG 4 Jan 1853)

MOFFIT, Martha, see **GILPIN**, Josiah H.

MOFFIT, William, see **GILPIN**, Josiah H.

MOFFITT, Jane, see **KIRKBRIDE**, Richard

MOGEE, Elenora, see **BRADFORD**, William Jr.

MOGEE, William, of Wilm, to **KILPATRICK**, Eliza Ann, Miss, of Phila, in Phila, 7 May 1846, by Rev.Mr. Tudhope (DG 15 May 1846)

MOLLESTON, Henry, see **TEMPLE**, Mary, Mrs.

MOLLESTON, Mary, see **TEMPLE**, Mary, Mrs.

MOLSTER, Benjamin F., near Middletown,

of consumption, 5 July 1835, aged 25 yrs
(DG 14 Jul 1835)

MONAGHAN, James, to O'DONNELL,
Mary, Miss, all of Wilm, 14 Nov 1846, at
Brandywine by the pastor of St. Joseph's
Church (DG 17 Nov 1846)

MONAGHAN, James J., formerly of Balt,
to McGOVERN, Julia A. F., dau of Hugh
McGOVERN of Wilm, 18 Nov 1852, by
the Rev. J. O'Conner of St. John's
(DG 3 Dec 1852)

MONAHAN, Michael, convicted at New
Castle of the murder of Mrs. ZEBLEY, of
Wilm, date set for execution, 2 May 1826
(DG 7 Apr 1826)

MONCKTON, Anna,
see ROBINETT, Benj. F.

MONGES, ____, Dr.,
see MONGES, John Armand

MONGES, John A.,
see MONGES, Sidney Louisa

MONGES, John Armand, eldest son of the
late Dr. MONGES of Phila, to GORDON,
Sidney Ann Cecelia, eldest dau of John
GORDON of Wilm, 24 Oct 1827, by the
Rev. Peirce Connelly (DG 30 Oct 1827)

MONGES, Sidney Louisa, dau of the late
John A. MONGES, 14 Dec 1840, aged 7 yrs,
in Wilm. (DG 25 Dec 1840)

MONRO, George, Dr.,
see DARRACH, William, Dr.
see BOYD, Thomas J.

MONRO, George, only son of the late Dr.
George MONRO of Wilm, in Wilm, 10 Oct
1822, aged 17 yrs (DG 11 Oct 1822)

MONRO, Margaretta,
see DARRACH, William, Dr.

MONRO, Mary Ann, see BOYD, Thomas J.

MONROE, George,
see MARSHALL, David
see DARRACH, William, Dr.

MONROE, Haslet, of yellow fever
(DE 17 Sep 1798)

MONROE, Margaretta,
see DARRACH, William

MONTGOMERY, Alexander,
see MONTGOMERY, Elizabeth

MONTGOMERY, Eliza,
see HARLAN, C., Dr.

MONTGOMERY, Elizabeth, inf dau of
Alexander and Maria MONTGOMERY,
22 Sep 1848 (DG 3 Oct 1848)

MONTGOMERY, Fidelia,
see VAN DYKE, Kinsey Johns, Esq.

MONTGOMERY, James,
see SHIPLEY, Esther

MONTGOMERY, James, Jr., of New York,
to LUCAS, Eliza, 3 Jul 1844, at Lewes, by
Rev. Walter B. Franklin (DG 19 Jul 1844)

MONTGOMERY, John, late of Christiana
Bridge. Notice given by Thomas DUNN and
Thomas MONTGOMERY (PG 11 Jul 1765)

MONTGOMERY, John, to ROBINSON,
Hanah (sic) Jane, Miss, all of Wilm,
10 Jun 1851, by Rev. Andrew Manship
(DG 17 Jun 1851)

MONTGOMERY, Margaret Ann,
see GEBHART, Benjamin F.

MONTGOMERY, Maria,
see MONTGOMERY, Elizabeth

MONTGOMERY, Sarah, see BALL, George

MONTGOMERY, Thomas,
see MONTGOMERY, John
see BLACK, James

MONTGOMERY, William,
see VAN DYKE, Kinsey Johns, Esq.

MOODY, David L., see HOSACK, Sarah
see MOODY, David Lewis
see MOODY, Sarah Elizabeth

MOODY, David Lewis, son of David L
MOODY, in Wilm, 24 May 1845, aged c 2 yrs
(DG 27 May 1845)

MOODY, Eliza R.,
see BRAMBLE, George M.

MOODY, Elizabeth, see COCHRAN, R. T.

MOODY, John, Esq.,
see MOODY, Lucinda

MOODY, John, see CROW, John, Esq.

MOODY, Lucinda, wife of John MOODY
Esq., 21 Mar 1841, at New Castle
(DG 26 Mar 1841)

MOODY, Mary, formerly Mary JEHU, dec'd,
late of Appoq. Hd, sale by sheriff, William
Herdman (DG 28 Dec 1827)

MOODY, Mary Jane,
see SAUNDERS, Amos Jr.

MOODY, Rachel Rebecca,
see GORDON, William H.

MOODY, Sarah A.,
see MOODY, Sarah Elizabeth

MOODY, Sarah E., see HAYES, Myers

MOODY, Sarah Elizabeth, dau of David L. and Sarah A. MOODY, 12 Apr 1850, in Wilm (DG 16 Apr 1850)

MOODY, William, dec'd, late of Christiana Hd, notice given by Henry LATIMER, adm'r (DG 2 Dec 1823)

MOON, Ann, Mrs., wife of Mr. James MOON of Wilm, 20 Dec 1835 (DG 22 Dec 1835)

MOON, James, to QUINBY, Martha Ann, Miss, both of Wilm, 28 Jan 1827, by the Rev. Lawrence McCombs (DG 30 Jan 1827)

MOON , James. see MOON, Ann, Mrs.

MOOR, Matilda, Miss,
see WILLIAMS, Samuel

MOORE, Ann,
see ANDERSON, Elizabeth Jane
see FLAMER, Solomon

MOORE, Ann Eliza,
see ORPWOOD, Thomas

MOORE, Caroline J.,
see VERNON, Samuel

MOORE, Catharine, Mrs.,
see COOK, James

MOORE, Charles T., to BLACKWOOD, Mary W., Miss, both of Wilm, in Chester PA, 21 Sep 1850, by Rev. Newton Heston (DG 1 Oct 1850)

MOORE, Edward, to HOOPES, Mary Ann, Miss, 22 Jan 1835, by Elder John P. Peckworth, all of Wilm (DG 27 Jan 1835)

MOORE, Elenor, 26 Oct 1798, on list of yellow fever victims (DG 27 Oct 1798)

MOORE, Eliza, Miss, in Wilm, 16 Jul 1849, aged c 55 yrs. Aunt of James V. MOORE, Esq., of Appoq. Hd (DG 20 Jul 1849)

MOORE, Eliza Jane Magee,
see HERDMAN, John

MOORE, Eliza Jane, see MAGEE, John

MOORE, Eliza S., see PHILLIPS, Evan C.

MOORE, Elizabeth,
see GARRETSON, Elizabeth M.
see GARRETSON, William
see MOORE, Francis James Loper
see COVEY, Joshua
see BRADLEY, John F.

MOORE, Emeline, see SAWDON, Thomas

MOORE, Ester, see SHAW, John H.

MOORE, Francis James Loper, youngest child of James and Elizabeth MOORE, in Wilm of dysentery, 50 (sic) Jul 1848, aged 3 yrs 7 mos 11 days (DG 28 Jul 1848)

MOORE, George H., of Phila, to NOBLIT, Elizabeth B., Miss, dau of Hamilton NOBLIT of Wilm, 6 Apr 1846, by Rev. John L. Grant (DG 14 Apr 1846)
see SWAYNE, Jacob

MOORE, George K., to HANDY, Margaret, both of NC Co, at Marcus Hook, 12 Oct 1852, by the Rev. J. Walker (DG 26 Oct 1852)

MOORE, George, see MOORE, Sarah

MOORE, George W., son of Outerbridge H. MOORE, in Wilm, 6 Jun 1848, aged 10 mos (DG 13 Jun 1848)

MOORE, George W., to McKINSEY, Susan Ann, Miss, both of NC Co, 25 Mar 1852, by Rev. S. R. Wynkoop (DG 30 Mar 1852)

MOORE, Henry, see JONES, Isaac

MOORE, Hester, Mrs., relict of Jacob MOORE, Esq., at the res. of George BATSON in Lewis, 14 Oct 1827, in her 85th yr (DG 19 Oct 1827)

MOORE, Isaac, Capt, at Frederica DE, 4 Mar 1851, na (DG 11 Mar 1851)

MOORE, J. V., see PALMATORY, Robert

MOORE, Jacob, M. D., in Glasgow, Pencader Hd, 5 May 1829, aged 32 yrs; leaves a widow and 4 young children (DG 15 May 1829)

MOORE, Jacob, see MOORE, Hester

MOORE, James,
see MOORE, Francis James Loper

MOORE, James A., Dr., of typhoid fever, at the res. of his father near Cantwell's Bridge, 24 Apr 1853, aged less than 25 yrs, just starting to practice medicine (DG 29 Apr 1853)

MOORE, James, B., Col., of St. Paul's M. E. Church, to POTTER, Margaret J., Mrs., of

Asbury M. E. Church, both of Wilm, 8 Jan 1846, by Rev. Mr. Atwood (DG 9 Jan 1846)

MOORE, James V., see MOORE, Eliza

MOORE, John, of Baltimore, 12 Mar 1849, in his 75th yr (DG 23 Mar 1849)

MOORE, John of Leipsic, to NOWELL, Mary Jane, Miss, of Little Creek, 27 Apr 1853, by Rev. J. P. Walter (DG 3 May 1853)

MOORE, John, see HERDMAN, John
see MAGEE, John

MOORE, John C., at the res. of his mother in Wilm, 16 Jan 1834, aged 24 yrs (Pittsburgh papers please copy) (DG 21 Jan 1834)

MOORE, John D., to McCANDLES, Eleanor, both of Wilm, 21 Aug 1849, by the Rev. A. S. Patton (DG 31 Aug 1849)

MOORE, Margaret, see BUTLER, William
see GARRETT, Gideon M.,

MOORE, Margaret Ellen, in Brandywine Village, 3 Sep 1853, aged c 36 yrs (DG 6 Sep 1853)

MOORE, Mary Ann, see SHUTE, Asa M.

MOORE, Minerva W.,
see MENDENHALL, Cyrus Jr.

MOORE, Outerbridge H.,
see MOORE, George W.

MOORE, Peter, to CHE, Ann, of NC Co, 24 Jul 1847, by Rev. M. J. Rhees (DG 3 Aug 1847)

MOORE, Rebecca S., see GRAY, Wm.

MOORE, Samuel E., to RASH, Margaretta, Miss, both of Kent Co, 23 Dec 1852, by the Rev. H. E. Gilroy (DG 14 Jan 1853)

MOORE, Samuel, Esq.,

MOORE, Samuel, Esq., Justice of the Peace for NC Co, and Rev. War officer, in NC Co, 16 Jul 1826, na (DG 18 Jul 1826) dec'd, late of New Castle Hd, notice given by Washington E. MOORE, adm'r (DG 4 Aug 1826)

MOORE, Samuel, son of Washington E. MOORE, Esq., late of NC Co, at Niles Ml, ndd, aged 23 yrs 7 days (DG 14 May 1852)

MOORE, Samuel, to PRITCHARD, Susanna A., Miss, 5 Feb 1846, in Wilm, by Bishop Lee (DG 10 Feb 1846)

MOORE, Sarah Ann, see BOOTH, John

MOORE, Sarah, Mrs., relict of George MOORE, 27 Apr 1827, near Laurel, aged 84 yrs. She had 14 children, 78 gch, 76 ggch (DG 10 Jul 1827)

MOORE, Shadrack D., of Wilm, to PAINTER, Sarah Ann, of Phila, in Phila, 27 Dec 1850, by the Rev. F. Swentzel (DG 7 Jan 1851)

MOORE, Thomas, at his farm below New Castle, 23 Feb 1790, aged 67 yrs (DG 6 Mar 1790)

MOORE, Thomas, Capt., who commanded the Revenue Barge of this district, 6 Jan 1793, aged 53 yrs. Buried Episcopal Burying Gr'd, Marcus Hook, PA (DG 12 Jan 1793)

MOORE, Thomas L. of VA, to ADAMS, Janet K., dau of T. Jenifer ADAMS, of Wilm, 16 Jun 1853, by Rev. Charles Breck (DG 21 Jun 1853)

MOORE, Thomas. Naamans Creek Mills and 85 acres of land being sold by Joseph CLOUD, adm'r (PG 28 Nov 1745)

MOORE, Thomas,
see GARRETSON, Elizabeth M.
see GARRETSON, William
see MARTIN, Rebecca
see MOORE, Washington E.,
see MOORE, Samuel, Esq.

MOORE, Washington E.,
see MOORE, Samuel

MOORE, William E., Rev., to FOOT, Harriet, Miss, all of Newark, 13 Sep 1850, by Rev. George FOOT (DG 1 Sep 1850)

MOORE, William H., 1 Apr 1852, in his 54th yr (DG 6 Apr 1852)

MORAN, Elizabeth G.,
see HADDOCK, John G.

MORELAND, Margaretta A.,
see CROZIER, Eli

MORETON, John, merchant of Phila, to CANBY, Margaret, Miss, of Brandywine, 18 Feb 1808, at Friends Meeting (MU 20 Feb 1808)

MORGAN, Evan F., at the res. of his mother, in Pencader Hd, 31 Aug 1850, in his 19th yr (DG 10 Sep 1850)

MORGAN, Ezekiel, to WEBB, Ellen, Miss, both of Kent Co, DE, 13 Mar 1849, by the Rev. T. P. McColley (DG 10 Apr 1849)

MORGAN, James H., of Elkton, to WATSON, Elizabeth W., of Wilm, 27 Oct

1850, in Phila, by Rev. J. Mason (DG 1 Nov 1850)

MORGAN, James T., to OSGOOD, Delia C., Miss, both of Wilm, in Phila, 16 Jan 1848, by Rev. Geo. Chandler (DG 26 Jan 1848)

MORGAN, Mary Ann, of Pencader Hd, in Wilm, 2 Feb 1853, aged c 25 yrs (DG 8 Feb 1853)

MORGAN, Solomon, to SIMPSON, Rachel, Mrs., widow of the late Thomas SIMPSON, dec'd, 13 Dec 1841 by the Rev. Henry Graham (DG 24 Dec 1841)

MORGAN, Thomas, to SAWDON, Ann E., Miss, all of NC Co, 27 Dec 1849, by Rev. P. Coombe (DG 1 Jan 1850)

MORIS, Evan, of Chester Co, PA, to STONE, Amelia Terissa, Miss, of New Port, 22 Jan 1807, by Rev. Mr. Pryce (MU 24 Jan 1807)

MORIS, Wm H., of Delaware City, near Newark at the res. of his uncle, Robert ARMSTRONG, 17 Oct 1853, aged 6 yrs 5 mos 28 days (DG 8 Nov 1853)

MORRELL, Charles, baggage agent, fell under wheels of baggage car, in Phila, 20 Mar 1851 (DG 21 Mar 1851)

MORRELL, R. E., see BLACKWELL, George

MORRIL, Mary A., see CLOSBY, Robert

MORRIS, Amelia T., Mrs., in Wilm, 4 Jul 1834, na (DG 8 Jul 1834)

MORRIS, Ann, Mrs, consort of Robert MORRIS, and dau of the late Col. William D. WAPLES, after an illness of 8 weeks, 21 Sep 1844, aged 45 yrs (DG 1 Oct 1844)

MORRIS, Bevan, Capt., to COLLINS, Ann, Mrs., at Milton, 25 Jun 1829, by Rev. Daniel Jester (DG 3 Jul 1829)

MORRIS, Cad., see SERRILL, Isaac

MORRIS, Daniel A., of Madison Co OH, to BROOMALL, Mary R., Miss, formerly of DE, 29 May 1848, by Rev. P. Combe (DG 2 Jun 1848)

MORRIS, F. Ann, see STEVENSON, James H.

MORRIS, Governeur, the Hon., at Morrisiana (NY), 6 Nov 1816 (AW 9 Nov 1816)

MORRIS, James P., Capt., see COVER, Robert

MORRIS, John, dec'd, late of Wilm, notice given by Cyrus LAMBORN, adm'r (DG 3 May 1833)

MORRIS, John L.,
see NICHOLSON, Henry
see GARRETSON, Henry
see SHEPHERDSON, Richard
see PHILLIPS, John

MORRIS, Lydia L., see GOVER, Robert

MORRIS, Maria, see DUFFIELD, Samuel, Dr.

MORRIS, Mary Jane, see TAYLOR, John

MORRIS, Mary R., Mrs., dau of the late Robert and Sarah BROOMALL, of Del Co PA, in Rock Island IL, of cholera, 31 Jul 1851, aged 24 yrs (DG 12 Aug 1851)

MORRIS, Robert, see MORRIS, Ann

MORRIS, Samuel, Jr., of Chester Co, PA, to BRIAN, Sarah H., Miss, dau of James BRIAN, Esq., of Wilm, 4 Apr 1833, by Rev. E. Cooper (DG 5 Apr 1833)

MORRIS, Sarah, see ROE, John
see LAYTON, John M.

MORRIS, Sarah B., see LEWIS, James W.

MORRIS, Susanna, see ATKINS, John

MORRISON, Ann Eliza, see STARR, Jacob

MORRISON, Charlotte, see BOTHERMEL, Daniel

MORRISON, David, to CANN, Rachel, Miss, both of NC Co, 6 Mar 1833, by Elder John P. Peckworth (DG 8 Mar 1833)
see MORRISON, Douglass

MORRISON, Douglas, see McCOY, James

MORRISON, Douglass, to MORRISON, Jane, Miss, both of NC Co, 17 Oct 1843, by Rev. W. R. Work (DG 27 Oct 1843)

MORRISON, Douglass, late of White Clay Creek Hd. David MORRISON, exec'r (DG 14 Sep 1849)

MORRISON, Elizabeth, see McCOY, James

MORRISON, George, the Rev., of Belle-Air, MD, formerly of Newark, DE, to LOVELL, Eliza A., Miss, dau of William LOVELL, Esq., of Baltimore, at Baltimore, 5 Jun 1823, by the Rev. Mr. Nevins (DG 13 Jun 1823)

MORRISON, Henry, to GREEN, Mary, Miss, both of Delaware, in Phila, 15 Jan 1846, by

Rev. John Chambers (DG 20 Jan 1846)

MORRISON, Isabella,
see **EDWARDS**, Joseph

MORRISON, Jane,
see **MORRISON**, Douglass

MORRISON, John, to **IRVIN**, Ellen, Miss, both of Wilm, 26 Dec 1853, by th Rev. T. R. Wynkoop (DG 30 Dec 1853)

MORRISON, Joseph, to **DAVIS**, Jane, Miss, all of NC Co, 20 Jul 1846, in Wilm (DG 24 Jul 1846)

MORRISON, Mary,
see **MORRISON**, Moses

MORRISON, Mary Ann, see **HAMON**, Jacob

MORRISON, Moses, merchant of Wilm, 17 Dec 1829, na (DG 18 Dec 1829) notice given by Mary MORRISON, adm'x (DG 12 Jan 1830)

MORRISON, Moses, to **BLACK**, Mary, Miss, both of Wilm, 25 Jun 1818, by Rev. E. W. Gilbert (AW 27 Jun 1818)

MORRISON, Robert, in Mill Creek Hd, 30 Sep 1848, aged 70 yrs (DG 10 Sep 1848)

MORRISON, Robert, to **BURNS**, Catharine, Miss, both of Wilm, in Phila, 29 Aug 1853, by the Rev. Andrew Manship (DG 6 Sep 1853)

MORRISON, Sally A.,
see **CARNAHAN**, M. K.

MORRISON, Samuel, to **McMANN**, Susan, Miss, all of Newark, 12 Dec 1850, by Rev. George Foote (DG 31 Dec 1850)

MORRISON, Thomas, in Wilm, after a lingering illness, 14 May 1842 (DG 20 May 1842)

MORROW, Bethiah E.,
see **MORROW**, Mary Elizabeth

MORROW, Franklin Turner, son of William and Sarah Ann MORROW, in Wilm, 12 Nov 1849, in his 3rd yr (DG 16 Nov 1849)

MORROW, James,
see **MORROW**, Mary Elizabeth

MORROW, James, of Wilm, to **EVES**, Bethia F., dau of William D. EVES of New London, Chester Co PA, 27 Apr 1847, by Rev. Robert DuBois (DG 30 Apr 1847)

MORROW, James L., to **ROBINSON**, Anna E., Miss, dau of Edward P. ROBINSON, Esq., all of Wilm, 30 May 1850, by Rev.

A. Atwood (DG 4 Jun 1850)

MORROW, John, of Brandywine Village, to **HAWKINS**, Sarah, Miss, of Wilm, 24 Jan 1824, by the Rev. J. Potts (DG 27 Jan 1824)

MORROW, Mary Elizabeth, dau of James and Bethiah E. MORROW, at the res. of her father in Wilm, 9 Dec 1850, aged 1 yr 4 mos (DG 10 Dec 1850)

MORROW, Robert B., of Brandywine DE, to **JORDON**, Emily H., of Phila, 16 Dec 1852, by Rev. John Chambers (DG 21 Dec 1852)

MORROW, Sarah A.,
see **FREEZE**, Edward M.

MORROW, Sarah Ann,
see **MORROW**, Franklin Turner
see **MORROW**, William Thomas

MORROW, Thomas, a native of Ireland, res. for many years at Cantwell's Bridge and the last 10 or 12 years in Wilm or vicinity, 18 Mar 1824, aged 64 yrs (DG 23 Mar 1824)

MORROW, William,
see **MORROW**, Wiliam Thomas
see **MORROW**, Franklin Turner

MORROW, William Thomas, son of William and Sarah Ann MORROW, in Wilm, 30 Jun 1848, aged 5 yrs 8 mos 9 days (DG 4 Jul 1848)

MORTEN, Edward, long a member of the Methodist Ch, in Appoq. Hd, on his 75th birthday, ndd (DG 20 Nov 1821)

MORTIMER, Clara, inf dau of George W. and Hannah MORTIMER, in Wilm, 16 Jul 1850, aged 18 mos (DG 23 Jul 1850)

MORTIMER, George W.,
see **MORTIMER**, Clara
see **MORTIMER**, Henry A.

MORTIMER, Hannah,
see **MORTIMER**, Clara

MORTIMER, Hannah Ann,
see **MORTIMER**, Henry A.

MORTIMER, Henry A., inf. son of George W. and Hannah Ann MORTIMER, 10 Aug 1845, in Wilm (DG 12 Aug 1845)

MORTON, Andrew, dec'd, late of Pencader Hd, notice given by James McCULLOUGH, atty-in-fact (DG 16 May 1826)

MORTON, Ann, see **MEREDITH**, James

MORTON, Elizabeth, see **GILPIN**, Samuel S.

MORTON, Emeline, see HALL, Joel

MORTON, Henry, see CHESTNUT, William

MORTON, Isaac H., to HITCHINGS, Lucinda, Miss, both of Wilm, 19 Sep 1841, at the house of S. A. PRICE, Esq., in the borough of Chester, PA, by the Rev. M. R. Talbot (DG 24 Sep 1841)

MORTON, Jacob G., of Guernsey Co, OH, to ARMSTRONG, Rebecca, Miss, of Newark, DE, in Newark, 24 Mar 1835, by the Rev. A. K. Russel (DG 27 Mar 1835)

MORTON, Morton, Dr., to BROTHERS, Rachel, Miss, 10 Jan 1821 (DG 12 Jan 1821)

MORTON, Norton, Captain, 4 Mar 1790. Buried Trinity Ch (DG 6 Mar 1790)

MORTON, Thomas, see GILPIN, Samuel S.

MOTE, Eli, see GILBERT, Joseph S.

MOULDER, Hannah W., see GARDEN, W. A.

MOULDER, John N., see GARDEN, W. A.

MOULDER, Sarah Jane, see HAUGHEY, James

MOULDER, William, see HAUGHEY, James

MOUNT, William G., of New London Crossroads, Chester Co PA, to EGBERT, Rachel, Miss, of Wilm, 2 Sep 1847, by Rev. Mr. Rockwell (DG 7 Sep 1847)

MOUSLEY, Alice, see MIRLER, George E.

MOUSLEY, George W., to WAY, Elizabeth, Miss, both of NC Co, 28 Oct 1851, by Rev. S. G. Hare (DG 4 Nov 1851)

MOUSELY, Joseph M., to SALLY, Charity, both of NC Co, 24 Oct 1850, at the parsonage at Village Green, by Rev. J. B. Maddux (DG 8 Nov 1850)

MOUSLEY, William, to DAY, Mary, Miss, all of Brandywine Hd, 3 Jan 1822, by the Rev. L. Lawrenson (DG 8 Jan 1822)

MULLEN, Arphe Elixa Jane, dau of P. J. and Prudence MULLEN, in Wilm, 13 Aug 1848, aged 16 mos (DG 15 Aug 1848)

MULLEN, Charles, near Henry Clay Factory in Christiana Hd, 28 May 1850, aged c 40 yrs (DG 4 Jun 1850)

MULLEN, P. J., see MULLEN, Arphe Elixa Jane

MULLEN, Prudence, see MULLEN, Arphe Elixa Jane

MULLEN, Robert, of New Castle, to ROBINSON, Mary, 21 Feb 1846, by Rev. S. R. Wynkoop (DG 24 Feb 1846)

MULLEN, William, Rev., of Phila Conf. to TRUITT, Margaret E., Miss, of Georgetown, 5 Oct 1848, in Union M. E. Church, by Rev. Dr. Kenneday (DG 20 Oct 1848)

MULLIN, Isaac, to KEENAN, Mary Ann, dau of Mark KEENAN, Esq., of Kensington, 20 Oct 1847, by Rev. P Reilly (DG 29 Oct 1847)

MUNDOON, Mary Elizabeth, see BLEASDALE, John

MURCH, John, in New Castle, 26 Jan 1829, aged 35 yrs; Mason, member of New Castle Guards (DG 3 Feb 1829)

MURDAUGH, Alexander, of Christiana Bridge, to McCOY, Jane, Miss, of White Clay Creek, 4 Apr 1833, by the Rev. A. K. Russel (DG 12 Apr 1833)

MURDOCK, James Jr, to GRAHAM, Sarah Ann, Miss, 3 June 1841, by Elder John Miller, all of Wilm (DG 11 Jun 1841)

MURDOCK, Susanna, see SEELEY, John A.

MURGATROYD, Benjamin, to EDMUNDSON, Clarissa A., Miss, all of Wilm, 22 Dec 1853, in Wilm (Cecil Co papers please copy) (DG 30 Dec 1853)

MURGATROYD, Sarah, see PICKELS, Henry

MURGIONDO, Lola, see LAMMOT, D., Jr.

MURGUIONDO, Prudencio, see LAMMOT, D., Jr.

MURPHEY, Ann, Mrs., wife of Samuel MURPHEY, Esq., formerly of DE, in Phila, 24 Jun 1851, in her 73rd yr (DG 27 Jun 1851) see TAYLOR, James

MURPHEY, George, see MURPHY, Wm. Jr.

MURPHEY, John, near Newark, 31 Jan 1825, aged 91 yrs 4 mos (Cl 16 Feb 1825)

MURPHEY, John B., to McKEE, Marian J., Miss, both of Brandywine Hd, in Phila, 12 Mar 1850, by Rev. Dr. William Neill (DG 22 Mar 1850)

MURPHEY, Samuel, see MURPHEY, Ann

MURPHY, Arthur, in Wilm, 5 Nov 1825, na (DG 8 Nov 1825)

MURPHY, Arthur, dec'd, late of Wilm, notice given by Peter JOHNSON, surviving exec'r (DG 6 Mar 1829)
see MURPHY, Eleanor

MURPHY, Bernard, in New Castle, 7 Apr 1849, in his 80th yr (DG 13 Apr 1849) late of New Castle, John MURPHY or Elizabeth MURPHY, exec'r (DG 1 May 1849)

MURPHY, Bernard, of Phila, to McCANLESS, Susan, Miss, of Wilm, 23 Apr 1849 by Rev. P. Riley (DG 1 May 1849)

MURPHY, Bernard, see MELLEN, Patrick

MURPHY, Catherine Ann, see KELLY, Luke

MURPHY, Daniel J., to ROTHWELL, Ann E., both of Delaware, 7 Jun 1842, in Phila, by Rev. G. Foot (DG 10 Jun 1842)

MURPHY, Eleanor, Mrs., relict of the late Arthur MURPHY, 19 Feb 1829, na (DG 27 Feb 1829)
see MURPHY, Arthur

MURPHY, Elizabeth, see MURPHY, Bernard
see MAGEE, George

MURPHY, John, see MURPHY, Bernard
see KELLY, Luke

MURPHY, Martha, see HURLEY, George

MURPHY, Mary, see FULLERTON, James

MURPHY, Samuel, to FLEMING, Anna J., both of Wilm, in Phila, 27 Feb 1851, by the Rev. Mr. Coleman (DG 7 Mar 1851)

MURPHY, Susan M., see MANY, James,

MURPHY, William, Jr., of Wilm, to TEMPLE, Sarah, Miss, of Chester Co PA, 7 Mar 1850, by Rev. Newton Heston (DG 22 1850)

MURPHY, William, Jr., in Wilm 22 Aug 1853, aged c 31 yrs (DG 26 Aug 1853) late of Wilm City, George MURPHEY, adm'r (DG 6 Sep 1853)

MURRAY, Alexander, dec'd, late of PA, notice given by Thomas A. ROGERS, adm'r (DG 21 Jul 1826)

MURRAY, John, of Elkton, of injuries, carriage accident (DG 11 Sep 1790)

MURRAY, John, of chronic diarrhea, in New Orleans, 9 Jul 1848, in his 32nd yr. He enlisted in the Navy Feb 11 1847, and had been in Mexico since. He was on his way home when attacked (DG 19 Sep 1848)

MURRAY, Margaret, see KNOWLES, Ephraim

MURRAY, Martha J., see HIGGINS, Jacob K.

MURRY, Mary, see KNOX, James

MUSGROVES, James, to THOMPSON, Elizabeth, Miss, both of Wilm, 2 Apr 1829, by the Rev. E. W. Gilbert (DG 7 Apr 1829)

McKINLEY, Daniel S., formerly of DE, to LOCK, Sarah E., of Kensington, in Phila, 6 Aug 1851, by the Rev. J. L. Grant (DG 23 Aug 1851)

MYERS, Alexander, to HENDERSON, Mary, Miss, both of Brandywine Hd, near duPont's Factory, 25 Dec 1822, by the Rev. E. W. Gilbert (DG 27 Dec 1822)

MYERS, Alexander, to PORTER, Nancy, Miss, both of Brandywine Hd, 16 Apr 1842 by Rev. S. M. Galey (DG 27 May 1842)

MYERS, Phebe, in Wilm, 4 Jun 1852, in her 83rd yr (DG 8 Jun 1852) (Del Co and West Chester papers please copy)

MYNICH, Daniel of Phila, to WOODCOCK, Ann C., Miss, of Wilm, 15 Jun 1823, by the Rev. J. Potts (DG 20 Jun 1823)

NAFF, Catherine, Mrs., at her res. near Wilm, 18 Sep 1817, aged c 90 yrs (AW 1 Oct 1817)

NAFF, Elizabeth, see WELSH, James

NAFF, Hance, 9 Oct 1841, near Wilm, aged c 86 yrs (DG 15 Oct 1841)

NAFF, Joanna, see JONES, George

NAFF, Mary, wife of Hance NAFF, near Wilm, 14 Dec 1835, aged 79 yrs (DG 1 Jan 1836)

NAGEL, Michael, see DAWSON, William

NASSAU, Charles W., Rev., see HANDY, Isaac Henry, M. D.

NASSAU, Mary Ann, see HANDY, Isaac Henry, M. D.

NASSAU, William, see HANDY, Isaac Henry, M. D.

NAUDAIN, _____, Miss, dau of the late Arnold D. NAUDAIN, in Wilm, 24 Jul 1848, aged 20 yrs (DG 1 Aug 1848)

NAUDAIN, A., Dr., see HAMILTON, A. Boyd

DELAWARE MARRIAGES AND DEATHS FROM NEWSPAPERS, 1729-1853   177

NAUDAIN, A., see **NAUDAIN**, Andrew S.

NAUDAIN, Andrew S., son of the Hon. A. NAUDAIN, to **CORBIT**, Mary P., Miss, of Cantwell's Bridge, in New Castle, 6 Mar 1833, by the Rev. E. W. Gilbert (DG 12 Mar 1833)

NAUDAIN, Ann, see **NAUDAIN**, James S.

NAUDAIN, Ann Elizabeth, late wife of James S. NAUDAIN, M.D., in Middletown, 20 Apr 1843, aged 32 yrs (DG 28 Apr 1843)

NAUDAIN, Arnold, dec'd, late of Appoq. Hd, notice given by Elias NAUDAIN, adm'r (DG 1 Mar 1797)

NAUDAIN, Arnold, see **NAUDAIN**, Caroline see **COWGILL**, Daniel

NAUDAIN, Arnold D., see **NAUDAIN**, _____, Miss

NAUDAIN, Caroline, youngest dau of Hon. Arnold NAUDAIN, M. D., late of Wilm, 14 Apr 1848, in Phila (DG 18 Apr 1848)

NAUDAIN, Catharine, see **HAMILTON**, A. Boyd

NAUDAIN, Cornelius, at his res. in Appoq. Hd, 23 Feb 1847, na (DG 5 Mar 1847)

NAUDAIN, Elias, see **NAUDAIN**, Arnold

NAUDAIN, James S., dec'd, late of White Clay Creek Hd. Notice given by Ann NAUDAIN, exec'x (DG 9 Dec 1842) see **NAUDAIN**, Ann Elizabeth

NAUDAIN, Lawrence M., in Appoq. Hd, last week, aged c 30 yrs (DG 2 Sep 1853)

NAUDAIN, Mary, Mrs, at her res. in Throughfare Neck, after a short illness, 28 Feb 1847 (DG 5 Mar 1847)

NAUDAIN, Mary, see **COWGILL**, Daniel

NAUDAIN, Matthew M., to **TORBERT**, Susan, dau of the late John TORBERT, Esq., of Wilm, 2 Oct 1849, by the Rev. Pennel Coombs (DG 9 Oct 1849)

NAUDAIN, Nicholas F. C., to **RATLIGE**, Rebecca C., Miss, both of NC Co, 15 Jun 1847, by Rev. L. Scott (DG 25 Jun 1847)

NAUMAN, Ann Mary, see **KUHNS**, Benjamin

NEAL, Ann, see **CROMPTON**, John

NEALIS, Anne E., see **GARRETSON**, Charles

NEALS, Rachel, see **CAMPBELL**, William

NEALS, Rebecca Ann, see **SHULL**, James B.

NEBEKER, Acquilla, in the village of Stanton, 19 Aug 1846, aged c 55 yrs (DG 21 Aug 1846)

NEELY, A., Esq., see **JUSTIS**, Augustus

NEIL, Lewis, see **FINNEY**, Washington L.,

NEILS, Mary, see **DARLINGTON**, Abel

NELSON, Charles, of New Castle, to **SHERIDAN**, Margaret, Miss, of Wilm, 13 Nov 1851, by the Rev. Andrew Manship (DG 18 Nov 1851)

NELSON, John, tanner, 13 Aug 1853, in his 64th yr (DG 19 Aug 1853)

NELSON, Mary, see **ROSELL**, John P.

NELSON, see **GREGORY**, William

NELSON, Robert, to **DEMPSEY**, Margaret, all of NC Co, 11 Jun 1846, by Rev. M. J. Rhees (DG 19 Jun 1846)

NETHERY, Lea J., to **HOFFMAN**, Caroline, Miss, both of Delaware, 29 Nov 1842, in Chester PA, by Rev. George W. Bartram, J. P. (DG 2 Dec 1842)

NEW, David, to **WELCH**, Rachel Ann, Miss, all of Wilm, 21 Feb 1850, by Rev. William Cooper (DG 1 Mar 1850)

NEWBOLD, Joshua, of Byberry, Phila Co, to **MIFFLIN**, Elizabeth Johns, dau of the late Warner MIFFLIN, near Camden DE, 12 Oct 1848, by Friends ceremony (DG 20 Oct 1848)

NEWELL, Elia G., see **WAIT**, Francis D., M. D.

NEWITT, Alexander, to **LEWIS**, Mary, Miss, of Wilm, in Wilm, 3 Jul 1825, by the Rev. Thomas H. Skinner (DG 5 Jul 1825)

NEWKIRK, James, to **THOMAS**, Sarah, Miss, both of Del. City, on board the steamboat *Cohansey*, 11 Oct 1851, by Rev. W. R. Durnett, of Cedarville NJ (DG 30 Jan 1852)

NEWLIN, Ann, see **HANSON**, John

NEWLIN, Eliza, see **CROW**, Thomas

NEWLIN, Elizabeth, see **RUSSEL**, Charles M.

NEWLIN, Elizabeth P., see **BREAER**, Abel

NEWLIN, Ellis J., Rev., of Lynchburg VA, formerly of Wilm, to BRILBANE, Catharine S., of Carlisle, at Carlisle, 23 Dec 1847, by Rev. E. W. Gilbert, D. D. (DG 31 Dec 1847)

NEWLIN, Jane, see HARMAN, Jacob

NEWLIN, Lydia, formerly of Wilm, in Phila, 11 Feb, 1850, aged 30 yrs (DG 1 Mar 1850)

NEWLIN, Samuel, see ALLEN, Robert

NEWLIN, Sarah E., see KEPLEY, Thomas L.

NEWLIN, T. S., see CHANDLER, Joseph F. see RICHARDSON, Ann

NEWLIN, Thomas, at Cantwell's Bridge, 16 Jul 1853, aged c 70 yrs (DG 22 Jul 1853)

NEWLOVE, Sina, see JOSHLIN, William

NEWSON, Alfred, to NOWEL, Mary, Miss, in Milford, 29 Jun 1852, by the Rev. T. P. McColley (DG 20 Jul 1852)

NEWTON, Thomas, Dr. of Norfolk VA, to DARRAGH, Margaret P., Miss, dau of Alexander P. DARRAGH, late purser in the US Navy, 21 Apr 1842, at New Castle by Rev. Mr. Spotswood (DG 29 Apr 1842)

NICHELSON, William, of Brandywine Hd, to WALRAVEN, Priscilla, Miss, of Wilm, 7 Jan 1830, by Rev. R. U. Morgan (DG 19 Jan 1830)

NICHOLESS, Emma, see YEATS, Abijah

NICHOLLS, Hannah, dec'd, late of Wilm, notice given by Joseph C. GILPIN, exec'r (DG 12 Jul 1825)

NICHOLS, John, of Newlin Twp, to DILWORTH, Adaline L., of Centreville DE, 29 Feb 1852, by the Rev. Wm. Moore (DG 5 Mar 1852)

NICHOLSON, Henry, dec'd, late of Newport, Isaac WALRAVEN and John L. MORRIS, exec'rs (DG 11 MAy 1827)

NICHOLSON, Isaac J., to MAXWELL, Margaret, Miss, both of NC Co, 9 Aug 1849, by the Rev. Thomas Barton (DG 31 Aug 1849)

NICHOLSON, Jane, see FOREMAN, Albert

NICHOLSON, John A., Esq., of Baltimore, to REED, Angelica K., dau of the late John REED, Esq., of Dover, at Dover, 2 Jul 1848, by Rev. Thos. J. Murphy (DG 4 Aug 1848)

NICHOLSON, William, Esq., to LAYMAN, Rachel, 7 Mar 1842, by Rev. William Rider (DG 18 Mar 1842)

NICKLE, Martha J., see BYLES, Thomas J.

NICOLS, James, of Caroline Co MD, to WINGATE, Hester, Miss, of Sussex, in North West Fork Hd, Sussex Co, 16 May 1848, by Rev. William Davis (DG 26 May 1848)

NIETZ, Henry, !0 Jan 1821, aged 89 yrs (DG 23 Jan 1821)

NILES, _____, Mrs., widow of the late Hezekiah MILES of Balt, 26 Jun 1852, aged 52 yrs (DG 2 Jul 1852)

NILES, Abel, see McCOOL, George see LAWRENCE, Andrew

NILES, Hetty Warner, see RUST, Luther C.

NILES, Hez., see BLACK, William

NILES, Hezekiah, dec'd, late of Wilm, notice given by Mary NILES, adm'x and Samuel NILES, adm'r (DG 31 Dec 1791)

NILES, Hezekiah, see NILES, _____, Mrs.

NILES, Hezekiah, to WARNER, Sally Ann, Miss, dau of the late John WARNER, Esq., in Balt, 20 Jun 1826, by the Rev. Mr. Henshaw (DG 27 Jun 1826)

NILES, Mary, see NILES, Hezekiah

NILES, Samuel, see NILES, Hezekiah

NIXON, Charles, see NIXON, Elizabeth

NIXON, Elizabeth, Mrs., of Dover, dau of John PRYOR, Esq., of Dover, dec'd. She m before her 17th yr, Vincent LOCKERMAN, by whom she had two children, Mrs. Thomas BRADFORD of Phila and Mr. Nicholas LOCKERMAN of Dover. Her husband died in 1785 and in 1788, she m Mr. Charles NIXON, who d in 1796, leaving three children, only one of whom survives her. Early in April, Mrs. NIXON was called to Cambridge, MD, to care for her sick dau, and it was there that she died, 9 May 1827, in her 71st yr (DG 25 May 1827)

NIXON, Isabella S., see BODINE, Samuel T.

NIXON, Jeremiah S., see BODINE, Samuel T.

NIXON, Thomas, see MILLER, Robert

NOBLE, Alexander, see NOBLE, Louisa

NOBLE, Louisa, Mrs, wife of Alexander NOBLE, 19 May 1848, in Caroline Co MD, near the Del. line (DG 28 May 1848)

NOBLE, Margaret, dec'd, late of Kent Co, notice given by Edward FOARD, adm'r, for demands to be "lodged with" William BURRELL (DE 2 Nov 1797)

NOBLE, William, of Phila, to **ZEBLEY**, Mary, Miss, of Brandywine, 7 Feb 1850, by Rev. William Cooper (DG 15 Feb 1850)

NOBLE, William, to **DINGEY**, Joanna B., both of NC Co, 18 Feb 1847, by Rev. M. J. Rhees (DG 23 Feb 1847)

NOBLE, William, to **KINDER**, Rhoda Ann, Miss, all of Sussex Co, 14 Jan 1851, by James Hargis (DG 28 Jan 1851)

NOBLET, Sarah Jane B., see **SWAYNE**, Jacob

NOBLIT, Dell, Esq., see **CHANDLER**, Gregg,

NOBLIT, Elizabeth B., see **MOORE**, George H.

NOBLIT, Hamilton, in Wilm, 15 Dec 1847, of consumption (DG 17 Dec 1847)
see **SWAYNE**, Jacob
see **MOORE**, George H.

NOBLIT, Maria Louisa, see **CHANDLER**, Gregg,

NOBLITT, John, to **CHANDLER**, Sarah H, dau of Benjamin CHANDLER, both of Wilm, 22 Apr 1841, by Rev. S. R. Wynkoop (DG 23 Apr 1841)

NOEL, Andrew, barber, colored, in Wilm, 20 Jan 1822 (DG 25 Jan 1822)

NOEL, Andrew, Jr., dec'd, notice given by Laurette NOEL, sole adm'x (DG 4 Dec 1828)

NOEL, Laurette, see **NOEL**, Andrew, Jr.,

NONES, Jefferson, Lieut, to **JOHNSTON**, Ellen, Miss, all of Wilm, 3 Mar 1853, by the Rev. Mr. Atwood (DG 4 Mar 1853)

NORMAN, Emily A., Miss, dau of Joseph and Jemima NORMAN of Wilm, in Phila, at the res. of her uncle, Mr. James F. GALBREATH, of inflammation of the lungs, 13 Mar 1835, aged 15 yrs (DG 20 Mar 1835)

NORMAN, Jemima, see **NORMAN**, Emily A.,

NORMAN, Joseph, see **NORMAN**, Emily A.,

NORRIS, Ann, Miss, in Wilm at the res. of her niece, Mrs. N. GREEN, ndd, aged 77 yrs (DG 18 Nov 1845)

NORRIS, George Pepper, of Phila. to **CAMPBELL**, Agnes, only dau of John H. PRICE of Wilm, in Wilm, 5 Oct 1852, by Rev. Mr. Van Deusen (DG 8 Oct 1852)

NORRIS, Lydia Ann, see **YOUNG**, Thomas T.

NORTH, George L., to **LUKENS**, Rebecca J., Miss, all of Kent Co, 4 Mar 1852, by the Rev. H. E. Gilroy (DG 16 Mar 1852)

NORTH, Joshua, see **EMPSON**, William

NORTON, Caroline G., see **NORTON**, William A.

NORTON, Nathaniel, see **NORTON**, William A.

NORTON, William A., youngest son of Nathaniel NORTON, dec'd., and Caroline G. NORTON, in Newark, of scarlet fever after 2 days illness, 21 Jun 1847, aged 2 yrs 3 mos (DG 29 Jun 1847)

NORWOOD, Elizabeth, see **McCRONE**, John

NORWOOD, Lucretia L. D., see **HANSON**, Benj. R.

NORWOOD, Thomas D., see **HANSON**, Benj. R.

NORWOOD, William, of Lewistown, to **TURNER**, Mary A., Miss, of Camden NJ, 18 Apr 1850, by Rev. Mr. Scott (DG 17 May 1850)
18 May 1850, by Rev. Mr. Scott (DG 28 May 1850)

NOWEL, Mary, see **NEWSON**, Alfred

NOWELL, Mary Jane, see **MOORE**, John

NOWELL, Phenor, see **SATTERFIELD**, M.

NOWLAND, Francis, see **KYLE**, Robert

NOXON, Thomas, late of Noxontown, NC Co. Property to be let by John ROSS in Phila or Abraham GOODING and John VANCE in NC Co (PG 28 Nov 1745)

NULL, William, of Dearfield NJ, to **HOLLAND**, Mary E., Miss, of Wilm, 16 Sep 1848, by Rev. S. R. Wynkoop (DG 15 Sep 1848)

NUTTER, Sophia Louisa, see **DAVIS**, James, Esq.

O'BRIAN, Bridget,
see SWARTZ, George C.

O'DANIEL, David F., 16 Apr 1845, in Wilm (DG 22 Apr 1845)

SPRINGER, Levi H., to FRIST, Esther Ann, Miss, all of Wilm, 17 Apr 1845, in Phila, by Rev. Daniel Dodge (DG 22 Apr 1845)

O'DANIEL, Eliza Ann, inf dau of William F. O'DANIEL, Thursday night, [6 Jun 1844] aged 8 mos and 11 days (DG 11 Jun 1844)

O'DANIEL, Elizabeth E.,
see O'DANIEL, Emma

O'DANIEL, Emma, dau of Wm. F. and Elizabeth E. O'DANIEL, 30 Jan 1851, na (DG 4 Feb 1851)

O'DANIEL, Francis, Esq., to ROBINETT, Rachel, Miss, both of Wilm, 12 Aug 1816, by Rev. William Wickes (AW 14 Aug 1816)

O'DANIEL, Francis, Esq., formerly of Wilm, in Phila, 12 Feb 1827, aged 59 yrs (DG 16 Feb 1827)
see JONES, Edward C.

O'DANIEL, George, to FILE, Mary, Miss, 7 Feb 1826, by the Rev. E. W. Gilbert, all of Wilm (DG 10 Feb 1826)

O'DANIEL, John, formerly of Wilm, a returned volunteer from the Mexican War, in Phila, 13 Oct 1848, in his 38th yr (DG 20 Oct 1848)

O'DANIEL, Maria Louisa B.,
see JONES, Edward C.

O'DANIEL, Mary B., see VANAKEN, William

O'DANIEL, Sarah, wife of William F. O'DANIEL, 23 Jan 1844 (DG 23 Jan 1844)

O'DANIEL, William F., to DePUY, Elizabeth Eves, Miss, dau of the late Dr. DePUY, all of Wilm, 12 Jun 1845, in St. Andrew's Church by the Rt. Rev. Bishop Alfred Lee (DG 13 Jun 1845)
see O'DANIEL, Eliza Ann
see O'DANIEL, Sarah

O'DANIEL, Wm. F., see O'DANIEL, Emma

O'DONALD, Martha, dec'd, late of Wilm, notice given by John GORDON, adm'r (AW 19 Nov 1817)

O'DONNELL, Mary,
see MONAGHAN, James

O'FLINN, Patrick, Capt., at Wilm, 7 Jul 1818, in his 70th yr; "Soldier of the Revolution and an honest man" (AW 15 Jul 1818) innkeeper, notice given by Alexander REYNOLDS, adm'r (DG 5 Aug 1818)

O'HANLEN, Mary, see RYAN, Patrick

O'NEIL, Mary Ann, Mrs, at Breck's Mill, Brandywine, 8 Jan 1848, aged 22 yrs (DG 21 Jan 1848)

O'NEILL, J., to CONNER, Margaret Anne, Miss, both of Wilm, 22 Sep 1851, by the Rev. Reilly, of St. Mary's Ch (DG 26 Sep 1851)

OCHELTREE, Hannah,
see BISHOP, Uriah C.

OCHELTREE, Isabella,
see McKENNON, Thomas

OCHELTREE, John, to DONNELL, Elizabeth, Miss, both of Mill Creek Hd, in Wilm, 18 Dec 1823, by the Rev. E. W. Gilbert (DG 19 Dec 1823)

OCHELTREE, John, watchmaker, at New Castle, 27 Aug 1824, na (DG 31 Aug 1824)

OCHELTREE, John J., aged 24 yrs, a native of New Castle, 12 yrs a resident of Phila, and last year a citizen of Galveston, of yellow fever in Galveston TX, 16 Oct 1847 (DG 5 Nov 1847)

OCHELTREE, Maxwell B., to LINDSEY, Elizabeth E., all of Mill Creek Hd, NC Co, 17 Apr 1845, by Rev. Thomas Love (DG 22 Apr 1845)

OCHELTREE, Robert,
see VANDEGRIFT, William
see REESE, Lewis

OCHELTREE, Robert, to VANDEGRIFT, Rebecca Ann, Miss, dau of William VANDEGRIFT, Esq., 4 Sep 1827, in Dragon Neck, by the Rev. S. W. Woolford (DG 18 Sep 1827)

ODLE, Benjamin, at Christiana, 29 Aug 1851, aged c 35 yrs (DG 5 Sep 1851)

OGDEN, Clarkson, to CANBY, Lydia, dau of Charles CANBY, Esq., in Wilm, 6 Feb 1851, by Friends ceremony in the presence of Hon. Joseph E. Driver, Mayor of Wilm (DG 7 Feb 1851)

OGDEN, Edward, to McINTYRE, Elizabeth, Miss, all of Wilm, 20 Sep 1846, by Rev. S. S. Southerland (DG 25 Sep 1846)

OGDEN, John, of consumption, 5 May 1843 (DG 12 May 1843)

OGDEN, John T., to SMITH, Sarah Ann, Miss, all of Wilm, 21 May 1846, by Rev. A. Atwood (DG 29 May 1846)

OGDEN, Orpha, see HALL, John

OGLE, Benjamin G., late of White Clay Creek Hd, William R. LYNAM, exec'r (DG 12 Sep 1851)

OGLE, Benjamin, to LYNAM, Ellen, Miss, both of White Clay Creek, NC Co, in Phila, 20 Dec 1848 (DG 5 Jan 1849)

OGLE, Elizabeth, see CURRENDER, John

OGLE, Esther, Mrs, relict of Peter L. OGLE, Esq., of Christiana Bridge DE, in Phila, 5 Mar 1848, in her 81st yr (DG 17 Mar 1848)

OGLE, Hannah Maria, see SIMPSON, Samuel

OGLE, Jane, see MARVIN, Ebenezer

OGLE, Peter, see SIMPSON, Samuel

OGLE, Peter L., see OGLE, Esther

OGLE, Thomas J., to McCOY, Isabella, Miss, both of NC Co, 8 Oct 1835, by the Rev. A. K. Russel (DG 13 Oct 1835)

OGRAM, Alice, see OGRAM, Mary

OGRAM. James, see OGRAM, Mary

OGRAM, Mary, dau of James and Alice OGRAM, in New Castle Hd, 19 Feb 1852, in her 5th yr (DG 24 Feb 1852)

OLDHAM, Edward, Major, of Bohemia Manor, eldest son of Col. Edward OLDHAM, 10 Feb 1849, in his 65th yr (DG 20 Feb 1849)

OLIVER, John, Capt., of yellow fever (DE 16 Sep 1798) dec'd, late of Wilm, notice given by Thomas MENDENHALL, adm'r (DE 10 Dec 1798)

OLIVER, Joseph, to WALKER, Sarah, both of Sussex Co, 6 Jul 1853 (DG 22 Jul 1853)

OLIVER, Thomas, Jr., of Phila, to HOWARD, Sarah Ann, Miss, dau of Thomas HOWARD, Esq., of Lewes, at Lewes, 9 Oct 1833, by the Rev. Michelmore (DG 18 Oct 1833)

OPIE, Margaret S., see RIDDLE, George Read

ORELL, James K., to KING, Lucretia, Miss, both of Cantwell's Bridge DE, in Phila, 24 Aug 1851, by the Rev. John W. Arthur (DG 29 Aug 1851)

ORPWOOD, Thomas, to MOORE, Ann Eliza, Miss, both of Wilm, 5 Oct 1848, by Rev. T. J. Thompson (DG 14 Oct 1848)

ORR, William P., of Lewes, to HUNTER, Emily, Miss, of Cool Spring, Sussex Co, 25 Oct 1850, by Rev. George Hall (DG 5 Nov 1850)

ORTLIP, Eliza W., see WALLACE, John A.

OSBORN, Martha, see OSBORN, William Cooper

OSBORN, Seleck, Esq., formerly editor of the *American Watchman*, in Phila, recently (DG 27 Oct 1826)

OSBORN, William Cooper, youngest son of William S. and Martha OSBORN, in Wilm, 14 Mar 1851, aged 6 mos (DG 18 Mar 1851)

OSBORN, William S., of Harford Co MD, to BUZINE, Martha, of Wilm, 6 Apr 1847, in Chester, by Rev. A. B. Hard (DG 9 Apr 1847) see OSBORN, William Cooper

OSBORNE, John W., of Kent Co MD, to THOMAS, Margaret Ann, Miss, of Wilm, 9 May 1843, by Rev. Mr. Hogarth (DG 12 May 1843)

OSGOOD, Delia C., see MORGAN, James T.

OSKINS, Jane M., see SIMPLER, George M.

OSKINS, William H., to HERRING, Margaret Ann, Miss, of Phila, in Phila, 20 Aug 1851, by Rev. Humphries (DG 29 Aug 1851)

OSLERE, Davis, see OSLERS, Davis

OSLERS, Davis, dec'd, late of B'wine Hd, sale of property by Joseph WALKER, Jr. and Amos SLAYMAKER, adm'rs (DG 31 Jul 1827) Obit on 24 Aug gives name as OSLERE, Davis

OSMOND, A. P., see OSMOND, William

OSMOND, Eliza, see OSMOND, Fanny

OSMOND, Fanny, youngest dau of Jesse and Eliza OSMOND, 17 May 1848, aged 18 mos and 5 days (DG 19 May 1848)

OSMOND, Jesse, see OSMOND, Fanny

OSMOND, Sarah, see OSMOND. William

OSMOND, William, eldest son of A. P. and Sarah OSMOND, of typhoid, 23 Oct 1850, aged 21 yrs 1 mo 23 days (DG 1 Nov 1850)

OTLEY, Abner, dec'd, late of Wilm, Ezra HOOPES, adm'r (DG 10 Jul 1827)

OVERLEY, Thomas W., in Georgetown DE, at the house of Philip C. JONES, Esq., 21 Jun 1853, na (DG 28 Jun 1853)

OWENS, David, , dec'd, late of Sussex Co, notice given by James OWENS and David PENNAWELL (DG 16 Sep 1818)

OWENS, Garrett, to CARPENTER, Sarah J., both of Milford, 30 Sep 1852, by the Rev. Daniel Godwin (DG 19 Oct 1852)

OWENS, James, see OWENS, David

OWENS, John, late of NC Co, OWENS, Mary, adm'x (DG 8 May 1827) see OWENS, Mary

OWENS, Margaret W., see WILLEY, Ezekiel

OWENS, Mary Ann, see WALLER, Stansbury W.

OWENS, Mary, widow of Dr. John OWENS, dec'd, late of Milford, near Milford, 12 Apr 1847 (DG 23 Apr 1847) see OWENS, John

OWENS, Virginia A., see TOUCHTINE, James

OWENS, Wm. H. to PRETTYMAN, Elizabeth W., both of Milford, 9 Feb 1853 (DG 11 Feb 1853)

OZIER, Martha, see BURGESS, Levi

O'CONNOR, J. Blight, see SHIPLEY, Thomas, Esq.

O'CONNOR, Sophia, see SHIPLEY, Thomas, Esq.

O'DANIEL, W. F., see HENRY, John J.

PAGE, Henry H., to STOOPS, Mary A., Miss, both of NC Co, 29 Sep 1852, by the Rev. J. A. Roche (DG 26 Oct 1852)

PAINTER, Rachel, see HAWKE, John

PAINTER, Sarah Ann, see MOORE, Shadrack D.

PAISLEY, Mary, see RIDGWAY, Jacob

PALMATORY, Robert, see COLLINS, William

PALMATORY, Robert, Esq., of Smyrna, to BEAUCHAMP, Sarah A., Mrs., of Cantwell's Bridge, 24 Jul 1848, at J. V. MOORE'S, by Rev. J. D. Perkins (DG 18 Aug 1848)

PALMATORY, Sarah A., see COLLINS, William

PALMER, Daniel C., of Kent Co DE, to ELLIOTT, Martha Georgiana, Miss, of Q. Anne's Co MD, 4 Jan 1853, by Rev. Charles Brown (DG 7 Jan 1853)

PALMER, Eliza, Miss, 21 July 1853, near Woollytown (DG 2 Aug 1853)

PALMER, Eliza, see RAYHOW, William

PALMER, John, dec'd, of Little Creek Hd, notice by James LAFFERTY, adm'r (FA 7 Feb 1803)

PALMER, John, of Wilm, to GRAY, Sarah B., dau of William GRAY of Brandywine Hd, 22 Feb 1848, by Rev. A. B. Hard (DG 7 Mar 1848)

PALMER, John, see PALMER, Sarah R.

PALMER, Levick, of Kent Co, to HARTLEY, Cornelia P., of Wilm, 27 Apr 1848, by Friends ceremony (DG 2 May 1848)

PALMER, Morris W., to WEBB, Mary, dau of Benjamin WEBB, all of Wilm, 7 Apr 1842 at Friends Meeting (DG 15 Apr 1842)

PALMER, Peter D., in Phila, 18 Jan 1851, in his 45th yr (DG 24 Jan 1851)

PALMER, Sarah R., wife of John PALMER, in Brandywine Village, 21 Mar 1853, aged c 28 yrs (DG 25 Mar 1853)

PALMER, William, to SIMPLER, Elizabeth, Miss, 3 Feb 1850, by Rev. J. R. Torbert (DG 12 Feb 1850)

PALMETORY, Lebena, see PRITCHETT, Edward R.

PANADER, Henry, to DELE VAN, Rosanna, both of Wilm, 4 Nov 1847, by Rev. Levi Stokes (DG 25 Nov 1847)

PANCOAST, Robert T., to ALCOCK, Rachel Ann J., both of Phila, 8 Jun 1848, by Rev. D. L. Carroll, D. D. of Newark (DG 20 Jun 1848)

PANCOAST, Samuel, see BYRNES, Thomas

PAPEL, Thomas, to WALKER, Martha, Miss, both of Chester Co, PA, 10 May 1821, by the Rev. E. W. Gilbert (DG 15 May 1821)

PARADEE, Charles, to PRETTYMAN,

Harriet, Miss, both of NC Co, at Christiana Bridge, 18 Jun 1846, by Rev. William Ryder (DG 7 Jul 1846)

PARADEE, Rachel, see **STOKES**, Priestly

PARADISE, Catharine, see **PARADISE**, Ellavene

PARADISE, Ellavene, inf dau of William H. and Catharine PARADISE, of bronchitis of the chest and brain inflammation, 9 Mar 1845, aged 10 mos (DG 14 Mar 1845)

PARADISE, William H., see **PARADISE**, Ellavene

PARDEE, Isaac, the Rev., Rector of Trinity Ch, Wilm, to **BENNETT**, Boadiciea (sic), Miss, dau of Caleb BENNETT, Gov. of DE, in Christ Ch, Phila, 1 May 1834, by Rt. Rev. Bishop White (DG 6 May 1834)

PARIS, William, to **McDANIEL**, Catharine, Miss,both of NC Co, 29 Aug 1833, by the Rev. A. K. Russel (DG 3 Sep 1833)

PARK, John, Col., at Poplar Grove in Kent, 10 Dec 1789, in his 36th yr. Buried Christ Ch (DG 26 Dec 1789)

PARKE, Francis, Esq., of Chester Co, PA, to **HUNTER**, Mary, Mrs., of Wilm, in Wilm, 3 Feb 1851, by the Rev. E. M. Van Duezen (DG 7 Feb 1851)

PARKER, Ala Anna, see **SHORT**, Allen

PARKER, Eliza B., widow of the late John E. PARKER, Esq., of Georgetown, and eldest dau of Dr. Wm. W. WOLFE of Milford, 9 Apr 1852, na (DG 16 Apr 1852)

PARKER, Emma, dau of Thomas and Lydia PARKER, in Wilm, ndd, aged 3 yrs (DG 13 Jun 1845)

PARKER, Hannah E., see **WILLIAMS**, Robert H.

PARKER, Henry L., of St. Louis MO, to **RUSSELL**, Jane, (or **HOWARD**, Jane Russell) dau of Thomas HOWARD, Esq., of Lewis, at Lewis, 17 Dec 1851, by the Rev. C. H. Mustard (DG 23 Dec 1851)

PARKER, James, at Georgetown, 15 May 1851, na (DG 20 May 1851)

PARKER, John, see **WARNER**, Frances B.

PARKER, John E., of Georgetown, to **WOLFE**, Eliza B., dau of William WOLFE, of Milton, at Milton, 24 Jan 1851, by Rev. John L. McKim (DG 7 Feb 1851)

PARKER, John E., young lawyer, at his res. in Georgetown, 12 Aug 1851, na (DG 19 Aug 1851) see **PARKER**, Eliza B.

PARKER, Joshua, see **LOBB**, Joseph

PARKER, Louisa White, see **WARNER**, Frances B.

PARKER, Lydia, see **PARKER**, Emma

PARKER, Peter S., merchant of Milton, Sussex Co, 23 Dec 1849, aged 56 yrs (DG 1 Jan 1850)

PARKER, Thomas, see **PARKER**, Emma

PARKER, Wm. C. to **CLEAVER**, Rachel, Miss, both of NC Co, at Port Penn. 6 Jun 1849, by Rev. J. W. K. Handy (DG 26 Jun 1849)

PARKES, Levina, see **STEWART**, Jno B.

PARKINSON, Richardson, to **CHANDLER**, Ellen, Miss, both of Newark, at Blockley, 4 Jul 1847, by Rev. John J. Baker (DG 16 Jul 1847)

PARMER, Julia A., see **SUTHEL**, William

PARMITER, James Clark, son of the Rev. S. C. PARMITER, 7 Oct 1852, na (DG 19 Oct 1852)

PARMITER, S. C., Rev., see **PARMITER**, James Clark

PARPER, Charlotte A., see **COOMBE**, Pennell

PARPER, James, see **COOMBE**, Pennell

PARRIS, Jane, see **HENDERSON**, Levi

PARRY, Ann, see **SWAYNE**, Henry

PARSONS, Adeline, wife of the late Charles PARSONS of Wilm, in Phila, 17 Oct 1851, in her 30th yr (DG 21 Oct 1851)

PARSONS, Adeline, see **PARSONS**, Charles

PARSONS, Amelia, see **MEREDITH**, John

PARSONS, Charles, in Wilm after a short illness, 26 Jul 1848, in his 27th yr (DG 28 Jul 1848)

PARSONS, Charles, inf son of the late Charles and Adline F. PARSONS, in Phila, 13 Aug 1849, aged 6 mos (DG 17 Aug 1849)

PARSONS, Charles,

see **PARSONS**, Adeline

PARSONS, Henry R., of Smyrna, to **MAY**, Elenora, dau of Joshua MAY, Esq., of Queen Anne's Co MD, 18 Jan 1853, by the Very Rev. Samuel M. Cooper (DG 11 Feb 1853)

PARSONS, Isaac, see **HURLOCK**. Abraham

PARSONS, Sarah A., see **HURLOCK**, Abraham

PARSONS, Sarah, Miss, in New Haven, CT, brotherly prank results in sad death, ndd, na (DG 8 May 1827)

PARVIN, Theophilus, the Rev., of Buenos Ayres, to **RODNEY**, Mary, Miss, dau of the late Hon. Caesar A. RODNEY, Minister Plenipotentiary from the U. S. to Buenos Ayres, in Phila, 6 Jan 1826, by the Rev. William M. Engles (DG 10 Jan 1826)

PARVIS, John T., see **PARVIS**, Wilhelmina

PARVIS, Margaret, see **FORREST**, William

PARVIS, Mary, see **PARVIS**, Wilhelmina

PARVIS, Wilhelmina, dau of John T., and Mary PARVIS, in Milford, 8 Jul 1852, aged 11 mos 11 days (DG 27 Jul 1852)

PAS WATERS (sic), John, to **DICKENSON**, Mary, Miss, 27 Jan 1852, by Rev. Daniel Goodwin (DG 3 Feb 1852)

PASCHALL, Henry M., of Kingsessing, Phila Co, PA to **DIXON**, Mary Ann, of Wilm, 3 Dec 1840, at Friends Meeting (DG 4 Dec 1840)

PASS, Rebecca Ellen, see **McCORMICK**, Lewis

PASSWATERS, William to **SIMPSON**, Mary M., Miss, all of Wilm, 10 Sep 1846, by Rev. A. Atwood (DG 18 Sep 1846)

PATTEN, Ann, see **WALES**, Ann

PATTEN, John, Maj., see **WALES**, Ann

PATTEN, John, see **MILLER**, Joseph

PATTERSON, _____, Mrs., consort of Rev. Mr. PATTERSON, formerl;y of Wilm, 13 Jan 1786. Buried Christiana Church Burying Ground (DG 18 Jan 1766)

PATTERSON, _____. Rev. see **PATTERSON**, _____, Mrs.,

PATTERSON, Abigail, Mrs., see **ISRAEL**, George

PATTERSON, Alfred, Esq., atty at law, Union Town, PA, to **WHITELY**, Mary Caroline, Miss, eldest dau of Col. Henry WHITELY of Wilm, at Wilm, 20 May 1834, by the Rev. A. K. Russel (DG 23 May 1834)

PATTERSON, Amelia R., see **WEBSTER**, John A.

PATTERSON, Amey Eliza, see **ISRAEL**, George

PATTERSON, Helen L., see **PATTERSON**, Rosalie Sherron

PATTERSON, James, son of Thomas, of yellow fever (DE 17 Sep 1798)

PATTERSON, John, see **WEBSTER**, John A. see **WORTH**, Emmor

PATTERSON, John, 12 Feb 1836, aged 65 yrs (DG 16 Feb 1836)

PATTERSON, John C., see **ROBINSON**, Jacob see **PATTERSON**, Rosalie Sherron

PATTERSON, Margaret R., see **JONES**, James H.

PATTERSON, Mary, see **FRED**, Benjamin

PATTERSON, Robert, at his res. in Smyrna, 2 Mar 1852, aged 85 yrs (DG 16 Mar 1852)

PATTERSON, Rosalie Sherron, inf dau of John C. and Helen L. PATTERSON, 8 Apr 1850, in Wilm (DG 12 Apr 1850)

PATTERSON, Samuel, to **POWELL**, Mary, Miss, 25 Feb or Mar 1823, by the Rev. J. Canby, all of Kent Co, DE (DG 1 Apr 1823)

PATTERSON, Susannah Maria, see **KIRKPATRICK**, David M., M. D.

PATTERSON, Thomas, see **PATTERSON**, James

PATTON, Willliam J., near Newark, 28 Aug 1852, aged c 25 yrs (DG 10 Sep 1852)

PAUL, Camilla, see **SMITH**, Jacob J.,

PAULSON, Aaron, see **PAULSON**, Charles see **PAULSON**, Joel

PAULSON, Charles, dec'd, late of Newport, Aaron PAULSON, exec'r (DE 12 Apr 1798)

PAULSON, Joel, dec'd, late of NEWPORT, notice given by Aaron PAULSON, adm'r

DELAWARE MARRIAGES AND DEATHS FROM NEWSPAPERS, 1729-1853   185

(DE 22 Aug 1799)

PAULSON, Peter,
see PORTER, John B.

PAULSON, Peter, merchant of Wilm, to ROBBISON, Mary, Miss, near Newport, 18 Jan 1810, by the Rev. Mr. Pryce (DG 20 Jan 1810)

PAULSON, Susanna R., Miss
see PORTER, John B.

PAXSON, Ann, wife of William PAXSON of Wilm, and dau of the late Samuel CANBY, near W. Chester Pa, 10 Aug 1849, na (DG 21 Aug 1849)

PAXSON, Isaac, see MARRIOTT, Sarah

PAXSON, William, see PAXSON, Ann

PAYNTER, Alfred, to BROWN, Mary Jane, Miss, both of Wilm, 9 Sep 1846, in Marcus Hook PA by Rev. Mr. Walker (DG 18 Sep 1846)

PAYNTER, Alfred S., son of Samuel PAYNTER, Esq., near Lewis, of croup, 20 Sep 1822, aged 5 yrs 8 mos 20 days (DG 4 Oct 1822)

PAYNTER, Catharine,
see JANVIER, George

PAYNTER, David, see JANVIER, George

PAYNTER, John, carpenter, in Wilm, 16 Sep 1853, aged 79 yrs 8 mos (DG 27 Sep 1853)

PAYNTER, John P., son of Samuel PAYNTER, Esq., at the res. of his father after a protracted illness, 8 Aug 1845, aged 38 yrs (DG 22 Aug 1845)

PAYNTER, Margaret C., see PYLE, William

PAYNTER, Rebecca, see WILKINS, John

PAYNTER, Ruth C., see WHITE, John W.

PAYNTER, Sally A.,
see PAYNTER, Samuel R.

PAYNTER, Samuel,
see PAYNTER, John P.
see WILTBANK, John Cornelius
see PAYNTER, Alfred S.

PAYNTER, Samuel, Hon, at his res. at the Drawbridge, Sussex Co, 2 Oct 1845, aged 78 yrs (DG 14 Oct 1845)
see PAYNTER, Sarah A.

PAYNTER, Samuel R.,
see PAYNTER, Samuel S.

PAYNTER, Samuel R., at his res. Drawbridge, Sussex Co DE, 20 Feb 1851, in his 50th yr (DG 28 Feb 1851) late of Broadkiln Hd. Sally A. PAYNTER and Edward WOOTEN, adm'rs (DG 6 May 1851)

PAYNTER, Samuel S., son of the late Samuel R. PAYNTER, at Drawbridge DE, 22 Aug 1851, aged 16 yrs 9 mos (DG 26 Aug 1851)

PAYNTER, Sarah A., Miss, dau of the Hon. Sam'l PAYNTER, 11 Aug 1820, aged 17 yrs (DG 22 Aug 1820)

PAYNTER, William, see PYLE, William

PEACH. Eliza Y., Mrs., wife of John PEACH, Jr.,at the res. of her husband in Bohemia Manor, Cecil Co, MD, 10 Mar 1849, aged 33 yrs   (DG 27 Apr 1849)

PEACH, James, to PENOYERS, Sarah Ann, Miss, in New York, 18 Apr 1833 (DG 3 May 1833)

PEACH, John, see PEACH, Mary, Miss
see DALZELL, Mary Ann
see PEACH, Margaret
see PLUME, A. B.
see HASSAN, Peter

PEACH, John, to HAWTHORN, Emeline, Miss, all of NC Co, 7 Apr 1846, by Rev. Mr. Work (DG 21 Apr 1846)

PEACH, John, Jr., see PEACH, Eliza Y.
see PEACH, Margaret

PEACH, Margaret, Miss, dau of John PEACH, in New Castle Hd, 13 Dec 1842 (DG 16 Dec 1842)

PEACH, Margaret, Mrs., at the res. of her son John PEACH, Jr., in Mill Creek Hd, ndd, in her 83rd yr (DG 19 Apr 1853)

PEACH, Mary, Miss, dau of Mr. John PEACH, in New Castle Hd, 2 Aug 1825, aged 23 yrs (DG 9 Aug 1825)

PEACH, Phoebe Ann, see PLUME, A. B.

PEARCE, George, Esq., 1st Lt. U. S. Frigate *Macedonian*, at Graney Island, [7 Aug 1822] "Wednesday last "(DG 13 Aug 1822)

PEARCE, George, Esq., Justice of the Peace, at New Castle, 26 Feb 1826, na (DG 28 Feb 1826)
see PEARCE, Mary, Mrs.

PEARCE, James Alfred, Hon., U. S. Senator from MD, to RINGGOLD, Matilda C., dau of the late Richard RINGGOLD of Kent Co DE, 22 Mar 1847, in Kent Co MD, by Rev. G. F.

PEARCE, Lydia, see SNYDER, Samuel

PEARCE, Mary, Mrs., wife of PEARCE, George, Esq., 26 Feb 1826, na (DG 28 Feb 1826)
see PEARCE, George, Esq.

PEARSON, John, see WILLIAMS, William

PEARSON, Joseph
see ARMSTRONG, William

PEARSON, Rebecca,
see ARMSTRONG, William

PECKARD, Henry L., to CANN, Mary, Miss, both of Christiana Bridge, in Wilm, 29 Jan 1829, by the Rev. E. W. Gilbert (DG 3 Feb 1829)
see PECKARD, Mary Elizabeth
see PECKARD, Susannah

PECKARD, Mary Elizabeth, dau of Henry L. and Mary Elizabeth PECKARD, at the res. of her parents at Delaware City, 11 Jun 1848, in her 18th yr (DG 13 Jun 1848)
see PECKARD, Susannah

PECKARD, Susannah, only remaining dau of Squire Henry L. and Mary Elizabeth PECKARD, at Delaware City, 17 Dec 1850, aged 9 yrs 8 mos 17 days (DG 20 Dec 1850)

PECKWORTH, J. P. Rev., to SUMMERS, Mary, Mrs., of Phila, 12 Sep 1820 (DG 15 Sep 1820)

PECKWORTH, John P., Rev., in Wilm, 7 Mar 1845, aged 75 yrs (DG 14 Mar 1845)

PECKY, Esther C., see CLARK, Esther C.

PECKY, Samuel, see CLARK, Esther C.

PEDRECK, Isaac,
see PEDRECK, Joshua

PEDRECK, Joshua, dec'd, late of Wilm, notice given by Isaac PEDRECK, Gideon SCULL and Stephen HAYES, exec'rs (DE 22 Aug 1799)

PEDRICK, Hannah,
see PEDRICK, Jane Kennaday

PEDRICK, Jane Kennaday, 4th dau of Mark and Hannah PEDRICK, in Wilm, 27 Aug 1850, aged 4 yrs 5 mos 10 days (DG 27 Aug 1850)

PEDRICK, Mark,
see PEDRICK, Jane Kennaday

PEDRICK, T. Sargent, to McKINLEY, Mary Jane, Miss, all of Phila, 19 Jun 1853, by Rev. J. A. Roche (DG 24 Jun 1853)

PEDRICK, William H., to FIRESTONE, Sarah, Miss, both from NJ, in Wilm, 2 Apr 1829, by the Rev. E. W. Gilbert (DG 7 Apr 1829)

PEEKY, Anna Lareine, see STOTSENBURG, Evan C.

PEERY, James C., see PEERY, Margaret

PEERY, Margaret, wife of James C. PEERY, 29 Oct 1847, aged 39 yrs (DG 16 Nov 1847)

PEIRCE, Caleb, of Chester, PA, to MAY, Mary A., Miss, of Wilm, dau of the late Rev. Thomas P. MAY of Norristown, 10 Dec 1835, by Samuel T. Walker (DG 18 Dec 1835)

PEIRCE, George, Esq.,dec'd, late of New Castle, notice given by James COUPER, adm'r (DG 18 Apr 1826)

PEIRCE, John Lee, to HOWELL, Margaret, Miss, 27 Aug 1835, by Elder John P. Peckworth, all of Wilm (DG 4 Sep 1835)

PEIRCE, Joseph W., of NC Co, to ESHER, Sarah Anna, of Phila, 18 Feb 1853, by Rev. B. R. Loxley (DG 25 Feb 1853)

PENINGTON, Caroline, at the res. of her father, Mr. Fredus PENINGTON, near Christiana Bridge, DE, of whooping cough and measles, 13 May 1829, aged 6 yrs 4 mos (DG 22 May 1829)

PENINGTON, Edmund, son of Hyland B. Jr and Eliza Ann PENINGTON, 31 Mar 1846, aged 3 yrs 19 days (DG 3 Apr 1846)

PENINGTON, Eliza Ann,
see PENINGTON, Edmund

PENINGTON, Fredus,
see PENINGTON, William,
see PENINGTON, James Munro
see PENINGTON, Caroline.
A fourth child, unnamed, survived

PENINGTON, Hyland B.,
see RICE, Thomas B.
see CROOKSHANKS, Mary Ann
see PENINGTON, Edmund

PENINGTON, James Munro, at the res. of his father, Mr. Fredus PENINGTON, near Christiana Bridge, DE, of whooping cough and measles, 4 May 1829, aged 3 yrs 9 mos (DG 22 May 1829)

PENINGTON, Martha Elizabeth,
see RICE, Thomas B.

PENINGTON, Mary Ann, see
CROOKSHANKS, Mary Ann

PENINGTON, William, at the res. of his
father, Mr. Fredus PENINGTON, near
Christiana Bridge, DE, of whooping cough
and measles, 3 May 1829, aged 17 mos
(DG 22 May 1829)

PENNAWELL, David, see OWENS, David

PENNELL, Rebecca, see TRUITT, Zadoc

PENNEPACKER, Margaret A.,
see FLINN, Daniel B.

PENNEVILL, Roberto, Esq., to CLARKE,
Elizabeth, Miss, dau of the late John
CLARKE, Esq., formerly Register of Kent Co,
at Dover, 2 Mar 1827, by the Rev. Solomon
Higgins (DG 6 Mar 1827)

PENNEWELL, Robert O., Esq.,
(DG 20 Aug 1850)

PENNEY, Ann,
see DERICKSON, Sarah Ann

PENNEY, David,
see DERICKSON, Sarah Ann

PENNEY, Sarah Ann,
see DERRICKSON, Joseph S.

PENNINGTON, Alrich, of St. Georges Hd, to
WAITHMAN, Mary, Mrs., of Port Penn, in
Bridgeton, 23 Jul 1826, by the Rev. J. Potts
(DG 11 Aug 1826)

PENNINGTON, Augustus Hyland, merchant
of Middletown, to COOMBE, Mary Ann,
Miss, eldest dau of Benjamin COOMBE,
Esq., of Smyrna, 20 Apr 1824
(DG 27 Apr 1824)

PENNINGTON, H. B.,
see PENNINGTON, Samuel Moody

PENNINGTON, Henrietta, Mrs., consort of
Noble PENNINGTON, Esq., of Sassafras
Neck. ndd, na (DG 3 Feb 1852)

PENNINGTON, Hyland B.,
see PENNINGTON, Josephus Francis

PENNINGTON, Hyland B., Jr., to DUNOTT,
Eliza Ann, Miss, both of Wilm, in Phila,
15 Nov 1835, by Rev. Samuel Keppler
(DG 17 Nov 1835)

PENNINGTON, Isaac, to MILLER, Mary,
Miss, both of Brandywine Hd, in Aston, Pa,
12 Jul 1849, by the Rev. Phineas Price
(DG 27 Jul 1849)

PENNINGTON, James, to GIBERSON,
Mary, Miss, both of Brandywine Hd,
29 May 1828, by Elder John P. Peckworth
(DG 6 Jun 1828)

PENNINGTON, John, to MACKEY, Maria,
Miss, both of NC Co, in Wilm 20 Jan 1850,
by Rev. A. Lee (DG 25 Jan 1850)

PENNINGTON, John B., to ROWAN,
Rebecca, Miss, both of NC Co, 8 May 1849,
by the Rev. Joseph Barr (DG 15 May 1849)

PENNINGTON, Josephus Francis, son of
Hyland B. PENNINGTON, merchant of Wilm,
3 Jan 1834, aged 7 yrs 2 mos
(DG 7 Jan 1834)

PENNINGTON, Lewis E., to PENNINGTON,
Portia Ann, Miss, both of New Castle, nmd,
by Rev. William Rider (DG 13 May 1842)

PENNINGTON, Lydia, see STIDHAM, John

PENNINGTON, Noble,
see PENNINGTON, Henrietta

PENNINGTON, Otho, formerly of Kent Co
DE, near Indianapolis, IN, 11 Dec 1852, in
his 65th yr (DG 11 Jan 1853)

PENNINGTON, Portia Ann,
see PENNINGTON, Lewis E.

PENNINGTON, Samuel Moody, son of
H. B. PENNINGTON, of Wilm, at
Pennington Seminary NJ, 4 Sep 1844,
aged 15 yrs (DG 10 Sep 1844)

PENNINGTON, Samuel, of Appoq. Hd, to
McCONEGHAY, Mary, Miss, of New Castle,
13 May 1810, by Rev. Mr. Burton
(DG 16 May 1810)

PENNINGTON, Sarah,
see PROVOST, William

PENNINGTON, Thomas McDonough,
nephew of Commodore McDONOUGH,
to BARR, Henrietta, Miss, both of New
Castle Hd, 23 Mar 1825, by the Rev. A. K.
Russel (DG 29 Mar 1825)

PENNINGTON, William R., to CLARK, Mary
J., dau of the late Thomas CLARK, both of
Wilm, 12 Dec 1843 by Rev. John Kennaday
(DG 15 Dec 1843)

PENNOCK, _____, Dr., see BRECK, Mary

PENNOCK, Harriet,
see PENNOCK, Isaac W.

PENNOCK, Isaac W., dec'd, notice given by
Harriet PENNOCK, adm'x, Doe Run, PA
(DG 17 May 1833)

PENNY, Francis Elliott, only son of Jane PENNY, of Wilm, at Jersey City, 3 Aug 1848, after an illness of 2 days (DG 8 Aug 1848)

PENNY, Jane, see PENNY, Francis Elliott

PENNY, Mary, see McCORKLE, George

PENNYPACKER, John, formerly of Wilm, at Beacon Hill MD, 4 May 1853, aged c 33 yrs (DG 10 May 1853)

PENOYERS, Sarah Ann, see PEACH, James

PENROSE, Barton, of Phila, to MEGONIGAL, Narcissa, Miss, of Milton,DE, in Phila, 14 May 1849, by Alderman C. Brazer (DG 25 May 1849)

PENROSE, H., of Phila, to DALBEY, Sarah, of Wilm, 10 Apr 1845, in Phila, by the mayor, Peter McCall (DG 2 May 1845)

PENTON, James, of Sussex Co, to COOK, Mary Ann, Miss, dau of Henry COOK, Esq., of Hill's Point, Dorchester Co MD, 21 Mar 1848, by Rev. E. Miller (DG 28 Mar 1848)

PEOPLES, John, to WHITE, Jane, Miss, both of NC Co, 17 Jun 1846, by Rev. S. M. Gayley (DG 19 Jun 1846)

PEPPER, Henry J., formerly of Wilm, in Phila, 17 Jul 1853, in his 64th yr (DG 22 Jul 1853) see PEPPER, Sarah B.

PEPPER, Peter J., to JOHNSON, Lavenia Jane, Miss, of Sussex Co, 28 Oct 1841, by Rev. Jno. R. Torbert (DG 5 Nov 1841)

PEPPER Sarah B. wife of Henry J. PEPPER, in Phila, 24 Mar 1849, in her 49th yr (DG 3 Apr 1849)

PEPPER, William S., to PRETTYMAN, Mary, Miss, dau of John PRETTYMAN, at Georgetown, 3 Sep 1834, by Rev. Jonathan Torbert (DG 12 Sep 1834)

PERCE, John, to RUSSELL, Harriet A., of DE, 28 Dec 1852, by Rev. Mr. Brooks (DG 18 Jan 1853)

PERKINS, ____, Dr., see PERKINS, ____, Mrs.

PERKINS, ____, Mrs., wife of Dr. PERKINS of Smyrna, 11 Jan 1848, at Smyrna (DG 26 Jan 1848)

PERKINS, Ann, see GRUBB, James

PERKINS, Catharine, see HARLAN, Thomas W.

PERKINS, Elizabeth, see BALDWIN, Charles H.

PERKINS, Ellen, see BAILY, Isaac

PERKINS, Francis Laura, one of twin daus of John and Sidney Ann PERKINS, at the res. of her father on Orange St, 24 Jun 1843, aged 3 mos 17 days (DG 7 Jul 1843)

PERKINS, Hannah, 29 Jul 1847, in her 55th yr (DG 10 Aug 1847)

PERKINS, Hannah A., see COUNTISS, James H.

PERKINS, J. D., Rev., of Smyrna, to HENDRIX, Eliza Ann, Mrs. of Q. Anne's Co MD, in Phila, 11 Jun 1849, by Rev. Joseph Mason (DG 19 Jun 1849)

PERKINS, John, see PERKINS, Francis Laura

PERKINS, Rachel, see QUIGLEY, Joseph

PERKINS, Reece, Sr., see QUIGLEY, Joseph

PERKINS, Sidney Ann, see PERKINS, Francis Laura

PERKINS, Thomas, Esq., dec'd, late Sheriff of NC Co, notice given by John MERRITT (DS 20 May 1812)

PERRIGO, Caroline, see TWEEDY, Jacob

PERRY, Charles. Sale of fulling mill, stone house, by Joseph BAILY of Lewistown (PG 8 Aug 1761) (PG 3 Dec 1761)

PERRY, Charlotte, see FIPPS, Cornelius

PERRY, Henry C., to THOMAS, Clarissa J., Miss, both of Wilm, 3 May 1853, by the Rev. S. R. Wynkoop (DG 6 May 1853)

PERRY, Henry C., of Wilm, to JEFFERIS, Malinda, Miss, in Chester PA, 9 Nov 1848, by Rev. Mr. Phillips (DG 21 Nov 1848) see PERRY, Malinda B.

PERRY, Jane, see HENDRICKSON, John S.

PERRY, Malinda B., consort of Henry C. PERRY, of Wilm, at the res. of her father, James JEFFERIS, in Newlin, Chester Co PA, aged 25 yrs, leaves twins (DG 26 Jul 1850)

PERRY, William H., of NC Co, to JESTER, Else A., of Wilm, 17 Jan 1850, by Rev. William Cooper (DG 25 Jan 1850)

PETERKIN, Mary, see WEBB, James

PETERS, Rebecca C.,
see PETERS, William H.

PETERS, Richard,
see HOPKINSON, Thomas

PETERS, William H. of Del Co PA, to PETERS, Rebecca C., of Wilm, 26 Oct 1852, by Friends ceremony, in the presence of the Mayor (DG 2 Nov 1852)

PETERSON, Almira,
see WAPLES, James W.

PETERSON, Charles B., of Wilm, to MAXWELL, Mary, Miss, of Phila, in Phila, 25 Oct 1829, by Rev. Thomas Allen (DG 3 Nov 1829)

PETERSON, Elizabeth, wife of Israel PETERSON, in Smyrna, 10 Sep 1849, aged 73 yrs (DG 2 Oct 1849)
see PETERSON, Israel

PETERSON, George F., to ROBINSON, Amelia, Miss, all of Wilm, 14 Nov 1848, by Rev. J. E. Rockwell (DG 21 Nov 1848)

PETERSON, H. W.,
see PETERSON, Harriett

PETERSON, Harriet, wife of H. W. PETERSON, Esq., dau of the late James CLAYTON, sister of (illegible)
(DG 27 Apr 1852)

PETERSON, Henry, Esq., property near Middletown to be sold by exec'rs, James BOOTH and Nicholas HAMMOND
(DG 15 Jun 1827)

PETERSON, Henry W., late editor of the Circular, to JONES, Hannah Ann, Miss, both of Wilm, 9 Jun 1825, by the Rev. E. W. Gilbert (DG 14 Jun 1825)

PETERSON, Israel, aged 72 yrs, in Smyrna, 21 Sep 1849 (DG 2 Oct 1849)
see PETERSON, Elizabeth

PETERSON, John, in Wilm, 14 Sep 1849, aged 75 yrs (DG 25 Sep 1849)

PETERSON, Margaret, see HIGBEE, James

PETERSON, Mary, of consumption, in Wilm, 9 Mar 1850, aged 34 yrs (DG 19 Mar 1850)

PETERSON, Miles, late of Christiana Hd. Rebecca PETERSON, widow, is adm'x (DG 5 Jun 1849)

PETERSON, Rebecca,
see PETERSON, Miles

PETERSON, Sarah Ann, see SINK, John

PETERSON, Sarah, in Wilm, 16 Jul 1844 (DG 19 Jul 1844)

PETIT, William, to SPENCER, Mary, Miss, both of NC Co, 10 May 1827, by Rev. John P. Peckworth (DG 22 May 1827)

PETITDEMANGE, John, to HAULEY, Harriet, Miss, both of Brandywine Hd, 4 Dec 1851, by the Rev. J. Clemson (DG 12 Dec 1851)

PETTIDEMANGE?, Mary Ann,
see HOLLAND, John

PETTIMAGUE (sic) (PETTIDEMANGE?), Mary Ann, see HOLLAND, John

PETTIT, Hannah, see EVANS, Purnell

PETTIT, Peter, late of Brandywine Hd, William PETTIT, John WELDIN, adm'rs (DG 2 Mar 1827)

PETTIT, William, see PETTIT, Peter

PHELPS, Francis P., M. D., of Federalsburg, MD, to WHITE, Hannah, Miss, dau of Dr. John WHITE of Lewistown, DE, at Lewistown, 15 Nov 1824, by the Rev. Mr. Ogden (DG 30 Nov 1824)

PHELPS, S., see BRATTAN, Caleb

PHILE, Eliza Jane, see ENGLISH, Henry

PHILIPS, Albert G., son of Thomas PHILIPS, Esq., of White Clay Creek Hd, 19 Sep 1816, in his 18th yr (AW 5 Oct 1816)

PHILIPS, Anne, alias SPRINGER,
see CHEESELY, Joseph

PHILIPS, Elizabeth Lester, dau of George and Maria PHILIPS, in Wilm, 12 Dec 1851, in her third yr (DG 19 Dec 1851)

PHILIPS, George,
see PHILIPS, Elizabeth Lester

PHILIPS, Isaac J., to FULTON, Maria, Miss, both of Cecil Co MD, 3 May 1827, by Rev. John P. Peckworth (DG 8 May 1827)

PHILIPS, James, see PHILIPS, Nancy

PHILIPS, Maria,
see PHILIPS, Elizabeth Lester

PHILIPS, Nancy, Mrs., relict of the late James PHILIPS, Esq., at her res. near Laurel DE, 27 Feb 1851, in her 69th yr

(DG 7 Mar 1851)

PHILIPS, Thomas, Esq.,
see PHILIPS, Albert G.

PHILLIPS, Ann, see KEERS, John

PHILLIPS, Ann Maria,
see LOWE, Ann Maria

PHILLIPS, Eliza, see DICKENSON, Morris

PHILLIPS, Evan C., of NC Co, to MOORE, Eliza S., of Chester Co PA, at West Chester PA, 3 Sep 1846, by Henry Fleming, Esq. (DG 15 Sep 1846)

PHILLIPS, George, to WHITE, Elizabeth, Miss, both of Rockland, 11 May 1843, by Rev. S. M. Gayley (DG 26 May 1843)

PHILLIPS, George Washington, son of Capt John M. PHILLIPS, near Laurel, Sussex Co, 25 Jun 1851, in his 15th yr (DG 4 Jul 1851)

PHILLIPS, James W., Esq., at Seaford, 23 Aug 1850 (DG 10 Sep 1850)

PHILLIPS, Jane, see CAMERON, William

PHILLIPS, John, dec'd, late of Mill Creek Hd, notice given by John L. MORRIS, adm'r (DG 9 Jun 1829)

PHILLIPS, John, to BOULDEN, Susan, Miss, both of Wilm, 12 Feb 1852, by Rev. A. Manship (DG 2 Mar 1852)

PHILLIPS, John C., see PHILLIPS, Robert

PHILLIPS, John M., Capt, near Laurel DE, to HARRIS, Hetty Ann, Miss, of Georgetown, at Georgetown, 25 May 1852, by the Rev. John McKim (DG 11 Jun 1852)--reported as DAVIS, Hetty Ann (DG 15 Jun 1852)
see PHILLIPS, George Washington
see LOWE, Ann Maria

PHILLIPS, John R., to JUSTISSON, Rebecca, Miss, of NC Co, at Marcus Hook, PA, 27 Aug 1833, by the Rev. Joseph Walker (DG 10 Sep 1833)

PHILLIPS, Lewis, to FORWARD, Margaret, Miss, both of NC Co, in Phila, 21 Oct 1847, by Rev. Francis Hodgson (DG 14 Dec 1847)

PHILLIPS, Martha J.,
see BANNING, George W.

PHILLIPS, Mary Ann, see SHAW, James

PHILLIPS, Nathaniel, dec'd, late of Wilm, notice given by Juliana CHASE, adm'x (DE 6 Aug 1798)

PHILLIPS, Robert, dec'd, late of Christiana Hd, notice given by John C. PHILLIPS and William HERDMAN, exec'rs (DG 10 Mar 1829)

PHILLIPS, Sarah, see MASSEY, Joshua

PHILLIPS, Thomas, dec'd, late of Brandywine Hd, notice given by Abner CLOUD, exec'r (DG 10 Mar 1829)

PHILLIPS, William W., to HORN, Sarah Jane, Miss, both of Wilm (DG 23 Nov 1848)

PHILLIPS, Wm. G., of NC Co, to WATSON, Hannah J., of Phila, 1 May 1849 by Friends ceremony (DG 8 May 1849)

PHISTER, Benjamin, merchant of Phila, to THOMAS, Ann Jane, Miss, dau of Mr. John B. THOMAS, dec'd, at Rockville Farm, late res. of Judge WAY, dec'd, 1 Oct 1833, by Rev. Joseph Lybrand (DG 4 Oct 1833)

PHLEGER, Anna A., see FORD, Franklin

PHYSICK, Henry W.,
see BRINCKLE, William D., Dr.

PHYSICK, Sarah T.,
see BRINCKLE, William D., Dr.

PICHCITI, Andrew, 11 Sep 1847, in his 68th yr(DG 28 Sep 1847)

PICKELS, Henry, to MURGATROYD, Sarah, Miss, all of Wilm, 25 Jul 1853, by the Rev. J. Humphries (DG 2 Aug 1853)

PICKEN, Ann, see THOMSON, William

PIERCE, Albert, of Pennsbury Twp PA, to STEDHAM, Catherine, Miss, dau of Aaron KLAIR of Christiana Hd, NC Co, 20 Nov 1851, by the Rev. John Miller (DG 25 Nov 1851)

PIERCE, Alfred, of New York, to FISHER, Hannah C., Miss, of Wilm, 6 Apr 1835, by Elder John P. Peckworth (DG 10 Apr 1835)

PIERCE, Edward B., of Wilm, to LOYD, Mary Ann, Miss, of Christiana, 2 Aug 1848, by Rev. T. J. Thompson (DG 4 Aug 1848)

PIERCE, Elias, to POOLE, Elizabeth, Miss, both of NC Co, 10 Mar 1842, by Rev. Ignatius T. Cooper (DG 18 Mar 1842)
see PIERCE, Elizabeth

PIERCE, Elias, to WALKER, Jane I., both of Wilm, 24 Apr 1845, by Rev. Bishop Lee (DG 29 Apr 1845)

PIERCE, Eliza J., see BROOKS, Charles W.

DELAWARE MARRIAGES AND DEATHS FROM NEWSPAPERS, 1729-1853

PIERCE, Elizabeth, late wife of Elias PIERCE, 5 Sep 1843 (DG 8 Sep 1843)

PIERCE, George, Esq., dec'd, late of New Castle, notice given by James COOPER, adm'r (WN 27 Apr 1826)

PIERCE, Henrietta, see **BARTLEY**, James

PIERCE, Isabella, found dead in bed, in Brandywine Hd, inquest 12 Apr 1852, na (DG 27 Apr 1852)

PIERCE, Ruth Ann, see **ELDRIDGE**, Tustin

PIERCE, Sarah G., see **ABBOTT**, Cyrus

PIERCE, Sarah M., see **BALDWIN**, Robert

PIERCE, Silas, formerly of NC Co, near New Albany IN, 16 Feb 1849, aged 67 yrs (DG 13 Mar 1849)

PIERCE, Thomas, of Cecil Co, MD, to **CLARK**, Sarah Ann, Miss, of Elm Grove near New Castle, at that place, 4 Mar 1828, by the Rev. Mr. Prestman (DG 7 Mar 1828)

PIERCE, Thomas, to **BROWN**, Sarah Jane, both of Brandywine Hd, at Marcus Hook PA, 23 Dec 1852, by Rev. J. R. Anderson (DG 14 Jan 1853)

PIERCE, Walter, to **ENOS**, Charity B., Miss, all of NC Co, 10 Oct 1845, at Village Green by Rev. John W. Arthur (DG 21 Oct 1845)

PIERCE, William H., of Wilm, to **ELDRIDGE**, Mary M., Miss, of Phila, 2 Oct 1845, in Phila, by Rev. J. L. Grant (DG 7 Oct 1845)

PIERSON, Emma, only dau of Joseph PIERSON, Esq., 22 Mar 1850, aged c 9 yrs (DG 2 Apr 1850)

PIERSON, Joseph, see **PIERSON**, Emma

PIERSON, Jane A., see **RAPP**, Adam W.

PIERSON, Robert L., to **WOTTRESS** (sic), Sarah Elizabeth, Miss, both of Kent Co DE, in Phila, 4 Sep 1849, by the Rev. George Chandler (DG 11 Sep 1849)

PIERSON, Sarah, see **MALONE**, John S.

PIERSON, Wilson, to **BERRY**, Mary, Miss, 6 Nov 1828, by Rev. Solomon Higgins, all of Wilm (DG 11 Nov 1828)

PINE, Adaline, dau of William S. and Anna Maria PINE, in Wilm, 14 Jan 1847, aged 7 yrs 6 mos (DG 15 Jan 1847)

PINE, Anna Maria, see **PINE**, Adaline

PINE, George, to **STILLEY**, Sarah, Miss, 23 Feb 1827, by the Rev. John P. Peckworth, all of Wilm (DG 27 Feb 1827)

PINE, William S., see **PINE**, Adaline

PINKERTON, David, of Phila, to **WELDE**, Phebe, Miss, dau of Mr. William WELDE of Wilm, 5 May 1834, by Rev. C. S. Hedges (DG 6 May 1834)

PIPER, William, to **PRETTYMAN**, Mary, Miss, both of Georgetown, 18 Sep 1853, by Rev. J. R. Torbert (DG 27 Sep 1853)

PIPPEN, William, to **ASPRIL**, Hannah, Miss, both of Cantwell's Bridge, 13 Dec 1821, by the Rev. John Burton (DG 18 Dec 1821)

PIPPIN, Rebecca Jane, see **TERRY**, Howell J.

PIPPIN, William, see **TERRY**, Howell J.

PITT, Emma, see **FISHER**, William H.

PITTMAN, Joseph, of consumption, 25 Mar 1850, aged c 30 yrs (DG 2 Apr 1850)

PLANK, Thomas, to **COX**, Ellen, Miss, dau of Edward COX, all of Wilm, 22 Jul 1851, by Rev. J. G. Collom (DG 25 Jul 1851)

PLANKINTON, Catharine, see **PLANKINTON**, Jesse

PLANKINTON, Jesse, dec'd, late of Brandywine Hd, notice given by Catharine PLANKINTON, Peter PLANKINTON and Amor TALLEY, exec'rs (MU 5 Mar 1808)

PLANKINTON, John, of Pittsburgh PA, to **BRACKEN**, Elizabeth, Miss, of Brandywine Hd, 9 Mar 1843, by Rev. Mr. Hambleton (DG 17 Mar 1843)

PLANKINTON, Peter, see **PLANKINTON**, Jesse

PLANTON, Sarah, Mrs., in Phila, 16 Apr 1849, in her 69th yr (DG 24 Apr 1849)

PLATER, J. Rousby, of Talbot Co Md, to **PRICE**, Margaret, dau of Jos. T. PRICE, Esq., of Wilm, 11 May 1852, by the Rt. Rev. Alfred Lee (DG 18 May 1852)

PLATT, Ann H., **PLATT**, Anna Jane

PLATT, Anna Jane, dau of George and Ann H. PLATT, 2 Oct 1845, at Handen Farm, aged 16 yrs and 2 mos (DG 7 Oct 1845)

PLATT, George, Esq., to **GEMMILL**, Ann E., Miss, dau of Capt. Hugh GEMMILL, all of NC Co, 18 Sep 1821, by the Rev. John E. Latta

(DG 21 Sep 1821)

PLATT, George, see PLATT, Anna Jane see SMITH, Richard E.

PLATT, John, to JACKSON, Mary, Miss, both of New Castle Hd, 2 Mar 1826, by the Rev. Mr. White (DG 7 Mar 1826) see ELLIOT. J. Cloud

PLATT, Lavinia, see ELLIOT. J. Cloud

PLATT, Mary, Mrs., in Wilm, of apoplexy, 27 Mar 1848, aged 72 yrs (DG 4 Apr 1848)

PLATT, Samuel, Jr., dec'd, late of Newark, notice given by George RUSSELL, exec'r (DE 10 May 1796)

PLATT, Samuel, see McMANUS, Phillip

PLEASANTON, John, to CUMMINGS, Lydia A., Miss, all of Kent, 23 Nov 1848, by Rev. E. G. Asay (DG 5 Dec 1848) see HILL, Jacob M.

PLEASONTON, Hannah M., see COWGILL, William

PLUME, A. B., of Newark, NJ, to PEACH, Phoebe Ann, dau of John PEACH, Esq., of NC Co, 22 Nov 1853, in St, Georges Ch, NY, by the Rev. Stephen H. Tyng DD (DG 29 Nov 1853)

PLUMLY, Alfred DuPont, inf son of Thomas C. and Sally D. PLUMLY, 26 Feb 1850. aged 16 mos (DG 1 Mar 1850)

PLUMLY, Charles, dec'd, late of Wilm, notice given by Robert PLUMLY and Joseph PLUMLY, exec'rs (AD 18 Oct 1822)

PLUMLY, Ellen Jane, inf dau of Thomas C. and Sally D. PLUMLY, 22 Feb 1848 (DG 29 Feb 1848)

PLUMLY, James, inf son of Thomas C. and Sarah PLUMLY, 17 Feb 1846, aged 7 mos, 2 days (DG 20 Feb 1846)

PLUMLY, Jane, see WILKINSON, Nathan

PLUMLY, Joseph, see PLUMLY, Charles

PLUMLY, Robert, see PLUMLY, Charles

PLUMLY, Sally D., see PLUMLY, Alfred DuPont see PLUMLY, Ellen Jane

PLUMLY, Sarah, see PLUMLY, James

PLUMLY, Thomas C., to DUNCAN, Sally S., Miss, of New Castle, 4 Feb 1835, by the Rev. E. W. Gilbert (DG 26 Jun 1835)

see PLUMLY, Ellen Jane
see PLUMLY, James
see PLUMLY, Alfred DuPont

PLUMMER, Mary Ann, see COLE, Elisha

PLUMMER, Silas, to WEBB, Sarah Ann, all of S. Milford, 16 Sep 1852, by the Rev. T. P. McColley (DG 28 Sep 1852)

PLURIGHT, Margaret, see COCHRAN, William

PLURIGHT, Rachel, see BRACKIN, Benjamin

PLURIGHT, William, to SHEWARD, Lydia, Miss, both of Wilm, 17 April 1804, by Rev. Dr. Read (FA 21 Apr 1804)

POGUE, David, to GILL, Rachel Miss, both of Wilm, 13 Mar 1851, by Rev. E. M. Van Dusen (DG 18 Mar 1851)

POGUE, John, in Wilm, 3 Apr 1825, na (DG 8 Apr 1825) dec'd, late of Wilm, notice given by Joseph POGUE, surviving exec'r (DG 17 May 1825)

POGUE, Joseph, see POGUE, John

POGUE, William Jr, to SHIPLEY, Elizabeth, Miss, both of Christiana Hd, 20 Mar 1851, by Rev. Newton Heston (DG 22 Apr 1851)

POGY, Mary E., see DeSANDRAN, Alexander Gardon

POINSETT, Ann, late wife of Asa POINSETT, 23 Apr 1843, in Wilm (DG 28 Apr 1843)

POINSETT, Ann Eliza, see READ, Henry

POINSETT, Anna Bella, inf dau of Asa and Elizabeth POINSETT Jr, 22 Sep 1846 (DG 29 Sep 1846)

POINSETT, Asa, to McKENNAN, Elizabeth, 13 Nov 1843, by Rev. William Hogarth (DG 17 Nov 1843)
see POINSETT, Sarah Holmes
see POINSETT, Anna Bella
see POINSETT, Ann

POINSETT, Elizabeth, see POINSETT, Sarah Holmes
see POINSETT, Anna Bella

POINSETT, Mary, see SNYDER, George

POINSETT, Sarah Holmes, infant dau of Asa and Elizabeth POINSETT, 19 May 1853, aged 10 mos 12 days (DG 7 Jun 1853)

POLK, Charles T., see POLK, William

DELAWARE MARRIAGES AND DEATHS FROM NEWSPAPERS, 1729-1853

POLK, Cyrus, see POLK, William

POLK, John P., of Wilm, to KINKEAD, Amelia J., Miss, dau of the late William KINKEAD, Esq., of of Elkton MD, 30 Apr 1846, by Rev. William Hogarth (DG 8 May 1846)

POLK, Juliet M., see CUMMINS, David J.

POLK, Robert, to HOGG,Catherine, both of Wilm, 21 Sep 1789 (DG 23 Sep 1789)

POLK, Robert, to McDOWELL, Mary M., Miss, both of NC Co, 5 Aug 1852, by the Rev. J. A. Roche (DG 31 Aug 1852)

POLK, William, late of St Georges Hd, Cyrus POLK, Charles T. POLK, and John P. COCHRAN, exec'rs (DG 20 May 1853)

POLK, William, of Baltimore, formerly of DE, to CULLISON, Elizabeth, Miss, dau of Micajah CULLISON of Balt. Co, 13 Jan 1848, by Rev. Mr. William Hank (DG 21 Jan 1848)

POLK, William, see CUMMINS, David J. see MANN, James M.

PONDER, Anna, see SAULSBURY, Willard

PONDER, James, see SAULSBURY, Willard

POOL, Benjamin, of near Indian River, committed suicide by drowning, 7 Dec 1833, leaves a wife and child, married 10 or 11 mos (DG 17 Dec 1833)

POOL, Charlotte, see BAIL, James S.

POOLE, Elizabeth, see PIERCE, Elias

POOLE, Julia Ann, Miss, eldest dau of the late Richard POOLE, 20 Jun 1829, aged 18 yrs (DG 23 Jun 1829)

POOLE, Lydia M., late wife of William S. POOLE, in Wilm, 11 Feb 1844 (DG 16 Feb 1844)

POOLE, Mary, see WILSON, David

POOLE, Richard, 4 Apr 1828, na (DG 8 Apr 1828) notice given by William CHANDLER, adm'r (DG 18 Apr 1828) see POOLE, Julia Ann, Miss

POOLE, William S., see POOLE, Lydia M.

POPE, Elizabeth Hemphill, Mrs., wife of Col. John POPE, and dau of the late Morgan JONES of Wilm, at "Oak Grove", Shelby Co, TN, 23 Jun 1852, na (DG 13 Jul 1852)

POPE, John, see POPE, Elizabeth Hemphill

PORTER, Alexander, Esq., dec'd, late of NC Co, accounts to be presented to James BOOTH, Esq., of New Castle, or to Mary PORTER, the adm'x, now Mary FORMAN. Notice given by Thomas Marsh FORMAN and Mary FORMAN (DE 24 May 1798)

PORTER, Alexander, Hon, to KING, Emily, Miss, of Wilm, 22 Feb 1849, by Rev. Joseph Castle (DG 27 Feb 1849)

PORTER, Alexander, see HOCKER, William see PORTER, Elizabeth see ROOT, Mary L. see FRENCH, A. J.

PORTER, Angelina, see LOWTHER, Angelina S.

PORTER, Ann R., see GILPIN, Richard B.

PORTER, Benjamin, in Cedar Neck, Cedar Creek Hd, Sussex Co, 19 Jul 1850 (DG 30 Jul 1850)

PORTER, Charles, see LOWTHER, Angelina S.

PORTER, Charles, son of John and Sarah PORTER, at Marshall's Rolling Mill in Mill Creek Hd, 25 Oct 1849, aged c 12 yrs (DG 9 Nov 1849)

PORTER, Edward C., formerly of DE, at Denton MD, 11 Jan 1850, at an advanced age (DG 22 Jan 1850),

PORTER, Eleanor, see JOHNSON, John, Dr.

PORTER, Elizabeth, Mrs, wife of Hon. Alexander PORTER, Mayor of Wilm at the res. of her son-in-law, Alfred P. ROBINSON, Esq., of Lewistown, 17 Apr 1848 (DG 21 Apr 1848) Obit, 28 Apr see EVES, Spencer D.

PORTER, J. B., see PORTER, Maxwell Kennedy

PORTER, James, in Wilm, 11 Jan 1853, aged 78 yrs (DG 14 Jan 1853)

PORTER, James T., to LYNAM, Emma S., all of NC Co, 21 Dec 1852, by the Rev. A. Atwood (DG 24 Dec 1852)

PORTER, Joel, of Wilm, ndd, na, drowned at Spruce St wharf. Coroner's inquest (DG 31 Oct 1851)

PORTER, John, see PORTER, Charles

see **PORTER**, Mary R.

PORTER, John B., to **PAULSON**, Susanna R., Miss, dau of the late Peter PAULSON, 17 Oct 1833, by the Rev. Robert Adair, all of Wilm (DG 22 Oct 1833)

PORTER, Jonas, notice given by John STOCKTON (DE 15 Jul 1795)

PORTER, Margaret, Mrs., in Phila, 4 May 1831, in her 78th yr (DF 14 May 1831)

PORTER, Margareta, see **LOWTHER**, Angelina S.

PORTER, Martha, wife of Robert PORTER, cooper, in Wilm, 8 Jul 1848, aged 28 yrs (DG 18 Jul 1848) see **SIPPLE**, Caleb

PORTER, Mary, see **PORTER**, Alexander, Esq.

PORTER, Mary L., see **ROOT**, Mary L.

PORTER, Mary R., eldest dau of John B. PORTER, in Wilm, 27 Mar 1852, aged 16 yrs (DG 30 Mar 1852)

PORTER, Maxwell Kennedy, inf son of J. B. and S. R. PORTER, in Wilm, 21 Jul 1850, aged 1 yr 3 mos 20 days. Mr. Porter is proprietor and publisher of the *Delaware Journal* (DG 23 Jul 1850)

PORTER, Nancy, see **MYERS**, Alexander

PORTER, Permelia C., see **FRENCH**, A. J.

PORTER, Peter B., bookseller and stationer, in Wilm, 10 May 1844 (DG 14 May 1844)

PORTER, Robert, to **HENRY**, Martha, Miss, both of Wilm, 26 Aug 1847, by Rev. S. R. Wynkoop (DG 14 Sep 1847)

PORTER, Robert, to **HENRY**, Catharine, Miss, both of Wilm, 13 Sep 1849, by Rev. S. R. Wynkoop (DG 25 Sep 1849)

PORTER, Robert, see **BRYNBERG**, Peter, Esq. see **JOHNSON**, John, Dr. see **PORTER**, Martha

PORTER, S. R., [fem] see **PORTER**, Maxwell Kennedy

PORTER, Sarah, see **PORTER**, Charles

PORTER, Scott, to **HENRY**, Eliza, Miss, both of Wilm, 3 Oct 1850, by Rev. S. R. Wynkoop (DG 8 Oct 1850)

POSTLES, Elen P., see **ANDERSON**, John T.

POSTLES, James H., to **DAVIS**, Margaret L., Miss, both of Milford Hd, Kent Co, 5 Dec 1850, by Rev. T. P. McColley (DG 10 Dec 1850)

POSTLES, Stephen, of Kent Co, to **CASSON**, Margaret E., Miss, in Wilm at Mr. Thomas BAYARD's, 8 Jan 1850, by Rev. James Smith P. E. (DG 11 Jan 1850)

POSTLES, Wm. R., to **ELLINGSWORTH**, Sarah, all of Sussex Co. 21 Dec 1852 (DG 14 Jan 1853)

POTTAGE, Ann Rebecca, Mrs., wife of Benjamin POTTAGE, 16 Oct 1827, in her 29th yr (DG 12 Oct 1827)

POTTAGE, Benjamin, see **POTTAGE**, Ann Rebecca

POTTER, Edith, consort of Mr. Elijah POTTER, in Wilm, 31 Jan 1830, na (DG 5 Feb 1830)

POTTER, Elijah, 30 Mar 1842 (DG 1 Apr 1842)

POTTER, Elijah, see **POTTER**, Edith

POTTER, Elizabeth, see **GINN**, Isaac

POTTER, Margaret J., see **MOORE**, James B.

POTTER, Mary A., see **COLLINS**, Henderson

POTTER, Morgan, of Kent Co DE to **WOODLEY**, Mary A. Miss, of Phila, in Phila, 1 Nov 1849, by the Rev. Jas. Allen (DG 9 Nov 1849)

POTTER, Rachel A., see **DONAVAN**, James I.

POTTOGUE, Benjamin, of Wilm, to **CLARK**, Jane E., Miss, of Lancaster, PA, in Lancaster, 29 Jul 1829, by the Rev. Mr. Ashmead (DG 11 Aug 1829)

POTTS, Deborah, see **SHALLCROSS**, Thomas

POUGE, Joseph, merchant, of Wilm, to **COOPER**, Jane, dau of Hugh COOPER, merchant, of Phila, 18 Jul 1827, in Phila, by the Rev Dr. J. J. Janeway (DG 24 Jul 1827)

POULSON, Aaron, see **POULSON**, Margaret, Mrs.

POULSON, Margaret, Mrs., wife of Aaron POULSON, in Wilm, 4 Nov 1823, na (DG 11 Nov 1823)

POWELL, Barring, Esq., of Phila, to
BAYARD, Caroline, dau of Richard H.
BAYARD, of Wilm, 25 Jan 1847, by
Rev. Dr. Kennaday (DG 2 Feb 1847)

POWELL, DeVeaux, at Powelton at the res.
of his father, John Hare POWELL, 11 Jun
1848, in his 28th yr (DG 23 Jun 1848)

POWELL, Elizabeth,
see WHITAKER, Jacob
see CAZIER, John

POWELL, H. M., see GAUZE, O. B.

POWELL, Henry Baring, at Portland OR,
5 Apr 1852, aged c 34 yrs
(DG 24 May 1852)

POWELL, John Hare,
see POWELL, DeVeaux

POWELL, John, to McKEE, Lydia, Miss,
27 Oct 1825, by the Rev. Daniel D. Lewis,
all of Wilm (DG 1 Nov 1825)

POWELL, Martha, see HESS, Hiram R.

POWELL, Mary,
see PATTERSON, Samuel

POWELL, Sarah C.,
see TUNNELL, Edward S.

POWER, John, see BOYD, Margaret G.

PRATT, Enoch, dec'd, late of Appo-
quinimink Hd, notice given by Isaac F.
WALKER, adm'r de bonis non. (Not Enoch
PRATT of Baltimore) (DG 27 Jun 1834)

PREALL, Margaret, see PRICE, William C.

PRENDERGRAST, John, colored, cook on
the revenue cutter, fell from the vessel
29 Apr 1848 (DG 2 May 1848)

PRESS, Ellen, see DALE, Richard

PRESSTMAN, Ann, wife of Rev. Stephen
Wilson PRESSTMAN, at the parsonage near
New Castle, 29 Dec 1833, na
(DG 10 Jan 1834)

PRESSTMAN, Anne F., Mrs., in Wilm,
4 May 1849, aged 73 yrs (DG 8 May 1849)

PRESSTMAN, Maria T.,
see HAYWARD, James F.

PRESSTMAN, S. W., Rev., rector of the
Episcopal Church in New Castle for years,
1 Sep 1843, at New Castle
(DG 8 Sep 1843)

PRESSTMAN, Stephen Wilson, see

PRESSTMAN, Ann

PRETTYMAN, Elizabeth, Mrs., at her
late res. near Millsboro, 22 Jul 1850,
in her 93rd yr (DG 30 Jul 1850)

PRETTYMAN, Elizabeth W.,
see OWENS, Wm. H.

PRETTYMAN, George, to JOHNSON,
Sarah, Miss, 14 Oct 1841, by Rev. S. M.
Gayley, all of Sussex (DG 5 Nov 1841)

PRETTYMAN, Harriet,
see PARADEE, Charles

PRETTYMAN, Henry R., of Kent Co DE,
to ANDERSON, Sarah P., of Wilm,
21 Sep 1853, by Rev. Joshua Humphries
(DG 23 Sep 1853)

PRETTYMAN, John,
see PEPPER, William S.

PRETTYMAN, John S., M. D., to HUDSON,
A. Ella, Miss, dau of Henry HUDSON, Esq.,
of Milford, 24 Nov 1850, by Rev. S. C.
Palmiter (DG 6 Dec 1850)

PRETTYMAN, L. M., Rev.,
see RIDGEWAY, William H.

PRETTYMAN, Mary,
see PEPPER, William S.

PRETTYMAN, Mary Jane Pennewill, dau
of Mrs. S. PRETTYMAN of Wilm, in Phila,
where she had gone for medical aid,
28 Mar 1842, aged 19 yrs (DG 1 Apr 1842)

PRETTYMAN, Mary M.,
see RIDGEWAY, William H.

PRETTYMAN, Mary, see PIPER, William

PRETTYMAN, S., Mrs,
see PRETTYMAN, Mary Jane Pennewill

PRETTYMAN, Sarah, consort of the Rev.
Solomon Prettyman, 2 Nov 1847, after a
short illness (DG 5 Nov 1847)

PRETTYMAN, Solomon,
see PRETTYMAN, Sarah

PRETTYMAN, Thomas J., Rev., Pres.
of Wesleyan Female College, Wilm, to
GOWAN, Mary A., Miss, of Phila, 2 May
1850, in Union Church, Phila, by Rev.
Thomas J. Thompson (DG 7 May 1850)

PRETTYMAN, Wm, the Rev., of Baltimore,
to BARRETT, Eliza, Miss, of Camden,
at Camden, 6 Mar 1823, by the Rev.
Wm. Torbert (DG 14 Mar 1823)

PRETTYMAN, Zippy,
see DICKERSON, George,

PRETZNER, Henry, to HARKER, Margaretta, Miss, both of Wilm, in Wilm, 30 Jun 1848, by Rev. Mr. Van Dusen (DG 7 Jul 1848)

PREVOST, Lewis M.,
see EVANS, William D.

PREVOST, Mary J. M.,
see EVANS, William D.

PRICE, ___, Capt., see CREERY, William

PRICE, Agnes,
see NORRIS, George Pepper

PRICE, Betsy, see BUSH, David, Dr.

PRICE, David T., of Wilm, to SMEDLEY, Hannah, Miss, of Willistown, at Willistown, 21 Mar 1850, by Rev. John Jones (DG 29 Mar 1850)

PRICE, Edward, a pilot belonging to Cape Henlopen, jumped from the schooner *Gilbert Hartfield* near New Castle and was drowned, 25 Feb 1844. The act was committed while laboring under temporary derangement of mind. He left a family at Lewistown (DG 1 Mar 1844)

PRICE, Elizabeth, see SYNNIX, Jacob

PRICE, Elizabeth P. O.,
see LONGFELLOW, Wm. H.

PRICE, Elizabeth W.,
see PRICE, Hannah Margarett

PRICE, Francis T., at his father's res. in Red Lion, 2 Nov 1852, aged 28 yrs (DG 5 Nov 1852)

PRICE, Hannah, 11 Jun 1852, na (DG 15 Jun 1852)

PRICE, Hannah Margarett, dau of John and Elizabeth W. PRICE, in Brandywine Village, 10 Feb 1849, aged 2 yrs 10 mos (DG 16 Feb 1849)

PRICE, Hyland, to TODD, Eliza Jane, 30 Jul 1853, by the Rev. Wm C. Cooley, all of Christiana (DG 5 Aug 1853)

PRICE, Isaac,
see McMECHEN, Mary, Mrs.
see EVANS, Edward R.
see DICKSON, John H.

PRICE, Isaac S., to McDOWELL, Martha, Miss, 11 Mar 1848, by Rev. J. R. Wynkoop (DG 17 Mar 1848)

PRICE, Isaiah, of Chester Co PA, to HEALD, Lydia, of NC Co, nmd, by Friends ceremony at the res. of Jacob HEALD (DG 3 Mar 1846)

PRICE, James, Esq., see PRICE, Margaret
see SMITH, James

PRICE, James E., to GORDON, Catharine, second dau of John GORDON of Wilm, 5 Nov 1833, by the Rev. Isaac Pardee (DG 8 Nov 1833)

PRICE, James W., to ANKINS, Susanna, Miss, both of Wilm, in Chester, 16 Feb 1853, by the Rev. Mr. Maddox (DG 25 Feb 1853)

PRICE, John,
see PRICE, Hannah Margarett

PRICE, John, of Christiana, to UNDERWOOD, Jane, Miss, of Cecil Co, MD, in Wilm, 27 Apr 1826, by the Rev. Mr. ___ (DG 9 May 1826)

PRICE, John, to WOODWARD, Elizabeth B., both of Brandywine Village, 28 Nov 1844, at the Mansion House, Phila, by Rev. Thomas Allen (DG 3 Dec 1844)

PRICE, John E., in Frederica, 5 Feb 1840, na (DG 16 Feb 1849)

PRICE, John H.,
see NORRIS, George Pepper
see STOTHART, Agnes

PRICE, John L., of Wilm, to CHEFFINS, Margaret J., Miss, of Smyrna, in Phila, 27 Jun 1850, by Rev. J. B. Hagany (DG 4 Jul 1850)

PRICE, Jos. T., see PLATER, J. Rousby

PRICE, Joseph T., of Brandywine to SANDERSON, Matilda Louisa, Miss, dau of John SANDERSON, Esq., of Phila, in Phila, by Joseph Watson, Mayor, nmd (DG 7 Apr 1826)

PRICE, Luke C., see PRICE, Susan M.

PRICE, Marcellus, to RICHARDSON, Mary Ann, Miss, both of Wilm, 25 Nov 1836, by Rev. H. Adams, rector of Trinity Ch, Wilm (DG 1 Mar 1836)

PRICE, Margaret, relict of the late James PRICE, Esq., 21 Mar 1841, aged 74 yrs (DG 26 Mar 1841)
see PLATER, J. Rousby

PRICE, Martha R.,
see HANDY, Benjamin R.

PRICE, Mary, Mrs., in Wilm, 28 Jul 1853, in

her 55th yr (DG 2 Aug 1853)

PRICE, Mary A., wife of Samuel E. PRICE, and dau of George S. DOWNING, in Wilm, 26 Dec 1852, in her 25th yr (DG 31 Dec 1852)

PRICE, Mary Jane,
see BRADFORD, William
see COOPER, M. S.

PRICE, Mary S.,
see SHARPER, Benjamin W.

PRICE, Mary, see CREERY, William

PRICE, Mary T., see CANBY, Edmund

PRICE, S. A., Esq., see MORTON, Isaac H.

PRICE, Sally, see EVANS, Edward R.

PRICE, Samuel E., see PRICE, Mary A.

PRICE, Samuel, Jr., to DOWNING, Mary A., Miss, dau of Geo. S. DOWNING, all of Wilm, in Phila, 15 Mar 1852, by Hon Charles Gilpin, Mayor (DG 19 Mar 1852)

PRICE, Sarah,
see CHALLENGER, Thomas

PRICE, Susan A., see MASSEY, Henry P.

PRICE, Susan M., wife of Luke C. PRICE, formerly of Madison, Morris Co NJ, 17 Apr 1851, aged 39 yrs, res'd 213 Orange St (DG 18 Apr 1851)

PRICE, T. Roberts, of Wilm, to LORE, Anna Matilda, Miss, youngest dau of the late Capt. Seth LORE of Wilm, in Phila, 21 Mar 1850, by Rev. W. Bishop (DG 26 Mar 1850)

PRICE, Thos. T., of Phila to BARTHOLOMEW, Mary, Mrs., of NC Co, DE, 12 Jun 1849, by Rev. Thos. F. Billopp (DG 19 Jun 1849)

PRICE, William C., of Canterbury, to STEVENS, Mary, Miss, 3 Apr 1842, by Rev. Jno. Manlove (DG 15 Apr 1842)

PRICE, William C., of DE, to PREALL, Margaret, Miss, of Southwark, in Phila, 5 Jul 1826, by the Rev. Mr. Ashton (DG 11 Jul 1826)

PRICE, William, of Balt Co MD, to JOHNSON, Rachel, Miss, of Wilm, 30 Sep 1851, by the Rev. J. A. Roche (DG 3 Oct 1851)

PRICHARD, John, see PRICHARD, Maria

PRICHARD, Maria, of MD, wife of John

PRICHARD, murdered, husband suspected, 24 Nov 1852, na (DG 30 Nov 1852)

PRIDE, Elizabeth, see McGEE, Levin J.

PRIDE, Rachel, Mrs., at Georgetown, 13 Jun 1851, at an advanced age (DG 17 Jun 1851)

PRIDE, Sarah,
see KIMMEY, Abraham, Capt.

PRIDE, William, at Lewes, 26 Nov 1853, aged 19 yrs (DG 6 Dec 1853)

PRIMROSE, Catharine,
see IRVINS, Thomas

PRIMROSE, James, Capt.,
see PRIMROSE, Thomas

PRIMROSE, Thomas, son of Capt James PRIMROSE, in Wilm, 8 Aug 1851, aged c 2 yrs (DG 12 Aug 1851)

PRINCE, John, dec'd, notice given by Samuel JORDAN and Valentine ROBINSON, adm'rs (AW 9 Dec 1815)

PRIOR, John,
see MANSON, James

PRIOR, John, of Dover, to STANLY, Eliza, Miss, 5 May 1789 (DG 16 May 1789)

PRIOR, John, of Dover, died, buried Christ Church, Dover, 22 May 1789 [date of death or burial?, not certain] (DG 20 Jun 1789)

PRITCHARD, _____, Mrs., wife of John PRITCHARD, 30 May 1848, in Stanton (DG 6 Jun 1848)

PRITCHARD, James,
see PRITCHARD, Rachel

PRITCHARD, James, near North East, Cecil Co MD, of hemorrhage of the lungs, 16 May 1853, aged 53 yrs (DG 27 May 1853)

PRITCHARD, John,
see PRITCHARD, _____, Mrs.

PRITCHARD, John, to HUGHS, Maria, Mrs, both of NC Co, 31 Jul 1848, by Rev. T. J. Thompson (DG 4 Aug 1848)

PRITCHARD, Rachel, dau of the late James PRITCHARD, near North East, 6 Oct 1853, aged c 20 yrs (DG 7 Oct 1853)

PRITCHARD, Susanna A.,
see MOORE, Samuel

PRITCHETT, Edward R., of Denton MD, to PALMETORY, Lebena, Miss, of Kent Co

DE, 27 Feb 1842, in Dover
(DG 11 Mar 1842)

PRITCHETT, Jesse, dec'd, late of the firm of Star and Pritchet of Phila, notice given by Eli MENDENHALL, exec'r (MR 7 Aug 1806)

PROCTOR, George W., of Carlisle PA, to LOWERY, Sallie A., dau of the late Justus LOWERY, of Milford DE, 12 Aug 1852, by the Rev. E. B. Bruen (DG 17 Aug 1852)

PROVOST, Ann,
see PROVOST, Thomas Elwood

PROVOST, Thomas Elwood, youngest son of William and Ann PROVOST, in Brandywine Village, 24 Jan 1850, aged 7 yrs (DG 5 Feb 1850)

PROVOST, William,
see PROVOST, Thomas Elwood

PROVOST, William, to PENNINGTON, Sarah, Miss, at Brandywine 14 Mar 1821, by the Rev. J. Rusling (DG 20 Mar 1821)

PRYCE, Sarah Tabitha, dau of the late Rev. Wm. PRYCE, 19 Feb 1820, aged 23 yrs (DG 26 Feb 1820)

PRYCE, William,
see SAVOY, Rebecca, Mrs.
see STORY, James
see STORY, James

PRYCE, William, the Rev. ,
see BLACK, William
see PRYCE, Sarah Tabitha
see MENDINHALL, Hannah

PRYOR, Charles, see NIXON, Elizabeth

PRYOR, Elizabeth, see NIXON, Elizabeth

PUNCH, Ellen, see HYATT, John T.

PURCELL, William J. J., to BRADLEY, Sarah J., Miss, both of Wilm, 25 May 1852, by Rev. Mr. Cosgrave (DG 28 May 1852)

PURNELL, James S., of Elkton, to HAMM, Susan B., Miss, of Kent Co, DE, 29 Sep 1835, by Rev. John Durborah (DG 6 Oct 1835)

PURVIS, William,
see COLESBERRY, William

PUSEY, Hannah, see HEALD, Joshua T.

PUSEY, Henry, son of Joshua L. PUSEY, 26 Mar 1848, aged 2 yrs (DG 4 Apr 1848)

PUSEY, Jonas, 4 Oct 1851, in his 61st yr (DG 7 Oct 1851) sale of real estate

(DG 14 Jan 1853)

PUSEY, Jonas, see HEALD, Joshua T.

PUSEY, Joshua L., see PUSEY, Henry

PUSEY, Mary, see VERNON, George

PUSEY, Mary M., see PYLE, Cyrus

PUSEY, Samuel N., to RICHARDS, Mary T., dau of William RICHARDS, all of Wilm, 9 Jun 1853, by Friends ceremony (DG 21 Jun 1853)

PYLE, Cyrus, to PUSEY, Mary M., both of Wilm, 25 May 1843, by Nicholas G. Williamson, Mayor (DG 2 Jun 1843)

PYLE, Humphrey, see TALLEY, Charlotte

PYLE, Joseph, to HAINES, Elizabeth, both of Wilm, 12 Oct 1848, at White Hall Hotel, by T. J. Haines (DG 20 Oct 1848)

PYLE, Joshua, see WIER, Joseph

PYLE, Lizzie P., see WALBORN, Rufus C.

PYLE, Reece, to COLLEY, Lydia Ann, Miss, of Wilm, in W. Chester 25 Nov 1849 by Rev. J. L. Houston (DG 29 Nov 1849)

PYLE, William, to PAYNTER, Margaret C., youngest dau of William PAYNTER, Esq., all of Wilm, 30 Sep 1851, by Friends ceremony (DG 7 Oct 1851)

PYSER, Sarah Louisa,
see CLOAK, John, Esq.

QUANDRILLE, John, dec'd, notice given by John HALL, Jr., exec'r (MW 23 May 1801)

QUIGLEY, Joseph, to PERKINS, Rachel, Miss, eldest dau of Reece PERKINS, Sr., Esq., 25 Oct 1849, at W. Chester PA, by the Rev. Caleb J. Good (DG 6 Nov 1849)

QUIN, William, living with Robert ENOS, on the farm of Chancellor JOHNS, in N Castle Hd, kicked in the stomach by a horse, 13 Feb 1853, died next day, 14 May 1853, aged c 26 yrs, unmarried (DG 27 May 1853)

QUINBY, John, see MEREDITH, Samuel

QUINBY, Martha Ann, see MOON, James

QUINN, Eliza J., see CURRAN, John

QUINN, Elizabeth, see QUINN, Nicholas

QUINN, John, see QUINN, Nicholas

QUINN, John, dec'd, late of Brandywine Hd,

notice given by Andrew BRADLEY, adm'r (DG 24 Nov 1826)

QUINN, Margaret, see RUSSELL, Benjamin F.

QUINN, Nicholas, dec'd, late of Hare's Corner, notice given by Elizabeth QUINN and John QUINN, adm'rs (DG 4 Oct 1822)

QUINN, Nicholas, of pulmonary consumption, in Wilm, 9 Jul 1847, in his 49th yr (DG 27 Jul 1847)

RAINGROVE, Vandiver, in Camden DE, 3 Jan 1851, na (DG 31 Jan 1851)

RALPH, John E., of Q. Anne's Co MD, to WOODALL, Frances Ann, Miss, dau of the late John WOODALL of Smyrna, 13 Jan 1851, by the Rev. P. Mansfield (DG 28 Jan 1851)

RALSTON, John, Esq., severely ill for 7 days, at Milford, 15 Aug 1803, aged 55 yrs; leaves a wife and 4 children (FA 17 Aug 1803)

RAMBO, Jacob, to JOHNSON, Elizabeth, Miss, brother, John A. JOHNSON, Esq., all of Elkton, at Elkton, 27 Jan 1853, by Rev. J. D. Onins (DG 1 Feb 1853)

RAMBO, Margaret, see HARTES, Richard

RAMBO, Richard, see HUSTON, John

RAMEAU, John, to WOOD,Jane, Mrs., in Wilm, 29 Oct 1807 by Rev. Mr. Pryce (MU 31 Oct 1807)

RAMO, Eliza, see RAMO, John

RAMO, John, inf. son of John and Eliza RAMO, 5 Sep 1843 (DG 8 Sep 1843)

RAMO, Peter, to ROBERTS, Hannah, Miss, both of Brandywine, 17 Apr 1834, by the Rev. Isaac Pardee (DG 25 Apr 1834)

RAMSEY, Elizabeth, see RAMSEY, Samuel

RAMSEY, Samuel, to RAMSEY, Elizabeth, Miss, of St. John, NB, at Wilm, 14 Nov 1853, by the Rev. Nicholas Patterson (DG 18 Nov 1853)

RANDEL, John, Jr., see RANDEL, Richard Vareck DeWit

RANDEL, Richard Vareck DeWit, son of John RANDEL, Jr., at New Castle, 22 Jul 1834, aged 10 mos (DG 25 Jul 1834)

RANDERSON, James, to RISHTINE,

Sophia, Miss, all of NC Co, 4 Oct 1827, by the Rev. Solomon Higgins (DG 12 Oct 1827)

RANDOLPH, B. Harrison, of San Francisco, to MATHIEU, Anne M., eldest dau of Capt. J. E. MATHIEU, 10 Feb 1852, at Glenbrook DE, by the Rt. Rev. Alfred Lee DD (DG 13 Feb 1852)

RANKIN, Joseph, see SPRINGER, James

RANKIN, Maria J., see MARTIN, Eleuthere J.

RANKIN, Parker, of Portsmouth, Ohio, to HODSON, Mary, Miss, of Wilm, 17 Sep 1746, in Phila, by Rev. Mr. Burrows (DG 22 Sep 1846)

RANKIN, Sarah (Sallie) Maria, see SPRINGER, James

RAPP, Adam W., to PIERSON, Jane A., both of Phila, 11 May 1852, by Wm. Hemphill Jones, Mayor (DG 28 May 1852)

RASH, Daniel, fell from sloop *Matilda* near the mouth of the Brandywine, aged 18 yrs; inquest, accidental drowning (DG 9 Aug 1853)

RASH, Daniel, of Smyrna, to TORBERT, Rachel, Miss, of Wilm, 3 Aug 1820 (DG 11 Aug 1820)

RASH, Elizabeth, see IRONS, William

RASH, John, see RASH, Phebe Ann

RASH, Margaretta, see MOORE, Samuel E.

RASH, Phebe Ann, dau of John and Sarah RASH, in Smyrna, 8 Jan 1853, aged c 3 yrs (DG 18 Jan 1853)

RASH, Sarah, see RASH, Phebe Ann

RASIN, Margaret, sister of the late Caleb and Isaac STARR, in Wilm, 26 Nov 1852, in her 90th yr (DG 30 Nov 1852)

RATCLIFF, Elizabeth, see HAYS, John

RATCLIFF, Samuel, to FRANCIS, Mary, Miss, both of Appoq. Hd, 26 Feb 1804, by Rev. James Lattomus (FA 10 Mar 1804)

RATLIFF, William, to HAMMOND, Alexina, Miss, all of Milford, 29 Nov 1848, by Rev. Mr. Spottswood (DG 5 Dec 1848)

RATLIGE, Rebecca C., see NAUDAIN, Nicholas F. C.

RATTEN, Joseph T., of Newark DE, to

WILLIAMS, Elizabeth, Miss, of Roxborough, 17 Apr 1850, at the Roxborough Baptist parsonage, by Rev. Thomas Winter (DG 19 Apr 1850)

RATTLE, Francis, of Peoria IL, to RODNEY, Ellen, Miss, youngest dau of the late Caesar A. Rodney of Wilm, in Ottowa, IL, 11 Jul 1850, at the res. of William H. CUSHMAN, Esq., by Rev. Charles Kelly (DG 27 Aug 1850)

RAUGHLEY, James, to WOODALL, Sarah A., Mrs., all of Kent Co, 29 Nov 1849, by Dr. John Perkins (DG 11 Dec 1849)

RAUGHLEY, James, late of Duck Creek Hd, 16 Nov 1851, in Dover Hd, na (DG 25 Nov 1851)

RAUGHLEY, Rachel, see JONES, Robert M.

RAY, Edmonda Louisa Strachan, in Wilm, 13 Nov 1828, aged 16 mos (DG 25 Nov 1828)

RAY, Edmund Strachan, merchant of Phila, to SELLARS, Mary Louisa, Miss, of Wilm, in Wilm, 1 Nov 1826, by the Rev. E. W. Gilbert (DG 7 Nov 1826)

RAY, James H., see MAYDIN, Eunice

RAY, Jane, Mrs., see KINCAID, Blair

RAY, John T., Dr., of West Greenville PA, to EVES, Eliza J., dau of the late Abraham EVES of New Castle, 2 Jun 1844, by Rev. Edmund Neville, at St. Phillip's Church (DG 11 Jun 1844)

RAYBOLD, Clayton B., of DE,to BARRON, Catharine A., Miss, dau of George BARRON of Wilm, 29 Nov 1847, by Rev. Mr. Janeway (DG 30 Nov 1847)

RAYHOW, Eliza, see DIXON, Thos.

RAYHOW, William, to PALMER, Eliza, Miss, both of New Castle, 16 Dec 1846, by Rev. A. Atwood (DG 22 Dec 1846)

RAYHOW, William, in N. Castle, 3 Nov 1849, aged c 25 yrs (DG 6 Nov 1849)

RAYMON, Jacob, Pres. of the Bank of Smyrna, in Smyrna, 6 Oct 1852, in his 65th yr (DG 12 Oct 1852)

RAYMOND, Benjamin, Esq., Asst. Engineer of the Chesapeake and Delaware Canal, late from St. Lawrence Co, NY, at the res. of John HIGGINS near St. Georges, 26 Sep 1824, na (DG 15 Oct 1824)

RAYMOND, Jacob (see RAYMON) (DG 15 Oct 1852)

RAYMOND, John, see RAYMOND, William Henry

RAYMOND, Mary E., see MARTER, I. B.

RAYMOND, Seymore, formerly of York PA, to KENNARD, Anna F., Miss, of Wilm, 23 Dec 1852, by Rev. J. Humphries (DG 28 Dec 1852)

RAYMOND, T. C., see MARTER, I. B.

RAYMOND, William Henry, son of John RAYMOND, Esq.,of Kent Co, DE, 20 Apr 1824, na (DG 23 Apr 1824)

REA, Philemon D., mariner, 29 Aug 1820, aged 28 yrs (DG 8 Sep 1820)

READ, Agnes, see JONES, David H.

READ, Catharine Ann, see McLANE, Catharine Ann, Mrs.

READ, Charles P. near Old Swedes Ch, aged c 42 yrs, leaves wife and children; inquest 19 Mar 1853 (DG 22 Mar 1853)

READ, Ellen, see HARRIGAN, Wesley

READ, Emily, see AYERS. Edward, Capt.

READ, George,
see TRANBERG, Andrew
see McLANE, Catharine Ann, Mrs.

READ, George, The Hon., 21 Sep 1798, very suddenly, at New Castle (DE 1 Oct 1798)

READ, George, Jr., see READ, Louisa Dorothy, Mrs.

READ, Hannah, see SCHULTZE, George Washington

READ, Henry, Capt., see AYERS, Edward, Capt.

READ, Henry, to POINSETT, Ann Eliza, both of Wilm, 27 Sep 1846, by Rev. S. R. Wynkoop (DG 2 Oct 1846)

READ, Hugh, to COYLE, Jane, Miss, of NC Co, 16 Apr 1843, by Rev. J. W. McCullough (DG 5 May 1843)

READ, Isabella, see McINTIRE, John

READ, Joseph, see SHEWARD, Rest

READ, Louisa Dorothy, Mrs., wife of George READ, Jr., Esq., at New Castle,

16 Jul 1835, na (DG 21 Jul 1835)

READ, Mary, see BALDWIN, Eli

READ, Mary S., relict of the late Rev. Dr Thomas READ, at her res. near Wilm, 11 Dec 1845, aged 84 yrs (DG 16 Dec 1845)

READ, Sarah Ann, see JEFFERSON, James

READ, Thomas, see SCHULTZE, George Washington

READ, Thomas, the Rev., D. D., Presbyterian Ch, in Wilm, 14 Jun 1823, at an advanced age (DG 17 Jun 1823) see READ, Mary S.

READEL, Rebecca Ann, see MASSEY, William B.

READER, Rachel, see STEDMAN, Henry

READER, William J., to STEVENS, Ruth, Miss, both of Wilm, 9 Mar 1847, by Rev. S. R. Wynkoop (DG 12 Mar 1847)

READING, Philip, at his res. in Wilm, 1 Nov 1821, at the completion of his 33rd yr (DG 16 Nov 1821)

RECORDS, Edward, late of NC Co, at his res. in New Town MD, after a protracted illness, 16 Jul 1845, aged 42 yrs. Leaves wife and 3 children (DG 25 Jul 1845)

RECORDS, Edward J., M.D., of Blackwoodtown NJ, to BEE, Mary J., Miss, youngest dau of Thomas BEE, Esq., of Gloucester Co NJ, 4 May 1852, by Rev. H. Westcott (DG 11 May 1852)

REDDEN, Abraham, negro, shot by Jacob GREEN, negro, St. Georges Hd, 21 Jul 1850 (DG 26 Jul 1850)

REDDEN, George, see REDDEN, Stephen T.

REDDEN, Jane B., see REDDEN, Stephen T.

REDDEN, Stephen T., son of Jane B. and George REDDEN, in Kent Co, 13 Aug 1850, aged 1 yr 1 mo 9 days (DG 27 Aug 1850)

REDDINGS, John, to WISE, Sarah F. all of New Castle, 1 Nov 1852, by Rev. William B. Walton (DG 10 Dec 1852)

REDFIELD, Belen, see HUSTON, Edward S.

REDFIELD, Mary Ann, see HUSTON, Edward S.

REDGRAVE, Samuel, to FINCHER, Sarah, Miss, all of Balt, in Balt 14 May 1849, by Rev. William Evans (DG 18 May 1849)

REDGRAVES, Abraham, of Duck Creek, to HOLLIDAY, Nancy, Miss, 24 Jul 1789 (DG 8 Aug 1789)

REDING, Thomas, see KING, Catharine

REECE, Delia, see FINLEY, Joseph

REECE, John, millwright, 9 Nov 1847 (DG 12 Nov 1847)

REECE, Lucretia, see HALL, John

REECE, Mary Jane, see JOHNSON, Elijah

REECE, Sarah, see SHAFFER, James

REECE, Thomas, 25 Aug 1851, in his 76th yr (DG 26 Aug 1851)

REED, Abigail W., see REED, Mary Elizabeth

REED, Alexander W., see CHURCHMAN, Henry

REED, Angelica K., see NICHOLSON, John A.

REED, Ann, see WHITTENGTON, James

REED, Elizabeth, in Wilm, at the res. of her son-in-law Thomas HARVEY, 25 Dec 1853, na (DG 30 Dec 1853)

REED, James, to JACKSON, Mary, Miss, both of NC Co, 19 Dec 1850, by Rev. J. A. Roche (DG 31 Dec 1850)

REED, John, see REED, Mary Elizabeth see NICHOLSON, John A.

REED, John B., near Whiteleysburgh, Kent Co DE, 27 Nov 1850, aged 53 yrs 5 mos 7 days (DG 9 May 1851)

REED, John G., to JONES, Frances Ann, all of NC Co, 2 Mar 1852, by the Rev. P. Mansfield (DG 16 Mar 1852)

REED, Margaret, see TINDAL, John

REED, Martha, see FORD, Wm.

REED, Mary Elizabeth, dau of John and Abigail W. REED, 31 May 1849, aged 4 yrs 26 das (DG 8 Jun 1849)

REED, Sarah, see CHURCHMAN, Henry

REEDER, John, see KNOX, Rebecca

REEDER, Mary Ann, 29 Mar 1846 (DG 3 Apr 1846)

REESE, Lewis, dec'd, late of White Clay Creek Hd, notice given by Robert OCHELTREE, adm'r (DG 17 Feb 1824)

REESE, William T., of Chesapeake City, to BULLOCK, E. A., of Wilm, 19 Feb 1848, by Rev. Mr. Billop of NC Co (DG 14 Mar 1848)

REEVE, Samuel, to TINGLE, Janett, in Wilm, 1 Jan 1848, by Rev. J. E. Rockwell (DG 7 Jan 1848)

REEVES, Clement, to CLARK, Susan, dau of Thomas CLARK, Esq., all of NC Co, 30 Nov 1852, by Rev. James C. Stow (DG 3 Dec 1852)

REGISTER, Eunity, see CROCKETT, Robert B.

REGISTER, Francis, see CROCKETT, Robert D.

REGISTER, Malvina, see MARTIN, J. Willis

REGISTER, Robert, see MARTIN, J. Willis

REGISTER, Samuel B., of Phila, to DENNY, Mary S., dau of the late Collins DENNY of Wilm, in Wilm, 26 Nov 1850, by Friends ceremony (DG 13 Dec 1850)

REID, Hannah, at res. of Joseph CRANSTON, in Mill Creek Hd, 29 Dec 1851, aged 76 yrs (DG 9 Jan 1852)

REILEY, Mary Ann, see dosSANTOS, A. F.

REILY, Mary A., see YOUNG, Robert P.

REVILL, Joseph Henry, son of Wm. F. REVILL, at the res. of his father in S. Milford, 4 Jun 1852, aged 3 yrs 6 mos (DG 15 Jun 1852)

REVILL, Wm. F., see REVILL, Joseph Henry

REYBOLD, _____, Maj., see REYBOLD, Clayton B.

REYBOLD, Clayton B., of Red Lion, son of Maj. REYBOLD of NC Co, 19 Jan 1852, aged c 30 yrs. Bur. at Laurel Hill (DG 23 Jan 1852)

REYBOLD, Elizabeth, see CARTER, Edward J.

REYBOLD, Elizabeth, wife of Major Philip REYBOLD, in Red Lion Hd, 10 Aug 1852, na (DG 17 Aug 1852)

REYBOLD, Mary P., dau of Maj. Phillip REYBOLD, 26 May 1850, aged 32 yrs (DG 4 Jun 1850)

REYBOLD, Philip, see REYBOLD, Elizabeth

REYBOLD, Phillip, Maj, see REYBOLD, Mary P.

REYBOLD, Phillip Jr., of NC Co, 8 Mar 1853, in his 40th yr (DG 15 Mar 1853)

REYHOW, Jane, see CANNON, John D.

REYHOW, Sarah, see VINCENT, Tench T.

REYNOLDS, _____, child of Curtis REYNOLDS, fell in St. Jones Creek, and was drowned, 19 Sep 1851 (DG 30 Sep 1851)

REYNOLDS, _____, Mrs., near Georgetown, 8 Oct 1853, aged c 80 yrs (DG 21 Oct 1853)

REYNOLDS, Aaron, of NC Co, to FLEMING, Alexa Rebecca Ann, Miss, of Southwark, in Phila, 14 Sep 1848, by Rev. C. Carsner (DG 3 Oct 1848)

REYNOLDS, Alexander, see COLESBURY, Mary see O'FLYNN, Patrick

REYNOLDS, Andrew, at his res. near Stanton, Mill Creek Hd, 13 Feb 1846, aged 82 yrs (DG 24 Feb 1846)

REYNOLDS, Ann, see EDMONDSON, Lydia see GOLDSBOROUGH, G. W. Dr.

REYNOLDS, Benjamin, see SPAIN, George

REYNOLDS, Curtis, see REYNOLDS, _____.

REYNOLDS, Elizabeth, Miss, suddenly, in Wilm, 28 Oct 1847, of heart disease (DG 29 Oct 1847)

REYNOLDS, Elizabeth, relict of the late William REYNOLDS of St. Georges Hd, in White Clay Creek Hd, 25 Nov 1850, aged 67 yrs. (DG 29 Nov 1850)

REYNOLDS, Ellender, see BROWN, William

REYNOLDS, George, printer, to THOMAS, Catherine, Miss, both of Brandywine Village, 16 Oct 1823, by the Rev. J. Potts (DG 21 Oct 1823)

REYNOLDS, Hannah, see McKEE, James

REYNOLDS, J., see **GOLDSBOROUGH**, G. W., Dr.

REYNOLDS, John, Jr., 29 Sep 1820, aged 32 yrs (DG 10 Oct 1820)

REYNOLDS, John T., of Cecil Co MD, to **MENDINHALL**, Elizabeth W., of Chester Co PA, 5 Feb 1851, by the Rev. Dr. Ducachet (DG 21 Feb 1851)

REYNOLDS, Lydia Ann, see **FELL**, Watson

REYNOLDS, Margaret W, see **WILLIAMSON**, J. F.

REYNOLDS, Mary, see **COLESBURY**, Mary

REYNOLDS, Mary Jane, see **BROWN**, Elgar

REYNOLDS, Mary W., see **HUGHES**, William H.

REYNOLDS, Michael, a small boy, killed by an ox cart, near Willow Grove, Kent Co, 25 Oct 1851 (DG 4 Nov 1851)

REYNOLDS, Rebecca, see **TOWNSEND**, Zadoc

REYNOLDS, Richard, to **VINCENT**, Ellen, both of Wilm, 13 Mar 1843, by Rev. S. James of Phila (DG 15 Sep 1843)

REYNOLDS, Roger, to **DERICKSON**, Mary, Miss, in New Port, by Rev. Mr. Pryce (MU 28 Mar 1807)

REYNOLDS, Sarah, see **SMITH**, James

REYNOLDS, Taylor, at his res. near Rising Sun, MD, 23 Apr 1850, in his 50th yr (DG 17 May 1850)

REYNOLDS, Taylor, 23 May 1850, in his 56th yr (DG 11 Jun 1850)

REYNOLDS, Thomas P.,to **McGINNIS**, Rebecca, Miss, all of Kent Co, 6 Mar 1851, by Elder Meredith (DG 1 Apr 1851)

REYNOLDS, William, see **REYNOLDS**, Elizabeth

REYNOLDS, William, of a long and painful disease, 8 Jan 1848, at his res. in Appoq. Hd, aged 33 yrs and 3 mos. Leaves wife and children (DG 26 Jan 1848)

RHEIN, Frederick, to **SCHMIDT**, Mary J, Miss, all of Wilm, 2 Jun 1853, by the Rev. Mr Eacres (DG 3 Jun 1853)

RHIN, John, of Wilm, to **ROBB**, Maria, Miss, of Chester Co PA, 5 Aug 1850, by Alderman George W. Williams (DG 16 Aug 1850)

RHINEHOLT, Jacob, citizen of MD and PA, at the house of Mrs. Catherine HUSLER, in Newark DE, 9 Mar 1845 (DG 14 Mar 1845)

RHOADES, Robert, Esq., at his res. near Red Lion, 21 May 1852, in his 62nd yr (DG 25 May 1852)

RHODES, Enoch, see **YOUNKER**, Hannah

RHODES, Joseph T., of Wilm, to **SHEPHERD**, Mary Ann, Miss, of Chester Co PA, in Phila, 25 Mar 1852, by the Rev. J. T. Ward (DG 30 Mar 1852)

RHODES, Martha, see **COOK**, Joseph

RHODES, Mary, see **HOLMES**, Thomas

RHODES, Robert, see **LAWS**, John

RHODES, William, colored, of Christiana Hd, drowned in a brick pond near Broad and Washington St., Phila (DG 2 Aug 1850)

RHODES, William, of Wilm, to **CUMMINS**, Lydia, of Del. Co PA, at Marcus Hook PA, 25 Dec 1851 (DG 6 Jan 1852)

RIBLER, John, of Cecil Co, to **MARINOR**, Matilda, Miss, of New York City, in Wilm, 30 May 1850, by Rev. P. Coombe (DG 31 May 1850)

RICE, Jacob, to **JONES**, Sarah Jane, 8 May 1845, (DG 13 May 1845)

RICE, James, to **VIRTUE**, Mary Ann, Miss 13 Dec 1824, by Rev. E. W. Gilbert, all of Wilm (CI 14 Dec 1824)

RICE, Jane, dec'd, notice given by Henry BARRY, adm'r (DE 7 Aug 1797)

RICE, John, see TOLAND, Joshua

RICE, Matilda, see **DAY**, Joseph W.

RICE, Robert, dec'd, late of Brandywine Hd, miller, notice given by Daniel FRIEL, adm'r (DS 18 Nov 1812)

RICE, Sarah Ann F., Miss, see **ADAMS**, James F.

RICE, Thomas B., to **PENINGTON**, Martha Elizabeth, dau of Hyland B. PENINGTON, Esq., all of Wilm, 16 Sep 1845, by Rev. John Kennaday DD (DG 19 Sep 1845)

RICE, William, in Wilm, 5 Aug 1848, aged 20 yrs (DG 8 Aug 1848)

RICE, William, see DAY, Joseph W.

RICE, William W., to WHITE, Mary W., Miss, both of Wilm, 3 Aug 1828, by the Rev. A. K. Russel (DG 5 Aug 1828)

RICE, Wm. W., late of Mill Creek Hd. Farm sold, 152 acres (DG 20 Jan 1852)

RICHARDS, Ann Eliza, see WELCH, James

RICHARDS, Elizabeth, Mrs., see FORMAN, John, the Rev.

RICHARDS, Emma, see ROBINSON, Joseph

RICHARDS. F. De B, of Wilm, to ELLIS, Matilda, of Phila, 24 Feb 1853, by the Rev. Wm. B. Stevens, DD (DG 1 Mar 1853)

RICHARDS, Frances, see JONES, Evan

RICHARDS, Isaac, son of Nathaniel RICHARDS, 4 Oct 1833, na; interred in Friends Burial Ground (DG 8 Oct 1833)

RICHARDS, John, in Northwest Fork Hd, 17 Mar 1853, in his 49th yr (DG 29 Mar 1853)

RICHARDS, Lydia, wife of Nathaniel RICHARDS, suddenly, in Wilm, 2 Aug 1822 (DG 6 Aug 1822)

RICHARDS, Mary T., see PUSEY, Samuel N.

RICHARDS, Nathaniel, see RICHARDS, Isaac see RICHARDS, Lydia

RICHARDS, Nathaniel, one of the oldest and most respectble citizens of Wilm, at the res. of his son-in-law, James WEBB, 26 May 1850, aged 95 yrs (DG 4 Jun 1850)

RICHARDS, Rachel Ann, see RICKARDS, William L.

RICHARDS, Theodore W., of Sussex Co to WHITE, Mary H., Miss, of Phila, in Phila, 2 Jun 1851, by the Rev. J. Humphries (DG 10 Jun 1851)

RICHARDS, William, see PUSEY, Samuel N. see BERHANS, Hezekiah

RICHARDS, William, to McCOY, Eliza, Miss, both of Brandywine Hd, in Wilm, 17 Mar 1824, by the Rev. J. Potts (DG 19 Mar 1824)

RICHARDSON, Ann, dec'd, notice given by T. S. NEWLIN, adm'r (DJ 30 Mar 1832)

RICHARDSON, Anna, see BRINGHURST, Joseph

RICHARDSON, Ashton, in Christiana Hd, 19 Aug 1852 aged c 75 yrs (DG 13 Aug 1852)
see RICHARDSON, Mary
see TYSON, Thomas
see WALRAVEN, Walraven
see TATNALL, Joseph
see TATEM, John R.
see RICHARDSON, Richard

RICHARDSON, Jacob, to McCALL, Mary Jane, Miss, both of Wilm, 27 May 1846, by Rev. S. R. Wynkoop (DG 27 May 1846)
see RICHARDSON, Joseph Alonzo

RICHARDSON, James H., to SUMERVILLE, Parnall Ann, Miss, both of Newport, 20 Dec 1825, by the Rev. Mr. Page (DG 30 Dec 1825)

RICHARDSON, John, see BRINGHURST, Joseph see WILLIAMS, Peter

RICHARDSON, Joseph Alonza, inf son of Jacob RICHARDSON, 16 Mar 1849 (DG 27 Mar 1849)

RICHARDSON, Joseph, see RICHARDSON, Richard

RICHARDSON, Lucy, see TATEM, John R.

RICHARDSON, Mary, Miss, dau of Thomas RICHARDSON of Wilm, 20 Nov 1809, na (DG 13 Dec 1809)

RICHARDSON, Mary, relict of the late Ashton RICHARDSON, in Christiana Hd, 1 Feb 1853, in her 68th yr (DG 4 Feb 1853)

RICHARDSON, Mary Ann, see PRICE, Marcellus

RICHARDSON, Nancy, see LATIMER, Henry, Esq.

RICHARDSON, Richard, dec'd, late of Christiana Hd, notice given by Joseph RICHARDSON and Asthon RICHARDSON, exec'rs (DE 11 Jun 1798)

RICHARDSON, Richard, of DE, to WHITE, Hannah, dau of Josiah WHITE, 12 Aug 1841, at Friends Meeting House of Mulberry St. (DG 20 Aug 1841)

RICHARDSON, Sarah, see TATNALL, Joseph

RICHARDSON, Sidney, see WALTERS, William H.

RICHARDSON, Susan,
see HAMON, James H.

RICHARDSON, Thomas, see
RICHARDSON, Mary

RICHY, Robert, see VAUGHAN, J. F.

RICKARAW, Eliza, dau of Mr. Moulton
RICKARDS of Milford, very suddenly,
23 Aug 1816, in her 16th yr
(AW 31 Aug 1816)

RICKARDS, Annie Maria, only dau of Dr.
Wm. M. L. and Rachael Ann RICKARDS,
in Lewes DE, 15 Aug 1852, in her 8th yr
(DG 20 Aug 1852)

RICKARDS, Edward, see BARLOW, John

RICKARDS, Hannah H., see ZEBLEY, John

RICKARDS, Mary Jane, Miss, dau of Nelson
RICKARDS, 15 Oct 1848, in Milford
(DG 24 Oct 1848)

RICKARDS, Moulton,
see RICKARDS, Eliza

RICKARDS, Nelson,
see RICKARDS, Mary Jane

RICKARDS, Rachael Ann,
see RICKARDS, Annie Maria

RICKARDS, William L., M. D., to
RICHARDS, Rachel Ann, Miss, at
Georgetown, 19 Mar 1844, by Rev.
E. J. Way (DG 29 Mar 1844)

RICKARDS, Wm. M. L.,
see RICKARDS, Annie Maria

RICKETTS, P. C., editor of the Cecil Whig,
to GETTY, Eliza, dau of John A. GETTY,
Esq., of Elkton, 8 Sep 1851, by the Rev. H.
S. Howell (DG 16 Sep 1851)

RIDDEL, George, in White Clay Creek Hd,
21 Aug 1849, aged 35 yrs (DG 4 Sep 1849)

RIDDLE, Eliza, dau of James RIDDLE, Esq.,
of New Castle, at New Castle, 3 Sep 1823
(DG 9 Sep 1823)
see JEWETT, William H.

RIDDLE, Elizabeth Canby,
see BEEBE, John Wesley

RIDDLE, George Read, of Delaware, to
OPIE, Margaret S., of Millville, Jefferson Co,
VA, 14 Jan 1846, in Millville, by R. H. Wilmer
(DG 20 Jan 1846)

RIDDLE, James, aged c 18 yrs, train derailed
at Grubb's Landing, died 7 Jul 1853
(DG 12 Jul 1853)

RIDDLE, James, see RIDDLE, Eliza

RIDDLE, John, see RIDDLE, Richard K.
see JEWETT, William H.

RIDDLE, Mary, see HAUGHEY, William --
DENIED

RIDDLE, Richard K., Capt., son of John
RIDDLE, Esq., of New Castle, DE, at New
Orleans, of cholera, 12 Apr 1849, in his
29th yr. Bur. Cypress Grove cem
(DG 1 May 1849)

RIDER, Evans, of Wilm, to SLACK,
Elizabeth, of Balt, in Balt 19 Apr 1849,
by the Rev. Mr. Tippett (DG 1 May 1849)

RIDGELEY, Mary, Mrs., at her res. in Dover
28 Jul 1852, in her 94th yr (DG 3 Aug 1852)
in her 95th yr, widow of Nicholas RIDGELEY,
late Chancellor of the State of DE,
Episcopalian (DG 6 Aug 1852)

RIDGELY, Charles, Esq., lawyer, in
Georgetown, 15 Jul 1844, aged c 38 yrs.
Leaves a wife and family (DG 19 Jul 1844)

RIDGELY, Charles W.,
see BIDDLE, Rebecca

RIDGELY, H. M., the Hon,
see McKEE, _____

RIDGELY, Henry, see RIDGELY, Sallie

RIDGELY, Henry, M. D., of Dover, to
JENKINS, Virginia E., dau of Jonathan
JENKINS of Camden DE, 1 Nov 1843,
before his honor the Mayor of Phila
(DG 13 Nov 1843)

RIDGELY, Henry M., Hon, to COMEGYS,
Sally Ann, eldest dau of ex-Gov. COMEGYS,
18 May 1842, at Cherbourg, near Dover,
by Rev. John Manlove (DG 20 May 1842)

RIDGELY, Henry Moore, Esq., 7 Aug 1847,
aged 69 yrs. Long biography.
(DG 13 Aug 1847)

RIDGELY, N., Rev., in Wilm, 1 Dec 1849, na
(DG 4 Dec 1849)

RIDGELY, Nicholas, see RIDGELY, Mary

RIDGELY, Sallie, dau of Dr. Henry and
Virginia RIDGELY, 20 Sep 1853,
at the res. of her parents near Dover,
aged 2 yrs 4½ mos (DG 23 Sep 1853)

RIDGELY, Virginia, see RIDGELY, Sallie

RIDGEWAY, Elizabeth Ann,

see **BROWN**, William

RIDGEWAY, Harriet S.,
see **WADE**, Samuel

RIDGEWAY, Joseph, see **BROWN**, William

RIDGEWAY, Josiah, to **BIDDLE**, Matilda, Miss, 22 May 1834, by Elder John P. Peckworth (DG 23 May 1834)

RIDGEWAY, William H., of DE, to **PRETTYMAN**, Mary M., Miss, dau of the Rev. L. M. PRETTYMAN, late of Phila, 29 Jul 1852, by Dr. M. W. D. Ryan (DE papers please copy) (DG 3 Aug 1852)

RIDGWAY, Caroline,
see **MACY**, Silnamus J.

RIDGWAY, Jacob, to **PAISLEY**, Mary, Miss, both of Milford, DE, 5 Aug 1849, by the Rev. Silas C. Palmiter (DG 14 Aug 1849)

RIDGWAY, Thomas,
see **MACY**, Silnamus J.

RIGARD, Ezekial J., to **SKINNER**, Ann Elizabeth, both of Wilm, 24 Mar 1846, by Rev. J. A. Kennard (DG 31 Mar 1846)

RIGGS, Eliza, see **BAILEY**, Thomas

RIGHTER, ____, inf child of Evan RIGHTER, 3 May 1848 (DG 16 May 1848)

RIGHTER, Anderson, to **RIGHTER**, Ann Eliza, both of Wilm, 31 Jan 1848, by Rev. J. Castle (DG 4 Feb 1848)

RIGHTER, Ann Eliza,
see **RIGHTER**, Anderson

RIGHTER, Evan,
see **RIGHTER**, ____
see **RIGHTER**, Mary Jane

RIGHTER, John, see **RIGHTER**, Mary

RIGHTER, John, to **McALLISTER**, Margaret, Miss, both of Wilm, 6 Jan 1846, in Phila, by Rev. Joseph Jaquett (DG 9 Jan 1846)

RIGHTER, John, to **MIDDLETON**, Hannah, both of Wilm, in Marcus Hook PA, 8 Jan 1852, by Rev. J. Walker (DG 20 Jan 1852)

RIGHTER, Mary, Mrs., consort of John Righter, 31 Jan 1850, in her 56th yr (DG 12 Feb 1850)

RIGHTER, Mary Jane, Mrs, late consort of Evan RIGHTER, 5 May 1848 (DG 9 May 1848)

RIGHTER, William, to **COMER**, Rebecca, Miss, all of Wilm, 28 Jan 1847, by Rev. Dr. Kennaday (DG 2 Feb 1847)

RILER Nancy, Mrs., 27 Oct 1849, aged 79 yrs (DG 6 Nov 1849)

RILEY, Conrad, killed in explosion of steam powder mill of John P. Garesche, 8 Apr 1853, na (DG 12 Apr 1853)

RILEY, Hannah Mary, see **RILEY**, Peter

RILEY, Joseph, to **GOTT**, Mary Ann, all of Wilm, 31 Dec 1827, by Elder John P. Peckworth (DG 8 Jan 1828)

RILEY, Peter, late of NC Hd, Hannah Mary RILEY, adm'x (DG 25 Jul 1851)

RILEY, Philip, arrived from Ireland about 3 mos ago, found in the woods near Jones Neck, Dover Hd. Body much decomposed (DG 20 Aug 1850)

RILEY, Priscilla, see **BOONE**, Foster

RILEY, Thomas S., to **CROZIER**, Jane, Miss, both of Wilm, 23 Nov 1853, by the Rev. J. C. Humphries (DG 30 Dec 1853)

RILLEY, Ellen, see **WRIGHT**, Samuel

RINE, Rebecca, see **TRUITT**, William G.

RING, Ann, see **LOCKERMAN**, James C.

RINGGOLD, Louisa, Mrs, consort of William RINGGOLD, Esq., at Kenton, 18 Sep 1828, aged 29 yrs (DG 3 Oct 1828)

RINGGOLD, Matilda C.,
see **PEARCE**, James Alfred

RINGGOLD, Richard,
see **PEARCE**, James Alfred

RINGGOLD, Sarah Ann,
see **TEMPLE**, Sarah Ann

RINGGOLD, William,
see **RINGGOLD**, Louisa

RINGGOLD, William, one of the late elected members of the General Assembly of MD, from Kent Co, 12 Oct 1822 (DG 25 Oct 1822)

RINGGOLD, Wm.,
see **TEMPLE**, Sarah Ann

RISHTINE, Sophia,
see **RANDERSON**, James

RITCHEY, Ann J., see **WILLIS**, William

RITCHIE, A. A., see ROGERS, Robert Clay

RITCHIE, Anna, see TORBERT, Hugh

RITCHIE, Eliza, see HILT, William

RITCHIE, Eliza H.,
see ROGERS, Robert Clay

RITCHIE, Elizabeth Jane,
see DENNIS, Augustus H.

RITCHIE, Robert, in Wilm, 17 Aug 1853, in his 60th yr (DG 23 Aug 1853)

RITCHIE, Sarah, see HADDOCK, Henry

RITER, Sarah Jane, see WRIGHT, Duffas

RITTENHOUSE, William, to KELLY, Sarah, both of Wilm, 15 Jul 1842, in Chester PA by George W. Patram at his office (DG 22 Jul 1842)

ROACH, Eli, to CHASE, Mary, Miss, 20 Jan 1850, by Rev. J. R. Torbert (DG 12 Feb 1850)

ROACH, Margaret,
see MEEKINS, Robert, Capt.

ROACH, Mary, see SLACUM, J. W. E.

ROADS, Mary Jane, see COX, Thomas

ROBB, John, to KEEN, Nancy, Miss, 3 Jan 1822, by the Rev. Richard D. Hall (DG 8 Jan 1822)

ROBB, Maria, see RHIN, John

ROBBINS, Elizabeth, see LOGRAM, John

ROBBISON, Mary, see PAULSON, Peter

ROBERTS, _____, Rev.,
see ROBERTS, Lydia

ROBERTS, Eliza, see CONARD, Benjamin

ROBERTS, Emily, see LEWIS, Samuel G.

ROBERTS, George,
see CONARD, Benjamin

ROBERTS, Hannah, see RAMO, Peter

ROBERTS, Hugh, to GALLAGHER, Alice Ann, Miss, both of Wilm, 8 Aug 1842, by John M. Scott, Esq., Mayor of Phila (DG 12 Aug 1842)

ROBERTS, James, Jr., merchant, to VOSHELL, Mary A., all of Smyrna, 25 Jan 1853, by the Rev. H. E. Gilroy (DG 11 Feb 1853)

ROBERTS, John, of NY, to GREATRAKE, Mary, Miss, of NC Co, 12 Apr 1825, by the Rev. Mr. Walker (DG 18 Apr 1825)

ROBERTS, John, Capt., at sea on board the ship *Alexander* on her voyage from Calcutta to New York, a native of Delaware and master of that ship, 9 Apr 1842. Buried June 12 at quarantine ground, Staten Island, NY (DG 24 Jun 1842)

ROBERTS, Lydia, Mrs., aged 77 yrs, widow of Rev. Mr. ROBERTS, and sister of the late Comm. Thomas McDONOUGH, 24 May 1846, at her res. near Middletown. Buried in family burying ground. Episcopal. (DG 5 Jun 1846)

ROBERTS, Margaret A.,
see TRULENDER, Norris K.

ROBERTS, Rachel, see SANDERS, Ellis B

ROBERTS, Reese, in Brandywine Hd, aged 50 yrs (DG 5 Dec 1848)

ROBERTS, Samuel, to WILSON, Catharine, Miss, both of NC Co, 16 May 1850, by Rev. J. R. Anderson (DG 7 Jun 1850)

ROBERTS, Tabitha, a native of Sussex, in Wilm, 18 Dec 1844, aged 94 yrs (DG 24 Dec 1844)

ROBERTSON, Charlotte,
see GREENWOOD, William

ROBERTSON, George B., of Salem, NJ, to TOPHAM, Jane, Miss, of Wilm, 31 May 1848, by Rev. J. Castle (DG 2 Jun 1848)

ROBERTSON, John, Dr., Ass't Surgeon, US Army and formerly of Delaware City, on board the brig *Gen. Sumpter* on her passage from Charleston to Baltimore, 20 May 1842, aged 25 yrs (DG 3 Jun 1842)

ROBERTSON, John, of NC Co, to SHARP, Susanna, of same, 26 Feb 1852, by Elder Thomas Barton, Chester Co PA (DG 2 Mar 1852)

ROBESON, Alexander,
see WHITELY, Benj., Esq.,

ROBESON, Eliza M.,
see WHITELY, Benj., Esq.,

ROBESON, John L., to JANVIER, Mary G., Miss, youngest dau of Mr. Thomas JANVIER, 26 Nov 1829, by Rev. J. N. Danforth of Washington, D. C. (DG 1 Dec 1829)

ROBESON, Thomas Janvier, after a short illness, 1 Apr 1850, in his 20th yr. Long obit in 12 Apr issue (DG 5 Apr 1850)

ROBINETT, Allan McLane,
see WILLIAMS, Samuel
see ROBINETT, Lewis P.

ROBINETT, Ann Janem
see VERDON, Thomas

ROBINETT, Benj. F., to MONCKTON, Anna, Miss, both of NC Co, 13 Feb 1852, by the Rev. J. A. Roche (DG 24 Feb 1852)

ROBINETT, Capt., see ROBINETT, Sarah

ROBINETT, David, to DAVIS, Catharine, Miss, both of Wilm, 27 May 1843, by Rev. E. Covel (DG 2 Jun 1843)

ROBINETT, David, Capt., see ROBINETT, Hannah B.

ROBINETT, David, in Wilm, 17 Jan 1835, at an advanced age (DG 20 Jan 1835)

ROBINETT, David, Jr., to YATES, Kessiah, Miss, both of Wilm, at Chester, 30 Nov 1822, by David Caldwell, Esq. (DG 4 Dec 1822)

ROBINETT, Hannah B., dau of the late Capt David ROBINETT, in Wilm, after a protracted illness, 25 Nov 1847, na (DG 3 Dec 1847)

ROBINETT, Joseph, to BRANNON, Margaret, Miss, both of Wilm, 7 Jul 1850, by Rev. Newton Heston (DG 23 Jul 1850)

ROBINETT, Lewis P., inf son of Allen M. ROBINETT, in Wilm, 16 Aug 1846, na (DG 21 Aug 1846)

ROBINETT, Mary Livinia,
see WILLIAMS, Samuel

ROBINETT, Rachel,
see O'DANIEL, Francis, Esq.

ROBINETT, Sarah E.,
see MILWARD, Thomas

ROBINETT, Sarah, Mrs, widow of the late Capt. ROBINETT, in Wilm, 2 Aug 1842, aged 75 yrs (DG 5 Aug 1842)

ROBINETT, William, of apoplexy, 18 Jul 1848, aged 18 yrs (DG 28 Jul 1848)

ROBINETTE, Joseph K.,
see ROBINETTE, Sarah Ann V.

ROBINETTE, Sarah Ann V., dau of Joseph K. ROBINETTE, in Wilm, of smallpox, 14 Jan 1828, na (DG 18 Jan 1827)

ROBINSON, _____, dau of George ROBINSON, of Salem NJ, in Wilm, on a visit to Mr. SORDEN, as the result of a fall, 7 Sep 1851, aged c 3 yrs (DG 12 Sep 1851)

ROBINSON, _____. Judge,
see WOOTON, Edward, Esq.

ROBINSON, A. Gilbert, of Wilm, to METZ, Susan Amelia, dau of Mr. Geo. W. METZ, of Phila, 14 Dec 1851, by the Rev. J. R. Crooks (DG 30 Dec 1851)

ROBINSON, Albert, after a short illness, 4 Mar 1845, aged 51 yrs (DG 7 Mar 1845)

ROBINSON, Alfred P.,
see PORTER, Elizabeth

ROBINSON, Amelia,
see DICKERSON, Alfred A.
see PETERSON, George F.

ROBINSON, Ann,
see ROBINSON, Francis
see JEFFERIS, Emmor
see HEAZLITT, John

ROBINSON, Ann C., see CLELAND, Nelson

ROBINSON, Anna E.,
see MORROW, James L.

ROBINSON, Annie S., see TATEM, Samuel

ROBINSON, Charles, drowned, body found "on Sunday" (DG 24 Apr 1790)
see HANBY, Richard

ROBINSON, Ebenezer, to ANDERSON, Mary, Miss, both of Wilm, 1 Aug 1822, by the Rev. Dr. Read (DG 6 Aug 1822)
see ROBINSON, Margaret, Mrs.

ROBINSON, Edward P.,
see MORROW, James L.

ROBINSON, Edward P., 2 Dec 1852, in his 41st yr, Methodist (DG 3 Dec 1852) late of Wilm City, Hannah Ann ROBINSON, exec'x (DG 14 Dec 1852)

ROBINSON, Eleanor, see WILSON, Eli

ROBINSON, Elenor, see LYMAN, Thomas

ROBINSON Elizabeth, Mrs., widow of the late Jacob ROBINSON of Wilm, at the res. of her son-in law, Mr. Samuel MILLER (Oak Hill), 22 Sep 1849, in her 71st yr (DG 26 Oct 1849)

ROBINSON, Elizabeth, see FOOTE, James

ROBINSON, Elizabeth, in Wilm, 30 Jan 1853, aged c 75 yrs. Funeral from the res. of her son-in-law, Dr. F. ASKEW, corner of 7th and Market St (DG 1 Feb 1853)

DELAWARE MARRIAGES AND DEATHS FROM NEWSPAPERS, 1729-1853

ROBINSON, Elizabeth H., wife of George W.
ROBINSON, and second dau of the late
Matthew SCOTT of Wilm, in Balt. 16 Jan
1849, in her 32nd yr. (DG 18 Jan 1849)
see ALLMOND, George

ROBINSON, Elizabeth J.,
see HEATHCOTE, Andrew

ROBINSON, Elizabeth W., Mrs., member of
the M.E.Ch, near Newark, 12 Sep 1828, na
(DG 16 Sep 1828)

ROBINSON, Francis, tanner, dec'd, late of
Wilm, notice given by Ann ROBINSON,
adm'x (DG 3 Jan 1793)

ROBINSON, George,
see ROBINSON, _____.

ROBINSON, George W., to BIDDLE,
Elizabeth S., all of Wilm, 3 Jun 1844, by
Rev. M. J. Rhees (DG 7 Jun 1844)
see ROBINSON, Elizabeth H.

ROBINSON, Hanah Jane,
see MONTGOMERY, John

ROBINSON, Hannah Ann,
see ROBINSON, Edward P.

ROBINSON, J., of Delaware City, to FRIST,
Mary, Miss, of Wilm, 31 May 1846, by Rev.
Mr. Hard of Chester PA (DG 5 Jun 1846)

ROBINSON, Jacob,
see ROBINSON, Elizabeth

ROBINSON, Jacob, to BRADLEY, Sarah,
Miss, 14 Dec 1820 (DG 15 Dec 1820)

ROBINSON, Jacob, carter, in Wilm,
17 Oct 1833, "old" (DG 22 Oct 1833)

ROBINSON, Jacob, of Wilm, to LITTLE,
Rebecca, Miss, of York PA, 15 Oct, 1850,
in St. John's Church, in York by Rev. Mr.
Thompson (DG 25 Oct 1850)

ROBINSON, Jacob, late of Wilm, property
sold by John C. PATTERSON, Esq.
(DG 15 Jun 1852)

ROBINSON, James H., late of Christiana Hd,
David GRAVES, adm'r (DG 23 Mar 1852)
see ROBINSON, Mary Frances

ROBINSON, James R., tobacconist of Wilm,
thrown from carriage and dragged by horse,
3 Feb 1851, na. Leaves a wife and three
children (DG 7 Feb 1851)

ROBINSON, Jane E.,
see HYLAND, Thomas B.

ROBINSON, John, of yellow fever
(DE 20 Sep1798)

ROBINSON, John, to DUNNING, Julia A.,
eldest dau of William DUNNING of Dagsborough, 28 Sep 1841, at Dagsborough by
the Rev. Mr. Watson (DG 8 Oct 1841)

ROBINSON, John,
see DICKERSON, Alfred A.
see ROBINSON, Julia A.

ROBINSON, John L.,
see WHITELEY, Benjamin

ROBINSON, John P., to YARNALL, Sarah,
Miss, both of Mill Creek Hd, in Wilm,
8 Jan 1824, by the Rev. E. W. Gilbert
(DG 9 Jan 1824)

ROBINSON, John T.,
see TOWNSEND, Sylvester D.

ROBINSON, Jos. F., see TATEM, Samuel

ROBINSON, Joseph, dec'd, late of
Brandywine Hd, notice given by Penrose
ROBINSON, adm'r (FA 3 Mar 1804)

ROBINSON, Joseph, to CARTER, Amelia,
Miss, both of Brandywine Hd, 21 Dec 1809,
by Rev. Mr. Pryce (DG 23 Dec 1809)

ROBINSON, Joseph, Esq., formerly
merchant of Wilm, 3 Jan 1827; left a large
family (DG 5 Jan 1827) dec'd, property in
Mill Creek Hd for sale by sheriff, William
Herdman (DG 16 Oct 1827)

ROBINSON, Joseph, see GILPIN, Vincent

ROBINSON, Joseph, to RICHARDS, Emma,
both of Wilm, in Phila, 18 Apr 1849, by
Friends ceremony, in the presence of
Alderman J. Mitchell (DG 24 Apr 1849)

ROBINSON. Julia A., late wife of John
ROBINSON of Phila, dau of William
DUNNING of Dagsborough, at Dags-
borough, 14 Jan 1844 (DG 18 Jan 1844)

ROBINSON, Lewis H., formerly of Wilm,
17 Jan 1845, at Norwich, Conn
(DG 7 Feb 1845)

ROBINSON, Lydia Ann,
see BLOUNT, James

ROBINSON, Margaret,
see VINING, James Lisle

ROBINSON, Margaret Jane,
see FISHER, Henry

ROBINSON, Margaret, Mrs., wife of
Ebenezer ROBINSON, 1 Mar 1820, na
(DG 8 Mar 1820)

ROBINSON, Mary, Mrs., relict of the late Gen. Thomas ROBINSON of Naaman's Creek, at her res. in Phila, 18 Dec 1833, aged 72 yrs (DG 24 Dec 1833)

ROBINSON, Mary, at the res. of her son-in-law, Eli WILSON, 17 May 1847, aged 82 yrs (DG 17 May 1847)
see WOOTON, Edward, Esq.
see MULLEN, Robert

ROBINSON, Mary E.,
see TOWNSEND, Sylvester D.

ROBINSON, Mary Frances, inf dau of James H. and Mary Orpha ROBINSON, in Newport, 2 Feb 1850, aged 6 mos 7 days (DG 18 Feb 1850)

ROBINSON, Mary Hanson,
see ASKEW, Henry Ford, M. D.

ROBINSON, Mary Jane,
see FREEMAN, JOHN

ROBINSON, Mary Orpha,
see ROBINSON, Mary Frances

ROBINSON, Naomi, see GILPIN, Vincent

ROBINSON, Penrose,
see ROBINSON, Joseph

ROBINSON, Peter, to MITCHELL, Sarah, Miss, 10 Jan 1821 (DG 23 Jan 1821)
see MITCHELL, John

ROBINSON, Robert P.,
see McKEAN, James
see ROBINSON, William Naff

ROBINSON, Ruth Ann,
see WARNER, William

ROBINSON, S. P., Mrs,
see SORDEN, John, Maj.

ROBINSON, Sally Ann,
see MARTIN, James

ROBINSON, Sarah,
see COOMBE, Benjamin, Jr.

ROBINSON, Sarah N.,
see ROBINSON, William Naff

ROBINSON, Thomas,
see COOMBE, Benjamin, Jr.

ROBINSON, Thomas, Col.,
see ROBINSON, Thomas

ROBINSON, Thomas, Esq., of Naaman's Creek, DE, to BRACKETT, Maria, Miss, dau of Mr. James BRACKETT of Quincy, MA, at Quincy, 28 Jul 1825, by the Rev. Mr. Cutter

(DG 5 Aug 1825)

ROBINSON, Thomas, Gen., see
ROBINSON, Mary, Mrs.

ROBINSON, Thomas, son of Col. Thomas ROBINSON of Naaman's Creek, 27 Jul 1834, aged 23 mos 24 days (DG 29 Jul 1834)

ROBINSON, Valentine,
see PRINCE, John

ROBINSON, William,
see SHIPLEY, Rebecca
see BYRNES, Thomas
see BROWN, Abraham

ROBINSON, William B., at his res. in Delaware City, 18 Nov 1852, in his 31st yr (DG 18 Nov 1852)

ROBINSON, William F., formerly of Wilm, at Lexington KY, of typhoid fever, 10 Sep 1849, in his 40th yr (DG 18 Sep 1849)

ROBINSON, William J., to SHORT, Sarah Jane, Miss, both of Delaware City, in Wilm, 6 Feb 1851, by the Rev. Wm. Cooper (DG 14 Feb 1851)

ROBINSON, William Naff, son of Robert R. and Sarah N. ROBINSON, in Wilm, 14 Oct 1851, in his 10th yr (DG 17 Oct 1851)

ROBINSON, William P., to SAVIN, Rachel H., all of NC Co, 3 Jan 1850, by Rev. P. Coombe (DG 8 Jan 1850)

ROBSON, Michael, Jr., at the res. of his father near New Garden PA, 4 Sep 1851, aged 25 yrs (DG 16 Sep 1851)

ROBSON, Rosemanda,
see ROBSON, William

ROBSON, William, son of William and Rosemanda ROBSON, at his late res. in St. Georges Hd, of pulmonary consumption, ndd, aged 38 yrs (DG 6 Mar 1846)

ROCHE, Ann Eliza,
see LAZALERE, Benjamin F.

ROCHE, Edward, Esq.,
see ROCHE, Eliza, Mrs.

ROCHE, Edward, Esq., a Justice of the Peace and Notary Public, "on Friday morning last" [6th?] (DG 10 Apr 1821)

ROCHE, Edward, see RUMFORD, Marietta

ROCHE, Edward, see RUMFORD, John

ROCHE, Eliza, Mrs., consort of Edward

ROCHE, Esq., of Wilm, after a short but painful illness, 25 Nov 1818 (DG 28 Nov 1818)

ROCHE, James L., see ROCHE, Manning

ROCHE, James L., of Wilm, to MALONEY, Mary A., of Brooklyn, NY, in Wilm, 21 Mar 1844, by Rev. M. J. Rhees (DG 26 Mar 1844)

ROCHE, Manning, son of James L. ROCHE, 11 Mar 1848, in Wilm (DG 14 Mar 1848)

ROCHE, Marietta M., see RUMFORD, John

RODDLE, G. Bedford, in Wilm, 27 Oct 1848, in his 49th yr (DG 30 Oct 1848)

RODGERS, Elizabeth, at the res. of Mrs. GREY, 11 Nov 1850, aged c 65 yrs. (DG 15 Nov 1850)

RODGERS, John, see LARKIN, William

RODGERS, Thomas, Esq., of Dubuque IA, to BURTON, Anna, Miss, late of Nashville TN, formerly of Lewes DE, in Nashville, at the res. of John FINN, Esq., 21 Oct 1850 (DG 1 Nov 1850)

RODMAN, Simon, to SMART, Rebecca, Miss, both of NC Co, 22 Feb 1848, by Rev. S. R. Wynkoop (DG 25 Feb 1848)

RODNEY, _____. Mrs, late consort of Hon George B. RODNEY, member of Congress from the district of Delaware, at New Castle, 8 Feb 1844 (DG 13 Feb 1844)

RODNEY, C. A., see CUSHMAN, William H. W.

RODNEY, Caesar A, see RATTLE, Francis
see PARVIN, Theophilus, the Rev.
see BANNING, Henry G.
see ESCHENBERG, John, Esq.

RODNEY, Caesar A., dec'd, notice given by J. G. BRINKLE, atty-in-fact of Susan H. RODNEY (DG 7 Dec 1824)

RODNEY, Caleb, see LANDRETH, David, Jr.

RODNEY, Caleb, see HALL, Henry, Dr.

RODNEY, Daniel, see WHITE, Hannah, Mrs.

RODNEY, Eliza, see ESCHENBERG, John, Esq.
see LANDRETH, David, Jr.

RODNEY, Ellen, see RATTLE, Francis

RODNEY, G. B., Esq., of New Castle, DE, to TAYLOR, Eliza, Miss, only dau of Geo. W. TAYLOR of Phila, 24 Jun 1851, at St Andrews Ch, Phila, by Rev. J. C. Clay DD (DG 27 Jun 1851)

RODNEY, George B., see RODNEY, _____.

RODNEY, Hannah, see WHITE, Hannah, Mrs.

RODNEY, Hannah C., see CUSHMAN, William H. W.

RODNEY, Henry F., Esq., of Lewis (sic), to BURTON, Mary, Miss, dau of Mr. Robert BURTON, all of Sussex Co, 9 Oct 1821 (DG 23 Oct 1821) see RODNEY, Mary

RODNEY, Hester, see HALL, Henry, Dr.

RODNEY, John, Rev., see HALL, Henry, Dr.

RODNEY, John, see McCLUNG, Wm. Linn

RODNEY, John, the Rev., see LANDRETH, David, Jr.

RODNEY, Mary, see PARVIN, Theophilus, the Rev.

RODNEY, Mary, wife of Henry F. RODNEY, late of Phila, at Lewes DE, 16 Mar 1852, aged 49 yrs (DG 18 Mar 1852)

RODNEY, Simon, formerly of DE, in Phila, 2 Apr 1853, in his 65th yr (DG 8 Apr 1853)

RODNEY, Susan H., see RODNEY, Caesar A.

RODNEY, Thomas, of Lewistown, 7 May 1820, aged 46 yrs (DG 17 May 1820)

RODNEY, Thomas M., Esq., to FROMBERG, Susan Maria, Miss, 21 Oct 1841, by Rev. S. M. Gayley, all of Wilm (DG 29 Oct 1841)

ROE, Andrew B., of Caroline Co MD, to SKEEVIN, Kate R., of Smyrna, 30 Aug 1852, by Rev. H. E. Gilroy (DG 10 Sep 1852)

ROE, John, of Caroline Co MD, to MORRIS, Sarah, Miss, of Kent Co MD, 13 Aug 1850, on Bethel Camp Ground, by Richard H. Merriken (DG 27 Aug 1850)

ROGERS, Daniel, see BOOTH, William

ROGERS, Eliza J., see BARNEY, J. Nicholson

ROGERS, Eliza, see BARNEY, Eliza

ROGERS, James,
see BARNEY, J. Nicholson
see BARNEY, Eliza

ROGERS, James, to JOHNS, Delia, Miss, 1 Mar 1804, by Rev. Robert Clay, notice signed by N. JOHNS (FA 3 Mar 1804) DENIED (FA 7 Mar 1804)

ROGERS, James, Esq., to BOOTH, Maria, Miss, 16 Apr 1807, by Rev. Mr. Clay (MU 18 Mar 1807)

ROGERS, James, son of James B. ROGERS, Esq., one of twins, at the res. of his father, James B. ROGERS, Esq., near New Castle, aged 3 yrs 5 mos, 25 days (DG 29 Aug 1848)

ROGERS, James B., see ROGERS, James

ROGERS, James Booth, to ROGERS, Saran (sic) A., dau of Hon. M. C. ROGERS, at New Castle, 9 Feb 1835, by the Rev. S. W. Presstman (DG 17 Feb 1835)

ROGERS, John, see BECK, John

ROGERS, M. C., Hon.,
see ROGERS, James Booth

ROGERS, Mary, see BOOTH, William

ROGERS, Robert Clay, USN, to RITCHIE, Eliza H., dau of A..A. RITCHIE, Esq., at New Castle, 15 Apr 1852, by the Rev. Thomas F. Billopp, rector of Immanuel Ch, New Castle (DG 20 Apr 1852)

ROGERS, Sarah Alfonso, see BECK, John

ROGERS, Sarah A.,
see ROGERS, James Booth

ROGERS, Thomas A.,
see MURRAY, Alexander

ROGERS, Wilhelmina,
see LAMBDIN, Thomas J

ROGERS, William, the Rev., native of Rhode Island, moved to DE previous to the Revolution. Pastor of First Baptist Ch, Prof. of *Belles Lettres* at U. of PA, last surviving Chaplain of Rev. Army, 8 Apr 1824, aged 73 yrs (DG 9 Apr 1824)

ROLLAND, Elizabeth,
see BENNETT, Angelo

ROLLINS, Carlusine J., of Pittstown ME, to KERNS, Cassandra S., of Wilm, in Phila, 4 Aug 1851, by the Rev. J. Bales (DG 18 Aug 1851)

RONEY, John, to YOUNG, Susanna, Miss, both of NC Co in Wilm, by the Rev. Wm. Cooper (DG 20 Jul 1849)

ROOT, John B., see ROOT, Mary L.

ROOT, Mary Ann,
see MARSHALL, Henry W.

ROOT, Mary L., consort of John B. ROOT, and dau of Alex. PORTER, Esq., of Wilm, of yellow fever, in Galveston TX, 11 Oct 1853, na (DG 28 Oct 1853)

ROSE, David, to FOSTER, Ruth Ann, Miss, both of NC Co, at Cantwell's Bridge, 10 Jul 1845, by Rev. Thomas D. Ozanna (DG 15 Jul 1845)

ROSE, Serena Jane, see HYATT, Francis A.

ROSELL, John P. formerly of Brandywine Village, to NELSON, Mary, Miss, of Accomac VA, 30 Sep 1849, by Rev. Mr. Stokes (DG 22 Jan 1850)

ROSS, Ann T., see COCHRAN, Wm. H.

ROSS, Charles, son of Mr. Samuel ROSS, in Milford, 7 Jun 1852, of scarlet fever, aged 4 yrs 6 mos (DG 15 Jun 1852)

ROSS, Curtis J., to COLLINS, Martha, Miss, youngest dau of the late John COLLINS, Esq., all of Sussex Co, at Bridgeville, 2 Nov 1830, by Rev. Samuel Rauley (DF 20 Nov 1830)

ROSS, David, Capt., dec'd, farm near New Castle to be sold by Marcia G. ROSS, adm'x (DG 18 Jun 1827)

ROSS, David, to CUNNINGHAM, Mary, Miss, both of Wilm, 1 Oct 1848, by Rev. John M. Grant (DG 20 Oct 1848)

ROSS, Hannah H., see BALL, James

ROSS, John, see NOXON, Thomas

ROSS, Marcia G., see ROSS, David

ROSS, Martha, Mrs., Newark DE, 14 May 1851, in her 80th yr; Presbyterian (DG 30 May 1851)

ROSS, Nathaniel, at his res. in North West Fork Hd, Sussex Co, after a long illness, 13 Nov 1822, aged 42 yrs, leaving a wife and 6 children (DG 26 Nov 1822)

ROSS, Rebecca, see LESLIE, Alexander

ROSS, Richard, Capt., of Chester PA, to EVES, Rebecca, Miss, of Phila, late of New Castle DE, 5 Aug 1847, by Rev. Mr. Roatch (sic) (DG 20 Aug 1847)

ROSS, Samuel, see ROSS, Charles

ROSS, William, in Mispillion Hd, Kent Co, on the 25th inst (DG 1 May 1849)

ROSSELL, William, to FREEZE, Sarah, Miss, of Wilm, 3 Jan 1822, by the Rev. Richard D. Hall (DG 8 Jan 1822)

ROTHERAM, Joseph, dec'd, late of White Clay Creek Hd, notice given by Joel LEWIS, James STROUD and Abel GLASFORD, exec'rs (DG 15 Aug 1795)

ROTHWELL, _____, Maj., see ROTHWELL, William

ROTHWELL, Abraham, to BUCKINGHAM, Sarah J., Miss, both of NC Co, 11 Apr 1844 in Wilm, by Rev. M. J. Rhees (DG 18 Apr 1844)

ROTHWELL, Ann E., see MURPHY, Daniel J.

ROTHWELL, William, son of Maj. ROTHWELL, of Appoq. Hd., of the firm of Grayson, Guild and Co., late of St. Louis, but formerly of Wilm (DG 12 Feb 1850)

ROULENSON, John H., Esq., editor of the *Centreville Sentinel*, to WHITTINGTON, Ellen R., Miss, all of Q. Anne's Co MD (DG 6 Jan 1852)

ROWAN, Archibald Hamilton, "a historical character," in Dublin, no date, in his 84th yr (DG 9 Dec 1834)

ROWAN, Henry, see McMULLEN, Samuel

ROWAN, Henry, to McCOY, Mary Ann, Miss, 26 Oct 1825, by the Rev. R. Williston (DG 11 Nov 1825)

ROWAN, Mary, see BENNETT, Charles W.

ROWAN, Mary C., see McMULLEN, Samuel

ROWAN, Rebecca, see PENNINGTON, John B.

ROWAN, William, see BENNETT, Charles W.

ROWAN, William, dec'd, late of Wilm. Notice given by William ROWAN to pay debts to Jonathan BYRNES, Jr. (DG 2 Apr 1841)

ROWAN, William, merchant, 5 Sept 1842 (DG 9 Sep 1842)

ROWAN, William, [2] see ROWAN, William

ROWE, Lucinda, see CHANDLER, Reece E.

ROWE, Reuben, see CHANDLER, Reece E.

ROWENS, Francis R., to ELLEGOOD, Mary E., eldest dau of J. H. ELLEGOOD, Esq., both of Georgetown, 29 Dec 1845, by Rev. J. L. McKim (DG 16 Jan 1846)

ROWINS, Francis H., see ROWINS, Mary E.

ROWINS, Mary E., aged 18 yrs, consort of Francis H. ROWINS, 13 Oct 1846, at Georgetown (DG 30 Oct 1846)

ROWLAND, Isaiah, son of Joseph G. ROWLAND, 21 Mar 1826, aged 11 yrs 7 mos...resembled his brother Mifflin, who d 8 yrs ago (DG 28 Mar 1826)

ROWLAND, J. A., Dr., of Chester Co PA, to CAMERON, Margaret M., Miss, of Cecil Co MD, 20 Mar 1845, by Rev. E. Miller of West Chester PA (DG 28 Mar 1845)

ROWLAND, James E., of DE to LAFFERTY, Anne, of Phila, 4 Sep 1853, by Rev. Henry Bacon (DG 25 Oct 1853)

ROWLAND, John, 7 Oct 1833, in Lewes and Rehoboth Hd, 7 Oct 1833, na (DG 15 Oct 1833)

ROWLAND, Jonathan M., of Newark, to WEEKS, Elizabeth, Miss, of Cecil Co MD, 9 Apr 1846, Rev. Edward Kennard (DG 14 Apr 1846)

ROWLAND, Joseph G, see ROWLAND, Rebecca see ROWLAND, Isaiah

ROWLAND, Mifflin, see ROWLAND, Isaiah

ROWLAND, Rebecca, after a lingering illness,11 Mar 1804, na, wife of Joseph G. ROWLAND of Camden (FA 21 Mar 1804)

ROWLAND, Samuel J., of Camden, DE, to LAWS, Mary dau of Clement LAWS, dec'd, late of Phila, 22 Nov 1826, at Friends Meeting in Caroline Co (DG 1 Dec 1826)

ROWLAND Sarah, dec'd, late of Kent Co, property in Wilm to be sold by Joseph P. COMEGYS, trustee (DG 4 Feb 1851)

ROYAL, Catharine F., Mrs, at her res. in Wilm, 14 Dec 1850 (DG 17 Dec 1850)

ROZELL, Isaac of Phila, to DAISY, Mary, Miss, of Sussex Co DE, 17 May 1852, by Rev. A. Johns (DG 28 May 1852)

ROZELL, Joseph, see ROZELL, Mary Ann

ROZELL, Mary Ann, wife of Joseph ROZELL, 10 Mar 1851, aged 46 yrs 2 mos 15 days (DG 21 Mar 1851)

RUBINCAME, John R., to BALL, Mary, Miss, 29 Mar 1849, by the Rev. Joseph Barr (DG 3 Apr 1849)

RUDMAN, Richard, to CHANDLER, Elizabeth, Miss, dau of William CHANDLER, 26 Feb 1835, by Rev. James D. Pichan (DG 3 Mar 1835)

RUDMAN, Richard, native of England, 1 Jul 1851, in his 42nd yr (DG 8 Aug 1851)

RUDOLPH, Hannah, see STIDHAM, Peter

RUDOLPH, Margaret, in Wilm, 4 Jan 1848, aged 97 yrs (DG 7 Jan 1847)

RUDOLPH, William, to THOMPSON, Martha A., Miss, both of Wilm, in Phila, 23 Mar 1847, by Rev. Robert Gerry (DG 26 Mar 1847)

RUMER, John, to DERRICK, Ann, Miss, both of Brandywine Hd, 1 Jul 1841, by Rev. M. R. Talbot in Chester PA (DG 16 Jul 1841)

RUMER, Martha, see FOOTE, Benjamin

RUMFORD, Caroline, see BURROUGHS, George R.

RUMFORD, Emily, see WOLLASTON, Joshua H.

RUMFORD, Henrietta, dau of Lewis RUMFORD of Wilm, hatter, 5 Aug 1826, aged c 8 mos (WN 10 Aug 1826)

RUMFORD, Henrietta, wife of Lewis RUMFORD of Wilm, hatter, 7 Aug 1826 (WN 10 Aug 1826)

RUMFORD, John, to ROCHE, Marietta M., Miss, dau of the late Edward ROCHE, Esq., 13 Mar 1828, by the Rev. E. W. Gilbert (DG 21 Mar 1828)
see BENSON, James H.

RUMFORD, John G., to BROWN, Lydia Ann, Miss, both of Wilm, 4 Apr 1844, by Rev. S. R. Wynkoop (DG 16 Apr 1844)

RUMFORD, Lewis, see WOLLASTON, Joshua H.
see RUMFORD, Henrietta (2)

RUMFORD, Louisa, see BENSON, James H.

RUMFORD, Marietta, dau of the late Edward ROCHE of Wilm, in Phila, 11 Jun 1846, aged 57 yrs (DG 16 Jun 1846)

RUMFORD, Mary Ann, see GARDNER, Mary Ann

RUMFORD, Matilda, see WIGGINS, William B.

RUMFORD, Sarah Ann, see CHESNUT, John

RUMFORD, Thomas, see GARDNER, Mary Ann

RUMFORD, Washington, to MEEKINS, Sarah Ann, Miss, both of Wilm, 22 Jun 1848, by Rev. T. J. Thompson (DG 27 Jun 1848)

RUMMEL, John A., of Baltimore, in Wilm, 4 Dec 1844. IOOF attended funeral (DG 6 Dec 1844)

RUMMELL, ___, aged c 35 yrs, in Wilm, leaving 3 children. Her husband died about 2 yrs ago. They were from Baltimore. (DG 10 Mar 1846)

RUMOR, John F., at Rockland, Brandywine, 3 Feb 1848, aged 74 yrs (DG 8 Feb 1848)

RUMSEY, Ann, wife of Charles RUMSEY, and sister of the editor [Samuel HARKER, see WRIGHT, Ezekiel] of the Delaware Gazette, in Salem, NJ, 30 Aug 1823, aged 26 yrs (DG 2 Sep 1823)

RUMSEY, Charles, see RUMSEY, Ann

RUMUR, John, see RUMUR, Mary Ann

RUMUR. Mary Ann, Mrs, wife of John RUMUR, at Rockland, Brandywine Hd, 28 Feb 1846, aged 28 yrs (DG 24 Mar 1846)

RUPP, Catharine E., see GARRETSON, Cornelius L.

RUPP, Daniel, see GARRETSON, Cornelius L.

RUSH, Isaac J., to WALMSEY, Mary, Miss, both of B'wine Hd, 1 Jul 1827, by John P. Peckworth (DG 3 Jul 1827)

RUSHAM, Caroline, see ALLEN, Jesse

RUSLING, Joseph, the Rev., Pastor of St. John's Ch, Phila, to HUNTER, Sarah, Miss, of Wilm, 3 Jan 1822, by the Rev. L. Lawrenson (DG 8 Jan 1822)

RUSSEL, A. K., the Rev., see RUSSEL, Andrew J.
see RUSSEL, Washington, Dr.

RUSSEL, Andrew J., second son of the Rev. A. K. RUSSEL, at Newark, 6 May 1835, aged 11 yrs (DG 12 May 1835)

RUSSEL, Charles M. to NEWLIN, Elizabeth, Miss, of Birmingham PA, 1 Dec 1842, by Rev. Alfred Lee (DG 9 Dec 1842)

RUSSEL, John, to VAUX, Eliza E., both of Kent Co, in Kent Co, 13 Jan 1848, by Rev. John Bell (DG 26 Jan 1848)

RUSSEL, Martha A., see COYLE, William

RUSSEL, Milton C., 20 Sep 1843, at Brandywine Village (DG 22 Sep 1843)

RUSSEL, Sallie A., see DAY, John R.

RUSSEL, Washington, Dr., of Christiana, to THOMSON, Mary, Miss, youngest dau of John THOMSON, Esq., of Newark, at Newark, 1 Nov 1825, by the Rev. A. K. RUSSEL (DG 11 Nov 1825)

RUSSELL, Alexander W., a member of Capt. Morris' Co of Missouri Volunteers, and son the late Rev. A. K. RUSSELL of Newark, at Santa Fe, NM, 3 Feb 1847, of typhus fever, aged 25 yrs (DG 25 May 1847)

RUSSELL, A. K. the Rev.
see RUSSELl, Alexander W.
see RUSSELL, Catharine

RUSSELL, Benjamin,
see RUSSELL, Eliza Jane

RUSSELL, Benjamin F., to QUINN, Margaret, Miss, both of Wilm, 25 Nov 1852, by the Rev. A. A. Willits (DG 30 Nov 1852)

RUSSELL, Catharine, youngest dau of the late Andrew K. RUSSELL, 12 Apr 1850, na, at Newark (DG 16 Apr 1850)

RUSSELL, Christopher, formerly of Yorkshire, England, in Christiana Hd, 12 Apr 1847, aged 69 yrs (DG 27 Apr 1847)

RUSSELL, Eliza Jane, wife of Benjamin RUSSELL, formerly of Chester Co Pa, in Wilm, 30 Jul 1849 (DG 3 Aug 1849)

RUSSELL, George, to FORREST, Mary, Miss, 5 Sep 1841, by Rev. J. W. McCullough, all of NC Co (DG 17 Sep 1841) see PLATT, Samuel, Jr.

RUSSELL, Harriet A., see PERCE, John

RUSSELL, Jane, (or HOWARD, Jane Russell), see PARKER, Henry L.

RUSSELL, Levi, of New Castle DE to LLOYD, Mary Ann, Miss, of Pennsgrove NJ, 7 Apr 1852, by Rev. Andrew Manship (DG 13 Apr 1852)

RUSSELL, Margaret A.,
see TERRY, Benjamin F.

RUSSELL, Margaret A.B., Mrs., relict of the late William C. RUSSELL, of Wilm, at Alexandria, 15 Jun 1853, na (DG 24 Jun 1853)

RUSSELL, Ruth, see GREEN, James

RUSSELL, William C.,
see RUSSELL, Margaret A. B.

RUSSOM, Benjamin D., to TAPP, Emily, of Red Lion DE, 6 Jan 1853, by the Rev. John Thompson (DG 14 Jan 1853)

RUSSOM, Mary Jane, see HYLETT, James

RUST, Harriet Jane,
see LYNCH, James W.

RUST, Luther C., Esq., of Phila, to NILES, Hetty Warner, Miss, of Wilm, 15 Jan 1846, at St. Andrew's by Rev. Alfred Lee (DG 20 Jan 1846)

RUST. Lydia, see CRAIG, John

RUTH, Levi to VANSANT, Rebecca, Miss, both of NC Co, Mar 21 1843, by Rev. W. R. Work (DG 21 Mar 1843)

RUTHERAM, Catharine,
see HARPER, Joseph

RUTHVIN, Sarah E., see BRYANT, William

RUTTER, Isabella, in Brandywine Hd, 13 Feb 1853, aged 78 yrs; Methodist (DG 25 Feb 1853)

RUTTER, John, see DAY, Francis

RYAN, Mary, see BRINGHURST, James

RYAN, Patrick, to O'HANLEN, Mary, Miss, both of Ireland, 25 Jan 1846, by the Rev. Mr. Riley (DG 30 Jan 1846)

RYDER, Andrew, see RYDER, Emeline

RYDER, Emeline, Miss, dau of the late Andrew RYDER, Esq., of Milford, 1 Oct 1847, at the res. of A. W. TOMPKINS, 308 Chestnut St., Phila, after a lingering illness (DG 8 Oct 1847)

RYDER, Wm., Rev., at Christiana after a short attack of typhus pheumonia, 18 Jul 1847, in his 70th yr (DG 23 Jul 1847)

SACRISTE, Amelia, see WALTON, William

SALLY, Charity, see MOUSELY, Joseph M.

SALMON, James, in Milford Hd,

2 Aug 1850 (DG 16 Aug 1850)

SAMPLE, David,
see SAMPLE, Margaret, Miss

SAMPLE, Jane, see McCOY, Robert,

SAMPLE, Jesse, to JACKSON, Elizabeth, Miss, all of Wilm, 8 Dec 1852, by the Rev. Andrew Manship (DG 31 Dec 1852)

SAMPLE, Margaret, Miss, only dau of the late David SAMPLE, near Newark, 1 Aug 1835, aged 16 yrs, bur. White Clay Creek Ch Cem (DG 21 Aug 1835)

SANBORN, David M., see CLAY, David M.

SANDERS, Arabella, see FISHER, Edward

SANDERS, Ellis B., to ROBERTS, Rachel, Miss, 19 Jun 1828, by the Rev. A. K. Russel, all of NC Co (DG 27 Jun 1828)

SANDERS, John F., of Wilm to HEMPHILL, Margaret, Miss, of Elkton MD, at Marcus Hook, 18 Feb 1849 (DG 2 Mar 1849)

SANDERS, William, see FISHER, Edward

SANDERSON, John, see PRICE, Joseph T.

SANDERSON, Matilda Louisa,
see PRICE, Joseph T.

SANFORD, Mary D., see MILLIGAN, Jas. C.

SANFORD, Whitine, see MILLIGAN, Jas. C.

SANFORD, Whiting, Esq.,member of the Legislature of DE of Sussex Co, at Port au Prince, 1 Nov 1825, na (DG 20 Dec 1825)

SANGSTON, Thomas H., of DE, to CLOSE, Anna, Miss, of Southwark, Phila, 27 Feb 1848, by Rev. A. B. Hard (DG 7 Mar 1848)

SAPP, Elizabeth, see GRAHAM, Emory

SAPP, George W., formerly of Chester Co Pa, to DRAPER, Mary Malvina, Miss, of Wilm, in Phila, 24 Jan 1853, by the Rev. Dr. Durbin (DG 1 Mar 1853)

SAPPINGTON, Lambert, at his late res. in Kent Co, MD, 12 Dec 1822; leaves a wife and 7 children (DG 20 Dec 1822)

SAPPINGTON, Lambert, son of Samuel SAPPINGTON, 17 Sep 1823
(DG 19 Sep 1823)

SAPPINGTON, Samuel,
see SAPPINGTON, Lambert

SAPPINGTON, Samuel, to KEITH, Gennett,

Miss, 2 Jan 1821 (DG 2 Jan 1821)

SARING, Samuel, see SARING, Sarah

SARING, Sarah, wife of Samuel SARING, in Wilm, 27 Aug 1849, aged 35 yrs
(DG 4 Sep 1849)

SATTERFIELD, M., to NOWELL, Phenor, both of Kent Co, 17 Feb 1853, by the Rev. T. P. McColley (DG 8 Mar 1853)

SAULSBURY, Gove, M. D., of Dover, to SMITH, Rosina J., dau of Isaac P. Smith, Esq., late of Snow Hill MD, 1 Nov 1848, at Phila by Rev. Albert Barnes (DG 3 Nov 1848)

SAULSBURY, Mary Ann,
see STAMP, William

SAULSBURY, Mary Louisa,
see BURTON, Erasmus D.

SAULSBURY, Willard, Esq., Atty.- General of DE, to PONDER, Anna, Miss, dau of James PONDER, Esq., all of Sussex, in Phila, 15 May 1850 (DG 28 May 1850)

SAUNDERS, Amos Jr, to MOODY, Mary Jane, Miss, both of NC Co, 27 Jul 1843, at Christiana Bridge, by Rev. William Ryder (DG 4 Aug 1843)

SAUNDERS, Charles, to CROW, Sarah, Miss, both of Wilm, at Chester, 17 Apr 1823 (DG 22 Apr 1823)

SAUNDERS, Elizabeth C., dau of John SAUNDERS, formerly of Wilm, in Phila, 10 Aug 1849, na (DG 21 Aug 1849)

SAUNDERS, James A., of Wilm, to VONDERSMITH, Lizzie L., Miss, of Phila, in Phila, 10 Nov 1850, by the Rev. John L. Grant (DG 21 Jan 1851)

SAUNDERS, John,
see SAUNDERS, Elizabeth C.

SAUNDERS, John C., to WITSEL, Lavinia W., Miss, by the Rev. S. Higgins, all of Wilm (DG 25 Nov 1828)

SAUNDERS, Mary Ann, formerly of Wilm, in New York, 3 Oct 1833, na
(DG 11 Oct 1833)

SAVAGE, Francis A.,
see SAVAGE, Mary Elmira

SAVAGE, Francis E., 30 Jan 1852, in his 27th yr (DG 27 Feb 1852)

SAVAGE, John, of New Castle, riding in the dark struck his head on a tree and died a few hours later (PG 26 Feb, 4 Mar 1734-5)

SAVAGE, Mary Elmira, dau of the late Francis A. and Sarah Ann SAVAGE, 22 Jul 1852, aged 3 yrs 9 mos (DG 27 Jul 1852)

SAVAGE, Sarah Ann, at her res. in Phila, 19 May 1850, in her 27th yr (DG 31 May 1850) see SAVAGE, Mary Elmira

SAVILLE, David to VEACH, Edith, Miss, both of NC Co, 12 Sep 1833, by Elder John P. Peckworth (DG 17 Sep 1833)

SAVILLE, George, in Wilm, 10 Aug 1848, in his 35th yr (DG 22 Sep 1848)

SAVILLE, Harriet, see SAVILLE, Jonathan

SAVILLE, Johnathan, in his 78th yr, in Wilm, 16 Jul 1849, res. 6 E. 6th St (DG 17 Jul 1849) late of Wilm. Harriet SAVILLE, exec'x (DG 7 Aug 1849)

SAVILLE, Lewis, after a lingering illness, 9 May 1846, in Phila (DG 12 May 1846)

SAVIN, Joseph, of Duck Creek Hd, 26 Oct 1853, na (DG 1 Nov 1853) Joseph H., near Smyrna, in his 25th yr (DG 4 Nov 1853)

SAVIN, Rachel H., see ROBINSON, William P.

SAVIN, Susan A., see HOFFECKER, Joseph V.

SAVIN, Wm., see HOFFECKER, Joseph V.

SAVOY, Rebecca, Mrs., dec'd, late of Wilm, sale of property Front and King Sts., by William PRYCE, exec'r (MU 5 Mar 1808)

SAWDEN, Jane, see DEPUTY, Elias

SAWDON, Ann E., see MORGAN, Thomas

SAWDON Francis, insane, escaped from the Almshouse, drowned in Mill Creek. Body found 4 Oct 1853, na (DG 7 Oct 1853)

SAWDON, Francis, see ADDISON, William

SAWDON, Thomas, to MOORE, Emeline, both of NC Co, in Phila, 14 May 1846, by Rev. Mr. King (DG 22 May 1846)

SAWYER, Ann see HIGGINS, John

SAWYER, George, of New York, to MEGGISON, Rebecca, Miss, niece of Capt. Joseph SAWYER of New Castle, 5 May 1846, at New Castle, by Rev. J. B. Spotswood (DG 8 May 1846)

SAWYER, Joseph, at New Castle, 4 Aug 1847, in his 84th yr (DG 10 Aug 1847) see SAWYER, George

SAXON, Isaac G., to YATES, Letitia, Miss, all of Wilm (DG 25 Mar 1842)

SAXTON, Deborah, see JESTER, Jonathan

SAXTON, Isaac G., to CARR, Susanna, Miss, both of Wilm, 15 Jan 1852, by Rev. J. G. Collom (DG 20 Jan 1852)

SAYERS, George, see SAYERS, John

SAYERS, John, in Wilm, 7 Nov 1852, aged 32 yrs (DG 16 Nov 1852) late of Wilm Hd, George SAYERS, adm'r (DG 19 Nov 1852)

SAYERS, William, to McLAUGHLIN, Margaret, Miss, both of NC Co, in Trinity Chapel, 7 Mar 1850, by Rev. E. N. Van Deusen (DG 12 Mar 1850)

SAYMAN, Edward, to WILLIAMS, Margaret, Miss, both of Christiana, 4 Jun 1847, by Rev. William Ryder (DG 4 Jun 1847)

SCANLAN, Elizabeth, see WALKER, Samuel A.

SCAWLIN, Elizabeth, see WALKER, Samuel A.

SCHEE, James, Esq., of De, late consul of the US at Genoa, in Phila, 2 May 1827, na (DG 11 May 1827)

SCHEETZ, Caroline A., see JONES, George C.

SCHEETZ, George, Rev., see JONES, George C.

SCHERMERHORN, Cortland, Esq., of New York, to BAYARD, Mary Ellen, Miss, eldest dau of James A BAYARD, late of Wilm, now of New York, 10 Jan 1845, in New York by Rev. Dr. Taylor (DG 21 Jan 1845)

SCHIFFELY, Fred'k, see HOYT, Wm J.

SCHIFFELY, Susan M., Miss, see HOYT, Wm J.

SCHMIDT, Mary J., see RHEIN, Frederick

SCHNEIDER, Catherine, see BAKER, William, Dr.

SCHOFIELD, James, to MARTIN, Emma, Miss, both of Christiana Hd, 17 May 1850, by the Mayor (DG 24 May 1850)

SCHOFIELD, John, 29 Jan 1846, in Christiana Hd (DG 30 Jan 1846)

SCHOLEY, Elizabeth, see BROWN, Robert

SCHOTT, Nicholas, Esq., of Phila, to FULLMER, Anna, dau of John FULLMER, Esq., of Wilm, in Phila, 4 Oct 1847, by Rev. W. H. Trapnell (DG 18 Oct 1847)

SCHRADER, Abraham, see GALAGHER, Francina Schrader

SCHRADER, Gertrude, see COOPER, William C.

SCHRAIDER, Abraham, to CALDWELL, Ann, Miss, Wilm, 9 Oct 1817, by Rev. Dr. Reed (AW 11 Oct 1817)

SCHULEE, John M., dyer, dec'd, late of Brandywine Hd, notice given by Samuel DERICK, adm'r (DG 15 Dec 1829)

SCHULTZE, George Washington, of Brandywine Hills DE, to READ, Hannah, Miss, dau of Thomas READ of Upper Merion Township, Montgomery Co PA, 19 Sep 1841, at Germantown PA, by Rev. Mr. Stern (DG 1 Oct 1841)

SCHWARTZ, G. C., to WALRAVEN, Eliza Ann, Miss, both of Wilm, in Phila, 22 Jan 1852, by Rev. A. D. Gillete (DG 27 Jan 1852)

SCOFIELD, Elizabeth M., see GRAY, Andrew C., Esq.

SCOFIELD, Frederick, see GRAY, Andrew C., Esq.

SCOLTON, Jacob, colored. Verdict of coroner's jury, accidental drowning (DG 17 Mar 1846)

SCOTT, Arrabella, see McLAIN, Andrew L.

SCOTT, Catharine, see COYLE, John

SCOTT, Eliza Jane, see CARSWELL, Wilson

SCOTT, Elizabeth, see DEDFORD, Elizabeth

SCOTT, Elizabeth H., see ROBINSON, Elizabeth H.

SCOTT, Hector, see SCOTT, Mary T.

SCOTT, Henry, to HAND, Rachel, Miss, both of Sussex Co, 12 Jan 1851, by T. P. McColley (DG 28 Jan 1851)

SCOTT, J. W., see SCOTT, Susan

SCOTT, James, to CASHO, Elizabeth, Miss, 19 Nov 1805, by Rev. Francis Hindman, all of Elkton (MR 20 Nov 1805)

SCOTT, Joseph, Esq., of Wilm, to SWAIN, Betsy, Mrs., late of New York, 11 May 1848, by Rev. J. Castle (DG 19 May 1848) see THOMAS, Joseph

SCOTT, Mary M., see BUZBY, David T.

SCOTT, Mary T., Miss, eldest dau of the late Mr. Hector SCOTT, g'dau of Luther MARTIN, Esq., at Kalarama, near Washington City, 22 May 1826, na (DG 16 Jun 1826)

SCOTT, Matthew, see ROBINSON, Elizabeth H.

SCOTT, Serepta, see HICKMAN, John H.

SCOTT, Susan, dau of J. W. SCOTT, 12 Jun 1848, in Wilm (DG 16 Jun 1848)

SCOTT, Violet, Mrs., near DE State line in Chester Co, PA, 30 Dec 1834, aged 77 yrs (DG 6 Jan 1835)

SCOTT, William, see DEDFORD, Elizabeth

SCOTT, William, to LATTOMUS, Angeline, Miss, both of NC Co, 19 Dec 1850, by Rev. J. A. Roche (DG 31 Dec 1850)

SCOUT, Ann, Mrs., wife of Capt. Augustus SCOUT, in Wilm, 7 Jan 1830 (DG 12 Jan 1830)

SCOUT, Augustus, Capt., see SCOUT, Ann, Mrs.

SCOUT, Augustus, son of Mr. George SCOUT, accidental drowning in the Christiana, 26 Aug 1853, aged c 10 yrs (DG 30 Aug 1853)

SCOUT, George, see SCOUT, Augustus

SCOUT, Sarah Ann, see HOLSTEIN, James J.

SCULL, Gideon, see PEDRECK, Joshua

SCULPHER, G. W., see SCULPHER, Lewis Cass

SCULPHER, Lewis Cass, son of G. W. and Mary Jane SCULPHER, 26 Aug 1850, aged 1 yr 26 days (DG 30 Aug 1850)

SCULPHER, Mary Jane, see SCULPHER, Lewis Cass

SEAL, Elizabeth, see THOMPSON, John, Rev.

SEAL, Jos., see CARTER, Ann

SEAL, Joseph, to CARTER, Sarah T., Miss, both of Wilm, at Chester, PA, 3 Dec 1828, by

Samuel Smith, Esq. (DG 9 Dec 1828)

SEAL, Joshua, to **DEVOU**, Mary W., dau of James L. DEVOU, all of Wilm, 11 Apr 1850, by Rev. J. E. Rockwell (DG 16 Apr 1850)

SEARLES, Thos., to **CHIPPS**, Hannah, Miss, 14 Dec 1820 (DG 15 Dec 1820)

SEATON, William, see **VINING**, H., Mr.

SEBO, John, to **HARTLY**, Rebecca,.Miss, both of Wilm, at Newark, 4 Sep 1823, by the Rev. Mr. Bell (DG 12 Sep 1823)

SEEDS, Catharine Ann, see **SPARKS**, James A.

SEEDS, Joseph, see **SPARKS**, James A.

SEEDS, Joseph B., formerly of Wilm, in Phila, 10 Apr 1853, in his 78th yr (DG 15 Apr 1853)

SEEDS, Joseph C., see **SEEDS**, Joseph M. see **SEEDS**, Mary Jane

SEEDS, Joseph M., 24 Apr 1851, in his 16th yrs. Fun. from the res. of his father, Joseph C. SEEDS, King St, bet 5th and 6th (DG 25 Apr 1851)

SEEDS, Joseph R. D., of Wilm, to **JACKSON**, Elizabeth V., Miss, of Ohio, 4 Nov 1851, by the Rev. Ignatius T. Cooper DD (DG 14 Nov 1851)

SEEDS, Mary Jane, Mrs, late wife of Joseph C. SEEDS, 1 Jan 1842, in Wilm (DG 7 Jan 1842)

SEEDS, Phebe, see **THOMAS**, Aquilla

SEEDS, Phebe Ann, see **McINYTRE**, James A.

SEELEY, John A., of Wilm, to **MURDOCK**, Susanna, Miss, eldest dau of John MURDOCK of Q. Annes Co MD, at Salem NJ, 22 Jul 1827, by the Rev. Pharaoh A. Ogden (DG 27 Jul 1827)

SEELY, Zipporah W., Mrs., 2 Sep 1852, aged 54 yrs (DG 3 Sep 1852)

SEITE, Mary, Mrs., see **WALKER**, John

SEITZ, George, of Phila, to **HAINES**, Mary, Miss, of Wilm, 10 May 1821, (Thursday last) by the Rev. Dr. Read (DG 15 May 1821) see **SEITZ**, Sarah

SEITZ, Sarah, wife of George SEITZ, 10 Dec 1820, na (DG 15 Dec 1820)

SELAH, Amanda, dau of Robert SELAH, in Wilm, 28 Jul 1853, in her 11th yr (DG 2 Aug 1853)

SELAH, Robert, see **SELAH**, Amanda

SELBY, Cage, a native of Sussex Co, at the res. of William VANDEGRIFT in Red Lion Hd, NC Co, 10 Jan 1826, supposed to be aged 19 or 20 yrs (DG 17 Jan 1826)

SELLARS, Elizabeth, Mrs, in Wilm, consort of the late John SELLARS, Esq., 26 May 1841, aged 73 yrs (DG 28 May 1841)

SELLARS, John, Esq., see **SELLARS**, Elizabeth

SELLARS, John, Esq., of Wilm, Past Grand of the Masons in the state, 9 Feb 1828, "old and highly respectable citizen" (DG 12 Feb 1828)

SELLARS, Mary Louisa, see **RAY**, Edmund Strachan

SELLARS, William, of Phila, to **FERRIS**, Mary, dau of Zeba FERRIS, of Wilm, in Wilm, 19 Apr 1849, by Friends ceremony (DG 24 Apr 1849)

SELLERS. ____, widow, see **DEAN**, William

SELLERS, John, dec'd, notice given by W. R. SELLERS, adm'r (DG 7 Mar 1828)

SELLERS, John, see **WILSON**, Jane

SELLERS, W. R., see **SELLERS**, John

SELLERS, William R., see **VAUGHAN**, J. F.

SEMANS, Edward, to **MITCHELL**, Sallie, Miss, only dau of Charles MITCHELL, Esq., all of Phila, 6 Feb 1849, by Rev. Dr. Durbin (DG 9 Feb 1849)

SEMANS, Richard, see **COMEGYS**, Ruhamah

SENAX, Jacob, dec'd, notice given by William SENAX, adm'r (DG 5 Oct 1827)

SENAX, Thomas, dec'd, notice given by William SENAX (DG 5 Oct 1827)

SENAX, William, see **SENAX**, Jacob see **SENAX**, Thomas

SENEX, Nehemiah, to **DIXON**, Ann, Miss, all of Wilm, 11 Mar 1847, by Rev. A. Atwood (DG 16 Mar 1847)

SERGEANT, Benjamin E., to **SHAW**, Mary Jane, Miss, all of Wilm, 3 Dec 1850, by Rev.

Andrew Manship   (DG 6 Dec 1850)

SERRILL, Isaac, (DG Serrill & Co), dec'd, notice given by Cad. MORRIS, adm'r (DG 5 Jan 1793)

SESSENE, Martin, Capt of the sloop *Fame*, in Phila, 31 Mar 1827, na (DG 3 Apr 1827)

SETON, _____, see VINING, John

SETON, William, see VINING, John

SETTLER, John, to BRUNON, Elizabeth Ann, Miss, both of Wilm, 24 Dec 1850, by Rev. S. R. Wynkoop   (DG 27 Dec 1850)

SEVIL, Abel, see SEVIL, David,

SEVIL, David, late of NC Co, dec'd, notice given by Abel SEVIL, adm'r, and Mary SEVIL, adm'x (DG 18 Feb 1825)

SEVIL, Mary, see SEVIL, David,

SEVILL, Nathan T., of Kent Co to WELLS, Rebecca, Miss, of Appoq. Hd, 12 Feb 1850, by Rev. P. Meredith (DG 22 Feb 1850)

SEWALL, John, see SWAYNE, B. B.

SEWELL, Mary Ida, see SWAYNE, B. B.

SHACKLEY, Joseph, to MITCHELL, Ann, 26 Feb 1828, by Rev. J. N. Danforth (DG 29 Feb 1828)

SHAD, Amelia, see TURNER, Elijah

SHAFFER, Benjamin, see SHAFFER, Margaret C.

SHAFFER, James, to REECE, Sarah, Miss, both of NC Co, 8 Mar 1827, by the Rev. John P. Peckworth (DG 13 Mar 1827)

SHAFFER, Margaret C., wife of Dr. Benjamin SHAFFER, 22 Sep 1847, of consumption, aged 22 yrs (DG 12 Oct 1847)

SHAKESPEAR, Rebecca, see CRAWFORD, Alexander B.

SHAKESPEARE, Mary Ann, see HARRIS, Barney, Jr.

SHAKESPEARE, William M., to HAMAN, Catherine, Miss, both of NC Co, 21 Nov 1843, by Rev. N. Patterson (DG 24 Nov 1843)

SHALLCROSS, Catharine, see COCHRAN, Richard Washington

SHALLCROSS, Jacob, see COCHRAN, Richard Washington

SHALLCROSS, Jacob, see COCHRAN, Wm. A.

SHALLCROSS, Sarah Overington, see COCHRAN, Wm. A.

SHALLCROSS, Thomas, miller, of Brandywine, to POTTS, Deborah, Miss, of Wilm, 22 Oct 1789 (DG 24 Oct 1789)

SHANKLAND, _____, Mrs., after a lingering illness, in Lewes, at the res. of her husband, R. SHANKLAND, Esq., 5 Feb 1803 (FA 21 Feb 1803)

SHANKLAND, Ann May, see MARSH, Ann May

SHANKLAND, R., Esq., see SHANKLAND, _____, Mrs.

SHANKLAND, William, see MARSH, Ann May

SHANNON, Abraham P., see SHANNON, Elizabeth, Mrs.

SHANNON, Elizabeth, Mrs., wife of Abraham P. SHANNON, near Smyrna, 6 Sep 1825, aged 25 yrs (DG 16 Sep 1825)

SHANNON, Mary Ann, see ALLMOND, Charles M.

SHAPLEIGH, M. S., of Phila, to BLANDY, Elizabeth Martha, dau of Thomas BLANDY, Esq., of Newark DE, 20 May 1845, in Newark, by Rev. Walter E. Franklin (DG 30 May 1845)

SHARP, Ann Marian, Mrs., near Bridgeville, 2 Nov 1849 (DG 6 Nov 1849)

SHARP, Elizabeth J., Joseph DAVIS and Francis HOBSON, exec'rs (DG 18 Jul 1851)

SHARP, Elizabeth, wife of Dr. Solomon SHARP, USN, aged c 45 yrs, at Norfolk, 23 Jan 1851 (DG 31 Jan 1851)

SHARP, Evans J., of London, Britain, Chester Co, to JACOBS, Maria, Miss, of DE, 13 Feb 1849, at the Turk's Head Hotel, by the Rev. Alfred S. Patton (DG 23 Feb 1849)

SHARP, Jemima, Mrs, widow of Rev. Solomon SHARP, at the res. of her son, Dr. Solomon SHARP, Gosport Naval Yard VA, 30 Jun 1850, in her 73rd yr (DG 12 Jul 1850)

SHARP, Mary, wife of Jesse SHARP, near Milford, 10 Nov 1848, in her 31st yr (DG 28 Nov 1848)

SHARP, Solomon, see SHARP, Elizabeth

SHARP, Solomon, see **SHARP**, Jemima

SHARP, Susanna, see **ROBERTSON**, John

SHARP, William B., of Phila, to **CONAWAY**, Ann F., Miss, of Wilm, 1 Jun 1848, by Rev. M. J. Rhees (DG 6 Jun 1848)

SHARPE, Elizabeth, Mrs., wife of the Collector of the Port, 28 Sep 1853, burial from her late res. 48 King St (DG 30 Sep 1853)

SHARPE, Elizabeth, see **SHARPE**, Joseph

SHARPE, Jesse, see **SHARPE**, Joseph

SHARPE, Joseph, son of Jesse and Elizabeth SHARPE, 20 July 1844, aged 2 yrs 8 mos 20 days (DG 19 Jul 1844)

SHARPE, Samuel A., son of Thomas H. SHARPE, 21 May 1843, aged 3 yrs 10 mos 6 days (DG 2 Jun, 1843)

SHARPE, Solomon, M. D., of Christiana, to **HARRIS**, Catharine Marion, Miss, of Cecil Co, MD, in Phila, 22 Nov 1828, by the Rev. Thomas Dunn (DG 9 Dec 1828)

SHARPE, Thomas H., see **SHARPE**, Samuel A.

SHARPER, Benjamin W., to **PRICE**, Mary S., Miss, both of Wilm, 12 Aug 1847, by Rev. Thomas G. Allen (DG 20 Aug 1847)

SHARPLESS, Hannah M., see **HARVEY**. Lea R.

SHARPLEY, Elizabeth, Mrs., widow of Jacob SHARPLEY, and dau of Col. Wm. ELLIOTT, at her late res. in Brandywine Hd, 27 May 1853, in her 70th yr (DG 31 May 1853)

SHARPLEY, Esau, see **SHARPLEY**, William

SHARPLEY, Jacob, see **SHARPLEY**, Elizabeth

SHARPLEY, John, to **SPRINGER**, Mary Jane, Miss, both of NC Co, 7 Feb 1843, by Rev. J. W. McCullough (DG 10 Feb 1843)

SHARPLEY, William, dec'd, late of Brandywine Hd, notice given by Esau SHARPLEY, exec'r (DG 2 Dec 1828)

SHAW, David, see **SHAW**, Martha M.

SHAW, Elizabeth, Miss, 16 Jan 1810, aged 26 yrs. Services in Methodist meeting house, the Rev. Mr. Cooper (DG 20 Jan 1810)

SHAW, Elizabeth, see **SHAW**, Martha M.

SHAW, James, of Manayunk, PA, to **PHILLIPS**, Mary Ann, Miss, of Brandywine, 28 Oct 1849, by the Rev. S. M. Gailey (DG 9 Nov 1849)

SHAW, Jane Eliza, wife of William SHAW, in Wilm, 21 Sep 1846, aged 19 yrs (DG 29 Sep 1846)

SHAW, John H., to **MOORE**, Ester, Miss, 25 Nov 1828, by Elder John P. Peckworth, all of Wilm (DG 28 Nov 1828)

SHAW, Joseph, of Wilm, to **HUGHES**, Mary, Miss, dau of John HUGHES of Phila, 29 Dec 1849, by Rev. Charles W. Quick (DG 11 Jan 1850)

SHAW, Martha M., dau of David and Elizabeth Shaw, in Wilm, 31 Jan 1846, aged 5 yrs (DG 10 Feb 1846)

SHAW, Mary Jane, see **SERGEANT**, Benjamin E.

SHAW, William, to **KING**, Temperance R., both of Wilm, 17 Feb 1848, by Rev. Dr. Kennaday (DG 28 Mar 1848)
see **JOHNSON**, James
see **SHAW**, Jane Eliza

SHAWN, Joseph, dec'd, see ALLSTON, John, on adjoining land

SHEARER, Catharine, see **EARLY**, James

SHELLEY, Joseph, to **BIRD**, Sarah, Miss, 6 Mar 1820 (DG 8 Apr 1820)

SHEPHERD, Mary Ann, see **RHODES**, Joseph T.

SHEPHERDSON, Mary, see **SHEPHERDSON**, Richard

SHEPHERDSON, Richard, dec'd, late of New Castle Hd, notice given by Mary SHEPHERDSON, exec'x, New Castle, or John L. MORRIS, exec'r, Newport (DG 24 Oct 1826)

SHEPPARD, Edward, see **MILES**, John

SHEPPERDSON, Elizabeth, see **BAILEY**, John

SHERER, William, of Newark, merchant, to **WARREN**, Ellen J., Miss, of Laurel, Sussex Co, DE, 30 Jan 1822, by the Rev. Daniel Higbee (DG 5 Feb 1822)

SHERER, William, principal of the Ladies Academy, Newark, DE, to **FISHER**, Lavinia Rodney, Miss, eldest dau of the Hon. John

FISHER of Dover, in Wilm, 19 May 1825, by the Rev. A. K. Russell (DG 24 May 1825)

SHERIDAN, Laurence, innkeeper, in Wilm, 5 Nov 1835, aged 38 yrs (DG 10 Nov 1835)

SHERIDAN, Margaret, see NELSON, Charles

SHERMA, O. F., to YOUNG, Fannie C., Miss, both of Delaware City, 19 May 1853, by the Rev. A. A. Willits (DG 29 Nov 1853)

SHERWOOD, Hannah, see COOPER, B. B.

SHEWARD, Benj., of yellow fever (DE 18 Sep 1798)

SHEWARD, Caleb, dec'd, late of Wilm (DG 21 Aug 1790)

SHEWARD, James, merchant, dec'd, late of Wilm, notice given by James LEA, Jr., adm'r (DG 24 May 1797)

SHEWARD, Lydia, see PLURIGHT, William

SHEWARD, Rest, widow, dec'd, late of Wilm, notice given by Joseph READ, sole exec'r (AW 21 Aug 1816)

SHEWELL, Esther D. B., see YOUNG, J. Evans

SHEWELL, Thomas, see YOUNG, J. Evans

SHIELDS, Amos, 27 Aug 1848, in Wilm (DG 29 Aug 1848)

SHIELDS, Susanna, see ELLIOTT, John

SHILLING, Sidney, see GRUBB, H. W.

SHIMP, David S., to WYATT, Eliza Ann, of Kent Co DE, 21 Feb 1850, by Rev. Joseph Gaskill (DG 19 Mar 1850)

SHINN, John, to BARDSLEY, Sarah Ann, Miss, in Manayunk PA, 29 May 1852, by Rev. B. Wistar Morris (DG 1 Jun 1852)

SHIPLEY, ____, Dr., see SHIPLEY, Sarah Ann

SHIPLEY, Elizabeth, see POGUE, William Jr.

SHIPLEY, Esther, late of Wilm City, James MONTGOMERY adm'r (DG 28 May 1852)

SHIPLEY, Esther, widow of the late Robert SHIPLEY, in Wilm, 30 Apr 1852, aged c 58 yrs (DG 4 May 1852)

SHIPLEY, Joseph B., to TEST, Mary, Miss, both of Wilm, 16 Apr 1804, in Phila by Rev.

Frederick Smith (FA 18 Apr 1804)

SHIPLEY, Joseph, see SHIPLEY, Mary

SHIPLEY, Mary, widow of Joseph SHIPLEY, at her res. in Brandywine, 11 Dec 1843, aged 88 yrs (DG 15 Dec 1843)

SHIPLEY, Rebecca, dec'd, late of Wilm, notice given by James ANDREWS and William ROBINSON, exec'rs (DE 22 Jun 1797)

SHIPLEY, Robert, see SHIPLEY, Esther

SHIPLEY, Samuel, proprietor of one of the Brandywine flour mills, served in the city council, in Wilm, 18 Dec 1848, aged 72 yrs (DG 22 Dec 1848)

SHIPLEY, Sarah Ann, Mrs., relict of the late Wm. SHIPLEY, Jr, 20 Jun 1851, in Seaford, at the res. of her son, Dr. SHIPLEY, in her 61st yr (DG 27 Jun 1851)

SHIPLEY, Susanna, see GRINER, John

SHIPLEY, Thomas, Esq., of Wilm, to O'CONNOR, Sophia, only dau of Lt. J. Blight O'CONNOR of the British Army and niece of James AEUSPRATTS, Esq., of Liverpool, at New York, 23 Jun 1835, by Rev. Dr. McCaulley (DG 10 Jul 1835)

SHIPLEY, Thomas, of Wilm, member of the Society of Friends, 1 Nov 1789, in his 72nd yr (DG 4 Nov 1789)

SHIPLEY, Wm., Jr., see SHIPLEY, Sarah Ann

SHIPMAN, Joseph J., of Phila, to BECKLEY, Sally Ann, Miss, formerly of Wilm, in Phila, 11 Jun 1835, by Elder John P. Peckworth (DG 12 Jun 1835)

SHIPWAY, Charles, Esq., of Bedford Co PA, to BAILEY, Ann, of Smyrna, in Kingsessing PA, 17 Jan 1848, by Rev. Samuel R. Brinkle (DG 21 Jan 1848)

SHIRKEY, John, of Wilm, formerly of Brandywine, to CARPENTER, Josephine, Miss, of Phila, 4 Nov 1852, by the Rev. Michael Gordoni (DG 12 Nov 1852)

SHOAL, Andrew, dec'd, late of NC Co, notice given by K. JOHNS, exec'r (DG 18 Apr 1789)

SHOCK, George W., 4 Mar 1853, in his 30th yr (DG 15 Mar 1853)

SHOCK, Lydia, see TURNBULL, Adam

SHOCKLEY, Ann, Mrs., suddenly at Milford,

DELAWARE MARRIAGES AND DEATHS FROM NEWSPAPERS, 1729-1853

8 Oct 1847, aged 70 yrs (DG 12 Oct 1847)

SHOCKLEY, Catherine, Mrs., widow of the late Capt. SHOCKLEY, formerly of Wilm, in Phila, 3 Dec 1826, na (DG 5 Dec 1826) see SHOCKLEY, Elias, Capt.

SHOCKLEY, Elias, Capt., memb. of the M. E. Ch, 25 Sep 1826, na (DG 26 Sep 1826) see SHOCKLEY, Catherine, Mrs.

SHOCKLEY, Elias, to BRITTENHAM, Lydia, Miss, both of Sussex Co, 28 Nov 1850, by Rev. S. C. Palmiter (DG 10 Dec 1850)

SHOCKLEY, Elizabeth, see WATSON, Henry S.

SHOCKLEY, Nehemiah, a U. S. pensioner, 27 May 1850, aged 46 yrs (DG 31 May 1850)

SHOCKLEY, Sarah Ann, see COULTER, Cornelius

SHOCKLEY, Wm. H., to TWIGG, Catherine, Miss, all of Milford, in Milford, 4 Nov 1851, by the Rev. Silas C. Palmiter (DG 11 Nov 1851)

SHOEMAKER, Charles, see HILL, Samuel V.

SHOEMAKER, Charles, to GEDDES, Jane, Miss, 6 May 1824, by the Rev. Daniel D. Lewis (DG 18 May 1824)

SHOEMAKER, Hester Ann, see HILL, Samuel V.

SHORT, Abraham C., to McINTIRE, Mary, Mrs., both of Pencader Hd, in Wilm, 19 Jun 1834, by the Rev. E. W. Gilbert (DG 23 Jun 1834)

SHORT, Allen, to PARKER, Ala Anna, Mrs., 28 Oct 1841, by Rev. Jno R. Torbert, all of Sussex Co (DG 5 Nov 1841)

SHORT, Edward, see GODFREY, Mary E.

SHORT, Edward, to VICKERS, Leah, Miss, 16 Jan 1850, by Rev. J. R. Torbert (DG 12 Feb 1850)

SHORT, John, to FENWICK, Eliza A, Miss, both of Milton DE, 4 Aug 1853, by the Rev. A. Johns (DG 9 Aug 1853)

SHORT, Kitturah Burton, at Lewis DE, aged 16 yrs (DG 9 Oct 1849)

SHORT, Mary, see DUNNING, John W.

SHORT, Mary E., see GODFREY, Mary E.

SHORT, Peter, of Little Creek Hd, killed by falling with his head between the spokes of a wheel of a log carriage, ndd, na (DG 30 Sep 1851)

SHORT, Philip, Esq., at his res. near Georgetown, 28 Jun 1847, in his 72nd yr (DG 9 Jul 1847)

SHORT, Rebecca, see MESSIK, James B.

SHORT, Sarah, see WOOTREST, Perry

SHORT, Sarah Jane, see ROBINSON, William J.

SHORT, William, to BRITTINGHAM, Mary E., all of Sussex Co, 25 Dec 1852, by Rev. T. P. McColley (DG 14 Jan 1853)

SHORTS, George, to WINDLE, Sarah, Miss, both of Kent Co, 14 Feb 1850, by Rev. John A. Roche (DG 1 Mar 1850)

SHORTT, William H, see JACKSON, Resdon

SHOUP, Ann Maria, see JONES, John

SHROUDEN, Thomas, in Milford, 28 Feb 1851, na (DG 4 Mar 1851)

SHUBRICK, _____. Capt., see SHUBRICK, Francis D. P.

SHUBRICK. Francis D. P.,son of the late Capt. SHUBRICK of the U. S. Navy, died in the great fire in San Francisco on Christmas (DG 12 Feb 1850)

SHUBRICK, Irvine, Esq., of South Carolina, to DUPONT, Julia Sophia, Miss, dau of Victor DUPONT, Esq., 12 May 1824, by the Rev. Dr. Kenny (DG 18 May1824)

SHUBRICK, Irvine, Commander, of the U. S. Navy, in Wilm 5 Apr 1849, in his 52nd yr (DG 10 Apr 1849)

SHUDEL, Andrew J., of Wilm, to ALEXANDER, Loretta, of Phila, 7 Oct 1845, in Phila, by Rev. S. H. Gloucester (DG 10 Oct 1845)

SHUGART, George S., see McCALL, Louisa, Mrs.,

SHUGART, Louisa, see McCALL, Louisa, Mrs.,

SHULL, James, B., of Phila, to NEALS, Rebecca Ann, Miss, of Wilm, 15 Apr 1846, by Rev. O. Douglass (DG 21 Apr 1846)

SHUSTER, Harriet, see JEFFERIS, William R.

SHUSTER, John L., see SHUSTER, Mary

SHUSTER, Mary, consort of John L. SHUSTER, after a lingering illness, in Appoq. Hd, 29 Jan 1850, in her 59th yr (DG 5 Feb 1850)

SHUSTER, Mary, see DAVIS, John Wesley

SHUTE, Asa M., to MOORE, Mary Ann, Miss, 17 Oct 1850, by Rev. Newton Heston (DG 22 Oct 1850)

SIDDY, James, to HASTINGS, Ann, Miss, both of NC Co, 10 Apr 1851, by Rev. S. M. Gailey (DG 22 Apr 1851)

SILTER, William Jr, to GIBBS, Eliza Jane, Miss, all of NC Co, 23 Jan 1849, by Rev. Thos. Barton (DG 9 Feb 1849)

SILVER, Eliza J., see SILVER, William

SILVER, George B., son of William SILVER, at his father's res., Red Lion, 4 May 1845, aged 20 yrs (DG 13 May 1845)

SILVER, John M, son of William SILVER, Esq., at Red Lion, 25 Jun 1843, aged 6 yrs (DG 30 Jun 1843)

SILVER, Sarah Elizabeth, only dau of William SILVER, Esq., aged 19 yrs 4 mos (DG 28 Dec 1852)

SILVER, Sarah, see THOMPSON, Andrew

SILVER, William,
see SILVER, George B.
see SILVER, John M.
see SILVER, Sarah Elizabeth

SILVER, William, inf son of William and Eliza J. SILVER, in Smyrna, 10 Aug 1850, aged 5 mos 10 days (DG 20 Aug 1850)

SILVER, William, Rev.,
see THOMPSON, Andrew,

SIMKINS, Abigail, see DENN, George

SIMMERS, Sarah Ann,
see COFFEODE, David

SIMMONS, _____, inf son of George SIMMONS, near Dover, 17 Oct 1853, aged 1 yr 5 mos (DG 28 Oct 1853)

SIMMONS, Anna M., late wife of William SIMMONS, in Wilm, 19 Jun 1844, aged 40 yrs (DG 25 Jun 1844)

SIMMONS, Bauduy, see SIMMONS, John

SIMMONS, Elizabeth, Mrs., consort of Mr. William SIMMONS, in Wilm, 25 Dec 1822 (DG 7 Jan 1823)

SIMMONS, Elizabeth, formerly of Kennett PA, in Wilm, at the res. of her nephew, Joshua SIMMONS, Esq., 10 Oct 1846, aged 75 yrs (20 Oct 1846)

SIMMONS, Emma, see SMITH, Thomas R.

SIMMONS, George, to EVANS, Ruth, Miss, 9 Dec 1807, by Rev. Mr. Pryce (MU 12 Dec 1807)

SIMMONS, George,
see SIMMONS, _____.
see GAFFORD, Samuel
see SIMMONS, Lydia
see SMITH, Thomas R.
see SIMMONS, John

SIMMONS, George H. P., to BULLOCK, Margary, Miss, all of Wilm, 18 Dec 1845, at Marcus Hook PA by Rev. J. B. Ayers (DG 23 Dec 1845)

SIMMONS, Hannah H.,
see KENNARD, William Groom

SIMMONS, Hannah, see TODD, Alfred

SIMMONS, Hannah T., in Wilm, 28 Nov 1843, aged 32 yrs (DG 1 Dec 1843)

SIMMONS, John, of Christiana Hd, 12 Oct 1824, na (DG 19 Oct 1824) dec'd, late of Christiana Hd, notice given by George SIMMONS and John SIMMONS, adm'rs (DG 17 May 1825)

SIMMONS, John, dec'd, late of Christiana Hd, notice given by Harman TALLEY and Bauduy SIMMONS, adm'rs (DG 31 Oct 1828)

SIMMONS, John B., of DE, to WILCOX, Angelina E., of Phila, 1 Feb 1849, by Rev. J. H. Kennard (DG 6 Feb 1849)

SIMMONS, Joshua,
see SIMMONS, Elizabeth
see SIMMONS, Sarah

SIMMONS, Lydia, dau of the late George SIMMONS, in Christiana Hd at the res. of Jesse CREGG, 8 Jan 1850, aged c 17 yrs (DG 11 Jan 1850)

SIMMONS, Lydia Ann, see DIXON, Thomas

SIMMONS, Mary, Mrs., see FOSTER, William

SIMMONS, Mary Ellen, in Wilm, 13 Oct 1851, na (DG 17 Oct 1851)

SIMMONS, Sarah, Mrs, late wife of Joshua SIMMONS, in Wilm after a short illness,

20 Apr 1842 (DG 22 Apr 1842)
see **LEMON**, John

SIMMONS, Sophia, at the res. of her mother in Wilm (DG 10 Aug 1847)

SIMMONS, William,
see **SIMMONS**, Elizabeth
see **SIMMONS**, Anna M.

SIMMONS, William, to **JONES**, Mary, Mrs., all of Wilm, 27 Nov 1845, by Rev. Dr. Kennaday (DG 5 Dec 1845)

SIMMS, Lydia C., widow of the late Joseph B. SIMS, Esq., formerly of Phila, but for many years a citizen of Delaware, 8 Aug 1844, after a lingering illness (DG 23 Aug 1844)

SIMPLER, Elizabeth, see **PALMER**, William

SIMPLER, Elizabeth Jane,
see **JOHNSON**, Nathaniel H.

SIMPLER, George Edward, at Georgetown, 19 May 1853, aged c 3 yrs (DG 31 May 1853)

SIMPLER, George M., to **OSKINS**, Jane M., in Sussex Co DE, 23 Jan 1849, by Rev. T. P. McColley (DG 6 Feb 1849)

SIMPLER, Hester A.,
see **BENNETT**, Stephen

SIMPLER, Leah, Mrs., widow of the late Thomas SIMPLER, 9 Feb 1826, aged 78 yrs; m 58 yrs, had 14 children, 76 g'children and 56 gr g'children, member of the M. E. Ch last 30 yrs (DG 17 Feb 1826)
see **SIMPLER**, Thomas, Sr.,

SIMPLER, Mary Jane, Mrs, on Thursday last, in South Milford (DG 24 Sep 1850)

SIMPLER, Samuel, of Kent Co, to **BENNETT**, Eliza J., Mrs., of Sussex, 29 Nov 1848, by Rev. Mr. Spottswood (DG 5 Dec 1848)

SIMPLER, Thomas, Sr., at his res. near Georgetown, 7 Feb 1826, aged 84 yrs (DG 17 Feb 1826)
see **SIMPLER**, Leah, Mrs. (same issue)

SIMPSON, Eliza, see **BURRIS**, Lewis

SIMPSON, Elizabeth M.,
see **CAREY**, Cornelius M.
see **HUNTZBERGER**, Enos

SIMPSON, George C.,
see **SIMPSON**, Joseph L.

SIMPSON, James A., of Wilm, to **GALLAWAY**, Martha Jane, Miss, of

Brandywine Village, NC Co, 1 Jul 1852, by the Rev. H. Humphries (DG 16 Jul 1852)

SIMPSON, James Thomas, son of Matthew SIMPSON of Smyrna, 11 Jan 1853, in his 3rd yr (DG 1 Feb 1853)

SIMPSON, Jane, wife of John SIMPSON, at Newport, 10 Apr 1852, in her 40th yr; leaves a husband and 4 small children (DG 27 Apr 1852)

SIMPSON, John,
see **SIMPSON**, Jane
see **SIMPSON**, Margaret Jane

SIMPSON, Joseph L., son of George C. SIMPSON, in Wilm, 15 Jul 1847 (DG 27 Jul 1847)

SIMPSON, Margaret Jane, dau of John SIMPSON, at Newport, 15 Apr 1848, aged 18 mos (DG 25 Apr 1848)
see **DICKSON**, David

SIMPSON, Mary, see **FARRA**, David W.

SIMPSON, Mary M.,
see **PASSWATERS**, William

SIMPSON, Matthew,
see **SIMPSON**, James Thomas

SIMPSON, Rachel, Mrs.,
see **MORGAN**, Solomon

SIMPSON, Samuel, of Phila, to **OGLE**, Hannah Maria, Miss, eldest dau of Peter OGLE of Christiana DE, 8 Jul 1827, in New Ark, by the Rev. A. K. Russell (DG 13 Jul 1827)

SIMPSON, Sarah,
see **WILSON**, Theodore J.

SIMPSON, Thomas,
see **MORGAN**, Solomon

SIMPSON, Thomas, member elect to State Legislature, at his res. in Kent Co, a few days ago, na (DG 11 Dec 1829)

SIMPSON, Thomas, to **WHEATMAN**, Ellen. Miss, both of Kent Co DE, 10 Jul 1851, by Rev. H. E. Gilroy (DG 18 Jul 1851)

SIMPSON, William, to **MATTHEWS**, Eliza, Miss, all of Wilm, 27 Mar 1826, by the Rev. E. W. Gilbert (DG 28 Mar 1826)

SIMS, Joseph, see **SIMMS**, Lydia C.

SINCLAIR, Ellen,
see **DOUGLASS**, James C.

SINCLAIR, Samuel,

see **McCAULLEY**, William
see **McCAULLEY**, Sarah L.

SINCLAIR, Samuel, Esq., 22 Jan 1828, at his res. in Kennet Twp PA, aged c 75 yrs (DG 29 Jan 1828)

SINCLAIR, Sarah,
see **McCAULLEY**, William

SINCLAIR, Sarah L.,
see **McCAULLEY**, Sarah L.

SINCLAIR, William,
see **DOUGLASS**, James C.

SINEX, Jacob, at Newport, 11 Sep 1826, aged 26 yrs (DG 15 Sep 1826)

SINEX, John, see **SINEX**, Mary

SINEX, Mary, consort of John SINEX, Esq., in New Albany, 4 Jan 1853, in her 52nd yr (DG 18 Jan 1853)

SINEX, Sarah Jane, see **TAYLOR**, Joseph

SINEX, Thomas, to **FOULK**, Elizabeth, Miss, 8 Feb 1821 (DG 13 Feb 1821)

SINEY, Charles, to **JOHNSON**, Margaret L., Miss, both of Wilm, at Marcus Hook, 10 Dec 1846, by Rev. Mr. Humphries (DG 15 Dec 1846)

SINGER, John, see, **GILBERT**, E. W.

SINGER, Margaret,
see **JOHNSON**, Christopher

SINGER, Mary Ann, see **GILBERT**, E. W.

SINGLES, Edward, to **BOWEN**, Mary Ellen, all of Wilm, 12 Sep 1846, by Rev. A. Atwood (DG 18 Sep 1846)

SINK, John, of Phila, to **PETERSON**, Sarah Ann, Miss, of Wilm, 20 Aug 1822, by the Rev. Thos. Griffin (DG 23 Aug 1822)

SINNEX, Margaret, see **WILLIAMS**, John

SIPPLE, C. E., see **BARKER**, Joseph,

SIPPLE, Caleb, Capt., to **PORTER**, Martha, Miss, both of Kent Co, in Milford, 10 Jul 1849 (DG 20 Jul 1849)

SIPPLE, Caleb E., Esq., retired merchant, in Dover, 11 Apr 1851, aged c 52 yrs (DG 22 Apr 1851) late of Dover Hd, HARRINGTON, S. M., exec'r (DG 29 Apr 1851)

SIPPLE, Caleb H., of Dover, to **STOUT**, Sally Ann, Miss, dau of Judge J. STOUT of Raymond's Neck, Kent Co, 5 Jan 1848, by Rev. T. G. Murphy (DG 14 Jan 1848)

SIPPLE, Elizabeth,
see **HARDCASTLE**, Philip

SIPPLE, Elizabeth Ann,
see **WOOTTERS**, Abner E.

SIPPLE, Garret, see **HARDCASTLE**, Philip

SIPPLE, Garrett W., at St. Louis MO, 20 Jul 1849, aged 34 yrs (DG 13 Apr 1852)

SIPPLE, James, 17 Jun 1850, in his 69th yr (DG 21 Jun 1850)

SIPPLE, James D., to **HARRINGTON**, Sarah, Miss, all of Milford Neck, 30 Mar 1852, by the Rev. Daniel Godwin (DG 6 Apr 1852)

SIPPLE, James Matthew, son of Thomas B. and Mary R. SIPPLE, in Georgetown, 5 Mar 1844, aged 2 yrs 4 mos 4 days (DG 8 Mar 1844)

SIPPLE, Mary R.,
see **SIPPLE**, James Matthew

SIPPLE, Thomas, Esq., dec'd, late Treasurer of DE, notice given by Joseph TATNALL, Jr. (DE 26 Feb 1798) accounts to be presented to Daniel COWGILL, near Dover, notice given by Joseph TATNALL, Jr., Acting exec'r (DG 24 Mar 1798)

SIPPLE, Thomas B.,
see **SIPPLE**, James Matthew

SIPPLE, Walker, Esq., at his res. in Milford, 19 Mar 1825, aged 41 yrs; Methodist (DG 29 Mar 1825)

SIPPLE, Zadoc, in Milford, 13 Jul 1852, aged c 60 yrs (DG 20 Jul 1852)

SKEEVIN, Kate R., see **ROE**, Andrew B.

SKEGGS, Ann Malvina,
see **LYNCH**, Christoppher

SKIDMORE, Rachel W., Mrs., dau of Josiah BROOKS, of NC Co, in Phila, at the res. of her husband, 1 Apr 1853, aged 22 yrs 4 mos 16 days (DG 12 Apr 1853)

SKILLINGTON, Elijah, Capt., Port Penn, 9 Apr 1820 (DG 12 Apr 1820)

SKINNER, Ann Elizabeth,
see **RIGARD**, Ezakiel J.

SLACK, Enos, in Pencader Hd, 17 Jun 1853, aged c 67 yrs (DG 24 Jun 1853)

SLACK, Esther, see WOLLASTON, Joshua

SLACK, Jane, see BURCHALL, Robert

SLACK, Rebecca, see MASON, Washington

SLACK. Elizabeth, see RIDER, Evans

SLACUM, J. W. E., of Wilm, to ROACH, Mary, Miss, of North East, Cecil Co MD, 18 Apr 1847, by Rev. Mr. Cox (DG 20 Apr 1847)

SLANE, Agnes, 17 Oct 1798, on list of yellow fever victims (DG 27 Oct 1798)

SLAY, Louise, wife of Wm. SLAY, Esq., near Dover, ndd, in her 33rd yr (DG 9 Sep 1851)

SLAY, Wm., see SLAY, Louise

SLAYMAKER, Amos, see OSLERS, Davis

SLEEPER, Anna W., see HAMPTON, Edward H.

SLEVER, Esther, see SLEVER, Philip

SLEVER, Philip, dec'd, late of Wilm, notice given by Esther SLEVER and John DAWSON (DG 4 Feb 1797)

SLOAN, David R., of Balt, to ALLDERDICE, Jane E., dau of Abraham ALLDERDICE of Wilm, 22 May 1849 by Rev. Morgan J. Rhees (Balt papers please copy) (DG 25 May 1849)

SMALLEY, Henry L., Esq., at his res. in White Clay Creek Hd, 18 Feb 1852, in his 47th yr (DG 20 Feb 1852) see MILES, John

SMALLWOOD, ____, Mrs. consort of Wm. SMALLWOOD, in Dover, 3 Mar 1853, na (DG 8 Mar 1853)

SMALLWOOD, Wm., see SMALLWOOD, ____ Mrs

SMART, Alexander, to LECATT, Nancy, Miss, both of Sussex Co, 12 Jul 1853, by the Rev. J. R. Torbert (DG 26 Jul 1853)

SMART, Rebecca, see RODMAN, Simon

SMEDLEY, Hannah, see PRICE, David T.

SMETHURST, Charles H., of Wilm, to MELLIER, Lena P., only dau of Adolph MELLIER of Phila, in Phila, 12 Apr 1852, by the Rev. J.H. Kennard (DG 1 Jun 1852)

SMITH, ____, the Rev. Mr., to MILLER, Ellis M., Miss, at the res. of Lowder LAYTON,

Esq., in Milford, "recently" ...Methodists (DG 9 Sep 1828)

SMITH, Allen, of Wilm, to MATHEWS, Eliza, Miss, of Elkton Md, at the White Hall, Phila, 6 Mar 1851, by Rev. Mr Green (DG 14 Mar 1851)

SMITH, Amelia, wife of Azariah SMITH, in NC Co, 10 Feb 1853 (DG 15 Feb 1853)

SMITH, Ann P., Mrs., see WHITE, John, Dr.

SMITH, Anna Eliza, dau of Charles C. and Caroline SMITH, in Wilm, 20 Jul 1847, aged 21 mos (DG 30 Jul 1847)

SMITH, Anna M., see WALLS, James

SMITH, Annastatia, dau of Jared SMITH, at her mother's res. in Wilm, 17Jul 1846 (DG 11 Aug 1846)

SMITH, Azariah, see SMITH, Amelia

SMITH, Caroline, see SMITH, Anna Eliza

SMITH, Carrie G., see CLARK, Levi Hanry

SMITH, Catharine, Mrs., wife of Capt. Willliam T. SMITH, in Milford, 3 May 1849 (DG 8 May 1849)

SMITH, Charles B., of Phila, formerly of Smyrna, to VANNEMAN, Mary, Miss, of Wilm, in Wilm, 1 Jun 1851, by the Rev. Andrew Manship (DG 6 Jun 1851)

SMITH, Charles C., see SMITH, Anna Eliza

SMITH, Charles C., to McGLAUGHLIN, Caroline, Miss, both of Wilm, 23 May 1844, by Rev. Mr. Spooner (DG 26 May 1844)

SMITH, Charles S., to STAYTON, Mary Ann, Miss, both of Smyrna, 27 Jan 1842, by Rev. James L. Houston (DG 4 Feb 1842)

SMITH, Charlotte, see BOON, James, Esq.

SMITH, David P., to TOWNSEND, Esther, Miss, dau of the late Samuel TOWNSEND, Esq., all of NC Co, 6 Apr 1852, near Cantwell's Bridge, by the Rev. Isaac W. K. Handy (DG 9 Apr 1852)

SMITH, Ebenezer A., dec'd, late of Wilm, notice given by Sarah SMITH, adm'x and Isaac BRYAN, adm'r (AW 29 Jun 1816) Dr., dec'd, late of Wilm, notice to pay debts to Mrs. SMITH, adm'x, Thomas WITHERSPOON, Atty-in-fact, or Isaac BRYAN, adm'r, given by M. SMITH and I. BRYAN, adm'rs (AW 18 Mar 1818)

SMITH, Elizabeth, Miss, in New Castle,

21 Jan 1824, in her 18th yr
(DG 13 Feb 1824)

SMITH, Elizabeth, Mrs., consort of Joseph SMITH, Esq., at Laurel, 3 Jun 1847, aged 60 yrs (DG 11 Jun 1847)

SMITH, Elizabeth, at Rockland, 28 Aug 1847, aged 21 yrs (DG 7 Sep 1847)

SMITH, Elizabeth, see BOYD, John, Jr.

SMITH, Elizabeth A., see SMITH, Robert L.

SMITH, Elwood E., to HODGSON, Margaret B., both of Delaware City, 6 Mar 1850, by Rev. Thomas J. Johnson (DG 19 Mar 1850)

SMITH, F. Burin, of Calvert Co MD, to BRADLEY, Rebecca W., 4th dau of A. BRADLEY, Esq., of Newark, 14 Mar 1850, by J. P. Wilson, DD (DG 19 Mar 1850)

SMITH, Fanny, see BIRD, Thomas M.

SMITH, Francis, dec'd, late of Wilm, notice given by Andrew CATHERWOOD (DE 14 May 1798)

SMITH, Gabriel, late of Wilm Hd, Abel STOKES, adm'r (DG 18 Oct 1853)

SMITH, George, dec'd, late of St. Georges Hd, notice given by Milcah SMITH, adm'x and Thomas SMITH, adm'r (DG 14 Jun 1825)

SMITH, George, in Brandywine Hd, 21 Jul 1848, aged 20 yrs (DG 1 Aug 1848)

SMITH, Hannah, see BLEST, Brian W.

SMITH, Hannah Wager, see MILLES, John, Esq.

SMITH, Isaac P., see SAULSBURY, Gove

SMITH, Isaac, see FAUCETT, Henry

SMITH, Isabella, see FAUCETT, Nathan Y.

SMITH, J. F., see SMITH, James F.

SMITH, Jacob, in Brandywine Hd, 14 May 1844, aged 87 yrs (DG 21 May 1844)

SMITH, Jacob, at the res. of his father in Brandywine Hd, NC Co, 4 Jul 1852, aged 29 yrs 1 mo (DG 23 Jul 1852)

SMITH, Jacob J., of Southwark, to PAUL, Camilla, Miss, formerly of Wilm, 24 Dec 1840, by Rev. George Higgins (DG 29 Jan 1841)

SMITH, James, to REYNOLDS, Sarah, Miss, of Christiana Hd, 7 Mar 1821, by the Rev. Richard D. Hall (DG 9 Mar 1821)

SMITH, James, the Rev., late an eminent itinerant minister of the Gospel in the M. E. Church, in Baltimore, 9 Apr 1826 (AW 14 Apr 1826)

SMITH, James, in the Village of Brandywine, 30 Jun 1829, a long and valuable citizen of that place and a member of the Presbyterian Ch in Wilm (DG 3 Jul 1829) notice given by Edward TATNALL and James PRICE, exec'rs (DG 14 Jul 1829)

SMITH, James F., son of J. F. SMITH, in Wilm, 19 Mar 1848, aged 2 yrs (DG 28 Mar 1848)

SMITH, James L., to DENNY, Rebecca A., all of Kent Co, 26 Feb 1846, by Rev. Joseph Mason (DG 26 Feb 1846)

SMITH, Jane, see FORD, William
see SMITH, William

SMITH, Jared, see SMITH, Annastatia

SMITH, Jerusha, see HAZLET, Thomas S.

SMITH, John, to STROUD, Mary, Miss, both of NC Co, 9 Mar 1848, by Rev. Dr. Kennaday (DG 28 Mar 1848)
see STROUD, James B.

SMITH, John D., son of Wm. SMITH, Esq., senator from NC Co, to GARRETT, Anna, Miss, both of Cecil Co MD, 18 Jan 1853, by the Rev. Jas T. Brown (DG 28 Jan 1853)

SMITH, John Fleming, to HUXLEY, Martha, Miss, dau of Elisha HUXLEY, Esq., all of Wilm, 20 Feb 1849, by Rev. A. Pries (DG 23 Feb 1849)

SMITH, John L., see SMITH, Rebecca

SMITH, John M., formerly of Wilm, in Phila, 11 Dec 1853, in his 67th yr. Burial at Trinity burying ground (DG 13 Dec 1853)

SMITH, Joseph, Esq., dec'd, late of Brandywine Hd, notice given to meet at the res. of James DUTTON by Samuel C. SMITH, adm'r (DG 10 Feb 1824)

SMITH, Joseph, of Wlm, to DUBOIS, Hannah Ann, Miss, formerly of Phila, at Marcus Hook, 24 Aug 1828,by the Rev. Joseph Walker (DG 9 Sep 1828)

SMITH, Joseph, Esq., to EARL, Lydia, Miss, of NJ, at Laurel DE, 26 Oct 1847, by Rev. Henry C. Fries (DG 29 Oct 1847)

SMITH, Joseph, of Delaware City, to

DELAWARE MARRIAGES AND DEATHS FROM NEWSPAPERS, 1729-1853

JOHNSON, Abigail, Miss, of W. Chester, 21 Feb 1853 (DG 4 Mar 1853)

SMITH, Joseph, see SMITH, Elizabeth

SMITH, Joseph E., to EDMONDSON, Caroline R., Miss, all of Wilm, 18 May 1852, by the Rev. J.Humphries (Cecil Co Md papers please copy) (DG 24 May 1852)

SMITH, Julia Ann, Miss, oldest dau of Mr. Thomas SMITH, in Wilm, 11 May 1829, aged 19 yrs (DG 15 May 1829)

SMITH, Lavinia, see MILLER, Anthony

SMITH, Louis, of NC Co, to GAMBLE, Rebecca, dau of Robert N. GAMBLE of Delaware Co PA, 14 Apr 1842, by Rev. J. Walker (DG 22 Apr 1842)

SMITH, Lydia, see EASTBURN, Charles

SMITH, M., see SMITH, Ebenezer A., Dr.

SMITH, Martha Phedora, Miss, see HOLDING, Ebenezer B.

SMITH, Mary, see DIEHL, George S.
see MERCER, James R.
see STANTON, Benjamin

SMITH, Mary I., see KIMES, Benjamin F.

SMITH, Mary Jane, see CARPENTER, Benjamin

SMITH, Milcah, see SMITH, George

SMITH, Prudence J., see FAUCETT, Henry

SMITH, Purnell Fletcher, the Rev., Rector of Shrewsbury Parish, to EVERITT, Mary Wright, Miss, dau of the late Benj. EVERITT, Esq., of Georgetown Cross Roads, Kent Co, MD, in Georgetown, Kent Co, MD, 20 Feb 1821, by the Rev. Richard D. Hall (DG 27 Feb 1821)

SMITH, Rachel Ann, 9 Apr 1848 (DG 21 Apr 1848)

SMITH. Rebecca, Mrs., widow of the late John L. SMITH of Wilm, in Phila, 16 Oct 1849, in her 58th yr (DG 23 Oct 1849)

SMITH, Rebecca R., see GAUSE, Washington

SMITH, Richard E., dec'd, late of White Clay Creek Hd, notice given by George PLATT, adm'r (DG 29 May 1829) see BOON, James, Esq.

SMITH, Robert, see SMITH, Rob't L.

SMITH, Robert, Dr., in the village of Christiana, 24 Jul 1834, aged 73 yrs (DG 30 Sep 1834)

SMITH, Rob't L., son of Robert and Elizabeth A. SMITH, at the res. of his father in Brandywine Village, 10 Jun 1851, aged 11 yrs 2 mos 5 days (DG 20 Jun 1851)

SMITH, Rosina J., see SAULSBURY, Gove

SMITH, Samuel, Capt., to DAVIS, Elizabeth, Miss, all of Wilm, in Milford, by Rev. Mr. Palmater (DG 19 Nov 1848)

SMITH, Samuel C., see SMITH, Joseph

SMITH, Samuel P., to CROZIER, Sarah Ann, Miss, 21 Feb 1841, by Elder John Miller, all of Wilm (DG 26 Feb 1841)

SMITH, Sarah, see MALCOM, John
see SMITH, Ebenezer A.
see MAJOR, Thomas
see WELCH, Daniel

SMITH, Sarah Ann, see WOOD, John
see OGDEN, John T.

SMITH, Sarah E., see LAYTON, Henry A.
see FOX, Aaron

SMITH, T. Broom, see HICKMAN, William M.

SMITH, Tabitha N., see BAILEY, John

SMITH, Thomas, see SMITH, Julia Ann, Miss
see SMITH, George

SMITH, Thomas Jr, in Wilm, 5 Nov 1844, aged 22 yrs (DG 8 Nov 1844)

SMITH, Thomas J. F., of Kent Co MD, to LAMB, Margaret R., Miss, of Kent Co DE, 10 May 1852, by Rev. T. Newman (DG 24 May 1852)

SMITH, Thomas Mackie, M D, at his late res. on the Brandywine, 21 Jan 1852, aged 42 yrs (DG 27 Jan 1852)

SMITH, Thomas R., of Wilm, to SIMMONS, Emma, Miss, dau of George SIMMONS, both of NC Co, 19 May 1843, by Rev. J. W. McCullough (DG 26 May 1843) 17 May 1843 (DG 2 Jun 1843)

SMITH, Thomas W., of St. Georges Hd, to FOARD, Mary, Miss, dau of Mr. Chris. FOARD of North East, Cecil Co, MD, 15 Dec 1822, by Rev. Mr. Griffith (DG 18 Jan 1822)

SMITH, William, of Delaware Co, PA, to

BIRD, Rebecca Caldwell, Miss, of NC Co, Brandywine Hd, 8 Mar 1821, by the Rev. Richard D. Hall (DG 9 Mar 1821)

SMITH, William, to HINES, Sarah, Miss, 7 Aug 1823, by the Rev. J. Potts, all of Wilm (DG 12 Aug 1823)

SMITH, William, farmer of Brandywine Hd, to SMITH, Jane, Miss, of Delaware Co PA, 10 Aug 1841, in St. Paul's Ch, Chester PA by Rev. M. R. Talbot (DG 16 Jul 1841)

SMITH, William, see HADDEN, John
see CLARK, William
see LANDERS, John

SMITH, William B., merchant of Baltimore, to WORRELL, Priscilla B., Miss, dau of Edward WORRELL, Esq., cashier of the Bank of Delaware, in Wilm, 30 Apr 1829, by the Rev. French S. Evans (DG 5 May 1829)

SMITH, William F., merchant, in Wilm, 1 Mar 1848. Remains interred in cemetery on side of hill as it slopes to the valley of the Brandywine (DG 3 Mar 1848)

SMITH, William T., see SMITH,Catharine
see MILLES, John, Esq.

SMITH, Wm., see SMITH, John D.

SMITHERS, John N., to CORKIN,Sally Ann, Miss both of Murderkill Hd, 18 May 1826, by the Rev. Zedekiah Davis (DG 26 May 1826)

SMITHERS, Joseph,
see SMITHERS, Nathaniel B.

SMITHERS, Mary E.,
see SMITHERS, Nathaniel B.

SMITHERS, Nathaniel,
see SMITHERS, Susan F., Mrs.,

SMITHERS, Nathaniel B., Esq., of Dover, to SMITHERS, Mary E., Miss, dau of Joseph SMITHERS, Esq., of NC Co, 22 Mar 1853, by Rev. H. E. Gilroy (DG 29 Mar 1853)

SMITHERS, Susan F., Mrs., wife of Nathaniel SMITHERS, Esq., in Dover, 2 Mar 1824, in her 30th yr (DG 9 Mar 1824)

SMYTH, Lindley, son of Wm. C. SMYTH, in Wilm, 17 Feb 1853, aged 6 mos (DG 22 Feb 1853)

SMYTH, Robert, Dr., Wilm, of consumption, 18 Dec 1826 (WN 29 Dec 1826)

SMYTH, William C., to BETTS, Emily, dau of Mahlon BETTS, 28 Sep 1847, by Friends ceremony at the res. of her father (DG 1 Oct 1847)

see SMYTH, Lindley

SNYDER, George, to POINSETT, Mary, Miss, 20 Nov 1828, by Elder John P. Peckworth, all of Wilm (DG 25 Nov 1828)

SNYDER, Harriet,
see BETEHLER, Andrew J.

SNYDER, Samuel, to PEARCE, Lydia, Miss, in Wilm, 24 Oct 1807, by Rev. Mr. Pryce (MU 31 Oct 1807)

SOLOMON, George Geddes, inf son of Isaac and Sarah SOLOMON, 2 Feb 1846, aged 3 mos (DG 10 Feb 1846)

SOLOMON, Hannah,
see JONES, Hannah, Mrs.

SOLOMON, Isaac,
see MEGINNIES, Edward
see SOLOMON, George Geddes
see JONES, Hannah, Mrs.
see SOLOMON, Ruth

SOLOMON, Isaac, to CHANDLER, Sarah, Miss,dau of William CHANDLER, both of Wilm, 22 Apr 1841, by Rev. S. R. Wynkoop (DG 23 Apr 1841)

SOLOMON, Isaac, 1 Sept 1842, aged 80 yrs (DG 2 Sep 1842) dec'd, notice given by William SOLOMON and John SOLOMON, exec'rs (DG 8 Nov 1842)

SOLOMON, Jane, see JACKSON, Bryan

SOLOMON, John, formerly of Wilm, at West Chester PA, 16 May 1844, aged 47 yrs (DG 21 May 1844)
see SOLOMON, Isaac

SOLOMON, Leah,
see MEGINNIES, Edward

SOLOMON, Martha,
see HUNTER, Joseph A.

SOLOMON, Ruth, Mrs., wife of Isaac SOLOMON (DG 17 May 1820)
see KENNARD, Edward

SOLOMON, Sarah,
see SOLOMON, George Geddes

SOLOMON, Sarah Ann,
see MAGENS, William

SOLOMON, William,
see SOLOMON, Isaac

SOLOMON, William, Esq., at his res. near Smyrna, 20 Sep 1849, aged 55 yrs (DG 25 Sep 1849)

SOMERS, Chalkley, to McCONNELL, Eliza, Miss, both of Wilm, in Phila, 3 Aug 1824, by Joseph Watson, Mayor (DG 6 Aug 1824)

SORDEN, ___, Mr.,
see ROBINSON, ___.

SORDEN, Elizabeth D., Mrs., wife of James SORDEN, Esq., one of the burgesses of Wilm, 27 Jun 1824, aged 46 yrs (DG 2 Jul 1824)

SORDEN, James,
see SORDEN, Elizabeth D.

SORDEN, John, Maj., to ROBINSON, S. P., Mrs, dau of the late John CAREY, all of Sussex, at Bridgeville, 18 Apr 1850 by Rev. Mr. Hoskins (DG 30 Apr 1850)

SORDEN, Mary Ann, Mrs., wife of Robert SORDEN, Esq., 14 Mar 1853, near Willow Grove, Kent Co, in her 38th yr (DG 29 Mar 1853)

SORDEN, Robert,
see SORDEN, Mary Ann

SORDON, James, see SORDON, John

SORDON, John, son of James SORDON, Esq., of Wilm, in Phila, 10 Feb 1826, aged 20 yrs (DG 14 Feb 1826)
see STEWART, William W.

SORDON, Mary A.,
see STEWART, William W.

SOUTHWELL, William, in Wilm, 21 Jun 1847, aged 43 yrs (DG 7 Jul 1847)

SOWDERS, Mary,
see SOWDERS, Samuel

SOWDERS, Reuben,
see SOWDERS, Samuel

SOWDERS, Samuel, son of Reuben and Mary SOWDERS, formerly of Wilm, _ Oct 1847, in Massilon, Star Co, Ohio (DG 25 Jan 1848)

SPACKMAN, George, dec'd, late of Wilm, notice given by Thomas SPACKMAN (DE 10 Dec 1798)

SPACKMAN, Samuel, merchant of Wilm, to BELLERBY, Ann, Miss, of Phila, "a few days since" in Phila by J. Copperthwait, Esq. (FA 25 Feb 1804)
see STORY, Betty

SPACKMAN, Thomas,
see SPACKMAN, George

SPAIN, George, dec'd, late of Wilm, notice given by Benjamin REYNOLDS, adm'r (DE 10 Dec 1798)

SPARE, James, to MILBY, Catharine, both of NC Co, 13 Sep 1827, by John P. Peckworth (DG 18 Sep 1827)

SPARKS, Amy,
see DUBOIS, Susan Sparks

SPARKS, Amy, see DuBOIS, Edward

SPARKS, Christiana,
see JARETTE, Joseph

SPARKS, Dodo, see SPARKS, William

SPARKS, George, 20 Dec 1842, in Wilm, inf. son of John and Hanna SPARKS (DG 23 Dec 1842)
see DUBOIS, Susan Sparks

SPARKS, George, Sr., see SPARKS, Susan

SPARKS, George W., to MEACHEM, Sarah E., Miss, both of Wilm, 4 Apr 1850, by Rev. Morgan J. Rhees (DG 9 Apr 1850)

SPARKS, Hanna, see SPARKS, George

SPARKS, James A., to SEEDS, Catharine Ann, Miss, dau of Mr. Joseph SEEDS, all of NC Co, 20 Feb 1826, by the Rev. Henry White (DG 21 Feb 1826)

SPARKS, John, see SPARKS, George

SPARKS, Josiah,
see McGLAUGHLIN, James

SPARKS, Levin D.,
see SPARKS, Margaretta

SPARKS, Margaretta, dau of Levin D. SPARKS, in Wilm, 5 Jun 1848, aged 7 mos (DG 13 Jun 1848)

SPARKS, Mary Jane,
see CLAYTON, Henry
see BLIZZARD, Gideon W.

SPARKS, Samuel, formerly of Wilm , in Phila, 9 Dec 1852, aged c 40 yrs (DG 14 Dec 1852)

SPARKS, Susan, Mrs., wife of George SPARKS Sr, in Wilm, 9 Aug 1849, aged 62 yrs (DG 14 Aug 1849)
see JOHNSON, Robert W.

SPARKS, William, inf son of Dodo SPARKS of Wilm, 15 Jul 1848 (DG 28 Jul 1848)

SPARKS, William D., to WELDF(sic), Ann Eliza, both of Wilm, in Phila, 16 Mar 1848, by Rev. Mr. Page (DG 28 Mar 1848)

SPARKS, William, Jr, formerly of NJ, in Wilm, of typhoid fever, 27 Jan 1851, aged c 17 yrs (DG 7 Feb 1851)

SPEAKMAN, Ann, see ALLEN, Thomas

SPEAKMAN, Eber, to MASSEY, Elizabeth D., both of New Castle, DE, in Phila, 3 Apr 1849, by the Rev. Peter Hallowell (DG 6 Apr 1849)

SPEAKMAN, Edith, Mrs., relict of Thomas SPEAKMAN, at the res. of her son, John SPEAKMAN near New Castle, 29 Apr 1847, aged 79 yrs (DG 11 May 1847)

SPEAKMAN, James E., to KARR, Isabella, Miss, all of Wilm, 26 Sep 1847, by Rev. T. J. Thompson (DG 5 Oct 1847)

SPEAKMAN, John, see SPEAKMAN, Edith

SPEAKMAN, John N.. to LOWTHER, Mary, Miss, both of Wilm, 29 May 1849, at C. Lyon's Hotel by Rev. C. W. Quick (DG 8 Jun 1849)

SPEAKMAN, Lewis, of Del Co PA, to HICKMAN, Charlotte R., Miss, of Wilm, in Phila, 12 Oct 1853, by the Rev. Wm Bacon Stevens (DG 21 Oct 1853)

SPEAKMAN, Mary G., Miss, see HURST, James M.

SPEAKMAN, Thomas, see SPEAKMAN, Edith

SPEAR, Amelia, Mrs., wife of John C. SPEAR, in Appoq Hd, 19 Aug 1849, aged 23 yrs (DG 31 Aug 1849)

SPEAR, Isaac, in Wilm, aged c 50 yrs (DG 27 Apr 1849)

SPEAR, John C., see SPEAR, Amelia

SPEAR, Springer, of Chester Co Pa, to GREENHALGH, Ann, of NC Co, at Trinity Chapel, 4 Jul 1849, by the Rev. E. M. Van Dusen (DG 5 Jul 1849)

SPEARMAN, Elizabeth, see LANCASTER, Ignatius T.

SPEARMAN, Mary S., late wife of Simon SPEARMAN and dau of Presley SPEARMAN, dec'd, 10 Oct 1844, at Smyrna (DG 18 Oct 1844)

SPEARMAN, Presley, see SPEARMAN, Mary S.

SPEARMAN, Simon, see SPEARMAN, Mary S.

see LANCASTER, Ignatius T.

SPEARMAN, Simon, Esq., of NC Co, to DUNNING, Emma E., of Kent Co, 17 May 1847, at the res. of James DUNNING in Dover (DG 21 May 1847)

SPENCE, Benjamin D., to COLLUM, Lydia B., Miss, of Wilm, 29 Oct 1850, by Rev. Andrew Manship (DG 6 Dec 1850)

SPENCE, Charles, see SPENCE, Rachel

SPENCE, Rachel, wife of Charles SPENCE, 3 Aug 1852, in her 60th yr (DG 10 Aug 1852)

SPENCER, Anna, see MILLER, Richard

SPENCER, Elizabeth, see SPENCER, James

SPENCER, Elizabeth I., see HILL, George P.

SPENCER, James, inf son of Nicholas and Elizabeth C. SPENCER, 9 Jul 1848, in Wilm (DG 18 Jul 1848)

SPENCER, James, 18 Dec 1853, in his 22nd (sic) yr. Fun from the res. of his son-in-law, George P. HALL, near the old Kings Rd (DG 20 Dec 1853) [?]

SPENCER, John W., to ENNIS, Rebecca F., Miss, both of NC Co, 19 Feb 1829, by Elder John P. Peckworth (DG 27 Feb 1829)

SPENCER, Joseph, blacksmith, formerly of Wilm, found dead of intemperance and exposure at New Castle (DG 27 Jul 1852)

SPENCER, Joseph, to MILMAN, Eliza, Miss, all of Sussex Co, 16 Feb 1853, by Rev. McColley (DG 22 Feb 1853)

SPENCER, Mary, see PETIT, William

SPENCER, Nicholas, see SPENCER, James

SPENCER, Patrick, 23 Apr 1852, near Mllford, in his 67th yr (DG 4 May 1852)

SPENCER, Richard B., to JACKSON, Mary, Miss, both of Wilm, in Phila, 21 Sep 1848, by Rev. J. M. Coleman (DG 26 Sep 1848)

SPENCER, William, of Wilm, to CANNON, Angeline, Miss, formerly of Milford, 19 May 1850, by Rev. Edward Kennard (DG 14 Jun 1850)

SPICER, Geo. W., of Milford, to HARPER, Matilda J., eldest dau of Francis B. HARPER, Esq., of Dover, DE, 27 Sep 1853, by the

DELAWARE MARRIAGES AND DEATHS FROM NEWSPAPERS, 1729-1853

Rev. Daniel W. Bartine (DG 4 Oct 1853)

SPICER, Rhoda Jane, see STEEL, Ishmael

SPOONER, Charles A., Rev., of Norwich CT, to McDOWELL, Mary Collins, Miss, dau of McDOWELL, Thomas, Esq., of Wilm, 11 Jul 1851, in Trinity Chapel, by the Rector, Rev. E. M. Van Dusen (DG 12 Aug 1851)

SPRAGUE, Asa, see MILNOR, George A.

SPRINGER, Anna or John, both of Mill Creek Hd, dec'd, notice given by Justa JUSTIS, adm'r and exec'r (sic) (DG 14 Jul 1828)

SPRINGER, Anne, alias PHILIPS, see CHEESELY, Joseph

SPRINGER, Catharine, Mrs., relict of the late John SPRINGER, in Wilm, 8 Oct 1848, in her 90th yr. Bur. in Episc Churchyd at New Castle. Born in Pencader Hd in 1760; leaves 8 ch, 54 g'ch, 73 gg'ch and 5 gggch (DG 12 Oct 1849) ... late of Wilm. PETER SPRINGER, adm'r (DG 23 Nov 1849)

SPRINGER, George, Esq., at his late res. in Mill Creek Hd, of a severe paralysis, 20 Feb 1835, aged 56 yrs, leaving a wife and 12 children...ruling Elder in Presbyterian Ch for about 25 yrs (DG 3 Mar 1835)

SPRINGER, George, to GRAVES, Rebecca, Miss, 27 Apr 1841, by Rev. J. W. McCullough, all of NC Co (DG 30 Apr 1841)

SPRINGER, Isaac, of Mill Creek Hd. Lewis C. JUSTIS, adm'r (DG 16 Jan 1849)

SPRINGER, James, to RANKIN, Sarah Maria, Miss, both of NC Co, at Newark, 30 Mar 1852, by the Rev. Joseph Barr (DG 6 Apr 1852)... to RANKIN, Sallie Maria, Miss, dau of Mr. Joseph RANKIN, both of Mill Creek Hd... (DG 13 Apr 1852)

SPRINGER, John, see SPRINGER, Catharine

SPRINGER, John, dec'd, late of Wilm, notice given by Sarah SPRINGER, exec'x and Peter BRYNBERG, exec'r (DG 12 Jan 1793)

SPRINGER, John, in Wilm of consumption, ndd, aged 29 yrs (DG 21 Jan 1848)

SPRINGER, John or Anna, both of Mill Creek Hd, dec'd, notice given by Justa JUSTIS, adm'r and exec'r (sic) (DG 14 Jul 1828)

SPRINGER, John, see SPRINGER, Sarah

SPRINGER, John, to SPRINGER Sarah Ann, both of Wilm, 5 Aug 1851, at the Black Bear Hotel, by the Rev. G. B. Ide DD (DG19 Aug 1851)

SPRINGER, John, to ARMSTRONG, Sarah Jane, both of Mill Creek Hd, 23 Feb 1841, by Rev. Mr. Love (DG 5 Mar 1841)

SPRINGER, Joseph, to EVANS, Sarah, Miss, 24 Feb 1820 (DG 26 Feb 1820)

SPRINGER, Joseph W., of Wilm, to ARMSTRONG, Rachel, Miss, of NC Co, 24 May 1852, by the Rev. Mr. Van Deusen (DG 1 Jun 1852)

SPRINGER, Lewis C., to McMULLEN, Sarah P., Miss, all of NC Co, in NC Co, 27 Feb 1850, by Rev. M. J. Rhees (DG 1 Mar 1850)

SPRINGER, Margaret, late of Mill Creek Hd, Robert HANNA, adm'r (DG 11 Mar 1851)

SPRINGER, Mary Ann, see WARD, George C. see HOLLINGSWORTH, Ferdinand

SPRINGER, Mary Jane, see SHARPLEY, John

SPRINGER, Peter, see SPRINGER, Catharine

SPRINGER, Peter, Esq., of NC Co, to HYNOLDS Elizabeth, Miss, of Phila, in Phila, 3 Oct 1822, by the Rev. Dr. Staughton (DG 15 Oct 1822)

SPRINGER, Peter, to LOVELL, Anna Mary, Miss, both of Wilm, in Phila, Dec 10 1846, by Rt. Rev. Alfred Lee (DG 15 Dec 1846)

SPRINGER, Rebecca, see GILL, Joseph

SPRINGER, Samuel, in Wilm, after a long illness, 18 Aug 1853, aged c 45 yrs. Leaves a wife and family (DG 23 Aug 1853)

SPRINGER, Sarah, see SPRINGER, John

SPRINGER, Sarah Ann, see SPRINGER, John

SPRINGER, Sarah, dau of the late John SPRINGER, 7 Jan 1821, na (DG 12 Jan 1821)

SPRINGER, Sarah E., see LOGAN, E. H.

SPRINGER, Stephen, of NC Co, to LOVE, Mary E., Miss, dau of the Rev. Thomas LOVE, of Loveville DE, [NW of Wilm], 16 Nov 1848, by Rev. James Latta

(DG 17 Nov 1848)

SPRINGER, Susan,
see CATHCART, William

SPRUANCE, Enoch,
see WAKEMAN, Ruth

SPRUANCE, Enoch, Jr., to FRAZIER, Mary Elizabeth, dau of John FRAZIER, Esq., all of Kent, at Elm Cottage, 23 Nov 1848, by Rev. E. G. Asay (DG 5 Dec 1848)

SPRUANCE, Presley,
see SPRUANCE, William Ellison

SPRUANCE, Willie Ellison, inf son of Presley SPRUANCE, of Smyrna, 5 Oct 1852 (DG 12 Oct 1852)

SPURRIER, Eleanor,
see SPURRIER, John

SPURRIER, John, dec'd, late of Phila, notice given by Eleanor SPURRIER, adm'x (DE 22 Aug 1799)

SQUIBB, Ellen, see ALLMON, John

SQUIBB, Robert, see ALLMON, John

SQUIBB, Samuel F., of Mill Creek Hd, to BAILEY, Hannah P., Miss, of East Bradford, Chester Co, PA, in Marcus Hook, PA, 4 Feb 1830, by Benjamin F. Johnson, Esq. (DG 9 Feb 1830)

STAATS, James, of NC Co, to CAULK, Mary Ann, Miss, dau of Jacob CAULK, Esq., of Cecil Co MD, 31 Jan 1850, by Rev. John Henry (DG 8 Feb 1850)

STAATS, Rebecca, see WILDS, John

STAATS, Sarah E.,
see DEAKYNE, Wm. S.

STAM, John L.,
see HOLLINGSWORTH, Francis

STAMP, William, of Phila, to SAULSBURY, Mary Ann, Miss, of Wilm, in Phila, 29 Dec 1848, by Rev. A. Atwood (DG 28 Jan 1848)

STANHOPE, Jacob, of West Chester, PA, to BILLINGHAM, Hannah B., Miss, of Brandywine, 12 Jun 1834, by Rev. Mr. Adair (DG 17 Jun 1834)

STANLEY, Charles, to HARVEY, Mary, Miss, both of Middletown, in Wilm, 15 Jul 1827, by the Rev. Solomon Higgins (DG 17 Jul 1827)

STANLEY, Phoebe Ann,
see BALDWIN, Lewis H.

STANLY, Eliza, see PRIOR, John

STANTON, ____, Mrs., of Summit Bridge, fell into the fire while preparing supper, ndd, na. Leaves a husband. (DG 4 Mar 1853)

STANTON, Benjamin, to SMITH, Mary, Miss, both of NC Co, 26 Sep 1816, by Rev. William Wickes (AW 26 Sep 1816)

STANTON, Sarah Ann,
see CAMPBELL, Joseph

STAPLEFORD, Edward, in Milford, 26 Sep 1852, aged 72 yrs (DG 28 Sep 1852)

STAPLEFORD, William, to ECCLESTON, Sarah E., Miss, 30 Jun 1850, by Rev. Silas C. Palmiter (DG 16 Jul 1850)

STAPLER, Ann, dau of Stephen M. and Elizabeth STAPLER, at the res of her father in Brandywine Hd, 17 Jul 1847, in her 13th yr (DG 3 Aug 1847)

STAPLER, Elizabeth, see STAPLER, Ann

STAPLER, Esther, 20 May 1850, aged 62 yrs (DG 28 May 1850) sale of real estate (DG 14 Jan 1853)

STAPLER, John, Esq., Justice of the Peace of NC Co, 30 Aug 1793, aged 72 yrs (DG 31 Aug 1793) notice given by Samuel CANBY and Edward GILPIN, exec'rs (DG 28 Sep 1793)

STAPLER, Mary, see DOWNING, Samuel S.

STAPLER, Stephen M.,
see DOWNING, Samuel S.
see STAPLER, Ann
see STAPLER, William

STAPLER, Thomas,
see STAPLER, William

STAPLER, William, member of the Society of Friends, native of Bristol, PA, at his res. near Stanton, 18 Mar 1828, aged 77 yrs (DG 4 Apr 1828) late of Stanton, notice given by Thomas STAPLER and Stephen M. STAPLER, exec'rs (DG 30 Dec 1828)

STARLING, Martha, see HOLLAND, Henry

STARR, Amanda Wallace, dau of Lewis and Ruth STARR, in Wilm, 16 Nov 1851, aged c 10 yrs (DG 21 Nov 1851)

STARR, Caleb, see RASIN, Margaret

STARR, Eliza,
see STARR, John Toland

STARR, Elizabeth, in Wilm, 24 Nov 1852,

aged 33 yrs (DG 30 Nov 1852)

STARR, Elizabeth T.,
see BROBSON, William P., Esq.

STARR Isaac H., in Wilm, 15 Jun 1849, aged c 89 yrs (DG 19 Jun 1849)

STARR, Isaac, see RASIN, Margaret

STARR, Jacob to HUTTON, Sarah Ann, of Brandywine, 24 Apr 1823, by the Rev. R. Williston (DG 29 Apr 1823)

STARR, Jacob, Capt., to KIRK, Jane F., Miss, 21 Jan 1830, by Elder John P. Peckworth, all of Wilm (DG 26 Jan 1830) see STARR, John Toland

STARR, Jacob, to MORRISON, Ann Eliza, Miss, of Brandywine Hd, 11 Jan 1847, at the hotel of Maj. Price, Chester PA, by Rev. A. B. Hard (DG 22 Jan 1847)

STARR, John Toland, son of Capt Jacob and Eliza STARR, in Wilm, 22 Nov 1849, aged 2 yrs 14 das (DG 29 Nov 1849)

STARR, Joshua, in Christiana, 2 Feb 1853, aged c 85 yrs (DG 8 Feb 1853)

STARR, Lewis,
see STARR, Amanda Wallace

STARR, Margaret, see RASIN, Margaret

STARR, Mary, Miss, at Milford, 10 Jul 1824, aged 24 yrs (DG 20 Jul 1824)

STARR, Melinda,
see CROASDALE, Howard

STARR, Ruth,
see STARR, Amanda Wallace

STARRETT, Charles R., son of Thomas A. STARRETT, in Wilm, 1 Dec 1828, aged 20 yrs (DG 2 Dec 1828)

STARRETT, Thomas A.,
see STARRETT, Charles R.

START, Elijah, see WAUGH, Eliza P.

START, Ephraim D., son of Mr. Ephraim START, in Smyrna, 3 Nov 1851, aged 2 yrs (DG 7 Nov 1851)

START, Ephraim, see START, Ephraim D.

START, Hannah Ann, dau of William H. START of Smyrna, 12 Feb 1850, in her 2nd yr (DG 22 Feb 1850)

START, William H.,
see START, Hannah Ann

STATTEN, Milton, Dr, of Montoursville, Lycoming Co, PA, to DIXON, Hannah C., dau of Mr. Samuel DIXON of NC Co, in Clinton Twp, Lycoming Co, at the res. of Mr. Wm. BUCKLEY, 26 May 1853, by J. G. Rathmell, Esq. (DG 19 Jul 1853)

STAUNTON, Susanna,
see UNDERWOOD, Levi

STAYTON, Mary Ann,
see SMITH, Charles S.

STAYTON, Rhoda, see CASHILL, Thomas

STEDHAM, Catherine, see PIERCE, Albert

STEDHAM, Joanna, Mrs., wife of Lucas STEDHAM, dau of William VANEMAN, 28 Nov 1789. Buried in Old Swedes Cem (DG 5 Dec 1789)

STEDHAM, Lucas,
see STEDHAM, Joanna, Mrs.

STEDMAN, Henry, to READER, Rachel, Miss, both of Wilm, 10 Dec 1840, by E. W. Gilbert (DG 18 Dec 1840)

STEEL, Ishmael, to SPICER, Rhoda Jane, Miss, both of Sussex Co, 12 Jun 1853, by the Rev. A. Wallace (DG 24 Jun 1853)

STEEL, James, Sheriff, to MAULL, Penelope K., Miss, dau of James MAULL, Esq., all of Georgetown, 2 Jun 1841, by Rev. Jonas Bissey (DG 11 Jun 1841)

STEEL, James, Capt., at his res. near Georgetown, 18 Nov 1852, in his 50th yr (DG 30 Nov 1852)

STEEL, Margaret, Mrs., see DAVIS, Eli

STEEL, Milton, see WALKER, Josiah

STEEL, Sarah H., see HOSKINS, Edward B.

STEELE, Henry, innkeeper, at New Castle, 7 Jun 1827, na (DG 12 Jun 1827)

STEELE, John, in Phila, 27 Feb 1827, in his 69th yr (DG 2 Mar 1827)

STEELE, Rachel, Miss, at Frederica, 17 Jul 1834, aged 73 yrs, born near Newark, DE, survived by a sister (DG 29 Jul 1834)

STEPHENS, Alexander, at his res. near Wilm, 23 Jul 1852, na (DG 27 Jul 1852)

STEPHENS, Alexander, of Wilm, to EVANS, Margaret Jane , Miss, of Delaware Co, PA, at Marcus Hook, PA, 17 Jul 1834, by the Rev. Joseph Walker (DG 22 Jul 1834)

STEPHENS, Charles, 26 Sep 1852, aged 28 yrs (DG 28 Sep 1852)

STEPHENS, George W., to **FOX**, Anne Maria, Miss, dau of James FOX, Esq., all of Wilm, in Wilm, 23 May 1852 by the Rev. Mr. Cosgrave (DG 28 May 1852)

STEPHENS, Rebecca J., see **AIKIN**, Samuel M.

STEPHENS, Samuel, at the res. of Lewis CURLETT, Esq., in Wilm, 25 Feb 1847 (DG 2 Mar 1847)

STEPHENSON, Davis, in Brandywine Hd, 21 Aug 1849, aged c 60 yrs (DG 21 Aug 1849)

STEPHENSON, Eliza Ann, Mrs., of Milton DE, 8 Oct 1851, in her 42nd yr (DG 10 Oct 1851)

STEPTOE, Sarah, see **STEPTOE**, Thomas Forman

STEPTOE, Thomas Forman, son of Wm. H. and Sarah STEPTOE, at Rockland near Wilm, 27 Apr 1853, aged 15 yrs 10 mos 2 days (DG 6 May 1853) (Elkton papers please copy)

STEPTOE, Wm. H., see **STEPTOE**, Thomas Forman

STERBETT, Catharine, Mrs., in Wilm, after an illness of about two months, 17 Feb 1818, in her 67th yr (AW 18 Feb 1818)

STERLING, Benjamin, at Louviers on the Brandywine at the residence of his mother, 21 Jul 1847, in his 23rd yr (DG 3 Aug 1847)

STERN, Cyrus, to **WILSON**, Caroline, Miss, both of Wilm, 1 Apr 1849, by Rev. Thomas J. Thompson (DG 10 Apr 1849)

STERNE, I., see **WELDIN**, William R.

STERNE, Sarah, see **WELDIN**, William R.

STERRETT, Sarah, see **STERRETT**, Thomas A.

STERRETT, Thomas, see **STERRETT**, Thomas A.

STERRETT, Thomas A., Jr., son of Thomas and Sarah STERRETT, in Camden NJ, 14 Mar 1853, aged 21 yrs (DG 18 Mar 1853)

STERRETT. John, late of Wilm, 21 Aug 1751 (PG 24 Aug 1751)

STEVENS, Daniel, to **MILLIGAN**, Elizabeth, Miss, both of Cantwell's Bridge, N.C.Co DE,
in Salem, 5 Aug 1849 (DG 28 Aug 1849)

STEVENS, E. P., in Wilm, 1 May 1851, na. Fun. from the house of his mother, 2nd St between West and Washington (DG 2 May 1851)

STEVENS, Edwin J., Esq., of Talbot, to **ECCLESTON**, Sarah Hooper, Miss, youngest dau of Hon. J. H. ECCLESTON, of Dorchester Co MD, 14 Nov 1843, by Rev. James A. McKenny (DG 1 Dec 1843)

STEVENS, Mary, see **PRICE**, William C.

STEVENS, Ruth, see **READER**, William J.

STEVENSON, Ann, see **THOMAS**, Samuel

STEVENSON, Anna, see **McFARLIN**, Robert

STEVENSON, Edward L., see **ADAMS**, John

STEVENSON, Eliza, see **VERION**, William M.

STEVENSON, Elizabeth J., see **MILNER**, Thomas

STEVENSON, George, Dr., see **WRENSHALL**, Nancy, Mrs.

STEVENSON, George, son of T. Collins STEVENSON of Wilm, 5 Jul 1835, aged 15 mos (DG 10 Jul 1835)

STEVENSON, Isaac, see **GIVEN**, James see **GIVEN**, William

STEVENSON, Jacob, to **DAVIS**, Kessiah, Miss, 5 Nov 1820 (DG 7 Nov 1820)

STEVENSON, James, at Dover, 12 Sep 1849, na (DG 18 Sep 1849) see **LODGE**, Samuel W.

STEVENSON, James B., late of St. Georges Hd. William C. STEVENSON, adm'r (DG 17 Apr 1849)

STEVENSON, James H., to **MORRIS**, F. Ann, Miss, both of Dover, in Phila, 18 Apr 1833, by the Rev. Mr. Sneyd (DG 23 Apr 1833)

STEVENSON, Margaret, see **HIGGINS**, S., Dr.

STEVENSON, Margaret Ann, see **DUNNING**, James A.

STEVENSON, Mary, see **BANDERBRAAK**, Lawrence

STEVENSON, Mary B.,
see LODGE, Samuel W.

STEVENSON, Nancy,
see WRENSHALL, Nancy, Mrs.

STEVENSON, T. Collins,
see STEVENSON, George

STEVENSON, Thomas Collins of Wilm, to DUNCAN, Eliza, Miss, of Phila, 7 May 1833, by the Rev. Joseph Lybrand (DG 7 May 1833)

STEVENSON, Thomas,
see DUNNING, James A.

STEVENSON, William C.,
see STEVENSON, James B.

STEWARD, David T., of quinsy, 30 Nov 1849, in his 48th yr (DG 4 Dec 1849)

STEWART, _____, Master,
see MANSON, James

STEWART, Ann C.,
see STEWART, Joseph C.

STEWART, Catharine,
see McMARTIN, D. J.

STEWART, Eliza Ann, see KEEN, Joseph

STEWART, Elizabeth, see STEWART, John

STEWART, Ellen F,
see LESLEY, Henry Voorhees

STEWART, J.,
see LESLEY, Henry Voorhees

STEWART, James, at his res. near Summit Bridge, 25 Sep 1847, aged 80 yrs (DG 5 Oct 1847)

STEWART, Jno. B., to PARKES, Levina, Miss, 8 Sep 1849, by Rev. S. M. Gailey (DG 28 Sep 1849)

STEWART, John,
see STEWART, John Wesley

STEWART, John, of Brandywine, to STEWART, Elizabeth, of Phila, in Phila, 27 Nov 1851, by the Rev. A. Tudehope (DG 2 Dec 1851)

STEWART, John, Capt., in Middleford, 30 May 1853, aged 39 yrs (DG 7 Jun 1853)

STEWART, John Wesley, inf son of John and Rachel STEWART, in Wilm, 11 Jul 1851, aged 7 mos 3 days (DG 18 Jul 1851)

STEWART, Joseph C., son of Michael and Ann C. STEWART, at Middleford DE, 17 Dec 1852, in his 20th yr (DG 14 Jan 1853)

STEWART, Michael,
see STEWART, Joseph C.

STEWART, Rachel,
see STEWART, John Wesley

STEWART, Richard Thomas, of NC Co, to WILSON, Georgiana, Miss, of Easton MD, in Easton, 6 Nov 1849, by the Rev. W. J. Dale (DG 16 Nov 1849)

STEWART, Samuel, formerly of Middletown, DE, to HAYS, Mary Ann, Miss, dau of Mr. Addis HAYS of Penn Township, (PA) in Phila, 13 Feb 1834, by Rev. Mr. Kitts (DG 21 Feb 1834)

STEWART, Sarah, see BIDDLE, Thomas

STEWART, Sarah Ann,
see FLINTHAM, George

STEWART, Seth, native of Ireland, in Pencader Hd, 7 Feb 1845, aged 75 yrs Leaves a family. (DG 21 Feb 1845)

STEWART, William, see BIDDLE, Thomas

STEWART, William W., Dr., of Middleford DE, to SORDON, Mary A., Miss, dau of the late John SORDON, of St. Johnstown, 30 Sep 1845 (DG 7 Oct 1845)

STICHMAN, Casper, see BRITTS, Eliza

STICHMAN, Eliza, see BRITTS, Eliza

STIDHAM, _____, Mrs, in Christiana Hd, 27 Jan 1848, aged 60 yrs (DG 4 Feb 1848)

STIDHAM, Anna,
see MENDENHALL, William A.

STIDHAM, Catharine,
see HUTTON, Nehemiah B.

STIDHAM, Catherine,
see BRYAN, Catherine, Mrs.

STIDHAM, Charles Henry, son of John H. and Hannah STIDHAM, at the res. of his father in Wilm, 7 Dec 1850 (DG 10 Dec 1850)

STIDHAM, Daniel, to COVERDILL, Amelia, Miss, both of NC Co, 9 Feb 1828, by Elder John P. Peckworth (DG 15 Feb 1828)

STIDHAM, Hannah,
see STIDHAM, Charles Henry

STIDHAM, Ingebur, see FRAZER, John

STIDHAM, Ingeber Ann,

see **GREGG**, Edmund C.

STIDHAM, Isaac,
see **BRYAN**, Catherine, Mrs.
see **MENDENHALL**, William A.
see **STIDHAM**, Jonas

STIDHAM, Isaac, at his late res., Point Pleasant, N. C. Hd, 17 Oct 1821, in his 59th yr (DG 26 Oct 1821)

STIDHAM, Jacob, formerly of Wilm, last week on the Tamaque RR above Reading. Engineer of the road. Death caused by meeting of 2 trains (DG 3 Mar 1848)

STIDHAM, James, dec'd, notice given by John STIDHAM, adm'r (DE 26 Oct 1797)

STIDHAM, John, see **STIDHAM**, James

STIDHAM, John, to **PENNINGTON**, Lydia, Miss, all of Newport, DE, 16 Jan 1822, by the Rev. L. Lawrenson (DG 22 Jan 1822)

STIDHAM, John H.,
see **STIDHAM**, Charles Henry

STIDHAM, John K., 1 Apr 1843, aged 60 yrs (DG 7 Apr 1643)

STIDHAM, Jonas,
see **STIDHAM**, Jonas Spencer

STIDHAM, Jonas B., to **FOREMAN**, Ellen B., Miss, both of NC Co, 4 Mar 1851, by the Rev. E. M. Van Deusen (DG 7 Mar 1851)

STIDHAM, Jonas, dec'd, late of Christiana Hd, notice given by Isaac STIDHAM, adm'r (DE 10 May 1796)

STIDHAM, Jonas, to **EVES**, Sarah, Miss, dau of Mr. Abraham EVES of NC Hd, 24 Jun 1823, by the Rev. Samuel R. Greene (DG 27 Jun 1823)

STIDHAM, Jonas Spencer, son of Jonas and Sarah STIDHAM, at the res. of his grandmother, Mrs. Elizabeth EVES, 19 Feb 1847 (DG 2 Mar 1847)

STIDHAM, Joseph G.,
see **STIDHAM**, Samuel

STIDHAM, L. W., see **BAILEY**, Sarah

STIDHAM, Penrose, see **STIDHAM**, Samuel

STIDHAM, Peter, to **RUDOLPH**, Hannah, Miss, both of Wilm, "Thursday evening last" (DG 1 Nov 1821), by the Rev. Dr. Holcomb (DG 6 Nov 1821)

STIDHAM, Samuel, dec'd, late of Christiana Hd, NC Co, notice given by Joseph G. STIDHAM and Penrose STIDHAM, adm'rs (DG 28 Feb 1834)

STIDHAM, Sarah,
see **STIDHAM**, Jonas Spencer

STIEN, John, at his res. in Wilm, 7 Mar 1853, in his 70th yr (DG 15 Mar 1853)

STILL, William, while loading wood on board steamboat *Wilmington*, fell overboard and drowned, 1 Dec 1829, no age or other identification (DG 4 Dec 1829)

STILLE, John, to **CARTMEL**, Susanna, Mrs., 3 Mar 1808, by Rev. William Pryce (MU 5 Mar 1808)

STILLEY, Elizabeth, see **STILLEY**, John

STILLEY, Hannah, 18 Aug 1844, aged 82 yrs (DG 27 Aug 1844)

STILLEY, John, dec'd, late of Christiana Hd, notice given by Elizabeth STILLEY and Robert ARMSTRONG, exec'rs (MU 21 Feb 1807)

STILLEY, Sarah, see **PINE**, George

STILLEY, Thomas, to **CAMPBELL**, Eleanor K., Miss, both of Christiana Hd, in Wilm, 17 Feb 1825, by the Rev. E. W. Gilbert (DG 18 Feb 1825)

STILLMAN, Mary Ann, see **URCH**, James

STIMSON, S. L., of Camden NJ, to McMARTIN, Flora, Miss, in Wilm, 20 Mar 1848, by Rev. S. R. Wynkoop (DG 24 Mar 1848)

STIMSON, Samuel, Esq., at his res. in Saratoga Co NY, 20 Apr 1852, aged 70 yrs (DG 23 Apr 1852)

STOCKLEY, Anne T. dau of Nehemiah STOCKLEY, Esq., at Smyrna, 3 Mar 1842, aged 21 yrs (DG 11 Mar 1842)

STOCKLEY, Charles T., of the firm of N. and C. T. Stockley of Phila, at Smyrna DE, 24 Jan 1849, aged 30 yrs (DG 9 Feb 1849)

STOCKLEY, John,
see **STOCKLEY**, Sarah A.

STOCKLEY, Marg. D., dau of Nehemiah STOCKLEY, Esq., at Smyrna, 17 Jan 1842, , aged 28 yrs (DG 11 Mar 1842)

STOCKLEY, Nehemiah,
see **STOCKLEY**, Marg. D.
see **STOCKLEY**, Anne T.

STOCKLEY, Sarah A., eldest dau of the late

DELAWARE MARRIAGES AND DEATHS FROM NEWSPAPERS, 1729-1853   239

John STOCKLEY, Esq., dec'd, in Georgetown, 8 Oct 1833, aged c 23 yrs (DG 15 Oct 1833)

STOCKLY, Nehemiah, to WILSON, Ann, Miss, 30 Apr 1835, by Rev. Daniel Higbee (DG 12 May 1835)

STOCKTON, John,
see STOCKTON, Thomas
see BEDFORD, God.
see PORTER, Jonas

STOCKTON, Thomas, Gov. of Delaware, son of John STOCKTON, 2 Mar 1846. Born about 1781, aged 65 yrs (DG 6 Mar 1846)

STODDART, A. Louisa,
see KENDRICK, William G. W.

STOKELY, Job, Capt., of Seaford, Sussex Co DE, in Balt, 14 Nov 1849, na (DG 4 Dec 1849)

STOKES, Abel, see SMITH, Gabriel

STOKES, Ann Elizabeth,
see FRAME, Samuel

STOKES, John B., to GRIMES, Elizabeth Ann, Miss, all of Wilm, 7 Jan 1847, by Rev. Dr. McCullough (DG 12 Jan 1847)

STOKES, Priestly, to PARADEE, Rachel, Miss, both of Kent Co, 20 Dec 1849, by Rev. S. C. Palmiter (DG 15 Jan 1850)

STONE, Amelia Terissa, see MORIS, Evan

STONE, Christiana, Mrs., relict of Mr. Lewis STONE, in Newport, 7 Feb 1824, na (DG 10 Feb 1824)

STONE, Lewis, see STONE, Christiana

STOOPS, Aaron, see STOOPS, Samuel

STOOPS, Caroline,
see TAYLOR, Thomas J.

STOOPS, Eleanor,
see STOOPS, William Henry

STOOPS, Mary A., see PAGE, Henry H.

STOOPS, Samuel, to McCURDY, Ann, both of Wilm, 3 Feb 1842, by Rev. S. R. Wynkoop (DG 11 Feb 1842)

STOOPS, Samuel, son of Aaron STOOPS of New Castle Hd, near Smyrna, ndd, aged 18 yrs (DG 29 Sep 1846)

STOOPS, William,
see STOOPS, William Henry

STOOPS, William Henry, eldest son of William and Eleanor STOOPS of St. Georges Hd, 4 Sep 1850, in N C Hd, aged 9 yrs (DG 10 Sep 1850)

STOREY, Elizabeth, see FOULK, John

STORKS, Levi, Rev., at his res. in North East MD, of bilious dysentery, 1 Oct 1853, in his 60th year (DG 7 Oct 1853)

STORY, Betty, dec'd, late of Wilm, notice given by Samuel S. GRUBB, Esq., Wilm and Samuel SPACKMAN, Phila (DG 6 Jan 1829)

STORY, James, dec'd, late of Wilm, notice given by William PRYCE and Thomas JONES, exec'rs (FA 14 Jan 1804)

STOTHART, Agnes, Mrs., a native of Scotland, but for many years a res't of Wilm, at the res. of her son-in-law, John H. PRICE, 5 Oct 1850, aged 75 yrs (DG 8 Oct 1850)

STOTSENBERG, John, to CASWELL, Mary, 22 Jul 1826, by Rev. R. Williston (DG 25 Jul 1826)

STOTSENBURG, Evan C., Jr., to PEEKEY, Anna Lareine, both of Wilm, at the Upper Presb Ch, 30 Apr 1849, by the Rev. Thomas Cole (DG 8 May 1849)

STOUT, Emeline D.,
see WHARTON, George

STOUT, J., Judge, see SIPPLE, Caleb H.

STOUT, Robert D., see WHARTON, George

STOUT, Sally Ann, see SIPPLE, Caleb H.

STRADLY, John, Esq., at his res. in Frederica, no date, aged 47 yrs (DG 29 Jul 1834)

STRAIN, Isaac, to CRUMP, Sarah F., Miss, all of Wilm, 9 Nov 1847, by Rev. Edward Kennard (DG 16 Nov 1847)

STRATTAN, William R., late of NJ, to DENNY, Evelina M., Miss, youngest dau of Collins DENNY, 5 Aug 1847, before Mayor Porter by Friends ceremony (DG 10 Aug 1847)

STRATTON, Isaac, to JONES, Sarah Jane, Miss, both of Wilm, 3 Sep 1850, at Chester PA, by Rev. Frederick Fairlamb (DG 10 Sep 1850)

STREET, Samuel B., to TALLEY, Margaret Jane, both of NC Co, in Wilm, 25 Mar 1851, by Rev. J. G. Collomi (DG 28 Mar 1851)

STRICKLAND, Louisa,

see **JOURDAN**, John H.

STRIMPLE, Joseph, to **CHRISTIE**, Mary, Miss, all of Wilm, 29 Sep 1846, by Rev. Mr. Rhees (DG 2 Oct 1846)

STROP, Lewis D., of Elkton MD, to **DIXON**, Mary, Miss, of Newark DE, 17 Nov 1853, by the Rev. B. Maddox (DG 22 Nov 1853)

STROUD, _____, Mrs., widow of Samuel STROUD, at the res. of her son-in law, Jesse MENDINHALL, Esq., in Wilm, 5 Nov 1847 (DG 25 Nov 1847)

STROUD, Caleb, see **STROUD**, Joshua

STROUD, Edward, son of Samuel STROUD of Wilm, at Havana, Cuba, 25 Oct 1821, in his 22nd yr (DG 20 Nov 1821)

STROUD, Elizabeth, see **STROUD**, Joshua

STROUD, Esther, in Wilm, 1 Apr 1843, , aged 15 yrs (DG 7 Apr 1843)

STROUD, Esther, in Wilm, 9 May 1845, aged 60 yrs, (DG 13 May 1845)

STROUD, James, to **HEDGES**, Hannah F., Miss, both of Wilm, in Phila, 26 Feb 1835, by John Swift, Mayor (DG 3 Mar 1835)

STROUD, James, see **ROTHERAM**, Joseph

STROUD, James B., late of Mill Creek Hd, John SMITH, adm'x (sic) (DG 16 Jul 1852)

STROUD, Joshua, in Wilm, 4 Apr 1834, "an old and esteemed citizen" (DG 8 Apr 1834) dec'd, late of Wilm, notice given by Caleb STROUD and Elizabeth STROUD, adm'x (DG 9 May 1834)

STROUD, Mary, see **SMITH**, John

STROUD, Rachel, see **WINDAL**, Martin

STROUD, Samuel, see **STROUD** _____, Mrs. see **STROUD**, Edward

STROUD, Samuel, Jr., to **JONES**, Mary E., Miss, of Wilm, 5 May 1829, by Rev. Joseph Walker (DG 5 May 1829)

STROUD, Thomas, see **WINDAL**, Martin

STROUP, Eliza, see **FOWLER**, William M.

STROUP, Sarah, see **MAHANY**, James L.

STROUP, Uriah, to **HUSTON**, Ellen, Miss, 25 Jun 1843, by Rev. S. M. Gayley (DG 30 Jun 1843)

STROUP, Uriah, Esq., Overseer of the Poor House of NC Co, in Wilm, 6 Dec 1847, aged 80 yrs (DG 14 Dec 1847)

STUARD, Ann E., see **LOFLAND**, Isaac

STUART, Caroline Bounds, only dau of James STUART, at the res. of her father, 8 Nov 1842, aged 1 yr 6 mos (DG 18 Nov 1842)

STUART, David, of Port Penn, to **JOHNS**, Susan, Miss, dau of the Hon. Kensey JOHNS, Chief Justice of the Supreme Court of DE, at New Castle, 2 Jan 1812, by Rev. Mr. Latte (DS 8 Jan 1812)

STUART, Edward, late of New Castle. Notice given by Redmond CONYNGHAN, adm'r (PG 11 Sep 1746)

STUART, James, of Middleford, to **GIBBONS**, Caroline, C., Miss, all of Sussex, at St. Luke's Church, Seaford, by Rev. John Long (DG 27 Aug 1844) see **STUART**, Caroline Bounds

STUART, Margaret. see **McCLELLAND**, William

STUART, Mary, see **MATHESON**, Gilbert

STUART, Michael, Esq., late of Middleford, Sussex Co DE, in Balt., 23 Jan 1849, aged 44 yrs (DG 6 Feb 1849)

STUBBS, Sarah, see **CAMBWELL**, John

STUCKERST. William M., to **CAZIER**, Olivia Ann, dau of John CAZIER, Esq., of NC Co, 24 Jan 1850, by Rev. W. H. Elliott (DG 29 Jan 1850)

STURGES, Rebecca, see **COLLINS**, Isaiah

SUDLER, _____, Dr., see **SUDLER**, Sarah B., Mrs.

SUDLER, Harriet, Miss, dau of Dr. Joseph SUDLER of Milford, 3 Oct 1821, aged 12 yrs and 6 mos (DG 23 Oct 1821)

SUDLER, John R., Dr., see **LAYTON**, William Joseph

SUDLER, John R., see **SUDLER**, Joseph

SUDLER, Joseph, Dr., see **SUDLER**, Harriet

SUDLER, Joseph, inf son of Dr. John R. SUDLER, in Bridgeville, Sussex Co, 4 Sep 1849 (DG 18 Sep 1849)

SUDLER, Sarah B., Mrs.,wife of Dr. SUDLER of Milford, at Milford, 7 Nov 1802, aged 23 yrs (FA 16 Nov 1802)

SUDLEY, John R., see SUDLEY, Lizzie

SUDLEY, Lizzie, dau of Dr. John R. and Sarah Ann SUDLEY, in Bridgeville, Sussex Co, 15 Jan 1852, aged 14 yrs 3 days (DG 3 Feb 1852)

SUDLEY, Sarah Ann, see SUDLEY, Lizzie

SULLIVAN, John, see SULLIVAN, Mary

SULLIVAN, John, to FOX, Sophia E., Miss, dau of Lewis FOX of Wilm, in Phila, 21 Oct 1847, by Rev. Henry C. Fries (DG 19 Nov 1847)

SULLIVAN, John W., see SULLIVAN, John Wesley

SULLIVAN, John Wesley, son of John W. SULLIVAN, 7 Jun 1848, in Wilm (DG 13 Jun 1848)

SULLIVAN, Mary, only dau of Sophia and John SULLIVAN, in Wilm, of scarlet fever, 19 "ult" 1851, aged 3 yrs 3 mos (DG 23 Dec 1851)

SULLIVAN, Sophia, see SULLIVAN, Mary

SUMERVILLE, Parnall Ann, see RICHARDSON, James H.

SUMMERS, Mary, Mrs., see PECKWORTH, J. P., Rev.

SUMPTION, Charles, son of the Rev. T. SUMPTION, at the res. of Joseph HOFFECKER, Jr., 17 Sep 1849, in his 20th yr (DG 25 Sep 1849)

SUMPTION, T., see SUMPTION, Charles

SUPPLEE, Andrew, to LOURY, Mary Jane, Miss, both of Wilm, 11 Jan 1848, by Rev. Dr. Kenneday (DG 3 Mar 1848)

SUPPLEE, Franklin, see SUPPLEE, Sarah Ann

SUPPLEE, Harriet, see SUPPLEE, Sarah Ann

SUPPLEE, Sarah Anna, dau of Franklin and Harriet SUPPLEE, in Wilm, suddenly, of asthma, 15 Oct 1849 (DG 19 Oct 1849)

SUTER, Henry, see KIRK, Samuel

SUTER, Sarah, see KIRK, Samuel

SUTHEL, William, to PARMER, Julia A.,

Miss, in Milford, 7 Mar 1852, by the Rev. Daniel Godwin (DG 16 Mar 1852)

SUTTON, A. B., Mrs., wife of Dr. James M. SUTTON at St. Georges, 20 Mar 1849, in her 35th yr, (DG 23 Mar 1849)

SUTTON, Dr., see GAW, Chambers

SUTTON, Eliza Jane, only child of Dr. James E. SUTTON and his late wife, Eliza Jane JANVIER, at the res. of her g'father, John JANVIER, 23 May 1834, aged 2 yrs 5 mos 15 days (DG 30 May 1834)

SUTTON, Isaac F., to HENDRICKSON, Sarah Ann, Miss, both of Kent Co, 24 Dec 1849, by Rev. J. A. Roche (DG 1 Jan 1850)

SUTTON, James E., Dr., see SUTTON, Eliza Jane

SUTTON, James M., Dr., see SUTTON, A. B.

SUTTON, James N., Dr., of St. Georges, to JANVIER, Eliza Jane, Miss, dau of John JANVIER of New Castle, 16 Jul 1829, by the Rev. James Latta (DG 21 Jul 1829)

SUTTON, James N. Dr., to BARBOUR, Abigail B., Miss, all of NC Co, 25 Sep 1834, by Elder John P. Peckworth (DG 30 Sep 1834)

SUTTON, James N., Dr., of St. Georges, to GOSSLER, Susan, Miss, of Columbia PA, at Columbia, 16 Dec 1851, by the Rev. Mr. Erskine (DG 19 Dec 1851)

SUTTON, John, see GEMMILL, Margaret Ann see BIDDLE, Augustine F. see JONES, E. I.

SUTTON, John E., son of John SUTTON, Jr., at St Georges, 19 Aug 1851, in his 18th yr (DG 23 Aug 1851)

SUTTON, John Jr, see SUTTON, John E.

SUTTON, John Jr., see GRIFFITH, David B.

SUTTON, Julia Ann, see GRIFFITH, David B.

SUTTON, Margaret Ann, see GEMMILL, Margaret Ann

SUTTON, Margaret J., see JONES, E. I.

SWAIN, Betsy, see SCOTT, Joseph

SWAIN, John W., to HUBBARD, Elizabeth A., both of Georgetown, 18 Oct 1853, by the Rev. John Hough (DG 28 Oct 1853)

SWARTZ, George C., of Phila, to O'BRIAN, Bridget, of Down, Ire, 22 Mar 1853, by the Rev. Mr. Cheyney (DG 25 Mar 1853)

SWARTZ, J. A., Dr, of Mifflin Co PA, to LEWIS, Tillie, Miss, of NC Co, at the Union Club, 20 Dec 1852, by Rev. G. T. Kattell (DG 7 Jan 1853)

SWAYNE, B. B., formerly of Wilm, to SEWELL, Mary Ida, second dau of the late John SEWALL of Balt., in Balt., 23 Dec 1850, by Rev. James J. Hammer (DG 7 Jan 1851)

SWAYNE, Caleb T., see SWAYNE, Sarah

SWAYNE, Henry, of DE, to PARRY, Ann, Miss, of Chester Co PA, 30 Sept 1841, by Rev. A. D. Giliette (DG 15 Oct 1841)

SWAYNE, Huson (sic), see SWAYNE, Susan, Mrs.

SWAYNE, Jacob, of Chester Co PA, to NOBLET, Sarah Jane B., dau of the late Hamilton NOBLIT, of Wilm, 23 Mar 1853, at the res. of George H. MOORE, Esq., in Phila, at Friends ceremony, in the presence of Alderman George Erety (DG 29 Mar 1853)

SWAYNE, Rebecca, wife of William SWAYNE, formerly of Chester Co PA, in Wilm, 21 Mar 1852, aged 46 yrs (DG 30 Mar 1852)

SWAYNE, Sarah, consort of Caleb T. SWAYNE, in Wilm, 8 Jul 1853, aged 61 yrs (DG 15 Jul 1853)

SWAYNE, Susan, d. 20 Aug 1751 (PG 24 Aug 1751)

SWAYNE, Susan, Mrs., wife of Mr. Huson (sic) SWAYNE of Wilm, 20 Aug 1826, na (DG 22 Aug 1826)

SWAYNE, William, see SWAYNE, Rebecca

SWAYNE, William A., Esq., late merchant of the city of New York, at his farm near Campbellville, Christiana Hd, 7 Mar 1847 (DG 16 Mar 1847)

SWEETLAND, Daniel, to BURNS, Mary, Miss, 18 Jul 1826, by the Rev. R. Williston (DG 25 Jul 1826)

SWETT, Benjamin, see LEWIS, Stephen

SWIFT, Jane Galloway, see SWIFT, John,

SWIFT, John, of Wilm, to SWIFT, Jane Galloway Miss, dau of Samuel SWIFT, Esq., of Phila Co, PA, in Phila, 6 May 1834, by Rev. George Sheets (DG 9 May 1834)

SWIFT, Samuel, see SWIFT, John,

SWIFT, Sarah M., see ARMSTRONG, John B.

SWIGGET, William, to HARRIS, Ella A., both of Georgetown DE, 25 May 1853, in Seaford, by the Rev. Dr. William Morgan (DG 24 Jun 1853)

SWIGGETTE, Sarah J., see MARTIN, O. B.

SWOPE, Jacob, 11 Jul 1852, in his 43rd yr (DG 16 Jul 1852)

SYKES, James, M. D., at his res. in Dover, 18 Nov 1822, in his 62nd yr (DG 19 Nov 1822)

SYNNIX, Jacob, to PRICE, Elizabeth, Miss, both of Newport, DE, 13 Dec 1821, by the Rev. L, Lawrenson (DG 18 Dec 1821)

SYTHENS, Mary Ann, see BAILEY, Perry

TAGGART, Joshua, to WILLIS, Mary Jane, both of Wilm, at Tustin's Black Bear Hotel, 30 Mar 1848, by Alderman J. Mitchell (DG 4 Apr 1848)

TAGGART, Morton, Capt., formerly of Wilm, for many years of Cincinnati, where he died, 17 Jan 1851, aged 65 yrs. Served as Capt. in the War of 1812 and participated in the Battle of North Point (DG 28 Jan 1851)

TALEY, Nelson, to WILSON, Rachel A., Miss, all of Brandywine Hd, in Phila, 3 Sep 1846, by Elder George W. Morgan (DG 25 Sep 1846)

TALLEY, _____, only dau of Eli B. TALLEY, Esq., March 1843, aged 8 yrs (DG 7 Apr 1843)

TALLEY, Agnes, dau of Thomas L. TALLEY, in Brandywine Hd, 31 Mar 1849, aged 11 yrs (DG 10 Apr 1849)

TALLEY, Amor, see PLANKINTON, Jesse

TALLEY, Anne H., Mrs, wife of Rev. John TALLEY, in NC Co, near Wilm, 1 Mar 1850 (DG 12 Mar 1850)

TALLEY, Baldson, see TALLEY, Curtis

TALLEY, Caleb, to BROWN, Sarah, Miss, 5 Dec 1816, by Rev. Pryce (AW 11 Dec 1816)

TALLEY, Charlotte, dau of the late Lewis S.

TALLEY, of Brandywine Hd, at the res. of her brother-in-law, Humphrey PYLE , of consumption, 14 Oct 1850 (DG 22 Oct 1850)

TALLEY, Curtis, son of Baldson TALLEY, in Brandywine Hd, 18 Sep 1851, aged 23 yrs (DG 23 Sep 1851)

TALLEY, Eli B., see TALLEY, _____

TALLEY, Elihu, to TWADDLE, Ann, Miss, 3 Mar 1808, by Rev. William Pryce (MU 5 Mar 1808)

TALLEY, Elizabeth, see CAMPBELL, David

TALLEY, Elizabeth, wife of Samuel TALLEY, in Brandywine Hd, 16 Jul 1847 (DG 27 Jul 1847)

TALLEY, Ellen M., dau of Louis S. TALLEY, at the res. of her father in Brandywine Hd, 10 Jun 1842, aged 24 yrs (DG 22 Jul 1842)

TALLEY, Harman, see SIMMONS, John

TALLEY, Hezekiah, see TALLEY, Julia Ann

TALLEY, John, Esq., in Brandywine Hd, 7 May 1848, aged 84 yrs (DG 16 May 1848)

TALLEY, John, Rev., see TALLEY, Anne H.

TALLEY, John, see CLARK, George

TALLEY, John Henderson, to FISHER, Elizabeth R., all of Brandywine Hd, 30 Dec 1846, by Rev. A. Atwood (DG 5 Jan 1847)

TALLEY, Julia Ann, wife of Hezekiah TALLEY, of B'wine Hd, 2 Oct 1849, aged 42 yrs (DG 12 Oct 1849)

TALLEY, Julia Ann, see JOHNSON, William

TALLEY, Levi, 16 Jul 1844, in Wilm, after 7 yrs illness, aged c 45 yrs (DG 19 Jul 1844)

TALLEY, Lewis S., see TALLEY, Charlotte

TALLEY, Louis S., see TALLEY, Ellen M.

TALLEY, Margaret Jane, see STREET, Samuel B.

TALLEY, Mary, Mrs., in Brandywine Hd, 14 Aug 1847, aged 75 yrs (DG 24 Aug 1847)

TALLEY, Mary, see MARTIN, Arthur

TALLEY, Samuel, see TALLEY, Elizabeth

TALLEY, Sidney, see BURNS, Alexander

TALLEY, Susan, see BROWN, Benjamin

TALLEY, Thomas L., see TALLEY, Agnes

TALLEY, William T., to ELLIOTT, Anna Mary, Miss, both of NC Co, in Phila, 23 Dec 1835, by Rev. Thomas G. Allen (DG 5 Jan 1836)

TANKARD, Georgiana, see FITZHUGH, Philip Aylett

TAPP, Emily, see RUSSOM, Benjamin D.

TATE, William, Dr., of Laurenceburg, IN, to LEWIS, Luranah M. dau of Kendall M. LEWIS, Esq., of Laurel DE, in Laurenceburg, 28 Jun 1853 (DG 22 Jul 1853)

TATEM, John R. to RICHARDSON, Lucy, dau of Ashton RICHARDSON, all of NC Co, at Friends Meeting on 9th St, 15 Apr 1852 (DG 20 Apr 1852)

TATEM, Joseph E., formerly of Wilm, in Phila, 3 Feb 1851, aged 72 yrs (DG 7 Feb 1851)

TATEM, Maria, in Wilm, 24 May 1853, na (DG 27 May 1853)

TATEM, Samuel, USN, to ROBINSON, Annie S., eldest dau of the late Jos. F. ROBINSON, all of Wilm, in Phila, 21 Aug 1851, by the Rev. Dr. Graham (DG 26 Aug 1851)

TATEM, Thomas, USN, in Wilm, 3 May 1853, na. Funeral from Mother's res., 117 E 4th St (DG 6 May 1853)

TATLOW, Joseph, Esq., see JANVIER, Francis

TATMAN, Collins, Esq., at the res. of Manlove HAYS, Cantwell's Bridge, 12 Jan 1825, aged 55 yrs (DG 18 Jan 1825)

TATMAN, Cyrus, to LOCKWOOD, Sarah Frances, dau of Richard LOCKWOOD, Esq., of Cecil Co, 18 Dec 1851, in Cecil Co MD, by Rev. H. H. Harrold, Rector of St Anne's Ch Middletown (DG 25 Dec 1851)

TATMAN, Purnell, see HAYES, Manlove

TATNALL, Edward, see SMITH, James
see GILLIS, John P.
see FEBIGER, Christian
see BETTS, Edward

TATNALL, Sarah, see FEBIGER, Christian

TATNALL, Elizabeth, see GILLIS, John P.

TATNALL, Joseph, Jr., see SIPPLE, Thomas, Esq.

TATNALL, Joseph, of Brandywine Mills, to RICHARDSON, Sarah, dau of Ashton RICHARDSON, 10 Jun 1841 by Friends ceremony (DG 18 Jun 1841)

TATNALL, Mary A. R., see BETTS, Edward

TATTNALL, Henry L., of Brandywine, to GIBBONS, Caroline, all of Wilm, at Vernon Place, 4 Dec 1851, by Friends ceremony in the presence of the Mayor (DG 9 Dec 1851)

TATUM, Hephzibah, 16 Dec 1840, aged 57 yrs. Funeral from house of Samuel BUZBY (DG 18 Dec 1840)

TATUN, David, one of the members of the Wilm borough Council, 27 Nov 1822 (DG 29 Nov 1822)

TAYLOR _____, Mrs., wife of James TAYLOR of Milford, 5 Sep 1851, na (DG 9 Sep 1851)

TAYLOR, Amy, see MENDINHALL, Philip

TAYLOR, Ann Eliza, dau of John and Martha TAYLOR, near Loveville DE, 15 Sep 1849, aged 8 mos (DG 25 Sep 1849)

TAYLOR, Ann Elizabeth, only dau of William H. and Emeline TAYLOR, at Vernon DE, 12 Nov 1851, aged 5 mos 13 days (DG 25 Nov 1851)

TAYLOR, Bankson, see HOLCOMB, Rebecca

TAYLOR, Bayard L., see TAYLOR, Mary S.

TAYLOR, Deborah, formerly of Wilm, in Phila, 28 Dec 1852, in her 80th yr (DG 31 Dec 1852)

TAYLOR, Edward, to BUSH, Martha T., dau of David BUSH, Esq., both of Wilm, 28 Oct 1847, by Rev. Wm. W. Taylor (DG 29 Oct 1847)

TAYLOR, Edward W., M. D., to GIBBONS, Mary T., both of Seaford, 23 Dec 1846, in St. Luke's Chapel, Seaford, by Rev. Jacob B. Smith (DG 15 Jan 1847)

TAYLOR, Eliza, Miss, see RODNEY, G. B.

TAYLOR, Elizabeth, see CURRY, Robert

TAYLOR, Emeline, see TAYLOR, Ann Elizabeth

TAYLOR, Ewemon, see HANBY, Susana

TAYLOR, Franklin, to HAYS, Martha J., Miss, both of NC Co, DE, in Wilm, 12 Apr 1849, by Rev. Marcellus E. Keene (DG 24 Apr 1849)

TAYLOR, George W., see RODNEY, G. B.

TAYLOR, Isaac, Dr., of Chester Co., PA, to BAILY, Sarah Ann P. Miss, of Wilm, 2 May 1826, by Robert Miller, Esq., Justice of the Peace (DG 5 May 1826)

TAYLOR, J. Bayard, of New York, to AGNEW, Mary, of Kennett Square, 31 Oct 1850, at Kennett Square (DG 1 Nov 1850)

TAYLOR, James, see TAYLOR, _____, Mrs.

TAYLOR, James, to MURPHEY, Ann, Miss, both of Brandywine Hd, 24 Jan 1810, by Rev. Dr. Pryce (DG 27 Jan 1810)

TAYLOR, James, to KERSHAW, Betty, Miss, both of Wilm, 17 Mar 1846, at Capt. Howe's Hotel in Marcus Hook PA (DG 7 Jul 1846)

TAYLOR, James T., to McCLENNAN, Eliza, in Wilm, 26 Aug 1848, by Bishop Lee (DG 1 Sep 1848)

TAYLOR, John, to LOWLER, Jane B, Miss, 23 Jun 1853, by the Rev. P. Meridith (DG 16 Aug 1853)

TAYLOR, John, of NC Co to MORRIS, Mary Jane, of Phila, in Phila, 20 Jan 1853, by the Rev. D. W. Bartine (DG 28 Jan 1853) see TAYLOR, Ann Eliza

TAYLOR, Joseph, to SINEX, Sarah Jane, Miss, both of NC Co, in Phila, 7 Jan 1849 (DG 12 Jan 1849)

TAYLOR, Major, 25 Oct 1798, on list of yellow fever victims (DG 27 Oct 1798)

TAYLOR, Margaret, see TRASK, William Henry

TAYLOR, Margaret, Mrs., 19 Oct 1820 (DG 24 Oct 1820)

TAYLOR, Martha, see TAYLOR, Ann Eliza

TAYLOR, Mary A., see GUTHRIE, William A.

TAYLOR, Mary Jane, see DENORMANDIE, A. E.

TAYLOR, Mary Rebecca, see BICKING, Richard

TAYLOR, Mary S., wife of Bayard L. TAYLOR, and dau of Lydia AGNEW. at the res. of her parents in Kennett Twnshp, 21 Dec 1850, aged 23 yrs (DG 3 Dec 1851)

TAYLOR, Rebecca,
see HOLCOMB, Rebecca

TAYLOR, Robert, to GIBSON, Ann Jane, Miss, both of Wilm DE, in Phila, 26 Sep 1849, by the Rev. J. L. Grant (DG 9 Oct 1849)

TAYLOR, Robert, of Wilm, to HASTINGS, Sarah, Miss, of Phila, 5 Sep 1852, by the Rev. Mr. Gallagher of St. Augustine's Ch (DG 10 Sep 1852)

TAYLOR, S. D. to THARP, Elmira, all of Kent Co, 18 Nov 1852, by the Rev. P. F. Cox (DG 30 Nov 1852) Elmira is only dau of Lewellen THARP (DG 3 Dec 1852)

TAYLOR, Samuel, of Delaware, to METZ, Harriet, Miss, of Southwark, in Phila, 8 Dec 1846, by Rev. Geo. Higgins (DG 22 Dec 1846)

TAYLOR, Sarah, Mrs., wife of William TAYLOR, 22 Mar 1848, in Thoroughfare Neck, Kent Co (DG 4 Apr 1848)

TAYLOR, Sarah B.,
see McKOWAN, William Alvord

TAYLOR, William, see TAYLOR, Sarah

TAYLOR, Susana, see HANBY, Susana

TAYLOR, Thomas J., of Phila, to STOOPS, Caroline, Miss, of NC Co, 8 Jul 1847, by Rev. Thomas Barton (DG 13 Jul 1847)

TAYLOR, Thomas, to HOSKINS, Harriet C., both of Wilm, at White Hall Hotel, Phila, 14 Dec 1848, by Alderman J. Mitchell (DG 26 Dec 1848)

TAYLOR, William, to BOOTHE, Eliza, Miss, both of Christiana, married there, 28 Jul 1825, by the Rev. Robert Murray (DG 5 Aug 1825)

TAYLOR, William H.,
see TAYLOR, Ann Elizabeth

TEMPLE, ____ Miss, of consumption, at Rockland, 15 Jul 1848, aged 21 yrs (DG 28 Jul 1848)

TEMPLE, Frances Ann, in the village of Camden of dropsy of the brain, 12 Jan 1846, aged 6 yrs 10 mos 12 days (DG 23 Jan 1846)

TEMPLE, Hannah Ann, see TEMPLE, Hiram

TEMPLE, Henry M., to JENKINS, Harriet, both of Camden, Kent Co DE, in Phila, 16 Jan, 1849, by Friends ceremony in the presence of Alderman J. Mitchell (DG 19 Jan 1849)

TEMPLE, Hiram, son of Thomas D. and Hannah Ann TEMPLE, at Smyrna, of croup, 14 Jan 1835, aged 5 mos 5 days (DG 3 Feb 1835)

TEMPLE, Mary, Mrs., wife of Thomas L. TEMPLE and dau of the late Henry MOLLESTON, Esq., at Camden, DE, 16 Oct 1826, aged 26 yrs (DG 24 Oct 1826)

TEMPLE, Sarah, see MURPHY, William Jr.

TEMPLE, Sarah Ann, Mrs., wife of Wm. TEMPLE, Esq., dau of Wm. RINGGOLD, Esq., in Smyrna, 26 Oct 1851, aged 34 yrs (DG 31 Oct 1851)

TEMPLE, Thomas, to COOMBE, Hannah Ann, Miss, both of Camden, in Camden, 28 Oct 1828, by the Rev. Mr. Lamden (DG 7 Nov 1828)

TEMPLE, Thomas D., see TEMPLE, Hiram

TEMPLE, Thomas L.,
see TEMPLE, Mary, Mrs.

TEMPLE, William, of Smyrna, ex-Gov of DE, to LOWBER, Kate, Miss, dau of John LOWBER, Esq., of Alexandria VA, at Alexandria VA, 4 Aug 1852, by the Rev. J. B. Hyland (DG 10 Aug 1852)

TEMPLE, Wm., see TEMPLE, Sarah Ann

TENNANT, Christopher, 16 Dec 1840, aged 66 yrs (DG 18 Dec 1840)

TENNEY, Otis S., of Kentucky, to WARNER, Junia M., in Wilm, 18 May 1848, by Rev. Mr. Rockwell (DG 23 May 1848)

TERHUEN, Albert H., of Phila, to TOWNSEND, Elizabeth J., dau of Joseph R. TOWNSEND of Wilm, 16 Feb 1852, by Rev. J. G. Collom (DG 20 Feb 1852)

TERRY, Benjamin F., to RUSSELL, Margaret A., Miss, all of NC Co, 17 Sep 1846, by Rev. A. Atwood (DG 18 Sep 1846)

TERRY, Howell J., Esq., to PIPPIN, Rebecca Jane, dau of William PIPPIN, both of New Castle, 2 Oct 1845, at New Castle (DG 10 Oct 1845)

TEST, Mary, see SHIPLEY, Joseph B.

TETLOW, Henry F., to VANDERGRIFT, Mary Ann, both of New Castle DE, 16 Mar 1853, by the Rev. Mr. Ruth (DG 25 Mar 1853)

THARP, Elmira, see TAYLOR, S. D.

THARP, Lewellen, see TAYLOR, S. D.

THARP, Reuben, to DEWDELE, Francis (sic) Ann, Miss, in Milford, 11 Dec 1834, by Rev. Mr. Allen - credibility in question, see paper (DG 23 Dec 1834)

THATCHER, Samuel R., to WEBSTER, Sally Ann, Miss, both of Wilm, 22 Apr 1847, by Rt. Rev. Bishop Lee (DG 23 Apr 1847)

THAWLEY, Samuel Jr, of Kent Co, to MASON, Mary E., Miss, of Queen Anne's Co MD, 10 Nov 1842, by Rev. Mr. Bain (DG 18 Nov 1842)

THISTLEWOOD, Ann, see VINYARD, Henry

THOMAS, _____, Mrs., 6 Aug 1801, wife of Edward THOMAS of Wilm (MN 8 Aug 1801)

THOMAS, Ann Jane, see PHISTER, Benjamin

THOMAS, Aquilla, to SEEDS, Phebe, Miss, all of Wilm, at New Castle, 17 May 1827, by the Rev. Solomon Higgins (DG 29 May 1827)

THOMAS, Catherine, see REYNOLDS, George

THOMAS, Charles, dec'd, late of Smyrna, notice given by D. W. THOMAS, adm'r near Cantwell's Bridge (DG 5 Feb 1836)

THOMAS, Clarissa J., see PERRY, Henry C.

THOMAS, D. W., see THOMAS, Charles

THOMAS, Daniel, in Milford, 28 Feb 1850 (DG 12 Mar 1850)

THOMAS, Edward, of NC Co, to GIRTLER, Lydia, Miss, of Chester Co PA, 20 Oct 1841 by Rev. Asher Moore (DG 29 Oct 1841) see THOMAS, _____, Mrs. see THOMAS, William

THOMAS, Elizabeth FITZRANDOLPH, see THOMAS, Randolph

THOMAS, Elizabeth R., wife of John B. THOMAS and dau of John WAY, Esq., in Wilm, 9 Oct 1823, na (DG 21 Oct 1823)

THOMAS, Elizabeth R., Mrs., relict of the late Evan H. THOMAS, Esq., 26 Dec 1846, in her 73rd yr (DG 5 Jan 1847)

THOMAS, Enoch, see THOMAS, James,

THOMAS, Evan, Esq., cashier of Bank of Wilmington and Brandywine, 25 Nov 1825, aged 23 yrs (DG 29 Nov 1825) see THOMAS, Randolph

THOMAS, Evan C., of Phila, to BUNTING, Hannah G., of NC Co, 24 Dec 1851, by the Rev. Mr. Love (DG 30 Dec 1851)

THOMAS, Evan H., see THOMAS, Phebe Ann see THOMAS, Elizabeth R.

THOMAS, Evan Henry, Esq., of New Castle, to HAZARD, Phebe, Miss, of Norwich, CT, 8 Aug 1826, by the Rev. Alfred Mitchell (DG 18 Aug 1826)

THOMAS, Hannah M., see CALVERT, Albert L.

THOMAS, Hester A., see JONES, Ebenezer

THOMAS, Ira, see THOMAS, William E.

THOMAS, James, see LOCKERT, Margaret

THOMAS, James, dec'd, late of St. Georges Hd, notice given by Nathan THOMAS and Enoch THOMAS, adm'rs (DG 24 Mar 1798)

THOMAS, James, to WEBSTER, Jane, Mrs., all of Wilm, 14 Apr 1829, by Rev. Solomon Higgins (DG 21 Apr 1829)

THOMAS, James, to LEGG, Emeline, Miss, both of NC Co, in Wilm, 10 Feb 1834, by the Rev. E. W. Gilbert (DG 11 Feb 1834)

THOMAS, John B., see PHISTER, Benjamin see THOMAS, Elizabeth R.

THOMAS, John H., of Cecil Co, MD, to LINDSEY, Susan, Miss, of NC Co, DE, near Newark, DE, 31 Mar 1829, by the Rev. A. K. Russel (DG 3 Apr 1829)

THOMAS, Joseph, M. D., to LOCKERMAN, Sarah C, Miss, all of Wilm, 19 May 1829, by Rev. E. W. Gilbert (DG 22 May 1829)

THOMAS, Joseph, Dr., in Wilm, 27 Nov 1835, aged c 33 yrs (DG 1 Dec 1835) dec'd, notice given by Joseph SCOTT, adm'r (DG 15 Jan 1836)

THOMAS, Margaret Ann, see OSBORNE, John W.

THOMAS, Margaret H., see VEAZEY, Lambert, Dr.

THOMAS, Mary A., in Wilm, 5 May 1851. Leaves a husband and children (DG 13 May 1851)

THOMAS, Nathan, see THOMAS, James,

THOMAS, Phebe Ann, consort of Evan H. THOMAS, Esq., 22 Apr 1843, na

(DG 28 Apr 1843)

THOMAS, Priscilla, see **WELSH**, Thomas

THOMAS, Randolph, 3rd son of Evan THOMAS, Esq., and Elizabeth FITZ-RANDOLPH, his wife, 29 Nov 1827, at Puerto Cabello, South America, na. He was born in New Castle, 15 Mar 1802. (DG 12 Feb 1828)

THOMAS, Samuel, at his late res. in Cantwell's Bridge, 20 Apr 1829, aged 62 yrs; member of the Society of Friends (DG 1 May 1829) notice given by Daniel CORBIT, Cantwell's Bridge, and James BOOTH, New Castle,. exec'rs (DG 5 May 1829) notice given by Samuel THOMAS, surviving partner of Samuel Thomas and Son, for debts owed to the firm to be paid to him (DG 8 May 1829)

THOMAS, Samuel of Wilm, to **STEVENSON**, Ann, Miss, of Del Co PA, by the Rev. J. Kennedy (DF 30 Oct 1830)

THOMAS, Sarah J., see **HARRINGTON**, Jonathan

THOMAS, Sarah, see **NEWKIRK**, James

THOMAS, Sarah, see **KEE**, Joseph

THOMAS, Sena, Miss, 25 Mar 1850, in Milford (DG 2 Apr 1850)

THOMAS, Tristram, of Easton, MD, to **GEDDES**, Susan, Miss, dau of William GEDDES of Wilm, 30 Dec 1792, by the Rev. Mr. Clarkson (DG 12 Jan 1793)

THOMAS, William, to **DAVID**, Mary, Miss, both of Rich Neck, NC Co, 8 Jan 1824, by the Rev. D. Cronch (DG 20 Jan 1824)

THOMAS, William, son of Edward THOMAS, dec'd, of Wilm, 10 May 1831 (DF 14 May 1831)

THOMAS, William C., of Cantwell's Bridge, to **DAVIS**, Sarah Ann, Miss, dau of Mr. Outen DAVIS near Middletown, DE, 25 Oct 1825, by the Rev. Mr. Wellar (DG 4 Nov 1825)

THOMAS, William E., son of Ira THOMAS, in Wilm, 4 Jun 1848, aged 18 mos (DG 13 Jun 1848)

THOMPSON, Amelia Freeman, see **BAILEY**, Leonard F.

THOMPSON, Andrew, to **SILVER**, Sarah, Miss, dau of the Rev. William SILVER, all of Christiana, 22 Jan 1822, by the Rev. L. Lawrenson (DG 29 Jan 1822)

THOMPSON, Andrew, in Mill Creek Hd, 22 Apr 1849, aged 80 yrs (DG 8 May 1849)

THOMPSON, Ann M., see **HARRIS**, George S

THOMPSON, Anne Maria, see **CHRISTY**, John V.

THOMPSON, Cordelia, dau of Mary THOMPSON, of inflammation of the bowels, 14 Jul 1848, aged 11 mos (DG 28 Jul 1848)

THOMPSON, Elizabeth, see **MUSGROVES**, James see **DAVIS**, Samuel

THOMPSON, Emilie D., see **CARPENTER**, Samuel T.

THOMPSON, Helen D., Miss, see **JOHNSON**, T. Sheward

THOMPSON, James, Esq., of Pittsburg, to **GIBBONS**, Sarah Ellan, Miss, dau of the late William GIBBONS, MD, at Vernon Place, 15 Jul 1851, by Rev. S. R. Wynkoop (DG 22 Jul 1851)

THOMPSON, Jane, see **TYSON**, Levi L.

THOMPSON, John P., at his res. in Phila, 20 Jul 1851, formerly res'd near St Georges, sent as a missionary to the State of DE by the Baptist Soc. (DG 1 Aug 1851)

THOMPSON, John, Rev., of the Phila Conf, to **SEAL**, Elizabeth, Miss, of New London, PA, at New London, 7 Dec 1852, by the Rev. Anthony Attwood (DG 31 Dec 1852)

THOMPSON, John, see **LULL**, Nathaniel

THOMPSON, Joseph J., to **CALHOUN**, Eliza, Miss, both of NC Co, 6 Jan 1846, at Christiana Bridge, by Rev. William Ryder (DG 16 Jan 1846)

THOMPSON, Martha A., see **RUDOLPH**, William

THOMPSON, Mary, see **THOMPSON**, Cordelia,

THOMPSON, Mary Ann, see **GRAY**, George W.

THOMPSON, Mary E., see **LULL**, Nathaniel

THOMPSON, Robert, to **McCOY**, Catharine, Miss, of Wilm, 22 May 1828, by Elder John P. Peckworth (DG 27 May 1828)

THOMPSON, Sarah, see **JOHNSON**, William

THOMPSON, Stewart, dec'd, notice given by John COLHOUN, adm'r (DE 31 Aug 1797)

THOMPSON, Thomas, late of New Castle. Sale of house, smithy, and stable house on Market St. opposite Court House in New Castle by Francis JANVIER and John McGRA (sic), exec'rs. (PG 15 Oct 1741)

THOMPSON, William, see **ANDERSON**, John T.

THOMPSON, Wm, at Wilm, 16 Aug 1851, aged 44 yrs (DG 19 Aug 1851)

THOMPSON, Wm, Hon, of Kent Co, to **MILES**, Jane W., Mrs. of Wilm, 8 Mar 1853 by Rev. Wm. E. Moore (DG 11 Mar 1853)

THOMSON, Allan, of Wilm, to **McCALLMONT**, Anna, Miss, dau of the late Dr. James McCALLMONT of New Castle DE, 8 May 1827, at Crescentville, by the Rev. John H. Kennedy (DG 11 May 1827)

THOMSON, Allen, see **THOMSON**, Jane see **FLEMING**, John

THOMSON, Anna, late wife of Allan THOMSON, in Wilm, 13 Feb 1844 (DG 16 Feb 1844)

THOMSON, Barton Haxall, inf son of Dr. J. W. and S. P. THOMSON, 17 Aug 1845, aged 8 mos and 3 days (DG 19 Aug 1845)

THOMSON, Henry, inf. son of Dr. J. W. and Sarah P. THOMSON, in Wilm, 7 Sep 1843, aged 6 mos (DG 15 Sep 1843)

THOMSON, J. W., see **THOMSON**, Barton Haxall

THOMSON, J. W., Dr., see **THOMSON**, Henry

THOMSON, James W., see **HIGGINBOTHAM**, Edward G.

THOMSON, Jane, Mrs., wife of Allen THOMSON, Esq., in Wilm, 6 Feb 1824, aged 39 yrs (DG 10 Feb 1824)

THOMSON, John, see **RUSSEL**, Washington, Dr.

THOMSON, John, the Hon., Esq., Judge of the Court of Common Pleas for many years, at his res. near St. Georges, 31 Oct 1790, aged 61 yrs (DG 13 Nov 1790)

THOMSON, Julia A., see **HIGGINBOTHAM**, Edward G.

THOMSON, Margaret, see **JONES**, Israel D.

THOMSON, Mary, see **RUSSEL**, Washington, Dr.

THOMSON, S. P. [fem.], see **THOMSON**, Barton Haxall

THOMSON, Sarah P., see **THOMSON**, Henry

THOMSON, William, to **PICKEN**, Ann, Miss, both of Wilm, 3 Feb 1847, by Rev. S. R. Wynkoop (DG 9 Feb 1847)

THORNTON, Thos, of Phila, to **HILLMAN**, Mary Ellen, Miss, dau of Mr. Thomas HILLMAN of Milford, 8 Mar 1853, by the Rev. J. Humphries (DG 15 Mar 1853) Thomas, of Southwark, to **HILLMAN**, Mary Ellen, of Milford, 9 Mar 1853 (DG 29 Mar 1853)

THORP, Henry, of Phila, to **HERRING**, Elizabeth J., dau of Abner HERRING of DE, 28 Jan 1851, by he Rev. Mr. Humphreys (DG 31 Jan 1851)

THURLOW, J(ohn). J., see **WILSON**, Eli see **JONES**, Israel D.

THURSTON, Edward, to **WARD**, Emeline, Miss, both of Southwark, Phila, 11 Oct 1852, by the Rev. Dr. Greenbank (DG 19 Oct 1852)

TIBBITT, Sarah Ann, see **CALLOWAY**, George H.

TILGHMAN, William, Hon., Chief Justice of the Supreme Court of PA, in Phila, 29 Apr 1827, in his 71st yr (DG 1 May 1827)

TILL, Catharine, Miss, see **GARRETSON**, Jacob M.

TILL, Gertrude, see **TILL**, Thomas

TILL, Thomas, of Sussex Co., property to be sold by William TILL and Gertrude TILL, adm'rs... Negroes...etc, of Prime Hook Neck, Sussex Co. (PG 20 Nov 1760)

TILL, William, see **TILL**, Thomas

TILTON, James, Jr., Dr., see **TILTON**, Mary Elizabeth, Mrs.

TILTON, Mary Elizabeth, Mrs., consort of Dr. James TILTON, Jr., at Peach Blossom, Talbot Co, MD, 20 Oct 1817 (AW 1 Nov 1817)

TINDAL, John, to **REED**, Margaret, both of Sussex Co, in Georgetown, 14 Apr 1853, by Rev. J.R. Torbert (DG 26 Apr 1853)

TINDALL, Eleanor R., wife of Gideon F. TINDALL, from consumption, in Wilm,

DELAWARE MARRIAGES AND DEATHS FROM NEWSPAPERS, 1729-1853

28 Jul 1849, aged c 34 yrs (DG 31 Jul 1849)

TINDALL, Gideon, of Wilm, to TURNER, Elenor R., Miss, of Phila, in Phila, 3 Nov 1834, by Elder John P. Peckworth (DG 7 Nov 1834)

TINDALL, Gideon F., see TINDALL, Eleanor R.

TINDLE, Elizabeth, see AULD, Mary E.

TINDLE, Mary E., see AULD, Mary E.

TINDLE, Robert, see AULD, Mary E.

TINDLE, Sally Ann, see TODD, Eli

TINGLE, Janett, see REEVE, Samuel

TITUS, Reuben, RR fireman, unmarried, not more than 22 yrs old, engine derailed, ran into the Brandywine, 8 Jul 1853 (DG 12 Jul 1853)

TITUS, Thomas, to HIGGINS, Sarah, Miss, both of NC Co, 16 May 1828, by Elder John P. Peckworth (DG 20 May 1828)

TODD, Alfred, to SIMMONS, Hannah, Miss, both of Wilm, 19 Nov 1850, by Rev. S. R. Wynkoop (DG 22 Nov 1850)

TODD, Eli, to TINDLE, Sally Ann, Miss, 4 Apr 1833, by Elder John P. Peckworth, all of Wilm (DG 5 Apr 1833)

TODD, Eliza Jane, see PRICE, Hyland

TODD, James H., to VANDEVER, Ellen, Miss, dau of Peter VANDEVER, 9 Apr 1829, by the Rev. Isaac Pardee (DG 14 Apr 1829)

TODD, Levin, see TODD, Sarah

TODD, Martha, see MILLER, James

TODD, Sarah, Mrs., wife of Levin TODD, in Sussex Co, 22 Apr 1849 (DG 1 May 1849)

TODD, William, see WELDIN, George

TOLAND, Joshua, late of St. Georges Hd, John RICE, adm'r (DG 30 Mar 1827)

TOMLINSON, Elizabeth, Mrs., 1 Nov 1789, aged 25 yrs (DG 7 Nov 1789)

TOMPKINS, A. W., see RYDER, Emeline

TOPHAM, Harriet, see BELL, Hugh

TOPHAM, Ina, dau of Richard and Sarah J. TOPHAM, in Wilm, 21 Apr 1851, na (DG 13 May 1851)

TOPHAM, Jane, see ROBERTSON, George B.

TOPHAM, Richard, near Newark, 18 Oct 1853, in his 46th yr (DG 21 Oct 1853) late of White Clay Creek Hd, Sarah Jane TOPHAM, exec'x (DG 8 Nov 1853) see TOPHAM, Ina

TOPHAM, Sarah C., see McMULLEN, Robert

TOPHAM, Sarah J., see TOPHAM, Ina

TOPHAM, Sarah Jane, see TOPHAM, Richard

TORBERT, Catharine, see JEFFERIS, John C.

TORBERT, Hugh, to RITCHIE, Anna, 29 Apr 1845, by Rev. M. J. Rhees (DG 13 May 1845)

TORBERT, John, see TORBERT, Mary Jane see NAUDAIN, Matthew M.

TORBERT, John, Esq., for many years cashier of the Farmer's Bank of Wilm, suddenly, 2 Jun 1842 (DG 10 Jun 1842)

TORBERT, Mary, wife of Rev. Wm. TORBERT, 4 Apr 1820 (DG 8 Apr 1820) see BURTON, Benjamin

TORBERT, Mary Jane, dau of the late John TORBERT, Esq., in Wilm, 19 Sep 1846 (DG 29 Sep 1846)

TORBERT, Rachel, see RASH, Daniel

TORBERT, Stephen, to WHITEHEAD, Sarah, both of Kent Co, 30 Dec 1852 (DG 14 Jan 1853)

TORBERT, Susan, see NAUDAIN, Matthew M.

TORBERT, William, Rev., at his res. in Greensborough, Caroline Co MD, 3 Jun 1841, aged 63 yrs, in the 31st year of his ministry (DG 11 Jun 1841)

TORBERT, William, Rev., see BURTON, Benjamin

TORBERT, Wm., see TORBERT, Mary

TORBETT, Peter, to HAMBY, Ann R., of Newport, 22 Nov 1842, by Rev. R. Garey (DG 2 Dac 1842)

TOUCHTINE, James, to OWENS, Virginia A., all of NC Co, 25 May 1844, by Rev. M. J. Rhees (DG 28 May 1844)

TOWNSEND, Isaac,
see **TOWNSEND**, Samuel Sr.

TOWNSEND, Ann, Mrs., see **CLARK**, John

TOWNSEND, Catharine,
see **TOWNSEND**, Zadoc, Esq.

TOWNSEND, Edward, to **CLAYTON**,
Maianna, (sic) Miss, all of NC Co, at Port
Penn, 24 Jan 1850, by Rev. Isaac W. K.
Handy (DG 29 Jan 1850)

TOWNSEND, Elizabeth, see **CLARK**, John

TOWNSEND, Elizabeth Ann,
see **WHITELY**, Albert

TOWNSEND, Elizabeth J.,
see **TERHUEN**, Albert H.

TOWNSEND, Esther, see **SMITH**, David P.

TOWNSEND, James, at Cantwell's Bridge,
after an illness of 7 mos, 11 Nov 1842,
aged 63 yrs (DG 2 Dec 1842)

TOWNSEND, Job, see **WHITELY**, Albert

TOWNSEND, John,
see **TOWNSEND**, Rachel

TOWNSEND, John T., to **ANDERSON**,
Martha K., Miss, 28 Mar 1843, at Cantwell's
Bridge, by Rev. George Poor , all of NC Co
(DG 14 Apr 1843)

TOWNSEND, Joseph R.,
see **TERHUEN**, Albert H.

TOWNSEND, Joseph R., to **MATTHEWS**,
Artemissia, Miss, both of Wilm, 8 Dec 1824,
by the Rev. Daniel D. Lewis
(DG 14 Dec 1824)

TOWNSEND, Mary Ann,
see **DALZELL**, Mary Ann

TOWNSEND, Mary Maria, wife of Robert
TOWNSEND, and 2nd dau of Thomas
and Rebecca WOODS, 22 Apr 1847, na
(DG 30 Apr 1847)

TOWNSEND, Rachel, wife of John
TOWNSEND, in Appoq Hd, 28 Jan 1853,
aged c 43 yrs (DG 8 Feb 1853)

TOWNSEND, Robert,
see **TOWNSEND**, Mary Maria

TOWNSEND, Samuel, of NC Co, to **HART**,
Anna Maria, Miss, of Kent Co, MD, in Phila,
14 Jul 1835, by Evangelist Abel C. Thomas
(DG 24 Jul 1835)

TOWNSEND, Samuel, at his res. in
Cantwell's Bridge, 5 Feb 1852, in his 69th yr
(South Bend IN papers please copy)
(DG 13 Feb 1852)
see **SMITH**, David P.

TOWNSEND, Samuel, Sr., late of St
Georges Hd, Isaac TOWNSEND, exec'r
(DG 17 Feb 1852)

TOWNSEND, Stephen F.,
see **DALZELL**, Mary Ann

TOWNSEND, Susan,
see **LISTER**, James S., Dr.

TOWNSEND, Sylvester D., of New Castle
Hd, to **ROBINSON**, Mary E., dau of John T,
ROBINSON, Esq., of Wilm, in Wilm,
10 Mar 1853, by the Rev. Dr. Hodgson
(DG 15 Mar 1853)

TOWNSEND, Washington, of West Chester
PA, to **GIBBINS**, Elizabeth, dau of the late
William GIBBINS, M. D., at Vernon Place in
Wilm, 11 Dec 1850, by Friends ceremony
(DG 13 Dec 1850)

TOWNSEND, William,
see **HEDGES**, Hannah

TOWNSEND, William, Esq., member of the
city and borough councils, and chairman of
the Watering Committee, in Wilm,
15 Mar 1847, at an advanced age
(DG 19 Mar 1847)

TOWNSEND, Zadoc, Esq.,dec'd, late of NC
Co, notice given by Catharine TOWNSEND,
adm'x (DG 13 Jan 1826)

TOWNSEND, Zadoc, to **REYNOLDS**,
Rebecca, Miss, both of NC Co,
28 Feb 1828, by the Rev. Solomon Sharp
(DG 4 Mar 1828)

TOY, Mary, see **McKENNA**, James

TOY, Thomas, formerly of Phila,
17 Dec 1847, in Wilm (DG 21 Dec 1847)

TRAINOR, Joseph W., of Wilm, to **DAVIS**,
Sarah K., Miss, of Port Kennedy,
Montgomery Co PA, 5 Apr 1848, by
Rev. Isaac Price (DG 18 Apr 1848)

TRANBERG, Andrew, late of Wilm. Notice
given by Adolph BENZEL and wife,adm'rs.
Pay to George READ of New Castle
(PG 8 Mar 1759)

TRANOR, Mary, notice given by HINKSON,
Washington, exec'r.(DG 10 Aug 1847)

TRASK, William Henry, to **TAYLOR**,
Margaret, Miss, both of NC Co, 17 Mar 1847,
by Rev. S. R. Wynkoop (DG 26 Mar 1847)

TRAUX, Sarah, see KNIGHT, Diel

TRAYNOR, Thomas, to KENT, Margaret Louisa, both of Wilm, 5 Dec 1853, by the Rev. S. R. Wynkoop (DG 9 Dec 1853)

TRIMBLE, Harriett B., see CORBIT, John C., Esq.

TRIMBLE, I. R., see HAYWARD, James F.

TRIMBLE, Joseph, Esq., see CORBIT, John C., Esq. see CORBIT, Mary, Jr.

TRUEFIT, Emily V., na, wife of Lewis A. TRUEFIT, and dau of the late George VAUX, Esq., in Phila, 1 Jan 1851 (DG 7 Jan 1851)

TRUEFIT, Lewis A., to VAUX, Emily, dau of the late George VAUX, Esq., at St Philips Ch, Phila, by Rev. E. Neville, DD, 4 Oct 1849 (DG 5 Oct 1849) see TRUEFIT, Emily V.

TRUITT, Eliza, see HATFIELD, Joseph

TRUITT, Esther F., see ANDERSON, James R.

TRUITT, George, Esq., formerly Governor of DE, at his res. in Camden, DE, 8 Oct 1818, aged 62 yrs (DG 31 Oct 1818)

TRUITT, George, Esq., at the res. of William K. LOCKWOOD, near Dover, 25 Nov 1842, aged 80 yrs (DG 16 Dec 1842)

TRUITT, Lavinia C., youngest dau of William TRUITT, near Laurel, 26 Feb 1853, in her 13th yr (DG 8 Mar 1853)

TRUITT, Margaret E., see MULLEN, William

TRUITT, William, see TRUITT, Lavinia C.

TRUITT, William G., of Smyrna, to RINE, Rebecca, Miss, 17 Dec 1846, by Rev. S. R. Wynkoop (DG 22 Dec 1846)

TRUITT, Zadoc, of Campden, merchant, to PENNELL, Rebecca, of the same place, (nmd) (DG 27 Mar 1790)

TRULENDER, Norris K., of Salem NJ, to ROBERTS, Margaret A., of Delaware City, 15 Aug 1850, by Rev. R. F. Young (DG 27 Aug 1850)

TRUMAN, Thomas, to GARLAND, Rebecca, Miss, both of Wilm, at Marcus Hook, 17 May 1829, by Benj. F. Johnson, Esq. (DG 9 Jun 1829)

TRUMP, Jesse, at his farm in Mill Creek Hd, NC Co, 15 Aug 1822, aged 32 yrs (DG 27 Sep 1822)

TRUTE, Charles, dec'd, late of Brandywine Hd, 16 Nov 1807 (MU 21 Nov 1807)

TSCHUDY, Sarah, Miss, at her res. in Millington, 18 Dec 1834, aged 25 yrs (DG 26 Dec 1834)

TUCKER, Elizabeth Ann, see HUDSON, Asay

TUCKER, Nathaniel, to ALFORD, Sarah Ann, Miss, both of Camden DE, 5 Jan 1847, by Rev. John Bell (DG 2 Feb 1847)

TULL, Mary, relict of Whittington TULL, after a lingering illness, 29 Mar 1850, in her 76th yr (DG 5 Apr 1850)

TULL, Whittington, see TULL, Mary

TUMLIN, James, formerly of NC Co, 21 Oct 1852, in his 55th yr (DG 26 Oct 1852)

TUNNELL, ____, Mr, see DULANEY, William W.

TUNNELL, Ann, see DULANEY, William W.

TUNNELL, Edward S., of DE, to POWELL, Sarah C., Miss, of Phila, 11 Mar 1852, by the Rev. Jos. F. Berg DD (DG 16 Mar 1852)

TURNBULL, Adam, of DE, to SHOCK, Lydia, Miss, formerly of Baltimore Co, in Phila, 22 Jan 1852, by Rev. Okans (DG 27 Jan 1852)

TURNER, Elenor R., see TINDALL, Gideon

TURNER, Elijah, to SHAD, Amelia, Miss, both of Wilm, 6 May 1824, by the Rev. William Williston (DG 11 May 1824)

TURNER, Eliz., see COLESBERRY, John

TURNER, Eliza, see HANSON, Levi,

TURNER, Elizabeth E., see WHITELOCK, James

TURNER, Elizabeth G., see DAVIDS, James J.

TURNER, Elizabeth, Mrs, consort of Thomas TURNER, 11 Jul 1844, aged 64 yrs (DG 19 Jul 1844)

TURNER, George W., to CAULK, Marriet, (sic), Miss, dau of Jacob CAULK, Esq., at New Castle, 3 May 1842 by Rev. William Hogarth (DG 6 May 1842)

TURNER, J. M., see DAVIDS, James J.

TURNER, John N., to GARLAND, Mary,

Miss, all of Wilm, 24 May 1827, by Rev. Solomon Higgins (DG 29 May 1827)

TURNER, Joseph, to DELAPLAINE, Sarah, Miss, both of Brandywine Hd, 8 Apr 1846, by Rev. Mr. Mansfield (DG 10 Apr 1846)

TURNER, Mary, see ALEXANDER, Charles

TURNER, Mary A., see NORWOOD, William

TURNER, Solomon, to DOWNING, Elizabeth, Miss, both of NC Co, 9 Nov 1851, by the Rev. Andrew Manship (DG 18 Nov 1851)

TURNER, Thomas, in New Castle, 26 May 1846, aged 72 yrs (DG 29 May 1846)

TURNER, Thomas, see TURNER, Elizabeth see MILLER, William

TUSSEY, Hannah, see WELDON, Isaac

TWADDELL, James, see TWADELL, William

TWADDELL, William, of Birmingham Twp, Del Co PA, James TWADDELL and William TWADDELL, exec'rs (DG 3 Apr 1827)

TWADDLE, Ann, see TALLEY, Elihu

TWADDLE, Mary, Mrs., wife of Wm. TWADDLE, near Christiana Hd, 13 Sep 1853, aged 65 yrs (DG 20 Sep 1853)

TWADDLE, Wm., see TWADDLE, Mary

TWAX, Benjamin, to BROWN, Melvina, both of Kent Co, 2 Dec 1852 (DG 1 Feb 1853)

TWEED, Curtis, conductor of a freight train on the Phila, Wilm, and Balt RR, accidental RR death, ndd, aged 51 yrs. Leaves several children (DG 29 Jun 1852)

TWEED, Curtis, late of Wilm City, Philip JONES, adm'r (DG 21 Sep 1852)

TWEED, James, of the firm of Tweed and Scott, at his res. near Elk Iron Works, 4 Mar 1851 (DG 18 Mar 1851)

TWEEDY, George Washington, son of Washington TWEEDY, 30 Mar 1849, in his 4th yr (DG 24 Apr 1849)

TWEEDY, Jacob, of Wilm, to PERRIGO, Caroline, Miss, of Baltimore, 17 Jan 1850, by Rev. Joseph Shane (DG 22 Jan 1850)

TWEEDY, Samuel, of DE and late of Baltimore, at New Orleans "of the prevailing fever," 19 Sep 1824, na. Left a wife and child. (DG 29 Oct 1824)

TWEEDY, Washington, see TWEEDY, George Washington

TWEELY, Sabilda, see BABB, Thomas S.

TWIGG, Catharine, see SHOCKLEY, Wm. H.

TWINING, Isaac, to MEGATTAGAN, Phebe, Miss, all of NC Co, 7 May 1846, by Rev. M. J. Rhees (DG 12 May 1846)

TYLER, Robert, see COOPER, Thomas

TYNER, Louisiana, see HAZZARD, John F.

TYRREL, Olivia Ann, see McCAULEY, Absalom

TYSON, Elijah A., see TYSON, Mary Emma

TYSON, Isaac, dec'd, notice given by Abraham EGBERT, exec'r (DG 19 Oct 1824)

TYSON, Jacob, dec'd, late of Pencader Hd, notice given by Abraham EGBERT, adm'r (AD 18 Oct 1822)

TYSON, Jesse, dec'd, late of Mill Creek Hd, notice given by Samuel TYSON, adm'r (DG 4 Oct 1822)

TYSON, Levi L. to THOMPSON, Jane, all of Cecil Co, MD, at Lord's Factory MD, 6 Apr 1852, by the Rev. Jos. Barr (DG 20 Apr 1852)

TYSON, Mary, see TYSON, Mary Emma

TYSON, Mary Emma, dau of Elijah A. and Martha TYSON, in Wilm, 25 Nov 1851, aged c 4 yrs (DG 2 Dec 1851)

TYSON, Samuel, see TYSON, Jesse

TYSON, Thomas, dec'd, late of Christiana Hd, notice given by Ashton RICHARDSON, exec'r (DG 23 Dec 1823)

UNDERWOOD, Annabella, late of Pencader Hd, John W. EVANS, exec'r (DG 29 May 1849)

UNDERWOOD, Elizabeth, at the res. of Jesse GREGG, in Christiana Hd, 26 Jan 1851, aged between 80 and 90 yrs (DG 31 Jan 1851)

UNDERWOOD, George W., of Chester Co PA, to BAYARD, Susannah, Miss, of Cecil Co MD, 13 Apr 1841, in Wilm by Rev. J. W. McCullough (DG 16 Apr 1841)

UNDERWOOD, Levi, to STAUNTON,

DELAWARE MARRIAGES AND DEATHS FROM NEWSPAPERS, 1729-1853

Susanna, Miss, 19 Dec 1820 (DG 22 Dec 1820)

UNDERWOOD, Solomon, see HYATT, John

UNDERWOOD, William, dec'd, late of Christiana Hd, notice by Caleb KIRK and William DIXSON, adm'rs (FA 21 Oct 1803)

UNRUH, Abraham, of Wilm, to DEDIER, Elizabeth, Miss, of Bristol Township, 29 Aug 1841 at Germantown PA (DG 17 Sep 1841)

URCH, James, to STILLMAN, Mary Ann, Miss, all of NC Co, 17 Sep 1846, by Rev. A. Atwood (DG 18 Sep 1846)

URMY, Daniel, see URMY, Marietta

URMY, Marietta, inf dau of Daniel and Rebecca URMY, 1 Jul 1843, aged 4 mos. (DG 7 Jul 1843)

URMY, Rebecca, see URMY, Marietta

USHER, John, dec'd, notice given by John JEFFERS (DG 13 Oct 1792)

UUMAN, Emelia, see MARTIN, Pascal Allen

UUMAN, John James, see MARTIN, Pascal Allen

UXLEY, Elizabeth, see EAKIN, Robert

VAIL, Thomas, dec'd, late of St. Georges Hd, sheriff's sale (DG 5 Jun 1827)

VALE, Caroline F., see LODGE, Henry H.

VALE, George, see LODGE, Henry H.

VALENTINE, _____, Mrs., wife of William VALENTINE, painter, in Wilm, 19 Mar 1850, aged c 30 yrs (DG 26 Mar 1850)

VALENTINE, Joshua E., see HARKER, John Newton

VALENTINE, W. William, to McKAIG, Amy A., 7 Oct 1851, in Wilm, by the Rt. Rev. Alfred Lee (DG 31 Oct 1851)

VALENTINE, William, see VALENTINE, _____, Mrs.

VALUE, J. R., of NY, to CONCKLIN, Edith B., dau of Jos. T. BAILY, of Wilm, 19 Oct 1852, by the Rt. Rev. Alfred Lee DD (DG 22 Oct 1852)

VAN BURKELOW, John, of Camden, DE, to HICKMAN, Patience, Miss, dau of the late Joseph HICKMAN of NC Co, 2 Nov 1824, by the Rev. R. Williston (DG 5 Nov 1824)

VAN DYKE, _____, Mrs., relict of the late Hon. Nicholas VAN DYKE, at New Castle, 4 May 1831 (DF 14 May 1831)

VAN DYKE, Delia, Mrs., wife of Kensey J. VAN DYKE, Esq., at New Castle, of pulmonary disease, 6 Mar 1825, aged 27 yrs (DG 15 Mar 1825)

VAN DYKE, Dorcas Montgomery, see DUPONT, Charles Irenee, Esq.

VAN DYKE, Elizabeth, Miss, of DE, in Phila, "on Tuesday morning" (DG 1 Jun 1821)

VAN DYKE, Kensey J., see VAN DYKE, Delia

VAN DYKE, Kinsey Johns, Esq., of New Castle, to MONTGOMERY, Fidelia, Miss, dau of William MONTGOMERY, Esq., of Lancaster, PA, 10 Oct 1821, by the Rev. Mr. Clarkson (DG 30 Oct 1821)

VAN DYKE, N., Jr, 23 Jun 1820 (DG 24 Jun 1820)

VAN DYKE, Nicholas, see DUPONT, Charles Irenee, Esq. see VAN DYKE, _____, Mrs.

VAN DYKE, Nicholas, Esq., late president of the Delaware State, at his farm in St. Georges Hd, 19 Feb 1789, leaving a wife and numerous family (DG 28 Feb 1789)

VAN DYKE, Nicholas, the Hon., senator in Congress for Delaware, at New Castle, 20 May 1826, na (DG 23 May 1826) late of NC Co, dec'd, notice given by Kensey JOHNS, Jr., exec'r (DG 7 Jul 1826)

VANAKEN, William, of Phila, to O'DANIEL, Mary B., Miss, of Wilm, in Wilm, 11 Oct 1828, by the Rev. John P. Peckworth (DG 17 Oct 1828)

VANAMAN, Harriett, see LEES, Samuel

VANCE, Jane, in Wilm, 21 Jan 1851, aged c 82 yrs. Memb Asbury Methodist Ch (DG 24 Jan 1851)

VANCE, John, see NOXON, Thomas

VANDEGRIFT, Christopher, Jr., to VANDEGRIFT, Rebecca G., dau of Abraham VANDEGRIFT, Esq., all of NC Co, 9 Oct 1851, near McDonough DE, by the Rev. Isaac W. K. Handy (DG 14 Oct 1851)

VANDEGRIFT, James, to COCHRAN, Adaline, Miss, both of NC Co, at Trenton NJ, 21 Aug 1844, by Rev. John Hall, pastor of 1st Presb. Ch, Trenton (DG 27 Aug 1844)

VANDEGRIFT, Rebecca Ann,
see OCHELTREE, Robert

VANDEGRIFT, William, dec'd, late of Red Lion Hd, notice given by Robert OCHELTREE, adm'r (DG 21 Jan 1834)

VANDEGRIFT, William, see SELBY, Cage
see OCHELTREE, Robert

VANDERGRIFT, Abraham,
see WOODS, Isaac Jr.
see VANDERGRIFT, Christopher Jr.
see JANVIER, Edward G.

VANDERGRIFT, Mary Ann,
see TETLOW, Henry F.

VANDERGRIFT, Rebecca G., see VANDERGRIFT, Christopher Jr.

VANDERGRIFT, Sarah B.,
see WOODS, Isaac Jr.

VANDEVER, Ann Jane, see CLOUD, John

VANDEVER, Catharine,
see WASSON, David H.

VANDEVER, Ellen, see TODD, James H.

VANDEVER, Jacob B., Esq., to BENNETT, Eliza, eldest dau of Caleb P. BENNETT, dec'd, late Governor of Delaware and formerly of the Rev. Army, 16 Dec 1841, in Phila by Rev. Mr. Van Pelt (DG 24 Dec 1841)

VANDEVER, Margaret (alias Sarah WEAVER), committed suicide by taking opium (DG 21 Jun 1850)

VANDEVER, Perthena,
see JEFFRIES, James

VANDEVER, Peter B., to McCULLOUGH, Catharine, Miss, at New Castle, 19 Dec 1843 (DG 22 Dec 1843)

VANDEVER, Peter, see TODD, James H.

VANDEVER, Peter, to CLANDENIRY, Elizabeth, Miss, 25 Jan 1798, by Rev. Mr. Clarkson (DE 5 Feb 1798)

VANDEVER, Rebecca, see HOOTEN, Isaac

VANDEVER, Thomas, 16 Aug 1847, in Wilm (DG 24 Aug 1847)

VANDEVER, Thomas, see HOOTEN, Isaac
see JEFFRIES, James

VANDIVER, Ann, wife of Thomas VANDIVER, Christiana Hd, 24 Nov 1853, aged c 55 yrs (DG 29 Nov 1853)

VANDIVER, Thomas,
see VANDIVER, Ann

VANDYKE, Kensey J., Esq., at New Castle, 2 Mar 1829, na (DG 6 Mar 1829)

VANDYKE, William S., to MATTHEWS, Mary J., Miss, both of Appoq. Hd NC Co, 18 Sep 1849, by the Rev. Mr. Grey (DG 28 Sep 1849)

VANEMAN, Anna S., see WHITE, John D.

VANEMAN, Joanna,
see STEDHAM, Joanna, Mrs.

VANEMAN, Rebecca,
see McANALL, James

VANEMAN, William, (who is now 77 and has buried a wife and nine children),
see STEDHAM, Joanna, Mrs.

VANGASKY, Susan,
see ANDERSON, John

VANGESIL, Angeline,
see CLARK, Matthew J.

VANGESIL, John, see CLARK, Matthew J.

VANNEMAN, Dorcas,
see ARMSTRONG, Samuel F.

VANNEMAN, John S., Capt., of Delaware Co, PA, at Chester, 27 Feb 1833, na (DG 8 Mar 1833)

VANNEMAN, John S., in Wilm, of consumption, 27 Apr 1851, aged c 20 yrs (DG 29 Apr 1851)

VANNEMAN, Mary, Miss,
see SMITH, Charles B.

VANNEMAN, Mary, see ISAACS, W. G.

VANSANT, Rebecca, see RUTH, Levi

VARE, Japhet, to GARRISH, Mary A., both of Wilm, 5 Jan 1853, by Rev. Andrew Manship (DG 14 Jan 1853)

VAUGHAN, Charles, a native of DE, at Norfolk, VA, where he has lived for the last four years, 14 Jun 1829, aged 58 yrs (DG 23 Jun 1829)

VAUGHAN, Charles Richard, infant son of E. B. VAUGHAN, 29 Jul 1834, na (DG 1 Aug 1834)

VAUGHAN, E. B.
see VAUGHAN, Charles Richard

VAUGHAN, J. F. Dr., Pres. of the Medical

DELAWARE MARRIAGES AND DEATHS FROM NEWSPAPERS, 1729-1853

Soc. of DE, 7 Jul 1834, aged 32 yrs (DG 8 Jul 1834) Obit (DG 11 Jul 1834) notice given to make payment to Mr. Robert RICHY, by William R. SELLERS, adm'r (DG 27 Oct 1835)

VAUGHAN, John, Dr., of Wilm, of a nervous fever, 25 Mar 1807. Mr. Dodge of the Baptist Ch delivered the sermon. Prayer at the grave by Dr. Read (MU 28 Mar 1807) see VAUGHAN, Joshua, the Rev.

VAUGHAN, John D., to GILPIN, Lydia Z., Miss, 3 Nov 1820 (DG 7 Nov 1820)

VAUGHAN, John D., Esq., formerly of Wilm, in Richmond, IN, of Asiatic malaria, 23 Aug 1834, aged 34 yrs (DG 5 Sep 1834)

VAUGHAN, Joshua, the Rev., pastor of the Baptist Ch of Brandywine, Chester Co, PA, 30 Aug 1808... The death of a son, Dr. (John) VAUGHAN of Wilm in the year past so affected him that he resigned himself to the will of God.....(MU 10 Sep 1808)

VAUGHAN, Richard, of DE, to BELL, Margaret, Mrs., of Phila, in Phila, 11 Apr 1849, by Rev. Charles Brown (DG 24 Apr 1849)

VAUGHN, Hannah Jane, only dau of Levin D. VAUGHN, in Georgetown, 24 Mar 1853, in her 2nd year (DG 5 Apr 1853)

VAUGHN, Levin D., see VAUGHN, Hannah Jane

VAULES, Mary E., see CREED, John B.

VAUS, Rachel, see WHEELER, James H.

VAUX, Eliza E., see RUSSEL, John

VAUX, Emily, see TRUEFIT, Lewis A.

VAUX, Emily V., see TRUEFIT, Emily V.

VAUX, George, see CHANDLER, William Penn see TRUEFIT, Emily V. see TRUEFIT, Lewis A.

VAUX, Hannah S., see CHANDLER, William Penn

VEACH, Edith, see SAVILLE, David

VEACH, Elizabeth, see JEWELL, Isaac

VEASEY, _____, Col., see VEASEY, George Clinton

VEASEY, George Clinton, son of Col. VEASEY of Cecil Co, MD, to HIRONS, Lydia Gilpin dau of John HIRONS of

Wilm, in Wilm 21 Jan 1834, by the Rev. Isaac Pardee (DG 24 Jan 1834)

VEASEY, Nathan T., to WARRINGTON, Susan B., 14 Jan 1850, by Rev. J. R. Torbert (DG 12 Feb 1850)

VEAZEY, George Clinton, see VEAZEY, Mary Virginia

VEAZEY, Lambert, Dr., of Summit Bridge, to THOMAS, Margaret H., of Newark, 8 Dec 1842, in Phila by Rev. Albert Barnes (DG 16 Dec 1842)

VEAZEY, Lydia G., see VEAZEY, Mary Virginia

VEAZEY, Mary Virginia, dau of George Clinton and Lydia G. VEAZEY, in Wilm after a short illness, 29 Apr 1847, na (DG 7 May 1847)

VENT, Ella, see JOSEPH, George W.

VERDON, Thomas, to ROBINETT, Ann Jane, Miss, both of Wilm, 21 Oct 1821, by the Rev. John Hagany (DG 6 Nov 1821)

VERION, William M., of Upland, Del Co PA, to STEVENSON, Eliza, of Wilm, 15 May 1853, by the Rev. J. B. Maddux (DG 31 May 1853)

VERNON, Alfred. to LAIN, Mary, Miss, both of Wilm, 22 Feb 1849, by Rev. T. J. Thompson (DG 2 Mar 1849)

VERNON, Ann Maria, see HENDRICKSON. William H.

VERNON, Bennett H., 21 Feb 1850, aged 24 yrs (DG 26 Feb 1850)

VERNON, David A., of Wilm, to COOPER, Elizabeth M. D., of West Chester PA, in W. Chester, 3 Aug 1851, by the Rev. Mr. Moore (DG 8 Aug 1851)

VERNON, George, to PUSEY, Mary, Miss, both of NC Co, 28 Apr 1829, by Elder John P. Peckworth (DG 5 May 1829)

VERNON, George W., of Wilm, to GUTHRIE, Annie F., of Chester Co PA, in Phila, 23 Oct 1851, by the Rev. Mr. Mason (DG 28 Oct 1851)

VERNON, Jane, wife of Rufus VERNON, in Wilm, 11 Dec 1852, in her 54th yr (DG 14 Dec 1852) see VERNON, Joseph

VERNON, Joseph, son of Rufus and Jane VERNON, in Wilm, 16 Apr 1850, in his 11th yr (DG 19 Apr 1850)

VERNON, Lydia, see WILKINS, George W.

VERNON, Rufus, see VERNON, Joseph see VERNON, Jane

VERNON, Samuel, to MOORE, Caroline J., both of Brandywine Hd, in Chester PA, 14 Apr 1853, by the Rev. A. P. Hard (DG 3 May 1853)

VICKERS, Leah, see SHORT, Edward

VICKREY, Sarah Ann, see CANAL, Thomas Jr.

VINCENT, Ellen, see REYNOLDS, Richard

VINCENT, Francis, one of the editors of the Blue Hen's Chickens, to FARRA, Harriet F., Miss, dau of the late John FARRA, Esq., of Brandywine HD, 1 Jun 1848, by Mayor Swift, at Morris Hotel, Phila (DG 6 Jun 1848) see VINCENT, Louisa Jane

VINCENT, Harriet, see VINCENT, Louisa Jane

VINCENT, Josephine, see WALKER, Samuel

VINCENT, Louisa Jane, dau of Francis and Harriet VINCENT, in Wilm, 14 Jan 1852, in her 2nd yr (DG 23 Jan 1852)

VINCENT, Tench T., to REYHOW, Sarah, Miss, all of Wilm, 21 Feb 1847, by Rev. A. Atwood (DG 26 Feb 1847)

VINCENT, Thomas M., of NC Co, to MARSHALL, Ann, Miss, of Phila, 31 Mar 1845, in Phila, by Rev. M. Sorin (DG 4 Apr 1845)

VINCINGER, William, to HILL, Lavinia Ann, Miss, both of Cecil Co, MD, 24 Dec 1835, by the Rev. A. K. Russel (DG 1 Jan 1836)

VINING, Elizabeth, see VINING, John,

VINING, H., Mr., only surviving son of John Middleton VINING of DE, and grandson of the late William SEATON "of that city", at New York, 12 Aug 1822, aged 28 yrs (DG 27 Aug 1822)

VINING, Henry, printer, to LYLE, Rebecca, Miss, both of Wilm, 12 Oct 1809, by the Rev. Dr. Read (DG 18 Oct 1809) see BELVILLE, John

VINING, James, late carpenter of the ship Mary, formerly res. of New Castle, at Whampoa, [Hong Kong?]of "locked jaw," 3 Dec 1832, na (DG 9 Apr 1833)

VINING, James Lisle, to ROBINSON, Margaret, Miss both of NC Co, 4 Dec 1834, by Eld. John P. Peckworth (DG 9 Dec 1834)

VINING, John, dec'd, late of New Castle, blacksmith, notice given by Elizabeth VINING, exec'x (DE 6 Dec 1798)

VINING, John, the Hon., Member of the House of Representatives, to SETON, ____, Miss, dau of William SETON of New York, at New York, nmd (DG 4 Dec 1790)

VINING, John Middleton, see VINING, H., Mr.

VINYARD, Henry, to THISTLEWOOD, Ann, both of Kent Co, 15 Mar 1853 (DG 29 Mar 1853)

VIRDEN, Alexander, of Jackson, MI, to VIRDEN, Ruth Ann, Miss, dau of Samuel VIRDEN, Esq., at Lexington Mills near Frederica, 28 Aug 1849, na, by the Rev. Dr. Pitts (DG 4 Sep 1849)

VIRDEN, Emma Matilda, see YOCUM, Henry A.

VIRDEN, Ruth Ann, see VIRDEN, Alexander

VIRDEN, Samuel, see VIRDEN, Alexander

VIRDEN, Sarah Ann, see LUDWICK, James G.

VIRTUE, Mary Ann, see RICE, James

VOLLMAR, George, see VOLLMAR, Jacob C.

VOLLMAR, Jacob C., son of George and Jeanette VOLLMAR, in Wilm, 31 Jan 1846, aged 6 yrs 4 mos (DG 10 Feb 1846)

VOLLMAR, Jeanette, see VOLLMAR, Jacob C.

VONDERSMITH, Lizzie L., Miss, see SAUNDERS, James A.

VONHLE, Charles, to WHITE, Mary Ann, Miss, all of Dover, 9 Jul 1849 (DG 20 Jul 1849)

VOSHELL, John C., to LORE, Ann W., Miss, 2 Jan 1842, near Blackbird, by Rev. Epraim Jefferson (DG 7 Jan 1842)

VOSHELL, Mary A., see ROBERTS, James Jr.

VOSS, William H., to LANE, Mary E., Miss, both of Kent Co, 15 Aug 1850, by Rev. Daniel E. Godwin (DG 27 Aug 1850)

WADDINGTON, Mary Elizabeth,

DELAWARE MARRIAGES AND DEATHS FROM NEWSPAPERS, 1729-1853

see **GILPIN**, Charles L.

WADDINGTON, Wm.,
see **GILPIN**, Charles L.

WADE, Samuel, to **RIDGEWAY**, Harriet S., both of NC Co, 3 Mar 1853, by J. A. Roche (DG 11 Mar 1853)

WAGNER, John, 8 Aug 1848, aged 70 yrs (DG 11 Aug 1848)

WAGSTAFF, James, formerly of Wilm, 24 Jul 1841, aged 62, at the house of his brother, John WAGSTAFF, Esq., Staylbridge, near Manchester, England (DG 27 Aug 1841)

WAGSTAFF, John, see **WAGSTAFF**, James

WAIT, Francis D., M. D., of Cantwell's Bridge, to **NEWELL**, Eliza G., Miss, living near the same place, 4 Nov 1821, by the Rev. John Burton (DG 20 Nov 1821)

WAITE, Joseph T., to **BUTLER**, Elizabeth, Miss, both of Wilm, at New London PA, 20. Sep 1849, by the Rev. Mr. DuBoise (DG 25 Sep 1849)

WAITHMAN, Mary, Mrs., see **PENNINGTON**, Alrich

WAITSON, Benjamin, see **HUSLER**, John

WAKEMAN, Ruth, Mrs, at the res. of her son-in-law, Enoch SPRUANCE, Esq., in Smyrna, after a short illness, 28 Jan 1847 (DG 9 Feb 1847)

WALBORN, Rufus C., to **PYLE**, Lizzie P., both of Phila, in Phila, 1 May 1851, by the Rev. T. J. Thompson (DG 6 May 1851)

WALCOTT, C., see **CLOAK**, Ebenezer

WALDIE, Adam, see **GARDEN**, Francis R.

WALDIE, Annie see **GARDEN**, Francis R.

WALDIE, Mary A.,
see **MAYBIN**, Joseph A.

WALES, Ann, late wife of John WALES, and dau of Maj. John PATTEN, in Wilm, 11 Nov 1842 (DG 17 Nov 1843)

WALES, John, see **WALES**, Ann

WALKER, David, of DE, late merchant of the Island of St. Thomas, in Phila, 10 Aug 1829, aged 56 yrs (DG 11 Aug 1829)

WALKER, Eliza Ann, wife of George W. WALKER, in Pencader Hd, NC Co, 13 Mar 1849, in her 34th yr (DG 17 Apr 1849)

WALKER, Elizabeth, see **HATTON**, Enos see **MILLER**, William

WALKER, George, late of Appoq. Hd. Sale of property.(DG 2 Mar 1827)

WALKER, George W., to **HUTTON**, Mary E., Miss, both of NC Co, in Phila, 1 Nov 1849, by the Rev. Samuel Ashton (DG 16 Nov 1849)
see **WALKER**, Eliza Ann

WALKER, Hampton, a native of DE and many years resident of Chowan Co, NC, died "lately" at that place (AW 9 May 1818)

WALKER, Isaac, sale of real estate (DG 14 Jan 1853)

WALKER, Isaac F., see **PRATT**, Enoch

WALKER, Isaac P.,
see **WILSON**, Thompson

WALKER, Jane I., see **PIERCE**, Elias

WALKER, John, to **SEITE**, Mary, Mrs., both of Wilm, 1 May 1824, by the Rev. John Hagany (DG 4 May 1824)

WALKER, John, lately belonging to Wilm, a boy caught in the machinery and killed at Gloucester Point Factories, NJ, one day last week (DG 17 Sep 1847)

WALKER, John A., late of Wilm, in Commerce MO, 5 Dec 1840, aged 64 yrs (DG 25 Dec 1840)

WALKER, John W., of Lewes, to **HERDMAN**, Eliza Ann, of NC Co, in Phila, 20 Apr 1853, by Rev. Bishop Lee (DG 26 Apr 1853)

WALKER, Joseph, late of Phila, in Wilm, 9 Mar 1848, aged 32 yrs (DG 21 Mar 1848)

WALKER, Joseph Jr, see **OSLERS**, Davis

WALKER, Josiah, in Mill Creek Hd, 1 Oct 1849, aged 31 yrs (DG 9 Oct 1849) Milton STEEL adm'r (DG 30 Oct 1849)

WALKER, Martha, see **PAPEL**, Thomas

WALKER, Mary, see **McCOY**, Nathaniel see **MARSH**, John

WALKER, Mary Ann, see **McCALL**, Ralph see **LOCKARD**, Mathew

WALKER, Robert, to **WHITEMAN**, Sarah, Miss, both of NC Co in Phila, 5 Mar 1851, by the Rev. Thomas L. Janeway (DG 11 Mar 1851)

WALKER, Robert, in Mill Creek Hd, 3 Feb 1853, aged c 82 yrs (DG 15 Feb 1853) Robert WALKER, Jr., exec'r (DG 11 Mar 1853)

WALKER, Robert, Jr., to DENNEY, Sarah, Miss, both of NC Co, Nov 18 1841, by Rev. W. R. Work (DG 10 Dec 1841)
see WALKER, Robert
see LOCKARD, Mathew

WALKER, Samuel, to WHITE, Sally Ann, Miss, both of New Castle, 2 Apr 1829, by the Rev. E. W. Gilbert (DG 7 Apr 1829)

WALKER, Samuel, to VINCENT, Josephine, Miss, both of Wilm, 22 Apr 1852, by Rev. S. L. Wynkoop (DG 27 Apr 1852)

WALKER, Samuel A., to SCANLAN, Elizabeth, Miss, all of NC Co, 20 Sep 1849, by the Rev. Mr. Grey (DG 28 Sep 1849)

WALKER, Samuel C., formerly of DE at Clark's Ferry on the Susquehanna River, Dauphin Co PA, 25 Jun 1843 (DG 28 Jul 1843)

WALKER, Sarah, see OLIVER, Joseph

WALKER, Sarah Ann, see LAMPBUGH [?], Thomas

WALKER, William, blacksmith, after a long and painful illness, in Wilm, 20 Mar 1825, aged 63 yrs (DG 22 Mar 1825)

WALKER, William, 10 Apr 1844, in Wilm, (DG 12 Apr 1844)

WALKER, Wilson W., to DEAKYNE, Emily, both of NC Co, in Phila at Union M. E. Ch pars., by Rev. T. J. Thompson (DG 19 Apr 1850)

WALL, Joseph, to MILLER, Rebecca, both of Wilm, 8 May 1841, by Rev. I. T. Cooper of Marcus Hook (DG 18 Jun 1841)

WALLACE, A., Rev., of the Phila Conf, to LEWIS, Margaret W., Miss, of Laurel DE, 10 Nov 1852, by the Rev. James L. WALLACE (DG 19 Nov 1852)

WALLACE, Ann, Mrs., at the res. of her son in Christiana Hd, 1 Apr 1828, aged 71 yrs (DG 13 May 1828)

WALLACE, Ann H., see WALLACE, George Thomas

WALLACE, B. S., see WALLACE, George Thomas

WALLACE, Benjamin, see WALLACE, William Thomas

WALLACE, Elizabeth, Mrs, 23 Nov 1853, aged 34 yrs (DG 29 Nov 1853) see EVERSOLE, A. S.

WALLACE, George Thomas, son of B. S. and Ann H. WALLACE, in Baltimore, 24 Jun 1847, aged 6 yrs 6 mos (DG 29 Jun 1847)

WALLACE, James L., Rev.
see WALLACE, A., Rev.

WALLACE, John, dec'd, notice given by Andrew CATHERWOOD (DE 14 May 1798)

WALLACE, John, in Milford, DE, 21 Apr 1849, age 70 yrs (DG 1 May 1849)

WALLACE, John A., to ORTLIP, Eliza W., Miss, all of Upper Oxford, Chester Co PA, 26 Apr 1849, by Rev. Alfred Hamilton (DG 4 May 1849)

WALLACE, Sarah, Mrs., in Wilm, 2 Aug 1849, aged 35 yrs (DG 14 Aug 1849)

WALLACE, Thomas, dec'd, late of Milltown, Mill Creek Hd, NC Co, notice given by William JOHNSTON, adm'r (DG 5 Jan 1793) see MIDDLETON, Robert

WALLACE, William Thomas, son of Benjamin WALLACE, at Camden, 5 Jul 1853, aged 18 yrs (DG 22 Jul 1853)

WALLER, Amanda W., see HEARN, Joseph J.

WALLER, Stansbury W., to OWENS, Mary Ann, Miss, all of Sussex, 17 Dec 1847, near Laurel, by Rev. H. C. Fries (DG 8 Jan 1847)

WALLS, Campbell, Esq., to DEAN, Rachel, Miss, 3 Apr 1833, by the Rev. Ephraim Jefferson (DG 12 Apr 1833)

WALLS, Eliza A., see LINGO, Cornelius B.

WALLS, Harriet J., see WALLS, Purnell

WALLS, James, to SMITH, Anna M., Miss, near Georgetown, 16 Jul 1834, by the Rev. J. R. Torbert, all of Sussex Co (DG 29 Jul 1834)

WALLS, Lydia, see JOHNSTON, Samuel W.

WALLS, Purnell, of Kent Co, to WALLS, Harriet J., of Sussex Co, 23 Mar 1853, by Rev. J. R. Torbert (DG 29 Mar 1853)

WALLS, Sarah Ann, see EISONBRY, Charles S.

WALMSEY, Mary, see RUSH, Isaac J.

WALMSLEY, Robert, Jr. of Dubuque IA, to BARR, Carrie, D., Miss, of New Castle, in Wilm, 28 Jul 1853, by the Rev. A. D. Pollock (DG 2 Aug 1853)

WALRAVEN, Eliza Ann, see SCHWARTZ, G. C.

WALRAVEN, Elizabeth D., see WILSON, William C.

WALRAVEN, Esther Ann, see CHAPMAN, Joseph B.

WALRAVEN, Isaac, in Wilm, 14 Mar 1849, in his 61st yr (DG 23 Mar 1849)
see WALRAVEN, Walraven
see WALRAVEN, Jane
see NICHOLSON, Henry

WALRAVEN, Jane, Mrs., widow of the late Isaac WALRAVEN, in Wilm, 23 Mar 1849, in her 56th yr (DG 27 Mar 1849)

WALRAVEN, Jonas, to CHADWICK, Henrietta, Miss, both of Wilm, 12 Feb 1846, in Wilm, by Rev. Bishop Lee (DG 13 Feb 1846)

WALRAVEN, Priscilla, see NICHELSON, William

WALRAVEN, Sarah Jane, in Wilm, 15 Dec 1850, in her 18th yr (DG 17 Dec 1850)

WALRAVEN, Thomas, late of Brandywine Hd, Thomas WALRAVEN, adm'r (DG 14 Sep 1852)

WALRAVEN, Walraven, dec'd, late of Christiana Hd, notice given by Isaac WALRAVEN and Ashton RICHARDSON, adm'rs (DG 7 Mar 1826)

WALSH, Christopher, in Newark, 11 Jan 1853, aged c 30 yrs (DG 14 Jan 1853)

WALSH, John S., see FITZPATRICK, Thomas

WALTER, Ann, of NC Co, 4 Aug 1834, aged 58 yrs (DG 8 Aug 1834)

WALTER, Asenath A., see WHITCRAFT, John G.

WALTER, Ebe. Jr. to MILLER, Mary Ann, Miss, dau of the late Capt. James MILLER, Esq., of Sussex Co, 1 Sep 1841, by Rev. H. C. Fries (DG 24 Sep 1841)

WALTER, John, Esq., 12 Jan 1846, at his res. in Christiana Hd, aged 50 yrs. An industrious, enterprising man...exemplary citizen (DG 20 Jan 1846)
see WALTER, Richard Gilpin

WALTER, John H., of East Marlborough, Chester Co PA, to DUTTON, Eliza Jane, Miss, of NC Co, 2 Jun 1842, by N. Stickland, Esq. (DG 10 Jun 1842)

WALTER, Richard Gilpin, eldest son of John WALTER, late of Christiana Hd, from an accident at the saw-mill of his uncle, Thomas WALTER, died at the res. of his grandmother, Mrs HOBART, in Wilm, 13 Oct 1851, in his 14th yr (DG 28 Oct 1851)

WALTER, Thomas, see WALTER, Richard Gilpin

WALTERS, Elizabeth, see MATSON, George

WALTERS, Jemima M., see CARPENTER, Joseph C.

WALTERS, Maria, see WILLIAMS, Moses

WALTERS, William H., to RICHARDSON, Sidney, Miss, both of NC Co, 19 Aug 1847, by Hugh B. Passmore, Esq. (DG 24 Aug 1847)

WALTON. Alfred, to HOOK. Minerva, Miss, 27 Dec 1849, by Rev. P. Reilly (DG 1 Jan 1850)
see WALTON, Chandler
see WALTON, Maria

WALTON, Chandler, inf son of Alfred and Minerva WALTON, 18 Aug 1853, na (DG 23 Aug 1853)

WALTON, David, at an advanced age, in Milford, 17 Jan 1851 (DG 21 Jan 1851)

WALTON, David, see WALTON, Susan

WALTON, Maria, inf dau of Alfred and Susan M. WALTON, 12 Jun 1845 (DG 20 Jun 1845)

WALTON, Minerva, see WALTON, Chandler

WALTON, Susan, Mrs., wife of David WALTON, of Milford DE, 4 Mar 1851 (DG 11 Mar 1851)

WALTON, Susan M., see WALTON, Maria

WALTON, Thomas, to FILAR, Sarah A., Mrs., both of NC Co, 6 Dec 1853, by the Rev. J. C. Humphries (DG 30 Dec 1853)

WALTON, William, of East Fallowfield, to SACRISTE, Amelia, Miss, of Brandywine Hd, in Phila, 1 Aug 1833, by the Rev. Mr. Kenny (DG 9 Aug 1833)

WALTONE, (sic), Paynter, to KOLLOCK,

Penelope, Miss, youngest dau of Philips KOLLOCK, Esq., at her father's res. in Georgetown, by the Rev. Daniel Higbee (DG 6 Aug 1822)

WAPLES, Ann, see MORRIS, Ann

WAPLES, Ann Custis, see BARNARD, D____

WAPLES, Gideon, see WAPLES, Thomas Alexander

WAPLES, Gideon, merchant of Milton, DE, to COTTINGHAM, Sarah, Mrs., dau of Mr. Miles BURTON, merchant near Millsboro, 24 Mar 1829, by Rev. Daniel Higbee (DG 31 Mar 1829)

WAPLES, Henry Clay, son of the late Col. William D. WAPLES, at Dagsborough, 3 Dec 1847 (DG 14 Dec 1847)

WAPLES, James W., to PETERSON, Almira, Miss, both of Wilm, in Wilm, 25 Dec 1828, by the Rev. E. W. Gilbert (DG 30 Dec 1828)

WAPLES, Sophia, Mrs., wife of Col. Wm. D. WAPLES of Millsborough, member of the Baptist Ch., of a pulmonary and dropsical disease, 2 Jan 1823 (DG 14 Jan 1823)

WAPLES, Thomas Alexander, only son of Mr. Gideon WAPLES, merchant of Milton, in Milton, 30 Jun 1829, aged 2 yrs and 6 mos (DG 7 Jul 1829)

WAPLES, William D., Col. to WELLS, Rachel, Miss, dau of William H. WELLS, Esq., at Dagsborough, nmd, no minister (DG 2 Jul 1824)
see MORRIS, Ann
see WAPLES, Henry Clay
see WELLS, William Hill
see BARNARD, D____
see WAPLES, Sophia, Mrs.

WARD, Emeline, see THURSTON, Edward

WARD, George C., to SPRINGER, Mary Ann, Miss, both of Wilm, 15 Sep 1851, by the Rev. S. R. Wynkoop (DG 26 Sep 1851)

WARD, J. Parrish, to BRADLEY, Elenora, youngest dau of the late Thomas BRADLEY, all of Wilm, in Phila, 19 Aug 1850, by P. F. Mayer, DD (DG 23 Aug 1850)

WARD, John, son of Joseph and Sarah WARD, in Mispillion Hd, 2 Nov 1850, aged c 14 yrs (DG 5 Nov 1850)

WARD, John E., see WARD, Mary Ann

WARD, Joseph, near Vernon DE, of tyohoid fever, 2 Aug 1852, aged 58 yrs (DG 17 Aug 1852)
see WARD, John

WARD, Mary Ann, dau of John E. WARD, at Cantwell's Bridge, of bilious pleurisy, 21 Feb 1835, aged 7 yrs 3 mos 15 days (DG 27 Feb 1835)

WARD, Sarah, see WARD, John

WARD, Thomas, to JONES, Martha, 7 Oct 1841, by Rev. William Rider (DG 15 Oct 1841)

WARE, John, to HARRISON, Hester, Miss, both of Wilm, 17 Aug 1847, by Alderman J. Mitchell (DG 15 Oct 1847)

WARE, Robinson, to McCRACKEN, Amelia Jane, Miss, both of Christiana DE, in the borough of Chester, 21 Apr 1853, by R. R. POWELL, Esq. (DG 26 Apr 1853)

WARNE, John E., of Phila, to CAULK, Sue E., Miss, dau of the late Major John CAULK of DE, in Phila, 17 May 1853, by the Rev. John McDowell DD (DG 20 May 1853)

WARNER, Frances B., of Wilm, to PARKER, Louisa White, dau of the late John PARKER of DE, 6 Aug 1846, in Phila, by Rev. J. J. Kerr (DG 11 Aug 1846)

WARNER, Henry, of Wilm, formerly cashier of the Bank of Delaware, suddenly, 2 Jun 1845 (DG 6 Jun 1845)

WARNER, John, see NILES, Hezekiah

WARNER, Joseph, see WARNER, Mary

WARNER, Joseph T., of Wilm, to YOUNG, Jean Stroud, Miss, dau of William YOUNG, Esq., of Phila, 4 Oct 1827, by the Rev. Thomas Beveridge (DG 16 Oct 1827)

WARNER, Junia M., see TENNEY, Otis S.

WARNER, Lydia Ann, see HARRIS, Jesse

WARNER, Mary, formerly of Wilm, widow of Joseph WARNER, at Baltimore, 30 Apr 1823, in her 79th yr (DG 6 May 1823)

WARNER, Mary, Mrs., eldest dau of John GANT, 30 Jan 1848, in Wilm (DG 8 Feb 1848)

WARNER, Sally Ann, see NILES, Hezekiah

WARNER, Susan, see WOOLASTON, John

WARNER, Thomas J., in Smyrna, at the res. of his uncle, John S. LAMBDIN, after an illness of nearly 9 mos, Dec 25 1847, in his 20th yr (DG 31 Dec 1847)

WARNER, William, see YARNALL, Esther
see WOOLASTON, John,
see FEBIGER, Christian

WARNER, William, of Dover, to WHARTON, Nancy, Miss, of near Dover, 19 Jul 1789 (DG 8 Aug 1789)

WARNER, William, Hon., near Camden, DE, 15 Jan 1822 (DG 22 Jan 1822)

WARNER, William, from Smyrna, DE, suddenly, possibly of consumption, on board the steamboat *Thistle*, on her passage from NY to Brunswick, 2 Aug 1825, aged c 29 yrs...identified by papers in his possession (DG 9 Aug 1825)

WARNER, William, in Wilm, 5 Jun 1845, aged 72 yrs (DG 10 Jun 1845)

WARNER, William, to ROBINSON, Ruth Ann, Miss, all of NC Co, 11 Jul 1848, by Rev. M. J. Rhees (DG 14 Jul 1848)

WARREN, Caroline, see HALL, John W.

WARREN, Ellen J., see SHERER, William

WARREN, James, from Phila, a conductor on the Phila, Wilm, Balt RR, fell from train in Phila, leaves a wife and 6 children, 5 Oct 1852, aged 36 yrs (DG 8 Oct 1852)

WARREN, Mary, see DAY, C. H. B.

WARREN, Penelope, dec'd, Thomas LOCKWOOD, adm'r (DG 6 Feb 1852)

WARREN, Samuel, see HALL, John W.

WARRINGTON, Ann B.,
see HAYES, Samuel

WARRINGTON, David, to DAY, Eliza, Miss, both of Sussex Co, 2 Jun 1853, by the Rev. Jonathan R. Torbert (DG 24 Jun 1853)

WARRINGTON, James P., to HOPKINS, Betty, Mrs., both of Sussex Co, near Lewes Town, DE, by the Rev. J. R. Torbert (DG 17 Nov 1835)

WARRINGTON, Mary Ann,
see KELLAM, Arthur

WARRINGTON, Stephen, to MARSEL, Mary B., 17 Jan 1850, by Rev. J. R. Torbert (DG 12 Feb 1850)

WARRINGTON, Susan B.,
see VEASEY, Nathan T.

WARRINGTON, Thomas J., of Wilm, to ESTELL, Naomi, Miss, of Phila, 31 May 1846, by Rev. Mr. Grant (DG 16 Jun 1846)

WASHINGTON, Daniel, basket maker, found in a Newport marsh, 9 Mar 1845. Coroner decided it was an apoplectic fit. (DG 18 Mar 1845)

WASHINGTON, Mary Ann,
see GULEY, Lewis H.

WASHINGTON, Mary Elizabeth, Mrs, at her res., 11 Nov 1845. aged 81 yrs (DG 4 Nov 1845)

WASSEN, William, to LAUDERS, Mary Ann, Miss, both of Newport, in Wilm, 17 Mar 1825, by the Rev. E. W. Gilbert (DG 22 Mar 1825)

WASSON, David H., to VANDEVER, Catharine, Miss, both of Wilm, 15 Jun 1848, by Rev. S. R. Wynkoop (DG 30 Jun 1848)

WASSON, William, keeper of the Depot Hotel in Wilm , 9 Jan 1849, na (DG 12 Jan 1849)

WATKINS, Josiah, to DAVIS, Elizabeth, Miss, in N. W. Fork Hd, 27 Jul 1848 by Rev. William Davis (DG 8 Aug 1848)

WATSON, Beniah, youngest son of Bethuel and Ruth WATSON of Milford, 16 Jul 1852, aged 17 mos 3 days (DG 27 Jul 1852)

WATSON, Bethnel [?] Emerson, son of C. S. and Sarah C. WATSON, in S, Milford, 4 Aug 1849, aged 3 yrs (DG 14 Aug 1849)

WATSON, Bethuel, see WATSON, Beniah

WATSON, C. S.,
see WATSON, Bethnel [?] Emerson

WATSON, Curtis S., infant son of Curtis S. WATSON, in Milford, 26 Mar 1849 (DG 3 Apr 1849)

WATSON, Elizabeth W.,
see MORGAN, James H.

WATSON, Emeline Truitt,
see DEPUTY, John

WATSON, George W.,
see WATSON, Mary Jane

WATSON. Hannah J.,
see PHILLIPS, Wm. G.

WATSON, Henry S., to SHOCKLEY, Elizabeth, Miss, both of Cedar Creek Hd, Sussex Co, DE, 3 Apr 1849, by the

Rev. T. P. McColley (DG 10 Apr 1849)

WATSON, James, see **JOHNSON**, Samuel

WATSON, Jane, see **WILLARD**, James H.

WATSON, Jesse, see **WATSON**, Mary

WATSON, Jesse A., to **WIRT**, Mary E., both of Wilm, 27 Jan 1848, by Rev. J. Castle (DG 4 Feb 1848)

WATSON, Lewis, see **HYATT**, John

WATSON, Mary, wife of Jesse WATSON, died of consumption, 4 Jun 1847, aged 41 yrs (DG 11 Jun 1847)

WATSON, Mary B., see **WHARTON**, Job

WATSON, Mary E., see **WATSON**, Samuel, Capt.

WATSON, Mary Jane, consort of George W. WATSON, near Williamsville, Kent Co, 18 Jan 1853, in her 30th yr (DG 1 Feb 1853) see **BAIRD**, William

WATSON, Naomi, see **BLACK**, James

WATSON, Nathan B., late of Newark, committed suicide, 8 Sep 1848, by cutting his throat with a razor (DG 15 Sep 1848)

WATSON, Obediah, at his res. in Washington Co PA, 15 Mar 1853, in his 36th yr (DG 8 Apr 1853)

WATSON, Ruth, see **WATSON**, Beniah

WATSON, Samuel, Capt., to **WATSON**, Mary E., Miss, all of Sussex, 2 Nov 1848, in Phila (DG 10 Nov 1848)

WATSON, Sarah Agnes, Miss, formerly of Wilm, at Freeport PA, 23 Nov 1843, aged 24 yrs (DG 8 Dec 1843)

WATSON, Sarah C., see **WATSON**, Bethnel [?] Emerson

WATT, William, Esq., of Phila, to **McDANNIEL**, Emma, Miss, 22 Sep 1853, at Pleasant Hill, NC Co, by Rev. S. R. Wynkoop (DG 27 Sep 1853)

WATTERS, Michael, to **JAQUETT**, Jane, Miss, both of Brandywine, 17 Apr 1834, by Rev. Mr. Carvel (DG 25 Apr 1834)

WATTS, Elizabeth L., see **HOSEA**, James W.

WATTS, George, see **HOSEA**, James W.

WATTS, James, to **BEETLE**, Rebecca,

Miss, 3 Jun 1829, by Rev. David Daily, all of Wilm (DG 9 Jun 1829)

WAUGH, Catherine O., see **CAULK**, Oliver

WAUGH, Eliza P., at the res. of Elijah START, Esq., in New Castle, 12 Nov 1848, in her 49th yr (DG 21 Nov 1848)

WAUGH, Virginia C., see **CULLEN**, Chas. M.

WAY, _____, Judge, see **PHISTER**, Benjamin

WAY, Caleb, dec'd, late of Christiana Hd, notice given by Samuel GREGG, adm'r (MU 7 Feb 1807)

WAY, David B., to **BROOKS**, Mary, Miss, dau of Josiah and Mary BROOKS, all of White Clay Creek Hd, 6 Jan 1850, by Elder Elson Whipple, from the state of Deseret {Utah} (DG 11 Jan 1850)

WAY. Elizabeth, see **MOUSLEY**, George W. see **WAY**, Joshua

WAY, Elizabeth R., see **THOMAS**, Elizabeth R.

WAY, John, Esq., see **THOMAS**, Elizabeth R.

WAY, Joseph C., to **FORMAN**, Elizabeth, Miss, both of Wilm, 2 Dec 1850, in Chester PA, by Rev. J. W. Gibbs (DG 17 Dec 1850)

WAY, Joshua, late of Wilm. Sale of European and West India goods by Elizabeth WAY, Joseph HEWS, and David FERRIS, exec'rs (PG 7 Nov 1751)

WAY, Nicholas, M. D., dec'd, late of Phila, notice given by John WAY (DE 23 Oct 1797)

WAY, Rachel Hanna (sic), see **BARBER**, Peter

WAY, Thomas, of Maryland, to **DAVIS**, Elizabeth, Miss, of PA, 8 Apr 1847, in Wilm by the Mayor (DG 13 Apr 1847)

WEAVER, John L., of Wilm, to **BOCKIUS**, Mary Ann, Miss, of Phila, 26 May 1852, by the Rev. S. Harris (DG 22 Jun 1852)

WEAVER, Sarah, see **VANDEVER**, Margaret

WEBB, Benjamin, at his late res., Greenhill, near Wilm, 22 Feb 1851, in his 65th yr (DG 28 Feb 1851)

WEBB, Benjamin, colored man, dec'd,

notice given by Thos. GARRETT, exec'r (DF 29 Dec 1832)

WEBB, Benjamin, see PALMER, Morris W. see BATTERSBY, James

WEBB, Christian, the last of 17 children of Daniel and Sarah HOOPES, at Kennet, 31 Dec 1815, in her 94th yr, Her father and grandfather came from England with William Penn in 1682 (AW 6 Jan 1816)

WEBB, Elizabeth A., see HEVERIN, Outten L.

WEBB, Ellen, see MORGAN, Ezekiel

WEBB, James, see RICHARDS, Nathaniel

WEBB, James D., of Benton MD, aged 25 yrs, to PETERKIN, Mary, Miss, of Milford DE, aged 53 yrs, 26 Jul 1827, in Milford, by the Rev. W. Hickman (DG 4 Sep 1827)

WEBB, Joseph, of Ridley, to MARTIN, Elizabeth, Miss, of Wilm, at Chester, 6 Nov 1830 (DF 13 Nov 1830)

WEBB, Joshua, see WEBB, Sarah

WEBB, Mary, Mrs., in Wilm, 30 May 1849, aged 73 yrs (DG 5 Jun 1849) see PALMER, Morris W.

WEBB, Ruben, see JONES, Israel D.

WEBB, Sarah, widow of Joshua WEBB, in Sussex Co., 20 Feb 1853, in her 86th yr (DG 18 Mar 1853)

WEBB, Sarah Ann, see PLUMMER, Silas

WEBB, Wm. B., to WHEELER, Rhoda Ann, Miss, all of Sussex Co, 15 Feb 1853, by Rev. McColley (DG 22 Feb 1853)

WEBSTER, Albert, to COOK, Catharine, both of Camden DE, 5 Jun 1850, by Alderman J. Mitchell (DG 11 Jun 1850)

WEBSTER, Dickerson, Esq., at his res. in Appoq. Hd, aged 75 yrs (DG 16 Jan 1849)

WEBSTER, Elizabeth, in Wilm, 24 Feb 1850, aged c 75 yrs (DG 5 Mar 1850)

WEBSTER, Elizabeth, see BIRD, Lewis

WEBSTER, George, see HARTT, Dennis

WEBSTER, Henrietta, at Camden DE, 19 Oct 1849, aged 32 yrs (DG 30 Oct 1849)

WEBSTER, Jane, Mrs., see THOMAS, James

WEBSTER, John A., to PATTERSON, Amelia R., Miss, dau of the late John PATTERSON, Esq., in Wilm, 18 Jun 1852, by the Rev. E. W. Gilbert (DG 18 Jun 1852)

WEBSTER, Richard A., to DERRICK, Eliza, Miss, 30 Sep 1844, at Rocklin, NC Co, DE (DG 25 Oct 1844)

WEBSTER, Sally Ann, see THATCHER, Samuel R.

WEEKS, Elizabeth, see ROWLAND, Jonathan M.

WEEKS, William, an old U. S. Navy pensioner, at the Cecil Co Poorhouse, 11 Jun 1847 (DG 22 Jun 1847)

WEER, James, see WEER, Mary

WEER, Mary, consort of James WEER, Esq., and dau of the late Joseph EDWARDS, Esq., of Phila, at Urieville, 20 Mar 1849, in her 46th yr (DG 3 Apr 1849)

WEIR, Ellen, see WELSH, Hugh

WEIR, John H., to McCOY, Abigail E., both of Wilm, at Chester PA, 23 Dec 1852, by Rev. J. B. Maddux (DG 4 Jan 1853)

WEIR, Mercer, see DERRICKSON, James

WELCH, Daniel, to SMITH, Sarah, Miss, both of Wilm, at Chester PA, 19 Jan 1848, by Rev. L. Stokes (DG 26 Jan 1848)

WELCH, James, to RICHARDS, Ann Eliza, Miss, all of Sussex Co, 20 Dec 1849, by Rev. James Hargis (DG 15 Jan 1850)

WELCH, Rachel Ann, see NEW, David

WELCH, William, Sr., at Mispillion Neck, 20 Oct 1850, aged c 84 yrs (DG 5 Nov 1850)

WELDE, Lydia A., see DERRICK, John A. J.

WELDE, Morris, see WELDE, Thomas James

WELDE, Phebe, see PINKERTON, David

WELDE, Thomas James, inf son of Morris WELDE, 13 Mar 1849 (DG 27 Mar 1849)

WELDE, William, see PINKERTON, David

WELDEN, George, in Brandywine Hd, 5 Nov 1850, in his 56th yr (DG 8 Nov 1850)

WELDEN, Jacob, grocer, of Wilm, to WELDIN, Ann Eliza, Miss, of NC Co, 6 Oct 1842, by Rev. D. Dailey (DG 21 Oct 1842)

WELDF, Ann Eliza, see SPARKS, William D.

WELDIN, ____, child of Lewis WELDIN, 2 Jul 1841, aged 7 mos, leaving 2 g'mothers, 2 g'fathers, 1 gg'mother and 1 gg'father (DG 16 Jul 1841)

WELDIN, ____, son of Joseph WELDIN, residing on Shellpot Hill, c 10 yrs old, thrown from a horse, ndd (DG 19 Jan 1847)

WELDIN, Ann Eliza, see WELDEN. Jacob

WELDIN, Barbara Ann, see McKENNEY, Barbara Ann

WELDIN, Beulah, see WELDIN, George

WELDIN, George, died in Brandywine Hd (DG 3 Dec 1850)

WELDIN, George, late of Brandywine Hd, Beulah WELDIN and William TODD, exec'rs (DG 7 Jan 1851)

WELDIN, Hannah, see FORWOOD, Valentine

WELDIN, J. A., see McKENNEY, Barbara Ann

WELDIN, Jacob B., to CALDWELL, Sarah A., Miss, all of Wilm, 4 Nov 1847, in Wilm by Rev. T. J. Thompson (DG 30 Nov 1847)

WELDIN, John, dec'd, late of Brandywine Hd, notice given by William R. WELDIN, adm'r (DG 1 Apr 1828) see PETTIT, Peter

WELDIN, Lewis, see WELDIN, ____

WELDIN, William R., see WELDIN, John

WELDIN, William R., to STERNE, Sarah, Miss, dau of the late I. STERNE, Esq., all of NC Co, 13 Dec 1821, at Mr. John PLUMLEY's Hotel, by the Rev. Richard D. Hall (DG 18 Dec 1821)

WELDON, Christopher, to DOUGHERTY, Sarah Ann, Miss, of Wilm, 22 Sep 1823, by the Rev. P. Kenny (DG 26 Sep 1823)

WELDON, Isaac, to TUSSEY, Hannah, Miss, both of Brandywine Hd, 16 May 1820, by Rev. S. C. Brinckle (DG 20 May 1820)

WELDON, John A., to MARTIN, Eliza, Miss, 22 May 1817, by Rev. William Pryce (DG 24 May 1817)

WELLS, Ann, see WELLS, Arthur A., Capt.

WELLS, Arthur A., Capt., dec'd, late of the borough of Wilm, notice given by Thomas McDOWELL, for Ann WELLS, adm'x (DG 17 Feb 1824)

WELLS, Edward L., see WELLS, William Hill

WELLS, Harriet C., wife of John W. WELLS, in Wilm, 10 Sep 1852, aged c 28 yrs (DG 14 Sep 1852)

WELLS, John D., see WELLS, William Hill

WELLS, John W., see WELLS, Harriet C.

WELLS, Rachel, see WAPLES, William D. Col.

WELLS, Rebecca, see SEVILL, Nathan T. see CORBIT, John

WELLS, Sarah A., see WOODS, William C. see CLELAND, George D.

WELLS, Sarah E., see CUSTIS, George W. N.

WELLS, Seth, in Wilm, 4 Mar 1847, in his 67th yr (DG 5 Mar 1847)

WELLS, Sophia E., see CLELAND, Thomas R.

WELLS, William H., see WAPLES, William D., Col.

WELLS, William Hill, former U. S.. Senator, at the res. of his son-in-law, Col. William D. WAPLES, in Sussex Co, 11 Mar 1829, na (DG 24 Mar 1829) notice given by John D. WELLS, adm'r, for accounts to be presented to Edward L. WELLS at Georgetown, Sussex Co, DE (DG 8 May 1829)

WELSH, Hugh, to WEIR, Ellen, Mrs. 5 Jun 1817, by Rev. William Pryce (DG 7 Jun 1817)

WELSH, James, of Phila, to NAFF, Elizabeth, Miss, near Wilm, 11 May 1807, by Rev. Mr. Pryce (MU 16 May 1807)

WELSH, John, to ELLIOTT, Peggy, in Brandywine Hd, "lately" (DG 3 Apr 1790)

WELSH, Thomas, to be executed at New Castle, 20 Dec 1833, for the murder of Priscilla THOMAS (DG 17 Dec 1833)

WERKER, Ann, in Wilm, 5 May 1849, aged 72 yrs (DG 8 May 1849)

WERT, Mary Landreth, see CARPENTER, Thomas H.

WEST, Ann, see WEST, David

WEST, Anna E.,

see **WEST**, James B. Anderson

WEST, Charles C., of Phila, to **LAWS**, Lydia, Miss, dau of the late Clement LAWS of Wilm, in Wilm, 19 Aug 1835, by the Mayor (DG 21 Aug 1835)

WEST, David, notice given by Ann WEST, exec'x (FA 25 Feb 1804)

WEST, Edward W., merchant, to **CANNON**, Amanda, Mrs., formerly of Wilm, 18 Oct 1842, in Belleville, Ill, by Rev. William Mitchell (DG 18 Nov 1842)

WEST, Elizabeth, see **LOFLAND**, Purnell

WEST, George, see **WEST**, James B. Anderson

WEST, Harriet, Mrs., wife of John WEST, at Frederica, 1 Dec 1849, na (DG 11 Dec 1849)

WEST, James B. Anderson, son of George and Anna E. WEST, of Bridgeville DE in Frederica, 30 Sep 1853 (DG 21 Oct 1853)

WEST, Jane, dec'd, notice given by Peter HORN, adm'r (DG 1 Sep 1835)

WEST, John, see **WEST**, Harriet

WEST, John M., at Lewes, 7 Oct 1852, aged 32 yrs (DG 19 Oct 1852) see **WEST**, Sally

WEST, Joseph, member of the Society of Friends, at his home in Wilm, 7 May 1790, of the family of West the celebrated painter in England... Discourse by Daniel Offly of Phila (DG 15 May 1790)

WEST, Luke, to **LEVICK**, Mary, Miss, both of Wilm, 18 Jul 1844, at the hotel of Jesse M. Justis, in Marcus Hook PA, by Benjamin F. Johnson, Esq. (30 Jul 1844)

WEST, Mary, see **MARVIN**, Ebenezer

WEST, Richard, see **LOFLAND**, Purnell

WEST, Sally, wife of the late John M. WEST, formerly of Lewes, in Phila, 18 Jan 1853, aged 68 yrs (DG 28 Jan 1853)

WEST, Stockley, to **KING**, Margaret, Miss, both of Sussex Co, 22 Jul 1853 (DG 2 Aug 1853)

WEST, Thomas, late of Wilm. Notice given to bring accounts to Thomas WEST of Concord or to William WEST and Thomas CANBY of Wilm, adm'rs. (PG 17 Nov 1743)

WEST, William, see **WEST**, Thomas

WEST, Wrexham, Esq., merchant of Lewis, DE, to **FINLEY**, Martha G., Miss, dau of the Rev. John FINLEY, of Long Branch, Monmouth Co, NJ, at that place, 21 Jun 1825, by the Rev. James Moore (DG 28 Jun 1825)

WETHERALD, Anna, see **AHRENS**, Adolph

WETHERALD, Jos., see **AHRENS**, Adolph

WETHERELL, Jane, see **BAILY**, James

WEYANT, Peter, see **JONES**, Isaac

WHAN, John, see **HOLLAND**, Thomas

WHANN, John, see **ANDERSON**, Mary see **HOLLAND**, Thomas

WHARTON, George, to **STOUT**, Emeline D., Miss, dau of the late Robert D. STOUT of Georgetown, DE, in Phila, 9 Dec 1829, by Joseph Watson, Esq. (DG 11 Dec 1829)

WHARTON, Hester, Miss, 16 Jun 1851, in her 80th yr (DG 20 Jun 1851)

WHARTON, Hetty Ann, see **HOOK**, Thomas H. Jr.

WHARTON, Job, to **WATSON**, Mary B., Miss, both formerly of Sussex Co DE, near Court House Point, Cecil Co MD, 6 Jan 1852, by Rev. Isaac W. K. Handy (DG 9 Jan 1852)

WHARTON, Nancy, see **WARNER**, William

WHEATMAN, Ellen, Miss, see **SIMPSON**, Thomas

WHEELER, Hester Ann, see **WHEELER**, Lucy Ann

WHEELER, Isaac S., see **WHEELER**, Lucy Ann

WHEELER, James H., to **VAUS**, Rachel, Miss, both of Sussex Co, 27 Jan 1852, by Rev. T. P. McColley (DG 3 Feb 1852)

WHEELER, Lucy Ann, dau of Isaac S. and Hester Ann WHEELER, 6 Aug 1848, aged 4 yrs (DG 15 Aug 1848)

WHEELER, Rhoda Ann, see **WEBB**, Wm. B.

WHEELER, Sally Louisa, see **CONNER**, John

WHELDON, Richard, of Phila, to **McGEE**, Mary, Miss, of Wilm, at Phila, 3 Nov 1825, by the Rev. Mr. Harlan (DG 11 Nov 1825)

WHETSTONE, Samuel, to **EVERSON**,

Hanna, Miss, both of NC Co, 10 Feb 1846, by Rev. M. J. Rhees (DG 13 Feb 1846)

WHILBY, John, to BIDDLE, Eliza, Miss, of Port Penn, DE, at the res. of Elihu JEFFERSON in New Castle, 14 Apr 1835, by the Rev. Mr. Prestman (DG 28 Apr 1835)

WHILDIN, Jane C., see DANFORTH, Joshua N., the Rev.

WHILLDIN, Mary, Mrs., wife of Capt. Wilmon WHILLDIN, in Phila, 10 Sep 1835, aged 54 yrs (DG 15 Sep 1835)

WHILLDIN, Wilmon, Capt., at his res. in Phila, 2 Apr 1852, aged 80 yrs. Owned a number of ships on the Delaware River (DG 6 Apr 1852) see WHILLDIN, Mary, Mrs.

WHISTLER, Eliza, see WHITE, John B.

WHITAKER, Francis A., see CAMPBELL, William

WHITAKER, J. Addison, Rev., of Darby PA, to JANVIER, C. Louisa, Miss, eldest dau of Geo. JANVIER, of Fairview near Newark, at Fairview, 24 May 1853, by the Rev. W. S. F. Graham (DG 31 May 1853)

WHITAKER, Jacob, to POWELL, Elizabeth, Miss, both of Kent Co, 10 May 1842, by Rev. William Connelly (DG 13 May 1842)

WHITAKER, Rachel E., see CAMPBELL, William

WHITAKER, William M., of Phila, to DURBIN, Augusta, eldest dau of the Rev. Dr. DURBIN, 3 Apr 1851, at Trinity ME Ch, by the Rev. J. P. DURBIN (DG 11 Apr 1851)

WHITCRAFT, John G., to WALTER, Asenath A., Miss, both of NC Co, 16 Aug 1848 (DG 1 Sep 1848)

WHITE, Ada, see MERRILL, William, Rev.

WHITE, Alphonso, to LENTNER, Ura, dau of George C. LENTNER, Esq., of Phila, 18 Apr 1844, by Rev. J. L. Grant (DG 23 Apr 1844)

WHITE, Ambrose, see HOLMES, Edmund A.

WHITE, Ann, see WHITE, James Springer

WHITE, Ann Matilda, see HOLMES, Edmund A.

WHITE, Armanica, see LACKLIN, George

WHITE, Benj., of Sussex Co, to HOPKINS, Hetty E., of Phila, in Phila, 2 May 1847, by Rev. Robert Adair (DG 7 May 1847)

WHITE, Elizabeth, see PHILLIPS, George

WHITE, George P., see WHITE, Oliver Laws

WHITE, Hannah, Mrs., consort of Dr. John WHITE and dau of Daniel RODNEY, Esq., at Lewis, 28 Sep 1823, na (DG 6 Oct 1823) see PHELPS, Francis P., M. D. see RICHARDSON, Richard

WHITE, James S., formerly of Wilm, in Baltimore, 13 Jan 1850, in his 57th yr (DG 22 Jan 1850)

WHITE, James Springer, son of Nicholas and Ann WHITE, of Cecil Co MD, 31 Apr 1850, aged 14 yrs 11 mos (DG 10 May 1850)

WHITE, Jane, see PEOPLES, John

WHITE, John, see MAROT, Joseph see MASON, Wm.

WHITE, John, Dr., of Lewistown, to SMITH, Ann P., Mrs., of Milton, at Milton, 11 Aug 1825, by Rev. Benjamin Ogden (DG 19 Aug 1825)

WHITE, John, at the res. of his son-in-law in New Garden, PA, 3 Jul 1826, aged 73 yrs, vol. in the Battle of Germantown in the Rev. War; bur. 4 Jul 1826 at Mr. McCannon's meeting house (DG 11 Jul 1826)

WHITE, John, at the res. of his son-in-law, Parish of Assumption, LA, 24 Jul 1848. Native of St. Georges DE. Born St. George's Chapel, Sussex Co, 23 Jun 1771. Res. of LA for last 20 yrs (DG 28 Jul 1848)

WHITE, John, Dr., see PHELPS, Francis P., M. D. see WHITE, Hannah, Mrs.

WHITE, John B., of Southwark, to WHISTLER, Eliza, Miss, of Wilm, in Phila, 5 Jul 1849 (DG 31 Jul 1849)

WHITE, John D., to VANEMAN, Anna S,, Miss, of Marcus Hook, 6 Oct 1822, by Rev. Samuel Green (DG 11 Oct 1822)

WHITE, John W., to PAYNTER, Ruth C., Miss, both of Sussex DE, 9 Jun 1852 (DG 15 Jun 1852)

WHITE, Joseph, see WHITE, Robert

WHITE, Josiah, see RICHARDSON, Richard

WHITE, Margaret. see GREEN, James

WHITE, Mary A., see MASON, Wm.

WHITE, Mary Ann, see VONHLE, Charles

WHITE, Mary H., Miss,
see RICHARDS, Theodore W.

WHITE, Mary W., see RICE, William W.

WHITE, Nicholas,
see WHITE, James Springer

WHITE, Oliver Laws, youngest son of George P. and Sophia E. WHITE, 14 Jul 1852, in Bridgeville, aged 9 mos 18 days (DG 27 Jul 1852)

WHITE, Rachel, see BURNS, Samuel

WHITE, Robert, son of Joseph WHITE, at the res. of his father in Pumpkin Neck [S of Woodland Beach], 31 Jan 1850, in his 9th yr (DG 5 Feb 1850)

WHITE, Ruth Ann, in Wilm, 28 Aug 1849, in her 36th yr (DG 4 Sep 1849)

WHITE, Sally Ann, see WALKER, Samuel

WHITE, Sophia E., see WHITE, Olier Laws

WHITE, Susan, at the res. of her mother in Mill Creek Hd, 6 Mar 1846, aged 22 yrs (DG 10 Mar 1846)

WHITE, Thomas, of yellow fever (DE 18 Sep 1798)

WHITE, William, to FORREST, Martha, Miss, both of NC Co, 21 Mar 1845, by Rev. S. R. Wynkoop (DG 28 Mar 1845)

WHITE, William H., see YOUNG, Robert

WHITECARFT, Asaneth, wife of John G. WHITECARFT, in Wilm, 8 Jan 1852, aged 28 yrs (DG 20 Jan 1852)

WHITECARFT, John G.,
see WHITECARFT, Asaneth

WHITECRAFT, Isabella C.,
see McDANIELS, Albert G.

WHITEHEAD, Sarah,
see TORBERT, Stephen

WHITELEY, Benjamin, DE Legislator, at Newark, 25 Nov 1829, na (DG 1 Dec 1829) dec'd, late of White Clay Creek Hd, notice given by John L. ROBINSON, atty-in-fact for Eliza WHITELEY, adm'x (DG 22 Jan 1830)
see WHITELEY, Elizabeth Caroline

WHITELEY, Eliza,
see WHITELEY, Benjamin

WHITELEY, Henry, see MACBETH, John

WHITELOCK, Isaac, of Frankfort, PA, to MERROT, Ann, Miss, of Wilm, 14 May 1807, at Friends Meeting House (MU 16 May 1807)

WHITELOCK, James,
see WHITELOCK, Mary

WHITELOCK, James, to TURNER, Elizabeth E., Miss, both of Wilm, in Wilm, 23 Sep 1849, by the Rev. H. E. Atmore (DG 28 Sep 1849)

WHITELOCK, James to BLISS, Mary, Miss, both of Wlm, at Marcus Hook, 11 Nov 1830 (DF 20 Nov 1830)

WHITELOCK, John M., to LANE, Mary Jane, Miss, all of Phila, formerly of Wilm, in Phila, 24 Aug 1851, by the Rev. Joseph Marson (DG 5 Sep 1851)

WHITELOCK, Mary, Mrs. wife of James WHITELOCK, in Wilm, 16 Jul 1840, in her 39th yr (DG 27 Jul 1849)

WHITELY, _____, Col.,
see BRADFORD, Sidney George

WHITELY, Albert, M. D., of Caroline Co MD, to TOWNSEND, Elizabeth Ann, only dau of the late Job TOWNSEND, Esq., of Frederica DE, 6 Oct 1841, at Phila, by Rev. Thos. Brainard (DG 15 Oct 1841)

WHITELY, Benj., Esq., of Newark, to ROBESON, Eliza M., Miss, only dau of the late Alexander ROBESON, Esq., of Newport, at New Castle, 8 Nov 1825, by the Rev. A. K. Russel (DG 11 Nov 1825)

WHITELY, Elizabeth,
see BRADFORD, Elizabeth W.
see BRADFORD, Sidney George

WHITELY, Elizabeth Caroline, dau of the late Benjamin WHITELY, Esq., of Newark, 20 Oct 1846, aged 17 yrs 4 mos, at the res. of Dr. William ELMER in Bridgeton NJ (DG 27 Oct 1846)

WHITELY, Henry, at the res. of his brother, William G. WHITELY, Esq., of pulmonary consumption, 26 Jul 1846, aged 21 yrs (DG 31 Jul 1846)

WHITELY, Henry, Col. late collector of this port, at his res. in Wilm, 2 Oct 1841, aged 57 yrs (DG 8 Oct 1841)
see BRADFORD, Elizabeth W.
see PATTERSON, Alfred, Esq.

WHITELY, Mary Caroline, see PATTERSON, Alfred, Esq.

WHITELY, Mary Kirkwood, Mrs.,
see BOYER, William

WHITELY, William, of Wilm, to ELMER,
Nancy P, dau of the late Dr. William ELMER
of Bridgetown, 13 Jun 1844, by Rev. S.
Beach Jones in Bridgetown NJ
(DG 18 Jun 1844)

WHITELY, William G.,
see WHITELY, Henry

WHITEMAN, Amanda,
see HOLLINGSWORTH, Wm. Penn

WHITEMAN, Benjamin,
see WHITEMAN, Jane

WHITEMAN, Charles W., to HUTTON,
Susanna, Miss, all of Christiana, 24 Feb
1850, by Rev. Mr. Crouch (DG 5 Mar 1850)

WHITEMAN, Jane, consort of Benjamin
WHITEMAN, in Mill Creek Hd, 19 Jan 1851,
aged c 60 yrs (DG 31 Jan 1851)

WHITEMAN, John,
see HALL, Jacob

WHITEMAN, Sarah, see WALKER, Robert

WHITEMAN, Thomas, Esq., of Christiana
DE, to DOWN, Mary G., Miss, of Glasboro
NJ, in Phila, 23 Jan 1851, by Rev. Fingston
Goddard (DG 21 Feb 1851)

WHITEMAN, Wm.,
see HOLLINGSWORTH, Wm. Penn

WHITINGTON, James to REED, Ann, Miss,
both of Kent Co DE, 9 Jan 1851, by the
Rev. Thomas Newman (DG 28 Jan 1851)

WHITTAKER, George, to WILLIAMS,
Rachel, both of Brandywine Hd,
30 Dec 1852, by Rev. J. R. Anderson
(DG 14 Jan 1853)

WHITTINGTON, Ellen R.,
see ROULENSON, John H.

WHITTINGTON, Mary Ann,
see COMLY, Benjamin

WICKERSHAM, Ada Blanche, youngest dau
of Amos H. WICKERSHAM,. at New Castle,
31 Mar 1852, aged 6 mos
(DG 6 Apr 1852)

WICKERSHAM, Amos H.,
see WICKERSHAM, Ada Blanche

WIER, John W., to COOLINN, Alice A.,
Miss, both of Wilm, at Chester, 22 Jul 1849
(DG 31 Jul 1849)

WIER, Joseph, dec'd, late of Brandywine Hd,
notice given by Joshua PYLE, exec'r
(DG 18 Nov 1828)

WIGGINS, Alexander M., of New Castle, to
HILL, Caroline, youngest dau of George
HILL, Esq., of Phila, 23 Aug 1853, by the
Rev. Henry Darling (DG 2 Sep 1853)

WIGGINS, William A., Rev.,
see WIGGINS, William B.

WIGGINS, William B., to RUMFORD,
Matilda, Miss, of Phila, 9 Nov 1843, in
Phila, by Rev. William A. WIGGINS
(DG 13 Nov 1843)

WIGGLESWORTH, Joseph, to
MATTHEWS, Margaret Jane, Miss,
both of Wilm, 27 Jan 1825, by the
Rev. E. W. Gilbert (DG 1 Feb 1825)

WILCOX, Angelina E.,
see SIMMONS, John B.

WILCOX, Ann, see BROOKS, John R.

WILCOX, Hannah Ashbridge,
see COLLINS, George D.

WILCOX, William, see COLLINS, George D.

WILDON, Dirba Ann,
see CLEMENTS, Alexander

WILDS, John, to STAATS, Rebecca, of
Thoroughfare Neck, in Phila, 30 Dec 1852
(DG 14 Jan 1853)

WILDS, Mary, see FARSON, John

WILEY, John, Esq., at New Castle, 28 Dec
1842, aged c 70 yrs (DG 6 Jan 1843)
see WILEY, Olivia
see CANNON, John Wiley

WILEY, Olivia, late wife of John WILEY,
at New Castle, 5 Nov 1842, aged 77 yrs
(DG 23 Dec 1842)
see CANNON, John Wiley

WILEY, Samuel, in Wilm, 31 Jan 1849,
aged 51 yrs (DG 6 Feb 1849)

WILGUS, Imogene, dau of John and Mary
WILGUS, in Phila, 5 Dec 1849, in her 4th yr
(DG 11 Dec 1849)

WILGUS, John, see WILGUS, Imogene

WILGUS, Mary, see WILGUS, Imogene

WILKINS, Ellonra, dau of James and
Margaret WILKINS, 17 May 1852,
aged 9 mos 22 days (DG 25 May 1852)

WILKINS, George W., of Wilm, to VERNON, Lydia, F., Miss, of Chester Co PA, 23 Dec 1852, by the Rev. George Chandler (DG 31 Dec 1852)

WILKINS, Hannah A., see YARD, Robt. B., Rev.

WILKINS, James, see WILKINS, Ellonra

WILKINS, John, to PAYNTER, Rebecca, Miss, all of Wilm, 3 Apr 1846, by Rev. William Urie of Phila (DG 14 Apr 1846)

WILKINS, Margaret, see WILKINS, Ellonra

WILKINSON, James, of Phila, to McCARTNEY, Mary, Miss, of Brandywine DE, 1 May 1851, by the Rev. Mr. Windle (DG 9 May 1851)

WILKINSON, Nathan, to Jane PLUMLY, both of Wilm, at Chester, PA, 31 Dec 1835, by Samuel Smith, Esq. (DG 19 Jan 1836)

WILKINSON, Nathan, to GARRET, Sarah Ann, Miss, dau of the late William GARRET, 20 Aug 1844, at Elk Mills, Cecil Co MD, by Rev. E. Wilson (DG 27 Aug 1844)

WILLARD, James H., to WATSON, Jane, Miss, both of Wilm, 1 Jun 1852 (DG 8 Jun 1852)

WILLET, Allen W., of Baltimore, to EVES, Henrietta, Miss, dau of A. EVES, Esq., of Wilm, 21 Oct 1845, by Rev. S. R. Wynkoop (DG 21 Oct 1845)

WILLET, GIdeon W., to MAGINNES, Ellen B., Miss, all of Milford, 24 Feb 1852, by the Rev. Daniel Godwin (DG 2 Mar 1852)

WILLEY, Absolom, late of White Clay Creek Hd, Eliza WILLEY, adm'x (DG 1 Jul 1853)

WILLEY, Eliza, see WILLEY, Absolom

WILLEY, Ezekiel, to OWENS, Margaret W., all of Sussex Co, 10 Sep 1852, by the Rev. Daniel Goodwin (DG 28 Sep 1852)

WILLEY, Julia Ann, see LOE, William

WILLIAMS, ____, Capt, of Bridgeton NJ, bitten by a mad dog in Brandywine Village, of hydrophobia, ndd, na (DG 6 Aug 1852)

WILLIAMS, Athea, see WILLIAMS, Maria

WILLIAMS, Elizabeth,
see JACOBS, Thomas
see RATTEN, Joseph T.

WILLIAMS, Elizabeth B.,
see BIDDLE, Bobias R.

WILLIAMS, George W.,
see WILLIAMS, Joseph

WILLIAMS, Harding,
see WILLIAMS, Rebecca

WILLIAMS, Henry C. of Bart Twp, Lancaster Co PA, to BOYS, Susanna, Miss, of Wilm, 6 Sep 1852, at the Turk's Head Hotel, West Chester PA, by the Rev. Levi Parmely (DG 10 Sep 1852)

WILLIAMS, Joan J., late of Montgomery Co PA, Thomas WILLIAMS and Jonathan WILLIAMS, adm'rs (DG 25 Dec 1851)

WILLIAMS, Job, dec'd, late of North West Fork Hd, Sussex Co, sale of property by Noble WILLIAMS, exec'r (MU 16 Jan 1808)

WILLIAMS, John, of Phila, to FLEMING, Mary, Miss, of Wilm, 21 Apr 1834, by the Rev. Isaac Pardee (DG 25 Apr 1834)

WILLIAMS, John, to SINNEX, Margaret, Miss, both of NC Co, 27 Mar 1834, by Elder John P. Peckworth (DG 1 Apr 1834)

WILLIAMS, John, late of Appoq. Hd, Joseph WILLIAMS and Nathaniel WILLIAMS, exec'rs (DG 3 Aug 1849)

WILLIAMS, John, late of St. Georges Hd, Jonathan GROVES, adm'r (DG 21 Oct 1851)

WILLIAMS, Jonathan, to CLENDANIEL, Mary A., Miss, 27 Jul 1852, by Rev. Daniel Godwin (DG 10 Aug 1852) see WILLIAMS, Joan J.

WILLIAMS, Joseph,
see BAYARD, Empson
see ANDERSON, James
see WILLIAMS, John

WILLIAMS, Joseph, "an old and respectable farmer", murdered and robbed, allegedly by James ANDERSON and Bayard EMPSOM, negroes, 31 Dec 1850. A long-time res. of NC Co, originally from Susssex Co (DG 3 Jan 1851)

WILLIAMS, Joseph, late of St. Georges Hd. George W. WILLIAMS, adm'r, the widow having renounced (DG 10 Jan 1851)

WILLIAMS, Margaret,
see SAYMAN, Edward

WILLIAMS, Margaret E.,
see DERICKSON, Jehu F.

WILLIAMS, Maria, Miss, oldest dau of Plummer and Athea WILLIAMS, at Gibralter, the res. of her father, 15 Jan 1853, aged c 40 yrs (DG 1 Feb 1853)

WILLIAMS, Mary, see FOWLER, James

WILLIAMS, Mary W., Principal of the Female Department of Middletown Academy, and wife of Payson WILLIAMS, Superintendent of the Institution, of congestive fever, 8 Apr 1845, aged 51 yrs (DG 6 May 1845)

WILLIAMS, Moses, to WALTERS, Maria, both of Del Co PA, 10 Nov 1853, by the Rev. W. H. Burrell (DG 18 Nov 1853)

WILLIAMS, Nathaniel, of NC Co, to FRAME, Elizabeth, Miss, of Sussex Co, 10 Apr 1853, by the Rev. George Hall (DG 13 May 1853) see WILLIAMS, John

WILLIAMS, Noble, see WILLIAMS, Job

WILLIAMS, Payson, see WILLIAMS, Mary W.

WILLIAMS, Peter, Esq.,dec'd, late of Pencader Hd, notice given by Jacob FARIS, exec'r (DG 14 Oct 1825)

WILLIAMS, Peter, dec'd, late of the village of Newport, notice given by Vincent GILPIN and John RICHARDSON , exec'rs (DG 11 Dec 1835)

WILLIAMS, Plummer, see WILLIAMS, Maria

WILLIAMS, Rachel, see WHITTAKER, George

WILLIAMS, Rebecca, widow of the late Capt. Harding WILLIAMS, 11 Dec 1852, aged 84 yrs 11 mos (DG 24 Dec 1852)

WILLIAMS, Robert H., of Phila, to PARKER, Hannah E., Miss, all of Milton, in Milton, 12 Feb 1852, by the Rev. John L. McKim (DG 24 Feb 1852)

WILLIAMS, Samuel, of Chester PA, to ROBINETT, Mary Livinia, Miss, eldest dau of Allan McLane ROBINETT of Wilm, in Phila 12 Feb 1853, by the Rev. Newton Heston (DG 22 Feb 1853)

WILLIAMS, Samuel, to MOOR, Matilda, Miss, both of Wilm, 1 Nov 1847, by Rev. S. R. Wynkoop, (DG 5 Nov 1847)

WILLIAMS, Spencer, Esq., in Milford of nervous fever, 24 Oct 1829, aged 48 yrs (DG 27 Nov 1829)

WILLIAMS, Thomas, see WILLIAMS, Joan J.

WILLIAMS, William, late of Darby. Notice given by John PEARSON, exec'r (PG 13 Jan 1763)

WILLIAMSON, Charles, son of Nicholas G. WILLIAMSON, Esq., postmaster of Wilm, 17 Jul 1828, aged 19 yrs (DG 18 Jul 1828)

WILLIAMSON, Eliza, see WILLIAMSON, John

WILLIAMSON, Elizabeth R., dau of J. F. and Margaret W. WILLIAMSON, at Newark, 23 May 1850, aged 7 wks 2 days (DG 4 Jun 1850)

WILLIAMSON, Elvina, see HOWELL, Courtland

WILLIAMSON, Henry, of Smyrna, drowned at a dock near Walnut St., Phila, ndd, na (DG 22 Jun 1852)

WILLIAMSON, J. F., to REYNOLDS, Margaret W., of Newark, 23 Mar 1847 (DG 2 Apr 1847) see WILLIAMSON, Elizabeth R.

WILLIAMSON, John, of Cecil Co MD, in Wilm at the res. of his dau, Eliza HAGUE, 23 Dec 1847, in his 73rd yr (DG 7 Jan 1848) see BUCKLEY, Adam

WILLIAMSON, John F., see WILLIAMSON, William R.

WILLIAMSON, Margaret, see WILLIAMSON, William R.

WILLIAMSON, Margaret W., see WILLIAMSON, Elizabeth R.

WILLIAMSON, Maria J., see WILLIAMSON, Matilda

WILLIAMSON, Mary S., see GALLAWAY, John W.

WILLIAMSON, Matilda, inf dau of Samuel M. and Maria J. WILLIAMSON, 22 Oct 1846, aged 15 mos 3 days (DG 6 Nov 1846)

WILLIAMSON, Nicholas F., see WILLIAMSON, Vincent L.

WILLIAMSON, Nicholas G., Esq., atty-at-law, to LOCKERMAN, Sarah E., Miss, both of Wilm, 14 May 1807, by Rev. Dr. Reed (MU 16 May 1807) see HOWELL, Courtland

WILLIAMSON, Samuel M., to WOOD, Maria Irvine, Miss, dau of John D. WOOD, Esq., both of Wilm, 21 Oct 1844, in Wilm, by Rev. John Kenneday (DG 26 Nov 1844) see WILLIAMSON, Matilda

WILLIAMSON, Vincent L., U. S. Navy, only

son of Nicholas F. WILLIAMSON of Wilm, na (DG 9 Sep 1834)

WILLIAMSON, William P., to FRENCH, Mary Jane, Miss, both of Wilm, 6 Mar 1848, by Rev. T. J. Thompson (DG 14 Mar 1848)

WILLIAMSON, William R., son of John F. and Margaret WILLIAMSON, at Newark, 11 Jan 1852, aged 20 days (DG 23 Jan 1852)

WILLIER, Henry R., of Balt, to HERON, Mary Elizabeth, Miss, dau of Alexander HERON, Esq., of Balt, 9 Sep 1852 in St. Andrew's Ch, Wilm, by the Rt. Rev. Alfred Lee, Bishop of DE (DG 10 Sep 1852)

WILLING, Charles, see HOPKINSON, Thomas

WILLIS, Jane, see JEFFERIS, Oliver

WILLIS, Jane H, see CLARK, Robert S.

WILLIS, Jonathan, see MARRIOTT, Sarah

WILLIS, Mary, see GAISFORD, George see CROSSMORE, John

WILLIS, Mary Jane, see TAGGART, Joshua

WILLIS, William, to RITCHEY, Ann J., Miss, both of Wilm, at Chester, PA, 26 Apr 1833, by the Rev. John B. Clemson (DG 30 Apr 1833)

WILLISTON, A. M., Mrs., wife of the Rev. Ralph WILLISTON, 7 Jun 1825, na (DG 10 Jun 1825)

WILLISTON, Ralph, the Rev., see WILLISTON, A. M., Mrs.

WILLITS, Elizabeth M., see WILLITS, Horace C.

WILLITS, Horace C., youngest son of Horatio and Elizabeth N. WILLITS, near Middletown, 11 Sep 1853, aged 15 mos (DG 20 Sep 1853)

WILLITS, Horatio, see WILLITS, Horace C.

WILLITTS, Clarence, inf son of Horatio N. and Elizabeth N. WILLITTS, near Middletown, 3 Jun 1851, aged 4 mos (DG 13 Jun 1851)

WILLITTS, Elizabeth N., see WILLITTS, Clarence

WILLITTS, Horatio N., Esq., of Phila, to MERRITT, Elizabeth Noxon, Miss, at White Cottage, the res. of her father, Thomas Schee MERRITT, Esq., near Middletown, 30 Apr 1846, by Rev. Mr. Truman (DG 8 May 1846) see WILLITTS, Clarence

WILLLIAMSON, Nicholas G., Esq., see WILLIAMSON, Charles

WILLS, Henry, to GALIGNA, Mary, Miss, both of Wilm, in "Old Chester", at the house of M. W. DESHONG, 12 Jan 1852, by Frederick Fairlamb, Esq. (DG 20 Jan 1852)

WILMER, Grover Simon, see WILMER, Rebecca Frisby

WILMER, James C., to LONGFELLOW, Sarah C., Miss, both of Head of Sassafras, Kent Co, MD, 2 Jun 1829, by the Rev. John Smith (DG 5 Jun 1829)

WILMER, Rebecca Frisby, Mrs., consort of Grover Simon WILMER, Rector of Trinity Ch, Swedesborough, NJ, 22 Jul 1827, na (DG 31 Jul 1827)

WILSON, ____. Mrs, wife of the Rev. Mr. WILSON, and dau of Andrew GRAY, in Wilm, 12 Jul 1848, aged 30 yrs (DG 18 Jul 1848) see WILSON, Elijah, Rev.

WILSON, ____. Rev., see WILSON, ____

WILSON, Alexander, 22 Oct 1820, aged 27 yrs (DG 24 Oct 1820)

WILSON, Andrew, 29 Jun 1846, at his res. near Newark (DG 14 Jul 1846)

WILSON, Ann, see STOCKLY, Nehemiah

WILSON, Caroline, see STERN, Cyrus

WILSON, Catharine, see ROBERTS, Samuel see GARRET, David

WILSON, D. C., see JORDAN, Thomas J.

WILSON, David, of Cantwell's Bridge, to POOLE, Mary, Miss, 8 May 1823, at the Friends' Meeting in Wilm (DG 13 May 1823)

WILSON, David, see MAHON, Richard

WILSON, David, to LEGG, Frances, Miss, both of Wilm, in Phila, nmd (DG 12 May 1848)

WILSON, David C., see KIRK, William

WILSON, David J., of Pennsville, Chester Co PA, to BOOZER, Leah M., Miss, of Centreville DE, 9 Mar 1845, by Charles Henry Plummer, evangelist

(DG 11 Mar 1845)

WILSON, Eli, to ROBINSON, Eleanor, both of DE, at the house of J. J. THURLOW, 16 May 1833, by Samuel Smith, Esq. (DG 21 May 1833)
see ROBINSON, Mary

WILSON, Elijah, Rev., formerly of Phila, to GRAY, Ann, Miss, dau of Andrew GRAY, Esq., 29 Nov 1842, at Chestnut Hill near Newark, by Rev. Mr. Wynkoop (DG 2 Dec 1842)

WILSON, Eliza A., see JONES, G. W.

WILSON, Elizabeth, see CARY, Samuel

WILSON, George P., to BARTON, Mary Jane, Miss, both of Newark, 11 Dec 1845 by Rev. A. Atwood (DG 15 Dec 1845)

WILSON, George S., of Newark DE, on the Eastern Shore of MD, ndd, in his 27th yr (DG 15 Apr 1853)

WILSON, Georgiana, see STEWART, Richard Thomas

WILSON, Gustavus, at his res. near Leipsic, Kent Co DE, 17 May 1851, aged 71 yrs 1 mo 17 days (DG 6 Jun 1851)

WILSON, Henry, printer, formerly of Wilm, 15 Apr 1842, in Phila (DG 22 Apr 1842)

WILSON, James, to WOOD, Sarah Jane, Miss, both of NC Co, 24 Apr 1845, by Rev. S. R. Wynkoop (DG 25 Apr 1845)
see WILSON, Mary, Mrs.

WILSON, James, to CLENDANIEL, Anna, Miss, both of Kent Co, 25 Apr 1850, by Rev. J. Humphries (DG 3 May 1850)

WILSON, James F. MD, to HUXLEY, Elizabeth, dau of Elisha HUXLEY, Esq., all of Wilm, 8 Apr 1847, in Wilm, by Rev. J. W. McCullough (DG 20 Apr 1847)

WILSON, James P., to BROOKS, Elizabeth, Miss, all of Phila, in Phila, 2 Oct 1849, by the Rev. Mr. Atwood (DG 19 Oct 1849)

WILSON, Jane, dec'd, late of Wilm, notice given by John SELLERS, adm'r (DG 7 Sep 1824)
see JORDAN, Thomas J.
see HUSBANDS, Wm.

WILSON, John, see WILSON, Thomas

WILSON, John E., of Wilm, to KATES, Eliza A., of Salem NJ, in Salem Co NJ, 29 Nov 1846, by Rev. Socrates Townsend (DG 15 Dec 1846)

WILSON, Jonathan, to CARTER, Mary Ann, Miss, both of the Village of Cantwell's Bridge, 5 Feb 1824, by the Rev. Joseph WILSON (DG 10 Feb 1824)

WILSON, Jonathan, of Mill Creek Hd, in Wilm, 26 Feb 1850, aged c 55 yrs (DG 5 Mar 1850)

WILSON, Joseph, Rev.,
see WILSON, Jonathan

WILSON, Lewis, see McALLISTER, Sarah

WILSON, Lewis, to McALLISTER, Sarah, Miss, of Wilm, in Wilm, 11 Mar 1824, by the Rev. E. W. Gilbert (DG 16 Mar 1824)

WILSON, Lewis Alexander, 13 Nov 1843, aged 10 yrs (DG 17 Nov 1843)

WILSON, Manlove D., of NC Co, to FRAME, Mary Y., Miss, eldest dau of George FRAME, late of Sussex Co, 22 Jan 1852, by Rev. T. P. McColley (DG 3 Feb 1852)

WILSON, Margaret J., consort of Samuel J. WILSON, after an illness of 1 week, 20 Sep 1845, aged 30 yrs. Long eulogy, bylined Millsboro (DG 30 Sep 1845)

WILSON, Margaret Jane, Mrs., wife of Col. Thomas WILSON, of Kent Co, MD, dau of Thomas KEAN, late of Wilm, 26 Mar 1826, na; bur. Wilm (DG 5 May 1826)

WILSON, Mary, Mrs., wife of James WILSON, formerly proprietor of the American Watchman, in Wilm, 26 Jun 1835, aged 59 yrs, res. 105 Market St. (DG 26 Jun 1835)
see LOCKWOOD, Richard

WILSON, Mary C., see CORBIT, Daniel

WILSON, Matthew, the Rev. , D. D.,in Lewes, 31 Mar 1790, aged 61 yrs...studied under Francis Allison (DG 3 Apr 1790)

WILSON, Rachel A., see TALEY, Nelson

WILSON, Rebecca,
see GALLAGHER, Charles H.
see HARTLEY, Joseph C.

WILSON, Robert, to LITTLETON, Elizabeth, Miss, both of Dagsboro, 2 Nov 1842, by Rev. J. Bissey (DG 8 Nov 1842)

WILSON, Samuel J.,
see WILSON, Margaret J.

WILSON, Sarah, Mrs.,
see DAVIDSON, Richard C.

WILSON, Sarah, see CHASE, James R.

WILSON, Susan, see GREEN, Charles

WILSON, Theodore J., to SIMPSON, Sarah, Miss, near Bridgeville, 14 Jan 1851, by James Hargis (DG 28 Jan 1851)

WILSON, Thomas, son of Col. John WILSON, at his father's res. in Milton, DE, 2 Feb 1822, in his 18th yr (DG 19 Feb 1822) see WILSON, Margaret Jane, Mrs.

WILSON, Thomas, to BROWN, Mary A., Mrs., 16 Jan 1850, by Rev. J. R. Torbert (DG 12 Feb 1850)

WILSON, Thomas, to CARNAHAN, Mary Jane, Miss, both of New Castle, 13 May 1851, by the Rev. Andrew Manship (DG 20 May 1851)

WILSON, Thompson, dec'd, late of Appoq. Hd, notice given by Isaac P. WALKER, adm'r (DG 25 Jul 1834)

WILSON, William, dec'd, late of Wilm, notice given by Thomas KEAN, adm'r (DE 27 Dec 1798)

WILSON, William, at the res. of his parents near Georgetown, 11 Jul 1853, aged 23 yrs (DG 22 Jul 1853) see CANNON, Henry H.

WILSON, William C., of W Chester, to WALRAVEN, Elizabeth D., of Wilm, 12 Apr 1853, by the Rev. S. R. Wynkoop (DG 15 Apr 1853)

WILSON, William L., see MITCHELL, Thomas

WILSON, William M., of Newark, to MITCHELL, Martha E., Miss, 18 Mar 1852, by the Rev. Mr. S. F. Graham, pres. of Del College (DG 30 Mar 1852)

WILSON, Wilmore, to YOUNG, Ann, Miss, 5 Feb 1824, by the Rev. J. Potts, all of Wilm (DG 13 Feb 1824)

WILTBANK, Alfred S., M.D., to WOLFE, Hannah R., dau of Reece WOLFE, Esq., all of Lewes, 28 Jan 1852, at the res. of her father, by the Rev. J. L. McKiny (DG 13 Feb 1852)

WILTBANK, Cornelius, to ARMSTRONG, Rebecca J., all of Wilm, 5 Dec 1853, by the Rev. J. C. Humphries (DG 30 Dec 1853)

WILTBANK, Isaac, at his res. in Mill Creek Hd, 23 Sep 1844, aged 56 yrs, Leaves a wife and 10 children (DG 8 Oct 1844)

WILTBANK, James T., of hydrocephalus internus, 27 Jan 1825, aged 16 yrs 11 mos 4 days (CI 16 Feb 1825)

WILTBANK, John, see WILTBANK, John Cornelius

WILTBANK, John Cornelius, youngest son of Mr. John WILTBANK and grandson of Samuel PAYNTER, Esq., at the res. of his father near Lewistown, DE, 9 Sep 1829, na (DG 15 Sep 1829)

WILTBANK, John, Esq., at his res. near Lewes, of asthma, 13 Feb 1830, aged 35 yrs (DG 19 Feb 1830)

WILTBANK, John, in Brandywine Hd, 10 Apr 1852, in his 69th yr (DG 16 Apr 1852)

WILTBANK, Samuel, of White Clay Creek Hd, 24 Feb 1833, aged 74 yrs 3 mos 18 days (DG 8 Mar 1833)

WILTBANK, Samuel Rowland, near Lewes, 9 Jul 1853, aged 6 mos 15 days (DG 15 Jul 1853)

WILTBANKS, Augusta, Mrs, in Brandywine Village, 17 Apr 1842, aged 76 yrs (DG 29 Apr 1842)

WINDAL, Martin, to STROUD, Rachel, dau of Thomas STROUD, 10 Jun 1841, by Rev. R. Gerry, all of Wilm (DG 18 Jun 1841)

WINDELL, Jonathan, see DEDFORD, Elizabeth

WINDLE, C. F., Mrs., in New Orleans, dau of Rev. William A. ASHMEAD, of Charleston, SC, and wife of Geo. W. WINDLE of New Orleans, 11 Aug 1853, aged 28 yrs (DG 23 Aug 1853)

WINDLE, Elizabeth, see HOFFECKER, James

WINDLE, Geo. W., see WINDLE, C. F.

WINDLE, J. Martin, in his oyster saloon in the Wilson Buildings, heart disease, 10 May 1847....leaves a wife and several children (DG 14 May 1847)

WINDLE, Lydia A., see KINKEAD, George B.

WINDLE, Sarah, see SHORTS, George

WINGATE, Frances Ann, see BODDY, _____, Mr.

WINGATE, Hester, see NICOLS, James

WINGATE, John A., of Paducah KY, to McFADDON, Mary A., Miss, of Wilm, in Phila, 6 Mar 1851, by the Rev. Mr. Hagany

(DG 11 Mar 1851)

WINGATE, Luranah,
see KNOWLES, Isaac Henry

WINGATE, Thompson, to FOOTE, Eliza, all of Mill Creek Hd, at St James Ch, 25 Mar 1852, by Rev. Mr. Bachelor (DG 27 Apr 1852)

WINKS, Ann, see LEWIS, John

WINSLOW, Elizabeth,
see ALLDERDICE, William Hillary

WINSLOW, George,
see ALLDERDICE, William Hillary

WINTERHALTER, George,
see CURLEY, Henry R.
see WINTERHALTER, Mary

WINTERHALTER, Mary, dau of George WINTERHALTER, in Wilm, at the res. of her father, 28 Jan 1849, na (DG 30 Jan 1849)

WINTERHALTER, Sarah,
see CURLEY, Henry R.

WIRT, Mary E., see WATSON, Jesse A.

WISE, Elizabeth A.,
see COLEMAN, William L.

WISE, Samuel, see WISE, Sarah A.

WISE, Sarah A., widow of Samuel WISE of Dover, in Milford, 11 Jul 1848, in her 59th yr (DG 21 Jul 1848)

WISE, Sarah F., see REDDINGS, John

WITHERSPOON, Thomas,
see SMITH, Ebenezer A., Dr.

WITSEL, Lavinia, see SAUNDERS, John C.

WITSELL, Ann, see HYATT, Francis
see ADAMS, Samuel

WITSELL, Catharine,
see JOHNSON, William

WITSELL, Henry, 18 Jan 1846, aged 73 yrs (DG 23 Jan 1846)

WITSIL, Elizabeth S.,
see WOODWARD, Lewis B.

WITSILL, John E., cedar cooper, in Wilm, 10 Dec 1845, aged c 75 yrs. A venerable and respectable citizen. Leaves a widow and several children (DG 16 Dec 1845)

WITTENBERG, Emma C.,
see MERRITT, Caleb S.

WITTENBERG, F. C.,
see WITTENBERG, Harry McLane

WITTENBERG, Harry McLane, son of F. C. WITTENBERG, in Wilm, 5 Mar 1853, aged 7 yrs 6 mos (DG 8 Mar 1853)

WOELPPER, David,
see CHANDLER, Samuel P.

WOELPPER, Mary Ann,
see CHANDLER, Samuel P.

WOLFE, Daniel, at his res. near Lewis, 22 May 1824, aged 51 yrs (DG 1 Jun 1824)
see WOLFE, John F.
see GRAY, George W.

WOLFE, David R., to LACY, Eleanor, Miss, both of Georgetown, in Georgetown, 18 Dec 1834, by the Rev. Jonathan Torbert (DG 23 Dec 1834)

WOLFE, Eliza B., see PARKER, Eliza B.
see PARKER, John E.

WOLFE, Erasmus D., of Phila, to HAZZARD, Maria, Miss, dau of David HAZZARD, Esq., near Milton, 3 Feb 1829, by the Rev. Wm. Torbert (DG 6 Feb 1829)

WOLFE, Hannah R.,
see WILTBANK, Alfred S.

WOLFE, John F. son of Daniel WOLFE, Esq., of St Georges, 26 Dec 1852, in his 18th yr (DG 31 Dec 1852)

WOLFE, Michael, late of Wilm, in Phila, 17 Jan 1834, aged 70 yrs (DG 21 Jan 1834)

WOLFE, Mary Ann, see GRAY, George W.

WOLFE, Mary E., see CROW, Andrew J.

WOLFE, Reece, see WILTBANK, Alfred S.

WOLFE, William, of Phila, at New Orleans LA, of typhus fever 24 Jul 1852, in his 42nd yr (DG 17 Aug 1852)

WOLFE, William P., to DUNNING, Mary E., both of Sussex Co, in Georgetown, 8 Nov 1852, by the Rev. J. Hough (DG 16 Nov 1852)

WOLFE, Wm. W., Dr.,
see PARKER, Eliza B.

WOLLASTON, Caroline, dau of Joshua and Hester WOLLASTON, in Wilm, of croup, 5 Nov 1851, in her third yr (DG 11 Nov 1851)

WOLLASTON, Emily,
see WOLLASTON, Joshua H.

WOLLASTON, Hester,

see **WOLLASTON**, Caroline

WOLLASTON, Joshua,
see **WOLLASTON**, Caroline

WOLLASTON, Joshua, to **BLAKSHAIRE**, Margaret, Miss, both of Wilm, 4 Mar 1841, by Rev. George W. Carleton (DG 12 Mar 1841) see **WOLLASTON**, Margaret Ann

WOLLASTON, Joshua, to **SLACK**, Esther, Miss, 5 Oct 1843, by Rev. M. J. Rhees, all of Wilm (DG 13 Oct 1843)

WOLLASTON, Joshua H, in Wilm, 21 Jul 1849, in his 27th yr. He had been married but two months to RUMFORD, Emily, dau of Mr. Lewis RUMFORD, formerly of Wilm, subsequently of Chestnut St., Phila, but now of Bucks Co, Pa, and niece to Mr. Atty-general GILPIN (DG 24 Jul 1849)

WOLLASTON, Margaret Ann, wife of Joshua WOLLASTON, 18 Mar 1842, aged 23 yrs (DG 1 Apr 1842)

WOLLASTON, Philena, late wife of Samuel WOLLASTON, in Wilm, 30 Dec 1842, aged 50 yrs (DG 6 Jan 1843)

WOLLASTON, Samuel, see **WOLLASTON**, Philena

WOLLASTON, William, to **DORSEY**, Mary Agnes, both of Cantwell's Bridge, 19 Jan 1851 (DG 10 Feb 1852)

WOOD, Elizabeth, wife of John M. WOOD, Esq., in St. Georges Hd, on the 80th (sic) ult, aged 40 yrs (DG 10 Apr 1849)

WOOD, Jane, Mrs., see **RAMEAU**, John

WOOD, John, to **SMITH**, Sarah Ann, in Phila, 24 Feb 1853, by the Rev. Mr. Miller (DG 1 Mar 1853)

WOOD, John D., Esq., see **WILLIAMSON**, Samuel M.

WOOD, John M., see **WOOD**, Elizabeth

WOOD, Maria Irvine, see **WILLIAMSON**, Samuel M.

WOOD, Samuel, Rev., in Wilm, 30 Oct 1851, aged c 84 yrs (DG 4 Nov 1851)

WOOD, Sarah Jane, see **WILSON**, James

WOOD, W. Dewees, to **GILPIN**, Rosalind H., dau of R. B. GILPIN, Esq., 16 Mar 1848, by Rev. S. R. Wynkoop (DG 21 Mar 1848)

WOOD, William, dec'd, late of Brandywine Hd, notice given by James GRUBB, adm'r (DS 16 Sep 1812)

WOODALL, Alfred A., youngest son of William and Sarah WOODALL, late of Prince Georges Co MD, in Balt, 22 Aug 1849, aged 12 yrs (DG 28 Aug 1849)

WOODALL, Frances, see **RALPH**, John E.

WOODALL, John, suicide by hanging, no known cause, in Smyrna. Leaves a wife and 7 children (DG 21 Jun 1844) see **RALPH**, John E.

WOODALL, Lizzy, see **HARTING**, Cyrus

WOODALL, Mary D., see **ALLEN**, Thomas M.

WOODALL, Sarah, see **WOODALL**, Alfred A.

WOODALL, Sarah A., see **RAUGHLEY**, James

WOODALL, William, see **WOODALL**, Alfred A.

WOODCOCK, Ann C., see **MYNICH**, Daniel

WOODLAND, Mary Emma, see **BAILY**, Edward T.

WOODLEY, Mary A., see **POTTER**, Morgan

WOODROW, James, to **DANBY**, Sarah Ann, Miss, both of Wilm, 30 Nov 1847, by Rev. J. Walker (DG 14 Dec 1847)

WOODS, Isaac Jr., to **VANDERGRIFT**, Sarah B., Miss, dau of Abraham VANDERGRIFT, all of NC Co, near McDonough DE, 12 Jan 1852, by Rev. Isaac W. K. Handy (DG 20 Jan 1852)

WOODS, James, of NC Co, to **BROWN**, Jane, Miss, of Wilm, 8 Aug 1851, in Trinity Chapel, by the Rector, Rev. E. M. Van Dusen (DG 12 Aug 1851)

WOODS, James, of NC Co, to **HAYS**, Susan, Miss, of Phila Co PA, 17 Oct 1853 (DG 6 Dec 1853)

WOODS, Jane, Mrs. native of DE, in Baltimore, 29 Dec 1822, in her 73rd yr (DG 24 Jan 1823)

WOODS, John, to **FRAZER**, Elizabeth V., Miss, both of NC Co, at the Red Lion, 6 Mar 1827, by the Rev. Mr. Wilson (DG 13 Mar 1827)

WOODS, John, Esq., to **COURSE**, Rebecca E., Miss, 14 Jul 1829, by the Rev. E. W. Gilbert, all of New Castle, DE

(DG 17 Jul 1829)

WOODS, Mary Ann, see ALSTON, Joab S.

WOODS, Mary Maria,
see TOWNSEND, Mary Maria

WOODS, Rebecca,
see TOWNSEND, Mary Maria

WOODS, Samuel P., to CLEAVELAND, Susan H., Miss, in MO, 9 Mar 1852, by the Rev. William Gray (DG 13 Apr 1852)

WOODS, Sarah Ann, late of St Georges Hd, Samuel JEFFERSON, adm'r (DG 23 Dec 1853)

WOODS, Thomas,
see TOWNSEND, Mary Maria

WOODS, William C., of Wilm, to WELLS, Sarah A., of Elkton MD, 10 Feb 1846, by Rev. Mr. McIntyre (DG 20 Feb 1846)

WOODWALL, Allen, of Wilm, to FRARY, Emily Eliza, Miss, of Cayuga Co, NY, in St. Matthew's Episc Ch, Cayuga Co, by the Rev. Walter Myrault (DG 16 Oct 1849)

WOODWARD, Abnor, in Mill Creek Hd, 20 Apr 1846, aged 82 yrs (DG 28 Apr 1846)

WOODWARD, Elizabeth B.,
see PRICE, John

WOODWARD, Hannah,
see WOODWARD, William

WOODWARD, Isaac W.,
see WOODWARD, William

WOODWARD, Leonard, to YOUNG, Elizabeth J., Miss, 14 Dec 1826, by the Rev. John P. Peckworth, all of Wilm (DG 19 Dec 1826)

WOODWARD, Lewis B., of W. Chester, PA, to WITSIL, Elizabeth S., Miss, of Wilm, in Wilm, 26 Apr 1849, by Rt. Rev. A. Lee (DG 1 May 1849)

WOODWARD, Mary Elizabeth,
see BRACKEN, William

WOODWARD, Rebecca,
see WORRELL, Joseph

WOODWARD, Samuel, to BANE, Mary, 23 Feb 1741, by Nicholas J. Williamson, Mayor, all of Wilm (DG 26 Feb 1841)

WOODWARD, William, to BROWN, Hannah, Miss, 6 Dec 1807, by Rev. Mr. Pryce (MU 12 Dec 1807)

WOODWARD, William, son of Isaac W. and Hannah WOODWARD, 2 Aug 1849, aged 11 mos (DG 14 Aug 1849)

WOOLASTON, John, of Wilm, to WARNER, Susan Miss, dau of William WARNER, Esq., in Phila, 28 Mar 1821, by the Rev. J. J. Janeway (DG 3 Apr 1821)

WOOLFORD, Hiram R. G., youngest son of Rev. S. W. WOOLFORD, Pastor of the Welsh Tract Baptist Ch, 27 Nov 1827, in his 3rd yr (DG 30 Nov 1827)

WOOLFORD, S. W., Rev.,
see WOOLFORD, Hiram B. G.

WOOLSON, John L., of New Castle, to KELLEY, Mary E., of Chester PA, 15 Aug 1850, by Rev. J. Castle (DG 27 Aug 1850)

WOOLSON, William R., to DAVIS, Ruth Hannah, Miss, in Phila 15 Feb 1853, by the Rev. Mr. Ryan (DG 22 Feb 1853)

WOOLSTON, E. S. Mrs.,
see DUNCAN, J. W.

WOOLSTON, Jeremiah,
see WOOLSTON, John

WOOLSTON, John, dec'd, notice given by Jeremiah WOOLSTON and Samuel WOOLSTON (AW 14 Apr 1826)

WOOLSTON, Samuel,
see WOOLSTON, John

WOOLWORTH, Richard C., to GILPIN, Abigail W., Miss, dau of Edward GILPIN, 3 Sep 1820 (DG 5 Sep 1820)

WOOTEN, Edward,
see PAYNTER, Samuel R.

WOOTEN, Martha E.,
see DELANEY, Levin W.

WOOTEN, Sarah E., see DILL, Lemuel

WOOTON, Edward, Esq., to ROBINSON, Mary, Miss, dau of Judge ROBINSON of Georgetown, at Seaford, 11 Jun 1833, by the Rev. Mr. Kingsbury of the Episcopal Ch (DG 16 Jun 1833)

WOOTREST, Perry, to SHORT, Sarah, Miss, both of Milford DE, in Phila, 30 Sep 1847, by Rev. Mr. Taylor (DG 12 Nov 1847)

WOOTSTON, Anna W.,
see CRAIGE, William S.

WOOTTERS, Abner E., to SIPPLE, Elizabeth Ann, both of Kent Co, 3 Mar 1853 (DG 29 Mar 1853)

WORK, Mary Ann McBeth, late wife of Rev. W. R. WORK of Newark DE, 2 Feb 1845, aged 25 yrs (DG 11 Feb 1845)

WORK, W. R., Rev.,
see WORK, Mary Ann McBeth

WORRALL, Stephen, of Kennett, to BURTON, Mary Jane, of DE, 8 Feb 1849. (DG 2 Mar 1849)

WORRELL, Edward,
see COLLINS, James
see WORRELL, George W.
see WORRELL, Rebecca
see ALRICHS, John, Dr.
see SMITH, William B.

WORRELL, Edward, Dr.,
see WORRELL, Rodney

WORRELL, Edward, only son of Dr. Edward and Louisa WORRELL, at Port Penn, after an illness of 5 hrs, 28 Sep 1846, aged 5 yrs (DG 2 Oct 1846)

WORRELL, Elizabeth Nicosho,
see ALRICHS, John, Dr.

WORRELL, George W., Capt., of the Brig Orient, son of Edward WORRELL, Esq., at sea, 9 Jul 1828, aged c 35 yrs, Mason(ic) member (DG 22 Jul 1828)

WORRELL, Joseph to WOODWARD, Rebecca, Miss, both of NC Co, 15 Sep 1853, by the Rev. S. R. Wynkoop (DG 20 Sep 1853)

WORRELL, Louisa,
see WORRELL, Edward

WORRELL, Louisa,
see WORRELL, Rodney

WORRELL, Priscilla B.,
see SMITH, William B.

WORRELL, Rebecca, Mrs. consort of the late Edward WORRELL, Esq., and dau of the late Col. Allen McLANE, near Phila, of dysentery, 1 Sep 1851, aged 73 yrs (DG 5 Sep 1851)

WORRELL, Rodney, only son and youngest child of Dr. Edward and Louisa WORRELL, aged 3 yrs 4 mos 23 days, in Delaware City, 1 Jan 1851 (DG 7 Jan 1851)

WORTH, Emmor, in Wilm, at the house of John PATTERSON, Esq., 18 May 1824, aged 14 yrs (DG 21 May 1824)

WORTHINGTON, Seth, at Kennett Sq, 12 Oct 1849, aged c 27 yrs (DG 30 Oct 1849)

WOTTEN, Isaac, to GRAY, Elizabeth C., Miss, both of Sussex Co, 16 Jul 1853, by the Rev. J. R. Torbert (DG 26 Jul 1853)

WOTTRESS. Sarah, Elizabeth,
see PIERSON, Robert L.

WRENSHALL, John F.,
see WRENSHALL, Nancy, Mrs.

WRENSHALL, Nancy, Mrs., wife of John F, WRENSHALL of Pittsburg, PA, and dau of Dr. George STEVENSON of Wilm, at Carlisle, PA, 24 Aug 1825, na (DG 30 Aug 1825)

WRGHT, James, see WRIGHT, Hellen

WRIGHT, Charles, son of Capt. Charles and Elizabeth WRIGHT, at Laurence, near Seaford, 19 Jul 1850, aged 1 yr 7 mos 18 days (DG 30 Jul 1850)

WRIGHT, Crispus S., of Wilm, to LANE, Ruth Ann, Miss, of Springville, Chester Co PA, 5 Jul 1852, by the Rev. J. B. Knipe (DG 23 Jul 1852)

WRIGHT, Duffas to RITER, Sarah Jane, Miss, both of Wilm, in Phila, 23 Mar 1846, by Rev. Mr. Chambers (DG 24 Mar 1846)

WRIGHT, Elizabeth, see WRIGHT, Charles

WRIGHT, Emma J., wife of Thos. C. WRIGHT, in Phila, 31 Jul 1853, na (DG 5 Aug 1853)

WRIGHT, Ezekiel, a near relative of Samuel HARKER, editor of the Del Gaz, 7 Nov 1823 (DG 11 Nov 1823)

WRIGHT, Harriet P., see FIELDS, Daniel

WRIGHT, Hellen, consort of Mr. James WRIGHT, in Wilm, 7 Dec 1828, na (DG 9 Dec 1828)

WRIGHT, James R., to HUNTER, Elizabeth R., Miss, in Wilm, 3 Jan 1848, by Rev. T. J. Thompson (DG 7 Jan 1848)

WRIGHT, Josephine,
see BULLOCK, George

WRIGHT, Lydiamira,
see JOHNSON, Nathan

WRIGHT, Margaret A.,
see HATSEL, John V.

WRIGHT, Mary Ann, see BARNARE, Moses

WRIGHT, Mary G., late wife of Dr. R. N. WRIGHT and dau of Rev. Dr. GILBERT, in Newark, 12 Jun 1845 (DG 13 Jun 1845)

WRIGHT, R. N., Dr.,
see WRIGHT, Mary G.

WRIGHT, Robert, to HARGADINE, Julia Ann, both of Kent Co, 3 Feb 1842 by Rev. Levi Jester (DG 11 Feb 1842)

WRIGHT, Samuel, to RILLEY, Ellen, Miss, both of NC Co, 21 Aug 1852, by Rev. F. Hodgson (DG 31 Aug 1852)

WRIGHT, Susan Barlow,
see BARLOW, John

WRIGHT, Thos. C., see WRIGHT, Emma J.

WRIGHT, W. Roderick, to HAVILAND, Emma, youngest dau of the late Joseph HAVILAND, all of Phila, at Grace Ch, 12 Mar 1849 by Rev. William Suddard (DG 16 Mar 1849)

WRIGHT, W. W., merchant of Phila, to DAVIS, Eliza, Mrs., of Dover, at Dover, 28 July 1822 (DG 9 Aug 1822)

WRIGHT, William, see BARLOW, John
see COLE, Ann

WRIT, John W., Dr., to MERCER, Margaret S., Mrs., of Cecil Co MD, in Wilm, 1 Aug 1848, by Rev. Mr. Wiley (DG 15 Aug 1848)

WYATT, Eliza Ann, see SHIMP, David S.

WYNNE, Peter, to JONES, H. Sophia, Miss, both of Smyrna, 10 Mar 1850, by Rev. John A. Roche (DG 19 Mar 1850)

YARD, Robt. B. Rev., of Somerville NJ, to WILKINS, Hannah A., of Mt. Holly, in Mt. Holly, 6 Oct 1851, by Rev. Dr. Holdich (DG 21 Oct 1851)

YARNALL, Benj., in the country, of yellow fever (DE 18 Sep 1798) Benjamin, blacksmith, of Wilm, notice given by Jonathan YARNALL, adm'r (DE 10 Dec 1798)

YARNALL, Esther, notice given by William WARNER, exec'r (MU 18 Feb 1809)

YARNALL, Holton, of Mill Creek Hd, 28 Jan 1829, na. He left a widow and 7 children (DG 6 Feb 1829)

YARNALL, Jonathan,
see YARNALL, Benj.

YARNALL, Peter, an eminent preacher among the Quakers, at Phila (DE 26 Feb 1798)

YARNALL, Sarah, see ROBINSON, John P.

YARNALL, Susan, see BRACKEN, Henry

YATES, Charles, of Wilm, to BOWERS, Catharine Ann, Miss, of West Chester PA, 16 May 1850, in West Chester, by Rev. A. S. Patton (DG 28 May 1850)

YATES, Charles, tobacconist, 17 May 1824, na (DG 18 May1824)

YATES, John, see YATES, Williamina

YATES, Kessiah,
see ROBINETT, David, Jr.,

YATES, Letitia, see SAXON, Isaac G.

YATES, Margaret C.,
see CHANDLER, Alexander

YATES, Williamina, Mrs, relict of the late John YATES, 5 Jan 1852, on her 60th yr (DG 13 Jan 1852)

YEATES, George, late of NC Co. Notice given by Mary YEATES and John YEATES, adm'rs. (PG 1 Oct 1747) Property sale by adm'rs (PG 14 Apr 1748)

YEATES, John, see YEATES, George

YEATES, Letitia D., see HORN, William M.

YEATES, Mary, see YEATES, George

YEATMAN, Thomas J., 18 Aug 1851, aged 54 yrs, at his res. in Mill Creek Hd,. Had a wife and children (DG 29 Aug 1851)

YEATS, Abijah, to NICHOLESS, Emma, Miss, 25 Dec 1812, by Rev. Daniel Dodge (DS 30 Dec 1812)

YOCUM, Henry A., of Kingsessing, PA, to VIRDEN, Emma Matilda, Miss, formerly of Wilm, at Hestonville, 4 Apr 1847, by Rev. J. J. Baker (DG 4 Jun 1847)

YOUNG, _____, Maj. Gen.,
see YOUNG, _____, Mrs.

YOUNG, _____, Mrs, late wife of Maj. Gen. YOUNG, and dau of the Hon. Thomas CLAYTON, 3 Jun 1847, in New Castle (DG 8 Jun 1847)

YOUNG, Ann, see WILSON, Wilmore

YOUNG, Amy (colored), burned to death on a sand boat, intoxicated, 1 Jan 1846 (DG 6 Jan 1846)

YOUNG Catharine Row, dau of Hetty D. B. and the late J. Evans YOUNG, in Phila, 21 Dec 1852, in her 5th yr (DG 4 Jan 1853)

YOUNG, Elizabeth J.,
see WOODWARD, Leonard

YOUNG, Fannie C., see SHERMA, O. F.

YOUNG, Fanny L., see McFARLIN, Thomas

YOUNG, Hetty D. B.,
see YOUNG, Catharine Row

YOUNG, Hiram, drowned in the Brandywine (DG 13 Mar 1846)

YOUNG, J. Evans, of Rockland, DE, to SHEWELL, Esther D. B. dau of Thomas SHEWELL, Esq., of Phila, in Phila, 15 Oct 1833, by Rev. Dr. Brantley (DG 18 Oct 1833)

YOUNG, J. Evans, late U. S. Commercial Agent in Curacao, formerly of Rockland, in Curacao, of typhus fever, 11 Jul 1850, in his 41st yr (DG 20 Aug 1850)
see YOUNG, Catharine Row

YOUNG, Jean Stroud,
see WARNER, Joseph T.

YOUNG, Margaretta M.,
see HAMILTON, Thomas, the Rev.

YOUNG, Martha B., see JOHNSON, C. P.

YOUNG, Rachel, in Wilm, 30 Jan 1847 (DG 5 Feb 1847)

YOUNG, Rebecca, see DAVIS, James

YOUNG, Robert, Esq., at his res. near Frederica, 23 Apr 1825, aged 23 yrs (DG 3 May 1825)

YOUNG, Robert, in Wilm, 11 Jan 1853, aged c 57 yrs (DG 14 Jan 1853) late of Wilm Hd, William H. WHITE and Samuel P. JACKSON, adm'rs (DG 4 Feb 1853)

YOUNG, Robert P., of Cape May Co NJ, to REILY, Mary A., Miss, of Wilm, both mutes, at the house of Prof. Pyatt of the Deaf and Dumb Asylum of Phila, 23 Dec 1850, by Rev. A. D. Gillette (DG 31 Dec 1850)

YOUNG, Samuel B., in Phila, 9 Oct 1852, in his 45th yr (DG 12 Oct 1852)

YOUNG, Sarah, see ENGLAND, James

YOUNG, Sarah A.,
see JACKSON, Samuel P.

YOUNG, Stephen Decatur, to BLACK, Jane, all of DE, 8 Jun 1848, by Rev. A. D. Gillette (DG 30 Jun 1848)

YOUNG, Susanna, see RONEY, John

YOUNG, Thomas, of Chester Co, PA, to CARNAHAN, Margaret, Mrs., of Wilm,
in Wilm, 9 Mar 1824, by the Rev. E. W. Gilbert (DG 16 Mar 1824)
see COLE, Thomas,
see GROVES, John
see JOHNSON, C. P.

YOUNG, Thomas T., to NORRIS, Lydia Ann, Miss, 21 Feb 1828, by Elder John P. Peckworth, all of Wilm (DG 7 Mar 1828)

YOUNG, William, formerly of Rockland, DE, in Phila, 12 May 1829, aged 74 yrs (DG 15 May 1829)

YOUNG, William, see WARNER, Joseph T.

YOUNG, William, Esq.,
see HAMILTON, Thomas, the Rev.

YOUNG, William H., to FARR, Sarah H., Miss, 23 Nov 1826, by the Rev. E. W. Gilbert, all of Wilm (DG 28 Nov 1826)

YOUNG, Zeriah P.,
see BACON, James W.

YOUNKER, Hannah, Mrs, at the house of her son-in-law, Enoch RHODES, 26 Jan 1846, aged 88 yrs. She was born in Evesham NJ, and moved here with her dau in 1811 (DG 30 Jan 1846)

ZANE, Esther S., see GOODMAN, Esther S.

ZANE, Jesse S., see BONSALL, Stephen

ZANE, Jesse Z.,
see GOODMAN, Esther S.

ZANE, Mary E., see BONSALL, Stephen

ZEBLEY, _____, Mrs.,
see MONAHAN, Michael

ZEBLEY, J. F. see DEWEESE, Daniel

ZEBLEY, John, to RICKARDS, Hannah H., Miss, in Phila, 2 Sep 1847, by Rev. Dr. Kennaday (DG 28 Sep 1847)

ZEBLEY, John F., see GOODALL, Sarah

ZEBLEY, Jonathan, see ZEBLEY, Mary

ZEBLEY, Margaret,
see HAYES, Geo. Washington

ZEBLEY, Mary, wife of Jonathan ZEBLEY, in Brandywine Village, 30 Aug 1853, aged c 42 yrs (DG 2 Sep 1853)
see CARTER, Amos
see NOBLE, William

ZIMMERMAN, Charles W., of Phila, to GARRETSON, Susanna M, of Wilm, 17 Dec 1844, by Rev. J. S. Inskip (DG 20 Dec 1844)

MINISTERS FROM VOL 3, DGAN, 1729-1853

Name (Rev., or var)	Dates	Place(s)
Adair, Mr.	1829-41	Wilm, B'wine
Adams, H.	1835, 6	Wilm
Rector Trinity Ch, Episc.		
Allen, Mr.	1834	Kent Co
Allen, Thomas G.	1847	Wilm
Anderson, J. R.	1850-53	NC Co, .
Asay, E. G.	1848	Kent Co
Aspril, James	1850, 53	Kent
Aspril, Joseph	1853	NC Co
Atkins, Isaac T.	1853	Sussex Co
Atmore, H. E.	1849	Wilm
Atwood, Anthony	1845-52	NC Co
Bachelor, Mr.	1852	NCCo
James Ch, Mill Creek Hd Episc.		
Baker, John J.	1847	Newark
Barns, William	1833	Kent Co
Barr, Joseph	1849, 52	Milford, Newark
Barr, Mr.	1798	Christiana Bridge
Bartine, Daniel W.	1853	Dover?
Barton, Thomas	1847-51	NC Co
Bell, Mr.	1823	Newark
Bell, John	1847,8	Kent Co, Camden
Billop, Thomas F.	1849-52	NC Co
Rector of Immanuel Ch, New Castle		
Bissey, Jonas	1841-43	Georgetown
Boyer, Mr	1797	Dover
Brown, Joseph T.	1853	Newark(Meth.)
Brinckle, S. C.	1820	B'wine Hd
Bruen, E. B.	1852	Milford
Burrows, Mr.	1846	Wilm
Burton, John	1810-21	NC Co
Canby, J.	1823	Kent Co
Carleton, George W.	1841	Wilm
Carpenter, P.	1851	Smyrna
Carrow, G. D.	1850-53	Kent and NC Co
Carvel, Mr.	1834	B'wine
Castle, Joseph	184t-50	Wilm
St. Paul's M. E. Ch		
Chambers, Corry	1836-42	Sussex, NC Cos
Chandler, George	1849-53	Kent, NC Cos
Clarkson, Mr.	1792-98	Wilm
Clemson, John B.	1845-51	NC, Kent Cos.
Coit, G. H.	1829	Wilm
Cole, Thomas	1849	Wilm?
Upper Presbyterian Ch		
Coleman, J. M.	1848	Wilm
Collom, J. G.	1851, 2	NC Co
Connelly, Peirce	1827	Wilm
Connelly, William	1842, 3	Kent Co
Conwill, John J.	1835	Milton
Cooley, Wm. C.	1853	Christiana Hd
Coombe, Pennel	1850	NC Co
Cooper, Mr.	1810	Wilm, Meth.
Cooper, E.	1833	Wilm
Cooper, Ignatius	1842,3	B'ywine Hd
Cooper, William	1846-51	Wilm
Cosgrave, Mr.	1852	Wilm
Cox, P. F.	1852	Kent Co
Cronch, D.	1824	NC Co, Rich Neck
Cullen, John	1847	N.Castle, R.Cath.
Cunningham, James	1848	Cantwell's Bridge
Dale, Mr.	1825	Dover
Daley, Mr.	1830	NC Co
Danforth, Joshua N.	1826, 8	New Castle
Davis, William	1846, 8	Sussex Co
Davis, Zedekiah	1823, 6	Kent Co
Decker, Mr.	1841	Wilm
Dodge, Daniel	1809-12	NC Co
Dodge, William	1809	Wilm
Dorsey, Dr.	1846	Wilm St. Andrew's
Douglass, O.	1846	Wilm
Durbin, J. P., Dr.	1851	?Trinity M. E. Ch
Durborah, John	1823-35	Kent Co
Durborrow, George	1849	Wilm, Grace Meth.
Eacres, Mr.	1853	Wilm

Name (Rev., or var)	Dates	Place(s)
Elliott, W. H.	1850	NC Co
Ely, Ezra Stiles	1850	Del.
Evans, French S.	1829	Wilm
Fernley, T. A.	1851	NC Co
Fields, A. C.	1851	Newark
Flannery, J.	1848-51	Kent Co
Foot(e), George	1823-50	NC Co
Fort, George	1846	NC Co
Franklin, Walter B.or E.	1844,45	Lewes, Newark
Fries, Henry C.	1841, 47	Laurel
Furness, Dr.	1850	NC Co
Garey, R.	1842	Newport
Gaskill, Joseph	1850	Kent Co
Gayley, S. M.	1841-51	Wilm, B'wine
Gerry, Robert	1841-53	NC Co
Gilbert, E. W.	1821-52	NC Co
Gillette, A. D.	1841	Port Penn
Gilroy, H. E.	1851-3	Kent, NC Cos
Go(o)dwin, Daniel	1850, 2	Kent Co
Graham, W. S. F.	1852,3	nr Newark
Fairview, Pres of Del. College		
Graham, Emory	1853	Kent Co
Granger, Arthur	1835	NC Co
Grant, John M.or L.	1846, 8	Wilm
Greene, Samuel R.	1823	NC Co
Greer, Mr	1807	Christiana Hd
Grey, Mr.	1849	NC Co, App. Hd
Griffin, Thomas	1822	Wilm
Hagany, John	1821-9	NC Co
Hall, George	1850-53	Sussex Co
Hall, Richard D.	1821, 2	NC Co
Hallowell, Mr.	1848	New Castle
Hamilton, J.	1835-50	NC Co
Handy, Isaac W. K.	1849-52	NC Co
Hard, A. B.	1849	Wilm
Hare, S. G.	1851, 2	NC Co
Hargis, James	1850	Sussex Co
Harrold, H. H.	1851	Middletown
Rector, St. Anne's Ch		
Hedges, C. S.	1834	Wilm
Henry, John	1849	Middletown
Hera, E. R.	1846	Dover
Heston, Newton	1850	Wilm
Hickman, Wm.	1821, 7	Sussex Co
Higbee, Daniel	1822-35	Sussex, Kent Cos
Higgins, Solomon	1827-52	NC Co, Dover
Hodgson, F. A.	1851-3	Wilm, St. Paul's ME
Hogarth, William	1842-5	NC Co
Holcomb, Mr.	1821	Wilm
Holdick, Mr.	1824	New Castle
Hough, John	1852, 3	Sussex Co
Houston, James L.	1842	Smyrna
Howe, James	1841-51	NC Co
Humphries, J	1846, 53	NC Co, PA
Ide, G. B.	1851	Wilm?
Inskip, J. S.	1844	Wilm
Jaquett, Joseph	1846	Wilm
Janeway, Mr.	1847	Wilm
Jefferson, Ephraim	1833	Smyrna
Jester, Daniel	1829	Milton
Jester, Levi	1842	Kent Co
Johns, A.	1852, 3	Sussex Co, Milton
Johnson, Thomas J.	1850	Del. City
Johnstone, Mr.	1797	Dover
Jones, John	1828	Milford
Karsner, Mr.	1848	Frederica
Keene, Marcellus E.	1849	Wilm
Keene, Samuel	1798	Dover
Kennaday, John	1842, 8	Wilm DD
Kennard, Edward	1844-50	NC Co
Kennedy, G. W.	1852	Milford
Kenney, Mr	1817	Red Clay Creek
Kenny, Patrick, Dr	1823, 4	NC Co
Kingsbury,	1833	Seaford, Episc.
Lamden, Mr.	1818	Camden

Name (Rev., or var)	Dates	Place(s)
Latta, James	1829-48	Wilm
Latta, John E.	1821, 2	NC Co
Kennedy, John H.	1827	New Castle
Crescentville		
Latte,	1812	New Castle
Lattomus, James	1804	Appoq. Hd
Lawrenson, L.	1821, 2	NC Co
Leach, S.	1841	Wilm
Lee, Alfred (Bishop)	1842-53	DE
St. Andrew's Ch, Wilm		
Lewis, Daniel D.	1824, 5	Wilm
Lewis, Joseph J.	1849	Kent Co
Long, John	1844, 5	Laurel, Seaford
St. Luke's Ch, Episc.		
Long, J. D.	1850	Del. City
Lord, W.	1849	Wilm
Love, Thomas	1841-51	Mill Crk Hd, NC Co
Lowe, Mr.	1842	NC Co
Lybrand, G. W.	1833	NC Co
Maddux, J. B.	1853	Wilm, Newark?
Manlove, John	1842	Dover
Mansfield, Pinor	1846-53	Kent Co
Manship, Andrew	1849-52	NC Co
Mason, Joseph	1846	Kent Co
May, E. J.	1852	Del. City
Maybin, A. W.	1853	NC Co
McCombe, Lawrence	1826-52	Wilm
McColley, T. P.	1849-53	Sussex, Kent Cos
McCullough, J. W.	1836-47	NC Co, Wilm
Trinity ch		
McIntire, James	1844-45	NC Co
McKean, John	1852	Wilm
McKee, Mr.	1798	Camden
McKim, John L..	1846-52	Sussex
Meredith, Peter, Elder	1850-3	App. Hd, Kent Co
Merriken, Richard H.	1852	NC, Kent Cos
Merrill, Isaac	1853	Sussex Co
Michelmore, Mr.	1833	Lewes
Miller, John, Elder	1841	Wilm
Moore, Jacob	1826	Dover
Moore, Wm. E.	1853	Wilm
Morgan, Mr.	1830	NC Co
Morgan, M. M.	1852	Sussex Co
Morgan, R. U.	1830	NC Co
Morgan, William	1853	Seaford
Murphey, Thomas J.	1848	Dover
Murphy, Thomas G.	1845, 8	Kent Co
Murph(e)y, Thomas C.	1853	Smyrna
Murphy, Theodore	1848, 50	Dover
Murray, Robert,	1825	Christiana
Mustard, Cornelius H.	1841, 2	Sussex Co
Neville, Edmund	1844	New Castle
St. Phillips Ch R.C.		
Newman, T.	1851, 2	Kent Co
Nickets, G. S.	1847	Kent Co
Ogden, Benjamin	1824, 5	Milton, Suss. Co
Ozanna, Thomas D.	1845	Cantwell's Bridge
Page, Mr.	1825	Newport
Palmiter, Silas C.	1845-51	Suss. Co, Milford
Pardee, Isaac	1829-34	B'ywine, Wilm
Rector, Trinity Ch Wilm		
Patterson, Nicholas	1850, 3	NC Co
Patton, A. S.	1849, 50	NC Co
Peckworth, John P.	1820-41	NC Co Elder
Perkins, John, Dr.	1849	Kent Co
Pichan, James D.	1835	
Piggot, Mr.	1829	Kent Co
Pitts, Dr.	1849	nr Frederica
Plummer,	1845	Centreville, DE
Charles Henry, evangelist		
Pollock, A. D.	1853	Wilm
Poor, George	1843	NC Co
Potts, John	1823, 5	Wilm
Presstman, S. W.	1824-35	New Castle
Pries, A.	1849	Wilm
Pryce, William	1807,17	NC Co
Quick, Charles W.	1849, 50	Lewes, Wilm
Rauley, Samuel	1830	Bridgeville

Name (Rev., or var)	Dates	Place(s)
Read, Thomas	1807, 22	Wilm Dr.
Reilly, Patrick	1843-50	Wilm
St. Mary's Ch R. C.		
Rhees, Morgan J.	1842-50	Wilm, NC Co
Rider, William	1821-46	NC Co
Robinson, John	1828	Smtrna
Roche, John A.	1849-53	NC, Kent Cos
Rockwell, J. E.	1848, 50	Wilm, Presbyt.
Rogers, William	1824 d	Wilm
Pastor, First Baptist Ch, Rev. War Chaplain		
Rusling, Joseph	1821-47	NC Co
m1822, then Pastor St. John's, Ph[a]		
Russel, A. K.	1825-35	Wilm, Newark
d bef Feb 1847; son's death reported		
Ruth, Mr.	1851, 3	NC Co
Ryder, William	1828, 47	NC Co
Scott, L.	1847	NC Co
Sharp, Solomon	1824-28	NC Co
Shaw, Joseph	1849	Rockland
Shields, C. W.	1852	Del.
Silver, William	1822	Christiana
Skinner, Thomas H.	1825	Wilm
Smart, Joseph	1846	Hare's Corner
Bethel Bapt. Ch		
Smith, Jacob B.	1847-53	Sussex Co
Seaford, St. Luke's Chapel		
Smith, James	1850	Wilm
Smith, Joseph	1849-52	NC Co
Smith, William	1824	NC Co
Southerland, S. S.	1846	Wilm
Spooner, Mr.	1844	Wilm
Spottswood, J. B.	1845-8	NC, Sussex Cos
Staats, Mr.	1834	Wilm
Storks, Levi	1849	New Castle
Stow, James C.	1852	Wilm
Sumption, Thomas	1848, 9	NC Co
Sutton, H.	1847, 8	Dover
Taylor, John L.	1848	St. Georges
Taylor, Wm. W.	1847, 53	Wilm
Greenhill Presbyt. Ch		
Thompson, Thomas J.	1847, 9	NC, Kent Cos
Tibbles, F. B.	1843	
Middletown		
Torbert, Jonathan R.	1834-53	Sussex Co
Torbert, Wm.	1827, 9	Milton
Townsend, S.	1852	NC Co
Trapnell, W. H.	1850	Wilm, Trinity Ch
Truman,	1846	Middletown
Tyng, Mr.	1844	Cantwell's Bridge
Van Deusen, E. N.	1849-52	NC Co
Trinity Chapel, Wilm		
Walker, Joseph	1829, 47	NC Co
Wallace, A.	1853	Sussex Co
Wallace, James L.	1852	Laurel
Walsh, J. S.	1849, 50	NC Co
St. Joseph's Chapel, B'wine		
Walter, J. P.	1853	Kent Co
Walton, William B.	1852, 3	New Castle
Watson, Mr.	1847	Dagsborough
Way, E. J.	1844	Georgetown
Wellar,	1829	Middletown
Whipple, Elson	1850	White Clay Crk Hd
from the state of Deseret		
White, Henry	1825, 6	NC Co
Wickes, William	1816	NC Co
Williams, E. R.	1848	Kent Co
Williston, R.	1823, 6	B'wine
Williston, William	1824	Wilm
Willits, A. A.	1852, 3	Wilm, Del. City
Wilson, J. P., DD	1827, 50	Red Lion, Newark
Wilson, Joseph	1824	Cantwell's Bridge
Windle, Mr.	1851	B'wine Hd
Woolford, S. N.	1825	Millsboro
Work, W. R.	1841, 3	NC Co
Wright, Mr.	1849	Kent Co
Wyncoop, S. R.	1841-53	Wilm, 1st Presb Ch
Young, R. F.	1829	Del. City

www.ingramcontent.com/pod-product-compliance
Lightning Source LLC
Chambersburg PA
CBHW070725160426
43192CB00009B/1324